S0-AYA-305

Dimensions of DENTAL HYGIENE

PAULINE F. STEELE, B.S., R.D.H.,
B.S. (Educ.), M.A.

Director of Dental Hygiene and Assistant Professor
West Virginia University

14 CONTRIBUTORS

258 Illustrations

Lea & Febiger Philadelphia

ISBN 0-8121-0228-2

Reprinted March 1968

Reprinted November 1970

Library of Congress Catalog Card Number 66:16616

Printed in the United States of America

"To My Parents"

Contributors

JAMES K. AVERY, B.A., D.D.S., Ph.D.
Professor of Dentistry, University of Michigan

HAROLD R. ENGLANDER, D.D.S., M.P.H.
Dental Director, United States Public Health Service in the Epidemiology and Biometry Branch, NIDR.

SHERWIN R. FISHMAN, D.D.S., M.P.H.
Instructor, Department of Community Dentistry, University of Kentucky

HAROLD W. HELD, B.S., M.A., D.D.S.
Professor of Dentistry, University of Michigan

ELMER E. KELLN, B.S., D.D.S., M.S.D. (Pathology), F.A.C.D.
Associate Professor, School of Dentistry, Loma Linda University
Coordinator of Hospital Services, Orange County General Hospital, Los Angeles, California

PAUL H. KEYES, D.D.S., M.S.
Dental Director, United States Public Health Service in the Laboratory of Histology and Pathology, NIDR.

GILBERT V. OLIVER, D.M.D.
Assistant Professor and Vice-Chairman, Division of Periodontology, University of California

PERRY A. RATCLIFF, D.D.S.
Professor and Chairman, Division of Periodontology, University of California

MARGARET M. RYAN, R.D.H., B.S., M.S.
Director of Educational Services American Dental Hygienists' Association, Chicago, Illinois

RICHARD E. STALLARD, D.D.S., Ph.D.
Associate Professor and Chairman, Division of Periodontology, University of Minnesota

PAULINE F. STEELE, B.S., R.D.H., B.S. (Education), M.A.
Director of Dental Hygiene and Associate Professor, University of Cincinnati

MARGARET E. SWANSON, B.S. (Education), R.D.H.

Formerly Executive Secretary, American Dental Hygientists' Association, Chicago, Illinois

PATRICIA McCULLOUGH WAGNER, R.D.H., B.S., M.Ed.

Assistant Professor of Dental Hygiene, University of Washington

ELIZABETH M. WARNER, R.D.H., B.A., M.P.H.

Associate Professor and Chairman, Department of Dental Hygiene, University of Nebraska

WESLEY O. YOUNG, D.M.D., M.P.H.

Associate Professor and Chairman, Department of Community Dentistry, University of Kentucky

Preface

THE heritage of this book is distinctive because it was originally the only text devoted to the instruction of dental hygienists. Dr. A. C. Fones, the "Father of Dental Hygiene," was the first editor. The content was presented in lecture form by Dr. Fones and colleagues at his school for dental hygienists. Initially this text was titled *Mouth Hygiene* and was first printed in 1916.

Later, Dr. Russell Bunting, Dean Emeritus of the University of Michigan School of Dentistry, was designated the second editor. The book was no longer a composite of lectures but those contributing were experts in their respective specialties. At this time the title was changed to *Oral Hygiene*.

This textbook has contributed to the education of dental hygienists for approximately fifty years. It is a distinct privilege to be selected the third editor for this classic text. Since there has developed an extension in the educational scope for the dental hygienist, it was thought appropriate that the title for this book be *Dimensions of Dental Hygiene*.

Since this book is a successor to a well established text, there has been a concerted effort to perpetuate the tradition of definitive excellence. With each revision, the editor has reflected the advancements which have occurred within the profession. Each contributor is highly qualified in his respective area.

The purpose of this book is to present a concise authoritative composite of information. Several specialty subject books exist, but currently there is a need for a text which will provide a general review of pertinent data especially compiled for dental hygienists. In this edition, new chapters have been included and all previous material has been thoroughly revised.

The format is philosophically structured to present modern principles and procedures applicable in dental hygiene practice. Emphasis throughout the book is directed toward advancing knowledge purposeful to the dental hygienist. These concepts have been integrated with practical illustrative diagrams and photographs whenever possible.

Many individuals have given invaluable assistance directly and indirectly in the preparation of this book. Special acknowledgment is extended to all contributors for the excellent manuscripts which were submitted. The co-operation which this project has received is gratefully appreciated.

Both dentists and dental hygienists have assisted in this important endeavor; therefore, various professional groups should find different aspects of the book useful. The text is valuable to dental hygiene instructors, dental hygiene students, practicing dental hygienists as well as dentists and allied health professions. It is intended that dental hygienists, in particular, will obtain distinct benefit from the material contained in this book.

PAULINE F. STEELE

Morgantown, West Virginia

Contents

Chapter 1. PREVENTIVE DENTISTRY
By Wesley O. Young and Sherman R. Fishman

Introduction 15
Basic Concepts of Preventive Dentistry 17
Major Oral Health Problems 21
Community Preventive Programs 29
Preventive Dentistry in the Dental Office . . . 30

Chapter 2. ORAL AND DENTAL ANATOMY
By Harold W. Held

Anatomy of the Skeletal System 35
Muscular Anatomy 42
Neuroanatomy 46
Circulatory System 50
The Oral Region and Associated Structure . . . 55
Anatomy of the Teeth 70
Nomenclature 80
Morphology of the Teeth 83

Chapter 3. ORAL PHYSIOTHERAPY
By Patricia McCullough Wagner

Oral Physiotherapy Objectives 104
Instruments and Aids 104
Toothbrushes, Manual and Automatic, Denture 105
Denture Brushes 110
Dental Floss and Tape 110
Interdental Stimulators 114
Rubber Cup Polisher and Stimulator 117
Oral Hydrotherapeutic Devices 119
Dentrifices 119
Denture Cleansers 121
Mouthwashes 121
Disclosing Agents 123
Toothbrushing Methods 123
Oral Physiotherapy Recommendations 136
Oral Physiotherapy Instruction 138
Summary 142

Chapter 4. ORAL PROPHYLAXIS
By Margaret M. Ryan

Armamentarium . . . 146
Sterile Technique . . . 146
Medical and Dental History . . . 153
Patient and Operator Positioning . . . 158
General Principles of Oral Prophylaxis . . . 162
Instrumentation . . . 162
The Oral Inspection . . . 165
Instruments . . . 166
Mouth Mirror . . . 166
Air Syringe . . . 168
Periodontal Probe . . . 169
Explorers . . . 171
Instruments and Techniques of Scaling and Root Planing . . . 174
Ultrasonic Scaling Devices . . . 193
Armamentarium and Techniques of Polishing . . . 194
Cleaning the Removable Denture . . . 202
Topical Anesthetics . . . 204
Postoperative Procedures to Promote Healing . . . 205
Desensitization of Hypersensitive Dentin . . . 205
Application of Topical Fluoride Preparations . . . 207
Instrument Sharpening . . . 210

Chapter 5. DENTAL CARIES: ETIOLOGICAL FACTORS, PATHOLOGICAL CHARACTERISTICS, THERAPEUTIC MEASURES
By Harold R. Englander and Paul H. Keyes

Introduction . . . 220
Etiological Mechanisms . . . 221
Flora and Bacterial Factors . . . 223
Dietary Substrates, Nutrition and Dental Caries 230
Factors in the Host and Teeth . . . 237
Effects of Fluorides . . . 238
Mechanism of Fluoride Action . . . 241
Pathological Characteristics . . . 242
Pit and Fissure Caries . . . 243
Smooth Surface Coronal Cavitation . . . 243
Root Surface Caries . . . 244
Pit and Fissure Lesions . . . 244
Smooth Surface Caries . . . 246

Coalesced Lesions 251
Root Surface Caries and Erosion 253
Arrested Carious Lesions 256
Control and Prevention of Dental Caries 258
Dietary Recommendations 258
Oral Hygiene 261
Fluoride Therapy 263
Antibacterial Measures 263
Epilogue 269

Chapter 6. THE HISTOLOGY AND EMBRYOLOGY OF THE FACE AND ORAL STRUCTURES
By James K. Avery

Introduction 275
Development of the Human Face 276
Development of the Jaws 280
Development of the Palate 283
Development of the Tongue 285
Histogenesis of Salivary Glands 287
Histogenesis of the Teeth 288
Eruption Process 296
Histology of the Oral Mucosa 302
Histology of the Teeth 307
Histology of the Supporting Structures 311
Histology of the Salivary Glands 314
Histology of the Temporomandibular Joint . . . 316

Chapter 7. ORAL PATHOLOGY
By Elmer E. Kelln

Oral Developmental Disturbances 318
Oral and Related Cysts 329
Diseases of the Oral Mucosa and Jawbones . . . 332
Disturbances of the Salivary Glands 343
Oral Neoplasia 346

Chapter 8. DENTAL DEPOSITS
By Richard E. Stallard

Introduction 354
Dental Plaque 355
Formation 355
Clinical Significance 356

Dental Calculus . . . 358
Formation . . . 360
Clinical Significance . . . 363
Calculus Prevention . . . 364
Dental Stains . . . 364
External Stains . . . 365
Metallic Stains . . . 365
Non-metallic Stains . . . 365
Clinical Significance . . . 366
Internal Stains . . . 366
Clinical Significance . . . 368

Chapter 9. PERIODONTICS
By Perry A. Ratcliff and Gilbert V. Oliver

Introduction . . . 370
Philosophy of Patient Care . . . 371
Healthy Gingiva . . . 371
Histology of Clinically Healthy Gingiva . . . 374
Classification of Periodontal Diseases . . . 376
The Periodontal Pocket . . . 392
Etiology of Inflammatory Periodontal Disease . . . 408
Diagnosis . . . 416
Treatment Plan . . . 418
Prognosis . . . 425
Necrotizing Ulcerative Gingivitis . . . 430
Therapy in Dental Practice . . . 436

Chapter 10. DENTAL HEALTH EDUCATION
By Pauline F. Steele

Introduction—Historical Background . . . 439
School Dental Health Education Development . . . 441
Health Concepts . . . 442
Dental Health Knowledge and the Behavioral Sciences . . . 444
Motivation . . . 445
Dental Health Education—Its Necessity . . . 447
Fundamental Educational Principles . . . 449
Health Education—Laws of Learning . . . 450
Characteristics of Children . . . 450
The Dental Hygienist—An Educator . . . 453
Formal Teaching Approaches . . . 454

Communication 456
Summary 458

Chapter 11. PUBLIC HEALTH
By Elizabeth M. Warner

Characteristics of Public Health Practice . . . 460
Dental Public Health Programs 461
The Role of the Dental Hygienist in Public Health 462
Public Health Responsibilities of Dental Hygienists in Private Practice 464
The Dental Survey 464
Measurements of Other Dental Diseases and Conditions 471
Dental Fluorosis Index 471
Malocclusion Indexes 471
Indexes of Periodontal Disease 472
Oral Hygiene Index 474
Emerging Problems of Public Health Concern . . 478

Chapter 12. HISTORY AND ORGANIZATION OF DENTAL HYGIENE
By Margaret E. Swanson

Introduction 483
Historical Background 484
Dental Hygiene Education 486
Dental Hygiene Student Enrollment 489
Licensure 490
National Board Dental Hygiene Examination . . 490
Professional Association 493
Structure of the American Dental Hygienists' Association 498
Status of Membership 503

1

Preventive Dentistry

Wesley O. Young

and Sherwin R. Fishman

PRIOR to 1840, oral health care was provided by preceptor-apprentice trained individuals whose skills were mechanical in nature and largely limited to restoration of simple cavities, tooth removal, and replacement of lost parts. Although three of the principal hallmarks of a profession appeared at about this time (a school of dentistry, a professional journal, and a dental society), a considerable period elapsed before the majority of practitioners had received formal instruction and the transition from a trade or vocation to a true profession took place. Even then, standards of professional preparation varied widely and were often grossly inadequate. Furthermore, even in the best schools, the primary emphasis was placed on acquiring mechanical and technical abilities.

Major advances in educational standards occurred in the second decade of this century. Efforts of the Council on Dental Education of the American Dental Association (and its predecessor—the Dental Educational Council of America) to improve professional preparation for dentistry were spurred by the findings of the Gies Report which pointed out the inadequacies of many schools, particularly those being operated for profit. In time, many of the poorest institutions closed their doors and the remainder raised their standards. Dental education became a university discipline and the technical training was accompanied by a background in the biological sciences. This development eventually made possible a shift in emphasis from merely restoring the ravages of disease to a concern for preventing the occurrence or progression of disease.

Throughout its relatively short history, the dental hygiene profession has maintained a strong commitment to prevention, generally exceeding that of its parent profession of dentistry. In part, this fact reflects the circumstances of the profession's origin.

At the turn of the century, the belief that oral cleanliness was a major factor in preventing caries attack led many dentists to promote regular oral prophylaxis as a caries-preventive measure. Alfred C. Fones, an enthusiastic supporter of this view, trained a laywoman to provide oral prophylaxis and employed her in his practice for this purpose. Anxious to extend this service to a greater segment of the community, he undertook a campaign to provide a prophylaxis service for children in the Bridgeport, Connecticut school system. The first formal training course for dental hygienists was inaugurated in 1913 to provide personnel for this school program. Thus, the moving force behind the creation of the dental hygiene profession was a desire to increase the availability of a preventive service. Other factors have reinforced the emphasis on prevention. Dental hygiene experienced major expansion during a period when dentists were exhibiting increasing interest in prevention and when preventive technics particularly suited for dental hygiene practice (such as topical applications of fluoride) were developed. Finally, it can be assumed that the fact that hygienists have never been legally permitted to play a major role in restorative dentistry has insulated them from the dilution of interest in prevention that may occur when one becomes preoccupied with the technical aspects of dental care.

The greater emphasis on the biological aspects of clinical practice should assure that graduates of today are better prepared to practice preventive dentistry than those of the past. In recent years, there has been a growing interest in developing more effective methods of teaching "preventive dentistry" as such. An expanded research effort has resulted in new methods of preventing the occurrence or progression of disease. During the past three decades there has been a steady increase in the amount of dental care sought per individual. It would appear that progress is being made toward the eventual goal of the dental and dental hygiene professions: that every individual should preserve a functioning, esthetically pleasing, natural dentition for life.*

Despite the advances that have been made, however, it is clear that present efforts are far from adequate. A discouragingly large segment of the population seeks only emergency care and is either unable or unwilling to obtain the treatment necessary to maintain a normal mouth. The knowledge that is currently available is not completely utilized and many patients receive "supervised neglect" from their

*For a more comprehensive treatment of the background of the problem and appropriate references, the reader is referred to *The Dentist, His Practice, and His Community*[16] (p. 140–201) and *The Survey of Dentistry: The Final Report*[17] (p. 13–46, 95–112, 239–249).

dentist rather than comprehensive oral health care. The failure to utilize preventive measures adequately is demonstrated by the findings of the National Health Survey which indicate that 60 per cent of the population did not claim that they had visited the dentist in the year preceding an interview.[1]

BASIC CONCEPTS OF PREVENTIVE DENTISTRY*

Of necessity, oral health care requires the utilization of a variety of technical procedures such as the exposure and development of a radiograph, the removal of calculus from a specific area of the mouth, or the preparation of a cavity to receive a restoration. The skills necessary for each of these procedures benefit the patient, however, only as they contribute to the ultimate objective in dental practice—the maintenance of optimum oral health for each patient. The identification of the components of dental practice that should be classified as "preventive" is not simple. The provision of topical applications of fluoride to reduce caries attack quite obviously merits inclusion. On the other hand, the extraction of a tooth necessitated by the ravages of dental caries or periodontal disease represents a failure in oral health service and would probably ordinarily not be listed as a preventive service. Yet an extraction may eliminate a source of acute or chronic infection that could become a severe health hazard and, in this light, can be viewed as a form of prevention. This dilemma in definition is sometimes solved by separating those services which *prevent the occurrence of disease* from those *control technics* which are corrective in nature and *prevent the development of more serious sequelae.*[16]

A more useful approach is to include all aspects of clinical practice in the definition of prevention and to categorize them according to the point in disease progression at which they are appropriately used. The entire range of services can be viewed in terms of what have been called "levels of prevention." These levels extend from the prepathogenic period before disease has occurred through the period of rehabilitation when the active disease process has ceased but has left disability in its wake.[7]

*The basic ideas contained in this section were developed in a series of seminars conducted by Dr. Robert Weiss of the Training Branch, Dental Health Center, Public Health Service. They have since been revised and expanded as unpublished teaching aids by the Center and the Department of Community Dentistry, College of Dentistry, University of Kentucky.

Periodontal Disease		Dental Caries	
Levels of Prevention	Process	Process	Levels of Prevention
Primary Prevention (Reversible periodontal changes)	Tissue susceptible to break down ↓ Oral structures predisposing to accumulation of oral debris ↓ Dental plaque ↓ Calculus ↓ Inflammatory changes (reversible) ↓	Tooth susceptible to caries ↓ Carbohydrate intake and other nutritional factors ↓ Dental plaque present on the tooth surface ↓ Enzyme system which facilitates break down of starches to sugars ↓	Primary Prevention
Secondary Prevention (Irreversible changes and moderate destruction)	Soft tissue break down ↓ Bone resorption ↓ Loss of tooth support ↓	Initial cavitation ↓ Advanced cavitation ↓	Secondary Prevention
Tertiary Prevention (Advanced disease and destruction)	Increased difficulty in eliminating local irritants ↓ Increasing tissue and bone loss ↓ Tooth loss	Invasion of pulp ↓ Systemic invasion ↓ Tooth loss ↓ Drifting and malposition of other teeth	Tertiary Prevention

FIG. 1–1. Diagrammatic outline of the disease process in periodontal disorders and dental caries and levels of prevention.

PRIMARY PREVENTION

Primary prevention occurs in the period before disease attack. Methods for primary prevention may involve either general health promotion or specific protection against a particular disease and may be applicable to individual patients or entire communities.

Measures for *health promotion* are those designed to raise the general level of oral health. Examples of this level of prevention would include health education about optimum diet, the promotion of regular visits to a dentist on a recall basis, and the teaching of effective methods of oral hygiene. Hopefully, the dental hygienist will also seek ways in which to promote the total health of patients such as making available information to a mother about the care of her children or actively supporting community efforts to improve standards of education or housing. The common characteristic of all these health promotion efforts is that they are not directed at a specific disease but at raising the over-all level of health, either general or oral.

On the other hand, measures for *specific protection* represent prevention in its strictest sense. Again, these are measures that operate during the prepathogenic period and are taken against a particular disease or group of diseases to intercept their course before they attack man. Some measures for specific protection may be applied to the environment, such as shielding the moving parts of a machine in a factory to reduce accidental injury or adding fluorides to a fluoride-deficient water supply. Others may be applied to man himself, such as the use of immunization against communicable diseases or the topical applications of fluorides.

Primary prevention of oral diseases through specific protective measures has been divided into three basic categories according to the mechanisms of action. According to this concept, preventive procedures:

(1) affect the oral environment (oral cleanliness—particularly in relation to periodontal diseases—and intraoral actions of diet).

(2) involve local protection of the tooth (preventive aspects of restorative dentistry, topical application of fluoride solutions).

(3) involve developmental protection of structures in the mouth (fluoridation and nutritional effects of diet operating through the blood stream).

SECONDARY PREVENTION

Secondary prevention occurs in the early period of disease attack and involves *early recognition* and *prompt and effective treatment.*

Early recognition and prompt treatment are the best preventive measures for diseases where there is yet no specific protection, as in oral cancer. They are needed also when for one reason or another specific preventive measures were not applied, as in dental caries attack. A wide variety of clinical procedures are involved in secondary prevention, including:

(1) Oral prophylaxis provided for patients with early reversible changes in the investing tissues.

(2) A cavity outline for restoring incipient occlusal carious lesions which is extended to include all susceptible developmental grooves.

(3) Proper contour of the proximal surface of a compound restoration to protect against recurrent decay and damage to the gingiva.

(4) Removal of impacted or supernumerary teeth at the proper time with a minimum of trauma.

(5) Minor tooth movement to correct the position of a maxillary incisor locked in a lingual position.

TERTIARY PREVENTION

Even after oral diseases have reached an advanced stage with marked destruction and disability, tertiary preventive procedures can *limit disability* or *restore function.* When several teeth have been lost, for example, the placement of a fixed prosthetic appliance can prevent the drifting and malpositioning of other teeth and, thus, prevent further complications and sequelae. Furthermore, prosthetic appliances serve to protect the normal muscle tone and harmony of the temporomandibular joints and facial muscles. The same procedure will restore masticatory function.

In this context, the practitioner who is concerned about preventive dentistry is interested in a wide range of services and clinical procedures. For example, practitioners should consider fluoridation of the public water supplies and the effectiveness of dental health teaching in the schools as among their important community services. On the other hand, the utilization of topical applications of fluorides, the elimination of over-hanging restorations, the replacement of lost teeth, the provision of oral prophylaxis on a regular basis, and the maintenance of a recall system in clinical practice share equally in providing a preventive oral health service to the public.

MAJOR ORAL HEALTH PROBLEMS

Dental Needs and Dental Demand

The magnitude of a disease is customarily measured either in terms of its incidence or its prevalence. The incidence of a disease is a measure of the number of new cases occurring in a population during a given period of time, while the prevalence represents the total number of cases existing in a population at one time. In chronic diseases of long duration, the prevalence may be anticipated to be much higher than the incidence since the population exhibits evidence of disease processes that have been initiated over a considerable period of time and which linger in the group under study.

Dental diseases generally are chronic and recurring. Once a tooth has been attacked by caries, for example, the evidence remains in the mouth, either as an open cavity, a restoration, or as a space resulting from a tooth extraction because of a long neglected lesion. Similarly. loss of the supporting bone due to periodontal disease is generally irreversible and can be demonstrated in the mouth as long as the tooth remains, whether or not active destruction is taking place. (As an individual becomes older, of course, it becomes progressively more difficult to differentiate between teeth extracted because of caries attack—the major cause of tooth loss in the first three decades of life—and those lost during the later adult years because of periodontal disease.)

The occurrence of dental diseases is studied most frequently by oral examinations of population groups that provide data on the total number of lesions present. Because of their chronic nature, the number of oral lesions accumulates over the years, resulting in regularly increasing prevalence rates with advancing age. This factor is compounded by the widespread failure to seek regular treatment.

The *need* for treatment can be measured with some precision by an examination of a population group. This "need," however, represents an assessment based on professional standards of oral health care. In fact, however, patients' concepts of acceptable dental health often may differ radically from professional norms and they may not seek dental care. Or, even if they desire optimum care, they may not have the resources to obtain service. Therefore, "need for care" and "demand for service" are often quite different. This discrepancy is illustrated by the fact that less than 40 per cent of those interviewed in the National Health Survey even claimed to have visited a dentist in the year preceding the time they were interviewed. One out of three admitted not visiting a dentist in the preceding five years, including 18 per cent who said they had never been in a dental office.[1] It has been estimated that only about 15 to 20 per cent of the population utilizes dental services on a routine periodic basis.[6]

Dental diseases attack almost the entire population. They are generally chronic and irreversible. They cannot be treated by advice or prescription but require time-consuming and demanding professional services by a dentist or dental hygienist. These factors, compounded by widespread failure to seek treatment, result in an accumulated backlog of unmet treatment needs of major proportions. The 111 million adults in the United States, for example, are estimated to have the staggering total of 2.25 billion decayed, missing, and filled teeth. The majority of these teeth are missing or decayed rather than filled.[8]

Dental Caries

Dental caries is probably the most prevalent disease of mankind. Less than five out of a hundred persons escape its attack. It is not uncommon for carious lesions to appear soon after the primary teeth erupt at the age of two or three. The prevalence of carious lesions increases steadily until about six to eight years of age when the average rate starts to drop due to the natural exfoliation of the primary teeth. Calculated in terms of the "essential" teeth that should normally be present in the mouth at a given age, however, the attack of caries appears to continue unabated as long as primary teeth remain in the mouth.[2]

Similarly, carious lesions appear in the permanent dentition soon after the eruption of the first permanent molars around six years of age. Once the permanent teeth come into the mouth, they are continually subject to attack until the individual has run out of teeth or out of time itself. The prevalence of dental caries in permanent teeth is expressed as the average number of unrestored decayed teeth (*D*), the number of missing teeth (*M*), and the number of filled teeth (*F*). See Chapter 11. Figure 1–2 illustrates the pattern of lifetime disease attack and demonstrates the marked reduction in caries experience among those fortunate enough to live in an area where the water contains optimum amounts of fluorides.

In children and young adults, the count of decayed, missing, and filled teeth closely approximates an expression of the cumulative impact of dental caries. Older adults have an increasing number of teeth lost because of periodontal disease so that the "D" component provides a summary of the lifetime tool of dental disease in the permanent dentition. The magnitude of this loss is shown in Figure 1–3 which indicates that above the age of fifty-five at least 20 permanent teeth are missing.

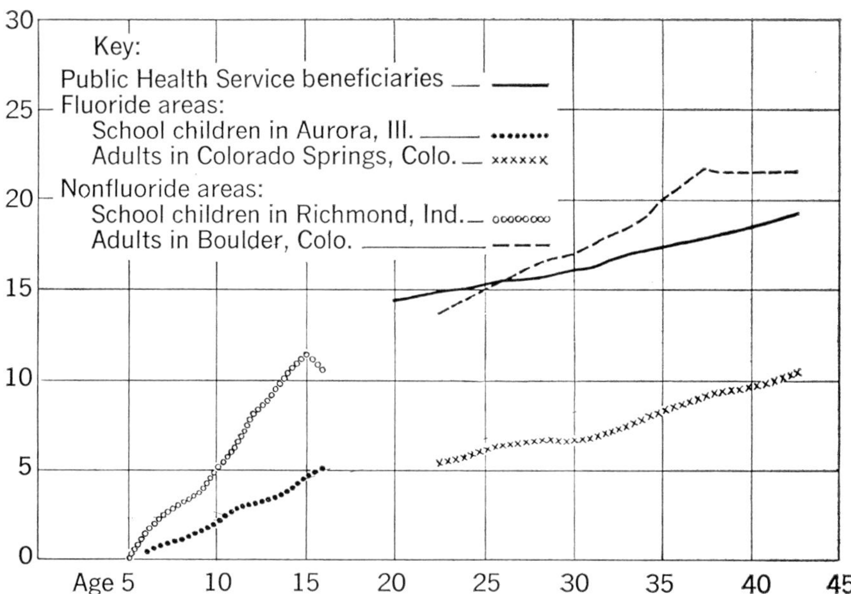

FIG. 1–2. Average number of decayed, missing, and filled teeth in two school and three adult populations (Young[17]).

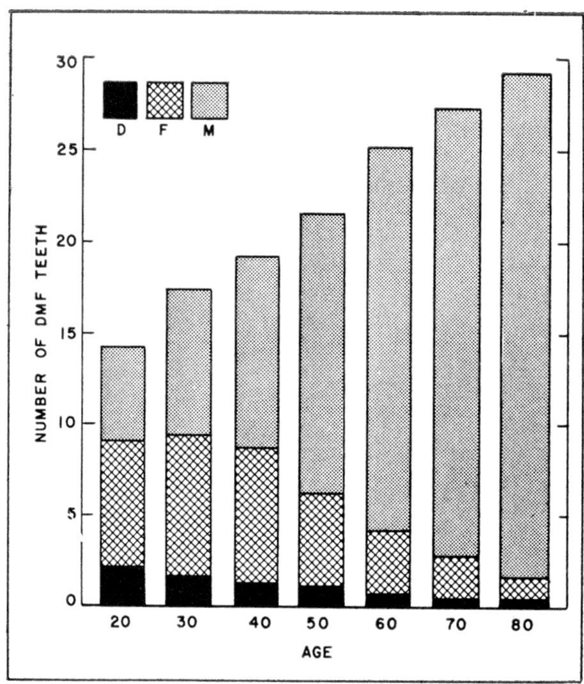

FIG. 1–3. Average number of decayed, missing, and filled teeth among 6,653 persons examined in the National Health Survey.[8]

Fortunately, dental research has developed an effective method for reducing the intensity of caries attack on a community basis through water fluoridation. This procedure is safe and effective. Its effects are long lasting, it reaches all individuals in a community, and is effective regardless of parental or patient cooperation. Despite the overwhelming scientific evidence supporting the merits of fluoridation and the active efforts of the health professions to promote its use, unseemly and unwarranted controversies have arisen to block its acceptance in many communities.

In areas without fluoridated water, some dentists and physicians prescribe tablets or drops which, if taken regularly, are thought to provide considerable protection. For children who do not receive the benefits of water fluoridation, topical applications of a fluoride solution are recommended, a preventive procedure particularly suited to dental hygiene practice. Several different fluoride solutions, applied in varying ways, have shown considerable inhibition of caries attack (in the neighborhood of 40 per cent). Two caries-inhibiting dentifrices containing fluorides have been classified by the Council on Dental Therapeutics of the American Dental Association and others are being tested.[11]

Even if all known methods of partially preventing the attack of dental caries were fully utilized (a possibility that appears remote at this time), carious lesions would still occur. If neglected, the disease will progress, the pulp will become involved, and the tooth lost. Early and regular oral examinations along with providing complete restorations remain, therefore, a key part of preventive dentistry.

Periodontal Diseases

Acute Gingivitis. Ulcerative necrotizing gingivostomatitis (Vincent's Disease) tends to occur in individuals past adolescence. The condition is usually of rapid onset and symptoms include pain, acutely inflamed interdental papillae and gingiva which bleeds at the slightest touch. Although individual cases are not unusual, the disease has been considered communicable since it not infrequently attacks groups of people in an apparently epidemic fashion. The etiology is more likely a combination of poor oral hygiene and conditions which lead to a general lowering of systemic resistance. It is for the latter reason that groups of individuals living under a common source of stress, such as in dormitories or in the armed forces, may experience the disease concurrently. In all probability, therefore, it is *not* a communicable disease.

Groups of young children sometimes experience outbreaks of acute gingivitis. As a general rule, these epidemics in young children are due to acute viral infections with incubation periods ranging up to nine days. Isolation or quarantine measures are relatively ineffective because the virus is usually well transmitted throughout the population group before the first case is apparent. Treatment is largely supportive.[12]

Chronic Destructive Periodontal Disease. Teeth which are not extracted due to caries usually will be attacked by periodontal diseases, the major cause of tooth loss after the age of thirty-five (Fig. 1–4). The National Health Survey findings showed that the per cent of persons with frank evidence of disease—pocket formation—rose rapidly with age, from one in ten for the eighteen-to-twenty-four-year-old group to more than half in the oldest age groups. The prevalence of disease was higher for men than for women and higher for Negroes than for Caucasians (Fig. 1–5).

Knowledge about the etiology of periodontal disease has been advanced by the development of several indices suitable for epidemiological studies and the field surveys that have been done using these tools. Of particular value have been the Periodontal Index and the Oral Hygiene Index, discussed in detail in Chapter 11. Russell's Periodontal Index (PI) provides a numerical score for overt signs of periodontal diseases by visual appraisal of the tissues supporting each tooth. The Oral Hygiene Index (OHI) of Greene and Vermillion yields a numerical score for the presence of both debris and calculus.

Early studies indicated an association between a variety of factors related to social status and the severity of periodontal disease as measured by the PI. Negroes, for example, experienced more disease than did whites; rural children more than those in cities. Men in the higher status incomes had less evidence of destruction than did those in lower class positions and incomes. Further analysis indicated that oral debris (as measured by the OHI) was the single most deleterious factor. Apparently, the relation between social factors and periodontal disease was an indirect one, functioning through their effect on oral hygiene habits. Studies throughout the world have confirmed this observation leading Russell to comment, "They . . . establish an association between mouth cleanliness and periodontal disease in population groups, which is as definite and predictable as the association between waterborne fluorides and dental caries."[13]

This evidence clearly establishes the important role of the dental hygienist in preventive practice. The prevention of periodontal diseases will require more effective patient education in oral hygiene practices and the provision of oral prophylaxis on a routine basis to all individuals in the population—two functions that constitute the major clinical skills of the hygienist.

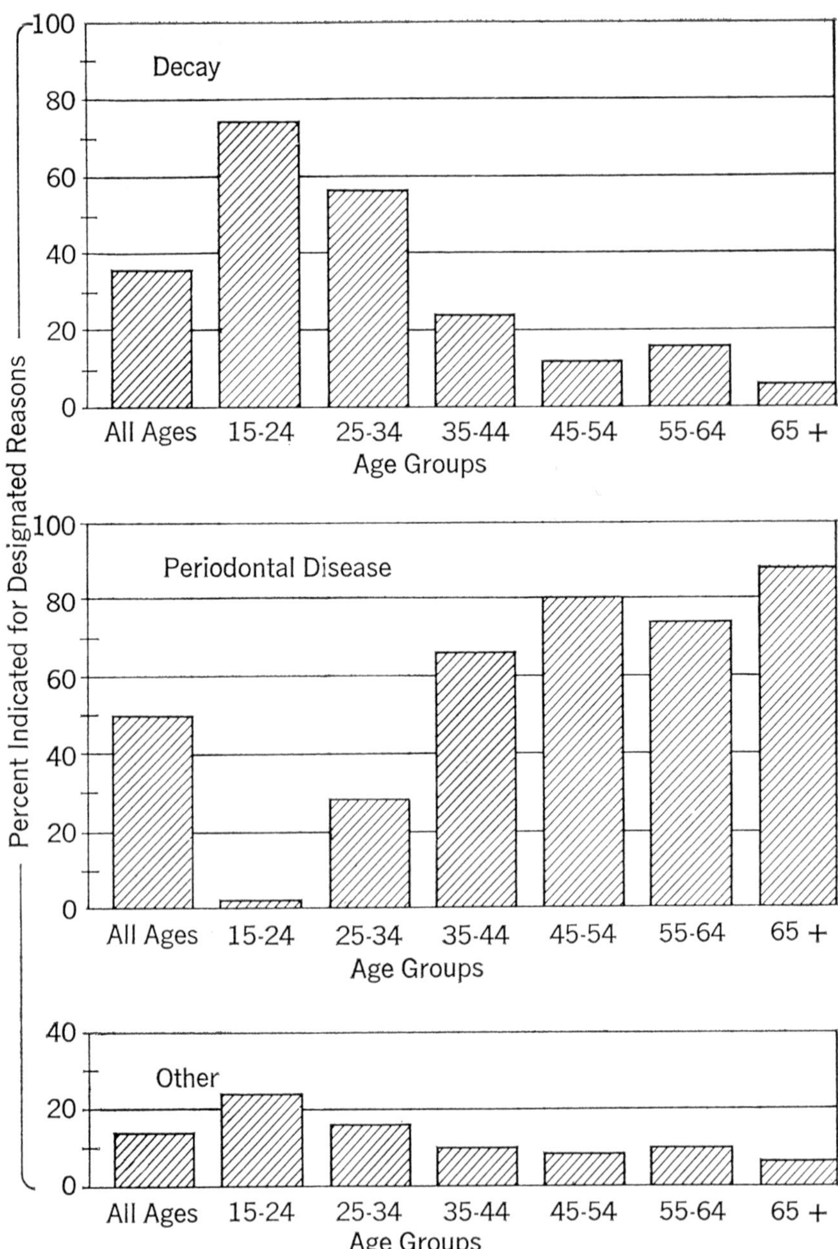

FIG. 1–4. Teeth indicated for extraction because of decay, periodontal disease, and others reasons. (Pelton, Pennell, and Druzina, courtesy of J.A.D.A.)

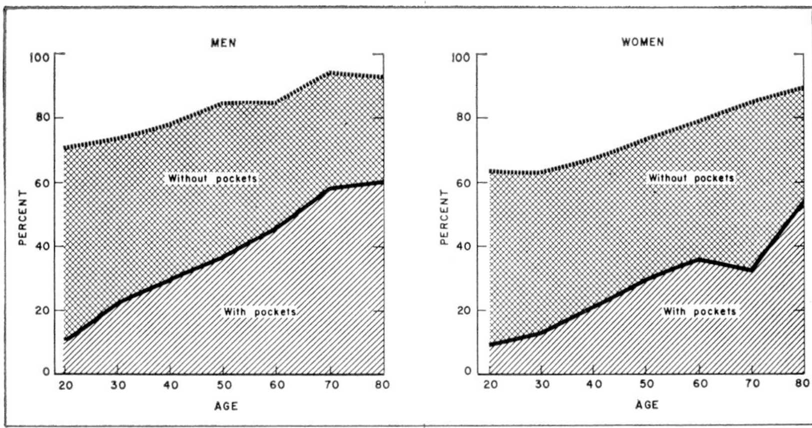

FIG. 1–5. Percent of men and women with periodontal disease, with and without pockets, by age, among adults examined in the National Health Survey.[8]

Oral Cancer

More than six thousand persons die each year from oral cancer, nearly as many as die from being hit by a car.[5] The seriousness of this disease and the necessity for early recognition and treatment are apparent. The only known preventive measure is early recognition of the lesion. This means that a thorough oral exam is essential, for to detect an early lesion, one must first find it! All parts of the oral cavity are easily accessible to examination which makes early detection of cancer possible. A large number of lesions are curable if treatment is initiated early. Unfortunately, most mouth cancers are detected and brought to treatment at a relatively late stage in the disease process. Even in areas where the best medical care is available, the cure rate does not exceed 30 per cent.[5] It is reasonable to estimate that this rate of cure could be at least doubled by more prompt detection.

Clinical examination of the lesion is usually supplemented with a biopsy and microscopic examination by a qualified pathologist. Recently exfoliative cytology has been developed as an aid in the early detection of surface lesions. In this technic, cells are gathered from the surface by scraping with a spatula or tongue blade, transferred to a clean microscopic slide, fixed, and examined by a qualified pathologist.[10]

Oral Clefts

Oral clefts result from a complete or partial failure of the segments forming the lip and the roof of the mouth to unite along a line beginning at the lip and extending through the hard and soft palates. The defects range in severity from a slight cleavage in the vermillion border of the lip, which can easily be repaired surgically, to bilateral clefts of the lip with complete separation of the palatal segments. In the latter case, the resulting deformity creates a grotesque facial appearance and, because there is no partition between the oral and nasal cavities, difficulty in eating and coherent speech result.

In studies reported since 1940, the incidence of cleft lip and palate has ranged from 1.06 per 1,000 live births to 1.97. Assuming a frequency of 1.3 cleft births per 1,000 live births, Greene has estimated that nearly 6,000 children are born each year in the United States with lip and palatal clefts.[4]

Reduced to the barest essentials, the treatment of a child with a cleft of the lip and palate is directed toward five objectives; 1) to repair the lip surgically and, in so doing, restore a normal contour to the upper lip and the nose; 2) to close the hard palate in order to restore the separation between the nasal and oral cavities; 3) to create a functioning palatopharyngeal mechanism adequate to close off the nasal cavity during speech; 4) to teach the child compensatory speech technics to overcome any deficiencies in the structure resulting from other procedures; and 5) during all of these procedures, attempt to allow and encourage normal growth of the maxilla.

Although these objectives may be stated simply, they are often difficult to attain. Successful therapy requires the coordinated efforts of many specialists over an extended period of time. Dentists and dental hygienists can play a key role in the team approach to habilitation of the cleft patient. It is vitally important, for example, that as many of the natural teeth as possible be retained in order to aid the child in speech, to be used during orthodontic treatment, and to be available for the retention of speech devices and partial dentures. Oral prophylaxis and patient education can play an important role in maintaining the normal health of the oral structures that remain.

Malocclusion

Malocclusions range from relatively insignificant deviations from normal to severe and disfiguring malrelation of the teeth, dental arches, and face. It has been estimated that about half of the school age children need some kind of treatment and that one out of five has an orthodontic problem that can be considered severe. Other estimates of "severe" malocclusion place more than a third of the child population in this category.[3] The impact of severe malalignment on personality development has not been clearly defined. However, it seems reasonable to assume that the individual with a pronounced and disfiguring malocclusion may be less likely to make an adjustment to his surroundings than an individual not so deformed.

The occurrence of some malrelation can be prevented by avoiding the drifting of teeth that may result from their premature loss. Others may be corrected (secondary prevention) rather simply by prompt movement of teeth at the proper time during the development of the arch. In many instances, however, complex, time-consuming, and expensive treatment by an orthodontic specialist is necessary.

The hygienist plays an important role in helping patients undergoing treatment to maintain optimum oral hygiene practices made more difficult by the appliances necessary for therapy. It is also important to be conscious of the need to observe the occlusion of children and young adults, so that prompt referral can be made when necessary.

Fluorosis and Other Enamel Defects

In most areas of the United States, the optimum concentration of fluorides in drinking water is approximately 1.0 ppm (parts per million). A significant number of individuals live in areas where the water contains excessive amounts of fluorides, sometimes ranging as high as 10 ppm or more. Children whose teeth are calcified while consuming excessive amounts of fluorides will develop mottled enamel (endemic fluorosis). Excess fluorides can be removed from a community water supply but it is a costly and difficult process. Where this is not practical, the condition can be prevented by limiting a child's daily fluoride intake to 1 milligram a day through the use of fluoride-free water from another source or milk. After the crowns of the permanent teeth have calcified, they cannot be mottled by subsequent exposure to fluorides.

Enamel opacities and other types of defects are not necessarily associated with excessive fluoride intake since they frequently are found in areas with fluoride-deficient water supplies. Many of these conditions are hereditary and cannot be prevented by alteration of the physical environment.[14] In recent years, a preventable hypoplastic enamel (which stains yellow to brown) has been identified in cases of children who have been given tetracycline, a broad-spectrum antibiotic, during the period of tooth formation.[15]

COMMUNITY PREVENTIVE PROGRAMS

Although the dental hygienist's most immediate opportunities in preventive dentistry are in the dental office, a professional concern for improving oral health should extend to providing leadership in developing more adequate community programs. Only a minority of the public receive routine care in dental offices; the remainder will be affected by community programs or not at all.

The first priority for preventive procedures should be given to controlled fluoridation, if the water supply is naturally deficient. In some instances, however, a fluoridation campaign may not be immediately practical, or there may not be a satisfactory central water supply that can be fluoridated. In such instances, the organization of a community program for the provision of topical fluoride applications is the method of choice. The effectiveness of fluorides is limited largely to the prevention of dental caries. The promotion of correct health habits of toothbrushing, good oral hygiene, and correct diet is important for the reduction of both caries and periodontal disease. The effectiveness of these preventive measures is determined by the adequacy of a health education program.

A major objective of dental health education is to teach correct health habits which will enable an individual to take care of his own mouth properly. It is also important to teach facts about dentistry which will assure rational decisions about dental care. Health education activities in the past probably have concentrated too exclusively on the problems of dental caries. Whereas this is the primary problem during childhood and adolescence, it would seem that school and community health programs should also emphasize the problems of periodontal disease, so that adults are aware of the hazards of periodontal disturbances.

Although modern preventive procedures can reduce the attack of dental disease, teeth will still decay and gingival tissues become inflamed. Consequently, unless early and regular dental care is instituted, the loss of teeth and function is inevitable. The promotion of dental care, therefore, becomes an important component of any community dental health program. Unfortunately, there are still many individuals in the community who cannot obtain care for financial or other reasons. The largest segment of these individuals is the medically indigent. A smaller, but perhaps more dramatic group, are those persons afflicted with handicaps such as cerebral palsy and mental retardation which make the provision of care in routine practice difficult and expensive.

PREVENTIVE DENTISTRY IN THE DENTAL OFFICE

Previous sections have noted some of the important contributions the dental hygienist can make at all levels of prevention. In particular, the critical part that the hygienist can play in the primary and secondary prevention of periodontal disease has been noted, as well as the special role in the provision of topically applied preventive agents for dental caries control. In the broadest sense, however, the hygienist can contribute most to improved oral health through patient education.

Water fluoridation accomplishes its mission without the necessity for parental or patient cooperation or the changing of health habits. Parental acquiescence is sufficient to permit children to receive topical applications of fluorides through school programs. All other preventive measures require active cooperation by the patient and the willingness to change established habits, accept treatment procedures that are at the least inconvenient, or to devote time or money to dental health rather than to other, perhaps more immediately desirable, goals. Preventive dental practice is contingent on the effectiveness of efforts to motivate and educate patients.

The dental hygienist should be prepared to function as an effective educator in the office. Patients are seen by the hygienist at a time when their interest in oral health should be at a peak. Patients usually seek care when they have a problem which has focused attention on oral health and they often are seeking answers to immediate questions, answers which can be used to build a framework for a discussion of preventive dentistry.

To serve as a dental health educator, the hygienist should possess skills in communication, know the basic principles of learning, and practice in an office that is organized to allow effective use of this knowledge.

The dental hygienist should know the operating technics of the dentist and the type of procedures which are usually recommended or performed. A hygienist is then in a position to explain the treatment recommendations to patients and give the reasons why specific clinical procedures are best adapted to meet the patient's need. Also, hygienists can educate the patient about the cause of disease and ways in which it can be prevented, especially about the importance of toothbrushing and the use of oral hygiene aids such as dental tape, interdental stimulators, and plaque-disclosing dyes. In some dental offices, the hygienist may analyze a diet record, and in consultation with the dentist, explain dietary recommendations. It is frequently the responsibility of the hygienist to suggest that the patient be placed upon a recall system as well as advise and provide (in most states) topical applications of fluoride.

With these special skills in dental health education, the dental hygienist can help develop individualized teaching materials for the dental practice in which employed. Visual aids specifically designed by the dental hygienist for use both in the prophylactic operatory and that of the dentist can be particularly useful. It is also helpful to develop individualized leaflets and printed material specifically for the dental practice.

The ultimate responsibility for the conduct of the practice rests with the dentist. He must create an atmosphere in his office which is conducive to patient education. The dentist must set the example in providing patient education and he must organize the office so that the dental hygienist has adequate time for patient education and the necessary materials. It is also important that the dentist establish consistent policies in the office so that the personnel who work with him will be confident that they can give a consistent and accurate reflection of the philosophy of the dental practice when talking with patients.

BIBLIOGRAPHY

1. Division of Public Health Methods, Public Health Service. Health Statistics from the U.S. National Health Survey: dental care; interal and frequency of visits; United States, July 1957–June 1959. Washington, Government Printing Office, 1960. 42 pp.
2. FULTON, J. T.: Dental caries experience in primary teeth. J. Dent. Res., *31*, 839-843, Dec. 1952.
3. GALAGAN, D. J.: Why a community dental health program? A dentist's viewpoint. J. New Jersey S. Dent. S., *26*, 65-72, Jan. 1955.
4. GREENE, J. C.: Epidemiology of congenital clefts of the lip and palate. Pub. Health Rep., *78*, 589-602, July 1963.
5. HAYES, R. L.: Oral cancer and occupational health. J. Occup. Med., *5*, 342-7, July 1963.
6. KEGELES, S. S.: Why people seek dental care: a review of present knowledge. Amer. J. Pub. Health, *51*, 1306-11, Sept. 1961.
7. LEAVELL, H. R. and CLARK, E. G.: *Preventive Medicine for the Doctor in His Community: An Epidemiologic Approach.* 2nd ed. New York, McGraw-Hill, 1958. xiv + 689 pp.
8. National Center for Vital Statistics, Public Health Service. Vital and health statistics data from the National Health Survey: selected dental findings in adults by age, race, and sex; United States, 1960-1962. Washington, Government Printing Office, 1965. 35 pp.
9. PELTON, W. J., PENNELL, E. H., and DRUZINA, ANTON: Tooth morbidity experience of adults. J.A.D.A., *49*, 439-45, Oct. 1954.
10. ROVIN, SHELDON: The role of biopsy and cytology in oral diagnosis. Dent. Clin. North America, July 1965, pp. 429-34.
11. RUSSELL, A. L.: Measures available for the prevention and control of dental caries. p. 95-124. (In Young, W. O. and Striffler, D. F. *The Dentist, His Practice, and His Community*. Philadelphia, W. B. Saunders Co., 1964. 318 pp.)
12. ————: Measures available for the prevention and control of periodontal and other oral diseases. Pp. 125-139. (In Young, W. O. and Striffler, D. F. *The Dentist, His Practice, and His Community*. Philadelphia, W. B. Saunders Co., 1964. 318 pp.)
13. ————: The epidemiology of dental caries and periodontal diseases, p. 80-9. (In Young, W. O. and Striffler, D. F. *The Dentist, His Practice, and His Community*. Philadelphia, W. B. Saunders Co., 1964. 318 pp.)

14. Witkop, C. J., Jr.: Genetic diseases of the oral cavity. Pp. 786-843. (In Tieche, R. W., ed. *Textbook of Oral Pathology.* New York, McGraw-Hill, c1965. xii + 873 pp.)
15. Witkop, C. J., Jr. and Wolf, R. O.: Hypoplasia and intrinsic staining of enamel associated with tetracycline therapy. J.A.M.A., *185,* 1008-11, Sept. 28, 1963.
16. Young, W. O. and Striffler, D. F.: *The Dentist, His Practice, and His Community.* Philadelphia, W. B. Saunders Co., 1964. 318 pp.
17. Young, W. O.: Dental health. p. 5-94. (In Hollinshead, B. S., dir. *The Survey of Dentistry; the Final Report.* Washington, American Council on Education, c1961. xxxiv + 603 pp.

2

Oral and Dental Anatomy

Harold W. Held

THE RELATIONSHIP between oral and dental anatomy is essential to the basic knowledge of the dental hygienist. Oral anatomy is that branch of anatomy that deals with the study of the internal and environmental structures of the oral cavity and with its blood and nerve supply, while dental anatomy deals with the study of the structure, form and functions of the teeth and the supporting tissues of the dentition.

In analyzing these two definitions it will be noted that the subject "oral anatomy" covers a much broader field of study than does that of dental anatomy. This chapter is written to give the hygienist a broad aspect of both subjects of fundamental knowledge that has a very important bearing on an intelligent understanding of the structural parts that are closely associated with the teeth and provide nourishment, nervous control, support, protection and functional powers to the dental units.

As today's philosophy emphasizes a broader concept of basic knowledge, the dental hygienist can better comprehend that the field she is especially interested in, is not an entity unto itself but a very important part of the entire body and depends upon the various bodily systems for its existence. Although the fact is emphasized that the dental hygienist must know more about her own special field of activity than any other portion of the body, she must not lose sight of the correlation of this area with the various bodily systems.

A unified understanding of the relationship between oral and dental anatomy is essential for the student of dental hygiene. Too often these subjects are separated so that the student loses continuity which must exist in order to ensure complete understanding.

This chapter is divided into two parts, first a systematic approach to the study of related structures of the oral cavity and regional associated structures and second, the study of dental anatomy of both primary and permanent teeth, occlusion, temporomandibular articulation and supporting structures.

ANATOMY OF THE SKELETAL SYSTEM

The skeletal system forms a solid framework around which the body is built. It is composed of bones and cartilage. It supports the softer tissues and provides protection for them. It also furnishes surfaces for attachment of muscles, tendons and ligaments.

Bones are not solid structures; within each bone there is a central cavity filled with bone marrow, which is yellow in some locations and red in others. Special cells in the red bone marrow produce the blood corpuscles. The skeletal system is far from being an inert system.

Formation of Bone

Bone begins to be formed in the embryo at an early age. It is formed by two methods: the *intramembranous* and the *cartilaginous* or endochondrial. Bones of the skull are formed by the intramembranous method and the ossification of the skull bones is not complete at birth, but eventually it is completed, and the cranial bones then consist of hard, strong, outer and inner plates of compact bone, with soft, spongy bone between, known as "diploi."

Most of the bones of the body are formed by the cartilaginous, or endochondrial method in which there are cartilage models of future bones. There is a skeleton of hyaline cartilage fully formed by the second month of embryonic life. The final stages in replacement of cartilage occur long after birth in some bones.

Types of Bones

Bones may be classified according to their shape:

Long bones are found in the extremities.

Short bones are cube-shaped such as the wrist bones (carpal bones).

Flat bones are thin, being made up of two plates of compact bone enclosing a layer of spongy bone. The scapula or shoulder blade, and the bones of the skull are examples of flat bones.

Irregular bones are of various shapes such as the vertebrae, ethmoid, and other skull bones.

Sesamoid bones are very small rounded bones that develop in the capsules of joints or in tendons. Their function is to eliminate friction.

Division of the Skeleton

For the purpose of study the skeleton is divided into two main subdivisions. These are: (1) the *axial skeleton,* including the bones of the head, the neck, and the trunk, comprises a total of 80 bones.

and (2) the *appendicular skeleton,* which includes the bones of the upper and lower extremities, the shoulder and pelvic girdles, numbers a total of 126 bones.

The total number of bones in the skeleton is 206.

The *skull* is the skeleton of the head and face. It is composed of flat bones united by interlocking or overlapping structures with the cranium, and a group of irregular bones forming the bony framework of the face and the base of the cranium.

Eight bones form the cranium and 14 bones form the face. The *cranial bones* are frontal, occipital, sphenoid, ethmoid, paired zygomatic, lacrimal, nasal, maxillae, inferior nasal conchae, palatine, and the unpaired vomer and mandible. There are also three small ossicles in each middle ear and one hyoid bone in the neck.

The *anterior aspect of the skull* (Fig. 2–1) shows most of the bones of the face and some of those of the cranium. The *frontal bone* is noted at the front of the skull forming the forehead, the upper

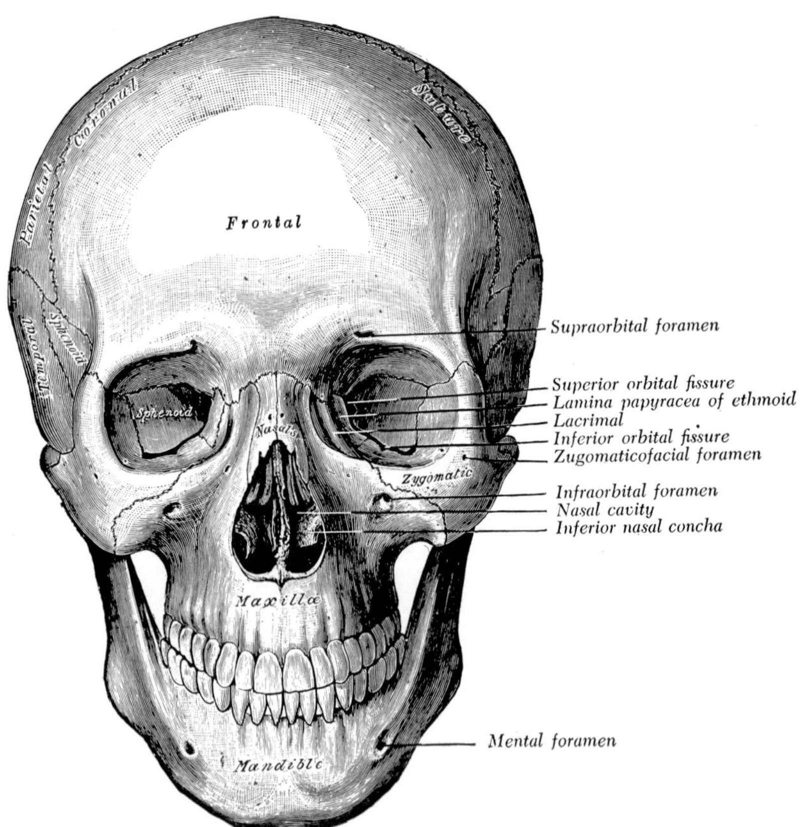

FIG. 2–1. The skull from the front. (*Gray's Anatomy.*)

part of the orbit, the anterior portion of the anterior cranial fossa and a part of the septum between the brain case and nasal cavity. Inside the bone are cavities known as the *frontal sinuses.* The sinuses communicate with the nasal cavity.

The *orbits* are the bony sockets for the eyeballs and are formed by parts of the following cranial and facial bones: frontal, maxilla, zygomatic, sphenoid, ethmoid and the small lacrimal bone.

The *ethmoid bone* is a light spongy bone located at the base of the cranium between the orbits at the base of the nose.

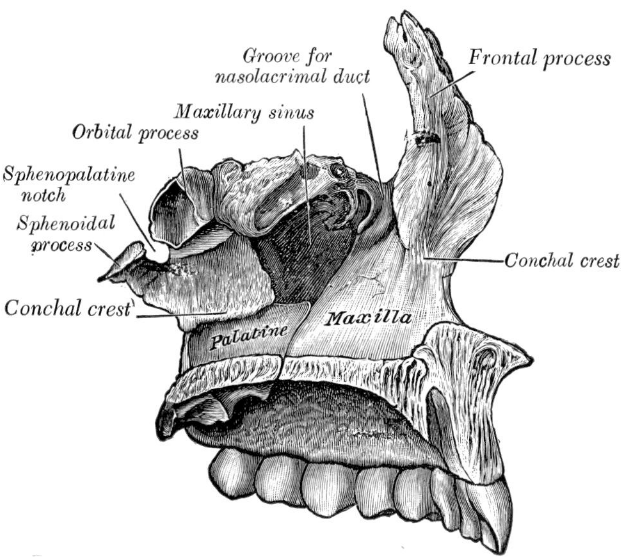

FIG. 2–2. Articulation of left palatine bone with maxilla. *(Gray's Anatomy.)*

The ethmoid has canals in it through which the fibers of the *olfactory* nerve pass. It also contains air cells which open into the nasal cavity.

The *lacrimal bones* are small, thin, scale-like bones present in the medial wall of the orbit on the ethmoid bone. Each lacrimal bone contains a groove which is part of the *lacrimal canal* from the orbit to the nasal cavity. The tear duct passes through the canal.

The *palatine bone* is paired and L shaped (Fig. 2–2). The perpendicular portion forms a part of the lateral wall of the nasal cavity. The *horizontal piece* (palatal process) forms part of the floor of the nasal cavity and part of the roof of the mouth. Each palatine bone is between the maxilla and the pterygoid process of the sphenoid bone.

The *nasal cavity* is prominent in the front view of the skull. The *nasal septum* separates the two halves of the nasal cavity. The septum is formed by the ethmoid and the *vomer* bones.

Facial Bones

The *maxilla* (Fig. 2–3) or upper jawbone is formed by the fusion of the two maxillae which articulate with the *frontal bone.* The maxilla forms part of the floor of the orbit and most of the roof of the mouth, the lateral walls of the nasal cavity and part of the wall of the nasolacrimal duct. Each maxilla consists of a *body* and *several processes.* A large single cavity inside the body, the *maxillary sinus,*

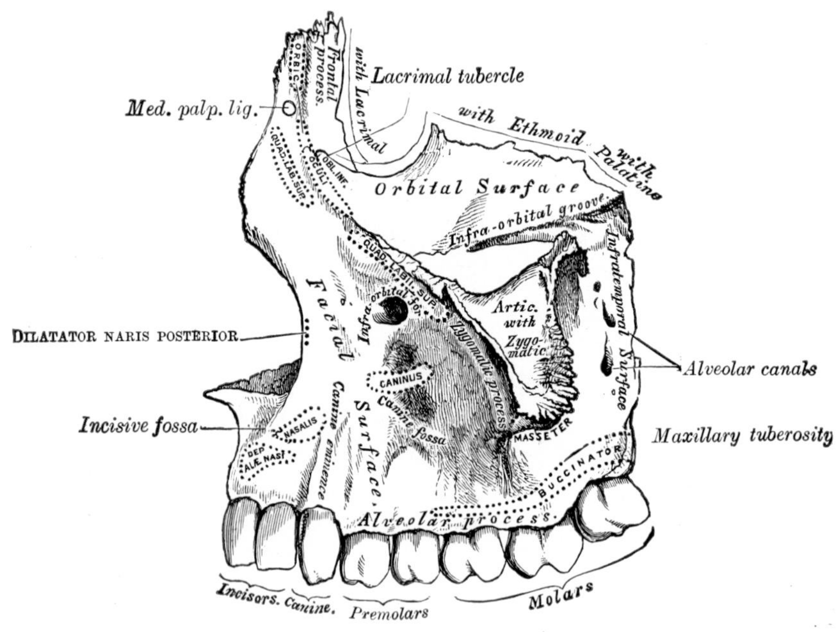

FIG. 2–3. Left maxilla. *(Gray's Anatomy.)*

communicates with the nasal cavity. The *alveolar* process contains the maxillary teeth. The palatine processes form the anterior and larger portion of the hard palate.

The *mandible* (Fig. 2–4). In form this bone resembles a horseshoe and is composed of a body and two rami. The latter arise from the posterior ends of the body. The angle formed between the rami, the vertical portion, and the body varies in degree according to race, type and age. The mandible is the only bone in the skull that is movable, having no osseous union with the skull proper. It is the heaviest and strongest bone of the head, gives support to the sixteen mandibular teeth, and serves as a framework for the lower half or floor of the mouth.

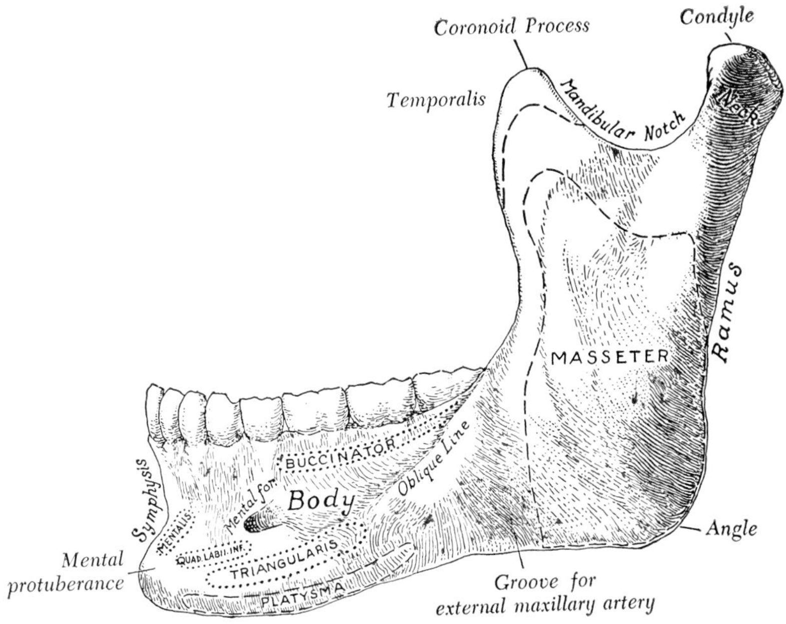

FIG. 2–4. Left half of mandible. Lateral aspect. *(Gray's Anatomy.)*

The *body,* or horizontal portion, consists of two identical halves which meet at the median line and form a slight vertical ridge, the symphysis. Midway between the borders of the body, and usually below the second bicuspid tooth, is a large foramen giving passageway to the mental branches of the inferior dental nerve and accompanying blood vessels. The buccinator muscle, which forms a large portion of the lateral wall of the mouth, has its origin from the facial surface of the mandible, being attached to the alveolar portion below the molar teeth.

The internal surface (Fig. 2–5) of the body presents in the median line four tubercles for the attachment of the genioglossi and genio-hyoid muscles. Along the body of the bone, about half-way between its borders, is a ridge called the mylohyoid ridge. This serves for the attachment of the muscle by the same name, which forms the floor of the mouth. Above this ridge, on either side of the median line, is a shallow smooth depression, the sublingual fossa. One of the salivary glands, the sublingual, is partially embedded in this fossa. Near the center of this surface, between the mylohyoid ridge and the lower border of the bone, is an oblong depression, the submandibular fossa. In this fossa rests another of the salivary glands, the submandibular.

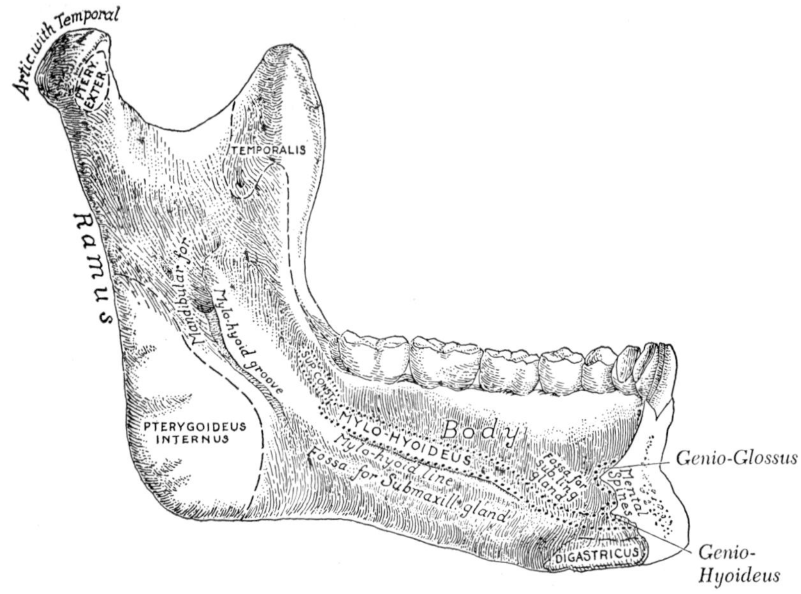

FIG. 2–5. Left half of the mandible. Medial aspect. (*Gray's Anatomy*.)

These glands pour their secretions into the mouth through a common duct, Wharton's, the openings of which are on either side of the frenulum of the tongue.

The *rami,* or vertical portion of the mandible, presents two surfaces, external and internal; four borders: superior, inferior, anterior and posterior; and two processes: the condyloid and the coronoid.

The external surface is flat and smooth. Near the center it is slightly concave where one of the muscles of mastication, the masseter, is attached.

The internal surface presents near the center an oblong opening: the inferior dental or mandibular foramen. It transmits the inferior dental artery and nerve which furnish the blood and nerve supply to the mandibular teeth. This surface also serves as a place of attachment for certain of the muscles of mastication, *i.e.,* the internal pterygoid and the temporal.

The superior border of each ramus is crescent-shaped and is known as the sigmoid notch. Anteriorly, there is a cone-shaped process, the coronoid process. Posteriorly, there is a rounded or oblong eminence, the condyloid process, which enters into the formation of the temporo-mandibular joint.

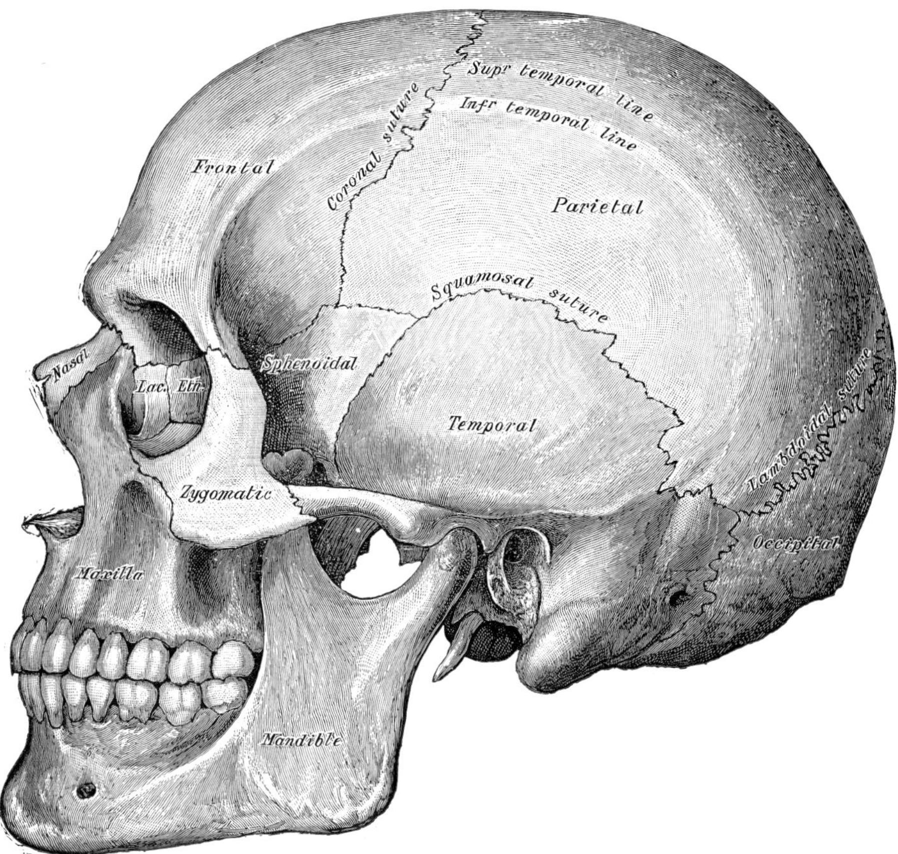

FIG. 2–6. Side view of the skull. *(Gray's Anatomy.)*

The *zygomatic* bone is the cheek bone, situated at the upper and lateral part of the face. It forms the prominence of the cheek.

The *nasal* bones are small flat bones which form the upper part of the bridge of the nose.

The lateral aspect of the skull (as seen in Fig. 2–6) shows parts of the *frontal,* the *parietal,* the *temporal,* the *occipital* and the *sphenoid* bones. The *parietal* bones lie between the *frontal* and the *occipital* bones.

The *hyoid* bone lies at the root of the tongue just above the larynx. The hyoid bone is suspended from the tip of the styloid process of the temporal bones by the stylohyoid ligaments. It serves for the attachment of those muscles which move the tongue and aid in speaking and swallowing.

MUSCULAR ANATOMY

Muscular tissue is specialized for contractility. Its general functions are numerous and varied. Life is dependent on the function of muscle action and all of us should appreciate our normally functional muscular system.

There are different types of muscles for the performance of various functions. Three types of muscular tissue are present in the body.

The *first* is *skeletal,* which is attached to bones. This type is called *striated* or *voluntary* and is under the control of the will.

The *second* type is *smooth involuntary* or visceral and is not under the control of the will.

The *third* type is *cardiac* involuntary or heart muscle.

Skeletal muscles are attached to the bones. They cover the skeleton, surround the oral, the abdominothoracic cavities, and form the body of the tongue.

Smooth muscle is present in the walls of the blood vessels, the gastrointestinal tract, bladder.

Cardiac muscle is present only in the walls of the heart. All types of muscular tissue are supplied abundantly with blood and lymphatic vessels and with nerve fibers that carry messages from the muscle to the brain.

Skeletal muscles make up the so-called flesh of the body and comprise about 36 percent of the body weight in women and 42 percent in men. Skeletal muscles are responsible for the movements of parts of the body, or the body as a whole, and are used in both voluntary and reflex movements.

The two principal groups of skeletal muscles are *appendicular* and *axial.* The appendicular group comprises the muscles of the *upper* and *lower* extremities. The axial group comprises the muscles of the *trunk,* the *head* and *neck.*

The muscles of the *head* and *neck* function in the mechanisms of *mastication* and *deglutition, facial expression, speech, sight, respiration,* and *posture.*

The muscles of the scalp, of the face, of mastication and of the tongue comprise the muscles of the head (Fig. 2–7).

Muscles of the Scalp. The *epicranius* is the scalp muscle which is composed of the *frontalis* and the *occipitalis.* The *frontalis* lies over the frontal bone, and the *occipitalis* over the occipital bone. The two muscular portions are connected together by a fibrous sheet called the *galea aponeurotica,* which extends over and covers the whole upper part of the cranium.

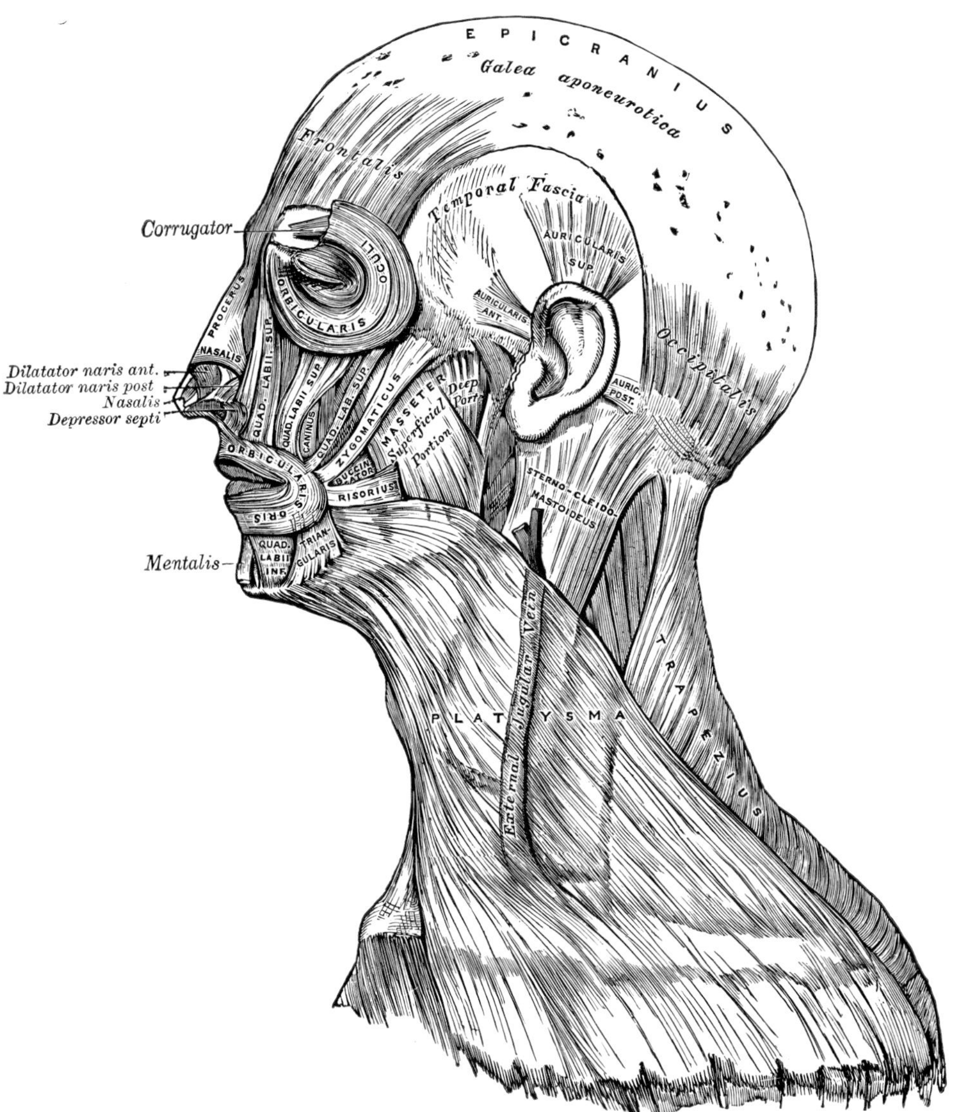

FIG. 2–7. Muscles of the head, face and neck. *(Gray's Anatomy.)*

Facial Muscles. The facial muscles are collectively known as the muscles of *expression,* since their activity permits an outward expression of the various emotional states. These muscles also contribute to the functions of mastication, respiration and vision. The facial muscles, innervated by the 7th cranial nerve, may be divided into *two* groups—those of orbits and eyelids and those of the lips and mouth.

Orbit and Eyelid. Muscles that encircle the orbit, constrict the entrance of the orbit, shut out light and protect the eye against the entrance of foreign bodies are orbicularis oculi, levator palpebrae and corrugator.

Mouth and Lips. The muscles that are directly associated with the mouth and lips may be divided into three groups:

A. *Depressors* of angle of the mouth and lips:
   1. Depressor anguli oris
   2. Risorius
   3. Depressor labii inferioris
   4. Some fibers of platysma

B. *Elevators* of angle of the mouth and lips:
   1. Levator labii superioris alaque nasi
   2. Levator labii superioris
   3. Levator anguli oris
   4. Mentalis
   5. Zygomaticus major and minor

C. *Sphincters* of angle of the mouth and lips.
   1. *Orbicularis oris* consists of numerous layers of muscle fibers that surround the opening of the mouth and extend in different directions. It is formed partly of fibers derived from other facial muscles which are inserted into the lips. The muscle causes closure of the lips by tightening the lips over the teeth, contracting them or causing the protrusion of one over the other.
   2. *Buccinator* is the muscle coat of the cheeks. It draws the corners of the mouth laterally, pulls the lips against the teeth and flattens the cheeks. It aids in mastication, swallowing, whistling and blowing wind instruments. It prevents food from being pocketed between the teeth and cheeks.

Muscles of the Nose. Around the nose are the following muscles: procerus; from nasal bone between the eyebrows, dilator naris and compressor nasi which surrounds the external nares facilitating respiration by dilating and constricting.

Muscles of Anterolateral Neck Region

1. *Superficial Cervical.* Platysma is a long, broad sheet of muscle, the principal muscle of this region.

2. *Lateral.* Trapezius and sternocleidomastoid draw the head toward the shoulder.

3. *Suprahyoid* and *Infrahyoid* muscles. Suprahyoid muscles extend from the base of the skull to the hyoid bone; they consist of the *digastric, stylohyoid, mylohyoid* and the *geniohyoid* muscles.

They assist in swallowing and mastication.

The infrahyoid muscles extend downward from the hyoid bone to the clavicle and scapula; they consist of the *sternohyoid, sternothyroid, thyrohyoid* and the *omohyoid.* They depress the larynx and hyoid bone after being drawn upward with the larynx and tongue during swallowing. Both sets of muscles aid in speaking.

The Muscles of Mastication. Four muscles which directly control the opening and closing of the mouth are usually classified as the *muscles of mastication.* The primary muscles of mastication are the *masseter,* the *temporal,* the *medial pterygoid,* and the *lateral pterygoid* (Fig. 2–8). If these muscles are unable to act, other muscles may effect an opening. These latter muscles are not designed to serve as masticators but rather to act upon the *hyoid bone* and are called the *supra* hyoid muscles.

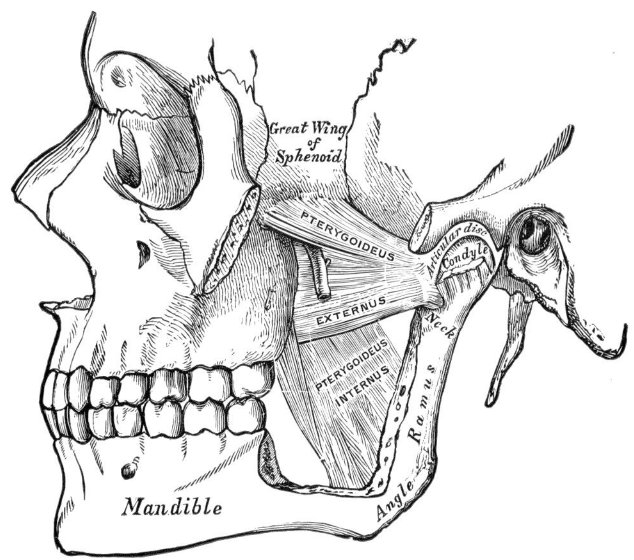

FIG. 2–8. The Pterygoid muscles, part of the ramus removed. *(Gray's Anatomy.)*

The *masseter,* the *temporal,* and the *medial pterygoid* act as a unit to effect closure of the mandible, while the weaker *lateral pterygoid* acts to open or depress the mandible. The *masseter* is among the most powerful muscles of the body and the combination of these three muscles can exert extreme force.

Blood Supply to Muscles of Mastication. To the muscles of mastication are branches from the *maxillary artery,* mainly the deep temporal, pterygoid, masseteric and buccinator.

Nerve Supply to the Muscles of Mastication. This is received from the mandibular branch of the trigeminal nerve of which a *motor branch* passes to the *medial pterygoid.* In the zygomatic fossa it divides into *anterior* and *posterior* divisions. The anterior division supplies motor nerves to the *masseter, temporal* and *lateral pterygoid muscles.* It has one sensory branch, the *long buccal.*

NEUROANATOMY

Nervous System

The nervous system is the mechanism concerned with the correlation and integration of various bodily processes and the reactions and adjustment of the organism to its environment.

It functions by means of conduction pathways or nerve fibers and centers. It is divided into two main divisions—(*a*) *central system* consisting of the brain and spinal cord and (*b*) *peripheral system* composed of nerves that carry messages to and from the *central nervous system.*

The nerves that carry impulses to and from the brain are called *cranial nerves;* those that carry impulses to and from the spinal cord are called *spinal nerves.* Peripheral nerves are of four types according to function.

(a) Somatic *afferent* nerves carry impulses from the skin, skeletal muscles, teeth, joints *to* the central nervous system.
(b) Somatic *efferent* nerves carry impulses *from* the central nervous system to the skeletal muscles.
(c) Visceral *afferent* fibers carry impulses from the viscera *to* the central nervous system.
(d) Visceral *efferent* fibers ("autonomic system") carry impulses *from* the central nervous system to smooth muscle, cardiac muscle and glands.

Spinal Nerves. There are 31 pairs of spinal nerves named from the segments that give them origin. Spinal nerves are attached to the cord by two roots known as the *anterior* and *posterior roots.* The *posterior* root shows a swelling called the *dorsal* ganglion. Functionally, the posterior root contains *afferent* sensory fibers carrying messages *from* the periphery to the cord; the *anterior root* contains *efferent* motor fibers carrying impulses *from* the cord to muscles and glands.

Cranial Nerves. There are 12 pairs of cranial nerves attached to the brain that have somatic and visceral sensory functions to perform. The *afferent* fibers arise from cell bodies outside the central nervous system in ganglia that correspond to the ganglia on the dorsal root of the spinal nerves. The somatic and visceral *efferent* fibers arise from nuclei within the brain (Fig. 2–9). These emerge from the skull through special foramina. Named in order, beginning with the most anterior, they are:

1. Olfactory (Sensory)
2. Optic (Sensory)
3. Oculomotor (Motor)
4. Trochlear (Motor)
5. Trigeminal (Sensory Motor)
6. Abducens (Motor)
7. Facial (Sensory Motor)
8. Acoustic (Sensory)
9. Glossopharyngeal (Sensory Motor)
10. Vagus (Motor Sensory)
11. Accessory (Motor)
12. Hypoglossal (Motor)

The cranial nerves associated with the oral cavity are: *(a)* Trigeminal, *(b)* Facial, *(c)* Glossopharyngeal and *(d)* Hypoglossal.

Trigeminal Nerve. This is the largest cranial nerve and the great sensory nerve of the head and the face. It is the motor nerve of the muscles of mastication.

It has two roots, a *sensory* and a *motor,* attached close together to the side of the pons. The sensory root passes into a *ganglion* (Semilunar or Gasserian). There are three (Fig. 2–9) large *sensory* branches which bring fibers into this ganglion: (1) the *ophthalmic,* bringing sensory impulses from the orbit, upper eyelid, bridge of nose, forehead and mucous membrane of the nasal cavity, (2) the *maxillary,* bringing sensory impulses from the lower eyelid, lower eyelid, lower part of the nose, cheek, upper jaw and teeth, lip and palate, and (3) the *mandibular* branch, the largest division, bringing sensory impulses from the lower lip, teeth, tongue, lower part of face and front of the ear. The ophthalmic nerve passes through the superior orbital fissure, the maxillary through the foramen rotundum and the mandibular through the foramen ovale.

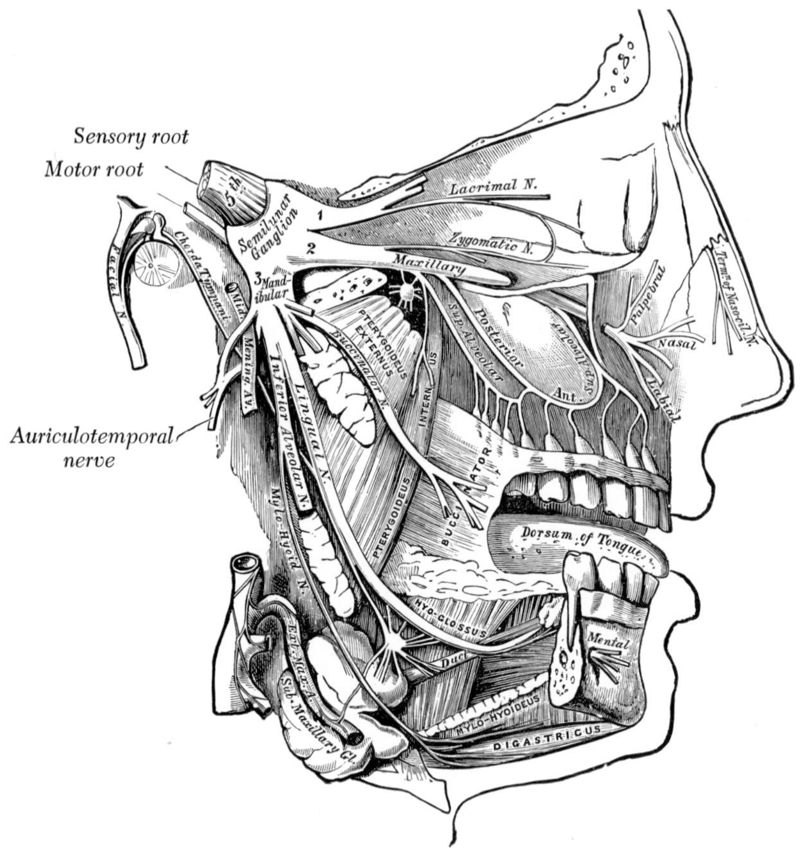

FIG. 2–9. Distribution of the maxillary and mandibular nerves and the submandibular ganglion. *(Gray's Anatomy.)*

The *motor root* passes beneath the semilunar ganglion and it continues into the *mandibular* nerve as it emerges through the foramen ovale. The motor fibers go to the muscles of mastication, namely the lateral and medial pterygoid, the masseter and the temporal muscles. Also the anterior belly of the digastric, mylohyoid, tensor veli palatine and tensor tympani muscle of the pharynx are supplied by the motor root.

The fifth nerve carries sensory fibers for heat, cold, pain and touch but not for taste.

Facial Nerve (Fig. 2–10). This nerve arises from the side of the brain stem just behind the pons close to the origin of the eighth nerve. Together they enter the internal acoustic meatus, continue through the facial canal and finally emerge through the stylomastoid foramen. Its fibers are distributed to the muscle of facial expression, secretory fibers to the submandibular and sublingual glands, and taste fibers to the anterior part of the tongue. It is also motor to the digastric posterior belly, stylohyoid, and stapedius muscles of the inner ear.

Glossopharyngeal Nerve. The glossopharyngeal nerve joins the side of the medulla and passes out of the skull through the jugular foramen into the neck forming the pharyngeal plexus. It distributes both motor and sensory branches to the tongue and pharynx. It is sensory to the mucous membrane of the pharynx, fauces, palatine tonsil and is the nerve of taste to the *posterior* third of the tongue.

Hypoglossal Nerve. This nerve arises from the medulla posterior to the eleventh nerve, leaves the skull through the hypoglossal canal, and supplies the muscles of the tongue.

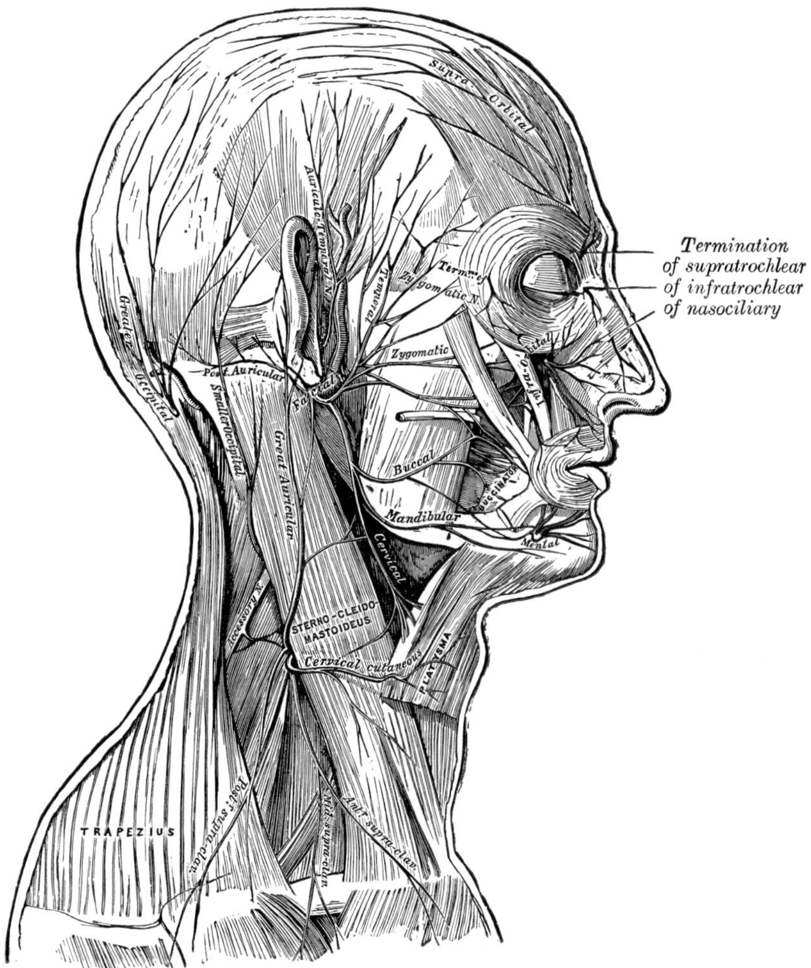

FIG. 2–10. The nerves in the scalp, face and side of neck. *(Gray's Anatomy.)*

CIRCULATORY SYSTEM

The circulatory system is composed of the heart and the blood vessels; it is known also at the *cardiovascular system.* The organization may be diagrammed as follows:

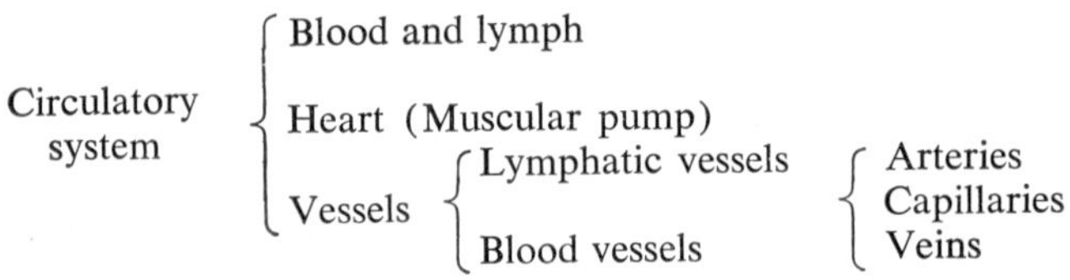

The heart is a pump composed of muscle, which drives the blood through the blood vessels, contracting about 72 times each minute. Leading off from the heart are two large *arteries* which distribute blood to two separate areas. One, the *pulmonary artery* supplies the lungs; the other, the *aorta,* gives off many branches over a long course, furnishing a circulation to the entire body, except the lungs. The former is called the *pulmonary circulation,* the latter the *systemic circulation.* From both of these circulations, the blood is returned to the heart by a system of vessels called the *veins.*

The *aorta* comes off the left ventricle of the heart and runs upward, backward, and to the left to form a curved tube and descends along the vertebral column. It passes through an aperture of the diaphragm and enters the abdomen to divide at the level of the fourth lumbar vertebra into the right and left common iliac arteries. The *aorta* is divided into the *ascending aorta,* the *arch of the aorta,* and the *descending aorta* (Fig. 2–11).

The *innominate* or *brachiocephalic artery* is the largest branch that arises from the arch of the aorta. It passes upward and divides into the *right common carotid* and the *subclavian arteries.* The *left common carotid artery* arises from the *arch* of the aorta.

The principal arteries (Fig. 2–12) of blood supply to the head and neck are the two *common carotid arteries.* They ascend in the neck lateral to the trachea and larynx to the upper border of the thyroid cartilage where each divides into two branches: (1) the *external carotid* supplying the exterior of the head, face and greater part of the neck; (2) the *internal carotid* supplying, to a great extent the parts within the cranial and orbital cavities. Near the origin of the *internal carotid* artery on either side is a dilatation called the *carotid sinus* (Fig. 2–13).

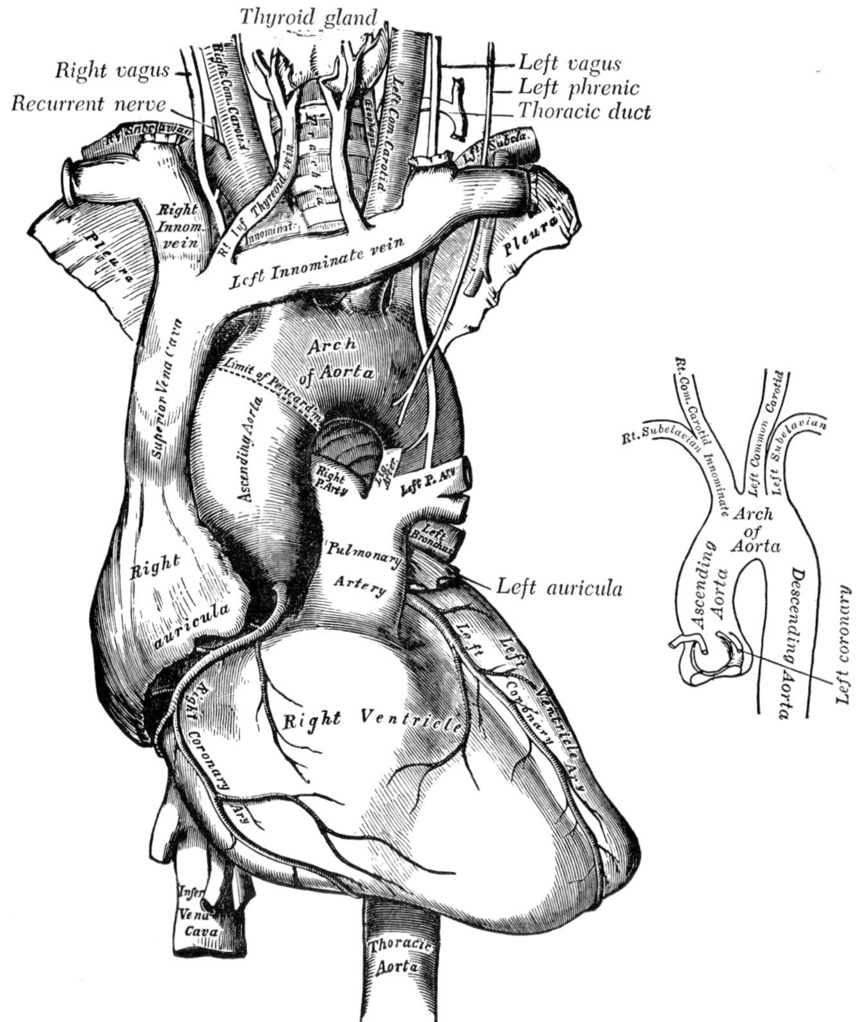

FIG. 2–11. The arch of the aorta and its branches. *(Gray's Anatomy.)*

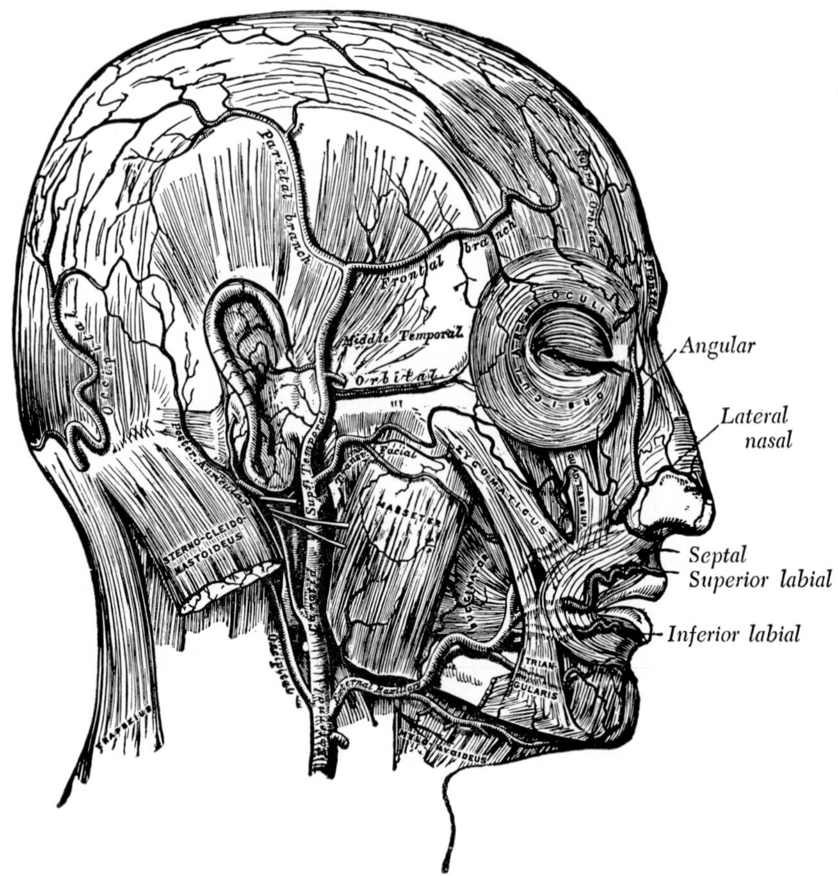

FIG. 2–12. Arteries of the face and scalp. *(Gray's Anatomy.)*

The *external carotid* artery ascends to the level of the neck of the mandible where it divides into the *superficial temporal* and the *maxillary arteries.* It gives off the following branches in its course: Superior thyroid, lingual facial, occipital, ascending pharyngeal, posterior auricular to supply such structures in the head and neck as pharynx, thyroid gland, tongue, teeth, gingiva, muscles of mastication, buccinator muscle, part of the ear, lining of maxillary sinus and the dura mater.

Maxillary artery, the largest of the two terminal branches, arises behind the neck of the mandible. This artery gives off alveolar branches to the teeth, gingiva, palatine glands, maxillary sinus, palatal mucosa, nasal cavity and branches to the muscles of mastication and the dura mater. The artery is usually divided into four divisions: (*a*) mandibular (*b*) pterygoid (*c*) maxillary (*d*) pterygopalatine.

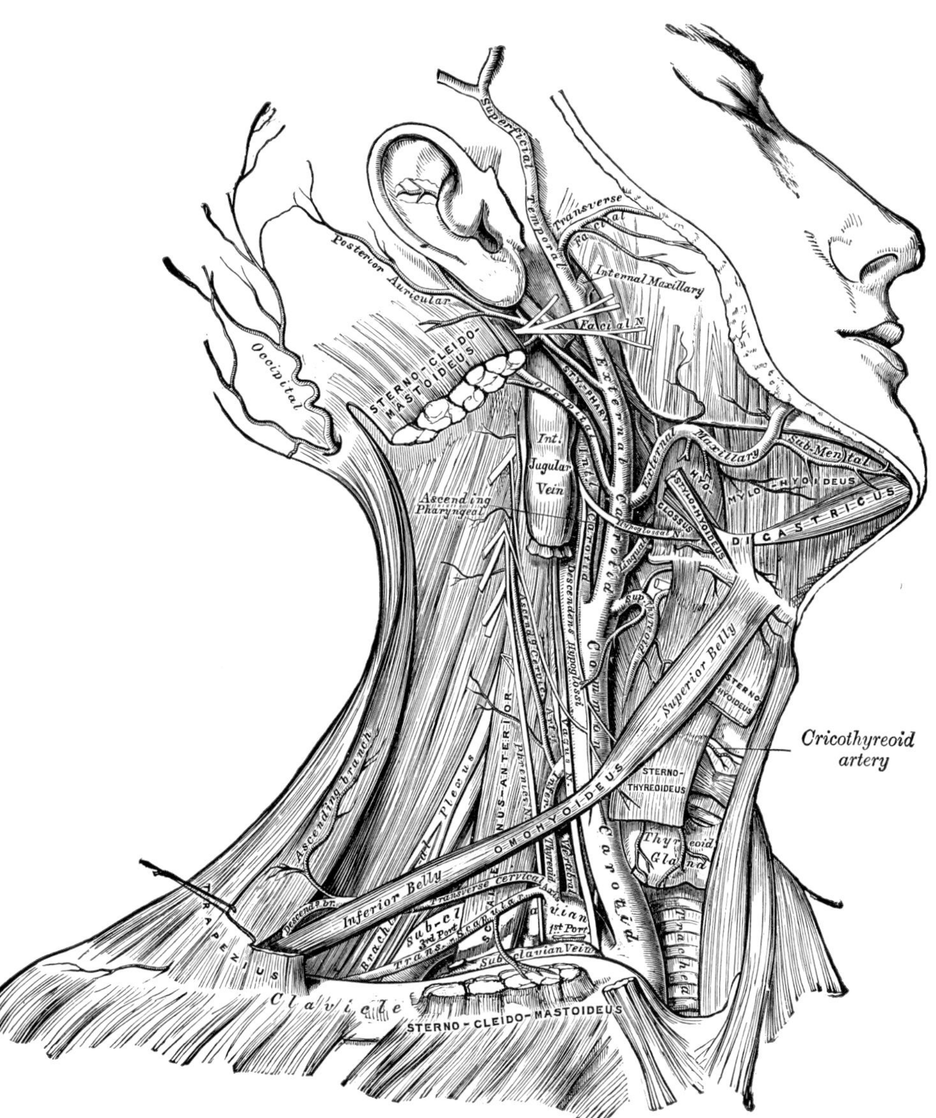

FIG. 2–13. Right side of the neck showing the carotid and subclavian arteries. *(Gray's Anatomy.)*

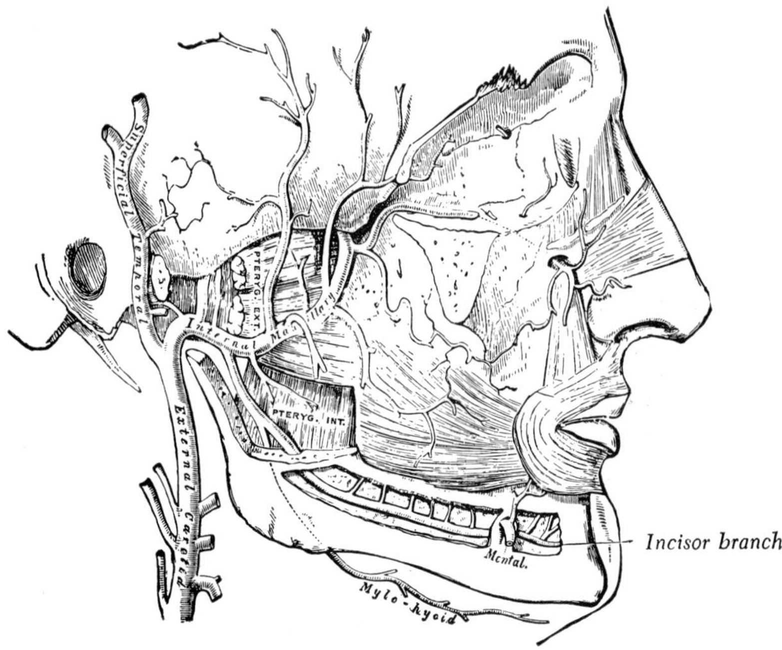

FIG. 2–14. Plan of branches of the maxillary artery. *(Gray's Anatomy.)*

Internal carotid artery supplies the anterior part of the brain, the eye and its appendages, and sends branches to the forehead and nose. At the base of the skull, the internal carotid artery enters the carotid canal and passes through it into the cranial cavity ending by dividing into the middle and the anterior cerebral arteries, and with the basilar artery form the "Circle of Willis" at the base of the brain.

Veins. The venous blood from the head and neck is drained almost entirely by the internal jugular vein which joins the subclavian vein to form the innominate vein. The two innominate (brachiocephalic) veins unite to form the superior vena cava.

The veins of the head and neck may be subdivided into three groups.

1. Veins of the exterior of the head and face.
2. Veins of the neck.
3. Veins of the brain and venous sinuses of the dura mater.

The blood, in returning from the teeth to the heart, is first taken up by the posterior and inferior dental veins, which in their course follow closely that of corresponding arteries. These veins, in conjunction with others, form the *pterygoid plexus.* From here the blood empties into the internal maxillary vein, then to the temporomaxillary vein which unites with the common facial vein and finally into the external jugular vein.

The Lymphatic System of the Head and Neck

As in all regions of the human body, lymph vessels and lymph nodes or glands are found in the head and neck. These are important because infection as well as malignant tumors may spread in lymph vessels.

The lymph system consists of a series of tubes (lymph vessels) leading to groups of solid bodies (nodes). Its function is to carry lymph and solid particles, not required by the tissues, from the tissues along lymphatic vessels, through lymphatic glands and finally along other vessels to the venous circulation at the root of the neck.

Lymphatic vessels are found in all tissues and are arranged into two groups:

1. *Superficial* beneath and draining the skin and mucous membranes.
2. *Deep* lymphatics.

The *thoracic duct* and the *right lymphatic duct* are the main lymphatic channels.

The mouth is well supplied with lymphatics which form rich networks of capillaries in the mucous membrane. Most of the lymphatic vessels from the mouth empty their contents into the cervical lymphatic glands.

The tonsils are lymphatic glands in close relationship with the mouth. The pharyngeal tonsil or adenoid tissue is located at the posterior wall of the nasal pharynx. The faucial tonsils are situated between the anterior pillars and posterior pillars of the fauces which are two pairs of muscles on either side of the opening leading from the mouth to the pharynx. The lingual tonsil is found at the base of the tongue. Some lymphoid tissue is found in the soft palate.

Knowledge of the regional coordinates of lymph nodes is of paramount importance in the therapy of inflammations and malignant tumors.

THE ORAL REGION AND ASSOCIATED STRUCTURES

The mouth (Fig. 2–15) is the entrance to the alimentary canal or digestive tube. The *digestive system* comprises that part of the body concerned with the preparation of food for assimilation. The alimentary canal may be divided into the following parts:

1. Mouth	Tongue Tonsils (Palatine) Salivary glands Teeth	4. Stomach
2. Pharynx		5. Small Intestine
3. Esophagus		6. Large Intestine

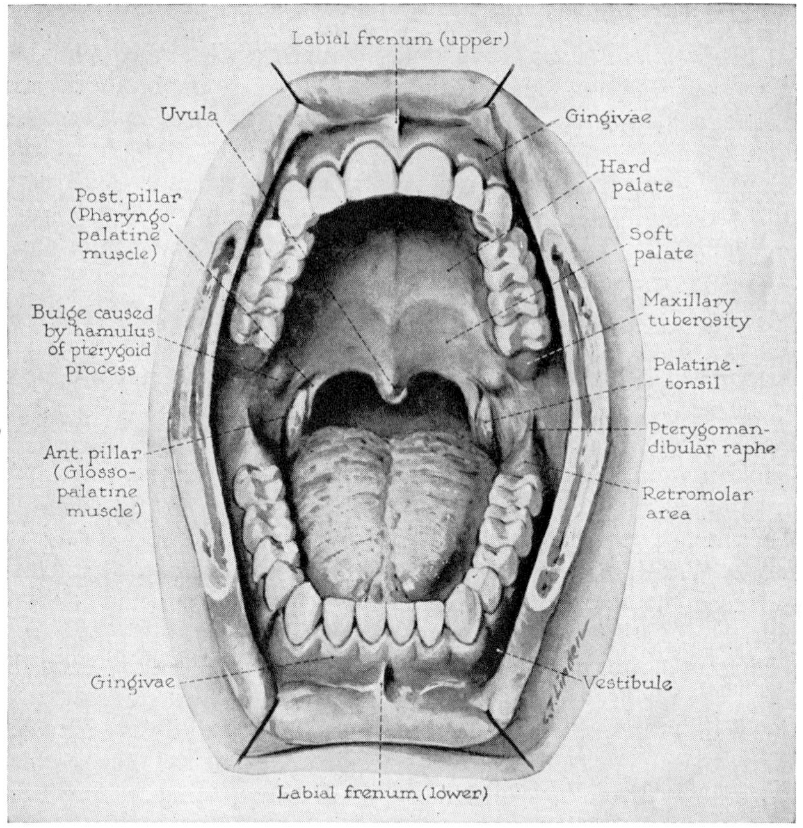

FIG. 2–15. The oral cavity. (From *Atlas of the Mouth,* by Massler and Schour. American Dental Association Bureau of Public Relations.)

Food undergoes two changes in the mouth: *(a)* a *mechanical one, mastication,* in which coarse food masses are ground into smaller pieces, and *(b)* a *chemical one,* in which digestive juices of the saliva cause certain changes in the chemical compounds of food.

Briefly then, the structures of the *oral cavity* to be studied are the maxillary and mandibular bones, lips, cheeks, tongue, facial muscles, pharynx, tonsils, teeth, supporting structures of the teeth, glands, blood and nerve supply to the oral regions, and the associated temporomandibular joint. All of these parts function together in *mastication, speech, respiration* and *deglutition.*

The Mouth

The mouth consists of two parts—the *vestibule* and the *mouth proper.* The vestibule is the narrow interval between the cheeks or lips and the teeth and gingiva, and communicates with the exterior through the orifice of the mouth. The mouth proper is limited laterally and in front by the alveolar arches and the teeth. The hard and soft palate forms the roof; the tongue and sublingual mucosa, the floor. The mouth is continuous with the *oropharynx* through the posterior opening called the *faucial isthmus* formed by the folds bounding the *palatine tonsil.*

The Lips (Labia)

The buccal orifice or entrance to the mouth is a transverse opening somewhat variable in extent, the extremities of which are known as the *corners* or *angles* of the mouth. It is bounded by two fleshy folds, the upper and lower lips (labia), the former usually being in the form of a double curve, coming together at the median line or center of the face and forming a tubercle (philtrum) while the latter is made up of a single curve extending from angle to angle. The lips are composed of muscles and glands, covered by skin on the outside and mucous membrane on the inside. The glands of the lips (labial glands) are located just under the mucous membrane.

The upper lip borders onto the nose and is separated from the cheek by a variable deep groove, *nasolabial groove,* which on either side starts at the wing of the nose and runs downward and laterally to pass at some distance from the corner of the mouth. In young individuals the lower lip has no boundary toward the cheek. Older people usually show a furrow extending from the corner of the mouth, in a curved arch medial to the nasolabial groove and extending toward the lower border of the mandible. It is known as the *labio marginal sulcus.*

The lower lip is separated from the chin proper by a more or less sharp and deep groove which is convex superiorly, the *labiomental groove.* The depth varies with the contour of the chin with each individual. The upper and lower lips are connected to each other at the corner of the mouth. The thin connecting fold, the *labial commissure,* is well visible when the mouth is opened and is a rather vulnerable area. *The red margin* of the lip is an intermediate zone; it is covered by a dry and nonglandular mucous membrane continuous with the moist mucosa of the vestibule. Its mucous membrane is translucent and transmits the color of the blood in the underlying capillaries. The lips are richly vascularized and are well supplied with sensory nerves. Under the skin of the lip is a layer of fatty subcutaneous tissue continuous with that of the face. The orbicularis oris muscle and many other associated facial muscle fibers insert into the skin of the lips. In the submucosa between the muscular layer and the mucous membrane lies an almost continuous layer of *labial glands.*

These small, nodular *mucous* glands, closely packed together, open through the mucous membrane by minute individual ducts. The mucous membrane, covered by stratified squamous epithelium, is continuous with that of the *gingiva.* At the midline a fold of mucous membrane, the *frenulum,* connects the mucous membrane of each lip with the corresponding gingiva.

The lips receive a rich blood supply from the labial branches of the *facial artery.* Their nerves are branches of the *infra-orbital* nerve for the upper lip and the *mental nerve* for the lower lip. The lymphatic vessels of the upper lip, and the lateral parts of the lower lip unite and pass to the *submandibular lymph nodes,* those vessels from the medial part of the lower lip descend through the chin to the *submental nodes.*

The Cheeks (Buccae)

The cheeks resemble the lips in their structure but have the *buccinator* muscle as their principal muscular component. The fatty subcutaneous tissue of the cheeks is very loose and transmits the ducts of the parotid gland. The *buccal pad of fat* is formed in the subcutaneous tissues. *Buccal glands,* similar in structure to but smaller than the labial glands, lie in the submucosa of the cheeks. The mucous membrane of the cheeks is reflected onto the gingiva. The external covering of the cheek is similar in structure to the skin covering other parts of the body.

The cheeks receive their blood supply through the *superior labial, inferior labial* and *transverse facial* branches of the *facial artery,* along with some branches of the *maxillary artery.*

The nerve supply reaches the cheeks through the buccal and infraorbital branches of the *facial nerve* and the buccal branches of the *mandibular nerve.*

The lymphatic drainage of the cheeks, gingiva, lower surface of the palate, and the anterior portion of the tongue pass to the *submandibular lymph nodes* and in turn drain to the *superior deep cervical nodes.*

Interior of the Mouth

The mouth proper is limited in front and at the sides by the lingual surfaces of all the teeth and their surrounding gingival tissue. Above it is limited by the roof of the mouth, the hard and soft palates, and below by the floor of the mouth, the tongue and the mucous membrane. Posteriorly, it communicates with the pharynx, the mucous membrane of the soft palate, merging with the mucous membrane of the pharynx.

For convenience of description, the interior of the mouth may be divided into a *superior portion* formed by the *hard palate, soft palate, the sixteen maxillary teeth* and the *muco-periosteum* (fused mucous membrane and periosteum) covering the oral surface of the bony palate and alveolar process and the *inferior portion* formed by the *tongue* and its muscles, the sixteen mandibular teeth and the mucous membrane which is reflected from the side of the tongue to the mandible where it is continuous with the gingiva. The right and left mylohyoid muscles form a diaphragm which stretches between the two halves of the mandible and the body of the hyoid bone.

Hard Palate. The bony framework of the hard palate (Fig. 2–16) forms the anterior two-thirds of the *roof of the mouth.* The posterior third, being a musculotendinous organ, called the "soft palate." The palate forms the *superior and posterosuperior* boundaries of the oral cavity, thus *separating* it from the nasal cavity and naso-pharynx. The palate is variably arched both anteroposteriorly and transversely, the transverse curve being more pronounced in the anterior portion.

The bony framework of the hard palate is formed by the union of the *palatal processes* of the two maxillae and the *horizontal processes*

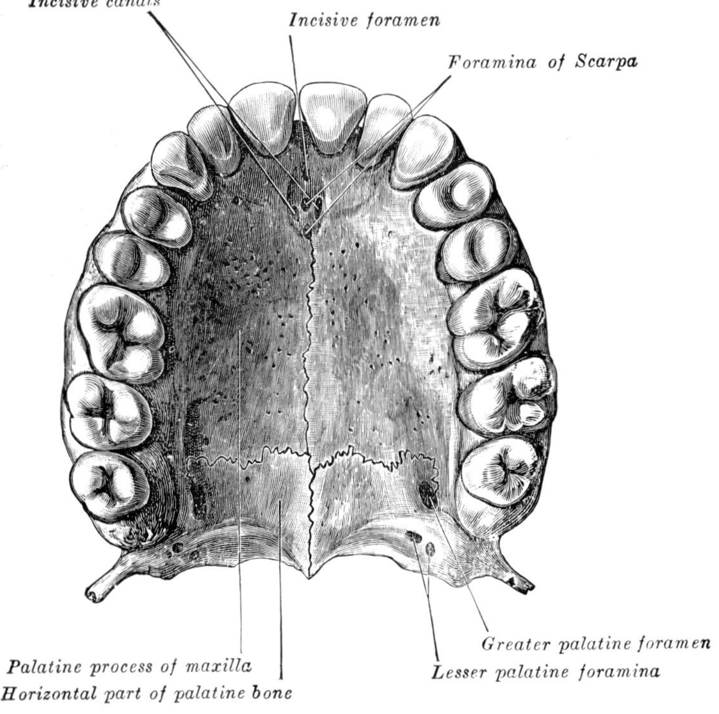

FIG. 2–16. The bony palate and alveolar arch. *(Gray's Anatomy.)*

of the two palatine bones. These bony structures also form the framework of the floor of the nasal cavity. This common bony wall is traversed near the midline anteriorly by the *incisive canal,* which transmits blood vessels and nerves from the mucous membrane of the nose to the mucous membrane of the roof of the mouth.

Usually one canal begins at each side of the midline on the upper or *nasal side* of the palate. Each of these canals then divides into two before reaching the oral side, where *four* canals open into a single midline fossa, the *incisive foramen.* Near the posterolateral angles of the palate, on each side, are located the *greater and lesser* palatine foramina for the transmission of the *greater and lesser palatine vessels and nerves.*

The oral surface of the bony palate is covered by mucoperiosteum which is very tough and adheres tightly to the bone. In the midline is a slight ridge, *the palatine raphi,* at the anterior end of which is a small elevation called *incisive papilla.* Running laterally from the interior part of the raphe are about six transverse ridges, *the transverse plicae or rugae.* The posterior border of the hard palate is continuous with the *soft palate.*

Blood Supply. Palatal branches of the maxillary artery.

Nerve Supply. Palatal branches from the nasopalatal nerve which arises from the sphenopalatal ganglion (Meckel's). All are sensory in function.

Soft Palate. The soft palate is continuous anteriorly with the hard palate. It ends posteroinferiorly in a *free margin,* which forms an arch with the *palatoglossal* and the *palatopharyngeal* folds on each side as its *pillars.* The *uvula,* greatly variable as to length and shape, hangs from the center of the free margin of the soft palate. A triangular space between the pillars on either side contains a small almond shaped body, *the palatine tonsil.* The space is known as the *tonsillar recess.*

The framework of the soft palate is formed by a strong, thin, fibrous sheet, known as the palatine aponeurosis, which is, at least in part, formed by the spread out tendons of the tensor veli palatini muscles. Also some of the thickness is made up of the palatine muscles, many mucous glands on the oral side, with mucous membrane covering both the oral and pharyngeal surfaces. The mass of glands extends forward onto the hard palate as far anteriorly as a line between the canine teeth.

Muscles of the Soft Palate

1. Levator palatine
2. Tensor veli palatine
3. Uvula

Fauces

1. Anterior wall Palatoglossus muscle
2. Posterior wall Palatopharyngeus muscle

Blood Supply

1. Superior palatal branches of the maxillary artery
2. Ascending pharyngeal branch of the external carotid
3. Palatal branches of the facial artery

Nerve Supply

1. Palatal branches of Meckel's ganglion
2. Glossopharyngeal nerve
3. Mandibular branch of the Trigeminal

The soft palate can be positioned as necessary for *swallowing, breathing* and *phonation* by the muscles that have been described. It can be brought into contact with the dorsum of the tongue, and can also be brought backward and upward against the wall of the pharynx to close off the nasopharynx during swallowing.

The Floor of the Mouth. The term "floor of the mouth" includes the structures which actually bound the cavity inferiorly such as the tongue, teeth and the mucous membrane which is reflected from the side of the tongue to the alveolar processes. It includes also the muscles and other structures which fill the interval between the mandible and the hyoid bone.

These structures include: (*a*) The right and left *mylohyoid muscles* form a diaphragm between the halves of the mandible and the hyoid bone, attaching along the mylohyoid line of the mandible. (*b*) Anterior belly of *digastric muscle* lies against the inferior surface of the mylohyoid muscle and extends from the digastric fossa to the hyoid bone and thence the posterior belly to mastoid notch of temporal bone. (*c*) *Stylohyoid* muscle lies closely to posterior belly of digastric and extends from the styloid process to the hyoid bone. (*d*) Right and left *genio-hyoid muscles* are on each side of the midline and lie on the superior surface of the mylohyoid muscle attaching at the *genial tubercles* of the mandible and extending to the hyoid bone.

The hyoid bone is hung in a muscular sling between the mandible and the stylomastoid area of temporal bone. All these muscles can elevate the hyoid bone and make the floor of the mouth quite mobile.

The hyoid bone is depressed and pulls the floor of the mouth downward by the infrahyoid muscles which extend between the hyoid bone above and the sternum, clavicle, and scapula below.

The mucosal boundary of the floor of the mouth consists of the mucous membrane which is reflected from the side of the tongue to the mandible, where it is continuous with the gingiva.

Blood Supply. Branches of the external carotid artery

Nerve Supply. Mandibular branch of 5th cranial, facial and cervical nerves.

The Oral Mucosa and Gingiva. A membrane is a sheet of tissue used to *cover* or *line* surfaces or to divide organs into lobes. Membranes are *epithelial* or *fibrous* in structure. *Mucous membranes* are of epithelial origin and have epithelium on the *free surface* and a layer of connective tissue called *lamina propria,* beneath. They line the *alimentary* canal (digestive), the *respiratory* (air passages), the *reproductive* and *urinary* tracts all of which open to the outside. The cells in the mucous membrane secrete mucus, absorb food material (in the intestine) and protect (mouth) underlying structures. Mucous membranes in different parts of the body differ so that their structure varies to suit the functions required. It is well to remember that the surface of the mucous membrane lining is always moist and smooth.

The oral mucous membrane lining the mouth is *heavier* and more *resistant* to injury than the mucosa of more protected cavities. Its structure enables the oral mucosa to withstand the wear and tear of ordinary oral functions and resist bacterial infection. The oral mucous membrane is composed of a combination of epithelial tissue and connective tissue. The epithelial tissue is composed of stratified squamous cells and in some parts of the mouth the surface epithelial cells form a tough layer called the keratin layer. The connective tissue portion or *sub-mucosa* is composed chiefly of fibrous connective tissue in which are blood vessels, nerves and glands. This layer of tissue of the oral mucosa varies in thickness at different parts of the mouth. Oral mucosa divides into regions and varies throughout the mouth according to thickness and attachment: (1) *Masticatory mucosa* covering the gingiva and hard palate having a thick firm hornified layer firmly attached. (2) *Lining mucosa* covering the remainder of the oral cavity except the dorsum of the tongue, is movable, elastic and no hornification of surface cells. (3) *Specialized mucosa* limited to the dorsal and base of the tongue.

THE GINGIVA is that part of the firm oral mucous membrane that surrounds the necks of the teeth and covers the alveolar process of the maxilla and mandible.

The gingiva can be divided into the (*a*) *free gingiva* and (*b*) the *attached gingiva.*

1. *Free gingiva.* Rests on the *enamel* of the young and the *cementum* of the old. It is very thin and knife edge and it may be divided into two parts.

(a) Marginal on labial and lingual.

The gingival line and cervical line should not be confused, the former referring to the free gingival margin of the gingivae which is variable, while the latter refers to a fixed dental anatomic landmark, the enamel border.

(b) Papillary or interdental gingiva located in the embrasure. (Smooth structure and keratinized.)

The gingiva also fills the space between the teeth (interproximal space) and is known as the gingival papilla. Positive contact of adjacent teeth in the arch protects the important gingival papilla provided the proximal surface form of each tooth in contact is also correct. According to Wheeler,[16] the teeth possess certain fundamental curvatures that serve to give proper degree of protection to the investing tissues that surround the teeth. These protective contours are physiologic, for any slight increase or decrease in dimensions at vulnerable areas would seriously affect the future of the tooth.

2. *Free gingival groove.* Dividing line between the *free gingiva* and the *attached.* Runs nearly parallel to the margin at a distance of 0.5 to 1.5 mm.

3. *Attached gingiva* (keratinized). Immovable and anchored to the underlying cementum and alveolar process. Extends from the *free gingival fold* to the *muco-gingival junction.* The tissue *is normally pink* sometimes with a grayish tinge characterized by high connective tissue papilla elevating the epithelium, the surface of which appears *stippled.* Stippled surface is a functional adaptation to mechanical impacts.

4. *Alveolar mucosa.* The attached gingiva ends in a *scalloped line* and the oral mucosa below this *muco-gingival junction* is *red, shiny* and *loosely attached* to the underlying tissue. The epithelium is non-keratinized.

The epithelial portion of the gingiva which is in direct contact with the surface of the tooth is called the *epithelial attachment.*

It normally extends from the bottom of the gingival crevice toward the cemento-enamel junction and often passes the latter.

It is characterized by a uniform width of stratified squamous epithelium which resembles closely that of the oral cavity.

5. *Gingival crevice.* The gingival crevice is the trough-like depression that results from the separation at the gingival crest of the epithelial attachment from the enamel surface. It is thus bounded on one side by the enamel surface and on the other side by the epithelium of the crevice. The apical end is called the bottom of the gingival crevice, and is limited by the level of the intact epithelial attachment. Ideally the crevice is very shallow or absent.

Function

1. Protects the underlying structures.
2. Attached firmly to the teeth at the bottom of the gingival sulcus.
3. Tissue is firm, tough and resists the forces of mastication.

Clinical Considerations. The intactness of the epithelium of the gingival sulcus and epithelial attachment is important to good periodontal conditions.

The characteristic form and color of the gingiva are altered by inflammation and other disease processes, and the changes are used as criteria for the diagnosis of periodontal disease. It is, *therefore,* essential that the normal appearance be remembered.

The Tongue. The tongue is a muscular organ composed of a root, a body and an anterior free extremity or tip. It is the principal organ of the sense of taste, and an important organ of speech; it also assists in the mastication and deglutition of food. The tongue is composed of both extrinsic (outward) and intrinsic (inward) muscles covered with mucous membrane.

The extrinsic muscles originate from the base of the skull, hyoid bone, and the mandible. They are the *hyoglossus, geniohyoglossus,* and *styloglossus.* The intrinsic muscles which make up the bulk of the tongue are two in number, the *superior lingual* and *inferior lingual,* with many fibers running transversely between the two. The under or inferior surface of the tongue is attached to the floor of the mouth by this membrane, the frenulum. The base of the tongue is attached to the hyoid bone and to the muscles of the pharynx.

The dorsum of the tongue (upper surface or that facing the roof of the mouth) is convex and contains papillae. These are composed of connective tissue covered by epithelium. They are thickly distributed on the anterior portion giving it a characteristic rough surface. There are three varieties; two are most important (*a*) *Circumvallate* papillae which are situated on the back part of the tongue, and arranged in the form of a letter V inverted. Usually they are from eight to twelve in number. (*b*) *Filiform* papillae are the smallest and most numerous. At the base of these papillae are located the taste buds, the end organs of the gustatory sense which are chiefly responsible for the sensation of taste.

On both margins of the tongue, the mucous membrane is thinner and for the most part devoid of papillae. On the posterior part of each margin, a variable number of vertical folds may be seen. These are called *"folia"* or *"foliate papillae."*

The posterior or pharyngeal part of the tongue is covered by a smooth mucous membrane overlying many nodules of lymphoid tissue *"the lingual tonsils."*

The receptor organs for the sense of taste, the *taste buds* are located in the epithelium of the tongue, soft palate, pharynx and epiglottis. The greatest number are located in the lining of the furrows surrounding the *circumvallate papillae.*

Nerve supply to the tongue is both motor and sensory through the hypoglossus (cranial 12th). Sensory through the *lingual* branch of the chorda tympani and the glossopharyngeal (9th cranial).

Blood supply is furnished by the lingual artery, a branch of the *external carotid.* Near the tip of the tongue this artery is called the *deep lingual* or *ranine artery.*

Lymphatic drainage of the tongue comes from a rich plexus of lymph vessels under the mucous membrane which drain into the submandibular, submental, and deep cervical lymph nodes.

The Pharynx. The *pharynx* (Fig. 2–17) is a musculomembranous tube-shaped cavity extending from the base of the skull to the level of the sixth cervical vertebra, where it becomes continuous with the *esophagus.* The pharynx lies in front of the cervical part of the vertebral column but behind the nasal and oral cavities and the larynx. It is about six inches in length and is divided into three parts. The anterior wall is incomplete because of wide openings with the *nasal, oral* and *laryngeal* cavities. Also found within the pharynx are the openings of the *auditory tubes* (Eustachian) which connect to the middle ear and are frequently blocked by the *adenoids* or *pharyngeal tonsils.*

The *nasopharynx* lies behind the nasal cavities and has two openings or *"choanae"* into the nose. The openings into these *auditory tubes* lie on the lateral walls. It becomes closed off from the oral pharynx when the soft palate is raised during swallowing.

The *oral pharynx* lies behind the pharyngeal surface of the dorsum of the tongue. The oral cavity communicates with the oral pharynx between the anterior pillars of the fauces. The mouth is closed off from the pharynx when the soft palate lies against the dorsum of the tongue. The *palatine tonsils* are located on the lateral walls. The oral pharynx is surrounded by the superior and middle constrictor muscles.

The *laryngeal pharynx* lies behind the epiglottis, the laryngeal openings and the cricoid cartilage. Inferiorly, the walls of the laryngeal pharynx continue into the walls of the *esophagus.* The *middle* and *inferior* constrictor muscles surround the laryngeal pharynx. The *hyoid bone* is an important element in the pharyngeal structure. Much of the framework of the lateral and posterior walls of the pharynx is formed by the pharyngeal musculature which is composed of an outer and inner layer. These layers are not completely separable throughout since in some areas they are definitely intermingled.

The *outer layer* is arranged in a somewhat circular fashion and is made up of the *three constrictor* muscles of the pharynx, namely the *superior, middle* and *inferior* pharyngeal constrictors which overlap each other from below upward.

The *inner layer,* which falls far short of being complete, is arranged more nearly longitudinally. It is composed of the *stylopharyngeus, palatopharyngeus* and the *salpingopharyngeus,* plus some other variable and irregular bundles of muscle fibers. In the act of swallowing, the constrictor muscles direct the passage of food downward into the esophagus. The other muscles assist the drawing of the larynx upward and forward out of the direct line of passage of food.

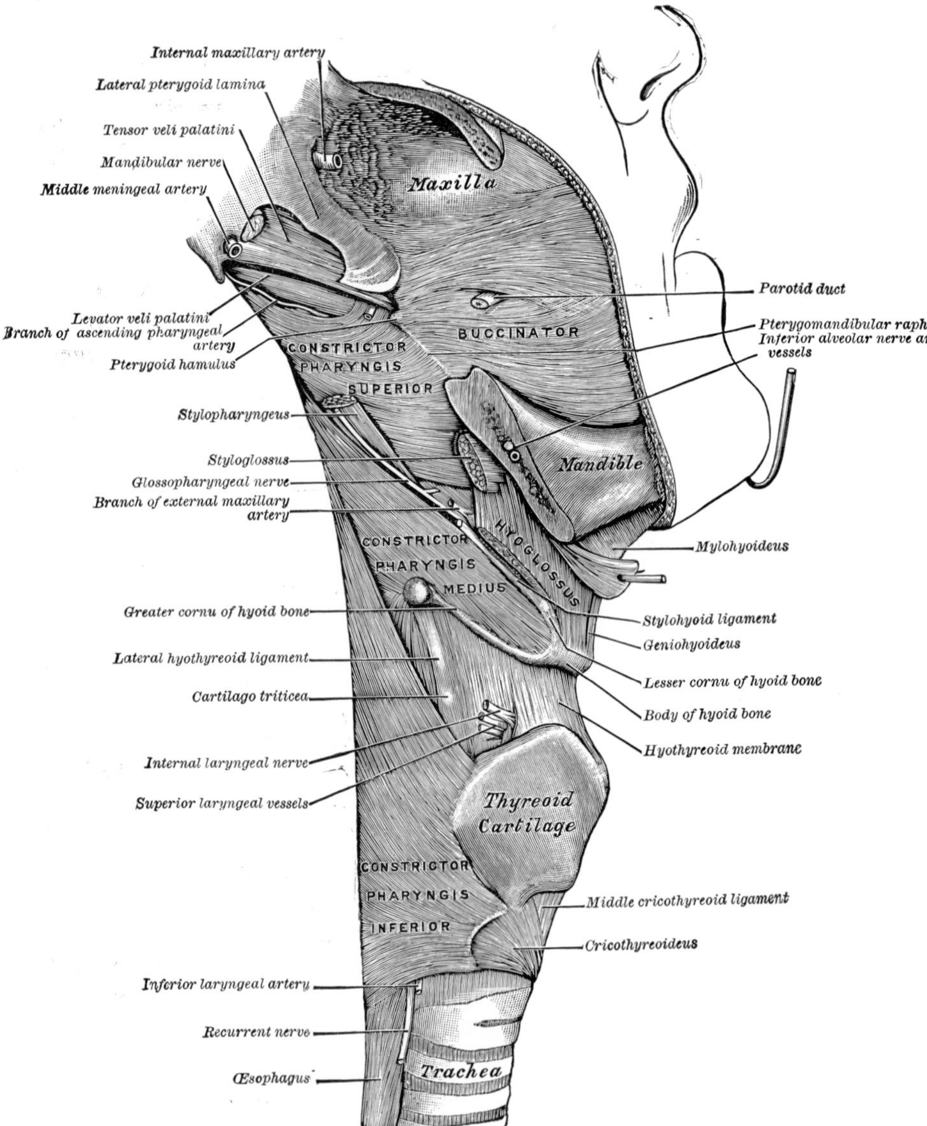

FIG. 2–17. The buccinator and muscles of the pharynx. *(Gray's Anatomy.)*

Blood supply is from ascending pharyngeal and superior thyroid branches of the external carotid artery.

Nerve supply is from branches of the maxillary, facial, glossopharyngeal, vagus and hypoglossal cranial nerves.

Lymphatic drainage enters the deep cervical lymph nodes.

The Salivary Glands. Three pairs of large salivary glands (Fig. 2–18) communicate with the mouth and pour their secretion into its cavity; they are the *parotid, submandibular* and *sublingual.* Saliva is the term applied to the accumulated secretory and excretory products discharged by the salivary glands into the oral cavity. The saliva is the first of many digestive fluids to act upon the food during mastication.

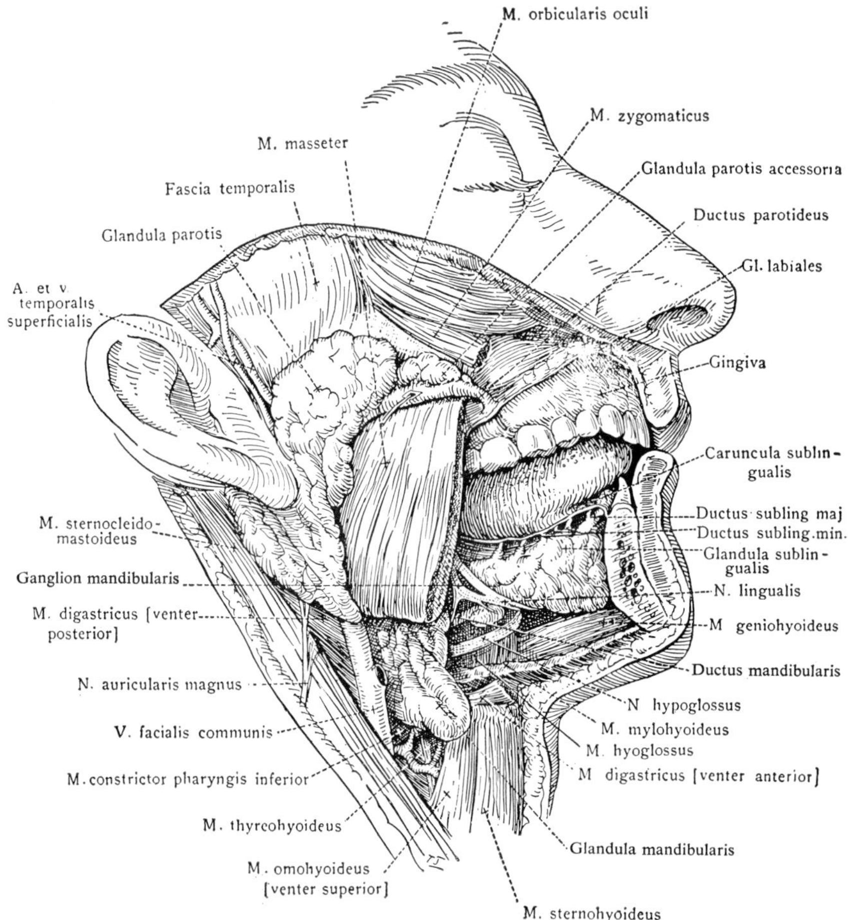

FIG. 2–18. The salivary glands in a dissection of the right side of the face. *(Gray's Anatomy.)*

The parotid glands, one on either side, are located below and in front of the ears. Their ducts, called Stenson's, open into the mouth opposite the maxillary molar teeth.

The submandibular glands are located below the floor of the mouth in the region of the bicuspid and molar teeth. The ducts from these glands enter the mouth on either side of the frenulum of the tongue.

The sublingual glands are very small and lie in the sublingual fossa of the mandible. Their ducts also open into the mouth on either side of the frenulum of the tongue. The ducts of both the submandibular and sublingual glands are known as Wharton's ducts.

The Tonsils. The name "tonsil" is commonly applied to the small masses of lymphoid tissue located in the oral cavity. They consist of lymph node groups bound together with fibrous tissue covered by a distinct fibrous capsule over which is mucous membrane. The surface of the tonsil is marked by openings leading to small pockets or crypts. In the head and neck, the tonsils lie in a ring supposedly guarding the entrance of the respiratory and digestive tubes. Waldeyer first described this ring of tonsillar tissue.

The tonsils which comprise this ring are: (1) The *pharyngeal tonsils* a mass of lymphatic tissue in the lamina propria of the mucous membrane lining the dorsal wall of the nasopharynx. When this mass is enlarged it is called *adenoids,* and it may obstruct the air passage of the auditory tube to the middle ear to such an extent that the child breathes through the mouth. (2) The *palatine tonsils,* invariably referred to as "the tonsils," are located on the sides of the posterior walls of the oral cavity between the pillars of the fauces. The palatine tonsils are oval, flat bodies much larger than the pharyngeal tonsil. Very little of the oral surfaces of these tonsils can be seen as they lie behind triangular folds of the mucous membrane which lie between the pillars of the fauces. (3) The *lingual tonsils* are located on the posterior portion of the tongue, between the circumvallate papillae and the epiglottis. The function of the various tonsils is to act as filters for contents of the lymphatic vessels and paranasal sinuses.

The Paranasal Sinuses. These are pneumatic areas in the *frontal, ethmoid, sphenoid* and *maxillary bones* which are lined by mucous membrane continuous with that of the nasal cavity. Beginning in the fourth fetal month, they develop as evaginations of the nasal mucosa which invade the bones surrounding the nasal cavities. Absorption of bone around the invading mucosal sacs establishes the air spaces known as the paranasal sinuses; their areas of evagination remain as the apertures by which communication is retained between the nasal cavity and the sinuses. Only the maxillary sinus exhibits a definite cavity at birth. The other sinuses are rudimentary until puberty, after which they develop to adult size. The principal value of the paranasal sinuses appears to be as resonating chambers for the voice and a means of lightening the bones of the head. The *maxillary sinuses* are the largest of the paranasal sinuses. Each maxillary sinus lies just external to the nasal wall and extends up to the orbital process of the frontal bone. Its floor is formed by the alveolar process of the *maxilla* and is usually marked by conical elevations over the roots of the first and second molars. The drainage of the maxillary sinus is very poor in the erect position. The branches of the *maxillary artery* and the *maxillary division* of the trigeminal nerve supply the lining of the maxillary sinus.

The Temporomandibular Joint. This is composed of the temporomandibular fossa, a depression in the temporal bone just anterior to each external auditory opening in which the condyles of the mandible are positioned and on the adjacent bony protuberance termed the articular tubercle. On opening the mouth, the condyles glide forward from their position in the anterior part of the fossa to the posterior aspect of the articular tubercle. The joint then is a combination hinge (ginglymoid) and sliding (arthrodia) movement of the condyles forward.

A loose fibrous sac, the *capsular ligament* (Fig. 2–19*A*) completely encloses the joint area, attached above to the perimeter of the fossa and articular tubercle and below around the necks of the condyles. The external portion of the capsular ligament is called the *external lateral ligament,* which offers lateral support to the joint. The synovial membranes line the capsule and form two loose sacs containing synovial fluid. Suspended horizontally from the inner surface of the capsule is the oval-shaped articular disk. This thin, fibrous plate divides the temporal fossa into an upper and lower cavity. The upper cavity is between the disk and temporal bone, the lower is between the disk and condyles. When the mouth is opened the condyle moves on the disk as the disk glides forward (Fig. 2–19*D*) on the articular tubercle. Other ligaments suspending the mandible and holding the condyles in the temporal fossa are the *sphenomandibular,* which gives medial support, and the *stylomandibular,* which gives posterior support. (Also see Muscles of Mastication.)

The movements of the joint are exceedingly complicated and have been placed in five main groups: (1) depression, (2) elevation, (3) protraction, (4) retraction, and (5) right and left lateral movements.

Blood Supply. Blood supply to the joint is derived from the *temporal, middle meningeal* and *ascending pharyngeal* branches of the *maxillary* artery.

Nerve Supply. (See for Muscles of Mastication.)

Lymphatics. Lymphatic drainage of the joint is to the *deep parotid* nodes.

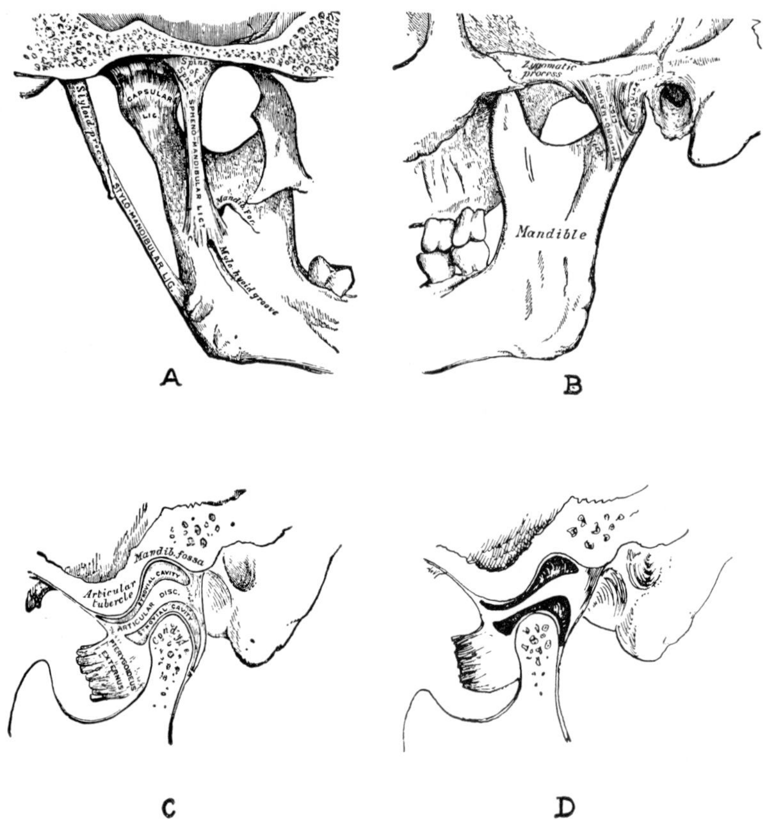

FIG. 2–19. Articulation of the mandible. *A,* Lateral aspect. *B,* Medial aspect. *C,* Section with condyle head in posterior position. *D,* Section with condyle head in forward position. (*A, B, C, Gray's Anatomy.*)

THE ANATOMY OF THE TEETH

Dental anatomy is a basic subject, necessary for the proper understanding of other dental subjects. It is important for the hygienist to have certain fundamental facts of dental anatomy at her disposal when she enters the clinical phase of her career.

Teeth possess certain fundamental anatomical curvatures and form that give proper protection to the periodontium by protecting the marginal gingiva from food impactions accumulating around the necks of the teeth. When well-formed teeth are in normal alignment with normal gingival attachment, they are quite self-cleansing, and the form of the teeth contributes toward proper dental hygiene.

The study of dental anatomy includes tooth morphology, the anatomical differences between the primary and permanent dentitions, the variability in size of human teeth, and the variation in root lengths which are of clinical importance.

The Teeth

Human teeth, the hard bodies found in the mouth, are derived from the ectoderm and mesoderm. They are attached to the skeleton, but do not form part of it. Teeth have one active function, that of mastication of food, and two passive functions: first, aiding in the production of sound and speech and second, adding to the esthetic harmony of the face. The teeth of man are classified as heterodont, meaning that all teeth of man are different in shape.

Mastication, however, is one of the remaining functions that teeth have come to serve. The teeth have served as weapons of combat. This persists today in the canines of the carnivora. The teeth have served as tools for securing food and building, as seen in the beaver. For long ages, the teeth served only for prehension of food. Thus, it will be seen that function determines the form of the tooth and its position in the jaw. Teeth concerned with obtaining food are restricted to the anterior part of the mouth, such as the tusks of the elephant or the gnawing chisels of the rodents. Teeth specialized as weapons take their position at the angles of the mouth where anchorage is the greatest. Those teeth used for mastication are always in the back of the mouth closest to the articulation joint where crushing power may be exerted.

In the lower vertebrates the teeth are usually homodont, that is, they are more or less similar to one another, as in reptiles. In the great majority of mammals they are heterodont, being of different forms and arranged in series.

Dentitions

The teeth of man are diphyodont, *i.e.*, he possesses two sets of teeth. The first set is known as the primary or deciduous dentition. The second, supposedly to serve man the remainder of his life, is known as the permanent dentition.

The primary dentition usually numbers twenty teeth; the permanent dentition thirty two teeth. The teeth of each dentition are originally arranged in a definite pattern. They form dental arches the size and shape of which vary with the individual. According to their original function, the teeth of man are divided into three groups: incisors to cut the food, cuspids and bicuspids (pre-molars) to seize and tear the food and molars to grind the food.

The superior dental arch (Fig. 2–20) which is attached to the maxillary bones is called a maxillary dental arch, and the teeth are called maxillary teeth.

The inferior dental arch (Fig. 2–21) is attached to the mandible and contains the mandibular teeth.

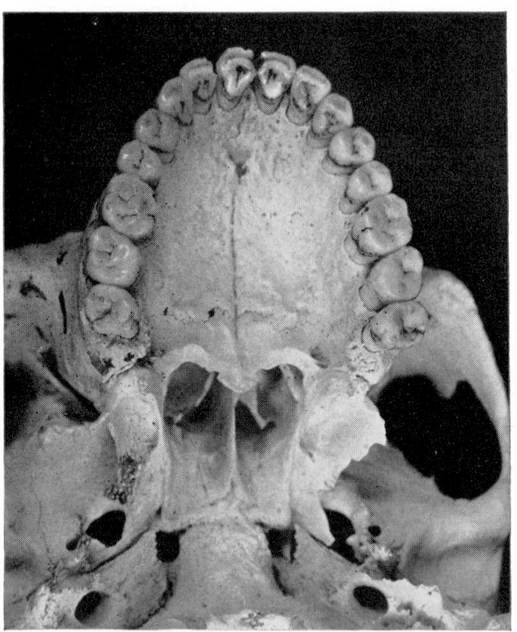

FIG. 2–20. The maxillary arch with the permanent teeth in position.

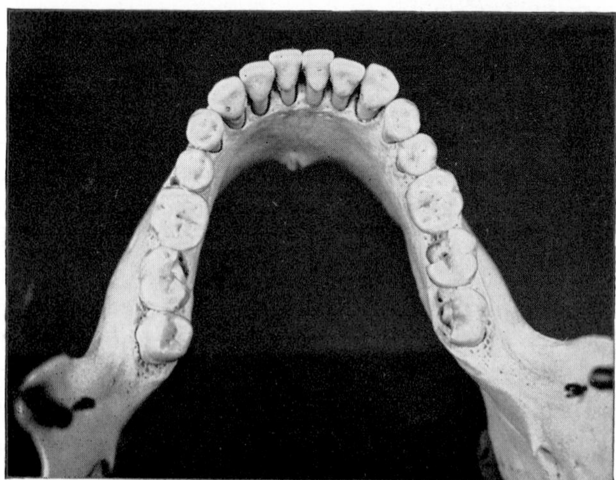

FIG. 2–21. The mandible with permanent teeth in position.

The teeth of the primary dentition on either side of the median line are named in order:

1. Central Incisor
2. Lateral Incisor
3. Cuspid
4. First Molar
5. Second Molar

The teeth of the permanent dentition are named:

1. Central Incisor
2. Lateral Incisor
3. Cuspid
4. First Bicuspid
5. Second Bicuspid
6. First Molar
7. Second Molar
8. Third Molar

The increase in number in the permanent set of teeth is accounted for by the fact that there are three molars on each side, instead of two as found in the primary dentition. All three permanent molars erupt posteriorly to the primary molars. The primary molars are replaced by teeth known as the bicuspids.

Collectively, the central and lateral incisors and the cuspids are referred to as the anterior teeth, and all the teeth posterior to the cuspids are called posterior teeth.

Dental Formula

A dental formula is a symbolic denotation of a dentition. The denomination of each tooth is represented by an initial letter (I, C, PM, M); each letter is followed by a horizontal line, and the number of each type of tooth goes above the line for the maxillary and below the line for the mandibular. The formula includes one side only:

The primary formula of man is: $I\frac{2}{2}\,C\frac{1}{1}\,M\frac{2}{2} = 10$

The permanent formula for man is: $I\frac{2}{2}\,C\frac{1}{1}\,PM\frac{2}{2}\,M\frac{3}{3} = 16$

Premolars or bicuspids have now been added to the formula, two upper and two lower.

Another system which is used extensively records the primary teeth from 1 to 20, beginning with the maxillary right second molar as tooth No. 1, and ending with the maxillary left second molar as tooth No. 10. The mandibular left second molar is tooth No. 11, continuing to the mandibular right second molar as tooth No. 20. This system can also apply to the permanent dentition. The maxillary right third molar tooth is No. 1, proceeding to the maxillary left third molar which is No. 16. The mandibular left third molar tooth is No. 17, and finally, the mandibular right third molar is tooth No. 32.

Occlusion

The teeth are arranged in two opposing series; one is fixed (maxillary) and the other movable (mandibular). Each series is made up of sixteen components arranged in two curving arches. *(See* Figs. 2–20 and 2–21.) Normally, the individual teeth of one arch do not meet those of the other in an end-to-end arrangement, but are dovetailed between each other. This brings broad surfaces in contact, instead of points. There are more than a hundred surfaces, known as "inclined planes," and it is the sliding together of their surfaces during mastication, in shear-like fashion, that comminutes the food for digestion (Fig. 2–22).

Normal tooth form and proper alignment of the inclined planes of the teeth when the jaws are closed is known as normal occlusion. This is the ideal, as will be seen in Figure 2–22, from which many individual and abnormal variations may occur. In centric occlusal relation of the normal denture *(when the teeth are in occlusion and at rest)* each tooth of one arch is in occlusal contact with portions of two others in the opposing arch, with the exception of the mandibular central incisors and the maxillary third molars. Each of these exceptions has only one antagonist in the opposing jaw. It is very important to

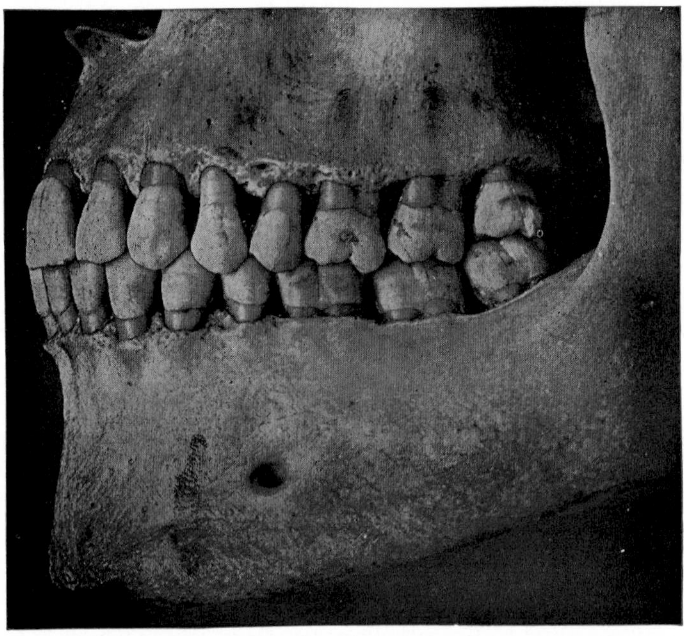

FIG. 2–22. Normal occlusion. Lateral aspect.

remember that the ultimate result of the loss of teeth means a gradual breakdown of the dental mechanism. The continuation of this breakdown ends in complete destruction through mechanical and pathologic changes such as migration of adjoining teeth, destruction of contact relations of the teeth in the same arch, changes of occlusal relations with teeth in the opposing arch, and also causes elongation of the tooth in the opposing arch immediately above or below the space left by the absent tooth (Fig. 2–23).

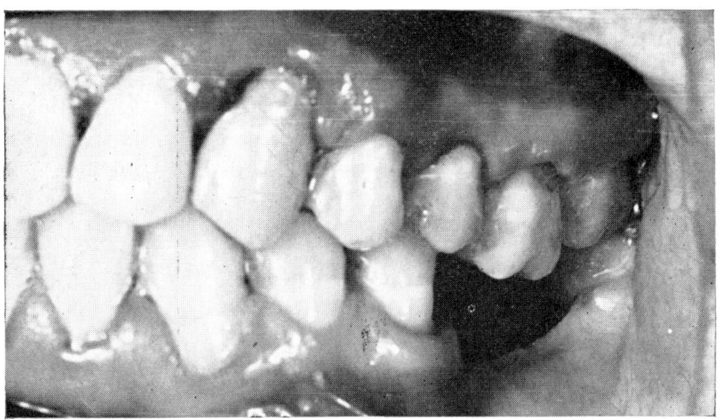

FIG. 2–23. Elongation of maxillary first molar by the loss of mandibular molar support.

Adequate mastication of food is an important function in the maintenance of optimum health of the individual. Anatomic characteristics of the teeth deflect food during mastication protecting the marginal gingiva, which insures the very life and stability of the tooth itself.

Contours of the teeth most prominently developed are on those surfaces over which food is normally propelled with the greatest force; namely, the buccal surfaces of the lower bicuspids and molars, labial surfaces of the lower incisors and the lingual surfaces of the upper teeth. Anatomic relationships of the adjoining teeth provide protection of the interdental gingival tissue by the interdental contact surfaces when the teeth are in normal approximal relationship (Fig. 2–22). The functions of the interdental embrasures formed by the interproximal contours of the teeth adjoining one another allow for the flow of food away from the occlusal surfaces of the teeth and the gingival tissues.

By careful observation, the student will see how the anatomical form and alignment of teeth contribute to the proper dental hygiene, as well as the function of mastication.

Anatomically, the tooth is divided into the crown and the root. The anatomical crown is covered by enamel, the anatomical root by cementum. The crown and root join at the cemento-enamel junction, also called the cervical line, which may be easily seen on a specimen tooth (Fig. 2–24). The cervical line is a fixed anatomic marking separating the enamel-covered crown from the root. The cervical line differs from the gingival line. Clinically, that portion of the tooth that is exposed to the oral fluids is called the clinical crown.

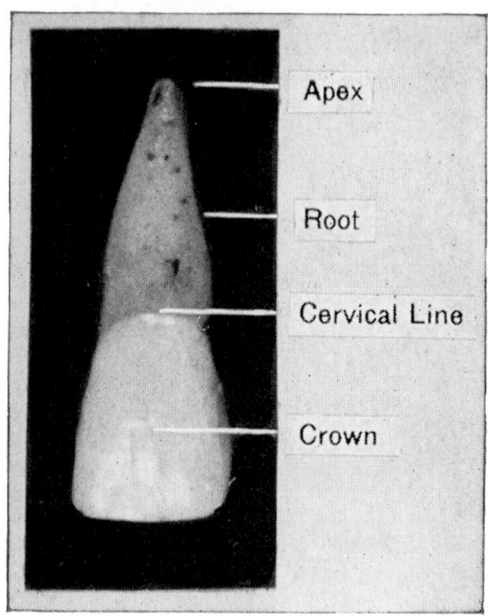

FIG. 2–24. Maxillary central incisor. Labial aspect.

In a cross-section, it may be seen that the main bulk of the tooth is composed of dentin (Fig. 2–25). Also, the section shows a pulp chamber which is within the crown and a pulp canal which is within the root. These are known collectively as the pulp cavity which normally contains the pulp tissue.

The tooth proper is composed of four tissues, three calcified tissues and one soft tissue as follows (*See* Fig. 2–25):

(1) *Enamel.* This smooth, hard substance covers the dentine on the anatomical crowns of the teeth of man, certain mammals, reptiles and fish. There are two types of enamel occurring in the vertebrate kingdom: (1) prismatic (man) and (2) tubular (fishes, rodents). It is the hardest tissue in the animal kingdom and contains a very small percentage of organic matter. In the normal human adult, the enamel contains less than 1 per cent organic matter. In some of the lower vertebrates, the enamel is entirely absent from the teeth.

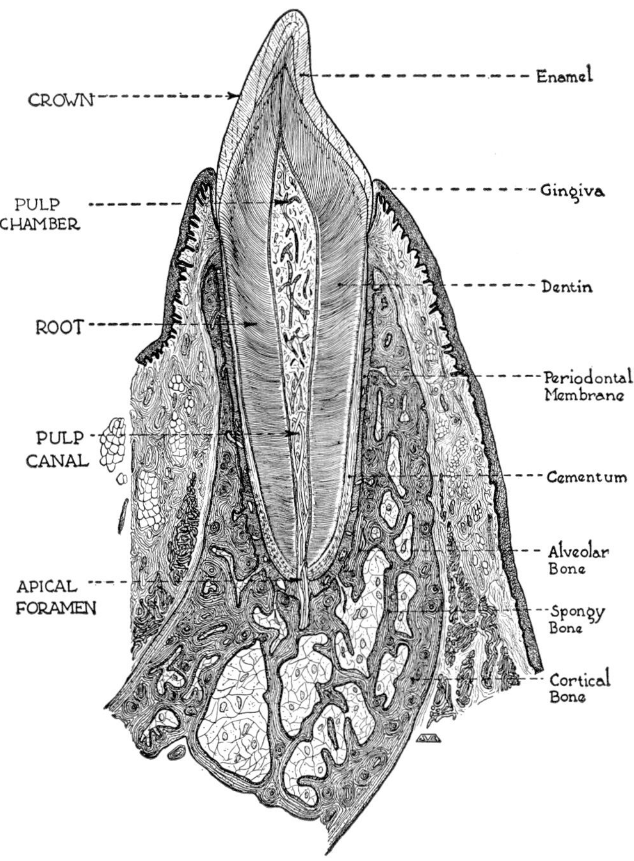

FIG. 2–25. Diagrammatic representation of the dental tissues. (Schour, *Noyes' Oral Histology and Embryology*.)

The functions of enamel are to resist the abrasion of mastication and protect the underlying dentin which it depends upon for support. The enamel in man is thickest over the molar cusps and incisal edges and gradually thins down to a very thin edge at the neck of the tooth. Hopewell-Smith[9] gave the following measurements: over the incisal edges of the incisors the enamel is 2 mm. thick, over the cusps of bicuspids 2.3 mm., and over the cusps of the molars 2.6 mm.

(2) *Dentin.* Dentin is calcified connective tissue penetrated by definitely arranged small canals which radiate from the pulp to the enamel. It forms the greatest bulk of the tooth and determines its morphological form. Also, it is the natural boundary of the dental pulp.

Dentin gives the tooth elastic strength. The enamel, being hard and brittle, is dependent upon the elastic support of the dentin. Normal dentin is yellowish in color, acellular and avascular. Tomes lists four variations of dentin.

(3) *Cementum.* This tissue is a slightly modified form of bone and arranged in layers around the tooth root. Cementum in man is confined to the roots of the teeth. It forms a continuous investment of the dentin, but in many animals, it forms the cementing substance between the enamel plates, as in the elephant and the horse. Cementum may in some cases overlap the enamel at the neck of the tooth or just meet the enamel, and in others a space of uncovered dentin may be present. In some mammals, the cementum may cover the entire crown before the tooth comes into use.

At the enamel border, it is a very thin layer about 20 μ thick and becomes thicker as it reaches the apex of the root. The chief function is to attach the tooth to the connective tissue fibers of the periodontal membrane which extends from the cementum to the bone and surrounding tissue thus supporting and making the tooth functional. The cementum is one of the most important of the dental tissues.

(4) *Pulp.* Connective tissue remains of the formative organ of the dentin provides the nervous and vascular supply to the dentin. The pulp is located in the center of the dentin in the pulp cavity. Extension of the pulp incisally or occlusally, corresponding with growth centers, are called pulpal horns, and the constricted portion in the root of the tooth, the pulp canal.

In teeth of continuous growth, the pulp grows actively throughout the life of the animal. However, in human teeth, the pulp becomes progressively smaller with age as development of dentin continues through the life of the tooth. It may become entirely calcified in old age.

The *crown* of an incisor tooth presents an incisal edge or ridge; on the cuspids there is a single cusp, and on bicuspids and molars there are two or more cusps.

The *root* portion of the tooth may present a single root with one apex as in normal anterior teeth and some bicuspids; or multiple roots as found in all molars and some bicuspids.

The teeth are made functional by the implantation of their roots in the bony processes of the maxilla and mandible which immediately surround the roots of the teeth as they erupt. In general, animals in the lower end of the vertebrate sub-kingdom all have teeth which are situated well above the jaw. As we rise, through the vertebrates to mammals and man, the teeth are gradually implanted lower in the substance of the jaws.

There are four main types of attachment of teeth to jaws:

(1) By fibrous membrane

(2) By hinge

(3) By anchylosis

(4) By gomphosis which is the mode of attachment seen in human and mammalian teeth generally. When a tooth is removed from its process, an opening is left that resembles in form the shape of the root (Fig. 2–26). This cavity, or socket, is called the *alveolus* (pl. alveoli). The tooth root is attached to the walls of the alveoli by a tough, vascular membrane or ligament, the *periodontal membrane* (Fig. 2–25). The periodontal membrane has four functions which are formative, supportive, sensory and nutritive in the life of the tooth.

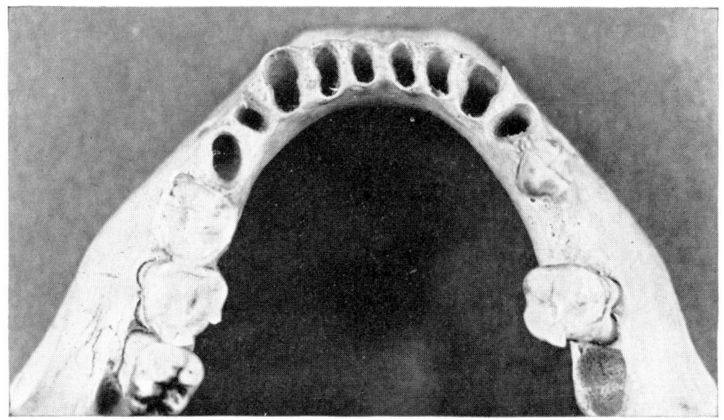

FIG. 2–26. Alveoli of mandibular anterior teeth.

The *alveolar process* is that part of the bone of the maxilla and mandible which surrounds and forms the sockets (Fig. 2–27) in which the roots of the teeth are held by periodontal membranes. The alveolar process consists of (1) outer cortical plate, (2) inner plate or alveolar bone proper and (3) intervening bone, or spongiosa. The function of the alveolar process is to support and attach the teeth.

The oral mucosa surrounds the necks of the teeth, covers the alveolar process and is known as the *gingiva.* It is continuous with the mucosa of other parts of the mouth.

The *cementum* of the root surface, the *alveolar bone* of the maxilla and mandible, the *periodontal membrane,* the *gingiva* which is a subdivision of the masticatory mucosa and the *epithelial attachment* collectively are known as the *supporting tissues* or periodontium of the teeth.

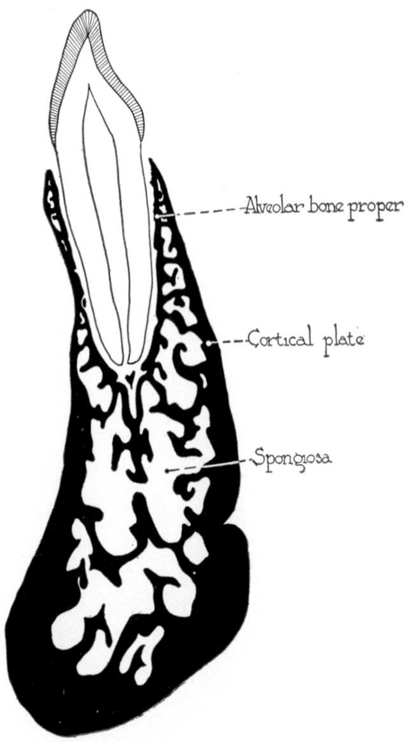

FIG. 2–27. Diagrammatic representation of the relationship of the alveolar process to both lower incisors and the mandible. (Schour, *Noyes' Oral Histology and Embryology.*)

Under normal conditions there is a harmonious relation between the different parts of the periodontium. An upset in this harmonious equilibrum will result in periodontal destruction.

The tooth form and the supporting structures are functional under all normal stresses to which they are subjected. When the relationship of tooth form and periodontium are disregarded, the normal physiology of the supporting tissue is disturbed. Understanding basic fundamentals of the supporting structures aids in comprehending its significance in clinical oral hygiene.

NOMENCLATURE

In describing the anatomy of various teeth, the student must become familiar with specific terms and should be able to recognize landmarks of importance by name.

The crowns of the incisors and cuspids present for examination four surfaces and a ridge (Fig. 2–28), and the crowns of the bicuspids and molars, five surfaces. The surfaces are named according to their positions and uses. The outer surfaces of the anterior teeth, because of their proximity to the labia or lips, are called the *labial surfaces.*

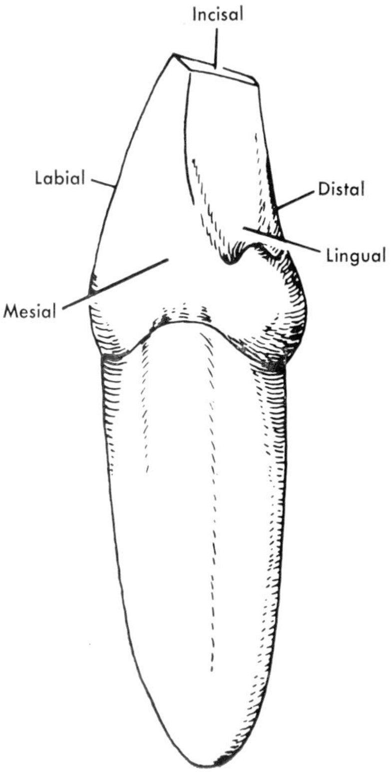

FIG. 2–28. Surfaces of an anterior tooth. (From Young: *Oral and Dentat Anatomy,* 1964.) Used by permission of McGraw-Hill Book Company, New York.

The same surfaces of the posterior teeth (Fig. 2–29), because of the proximity of the cheek, are called the *buccal surfaces.* The inner surfaces of the teeth which approximate the tongue are known as the lingual surfaces.

The surface of the tooth nearest to the median line is called the *mesial;* that farthest from the median line is called the *distal* surface. At the median line, two mesial surfaces of the central incisor teeth are adjacent to each other. In all other teeth the mesial surface of one tooth contacts the distal surface of its adjacent tooth. The mesial and distal surfaces are also referred to as *proximal* surfaces.

The surfaces of the teeth which come in contact with those in the opposite jaw during the act of closure are called *occlusal surfaces.* These surfaces on the incisors and cuspids are called *incisal* surfaces (*See* Figs. 2–20 and 2–21).

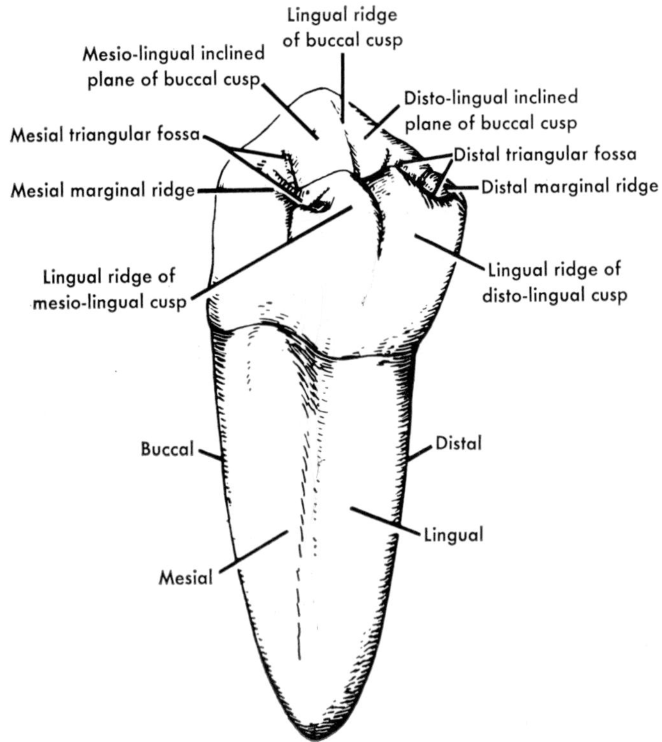

FIG. 2–29. Surfaces of a posterior tooth. (From Young: *Oral and Dental Anatomy,* 1964.) Used by permission of McGraw-Hill Book Company, New York.

The terms mesial, distal, labial, buccal, lingual and incisal, may be used to denote two or more surfaces and to indicate direction from one surface to another. Junctions of tooth surfaces are described as *line angles* and *point angles.* It must be pointed out that actually there are no angles or points or plane surfaces on the teeth anywhere. Rather they are curved or rounded except when sharpened by wear or "abrasion." For example, the junction of the mesial and labial surfaces is called the mesio-labial line angle; the junction of three surfaces, such as the mesio-buccal-occlusal surfaces of a molar form a point angle. It must be remembered that these terms are used for descriptive purposes only.

Other terms of importance to become familiar with are: *Cusp*–an elevation on the crown portion of a tooth, making a divisional part of the occlusal surface. *Cingulum*–the lingual lobe of an anterior tooth, the bulk of the cervical third of the lingual surface. *Marginal ridges*–those rounded elevations of the enamel which form the mesial and distal margins of occlusal surfaces of bicuspids and molars, and of the lingual surfaces of incisors and cuspids.

Lobes are primary centers of calcification formed in the development of the crown. Cusps are representative of lobes. A *developmental groove* is a shallow groove or line denoting evidence of coalescence between primary parts of the crown and root. *Pit faults* are incomplete calcified sharply pointed depressions usually located at points of junction of developmental grooves. A *sulcus* is a notably long depression or valley in the surface of a tooth between ridges and cusps, the inclines of which meet at an angle.

MORPHOLOGY OF THE TEETH

Primary Teeth

The twenty primary teeth consist of one central incisor, lateral incisor, cuspid, first molar and second molar in each quadrant (Fig. 2–30). These teeth are replaced by the permanent central incisors, lateral incisors, cuspids and first and second bicuspids, respectively.

The primary teeth with some exceptions closely resemble in form the corresponding permanent dentition. For a detailed description of the anatomy of the primary teeth, the student is referred to text books on dental anatomy.

The characteristic differences between the primary and permanent teeth may be noted as follows:

1. *Size.* The primary teeth are smaller in correspondence with the smaller jaw in which they must function. The thickness of the enamel and dentin is about one-half that of the permanent teeth.
2. *Color.* Enamel of the primary teeth is much whiter.
3. *Crowns.* Crowns are sharply constricted at the cervical margin. The labial or buccal surfaces show sharp inclinations to the lingual, occlusally, thus making the occlusal surfaces narrow. This results in the formation of distinct labio- or bucco-gingival ridges. In some instances, the mesio-distal diameter of the primary molar roots is wider than that of the corresponding crown.

4. *Roots.* The roots of the primary teeth are considerably more divergent than those of the permanent dentition. This accommodates the crowns of the underlying permanent successors. Usually the roots are more slender and tapering and are longer in proportion to the crown than is the case in the analogous permanent teeth.

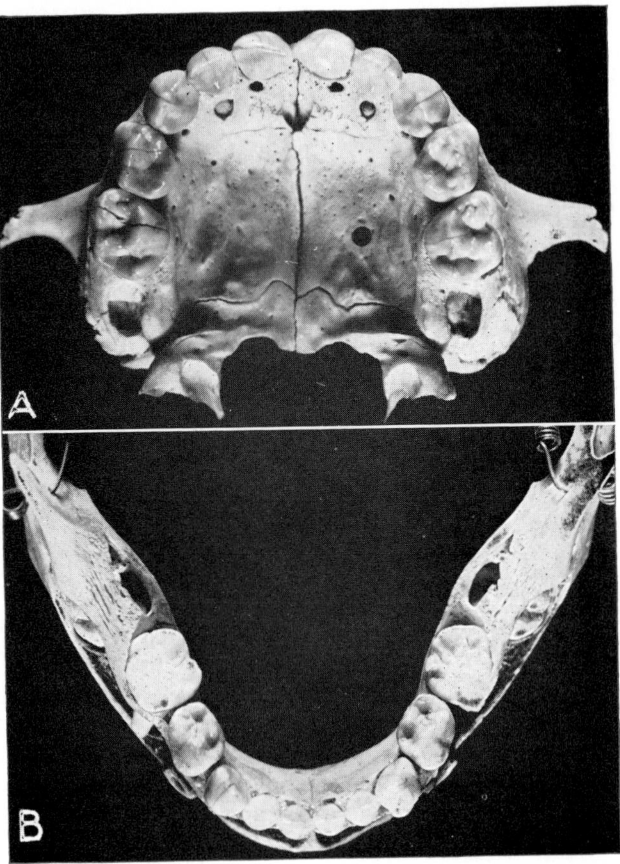

FIG. 2–30. Maxillary and mandibular primary dentition. *A,* Maxillary arch. *B,* Mandibular arch.

Primary Anterior Teeth

The incisor and cuspid teeth of the primary dentition are closely related in form to the corresponding permanent teeth. However, the crowns appear broader and lower. They are more rounded and not so angular as the permanent ones. The marked constriction and convexity of the crown near the cervical line is the result of a thickening of the dentin, rather than an increase in enamel thickness.

The lower central and lateral incisors, as well as, the upper lateral incisors, are more chisel-shaped and more slender (Fig. 2–31).

Primary Molars

The primary molars are smaller in size, have a marked gingival bulge, and a marked mesio-distal constriction. The occlusal surfaces of the primary molars are quite narrow bucco-lingually as compared to the permanent molars, and there is a close approximation of the sizes of their occlusal intra-cuspal area and surface. The contact between the primary molars tends to be an ellipsoid, flattened area.

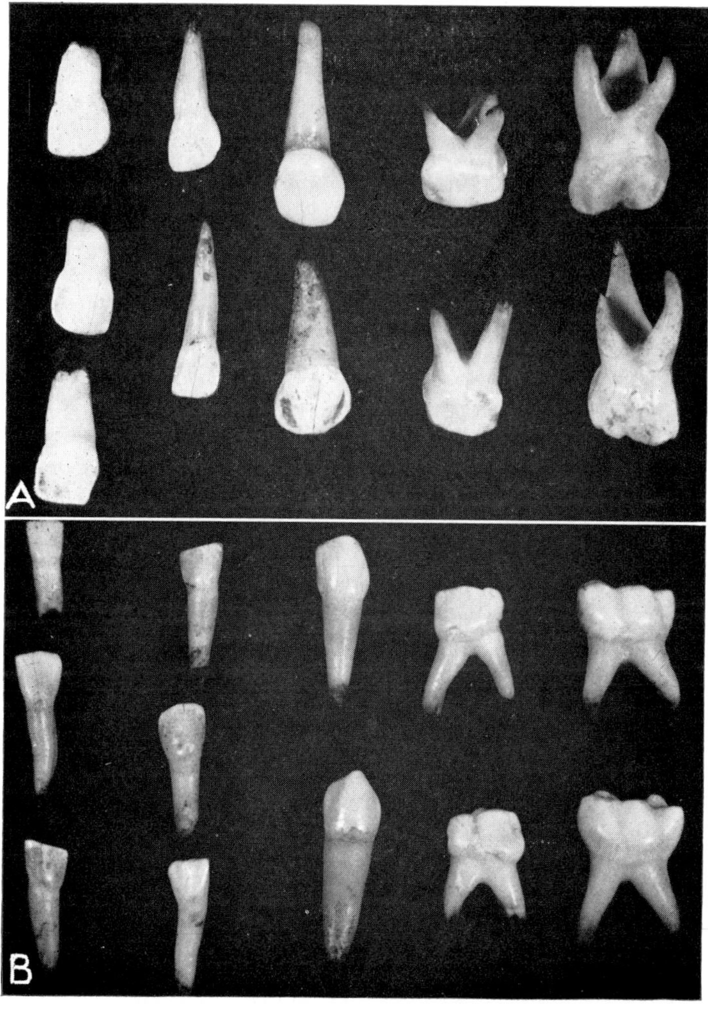

FIG. 2–31. *A,* Primary maxillary incisors, cuspids, and molars. *B,* Primary mandibular incisors, cuspids, and molars.

First Primary Molars

The maxillary first primary molar is a three-cusped tooth (Fig. 2–32), having two buccal cusps and a lingual cusp. This may vary by sometimes showing a small disto-lingual cusp. The surfaces are convex occluso-gingivally with the buccal and lingual surfaces converging toward the occlusal surface. The two most important anatomical features of this tooth are the deep central pit from which

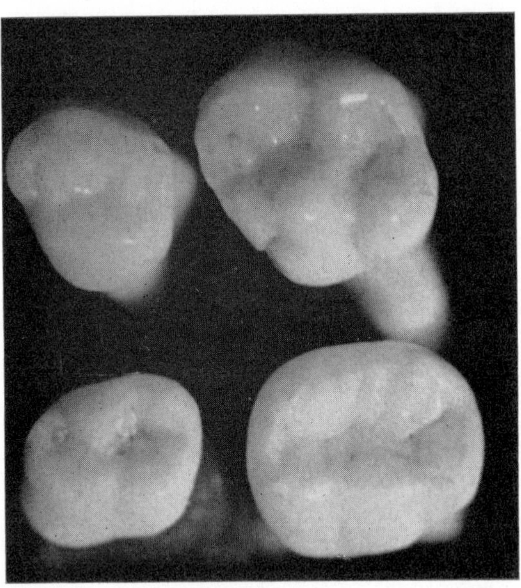

FIG. 2–32. Occlusal view primary molars. first and second maxillary and mandibular.

three grooves arise and the marked bucco-gingival ridge which is more prominent at the mesial border. The mesial and distal surfaces are less convex and converge toward the lingual.

The mandibular first primary molar does not resemble any of the other teeth, primary or permanent (*See* Fig. 2–30). It has four cusps, two buccal and two lingual. The mesial half of the crown is more developed and larger than the distal portion. The mesio-buccal cusp is the larger and forms about three-sevenths of the occlusal surface.

Constant anatomical features are the deep central pit from which four grooves originate and the marked bucco-gingival ridge. The buccal and lingual margins of the occlusal surface converge distally, making the distal margin ridge very short.

Second Primary Molars

The primary second molars are similar to the permanent first molars (*See* Figs. 2–31 and 2–32). However, they are smaller in all dimensions and show in the proximal aspect a marked gingival constriction at the cemento-enamel junction and bulge in the gingival third of the crown. The occlusal surface is narrowed bucco-lingually, but not so markedly as in the first primary molar. The second primary molars are larger than their permanent successors, the second bicuspids. These teeth frequently are mistaken for the first permanent molars. The primary second molar is the fifth tooth from the median line; this with the characteristic gingival ridge and the age of the individual should distinguish this tooth from the permanent molar.

About 50 per cent of the children show a physiologic spacing in the anterior teeth at about four to five years of age, as preparation for the eruption of the larger succeeding permanent teeth and in adjustment to the growth of the jaws.

PERMANENT TEETH

The Incisors (Fig. 2–33)

These teeth are adapted for incising or cutting the food. The upper incisors are positioned in the maxilla, and the lower incisors supported by the mandible oppose them. In both jaws, the tooth nearest the median line of the dental arch is known as the central incisor and the second tooth as the lateral incisor. These teeth are similar in anatomic form and supplement each other in function. These teeth possess incisal ridges and the crowns are wedge-shaped and present four surfaces for study. Incisors are normally the most prominent and noticeable teeth in the mouth.

Labial Surface. This is convex except for slight flattening in the incisal third portion of the maxillary incisors. The lateral incisors are more slender in every respect; the labial surface is flatter and triangular in outline. This surface usually shows two shallow longitudinal depressions which end at the cutting edge in slight notches or mamelons. All borders of these teeth are more or less convex, markedly so at the cervical line, which ends in a distinct ridge. The mesio-incisal angle is quite sharp, while the disto-incisal angle is usually rounded. The incisal edge of the mandibular central is at right angles to the long axis of the tooth and its incisal angles are acute and sharp. The crown of the mandibular lateral incisor appears twisted toward the lingual, following the curve of the arch.

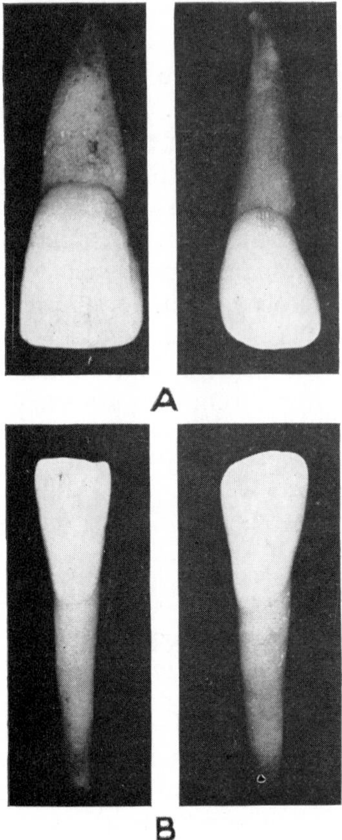

FIG. 2–33. *A*, Maxillary central and lateral incisors. *B*, Mandibular central and lateral incisors (labial aspect).

The maxillary lateral incisor is about one-third smaller than the central, while the mandibular lateral incisor is larger than the mandibular central.

Lingual Surface. This is irregularly wedge-shaped in outline and, in general, concave over the lingual surface. This surface is slightly smaller than the labial surface; the margins are outlined with ridges. The lateral incisor often shows a pit in the cervical ridge of the lingual fossa. The mandibular incisors rarely present a fossa, due to the lack of prominent marginal ridges.

Mesial and Distal Surfaces (Fig. 2–34). The general outline of the mesial and distal surfaces resembles a triangle with its lines curved, with the convexity toward the labial and with the sharpest angle at the incisal edge. These surfaces tend to be slightly convex except for the mandibular incisor where there is a tendency toward a concavity at or near the cervical line. Both mesial and distal surfaces converge from the incisal edge toward the apex of the root.

Roots. The roots are conical in shape, tapering from the crown to the apex. The labio-lingual diameter is greater than the mesio-distal. The mandibular incisor roots are more flattened mesio-distally than the maxillary incisor. The incisor roots are about one to one and one-half times as large as the crown.

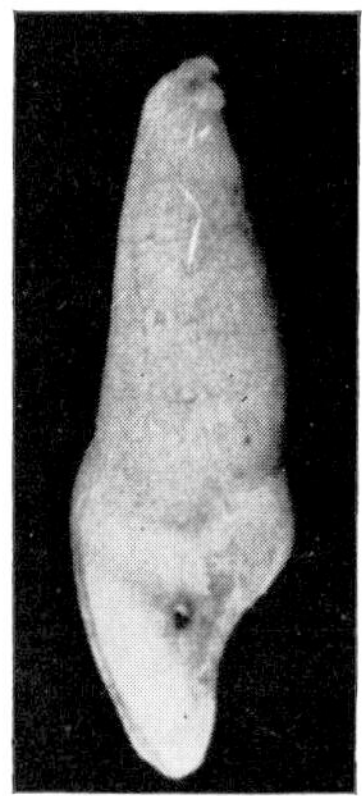

FIG. 2–34. Maxillary central incisor. Mesial aspect.

Special Characteristics of the Incisors

(1) The maxillary central is the largest of the incisors. (2) The crowns of the incisors are wedge-shaped. (3) Maxillary lateral incisor is about 1/3 smaller than the central incisor. The developmental grooves frequently are quite marked on the lingual side. (4) Lateral incisor is frequently malformed, peg-shaped or congenitally missing. (5) The incisal edge of the maxillary incisor forms a sharp angle at the mesial and slopes toward the distal, making a rounded angle with the distal surface. (6) Mandibular central incisors are the smallest of the incisors. (7) Mandibular lateral incisors are larger than mandibular central incisors. (8) Mandibular central incisors have sharp incisal angles. (9) Crown of mandibular lateral incisor appears rotated on its root.

The Cuspids

The first tooth situated behind the suture between the premaxilla and maxilla proper. The lower cuspid is the tooth which occludes directly in front of the upper cuspid. The crowns of these teeth present four surfaces and an incisal edge which becomes raised to a well formed point or cusp. The upper cuspid is a larger and stronger tooth than the incisors and is the longest tooth in the series.

Labial Surface (Fig. 2–35). The general outline of the labial surface is pentagonal in form. It is convex in all directions, but more convex in the mesio-distal direction than the maxillary incisor. The labial ridge is a strong elevation of enamel running from the point of the cusp to the cervical line. The distal margin of the labial surface is a little shorter than the mesial. There are two labial grooves or furrows which lie between the convexity of the labial ridge.

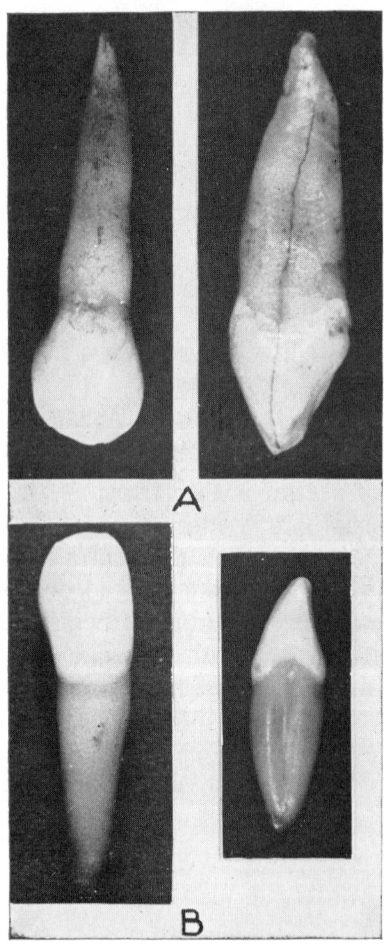

FIG. 2–35. *A,* Maxillary cuspid. Labial and mesial aspect. *B,* Mandibular cuspid. Labial and mesial aspect.

The mandibular cuspids closely resemble the maxillary cuspids, except that the crowns are slightly smaller with a slender appearance. The occlusion of the lower cuspid is such that the cusp with age is often reduced to a blunt conical form.

Lingual Surface. The lingual surface presents the same general outline as the labial, but is somewhat narrower toward the cervical line. It is usually straight from the point of the cusp to the lingual cervical ridge or cingulum. The lingual surface of the mandibular cuspid is smooth and the ridges are less prominent with a poorly developed cingulum.

Mesial and Distal Surfaces. These are triangular in outline, with the mesial surface larger and convex in all directions, but flattened or slightly concave near the cervical line. The mesial surface of the crown and root of the mandibular cuspid is usually flat and continuous for the entire length of the crown and root.

The *roots* are irregularly conical, tapering from neck to apex, and appear flattened in the mesio-distal direction. The maxillary root is the longest in the human mouth. The mandibular root is shorter and when viewed from the mesial aspect, the labial surface of the crown and root presents a somewhat regular convexity from the point of the cusp to the apex of the root.

Special Characteristics of the Cuspids

(1) The mandibular cuspid is smaller and has a more slender and longer crown than the maxillary. (2) The mesial surface of mandibular cuspids is quite straight over both crown and root. Right and left lower cuspids can be distinguished by this characteristic. (3) The distal surface bulges out to great prominence which makes the tooth appear bent, producing a considerable concavity in the cervical section of the distal surface. (4) The cervical margin of the maxillary cuspid is marked by a well developed cingulum.

The Bicuspids (Figs. 2–36 and 2–37)

The bicuspids are situated behind the cuspids which replace the primary molars. There are eight bicuspids, two on each side in the maxillary and two on each side in the mandibular arch. In man the bicuspids have two cusps, a buccal and a lingual, hence the name bicuspid. In the animal kingdom the number of cusps varies, hence the name *premolar*. The function of the bicuspids is to crush the food and assist in grinding, the true function of the molars.

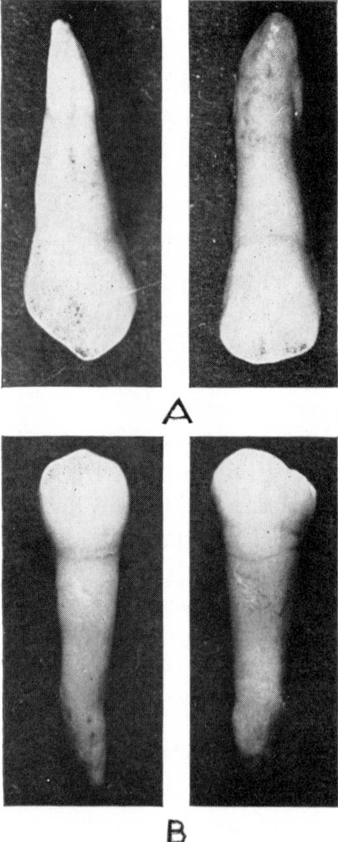

FIG. 2–36. *A*, Maxillary first and second bicuspids. *B*, Mandibular first and second bicuspids (buccal aspect).

The *buccal surface* is convex and is bound by five borders. It is similar to the labial surface of the cuspid, but is slightly shorter and narrower. The buccal cusp of the maxillary first bicuspid is larger, higher and more prominent than the lingual. The central inclination of the buccal surface of the mandibular first bicuspid is greater than that of the maxillary bicuspids. The buccal surface of the mandibular second bicuspid (*see* Figs. 2–36 and 2–37) does not differ from the other bicuspids except in being shorter, the cusp being lower.

The *lingual surface* is regularly convex but smaller than the buccal surface. The convexity of the lingual cusp forms the occlusal margin of the lingual surface. The lingual cusp of the mandibular first bicuspid is only about one-half as long as the buccal surface and all of the occlusal surface can be seen from the lingual aspect. The lingual cusp

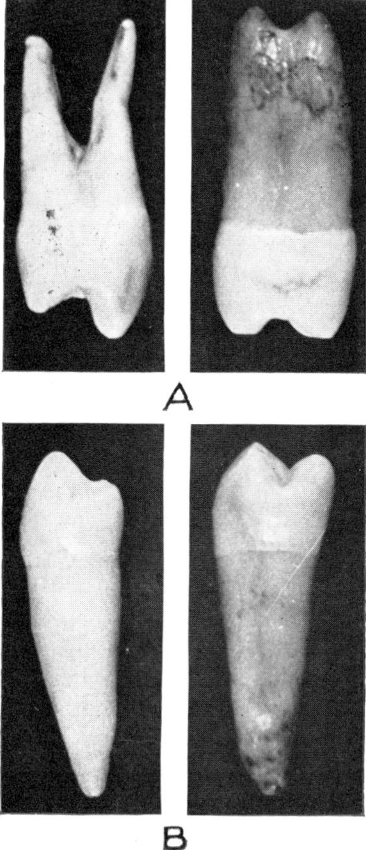

FIG. 2–37. *A,* Maxillary first and second bicuspids. *B,* Mandibular first and second bicuspids (mesial aspect).

of the mandibular second bicuspid is more nearly, but never quite, on a level with the buccal cusp. The lingual surface is about equal to the buccal in mesio-distal breadth.

The *mesial and distal* (Fig. 2–37) surfaces are irregularly quadrilateral and slightly convex. There is a marked concavity on the surface near the cervical third, extending upon the root surface of the maxillary first bicuspid. The occlusal border of the maxillary bicuspids is somewhat "V" shaped with the apex between the cusps.

The mesial and distal surfaces of the mandibular first bicuspid are convex from buccal to lingual and are bell-shaped from the occlusal border to the cervical line. Mandibular second bicuspids are nearly straight from the occlusal border to the cervical line.

Occlusal surfaces of the maxillary bicuspids (Fig. 2–38) are irregularly quadrilateral in form, while the mandibular first bicuspid is more circular. The second bicuspid (Fig. 2–39) may present two general forms, square and round.

They present for study two cusps (there are three cusps on some mandibular second bicuspids), a central groove and a mesial and

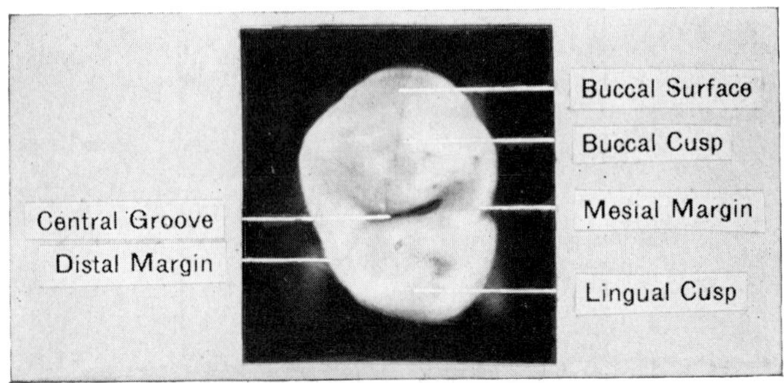

FIG. 2–38. Maxillary first bicuspid (occlusal aspect).

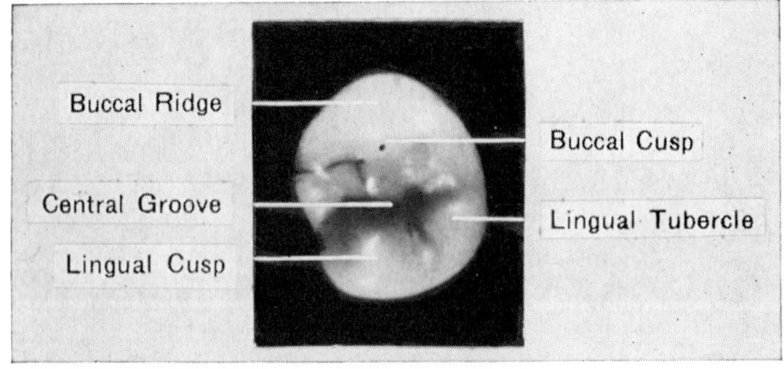

FIG. 2–39. Mandibular second bicuspid (occlusal aspect).

distal border. The cusps are placed buccally and lingually, the buccal being the larger one. There are four ridges leading down from the point of the buccal cusp. Two ridges form the cutting edges which slope toward the buccal point angles. The central groove extends mesio-distally and separates the cusps. The mesial and distal marginal ridges are prominent, strong elevations of enamel. Anatomic variations in the occlusal surface divide the mandibular second bicuspids into U, H, and Y shapes. All of the occlusal surface of the mandibular first bicuspid may be seen when the tooth is viewed from the lingual, because the lingual cusp is very rudimentary.

The Roots. The maxillary first bicuspids usually develop two roots, sometimes only one. When two roots are present, one is above the buccal and the other above the lingual half of the crown. They are named according to their position buccal or lingual. The second maxillary bicuspid usually presents a single root. The mandibular bicuspids usually present single roots which are straight, somewhat flattened on the mesial and distal side and taper gradually from the neck to the apex.

Special Characteristics of the Bicuspids

A. Maxillary: (1) The buccal cusp of the first bicuspid is higher in proportion to its lingual cusp than the buccal cusp of the second. (2) The occlusal surface of the first shows sharper buccal point angles, and more defined developmental grooves than the second which may show supplemental grooves on the occlusal surface. (3) The first bicuspid usually has two roots, bifurcated at the apical third. (4) The first bicuspid has a marked developmental depression on the mesial surface of crown and root. *B.* Mandibular: (1) First has a more triangular-shaped occlusal surface. (2) Second has a square-shaped occlusal surface. (3) First has a small lingual cusp which is variable in size. (4) The buccal surface of the first is markedly inclined toward the lingual, placing the point of the buccal cusp well toward the center of the long axis. (5) The second has two well developed cusps and may have three. (6) The developmental grooves on the occlusal surface of the second may be in the form of a U, Y or H. (7) The occlusal surface of the first generally has one well developed transverse ridge extending from the buccal to the lingual cusp with small fossae on either side.

The Maxillary Molars (Fig. 2–40)

These teeth are adapted for crushing and grinding the food. They are multi-cusped and multi-rooted. Molars have no primary predecessors. Fishes and reptiles have teeth of conical form, while Mammalia have multi-cuspidate teeth. In mammals, diet, customs and reduction in the size of the jaws have reduced the dentitions and the number of teeth. The forms of the teeth have become more complicated as a result. The crowns of these teeth are irregular cuboidal in shape, and in man the first molar is the largest of the series and the two posterior teeth decreasing in size.

The *buccal surface* is generally convex and is divided into a mesial and distal half. These two portions are quite similar in outline, and are separated from each other by the buccal groove which may termi-

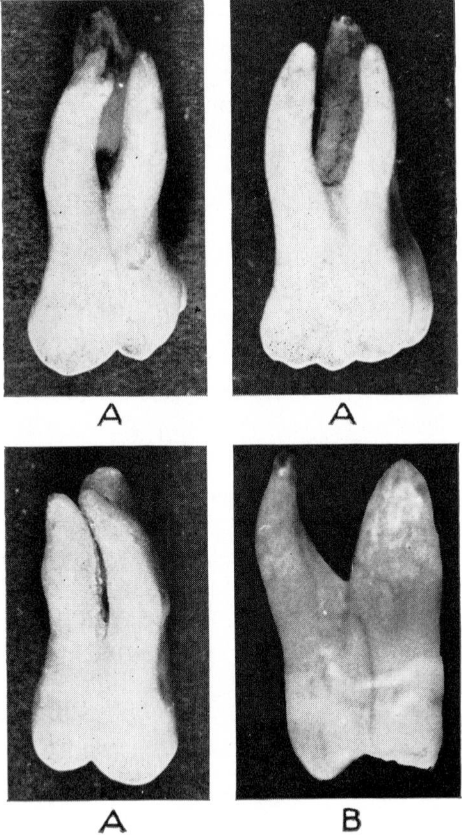

FIG. 2–40. *A,* Maxillary first, second and third molars (buccal aspect). *B,* Maxillary first molar (mesial aspect).

nate in a pit—*the buccal pit.* The margins of the surface, which form an irregular quadrilateral, are the mesial, distal, occlusal and cervical; of these, the occlusal is the most striking in that it is marked with two cusps.

The *lingual surface* is developed from two lobes, the mesio- and disto-lingual lobes. The line of union between the two is recorded by a well defined groove, *the lingual groove.* This groove usually ends near the center of the lingual surface in a well defined pit, *the lingual pit.* It is located a little to the distal of the center of the surface, thus making the mesial a trifle larger than the disal portion. The mesial and distal margins converge slightly in the direction of the root.

The *mesial surface* at the occlusal third is convex, while the gingival two-thirds is straight or concave.

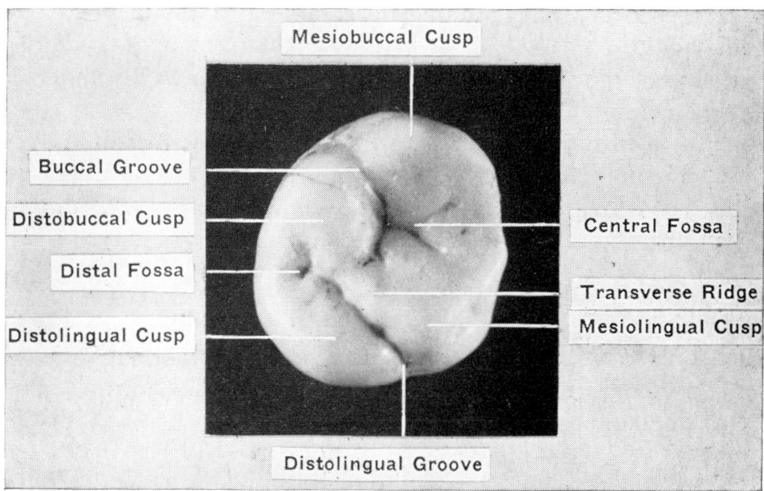

FIG. 2–41. Maxillary first molar (occlusal aspect).

The *distal surface,* in its entirety, usually presents a general convexity.

The *occlusal surface* of the maxillary molars (Fig. 2–41), when seen in a line with the long axis of the teeth, presents an outline of an irregular rhombic form with two convex sides at the buccal and lingual margins, and the mesial and distal margins are flattened. The surface is bound by these four margins which are nearly of equal length, the angles formed by their union being more or less rounded, two of which, the mesio-buccal and the disto-lingual, are acute angles. The surface is divided into four developmental portions—the mesio-buccal, disto-buccal, mesio-lingual and disto-lingual. Each one of these parts is surmounted by a well defined point or cusp, which is also named according to its location. These various parts are divided from one another by four developmental grooves—the mesial, the buccal, the distal and the disto-lingual. In the center of the triangle formed by the central incline of the mesio-buccal, disto-buccal and mesio-lingual cusps is a deep depression—the *central fossa,* while near the distal margin is a smaller depression—the *distal fossa.*

The Roots. These are three in number, two placed buccally and one lingually. The lingual root is the largest and the disto-buccal the smallest.

Special Characteristics of the Maxillary Molars

(1) The first molar is the largest of the maxillary molars. (2) The second is frequently flattened mesio-distal, with the disto-lingual cusp

less developed. (3) They are not preceded by primary teeth so are not succedaneous. (4) A fifth cusp may sometimes be found on the lingual side of the mesio-lingual cusp. It is known as the *tubercle of Carabelli.*

The Third Molar is variable in form. If typical, it should present three cusps, the disto-buccal cusp has all but disappeared. The roots may be fused into one, or again may present the typical maxillary molar roots of three.

The Mandibular First Molar (Fig. 2–42)

The lower first molar is the largest of the series. It is a trapezoidal rectangular tooth. The occlusal surface shows five cusps, three buccal and two lingual.

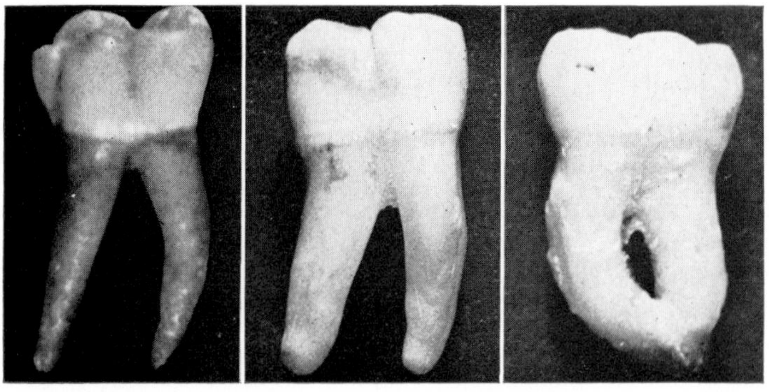

FIG. 2–42. Mandibular first, second and third molars (buccal aspect).

The *buccal surface* differs from the maxillary molar in that it is longer mesio-distally and presents two grooves instead of one. It is convex from mesial to distal, and also from the occlusal margin to the cervical line. The occlusal margin is made irregular by the presence of three buccal cusps. The cervical margin is nearly straight, and is surmounted throughout by a strong enamel fold, *the cervico-buccal ridge.*

The *lingual surface* is smooth and convex in every direction. The surface is nearly one-third less in extent than the buccal. The occlusal margin is formed by the double incline of the two lingual cusps separated by the lingual groove.

The *mesial surface* is inclined to flatness, with a slight bulging near the center, which marks the point of contact with the approximate tooth. The distal surface, unlike the mesial, is decidedly convex in every direction. It is surmounted by a portion of the disto-buccal cusp.

The *occlusal surface* (Fig. 2–43) differs considerably from that of the maxillary molars. It is trapezoidal in outline with the buccal margin the longest. The mesial and distal lines converge to meet the lingual. The buccal angles are acute in character, while the lingual angles are about equally obtuse. The surface is divided into five distinct or developmental lobes, each of which is surmounted by a cusp, named, as their location indicates, mesio-buccal, disto-buccal, mesio-lingual and disto-lingual. Separating these five parts are five developmental grooves—the mesial, the distal, the buccal, the lingual and the disto-buccal. The first four grooves cross the marginal ridges from the various surfaces and end in the central fossa, while the disto-buccal groove passes from the disto-buccal angle and joins the distal groove, which may end in a slight depression—*the distal pit*. The mesio-buccal cusp is the largest and the disto-buccal the smallest.

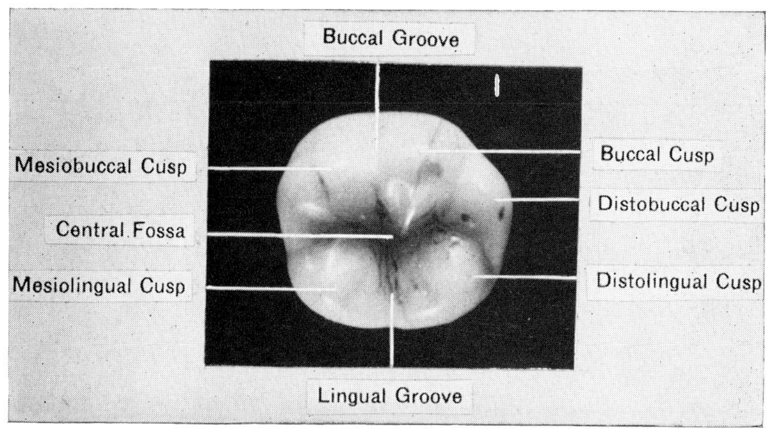

FIG. 2–43. Mandibular first molar (occlusal aspect).

The Roots. The roots of this tooth are two in number—one of which is placed beneath the mesial, and the other beneath the distal half of the crown—and are named the mesial and distal roots. The mesial root is the larger.

The Mandibular Second Molar (Fig. 2–44).

The most characteristic difference between the mandibular first and second molars is the absence of the fifth lobe (disto-buccal cusp). Mandibular second molars may have a fifth lobe, but its occurrence is quite rare. Generally, four equally proportioned cusps are observed, separated from each other by four developmental grooves radiating from a central fossa.

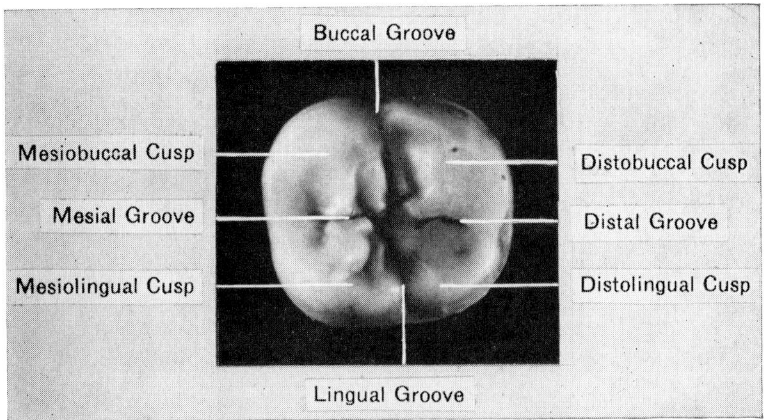

FIG. 2–44. Mandibular second molar (occlusal aspect).

The *roots,* like those of the first molar, are two in number, a mesial and distal. They are somewhat smaller in form, often nearer together, and in some instances united. The roots may show a marked distal inclination.

The Mandibular Third Molar

This tooth is probably subject to a greater variety in form than any other. There are, however, two types which are found most frequently. In one, the crown form is similar to the mandibular second molar, having four cusps. The other is similar to the mandibular first molar, having five cusps. While these forms are the most commonly met, the occlusal surface may be so marked by supplemental and developmental grooves that six or eight well-defined cusps may be present. One feature very common to the crown is its tendency to the circular form.

Special Characteristics of the Mandibular Molars

(1) First molar has five cusps, the second four, and the third molar variable, as it may have five cusps like the first or four like the second, or show an irregular occlusal surface of many cusps and grooves. (2) Frequently the third molars are congenitally missing, or when mandibular growth is lacking, they cannot erupt at all, and the term "impacted" third molar is used. (3) Partially erupted third molars are generally "food traps" so that extraction is indicated.

Average Measurements of Teeth

Given in millimeters and tenths of millimeters

PRIMARY

(According to G. V. Black)[2]

	Length over all	*Length of crown*	*Length of root*	*Mesio-distal diameter of crown*
Maxillary teeth				
Central	16.0	6.0	10.0	6.5
Lateral	15.8	5.6	11.4	5.1
Cuspid	19.0	6.5	13.5	7.0
First molar	15.2	5.1	10.0	7.3
Second molar	17.5	5.7	11.7	8.2
Mandibular teeth				
Central	14.0	5.0	9.0	4.2
Lateral	15.0	5.2	10.0	4.1
Cuspid	17.0	6.0	11.5	5.0
First molar	15.8	6.0	9.8	7.7
Second molar	18.8	5.5	11.3	9.9

Average Measurements of Teeth

Given in millimeters and tenths of millimeters

PERMANENT

(According to G. V. Black)[2]

	Length over all	*Length of crown*	*Length of root*	*Mesio-distal diameter of crown*
Maxillary teeth				
Central	22.5	10.0	12.0	9.0
Lateral	22.0	8.0	13.0	6.4
Cuspid	26.5	9.5	17.3	7.6
First bicuspid	20.6	8.2	12.4	7.6
Second bicuspid	21.5	7.5	14.0	6.8
First molar	20.8	7.7	13.2	10.7
Second molar	20.0	7.2	13.0	9.2
Third molar	17.1	6.3	11.4	8.6
Mandibular teeth				
Central	20.7	8.8	11.8	5.4
Lateral	21.1	9.6	12.7	5.9
Cuspid	25.6	10.3	15.3	6.9
First bicuspid	21.6	7.8	14.0	6.9
Second bicuspid	22.3	7.9	14.4	7.1
First molar	21.0	7.7	13.2	11.2
Second molar	19.8	6.9	12.9	10.7
Third molar	18.5	6.7	11.8	10.7

GROSS ABNORMALITIES IN THE TEETH

Teeth are subject to abnormal development and anomalies of form, the same as other parts of the body. Probably many teeth are lost prematurely due to failure of development of normal functional forms or the abnormal alignment of well formed teeth in the dental arches where protective factors are lost.

Abnormalities may affect the form and size of the teeth or their histologic structures. We are mostly interested in the gross malformations which consist of hyperplasias and hypoplasias of form. Hyperplasias of the teeth consist of such abnormalities of form as giantism, supernumerary teeth, supplemental cusps, supernumerary roots and hypercementosis.

Hypoplasias of the teeth result in such abnormalities as dwarfism, agenesia of the teeth, pitted and grooved enamel, opaque areas in the enamel, mottled enamel and Hutchinson's teeth.

Abnormal arrangement of the dental tissues may arise during their formative periods and result in many deformities which may be slight or so pronounced that the final result has no resemblance to a tooth. Such deformities as dilaceration, fusion of teeth, concrescence, enamel pearls and excessive formations of several dental tissues forming atypical enlargements known as odontomas may exist.

The student should refer to textbooks on oral pathology for illustrations of such abnormalities as they are encountered in their study of dental anatomy.

BIBLIOGRAPHY

1. Atchison, James: *Dental Anatomy and Physiology for Students.* 2nd ed. London, Staples Press, 1950.
2. Black, G. V.: *Descriptive Anatomy of the Human Teeth.* 4th ed., Philadelphia, S. S. White Co., 1902.
3. Broomwell, I. N., and Fischelis, P.: *Anatomy and Histology of the Mouth and Teeth,* 6th ed., Philadelphia, P. Blakiston's Son and Co., 450 pp., 1923.
4. Churchill, H. R.: *Human Odontography and Histology.* Philadelphia, Lea & Febiger, 1932.
5. Colby, Robert A., Kerr, Donald A., Robinson, Hamilton B. G.: *Color Atlas of Oral Pathology.* 2nd ed., Philadelphia, J. B. Lippincott Co., 1961.
6. Diamond, Moses: *Dental Anatomy.* 3rd ed., New York, The Macmillan Co., 1952.
7. Gray, Henry: *Anatomy of the Human Body.* 27th ed., Charles M. Goss, ed., Philadelphia, Lea & Febiger, 1959.
8. Held, H. W.: *A Syllabus of Human Dental and Comparative Anatomy for Dental Hygienists.* Ann Arbor, Overbeck Co., 1952.

9. HOPEWELL-SMITH, ARTHUR: *Dental Anatomy and Physiology.* Philadelphia, Lea & Febiger, 1913.
10. MCBRIDE, W. C.: *Juvenile Dentistry.* 5th ed., Philadelphia, Lea & Febiger, 1952, Chapter IV.
11. NOYES, F. B.: *Oral Histology and Embryology.* 8th ed., Isaac Schour, ed., Philadelphia, Lea & Febiger, 1960.
12. ORBAN, B. J., *Oral Histology and Embryology.* 5th ed., Harry Sicher, ed., St. Louis, C. V. Mosby Company, 1962.
13. SCHOUR, ISAAC: *Noyes' Oral Histology and Embryology.* 7th ed., Philadelphia, Lea & Febiger, 1953.
14. SIMKINS, C. S.: *History of the Human Teeth.* Philadelphia, P. Blakiston's Son & Co., 1937.
15. TOMES, CHARLES S.: *A Manual of Dental Anatomy, Human and Comparative,* 8th ed., H. W. M. Tims, ed., New York, The Macmillan Co., 1923.
16. WHEELER, R. C.: *A Textbook of Dental Anatomy and Physiology.* 3rd ed., Philadelphia, W. B. Saunders Co., 1958.
17. WOODBURNE, R. T.: *Essentials of Human Anatomy.* New York, Oxford University Press, 1957.

3

Oral Physiotherapy

Patricia McCullough Wagner

Oral physiotherapy is a term used to describe mechanical cleansing and massaging procedures performed by the patient to maintain oral health. These procedures include use of instruments such as the toothbrush, and aids such as dentifrices and dental floss. The manner in which an individual accomplishes his oral physiotherapy procedures constitutes his personal oral hygiene regimen. Because many factors influence an individual's susceptibility or resistance to disease, oral physiotherapy measures alone cannot guarantee oral health. However, combined with adequate dental health measures such as regular professional care and dietary regulation, a conscientious personal oral hygiene regimen will contribute materially to the maintenance of oral health.

OBJECTIVES

Thorough cleansing of the oral cavity promotes esthetics and comfort, prime objectives for patients of all ages in all walks of life. Improved gingival health results when debris and microorganisms and their metabolic products are removed from cervical surfaces of teeth next to gingival margins. When the gingiva is massaged, intermittent pressure and relaxation promote circulation in underlying tissues, and friction against the surface of attached gingiva stimulates keratinization or callousing. Removal of microbial colonies and debris from exposed surfaces of the teeth will assist in prevention of calculus accumulation since inorganic salts will deposit and calcify only when the organic matrix of this deposit is present. Mechanical removal of sugars immediately after they are ingested before they are fermented by acidogenic microorganisms may reduce dental caries activity.[19]

INSTRUMENTS AND AIDS

Oral physiotherapy instruments described in this section include manual and automatic toothbrushes, denture and clasp brushes, interdental stimulators, rubber polishing and stimulating cups, and hydrotherapeutic devices. Also described are aids that may be used by the patient in his personal oral hygiene regimen, including dental floss and tape, knitting yarn, gauze strips, digital massage, dentifrices, denture cleansers, mouthwashes and disclosing agents. Recommendations and procedures for use are given for each instrument or aid except the toothbrush. Toothbrushing methods are described in a separate section.

Toothbrushes

Mechanical devices to cleanse the teeth and massage the gingiva no doubt have existed as long as man has had teeth, and the instrument used most universally in civilized countries today for these purposes is the toothbrush. A toothbrush consists of bundles or tufts of natural swine bristles or synthetic nylon filaments inserted at right angles into one end of a long, flat stock of semi-flexible material called the handle (Fig. 3–1). Free ends of bristles form the working end or "head" of the brush. The handle, constricted near the head, is grasped with thumb and fingers, and wrist action is used to manipulate the brushing plane, or free ends of bristles, over oral structures.

The Council on Dental Therapeutics of the American Dental Association has recommended specifications for the toothbrush:

> "It must conform to individual requirements in size, shape and texture, and be easily and efficiently manipulated, readily cleaned and aerated, impervious to moisture, durable, and inexpensive. Prime functional properties are flexibility, elasticity, and stiffness in the bristles; strength, rigidity, and lightness in the stock."[2]

Manual toothbrushes are available in a wide variety of designs, but toothbrushes of professional design have these features in common: equal length of bristles, brushing plane large enough to cover approximately three adjacent teeth, and handle sufficiently long and narrow to be held firmly while the working end is inserted in the mouth and activated against teeth and gingiva. The handle should be in the same plane as the head to permit maximum control of bristle action. The Council recommends that adults use a brush with a brushing surface 1 to 1-1/4 inches long by 5/16 to 3/8 inch wide.[3] Children and others with smaller mouths should use smaller brushes with shorter brushing planes in proportion to the size of their oral cavities (Fig. 3–1).

Bristles of manual toothbrushes may be arranged in rows 5-to-12 tufts in length by 2-to-4 tufts in width (Fig. 3–2). A "tufted" brush is 2 or 3 rows of tufts wide by 5 or 6 rows long; a "multitufted" brush

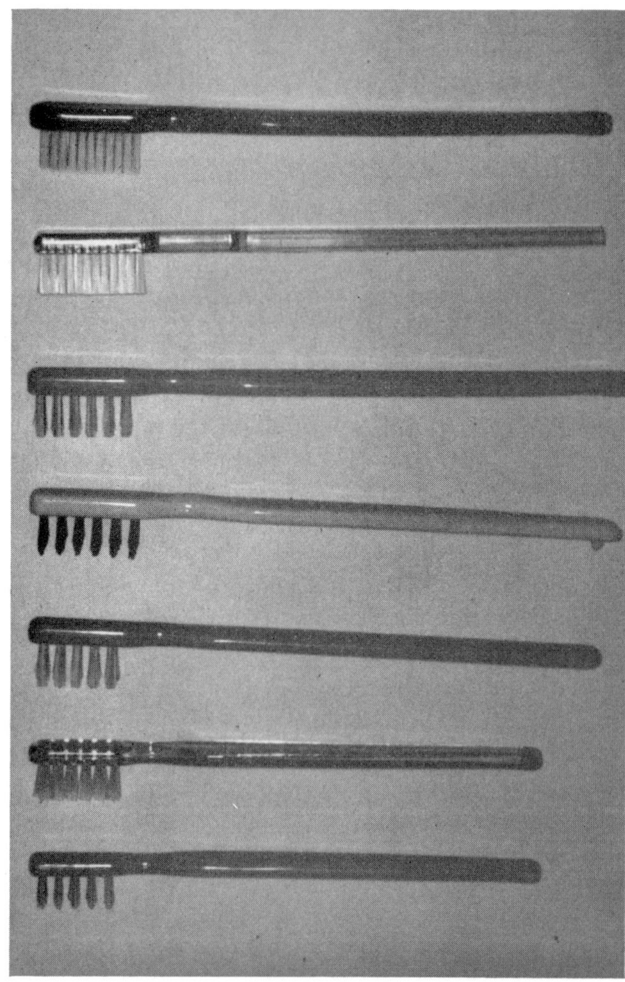

FIG. 3–1. Professional Toothbrushes.

The flat brushing plane is formed by equal-length bristles and the long, narrow handle is in the same plane as the brush head. From top to bottom: 2 adult size multitufted brushes; 2 adult size tufted brushes; 1 junior size tufted brush; 2 child size tufted brushes.

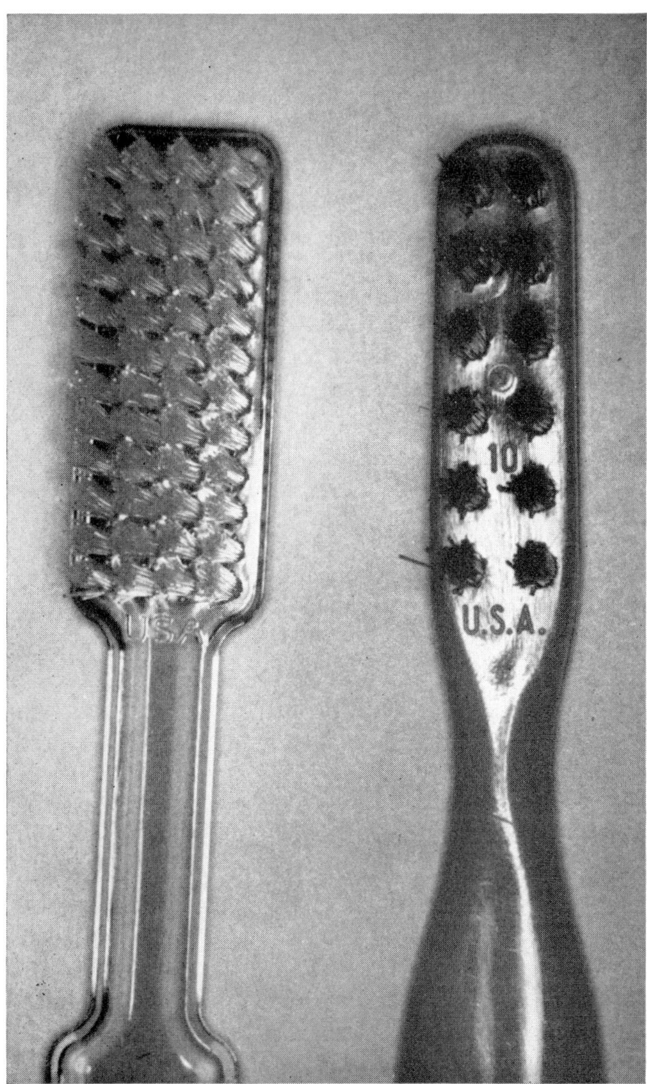

FIG. 3–2. Professional Toothbrushes.

Note constriction of handles near heads of brushes. *Left:* multitufted, soft-textured synthetic nylon filaments. *Right:* tufted, hard-textured unbleached natural bristles.

is 3 or 4 rows wide by 10 or 12 rows long. Bristles used in multitufted brushes are narrower, thus more bristles are used to form a tuft and more tufts used to form the brushing plane.

Bristle texture, graded as soft, medium, hard or extra-hard, is an important consideration in selection of a toothbrush that will cleanse teeth and massage soft tissues. Texture (resiliency) of synthetic filaments is determined by their length and diameter: longer and/or narrower filaments are more resilient, or softer. Length and diameter of natural bristles is determined by the portion used; the tip is narrower than the base, next to the swine's skin. Processing methods including boiling, sterilizing or bleaching may remove oils from centers of natural bristles and render them more resilient.[26]

The correct bristle texture for cleansing and/or massage cannot be assigned by rule-of-thumb since oral conditions, manual dexterity and method by which a brush is used vary with the individual. Generally, patients with hypersensitive or hemorrhagic gingiva, exposed root surfaces, malaligned teeth, or fixed appliances, and very young children or patients who cannot control the brush will be less apt to injure soft tissues with a soft-textured multitufted brush. Greater pressure can be exerted with medium and hard-textured bristles to remove soft deposits from teeth and to stimulate keratinization of attached gingiva, however.

The toothbrush should be cleaned thoroughly after each use as follows: hold bristles under a strong stream of cold water (hot water tends to soften bristles and loosen their attachments to the stock), tap handle against the sink rim to loosen debris and dentifrice, then rinse bristles and tap brush against sink to remove excess water. When bristles and stock are clean, the brush should be placed head upward to drain and dry in open air. At least two or three brushes should be available so each can dry completely before it is used again. Natural bristles, because of their hollow centers, take longer to dry than synthetic filaments. Adequate cleaning and drying of bristles prolong the service life of a brush and provide a more effective brushing plane. A toothbrush should be replaced when bristles start to shorten or bend, since brushing efficiency is lost and laterally protruding bristles may injure soft tissues.

Automatic Toothbrushes

Automatic toothbrushes provide powered movement of the brushing plane. Power may be supplied to a motor in the handle, either directly from an electrical outlet or indirectly through batteries (Fig. 3–3*A*). Tufts of bristles are attached to the end of a stock shorter than, but similar to that of a manual brush, and the interchangeable stock is

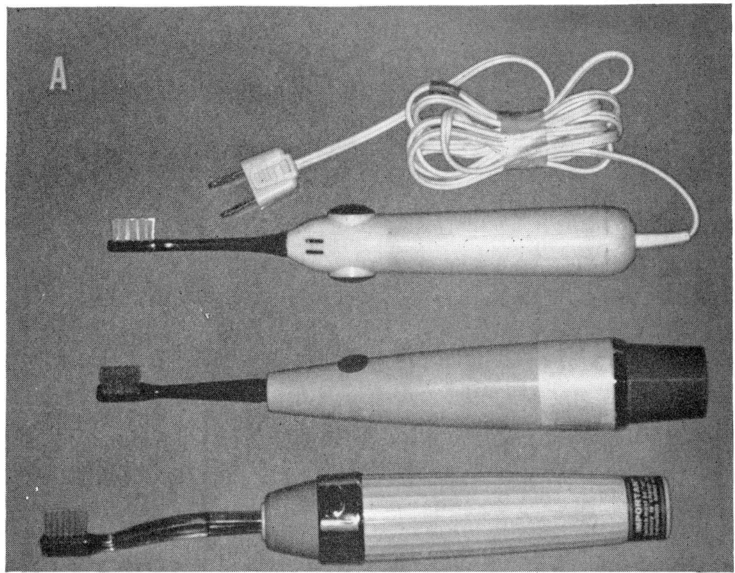

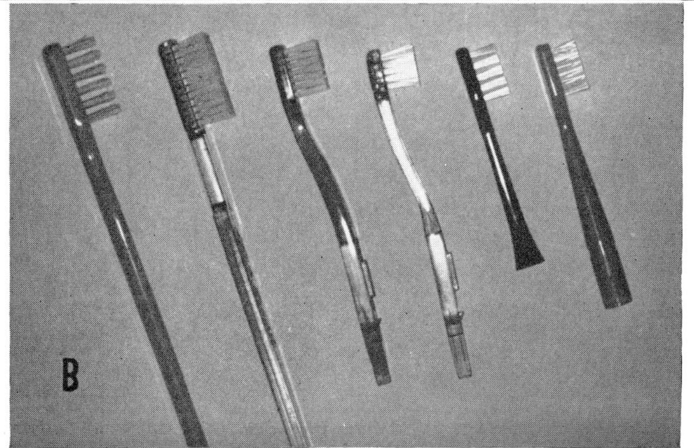

FIG. 3–3. *A,* Representative Automatic Toothbrushes.

Top: brush powered directly from electric outlet;* center† and bottom‡: battery-operated brushes, shown without their corresponding charging units.

B, Comparative Size of Manual and Automatic Toothbrush Heads.

Left to right: manual, adult size tufted; manual adult size multitufted; automatic, regular size; automatic, small; automatic, regular size; automatic, regular size. Note brushing planes of automatic toothbrushes are shorter than those of manual brushes.

*E. R. Squibb Company
†Oral B Company
‡General Electric Company

inserted into a power handle. Brushing planes are activated in orbital, back-and-forth, or arcuate strokes, or in combinations of these movements. Since bristle action of powered brushes is rapid compared with manual brushing, automatic brush heads are smaller, and bristles are of soft or medium texture (Fig. 3–3*B*).

Because automatic brushes can be purchased without prescription and their unsupervised use may be hazardous, the Council on Dental Therapeutics has been empowered to study these devices for acceptance. Criteria by which individual brushes will be evaluated include: *Brush characteristics:* durability, inexpensiveness, ability to be cleaned and aerated; shape of brush and bristle specifications compatible with motion and power characteristics of the brush; testing laboratory approval of safety if any possible hazard from electric shock exists; *Clinical effectiveness:* potential for cleansing oral structures efficiently when used according to instructions; proof that unsupervised use will not injure oral structures.[3]

Automatic brushes are cleansed, dried and replaced in the same manner as manual brushes. Brushes attached directly to an electric outlet should not be held immersed in water when the power is on, and cords leading from the brush handle or from the charging unit should be inspected periodically to determine that insulation is intact.

Denture Brushes

Brushes used to clean removable dentures are of two types: denture brushes, designed to cleanse complete dentures, and clasp brushes, designed to cleanse clasps of removable partial dentures. Denture brush handles are shorter and thicker than toothbrush handles. Hard-textured bristles are arranged in one or two groups of tufts, and longer tufts at the tip of the head are used to brush the denture surface that rests against the soft tissue ridge (Fig. 3–4*A*). Clasp brushes are shaped like miniature bottle brushes with bristles inserted at right angles spiralling down the length of a wire stem (Fig. 3–4*B*). Clasp and denture brushes should be cleansed and dried thoroughly after each use and replaced when bristles begin to bend or mat, thus losing cleansing efficiency.

Dental Floss and Tape

Dental floss is a thin strand of silk or nylon thread with or without wax coating; dental tape, thicker than floss, is flattened into a ribbon. Strands of either tape or floss may be worked over proximal surfaces of adjacent teeth or over gingival surfaces of fixed partial dentures and proximal surfaces of their abutments to loosen retained debris.

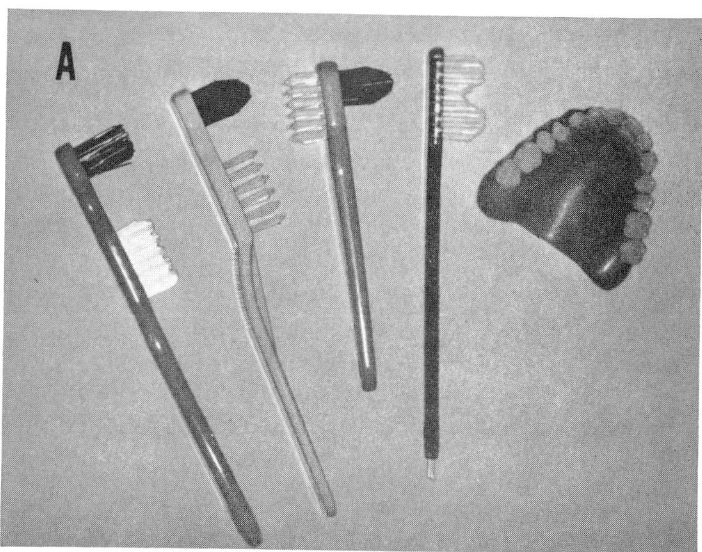

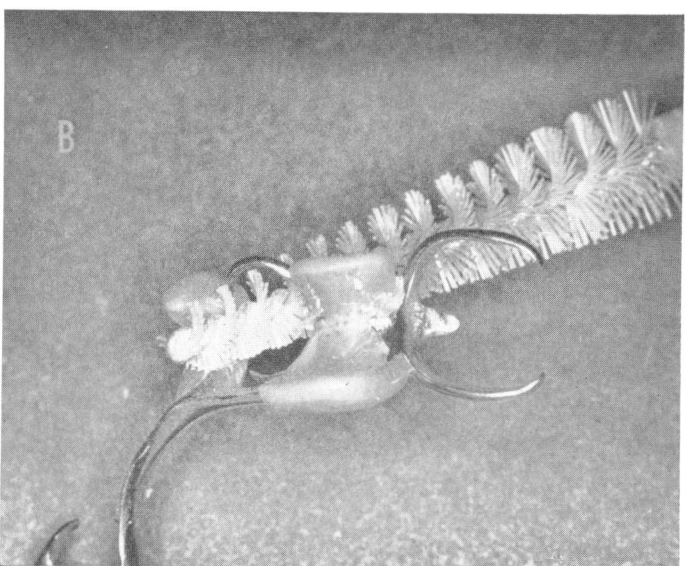

FIG. 3–4. *A,* Denture Brushes.

Longer bristles are used to brush the inner surface of the denture that rests along the soft tissue ridge.

B, Clasp Brush and Removable Partial Denture.

Bristles are inserted at right angles into a wire stem. Bristles are worked over inner surfaces of clasps to remove soft deposits.

Dental floss should not be used routinely to relieve food impaction caused by faulty tooth contour or in areas that require operative correction because this practice merely relieves symptoms of a defect that will continue to injure soft tissues. Only the individual who is adept and will follow instructions should be advised to use dental floss or tape, and he should be cautioned to follow instructions implicitly to avoid injuring the soft tissue.

To insert floss through the contact area, hold a 12-inch strand between thumbs and forefingers, with digits about 1 inch apart, then press the strand against the facial aspect of the contact and *gently* pull floss toward lingual surfaces (Fig. 3–5*A*). As soon as the strand clears the contact, release tension of grasp, then adapt the strand to the curved surface of one tooth (Fig. 3–5*B*). With gentle pressure, work floss apically along the tooth surface until the depth of the sulcus is reached, then back to the contact area. Pull an unused portion of the strand beneath the contact, adapt floss to the adjacent tooth surface and work strand to the sulcus depth and back. Slide a new, unused portion of the strand through the contact area to remove floss from the interdental embrasure.

Several precautions must be observed to avoid lacerating soft tissue: use a short grasp to maintain control as floss is activated; do not "snap" floss through the contact and onto the interdental papilla; avoid pulling strand against interdental papilla as strand is moved from one proximal surface to the other; curve strand over proximal surface to avoid pressing floss through marginal gingiva; do not remove floss by pulling it through the embrasure and against crest of papilla.

Since dental tape is flattened into a ribbon, it presents a greater working surface than floss, therefore is preferred for use with polishing agents to remove stains or soft deposits. A small amount of dentifrice

---

FIG. 3–5. Dental Tape.

A, Strand of tape is pressed against facial aspect of contact, then gently pulled toward lingual surfaces.

B, When strand clears contact, grasp is released, strand is adapted to curved surface of one tooth, and worked apically along tooth to base of the sulcus. The strand is worked back to contact area, then an unused portion is worked beneath contact and the stroke is repeated on the adjacent tooth surface. A new, unused portion of strand is worked between contact to remove tape from the embrasure.

C, Error to avoid: edge of tape is pressed into facial marginal gingiva and will lacerate the soft tissue.

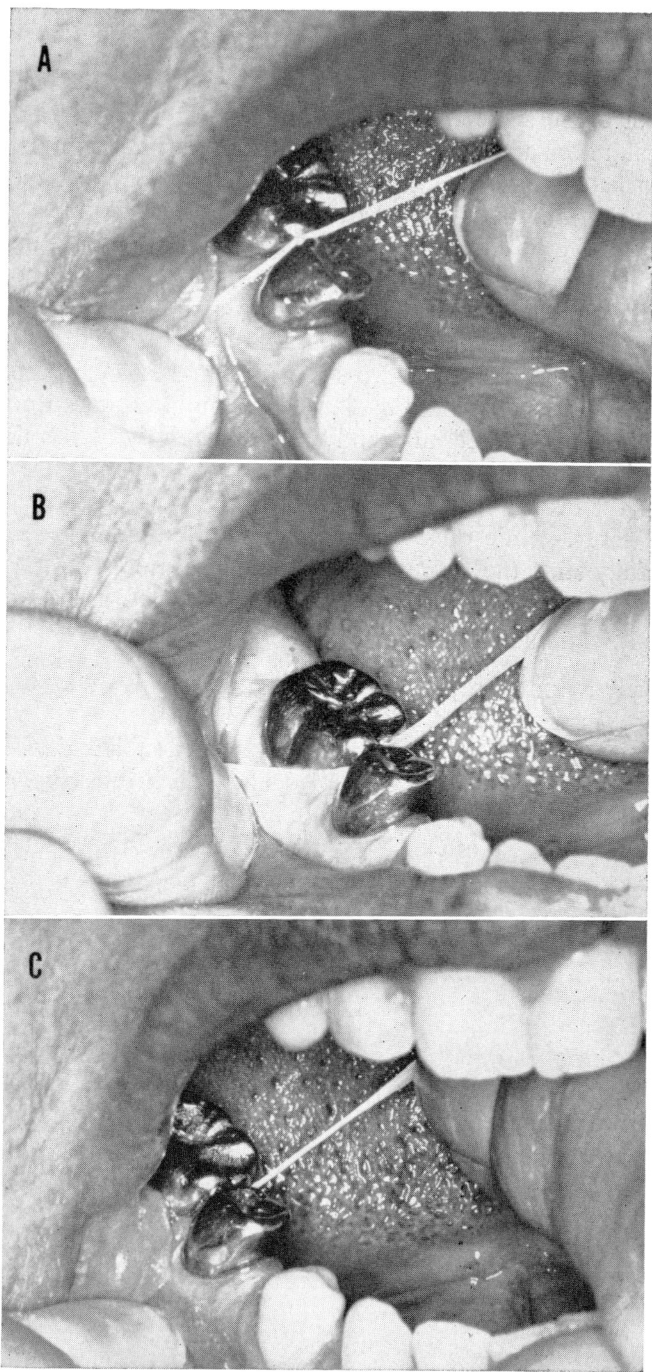

FIG. 3–5. *(Legend on opposite page.)*

8

is placed on the facial, occlusal or incisal aspect of the contact area, then worked through the contact and over each proximal surface with tape. Special precaution should be taken to adapt tape around curved surfaces of teeth, since ribbon edges of tape are even narrower and sharper than floss and present a greater potential hazard to soft tissue.

To use dental floss or tape over gingival surfaces of fixed partial dentures and proximal surfaces of abutment teeth, double the strand and thread the loop through an embrasure next to an abutment tooth from the facial to the lingual aspect. Grasp the loop and pull it through until the strand can be reduced to a single thickness. Adapt floss or tape to the abutment tooth at the joint between denture and abutment, and work strand across the proximal surface of the abutment to the sulcus depth and back. Gently pull an unused portion of the strand against the denture and work it carefully across the appliance to the other abutment. Polish the proximal surface of that abutment, then work the strand back across the appliance to its original position. Exert gentle pressure with the strand against the appliance and carefully slide the strand out of the embrasure.

Nylon or Rayon Knitting Yarn

Three-ply nylon or rayon (not wool) knitting yarn may be used to cleanse proximal surfaces of abutment teeth or teeth exposed by receded interdental gingiva. An 8-inch length of yarn is doubled; dental floss is drawn through the loop, then doubled and tied in position. Floss is threaded through the interdental space and the yarn drawn into working position. A single thickness of yarn is worked facio-lingually over proximal surfaces of adjacent teeth in the same manner as dental tape.[27]

Gauze Strips

If exposed proximal surfaces of teeth bordering edentulous areas are inaccessible to the cleansing action of toothbrush bristles or dental tape, these surfaces may be cleansed with strips of gauze. A 6-inch-length of 1-inch gauze bandage, folded down the center, is placed with the fold toward the gingiva, then curved around the proximal surface and worked back and forth until the fold extends to the base of the sulcus. The back and forth movement is repeated several times until debris is loosened and removed.[20]

Interdental Stimulators

Interdental stimulators are used to massage interdental gingiva and to remove debris from exposed proximal surfaces of teeth. These devices, made of rubber, wood or plastic, are used only when there has been moderate to severe recession of interdental papillae or when there is sufficient space in the interdental embrasure to insert stimulators without injury to the soft tissue.

A rounded or hexagonal rubber cone, attached to a handle such as the toothbrush handle, is inserted comfortably in an open interdental embrasure from the facial or lingual aspect, with the tip of the cone pointed slightly toward the occlusal plane (Fig. 3–6*A, B*). The tip is inserted until the cone fills the space and light pressure is exerted against the soft tissue, then the handle is rotated gently to a slow count of ten. Sides of the cone bump against the soft tissue, massaging it, and against the teeth, loosening debris. Normal interdental gingiva slopes away from the crest, and the side of the cone that rests against the soft tissue must be positioned to approximate this sloping contour. The stimulator should never be "jammed" uncomfortably or at a right angle into an embrasure in a manner that would cause further recession or breakdown of epithelial attachments (Fig. 3–6*C*).

A specially designed toothpick of soft balsam wood that does not splinter readily and is impregnated with a mild antiseptic* can be used to cleanse proximal surfaces as well as massage interdental gingiva. Longitudinally, one end of the toothpick is pointed and the other is flat where it has been detached from its matchbook-like holder; in cross-section, it is triangular in shape, with the base of the triangle shorter than its equilateral sides. The toothpick is moistened with saliva, then inserted *gently* several times into an open embrasure. During insertion, sides of the soft wood pick conform to contours of the proximal surfaces of teeth, cleansing them, and to the crest of the interdental gingiva, massaging it. The tip is directed toward the occlusal plane so the side formed by the base of the triangle will rest on interdental tissue at an angle approximating normal gingival contour (Fig. 3–7). In areas of limited access, for example, between posterior teeth or from the lingual aspect, the toothpick is broken in two and the pointed end used. When wood softens and loses its triangular contour, the stimulator should be replaced.

Plastic toothpicks similar in design to balsam wood stimulators are available and, although the plastic is flexible, sides of the picks cannot be contoured to walls of the interdental embrasure, therefore they are less effective for cleansing and potentially harmful to the soft tissue. Regular hardwood toothpicks should not be used because the wood may splinter, thus puncture or lacerate soft tissue.

*Stim-U-Dents, a product of Stim-U-Dents, Inc., 14035 Woodrow Wilson, Detroit, Michigan.

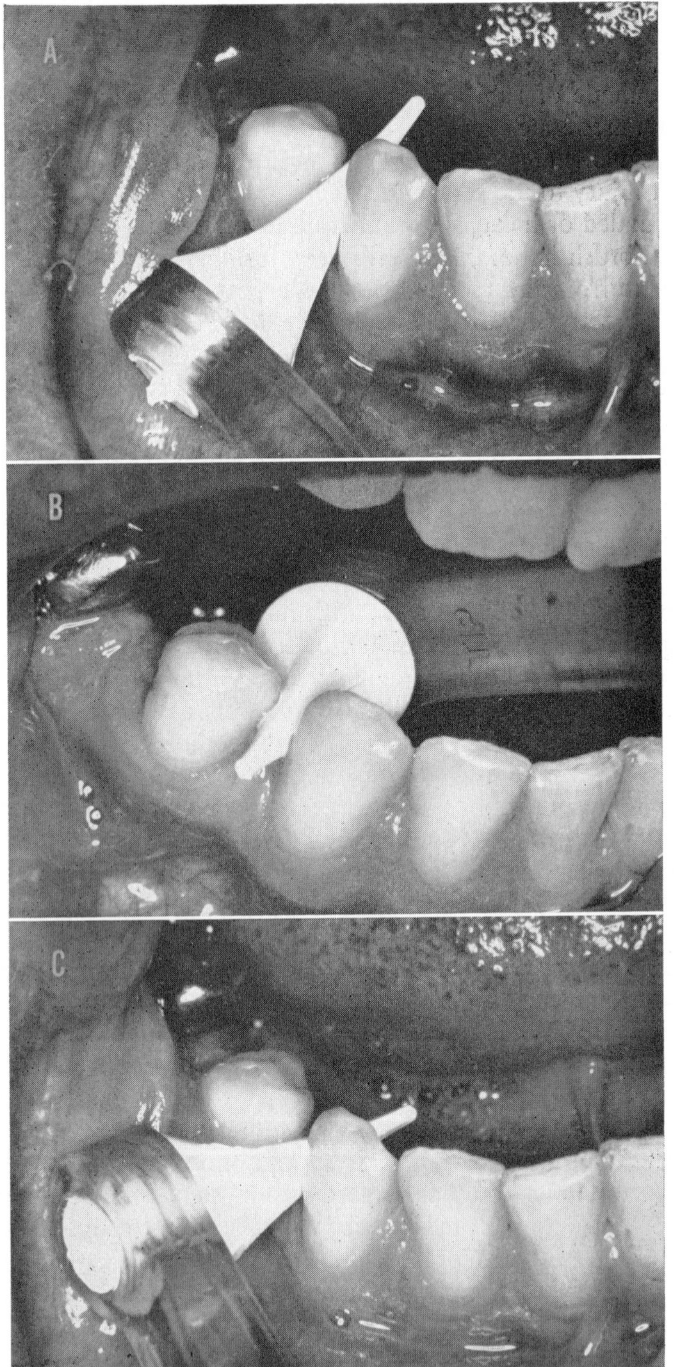

FIG. 3–6. Rubber Cone Interdental Stimulator.

A, Cone inserted in interdental embrasure from facial aspect: tip is directed toward occlusal plane, sides rest against crest of gingiva and proximal surfaces of teeth. Light pressure is exerted, then handle is rotated gently to count of ten.

B, Cone inserted in open interdental embrasure from lingual aspect.

C, Error to avoid: cone inserted at right angle to facial surfaces of teeth could cause further gingival recession or breakdown of epithelial attachments.

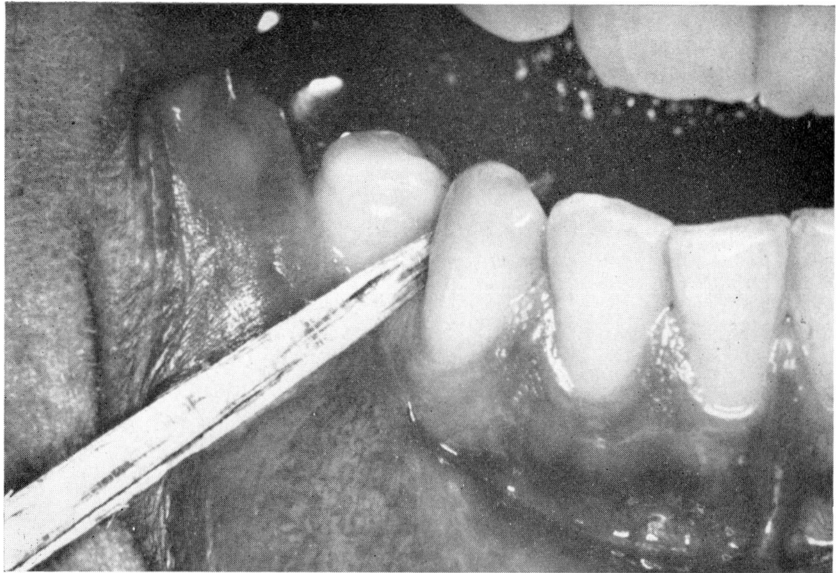

FIG. 3–7. Soft Balsam Wood Toothpick Interdental Stimulator.
The tip is pointed slightly toward occlusal plane, and the side formed by the base of the triangle in cross-section rests on interdental gingiva at angle approximating normal gingival contour.

Rubber Cup Polisher and Stimulator

One or more soft, natural rubber cups, similar to those used for professional polishing, and mounted on a handle, are used to cleanse cervical surfaces of teeth and to massage the gingiva. These devices are useful after gingival surgery or during an acute phase of a gingival disturbance when the patient cannot use a toothbrush because teeth and/or gingiva are hypersensitive. Only one cup is used to polish the teeth. The cup is moistened with dentifrice, then placed on a tooth next to the gingival margin, and sufficient pressure is exerted to splay the cup onto proximal and/or submarginal surfaces (Fig. 3–8*A, B*). The handle is rotated gently to move the inner surface of the cup over the tooth and, as the tooth is cleansed, marginal gingiva is massaged by pressure from the outer rim of the cup. Two or three cups are used when the gingiva is to be massaged. Cups are lubricated and placed over the soft tissue; sufficient pressure is exerted to spread the cup rims, then the handle is pumped or rotated slightly to a count of ten. Suction is created as the moistened inner surface of the cup is pressed against soft tissue, so the patient needs to use gentle pressure and rotate the handle with very small circular movements.

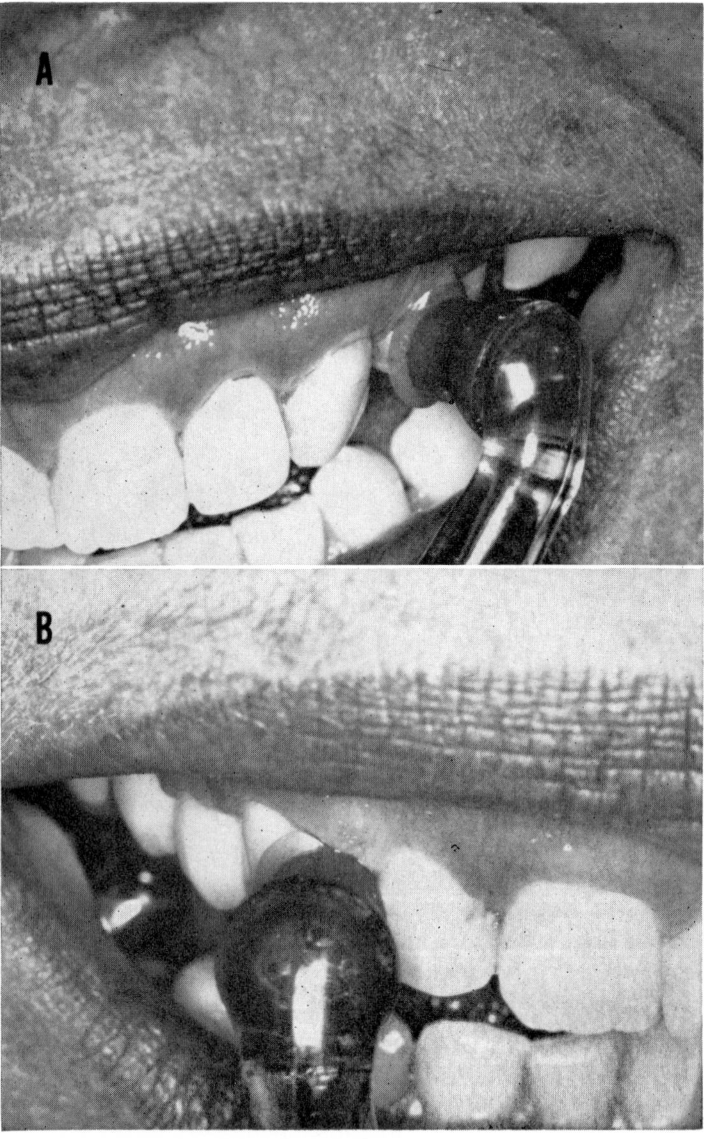

Fig. 3–8. Rubber Cup Polisher and Stimulator.

A, Rubber cup is moistened then placed with sufficient pressure to splay cup rim onto proximal and/or submarginal surfaces of tooth. Polishing is accomplished by rotating handle so inner surface of cup moves over the tooth. Massage occurs as outer surface of the cup rim presses against marginal gingiva and sulcular epithelium.

B, Rubber cup rim spread over submarginal and proximal surface provides cleansing and massaging actions.

Digital Massage

Digital or finger massage may be applied by the patient to improve tone of unstimulated or spongy gingiva. This type of massage is of particular value to stimulate soft tissue underlying removable dentures. The hands are washed and a dentifrice or lubricant is spread lightly on pads of the thumb and forefinger. Facial and lingual surfaces of the arch are kneaded gently between these digits several times in each position, beginning at the distal end of the arch and working to the midline.

Oral Hydrotherapeutic Devices

Instruments that spray fine pressurized streams of water on oral structures have been termed oral hydrotherapeutic devices.[29] One instrument that may be of value to loosen debris adhering to fixed appliances and supporting teeth consists of a tube attached at one end to the sink faucet and at the other to a toothbrush handle. Water passes through the tube into the handle, through a compartment containing replaceable tablets of dentifrice, and is emitted in fine streams through four tiny holes in the toothbrush head next to bases of bristle tufts.*

Another oral hydrotherapeutic device useful for interdental cleansing consists of a 1-quart liquid reservoir, an encased pump, and a plastic tube that transports the liquid to a hand-held, removable, adjustable tip.† The user adjusts pump pressure, then positions the tip so the stream will flow in the desired direction. He inserts the tip into his oral cavity, leans over the sink, turns the pump on and moves the tip so the intermittent pulsating stream passes interdentally and into gingival sulci. The liquid escapes the oral cavity through the user's open lips.

Other devices to achieve oral lavage can be assembled, for example: a water syringe; a 50-ml. glass hypodermic syringe with suitable nozzle; or a chip blower with bulb containing warm water or a saline solution.[30]

Dentifrices

Dentifrices may be regarded as cosmetic and/or therapeutic or prophylactic aids to dental health. Most dentifrices are marketed as toothpastes or tooth powders. Removal of soft deposits and stains from accessible surfaces of the teeth with the toothbrush may or may not require the aid of a dentifrice.[24] Conditions determining the need

*Ora-jet, a product of the Oral B Company, San Jose, California.
†Water Pik, a product of Aqua Tec Corp., Denver, Colorado.

for a dentifrice vary with the individual's tooth alignment, rate of formation of soft deposits and stains, and degree of exposure of root surfaces of the teeth. Probably the most important factor considered by the layman as he selects a dentifrice is the flavor of a particular brand.[17]

Cosmetic dentifrices contain flavors (essential oils) and noncarbohydrate sweetening agents (saccharin) to impart pleasant odors and tastes. Most dentifrices contain soap or synthetic detergents, although proof is lacking to demonstrate that detergents possess inherent ability to cleanse the teeth.[4]

Toothpastes and powders contain abrasives, the active ingredients that aid the toothbrush or dental tape in removal of soft deposits and stains. Some abrasives used in dentifrices are calcium carbonate, one or more of the calcium phosphates, calcium sulfate, insoluble sodium metaphosphate, hydrated aluminum oxide, magnesium carbonates and phosphates, sodium bicarbonate and sodium chloride.[5] Patients whose exposed cervical root surfaces need to be cleansed with the least abrasive method can be advised to use the toothbrush moistened with water. Sodium bicarbonate, a mild abrasive, can be placed on the toothbrush and used to remove stain if it occurs after ten days or two weeks of brushing without a dentifrice.[5]

Toothpastes contain binding agents to help the mixture retain moisture and desired consistency. Compounds commonly used for this purpose are glycerin, propylene glycol, sorbitol solution, or water and alcohol. Thickeners used in toothpastes are tragacanth, alginate, carrageenan and cellulose derivatives.[5]

Cosmetic dentifrices are not considered by the American Dental Association, Council on Dental Therapeutics for acceptance. Therapeutic dentifrices accepted by the Council include those containing stannous fluoride combined with ingredients that do not immobilize the fluoride ion. The Council qualified acceptance of these dentifrices with this statement:

> ". . . has been shown to be an effective decay preventive dentifrice that can be of significant value when used in a conscientiously applied program of oral hygiene and regular professional care."[12]

Although use of accepted dentifrices has been demonstrated to reduce incidence of dental caries in permanent teeth of individuals over a fairly wide age range, experimental studies did not include many older adults.[6]

Other proposed caries-preventive agents have been incorporated in dentifrices. Foaming detergents with claimed anti-enzyme or antibacterial properties, environmental modifiers, enamel modifiers and antibiotics have been considered by the Council, but reports of their effectiveness have been inconclusive, contradictory or so limited that they could not be evaluated with accuracy.[7] Topical administration of penicillin in the mouth is contraindicated because penicillin sensitivity could be produced, reactions could occur in the sensitized patient, or penicillin-resistant organisms could be developed locally in the mouth as well as elsewhere in the body.[8] Dentifrices applied with the toothbrush for prevention of calculus formation or to reduce hypersensitivity of exposed cementum and dentin have appeared on the market but their effectiveness has yet to be proven.

Denture Cleansers

When removable dentures are cleansed thoroughly immediately after the wearer ingests food, stains and deposits do not tend to adhere. Used with plain water, the denture brush will remove most soft deposits but if stains or deposits persist a mild abrasive and/or mild inorganic chemical denture cleanser may be used.

Cleansers suitable for use with the denture brush include toilet soap, bicarbonate of soda or precipitated calcium carbonate.[9] Commercial paste denture cleansers are similar in composition to toothpastes. Vigorous brushing with any abrasive should be avoided, particularly on the denture surface that rests against soft tissues, and kitchen cleanser abrasives are definitely too harsh for use on dentures.

Acrylic dentures may be soaked for a short time in a cupful of water with one of the following additives: 1 teaspoonful of 5 per cent sodium hypochlorite, 1 tablespoonful of mild white vinegar, 1 teaspoonful of 28 per cent ammonia, or 1/3 teaspoonful of trisodium phosphate. Removable denture wearers should be cautioned that metallic clasps, bars or rests made of chromium cobalt alloy will corrode if allowed to remain any length of time in a solution containing chlorine.[9]

Mouthwashes

Mouthwashes are liquids with pleasant tastes and odors used to rinse the mouth. Essentially a mouthwash flushes debris and microorganisms out of the mouth as the liquid is forced between the teeth, then expectorated. This flushing action can be achieved adequately with plain tap water, and should be performed routinely after toothbrushing, after use of dental floss or tape, and after eating, if the toothbrush cannot be used.

Nonmedicated commercial mouthwashes labeled as cosmetic agents are not considered by the Council on Dental Therapeutics for acceptance. Rinses recommended to soothe soft tissues following extensive instrumentation and to promote healing are: ½ teaspoonful salt in an 8-ounce glass of warm water, or ½ teaspoonful soda in ¾ of a glass of warm water.[10] If a flavored, colored mouthwash is preferred, the following is recommended: ½ teaspoonful salt, ¼ teaspoonful soda, 1 drop red food coloring, and a touch of peppermint oil in an 8-ounce glass of warm water.

Commercial mouthwashes that contain agents or medicaments with claimed germicidal, astringent, deodorant, buffering or therapeutic properties have been marketed for unsupervised use by the public but, to date, have not met acceptance standards outlined by the Council. Mouthwashes contain essential oils that impart a pleasant fragrance, temporarily masking the offensive oral odor. This masking effect depends on the intensity of the substitute fragrance and on the cause of the breath odor, which might be poor oral hygiene, oral disease, or a systemic disturbance. The patient who has a marked breath odor that persists after toothbrushing should be advised not to rely on effects of a mouthwash, and the cause of his halitosis should be investigated.[10]

Buffered mouthwashes, claimed to neutralize acids, impart a transient effect in the oral cavity as saliva quickly dilutes the buffer concentration. Astringent mouthwashes contain agents that precipitate protein material from mucous secretions and saliva. Patients who use astringent mouthwashes routinely should be cautioned to dilute concentrates according to directions on the labels because concentrated solutions may irritate soft tissues and gradually may decalcify tooth structure.

Since the exact role of microorganisms in oral disease has not been established, there is no reason to incorporate nonspecific germicidal agents in a mouthwash; in fact, it may be harmful to change the normal oral flora. Claims that mouthwashes exert an anti-bacterial effect are based on test-tube results and have not been substantiated in experiments with patients.

Unsupervised use of mouthwashes that claim to relieve pain or symptoms of oral disease is condemned strongly because the patient may rely on claimed curative effects of these products and fail to seek professional care until symptoms progress to a serious stage. The dentist may prescribe specific medicated mouth rinses in therapeutic management of oral disease but, in this case, he evaluates the need for a rinse and supervises its use by the patient.

Disclosing Agents

Disclosing agents are dyes used to color food debris, dental plaque, calculus and microbial masses in the oral cavity. Ideally, these agents stain extraneous material but do not impart permanent color to teeth, soft tissues or restorative materials. A disclosing tablet or solution can be used by the patient to visualize stains and deposits that need to be removed with the toothbrush or other oral physiotherapy aid.

Various formulæ for disclosing agents have been found effective but several seem particularly suited for home use: dilute basic Fuchsin solution, or dilute F.D.C. Red No. 3 solution,[11] flushed in the oral cavity for thirty seconds, then expectorated; or Compressed F.D.C. Red No. 3 tablets, chewed and mixed with saliva for thirty seconds, then flushed between teeth and expectorated.*

TOOTHBRUSHING

Frequency. Thorough toothbrushing immediately following ingestion of meals and snacks that contain refined carbohydrates is a habit that should be formed early in life. Removable appliances need to be cleansed as often as natural teeth, particularly inner surfaces of partial denture clasps that hold deposits against abutment teeth.

Folding toothbrushes can be carried to school or work and used when the individual is away from home. When the patient cannot brush, he can chew a raw, crisp, watery fruit or vegetable at the end of a meal to stimulate salivary flow. Another substitute measure is to rinse the mouth or "swish" with tap water or a noncarbohydrate liquid to dilute sugars and remove loosened particles of debris.

Sequence. If a routine order of brushing becomes an established habit, the individual is more likely to cleanse and massage all areas every time he brushes. When the patient's established routine produces satisfactory results, he should be advised to continue this practice rather than change the routine and perhaps reduce efficiency. However, if the patient's regimen is inadequate, a specific sequence of brushing should be instituted. The operator should show the patient the three major aspects of his dentition: facial, lingual and occlusal, or cheek, tongue and biting surfaces, as well as proximal, or adjacent surfaces. The patient will perform best when he first begins brushing, so the order recommended should start from the aspect where he has had least success, usually lingual surfaces of mandibular teeth. One

*Flavored disclosing tablets, labeled active ingredient erythrosine, distributed by Procter and Gamble, Cincinnati, Ohio.

sequence that could be recommended is: brush lingual surfaces of mandibular teeth, from the right most posterior tooth around the arch to the left most posterior tooth, then all facial surfaces from left to right. Repeat the procedure on the maxillary arch, then brush occlusal surfaces. Occlusal surfaces may be brushed last, but when softer bristles are desired for gingival massage, occlusal surfaces should be brushed first.

Bristle Placement. The length of the brushing plane covers approximately three teeth; the width, one anterior tooth. When a patient has a normal complement of teeth, the length of the brushing plane is used across molars, then bicuspids, cuspids, and central and lateral incisors on one side, then the other side of each arch. From the lingual aspect, most individuals' arches are too narrow from cuspid-to-cuspid to accommodate the full length of the brushing plane, so lingual surfaces of each anterior tooth are brushed individually with the narrower aspect of the brush head.

Bristle tips remove soft debris when they are drawn over smooth surfaces or worked into pits and fissures of the teeth. Thorough cleansing requires the brushing plane to be drawn over a tooth surface at least six times. When sides of bristles are drawn gently over facial attached gingiva, resultant friction promotes callousing or keratinization, thus makes gingiva more resistant to trauma. As sides of bristles are pressed against the gingiva, then relaxed, stagnant fluids are forced out and fresh fluids allowed into the tissue. Thorough massage requires intermittent pressure of sides of bristles against gingiva for at least ten seconds, or to a slow count of ten.

Limitations and Contraindications. Toothbrush bristles are straight and extend at right angles from the brush head to form a flat brushing plane, while teeth present curved surfaces, some of which are inaccessible to bristle tips. A combination of toothbrushing methods and supplementary aids may be required to accomplish adequate oral physiotherapy in the following areas: contact areas and proximal surfaces of crowded teeth with intact interdental papillae; convexities in proximal surfaces of teeth exposed by receded interdental gingiva; exposed proximal surfaces of teeth adjacent to edentulous areas; cervical surfaces from heights of contour to depths of gingival sulci; gingival surfaces of fixed partial dentures and adjacent proximal surfaces of abutment teeth; and teeth with fixed orthodontic bands and wires.

When gingiva is hypersensitive, for example after extensive instrumentation, or denuded, as in the acute phase of necrotizing ulcerative gingivitis or following gingival surgery, open lesions should not be irritated with the toothbrush. However, a warm saline solution rinse and either rubber cups or hydrotherapeutic devices can be used to remove debris from the teeth. After surface epithelization, gentle massage with a soft-textured brush will stimulate circulation and healing, then, as soon as epithelium is intact, a medium or hard-textured brush may be advocated to promote keratinization of attached gingiva. Measures to be used by the patient with an acute disturbance are always prescribed by the dentist who is responsible for the patient's welfare as a result of treatment.

Toothbrush Trauma. Patience and practice are required to develop skill necessary to cleanse teeth and massage gingiva, yet avoid injury. Careless brush placement and vigorous scrubbing can puncture, lacerate or bruise facial gingiva. Punctate lesions appear as red pin-point dots that correspond to tips of bristles. Lacerations appear as linear scratches where bristle tips were drawn over gingiva with excessive pressure. An overzealous patient with a new stiff-textured toothbrush may brush too long in one or two areas and remove surface epithelium, producing a raw, painful bruise.

Chronic, vigorous, horizontal or circular scrubbing with an abrasive dentifrice over a long period removes marginal gingiva, then abrades exposed root surfaces, producing smooth wedge- or saucer-shaped concavities bounded by marginal gingiva and the cervico-enamel junction. These abrasions occur on facial surfaces of teeth that extend beyond adjacent teeth, such as cuspids or teeth in bucco- or labio-version. Occasionally cervical enamel is abraded.

Chronic vigorous circular or vertical brushing of facial gingiva can produce narrow grooves or notches extending from the center of the marginal crest to the attached gingiva. Another characteristic reaction to chronic up and down or circular brushing is recession, then enlargement or "piling-up" of marginal gingiva in the shape of a collar, called "McCall's festoons."[21]

Rolling Stroke Method. The Rolling Stroke Method, named for the rolling or sweeping stroke of the brushing plane across gingiva and teeth, has been advocated by professionals for patients who have relatively normal tooth alignment and normal healthy gingiva.[13] To brush all facial surfaces and lingual surfaces of posterior teeth: position the brush head parallel to the occlusal plane with sides of bristle tips on the attached gingiva, exert gentle but firm pressure, and roll the brushing plane toward and over gingiva and teeth (Fig. 3–9*A*). To brush lingual surfaces of anterior teeth: insert the brush head longitudinally so its width covers the lingual surface of a tooth; place sides of bristle tips nearest the handle on attached gingiva, and exert gentle pressure to bend bristles against gingiva (Fig. 3–9*B*). Move the brush handle forward and down in an arc to bring the brushing plane across lingual surfaces of maxillary teeth and gingiva, and forward and up in an arc to brush mandibular teeth and gingiva. To cleanse occlusal surfaces: work bristle tips into pits and fissures with short, vibratory back and forth movements to a slow count of ten.

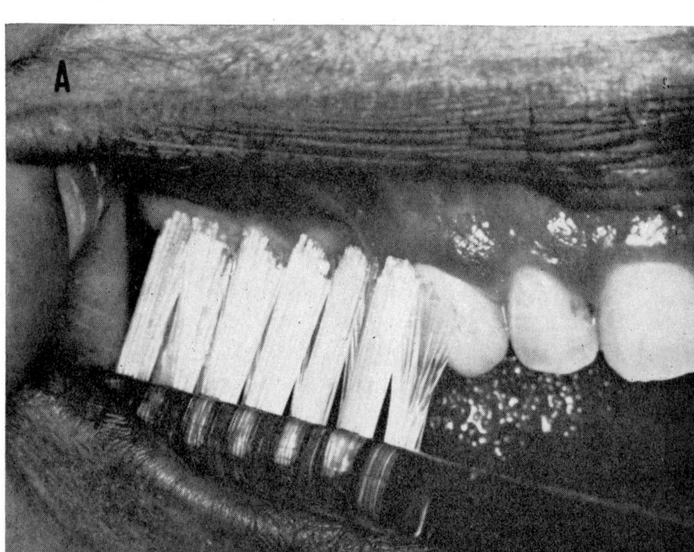

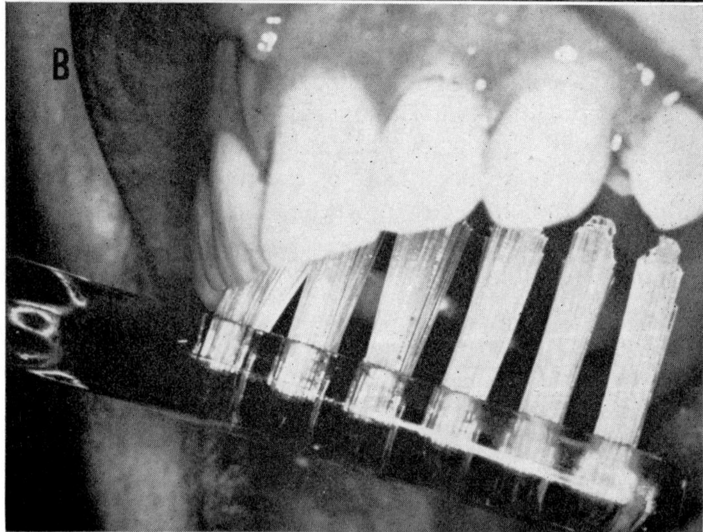

FIG. 3–9. Rolling Stroke Method of Toothbrushing.

A, Brush placement for facial surfaces and posterior lingual surfaces of teeth: *place* brush head parallel to occlusal plane with sides of bristle tips on attached gingiva; rotate head 45° toward teeth and *press* gently until tissue blanches; *roll* brushing plane slowly across gingiva and teeth.

B, Brush placement for lingual surfaces, anterior teeth: *place* brush parallel with long axis of tooth, with sides of bristles on attached gingiva; *press* gently until tissue blanches; *roll* brushing plane slowly across gingiva and tooth. Draw handle forward and down to cleanse maxillary teeth, forward and up to cleanse mandibular teeth.

Three discrete movements need to be emphasized as the patient learns and practices this method: *place* sides of bristle tips on gingiva; *press* until tissue blanches; *roll* brushing plane *slowly* so bristles reach cervical and proximal surfaces of teeth as well as interdental gingiva. Errors seen as the patient learns or becomes careless with this method include: bristle tips are directed at right angles into attached gingiva and produce punctures or lacerations; bristle tips are placed beyond mucogingival line and lacerate oral mucosa; the brush head is not positioned parallel with the occlusal plane so only a few toe-end bristles reach gingiva; too little pressure is used so bristles do not spread over cervical, proximal or interdental areas; too much pressure is used so bristle tips lacerate tissue; rolling stroke is accomplished too quickly so bristles do not loosen deposits or reach cervical or proximal surfaces; bristle tips are swept back and forth across occlusal surfaces, thus tips do not loosen particles deep in pits and fissures.

Modified Stillman's Method. Modified Stillman's Method, performed with a soft-textured multitufted toothbrush, may be more effective than the Rolling Stroke to massage slightly receded, hemorrhagic or spongy gingiva. Stillman's Method requires that bristles be placed and pressed gently against gingiva and teeth in the same manner as for the Rolling Stroke (Fig. 3–10*A, B*). When sides of bristle tips are positioned, gentle pressure is exerted to maintain tips in place on soft tissue while the brush is vibrated or rotated slightly to a slow count of ten.[32] Although bristle tips remain in position on the gingiva, those against tooth structure move slightly and remove soft deposits. Modification of the method incorporates the rolling stroke over facial and lingual surfaces. Occlusal surfaces are cleansed with bristle tips.

Five movements are emphasized as the patient learns and practices this method: *place* sides of bristle tips on gingiva; *press* until tissue blanches, turn brush 45° toward teeth until bristles *flex* over marginal and interdental gingiva; *vibrate* the brush to a slow count of ten; *roll* brushing plane slowly over gingiva and teeth. Errors seen as the patient learns or becomes careless with this method are those seen with the Rolling Stroke and, in addition, may include: too much pressure exerted during vibrations causes bristle tips to puncture gingiva, or over a period of time will promote further recession; too little pressure exerted during vibrations allows bristle tips to lacerate gingiva or fails to flex bristles over cervical and proximal surfaces.

Bass' Method. Bass' Method, carefully executed with a "Right Kind" brush (soft-textured, tufted, round-end nylon bristles) and "Right Kind" dental floss (thin, smooth, unwaxed), has been advocated to cleanse hard-to-reach cervical and proximal surfaces of teeth and to massage marginal gingiva. Bristles are directed apically at a 45° angle to long axes of teeth and, with short vibratory strokes, are

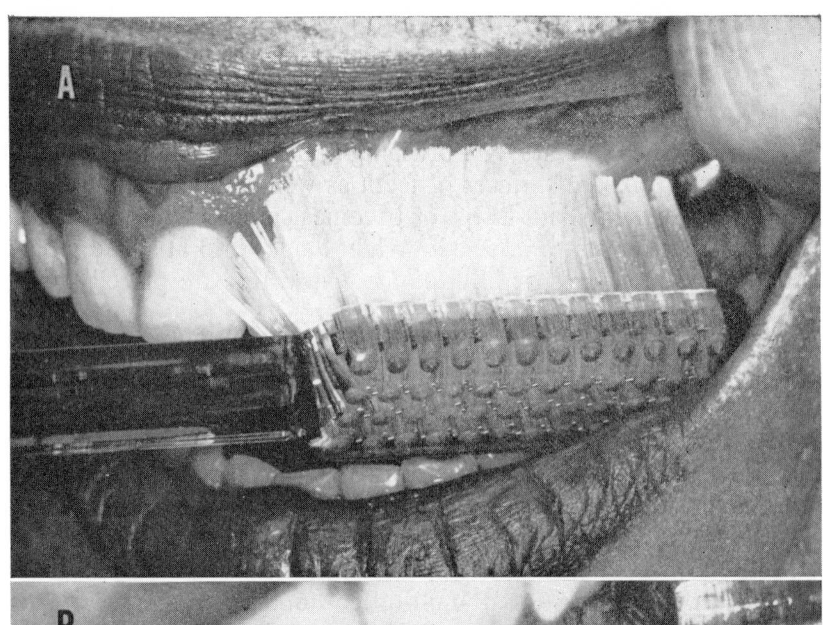

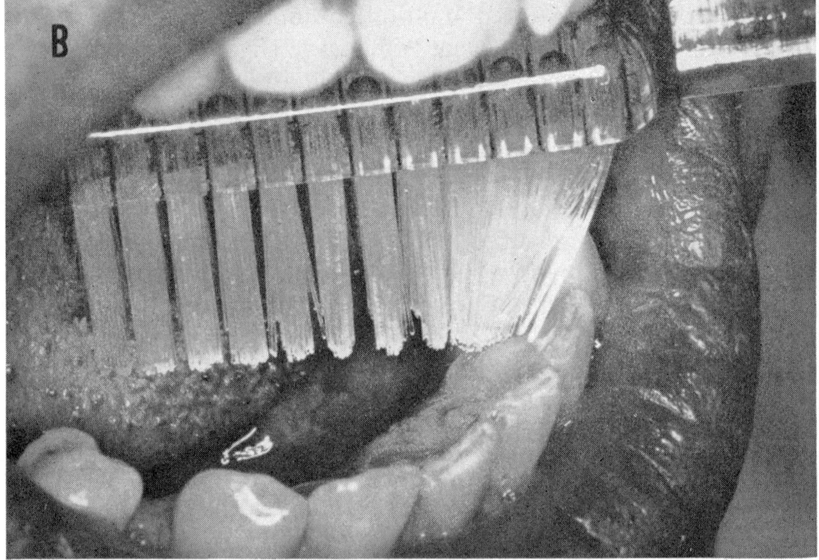

FIG. 3–10. Modified Stillman's Method of Toothbrushing.

A, Brush placement for facial surfaces: *place* brush head parallel to occlusal plane with sides of bristle tips on attached gingiva; rotate head 45° toward teeth and *press* gently until tissue blanches; *vibrate* brush to slow count of ten. *Roll* brushing plane slowly across gingiva and teeth. NOTE: entire length of brushing plane cannot be adapted to teeth and gingiva over cuspid eminences.

B, Brush placement for lingual surfaces, anterior teeth: *place* brush head parallel to long axis of tooth with sides of bristle tips on attached gingiva; *press* gently; *vibrate* brush to slow count of ten. *Roll* brushing plane slowly across gingiva and tooth; bring handle forward and down to cleanse maxillary teeth, forward and up to cleanse mandibular teeth.

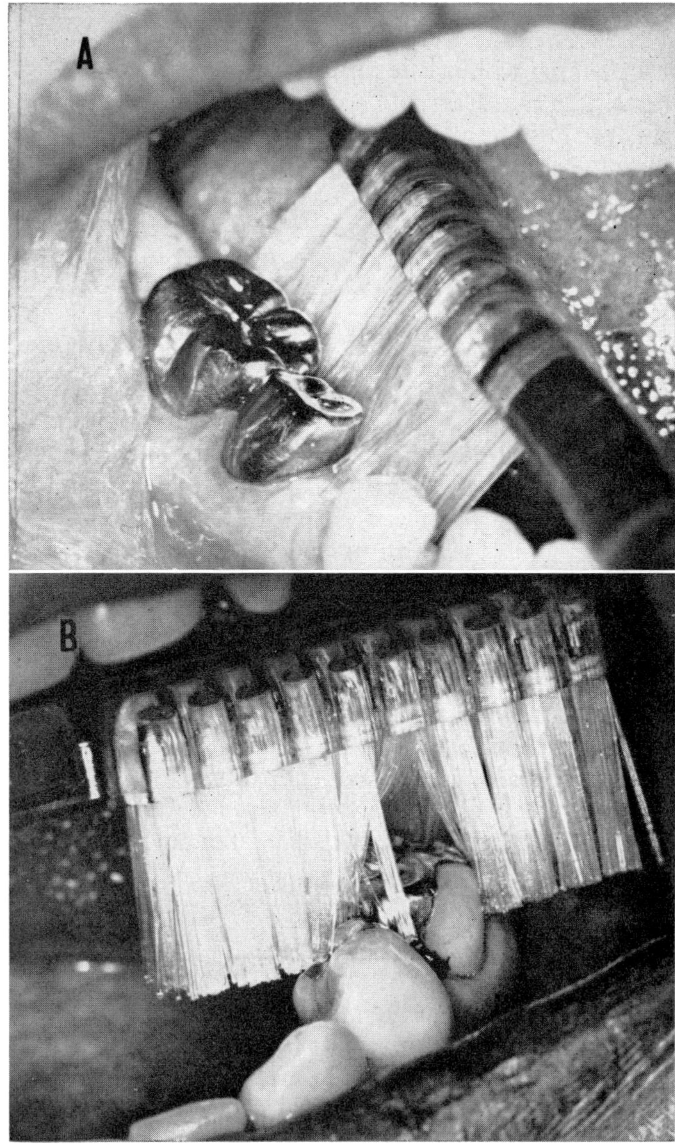

FIG. 3–11. Bass' Method of Toothbrushing.

A, Bristles are directed apically at a 45° angle to long axes of teeth and, with short vibratory strokes, are worked over marginal gingiva and cervical areas onto exposed submarginal surfaces of teeth.

B, Brush placement for hard-to-reach areas, for example, exposed proximal surfaces of teeth adjacent to edentulous areas: brushing plane is placed parallel to proximal surface; bristles are directed apically and at a 45° angle to proximal surface, then with short vibratory strokes, worked over marginal gingiva and onto exposed submarginal surfaces.

worked over marginal gingiva and cervical areas onto exposed submarginal surfaces of the teeth[14] (Fig. 3–11*A, B*). Occlusal pits and fissures are cleansed with bristle tips. Floss is used to cleanse proximal surfaces to depths of sulci.

The patient must be cautioned that too vigorous scrubbing with bristle tips on marginal gingiva or with a hard-textured brush will injure gingiva and gradually may cause recession. Use of an abrasive dentifrice on exposed cementum and dentin may abrade tooth surfaces.

Charters' Method. Charters' Method, performed with a soft-textured multitufted brush, is advocated for periodontal patients who have moderate to severe gingival recession and loss of interdental papillae. Although difficult to master, this method may massage interdental gingiva and cleanse exposed proximal surfaces more effectively than other methods. Charters' Method also is recommended for patients with fixed partial dentures to cleanse gingival surfaces of the appliances and proximal surfaces of abutment teeth. To brush facial surfaces: bristle tips are directed toward and parallel with the occlusal plane and sides of tips are placed against facial surfaces of teeth next to gingival margins. The brush head is turned 45° toward facial surfaces and gentle pressure is exerted to flex bristles over proximal surfaces of teeth and onto crests of interdental gingiva (Fig. 3–12*A*). Gentle pressure maintains bristles in position on gingiva while the brush is rotated slightly to a slow count of ten.[16]

To brush lingual surfaces of posterior teeth: bristles are directed toward lingual surfaces of teeth and toe-end bristles are inserted gently into an embrasure between contact area and interdental gingival crest. Gentle pressure is exerted to flex sides of bristles onto proximal surfaces

---

FIG. 3–12. Charters' Method of Toothbrushing.

A, Brush placement, facial surfaces: with bristles directed toward and parallel to occlusal plane, *place* sides of bristle tips to level of gingival margins; turn brush toward teeth, *flex* bristles over teeth and crests of interdental gingiva, maintain gentle pressure and *vibrate* brush to a slow count of ten. Brush placement, and activation on lingual surfaces (not pictured) are similar except only the toe-end bristles are used to cleanse teeth and massage tissue in one embrasure at a time.

B, Brush placement, lingual surfaces, anterior teeth: gently *place* toe-end bristles into interdental embrasure; *flex* bristles onto proximal surfaces and over crest of interdental gingiva, then *vibrate* brush to a slow count of ten.

C, Incorrect brush placement: brushing plane is not parallel with occlusal plane, thus some bristles are pressed too hard against gingiva, others do not reach soft tissues, or tips lacerate gingiva during vibratory movements.

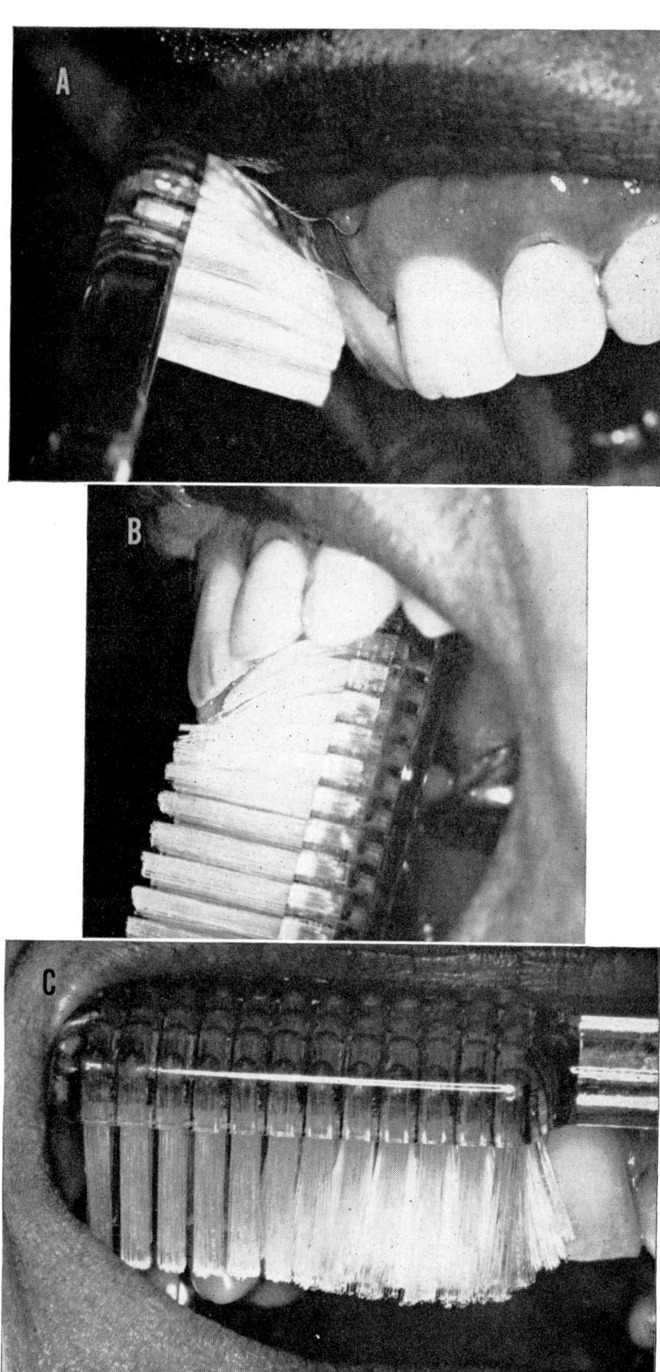

FIG. 3–12. *(Legend on opposite page.)*

of teeth and the gingival crest, and maintained while the brush is rotated to a slow count of ten. To brush lingual surfaces of anterior teeth: the brush head is inserted parallel with long axes of teeth, the brushing plane is directed toward a lingual interproximal embrasure, and toe-end bristles are inserted between contact area and crest of interdental gingiva (Fig. 3–12*B*). Gentle pressure is exerted to flex bristles, then maintained while the brush is rotated to a slow count of ten.[16]

The Rolling Stroke Method can be used to cleanse the teeth either preceding or following massage with Charters' Method. Modified Stillman's Method can be substituted to massage lingual surfaces if the patient cannot master this aspect of Charters' Method. The major difference between Charters' and the other two methods lies in the direction of bristle placement and, if the patient is instructed to use a combination of Charters' and another method, he may become confused unless this distinction is emphasized.

Movements emphasized as the patient learns and practices this method are: to brush facial surfaces, *place* sides of bristles on teeth so tips are near gingival margins, *flex* bristles over proximal surfaces of teeth and crests of interdental gingiva, then *vibrate* brush to a slow count of ten; to brush lingual surfaces of posterior teeth, use only the toe-end bristles, then *place, flex, vibrate;* to brush lingual surfaces of anterior teeth, insert brush head parallel to long axes of teeth, use toe-end bristles, then *place, flex* and *vibrate.*

Errors in the practice of Charters' Method include: the brush is not positioned parallel with the occlusal plane, so heavy pressure is exerted against tissue in one area and light or no pressure is exerted elsewhere (Fig. 3–12*C*); the brushing plane is placed too high or low so bristles do not reach crests of interdental gingiva; attempted use of entire length of brushing plane along lingual surfaces forces bristle tips into gingiva; too vigorous vibration of the brush moves bristle tips and lacerates soft tissues.

Hirschfeld's Method. Hirschfeld's Method of toothbrushing is similar to Charters' and can be used to achieve the same objectives on facial surfaces of teeth and gingiva by patients who lack manual dexterity to perform the more complex method. Teeth are occluded, and bristle tips are directed toward the occlusal plane. To brush facial surfaces of maxillary teeth, the brush head is rotated upward 45° so bristles are directed down toward the occlusal plane; to brush mandibular teeth, the brush head is rotated downward so bristles are directed up toward the occlusal plane. With the brushing plane in position, cheek and/or lip muscles are used to exert gentle pressure to flex bristles over proximal surfaces and crests of interdental gingiva. Cheek pressure is maintained to hold bristles in position on gingiva while the brush is rotated to a slow count of ten.[22] Lingual aspects of teeth and gingiva are brushed with Charters' Method or, if the patient is unable to perform this, with Modified Stillman's Method.

The potential advantage of Hirschfeld's over Charters' Method is the use of cheek and lip muscles to help flex and maintain bristles in position when the patient lacks manual dexterity. Since bristle placement and action should be observed by the patient in a mirror and this is not possible when the cheek covers the brush, it would seem advantageous to have the patient attempt to master Charters' Method.

Smith-Bell (Physiologic) Method. Advocates of the Smith-Bell Method contend that bristles should be drawn across teeth and gingiva in the same direction food passes over these structures during mastication, thus this is called the "Physiologic Method." A very soft-textured, multitufted camel's hair brush is used. With the brushing plane horizontal to the occlusal plane, bristles are directed at right angles to facial surfaces of teeth, then drawn upward over maxillary or downward over mandibular teeth and gingiva. Lingual surfaces are brushed in the same direction as facial surfaces, but a small rotary movement is used when bristle tips reach marginal gingiva. Bristle tips are worked up and down over cervical surfaces of mandibular anterior teeth from the lingual aspect. If arch width is constricted, the brush may be inserted vertically and toe-end bristles used. Bristles are drawn antero-posteriorly over occlusal surfaces to cleanse them.[15,28]

Camel's hair is very soft, thus bristle action is relatively ineffective for cleansing or massage. If stiffer bristles are used, marginal gingiva may be lacerated.

Fones' Method. Fones' Method is used by some youngsters who lack muscular coordination until they develop sufficient dexterity to manipulate the toothbrush. A soft-textured multitufted toothbrush must be used to avoid soft tissue injury. With teeth occluded, the brushing surface is applied in large circular movements over facial surfaces of opposing teeth, then the mouth is held open and lingual surfaces are brushed with smaller circular motions. Bristle tips are drawn back and forth over occlusal surfaces to cleanse them.[18]

Although Fones' Method is easy to perform, a child who learns to brush in this manner establishes an incorrect habit that must be replaced. A young child may use excessive pressure that will splay bristles and lacerate the gingiva. Haphazard movement of bristles against gingival margins may cause recession and eventual formation of McCall's festoons.

Leonard's (Vertical) Method. Leonard's Method, also called the Vertical Method because the brushing plane is drawn up and down over tooth surfaces, is simple to learn. With teeth occluded edge-to-edge, bristles are directed at right angles to long axes of teeth and drawn over facial surfaces from maxillary to mandibular gingival margins. When bristles reach marginal gingiva, the brush head is rotated slightly and bristles are flexed onto interdental gingiva.[25] The stroke is repeated six times in each brush position. A variation of this method or Fones' Method may be used to cleanse lingual surfaces. Excessive pressure exerted as bristles strike gingival margins or are flexed onto interdental gingiva may force free gingiva away from the teeth and press soft debris into gingival sulci. Acute and chronic soft tissue injuries are described under *Toothbrush Trauma.*

Horizontal Method. The Horizontal Method is named for the back and forth direction of the brushing stroke. With bristles directed at right angles to tooth surfaces, the brushing plane is drawn in long horizontal strokes across adjacent teeth. Debris removed from cervical surfaces is forced into interproximal spaces. Acute and chronic injuries that can result from overvigorous horizontal brushing are described under *Toothbrush Trauma.*

Automatic Brushing. No automatic brush action simulates exact bristle movement achieved with a manual brush used to perform one of the methods described in this section. Manufacturers of some automatic brushes may claim brush actions reproduce one or another method but, in analyzing effectiveness, the type of brush action is secondary to the way in which a brush is used by the patient. Automatic brushes that provide short back and forth or orbital strokes can be used to perform most toothbrushing methods described in this section (Fig. 3–13*A*). The patient is instructed to hold and move the brushing plane over teeth and gingiva in the same manner as he would if he were using a manual brush, except that most automatic brushes have shorter brushing planes that can be inserted lengthwise on lingual surfaces of anterior teeth (Fig. 3–13*B*). Until the patient gains proficiency in brush placement, he can be advised to turn the power off and observe bristle position in a mirror each time he moves the brush

---

FIG. 3–13. Automatic Toothbrushing.

A, Rolling Stroke Method with automatic brush. Most methods of toothbrushing can be performed with back-and-forth or orbital stroke automatic brushes. The patient is instructed to place the brushing plane in the same manner as for manual toothbrushing methods.

B, Bass' Method with automatic brush. One advantage some automatic brushes present is a shorter brushing plane with standard length bristles, allowing use of entire length of brushing plane on lingual surfaces of anterior teeth.

C, Arcuate, vertical action automatic brush: center brushing plane over gingival margins; draw brush over free gingiva, then over occlusal or incisal thirds of teeth, and back to gingival margins.

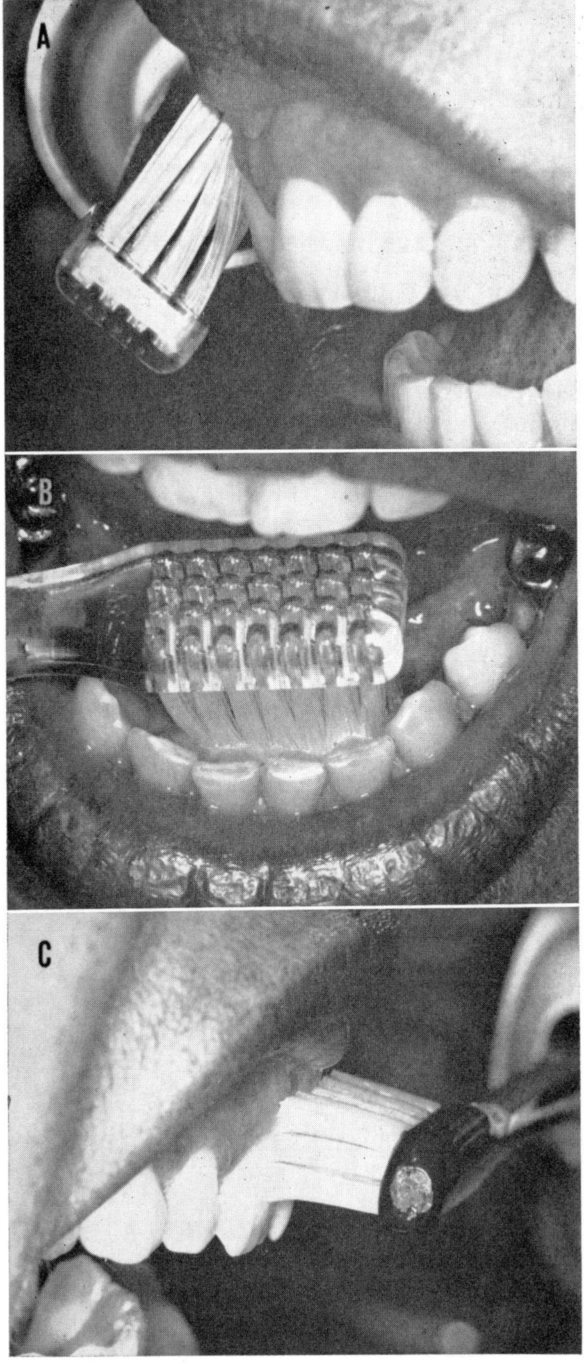

FIG. 3–13. *(Legend on opposite page.)*

to a new position. Patients who use arcuate, vertical-stroke brushes can be instructed as follows: center the brushing plane over gingival margins (Fig. 3–13*C*); draw the brush over free gingiva, then over occlusal or incisal one-thirds of teeth, and back to gingival margins. Repeat until all facial and lingual surfaces are brushed, then hold the brushing plane against occlusal surfaces to cleanse pits and fissures.

ORAL PHYSIOTHERAPY RECOMMENDATIONS

No one type of oral physiotherapy regimen can be recommended routinely because each patient possesses a unique combination of characteristics that may influence retention or clearance of debris from the oral cavity. Tooth morphology, occlusion, presence of natural teeth and dental appliances, gingival morphology and health, tongue size and position, and cheek musculature may affect an individual's rate and degree of deposit and stain accumulation. Other related factors include diet, salivary flow and consistency, oral habits, use of drugs or tobacco, and the patient's past personal oral hygiene program.

Recommendations included under Instruments and Aids and Toothbrushing are summarized in Table 3–1. The professional should regard these as general suggestions rather than inflexible rules. Supplementary aids recommended for all patients include thorough rinsing with tap water after eating and after use of oral physiotherapy devices, and use of a disclosing agent at least once a day, usually before retiring when sufficient time is available for thorough attention to results of brushing.

If a patient expresses preference for a particular bristle texture, no change is recommended unless inadequate cleansing or massage seems to be related to previous use of too hard or too soft bristle texture. A harder-textured brush may be recommended to assist in removing soft deposits or to improve gingival tone or keratinization. A softer-textured brush is recommended to massage receded gingiva, to cleanse exposed cervical and proximal surfaces of teeth, or to minimize trauma from too vigorous application of the brush. Inspection of a patient's used brushes will aid the operator in determining whether trauma was caused by a specific bristle texture or by use of worn, nonresilient brushes.

A new toothbrushing method is recommended only when the patient's present method is inadequate or has traumatized the oral tissues. Sometimes a patient's present method can be retained and supplemented in one or two areas by a change in bristle position or stroke that will massage spongy or enlarged gingiva or cleanse hard-to-reach surfaces of two or three teeth.

TABLE 3–1. ORAL PHYSIOTHERAPY RECOMMENDATIONS

Patient— Oral Condition	*Toothbrushing Method*	*Supplementary Aids*
ALL PATIENTS	Present method if adequate; partial supplement if possible; new method if indicated	Mouth rinse (tap water) Disclosing agent
GINGIVA: normal, healthy TEETH: normal alignment, occlusion	Rolling Stroke	Dental floss or tape (if necessary, and if patient will follow instructions)
YOUNG CHILD or HANDICAPPED PATIENT who cannot control brush	Rolling Stroke if possible, otherwise Fones' or Leonard's	(Supervision and assistance by parent or attendant)
GINGIVA: mild recession or mild disturbance	Modified Stillman's, Bass' or combination	Dental floss or tape Interdental stimulator
GINGIVA: moderate to severe recession, loss of interdental papillae	Charters', Hirschfeld's, Modified Stillman's or combination; supplement with Rolling Stroke	Dental floss or tape Interdental stimulator Knitting yarn, pipe cleaner Hydrotherapy
FIXED PARTIAL DENTURE	Charters' (over appliance and abutment teeth)	Dental floss or tape Hydrotherapy
ORTHODONTIC BANDS and WIRES	Modified Stillman's, Bass', Rolling Stroke or combination	Hydrotherapy
REMOVABLE PARTIAL DENTURE or ORTHODONTIC RETAINER	Modified Stillman's, Bass'	Clasp brush Dental floss or tape Gauze strips Hydrotherapy Interdental stimulator Denture cleanser or regular dentifrice
COMPLETE REMOVABLE DENTURES		Denture brush Denture cleanser or regular dentifrice Digital massage

ORAL PHYSIOTHERAPY INSTRUCTION

Oral physiotherapy instruction is the process by which the professional explains and demonstrates personal oral hygiene procedures the patient is to use. Each patient who comes to the dental office is ready, psychologically, for oral physiotherapy instruction but, before new methods of behavior will be learned, there must be a desire to change present practices and a readiness to act. The patient must be motivated.

Motives are impulses, emotions, desires or urges that cause one to respond in a certain way to a given situation. In a study of why people seek dental care, Kegeles found that before an individual will take a voluntary health action, he must believe that: he is susceptible to the disease; if he were afflicted, serious consequences would result; the need to take action is more important than a variety of other things he might do; there are beneficial actions he can take that will either prevent or alleviate the seriousness of the disease; and such actions do not cause greater disability than the illness itself.[23]

If these precepts are adapted to oral physiotherapy instruction, it follows that the patient needs to recognize abnormal conditions in his mouth that were caused by inadequate personal oral hygiene practices, realize that continued neglect could result in more serious problems, and be assured that these problems could be reduced or prevented if he improved his habits of personal oral hygiene. During this motivating phase of instruction, positive aspects of a change in behavior should be stressed rather than negative results of neglect, and the patient should be encouraged to want to participate in the maintenance of his oral health.

Setting

The dental operatory is the logical setting for oral physiotherapy instruction because adequate light, water and waste receptacles are available, and because the situation focuses attention on the patient's oral condition. The patient should be seated comfortably and put at ease. Although prolonged discussion of unrelated subjects merely wastes time, the operator needs to elicit information about the patient's attitude toward his personal oral hygiene habits. The patient's chance remarks about his past experiences, special interests, vocation, social status or children may indicate a unique factor upon which positive values of improved oral health can be based.

Motivation

Instruction should begin before the oral prophylaxis so the patient can be shown the results of his present oral physiotherapy regimen.

After the operator inspects the patient's oral cavity, disclosing solution is applied to the teeth. The patient is given a large hand mirror and asked to observe while the operator indicates stained deposits that need to be removed and/or abnormal gingival conditions related to inadequate or overvigorous toothbrushing. Then he is given a new toothbrush and asked to remove as much debris as possible. As he brushes, the operator observes the patient's technique and estimates his degree of manual dexterity.

When brushing has been completed, the patient again observes in the mirror while the operator inspects for cleanliness and/or for soft tissue trauma. If most debris has been removed without injury to the gingiva, the patient should be praised, but uncleansed tooth surfaces or abnormal gingiva need to be called to his attention. A minor change in brush placement or bristle flexion may be all that is required to help the patient cleanse hard-to-reach areas or to massage unstimulated gingiva.

If cleansing and massage are ineffective, a new method should be instituted. In selecting a toothbrushing method for the patient, the operator considers the patient's oral conditions, manual dexterity and apparent motivation. Obviously a complex method would not be mastered by a very young child, an infirm patient, or one who had little interest in maintaining his oral health.

Instruction

Explanation and demonstration should be as simple as possible to gain the patient's understanding and cooperation. First, the operator explains the design of the "professional toothbrush" the patient has received, then, with a demonstration brush of the same type, the new method of toothbrushing is demonstrated on a model of the teeth. The model may be a stone replica of the patient's mouth or a plastic model that can be altered to resemble the patient's dentition. The surfaces to be brushed are held directly in the patient's line of vision and the demonstration brush is applied to the model as though lips and cheeks surrounded the teeth. Bristles are placed and activated slowly and movements such as *place, press* and *roll* are emphasized visually as the brushing plane is stopped momentarily in each position. The operator explains why the brush is applied in this manner because the patient will be more likely to attempt correct performance if he knows why it is important.

After the method has been demonstrated on the model, the patient's brush is applied to his anterior teeth and gingiva to demonstrate correct bristle pressure and flexion. The patient is asked to practice brushing and to view his technique in a mirror. As the patient practices, the operator observes and encourages him, and tactfully corrects errors. The practice period should continue until the patient is able to manipulate the brush with reasonable proficiency in each area. If other oral physiotherapy instruments are recommended, their use is described in the same manner: demonstration on the model, demonstration in the mouth, then practice until the patient becomes proficient.

During the oral prophylaxis the operator has an opportunity to discuss other aspects of the recommended personal oral hygiene regimen. Thorough rinsing after eating or after cleansing the teeth, use of dentifrices and mouthwashes, and facts related to the patient's specific oral problems need to be explained, yet do not have to be demonstrated or do not require the patient's active participation. Every attempt should be made to answer the patient's questions throughout the appointment since his curiosity may be utilized to stimulate his desire to practice improved oral hygiene habits.

After the oral prophylaxis, disclosing solution is reapplied and the teeth and gingiva are compared to their preoperative state. Unless instrumentation has been extensive and the patient's tissues are hypersensitive, he should redemonstrate toothbrushing, particularly those phases with which he had difficulty during the first practice period. Written instructions or printed pamphlets from the American Dental Association[1] or a noncommercial source can be given to the patient and major points of his new oral physiotherapy regimen reviewed. These written instructions, posted in his home, will serve as reminders of the new program until procedures become a matter of habit.

Patients cannot be expected to retain all information or to master new oral physiotherapy procedures after only one period of instruction. Some patients need two or more periods of instruction to learn a simple method of toothbrushing, and most require at least two sessions to master more complex procedures. All patients need periodic review and reinstruction as time passes and they become less meticulous in following instructions or as their oral health problems change.

Instruction for Child and Parent

The young child in some ways is more receptive to instruction than his elders. He reacts favorably to deserved praise, desires to please adults, is interested in learning to perform skills, and has relatively few habit patterns that require retraining. On the other hand, he has a short attention span and undeveloped manual dexterity. He has not learned to strive for long-range goals; his desires are immediate and results of his behavior need to occur almost as soon as he acts. He has not been conditioned to learn from others' experiences, thus thinks only in terms of his own sphere of activity. Both parent and child need to be instructed in oral physiotherapy measures if these limiting factors are to be overcome and the child is to learn why and how his teeth are to be cleansed.

After the operator develops rapport with the child and has inspected his oral cavity, disclosing solution is applied. The child is given a hand mirror and the parent is asked to stand opposite the operator so he can see the child's teeth. The operator explains the relationship of oral deposits to development of dental caries and gingival disturbances as he shows the parent and child where deposits have accumulated. The child is given a new toothbrush, moistened with water, then he is asked to look in the mirror and to brush as much of the stain off his teeth as he can. When he has finished, the operator reinspects the teeth and shows the parent and child stained deposits that remain.

At this time the oral prophylaxis should be completed to change the pace of the child's activity. He is told that the rest of the stained debris will be removed and that he will be shown a new way to brush his teeth so he can keep them cleaner. After polishing, the teeth are redisclosed and the child and parent are shown the results. The toothbrushing method is demonstrated on a model in a slow and precise manner. This demonstration is primarily for the child but the parent should be positioned so he can observe and listen to instruction. The child must be shown how to brush every surface of every tooth because he will emulate the demonstration, emphasizing in his performance the procedures that were stressed. Recitation will aid the child to focus his attention on the demonstration, so he is asked to repeat instructions such as *place, press* and *roll* with the operator as brush action corresponds to these words. Counting numbers of strokes in each area helps the child remember how many times he should brush.

The child's brush is placed on his anterior teeth and gingiva, and correct bristle placement and pressure are demonstrated so he will feel the amount of pressure he is supposed to use when he brushes. Since his ability to control the brush is limited, he needs to practice grasping the handle firmly and using wrist action to turn the brushing plane before he places the brush in his mouth. When he learns how to turn the brush head, maintain a firm grasp, and use wrist action to move the brushing plane, he can begin practice in his mouth. As he practices the new method, he should be praised for correct performance and assisted where necessary.

After the child gains reasonable proficiency in brushing, the parent needs to become an active participant. The child is told that, although he knows what he is supposed to do, he needs to practice conscientiously for a long time before he will be able to clean every surface of every tooth. Until he can do this his parent needs to check his brushing to see that he is using the brush correctly and to brush those areas that are not cleansed. This assistance probably will be required until the child is at least ten years old, and sometimes until he is fourteen, thus both child and parent should be prepared to participate until the child learns to be self-sufficient.

The parent should be shown again where the child has not been able to remove deposits, usually on lingual surfaces of mandibular teeth and on labial surfaces of anterior teeth. At home, the parent will not have a dental chair or light so he should be shown how to support the child's head comfortably, yet see the teeth and use the toothbrush in all areas. The child is asked to stand in front of the operator and rest his head backward so his mouth is directed upward. The operator's left arm is crooked gently around the child's head, the left fingers are used to retract his lips and cheeks, and the right hand used to manipulate the toothbrush.[31] The parent repeats this demonstration, brushing the child's teeth in the recommended sequence. The parent needs to learn to position the brushing plane on lingual surfaces of molars without pressing the child's tongue and how to retract the cheeks to gain access for the brush on buccal surfaces of maxillary molars.

Summary. Oral physiotherapy instruction is the process by which personal oral hygiene measures are explained and demonstrated. Before the patient will accept recommended new procedures, there must be a desire to change personal oral hygiene habits. Each patient has similar but unique reasons for desiring oral health and these potential motives must be identified then strengthened until the patient is ready to act in accordance with professional recommendations.

Instruction should be simple to gain the patient's cooperation and understanding, and it needs to be repeated at more than one appointment before the patient can be expected to remember and follow directions. Explanations of each procedure should accompany demonstration, be repeated as the patient practices, and be reviewed after operative procedures are completed. Written instructions or pamphlets given to the patient to take home will help him follow directions and establish correct habit patterns.

Although the young child has some advantages in the learning process, limitations imposed by his youth must be considered and overcome if oral physiotherapy instruction is to be effective. The length of instruction time should be short and activities should be varied to keep the child's interest. The parent must be involved in all phases of instruction including motivation, demonstration and practice, because he is responsible for keeping the child's teeth clean and helping the child learn to perform this function.

Methods of instruction suggested in this section may be varied according to the operator's skill in working with patients and according to the individual patient's reactions to instruction. There is no "best" method of instruction that can be used by all professionals with all patients.

BIBLIOGRAPHY

1. American Dental Association, Bureau of Dental Health Education, 211 East Chicago Ave., Chicago, Illinois.
2. American Dental Association, Council on Dental Therapeutics: *Accepted Dental Remedies,* 30th ed. Chicago, American Dent. Assn., 1965, p. 189.
3. Ibid., p. 190
4. Ibid., p. 197.
5. Ibid., p. 209.
6. Ibid., p. 160.
7. Ibid., p. 210.
8. Ibid., p. 109.
9. Ibid., p. 188
10. Ibid., p. 211.
11. Ibid., p. 225.
12. American Dental Association, Council on Dental Therapeutics: Council Announces Classification of Additional Products, J.A.D.A., *61,* 274, August, 1960.
13. American Dental Association: *Toothbrushing.* Chicago, American Dental Assn., October, 1961. Pamphlet G6 200 M 10-61, 6 pp.
14. Bass, C. C.: An Effective Method of Personal Oral Hygiene. II., Louisiana S. Med. Soc. J., *106,* 100, March, 1954.
15. Bell, D. G.: Teaching Home Care to the Patient, J. Periodont., *19,* 140, October, 1948.
16. Charters, W. J.: Home Care of the Mouth. I. Proper Home Care of the Mouth, J. Periodont., *19,* 136, October, 1948.
17. Dudding, N. J., Dahl, L. O. and Muhler, J. C.: Patient Reactions to Brushing Teeth with Water, Dentifrice or Salt and Soda, J. Periodont., *31,* 386, October, 1960.
18. Fones, A. C.: *Mouth Hygiene,* 4th ed. Philadelphia, Lea & Febiger, 1934, p. 300.
19. Fosdick, L. S.: The Reduction of the Incidence of Dental Caries. I. Immediate Toothbrushing with a Neutral Dentifrice, J.A.D.A., *40,* 133, February, 1950.
20. Grant, David, Stern, I. B. and Everett, F. G.: *Orban's Periodontics,* 2nd ed. St. Louis, Mosby, 1963, p. 317.
21. Hirschfeld, Isador: *The Toothbrush: Its Use and Abuse.* Brooklyn, Dent. Items Interest Pub. Co., 1939, p. 262.
22. Hirschfeld, Isador: The Why and How of Toothbrushing, J.A.D.A., *32,* 80, January, 1945.
23. Kegeles, S. S.: Why People Seek Dental Care: A Review of Present Knowledge, Amer. J. Pub. Health, *51,* 1306, September, 1961.
24. Kitchin, P. C. and Robinson, H. B. G.: How Abrasive Need a Dentifrice Be? J. Dent. Res., *27,* 501, August, 1948.
25. Leonard, H. J.: Conservative Treatment of Periodontoclasia, J.A.D.A., *26,* 1308, August, 1939.

26. McCauley, H. B.: Toothbrushes, Toothbrush Materials and Design, J.A.D.A., *33,* 283, March 1, 1946.
27. Smith, J. H., O'Connor, T. W. and Radentz, William: Oral Hygiene of the Interdental Area, Periodontics, *1,* 204, September-October, 1963.
28. Smith, T. S.: Anatomic and Physiologic Conditions Governing the Use of the Toothbrush, J.A.D.A., *27,* 874, June, 1940.
29. Sorrin, Sidney, ed.: *The Practice of Periodontia.* New York, Blakiston Division, McGraw-Hill Book Co. Inc., 1960, p. 314.
30. Ibid., p. 316.
31. Starkey, P. E.: Instructions to Parents for Brushing the Child's Teeth, J. Dent. Child., *28,* 42, 1st Q., 1961.
32. Stillman, P. R.: A Philosophy of the Treatment of Periodontal Disease, Dent. Digest., *38,* 315, September, 1932.

4

Oral Prophylaxis

Margaret M. Ryan

The individual patient's needs and state licensure acts governing dental hygiene practice determine the procedures which are performed by the dental hygienist. Within the limitations of the practice act, the patient's needs are of primary concern. With the commencement of professional education, the hygienist assumes the moral obligation of providing service to dentistry and to the public through ethical performance of delegated responsibilities. There should be no violation of the law or professional principles in ethical practice. Performance of all procedures to the highest possible degree of excellence is imperative.

By reason of education, the dental hygienist is generally considered to possess a high degree of proficiency in the performance of oral prophylaxis procedures. Dentist employers rely upon the dental hygienist's skills and judgment to provide a particular phase of total patient service. This reliance requires that the hygienist work diligently to meet the needs of the patient and the practice.

Dictionaries agree in the definition of prophylaxis as the prevention of disease.[8,59] When the term is applied to the oral cavity, its definition becomes more complex. The broadest interpretation of oral prophylaxis includes all procedures performed in the oral cavity for prevention of disease. In its narrowest sense, oral prophylaxis is defined as a series of scaling and polishing procedures whereby deposits and stains are removed from the teeth for preventive purposes.[62] A third definition, which will be used here, explains oral prophylaxis as those clinical procedures performed by the dental hygienist. This definition includes: taking or reviewing the patient history, inspection of the oral cavity, recording existing oral conditions, removal of deposits and stains, application of topical agents for prevention of disease and sensitivity, and patient education. With the exception of patient education, the procedures included in the third definition will be explored.

ARMAMENTARIUM

The instruments, equipment and supplies used by the dental hygienist are referred to as the dental hygiene armamentarium. The armamentarium should be versatile and durable. In selection of an item, its usefulness and tolerance of optimum sterilization methods must be considered. Whenever possible, an item that can be subjected to heat and moisture is selected in preference to an item that cannot. Metals vary in their ability to withstand the attacks of chemicals, heat and moisture used in disinfection and sterilization. The type of metal used in the manufacture of cutting instruments will influence the operator's ability to attain and maintain a sharp cutting edge. Subjecting instruments and equipment to routine use, and to disinfection and sterilization is probably the most reliable means of determining durability.

Instruments have three parts: the handle, the shank and the working end. The shank joins the handle to the working end. Instruments are identified by their type, particular design and manufacturer. The type is determined by the use. The design usually is designated by the name of an individual or school. Many instruments also carry a number for more specific identification. A single number may be applied to more than one type or design of instrument. For example, the Columbia number 14 curet is a specific type and design of instrument used for removal of calculus. The University of Washington number 14 sickle is an instrument of another type and design which also is used for calculus removal.

Instrument handles may be permanently fixed to the shank and working end or they may be removable. Removable handles with threaded openings are called cone socket handles. The shanks of mouth mirrors and other instruments screw into the cone socket. The possibility of loosening the working end of cone socket instruments during their use must be considered in instrument selection and use.

Instruments may be termed single-ended or double-ended. Single-ended instruments have only one working end. Double-ended instruments have paired or complementary working ends attached to one handle. Care must be taken in the manipulation of double-ended instruments, as uncontrolled movement of the unemployed end could injure the patient or operator.

STERILE TECHNIQUE

In the performance of dental and dental hygiene techniques, specific procedures are directed toward the prevention of disease transmission.

The procedures include methods of sterilization, disinfection and sanitization. The composite of these methods is termed sterile technique. Maintenance of sterile technique is referred to as the sterile chain. When any item of the armamentarium comes in contact with an object or part of a person that has not been subjected to sterilization procedures the item is contaminated and the sterile chain broken. Measures of repair must then be taken. The patient's own oral cavity should not be considered as a contaminated area when operations are being performed for that individual.

Practice of sterile technique is a moral professional obligation, as neglect can result in disease transmission. Because diseases are not always recognized by the operator or indicated by the patient, sterile technique must be practiced constantly by any person preparing the armamentarium for, or performing, dental and dental hygiene procedures. Every available measure must be taken to avoid the transmission of disease producing organisms from one person to another. Diseases can be transmitted to the dental office personnel as well as to patients. The range of transmittible diseases runs from the relatively benign common cold to the debilitating and sometimes fatal bacterial endocarditis and serum hepatitis.

Sterilization[1,45]

Sterilization is the process by which all forms of life including bacterial spores are destroyed. Elimination of all microorganisms is desirable, but not always attainable in the dental office. Methods of sterilization should be employed whenever possible in preference to procedures less effective in reducing the potential for disease transmission. Of the two methods of sterilization, the use of moist heat or steam under pressure is more feasible than the use of dry heat.

The equipment manufactured for moist heat sterilization is commonly referred to as an autoclave. A pressure cooker may be used to achieve the same result, but does not have the reliability of the autoclave. Sterilization by moist heat is the product of heat plus moisture. The destructive force is the heat which is given up when steam condenses back to moisture. Therefore, all parts of an article should be exposed to the steam to assure the benefit of the heat produced by its condensation. Packages or items are placed in a single layer on the autoclave tray to provide for their complete exposure to steam.

The effectiveness of sterilization procedures is partially dependent upon the preparation of the articles to be sterilized. Removal of all debris is essential. As little as 0.00001 cc. of blood has proven to be the infectious agent in causing hepatitis.[36] Articles that have parts are disassembled before cleansing. Detergent or soap, water and a brush are used for removing debris from instruments and equipment that will tolerate them. A brush should be kept for the specific purpose of cleaning contaminated articles. Scrubbing is followed by complete rinsing and drying.

Cleansed instruments and other metal items may be coated with an emulsion if they are subject to corrosion. Commercial preparations are available for this purpose. Articles are placed between towels or muslin on the autoclave trays, or packaged. Paper autoclave bags provide a convenient method of packaging, but have the disadvantage of being easily penetrated by sharp instruments. A towel or muslin wrap can be used. If a straight pin is used to secure the wrap, the point is not exposed. Metal instrument tubes are available. Perforations in the tube allow penetration of steam, but make it unsuitable for instrument storage after sterilization. Articles are packaged loosely to insure their complete contact with steam. Sterilized packages of instruments and equipment can be stored without cover. Unpackaged items are covered with sterile towels for storage after sterilization. Sterile forceps are used for the removal of items from the autoclave, sterile package or sterile storage.

The time and temperature of the autoclave cycle varies with the type of material and its use. For sterilization of dental instruments, equipment and supplies the autoclave is usually operated at 250°F (121°C) and 15 to 20 pounds pressure for fifteen to twenty minutes. Higher temperatures would not be tolerated by some articles. The cycle is begun after a temperature of 250°F has been reached.

The moisture in steam under pressure sterilization places limitations upon its use. Powders and ointments cannot be autoclaved successfully. Gauze, cotton, wood and some glass, metal and rubber articles used in clinical practice are autoclavable. Heat produced by this method of sterilization does present some disadvantages since frequently mouth mirrors cannot tolerate the temperatures of the autoclave, The edges of fine cutting instruments are also dulled by the autoclaving process. But, these disadvantages are overridden by the advantages of moist heat sterilization. A number of instrument companies have been successful in manufacturing instruments which can withstand the heat and moisture of autoclaving with little or no corrosion or dulling of cutting edges.

The production of dry heat is the second method of sterilization. Heat alone produces sterilization. Commercial dry heat sterilizers or an oven may be used. The former is more reliable, because it provides better heat distribution and temperature control. Sterilization by dry heat is achieved by maintaining a temperature of 320°F to 355°F for at least one hour and preferably two.

Articles are wrapped loosely in cloth towels after cleansing and drying. Small packages allow access of heat to the articles. The possibility of contamination after sterilization is minimized if a package contains only those items required for a single operation.

The disadvantages of dry heat sterilization limit its usefulness in the dental office. Dry heat is difficult to control within limits. Long exposure periods are required because the heat penetrates materials slowly and unevenly. In dentistry, dry heat is used primarily for sterilization of the endodontic armamentarium and instruments with fine cutting edges. It is the only method of sterilization for materials such as oils and powders. Sterile forceps should be used to handle articles sterilized by dry heat. Sterile items are stored in the towel wrap used for the sterilization procedure.

Disinfection[2,46,63]

The process by which most microorganisms, but not necessarily bacterial spores, are destroyed is termed disinfection. Because this process usually does not kill bacterial spores, it is less desirable than sterilization.

Hot oils and silicone fluids are primarily used for disinfection of metal instruments with moving parts which require lubrication, such as the straight, contra-angle and right-angle handpieces. The instruments are cleaned according to the manufacturer's instructions before immersion into the disinfectant. Instructions for use of hot oil or silicone fluids should be followed strictly. Disinfection is achieved by heat. The temperature is maintained at 300°F (150°C) for 15 minutes or at 260°F (125°C) for 20 to 30 minutes. A temperature of 320°F (160°C) must be maintained for a minimum of one hour to kill anaerobic spore formers. Upon completion of disinfection, instruments are drained, cooled and wiped with a sterile towel.

There are disadvantages in the use of silicone fluids. Some silicones are irritating to tissue and cannot be used for disinfection. Handpieces with enclosed gears require cleaning with carbon tetrachloride and packing with silicone grease after every second or third disinfection. Cleaning agents other than carbon tetrachloride may contaminate the silicone. A silicone lubricated handpiece will run warmer than one lubricated by other means. The fact that silicone fluids darken after use has no bearing upon their effectiveness.

Boiling water has enjoyed popularity in disinfection procedures. However, with increased knowledge of diseases and their transmission, boiling water is employed less frequently. Because many spores and some viruses will survive hours of boiling this method cannot be used for sterilization, but will achieve disinfection. The usual cleansing methods are employed and the instruments placed in continually boiling water, 212°F (100°C) for a minimum of ten minutes. If instruments are added during the ten minute cycle, contamination occurs and timing must begin again.

The addition of trisodium phosphate or sodium carbonate will retard corrosion of the instruments and assist in the removal of debris. However, if articles to be disinfected are made of aluminum these compounds cannot be used, as strong alkalis will dissolve aluminum. The use of distilled water will help prevent corrosion.

Free flowing steam also is classified as a disinfectant. At a temperature of 212°F most vegetative forms of organisms are destroyed during a ten minute cycle. Because the steam may not reach all the contaminated areas, this procedure is less desirable than boiling water.

Disinfection by the use of chemicals is a more widely accepted method than others described. Inability to kill all bacterial spores, including those of pathogens, limits the use of chemical disinfectants. Chemical solutions do not effectively disinfect instruments and equipment with hinges and crevices. Soap will inhibit the action of chemical solutions, consequently thorough rinsing after cleansing procedures is imperative. Removal of all oil or grease is necessary, as it will protect the microorganisms from the attack of solutions. Articles are submerged for a minimum of fifteen to thirty minutes dependent upon the chemical. A twenty to thirty minute cycle will give a margin of safety. The cycle is timed from the insertion of the last item.

Drying before disinfecting will prevent dilution of the solution and reduction of its effectiveness. A major breakdown in the use of chemical disinfectants is the failure to submerge completely all articles. If forceps are not used for the removal of articles from the solution, the tray is lifted out of the container and the instruments and equipment turned onto the sterile surface of the drying towel.

The disinfectant container is cleaned and residual deposits removed at least once a week in the dental office. Accumulation of debris and microorganisms will reduce the effectiveness of the disinfectant.

Quarternary ammonium compounds are widely used disinfecting agents. Normal skin and oral mucosa are not irritated by these compounds; however some people exhibit an allergic reaction to continued contact with them. Careful attention must be given to instructions for preparation of the solution. Some commercial preparations include rust inhibitors, while others require the addition of an anti-rust compound.

Substances present in certain natural waters, particularly calcium, magnesium and aluminum will interfere with the effectiveness of quarternary ammonium compounds. In areas where the water is "hard," distilled water is used in the preparation of quarternary ammonium solutions.

Benzalkonium Chloride is a commonly used quarternary ammonium compound distributed under the commercial names: Zephiran Chloride and Benzalkonium Chloride. The names of other compounds and the solution concentrations for disinfecting procedures can be found in the current American Dental Association publication *Accepted Dental Remedies.*

Compounds of mercury, phenolic compounds and formaldehyde are included in the long list of substances used in the preparation of disinfecting solutions. Each of these has limitations which make the use of the quarternary ammonium compounds preferable. The odor and potential for irritation to the skin and oral tissues of formaldehyde solutions make them undesirable. Mercury preparations cause precipitation of protein, irritation and toxic effects. Phenolic compounds, particularly phenol, are irritating to tissue and consequently have been replaced by other disinfectants. Phenols do have the advantage of becoming soluble in water with the addition of soap. Hexachlorophene is used with soap and detergents for the surgical scrubbing of hands.

Disinfection by alcohol is possible. Some water must be present for alcohol to exert its most effective bacteriocidal action. A concentration of 70 per cent ethyl alcohol is preferred; however a concentration in the range of 50 to 95 per cent is acceptable. Isopropyl alcohol is most effective in a 90 to 95 per cent concentration.

Antiseptics[47,63]

Antiseptics are substances which either kill or prevent the growth of microorganisms and are used especially for application to living tissue. Although it is not possible to sterilize the skin, the number of bacteria on its surface can be significantly reduced by application of an antiseptic. Antiseptic soaps are employed for handwashing procedures during the performance of clinical techniques. The opportunity for transmission of microorganisms is lessened with the use of liquid rather than bar soap.

Thorough handwashing with particular attention to the fingernails is essential to the practice of sterile technique. A brush is used to scrub all sides of the fingers working from the fingertips toward the hand. Scrubbing proceeds to the palm and back of the hand and then to the wrist terminating at the forearm. The procedure is completed with rinsing from the fingertips to the wrist and drying with a sterile towel. If the water is not regulated by a foot or knee pedal, it is turned off with the wrist or forearm. The initial handwashing of the day requires a three minute scrub. From one to two minutes' time should be expended on each subsequent washing.

The hands are washed prior to commencing any procedure in the patient's mouth. If during the clinical procedures for the patient an item not within the sterile chain is touched by the operator, the hands must be washed again.

Sterilization and disinfection methods are defeated if sterile technique is not practiced in removal of instruments, equipment and supplies from sterile storage. Forceps placed upon the bracket table during procedures for a patient cannot be used for procuring sterile items. Storage of forceps with the tips between the folds of a sterile towel or in a disinfecting solution is suggested. Removal of an article from a sterile drawer or container with other than antiseptically washed hands or disinfected forceps contaminates all other contents. Soap and water and chemical agents should be used periodically to disinfect cabinets and containers used for sterile storage.

Sanitization[47,63]

Parts of the dental unit, chair, cabinet and x-ray machine are sanitized to assist in maintenance of the sterile chain. The term sanitization refers to the process by which the number of organisms on inanimate objects is reduced to a safe level. A sterile gauze sponge saturated with alcohol or another chemical disinfectant is used to sanitize all parts of the operatory equipment that will come in contact with the patient's mouth or operator's hands. The hands are washed before commencing sanitization procedures.

Sanitization of the air and water syringes and the saliva ejector outlet begins at the tip or opening. The sanitized portion can then be held with the free hand while the disinfectant is applied to other parts of the syringe or outlet. Removable syringe tips which can be disinfected should be used when possible. Saliva ejectors are always removed and discarded or disinfected after completion of each patient appointment.

The use of sterile towels and the removal of articles from sterile packages bears attention. Care must be taken to avoid contact of the contaminated outside surfaces of the towel or package with sterilized or disinfected storage. The use of forceps to remove articles from sterile packages lessens the possibility of contaminating the contents. The sterile surface of the towel always is folded inward. Separate towels are used for instrument and hand drying.

Prevention of disease transmission procedures include measures taken to avoid infection through inhalation, open wounds or foreign materials in the eye. A face mask is worn if the patient or operator has a respiratory infection. Because it is effective only when dry, the mask is changed frequently. An open wound in the operator's hand is sealed off to prevent cross infection. A surgical finger cot or glove will satisfactorily isolate a finger or hand wound. The use of a collodion solution is less desirable. Glasses can be worn to protect the operator's eyes from polishing abrasives and pieces of calculus.

Maintenance of sterile technique requires constant attention. Deviations from accepted procedures may seriously jeopardize the health of the patient and operator.

TABLE 4–1. ACCEPTED STERILE TECHNIQUE PROCEDURES

Technique	*Method*	*Temperature*	*Exposure*
Sterilization	Steam Under Pressure	250° F. (121° C.) 15–20 lbs. pressure	15–20 minutes
	Dry Heat	320°–355° F. (160°–180° C.)	1 hour
Disinfection	Boiling Water	212° F (100° C.)	10 minutes
	Hot Oil & Silicones	300° F. (150° C.) 260° F. (125° C.)	15 minutes 20–30 minutes
	Chemical Agents	Room Temperature	20–30 minutes
	Antiseptic Soaps: Initial handwashing Subsequent handwashings		 3 minutes 1–2 minutes
Sanitization	Chemical Disinfecting Agents		Complete contact

MEDICAL AND DENTAL HISTORY—THEIR SIGNIFICANCE[10,17,21,33,34,39,40,64]

Before commencing any intraoral procedures the patient history is taken or reviewed. If the initial history of a new patient has been taken by someone other than the dental hygienist, it is read carefully before the first oral prophylaxis. On all recall appointments, the history is reviewed with the patient and new information is recorded, A notation of the date upon which the history is taken or reviewed should be made. All patient records should be written in ink. Any allergy, sensitivity, disease or condition which might alter dental procedures is recorded in a manner that will receive the immediate attention of anyone referring to the patient chart. The importance of thoroughness and accuracy in recording or reviewing the medical and dental history cannot be overemphasized. For this reason, information for the history of the child and teenage patient should be given by the parent.

The use of tact, ingenuity and good judgment in the taking and utilization of the history will assure patient cooperation. Privacy should be respected, therefore information should not be taken where it can be overheard by other patients. To reveal information from a history to any person not concerned with the patient's treatment is a breach of professional ethics.

A typical history includes five categories of information: pertinent facts necessary for the business relationship of the dentist and patient; the past and present health status of the patient; the record of past dental treatment; the past and present oral health; and the treatment plan. As the plan of treatment is executed, the services rendered are recorded in the patient chart. The last four categories of the history are of vital concern to the hygienist in performance of oral prophylaxis techniques.

Medical History

The medical history is structured to reveal any health condition which has or may have a bearing upon the treatment procedures. The date of the last physical examination will indicate the reliability of the information. A record of medication being taken by the patient will indicate the past or present existence of disease or disability. Knowledge of the fact that a patient is under medication can also avert emergencies. Allergies or sensitivities must be carefully recorded, for reactions can be severe or fatal. The dentist and hygienist must know the ingredients of all compounds used in their procedures and closely check all labels. Patients under some types of medication or exhibiting certain allergies can have serious reactions to some of the compounds used in the dental office. Slight reactions in the past usually result in severe reactions if the drug evoking the reaction is administered again. The hygienist's knowledge of the composition of all agents used in oral prophylaxis procedures is imperative. A convenient source of information is the current edition of the American Dental Association publication *Accepted Dental Remedies.*

Heart and Kidney Disease. Recognition of a history of heart or kidney disease is of particular importance to the patient and the operator. Indication of a history of rheumatic fever, congenital heart disease or glomerular nephritis requires consultation with the dentist and physician to determine whether or not the patient will need antibiotic therapy prior to and after the oral prophylaxis appointment. Introduction of bacteria into the blood stream is always a potential hazard in operations which require the manipulation of the gingiva. Streptococcal infections resulting from oral prophylaxis procedures can cause a secondary bacterial endocarditis in patients with a history of rheumatic fever or congenital heart disease. The already weakened heart is attacked and the resultant disease process has a much higher mortality rate than the initial heart disease. The primary infection in glomerular nephritis is generally streptococcal in type, consequently reintroduction of streptococci into the blood stream can initiate a secondary streptococcal infection of the kidney, with fatal results. Under no circumstances should any dental hygiene procedure be performed for patients with a record of rheumatic or congenital heart disease or glomerular nephritis before the dentist and patient's physician have been consulted.

Strict attention is given to the prescription and administration of antibiotic therapy. Should oral medication be prescribed the hygienist assumes the responsibility of determining whether or not the patient has followed the prescription instructions. If the instructions have not been followed, further consultation with the dentist is necessary before commencing any procedure. The oral prophylaxis may be postponed until premedication requirements are met by the patient. After the oral prophylaxis the dentist or hygienist should contact the patient to determine whether or not the antibiotic prescription instructions have been followed to completion.

Heart disorders other than those mentioned above which are of concern to the dental hygienist are coronary occlusion and angina pectoris. The patient who has had a coronary occlusion may be taking a blood anticoagulant. The resultant increased blood clotting time presents a potential postoperative hazard in oral prophylaxis techniques. Therefore, the dentist and patient's physician should be consulted before commencing the oral prophylaxis appointment. If indicated, the patient's anticoagulant therapy will be altered prior to the appointment. Angina pectoris is manifested by choking or suffocation and severe pain (angina). It is caused by ischemia of the myocardium of the heart. Because the arteries lack the ability to circulate the blood, the heart either does not receive an adequate supply of blood or must do additional work. Acute angina pectoris is relieved almost immediately through dilation of the coronary arteries. Patients with a history of angina pectoris often will carry nitroglycerin capsules or amylnitrite tablets. The hygienist should question the patient to determine the possible need for, and presence of such medication. Office first-aid supplies should include nitrites. The supply should be replenished every few months. Nitroglycerin will deteriorate slowly, particularly if it is exposed to air, and thus lose its therapeutic potency.

Blood Dyscrasias. The presence of blood dyscrasias may alter or prohibit performance of oral prophylaxis procedures. Techniques are performed on a patient with hemophilia only under the direct supervision of a physician. People with a bleeding tendency or pseudo-hemophilia may hemorrhage for a prolonged period of time following dental or dental hygiene procedures. Therefore, consultation is required when the history reveals this condition. Purpura, manifested by small red spots resulting from extravasation of blood into the skin or mucous membrane, requires close medical supervision for performance of oral prophylaxis procedures. Patients with hemophilia, a severe bleeding tendency, or purpura should be hospitalized for required dental and dental hygiene procedures.

Hepatitis. A history of hepatitis will not prevent the performance of clinical techniques for the patient, but will require strict adherence to ideal sterilization procedures. Infectious hepatitis is transmitted orally, parenterally or fecally. Serum hepatitis is transmitted parenterally. Minute amounts of blood contacting an open wound on the operator's hand or carried on an instrument into the mouth of a patient can produce either type of hepatitis. Therefore, absolute thoroughness in covering wounds and in the scrubbing and sterilization of instruments is required. The fact that hepatitis can be carried by persons without disease manifestations is justification for the routine use of sterilization rather than disinfection procedures for oral prophylaxis instruments and equipment.

Respiratory Diseases. Diseases of the respiratory system may necessitate postponement of procedures. The list of respiratory diseases ranges from the relatively innocuous common cold to the debilitating tuberculosis infection. Infections of the throat, tonsils and ears are often streptococcal in type. Because of the possibilities of infection of the operator or spread of the infection in the patient via the blood stream, the oral prophylaxis appointment should be postponed when there is evidence of a throat, tonsil or ear infection.

During the active stage of tuberculosis, oral prophylaxis techniques are avoided. If there is sufficient reason for performing the oral prophylaxis for a patient with active tuberculosis, surgical technique in a hospital is employed. The person with undiagnosed tuberculosis presents a far greater hazard to the hygienist than does the person with diagnosed active, or arrested tuberculosis. Following procedures for a patient with active or arrested tuberculosis, expendable items of the armamentarium are destroyed and ideal measures of preventing disease transmission are employed for sterilization of unexpendable items.

Diabetes. A history of diabetes requires caution in the use of medicaments, awareness of emergency procedures for insulin shock and diabetic coma, and particular attention to prevention of periodontal disease. If the patient is on insulin therapy, a notation is made in the patient record. Because some of the symptoms of insulin shock and diabetic coma are similar, it is necessary to determine whether or not the patient has taken insulin prior to each appointment. Sudden nervousness, weakness, sweating, muscular incoordination and fainting are manifestations of insulin shock. A piece of candy, sugar cube or orange should be given at the onset of insulin shock to raise the blood sugar level and prevent a lapse into coma. If the patient has not had insulin and complains of headache, nausea, becomes listless and breathes deeply one should suspect diabetic coma and summon medical help immediately. The sweetish, acetone smell of the breath is a very significant danger signal of diabetic coma.

Because diabetic patients may manifest an allergy to iodine, the use of medicaments with this ingredient is avoided. The diabetic's tissue resistance is lowered and healing is impaired. Consequently, avoidance of tissue trauma during procedures and prevention of periodontal disease take on added significance. Patient education should include specific reference to the relationship of oral hygiene and the patient's vulnerability to periodontal disease.

Epilepsy. Epilepsy is not a disease, but a group of symptoms resulting from disordered functions of the central nervous system. Because of the social stigma attached to the condition, patients will sometimes withhold the fact that they are epileptic. The hygienist has the responsibility of accepting the condition matter-of-factly and of educating others to place it in proper perspective. Indication of epilepsy in the patient history should call attention to the necessary emergency procedures should a seizure occur. The degree of epileptic seizure ranges from the very short loss of consciousness, fixed posture and twitching of the head, eyelids or eyebrows of the petit mal to the loss of consciousness, contraction of the voluntary musculature, cyanosis, pupil dilation, peculiar epileptic cry, and intermittent muscular contractions of the grand mal. The patient with grand mal seizures may experience the warning signs of numbness, a strange feeling in the stomach, hallucinations and muscle twitching. Emergency procedures should be directed toward protecting the patient from injury. Equipment should be moved away and the patient helped to the floor if feasible. When possible the patient's mouth is propped open with a bite-block or towel wrapped instrument and the tongue held to prevent its falling into the throat.

Dilantin is a commonly used anticonvulsant drug. It has the unfortunate side effect of producing gingival enlargement in some patients. Dilantin hyperplasia contributes to poor oral hygiene, necessitating special adaptation of home care techniques.

History of Dental Treatment and Oral Health

The history of dental treatment will reveal the patient's concept of the importance of oral health. The patient who has not seen a dentist for several years will require more motivation for attaining and maintaining optimum oral health than the patient who has received regular dental care. Notation of the date and treatment of the last dental appointment before commenting upon existing oral conditions will prevent embarrassment to the dentist or dental hygienist.

The present state of oral hygiene will reveal the patient's attitude toward dental health. It must be remembered that exposure to dental health education influences the patient's attention to oral cleanliness.

The time lapse since the patient's last oral prophylaxis will indicate the rapidity of deposit and stain formation, and therefore assist in determining the optimum recall interval. The date and extent of the last radiographic survey will suggest the need for additional radiographic exposures. Radiographs should be studied and related to visual findings.

Knowledge of previous periodontal treatment, its type and extent, will assist the dentist in making a diagnosis and formulating a treatment plan. Notation of the date when appliances were made, placed and adjusted will also assist diagnosis and treatment planning. All aspects of the medical and dental history have significant bearing upon procedures performed for the patient. Therefore, the patient's history should be meticulously taken and recorded.

PATIENT AND OPERATOR POSITIONING EQUIPMENT ADJUSTMENT[65]

The relative positions of the patient, operator and dental equipment have a direct bearing upon the efficiency and comfort with which clinical procedures are performed. Incorrect positioning will result in patient discomfort, operator fatigue and inability to manipulate instruments effectively.

Placement of the Dental Chair and Unit. Placement of the dental chair in close proximity to the unit will enable the patient to use the cuspidor easily and the operator to reach the air and water syringes, engine arm and operating light readily.

Patient Position for Oral Prophylaxis Techniques. The same basic chair position may be used whether the operator intends to stand or sit for performance of clinical techniques. The dental chair is adjusted to the approximate position for the patient prior to seating. If the guide markers found on most dental chairs are followed, readjustments after seating will be minor for adult patients. Before seating the patient the bracket table, operating light, engine arm, rheostat and operating stool are moved from the individual's pathway. Preschool age children, aged and handicapped persons may need to be assisted into the chair. The seating of these patients is observed and assistance offered when necessary to prevent accidental injury. Safety requires that a small child never be left unattended in the dental operatory. There are times when the hygienist's judgment will require the application of this rule to other patients, such as the cerebral palsy patient or very elderly person.

Support of the patient's spinal column in the normal erect position provides comfort during extended appointments. When the backrest is positioned at greater than a right angle to the chair seat and the chair is tilted slightly back, the tendency for the patient to slump is lessened. Adjustment of the backrest to support the lumbar region of the back automatically places the upper edge of the backrest below the superior border of the scapulae on the average adult patient. While single unit contour chairs do not allow backrest adjustment, they are designed for patient comfort. When possible the dental chair footrest should be adjusted to accommodate the patient's height.

Strain on the neck will be prevented by careful placement of the headrest. The vertical adjustment of the headrest is used to position it behind the occipital protuberances of the skull. The headrest is moved in a horizontal plane to maintain straight alignment of the cervical vertebrae. When the head is positioned correctly all areas of the mouth are usually within the range of the operator's vision and accessible for instrumentation. An angle of approximately 40 degrees is formed by the line of the occlusal surfaces of the maxillary teeth and a horizontal plane when the head is positioned correctly and the mouth comfortably opened. At the same time, the line of the occlusal surfaces of the mandibular teeth and a horizontal plane form an angle of approximately 15 degrees (Fig. 4–1).

Positioning the head too far back will place strain on the neck, make swallowing and breathing more difficult and increase the possibility of gagging or swallowing debris. This error in head placement also will interfere with visibility of the lingual surfaces of the anterior teeth and inhibit instrumentation there and in other areas of the mouth. Positioning the head too far forward makes opening of the mouth difficult, causes pooling of saliva in the mandibular anterior area, and promotes tension of the sublingual muscles. Visibility and instrumentation is impaired, particularly in the area of the lingual surfaces of the maxillary anterior teeth, when the head is forward of the optimum position.

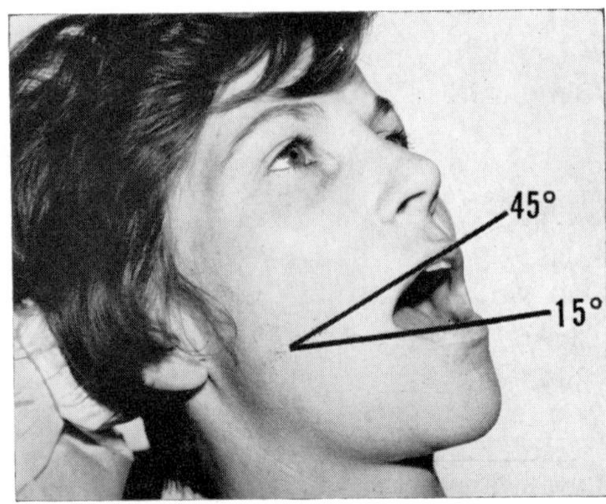

FIG. 4–1. The patient's head positioned correctly. With the mouth opened comfortably, an angle of approximately 45 degrees is formed by the line of the occlusal surfaces of the maxillary teeth and a horizontal plane. The line of the occlusal surfaces of the mandibular teeth and a horizontal plane form an angle of approximately 15 degrees.

Adjustment of the dental chair for the child patient requires adaptation of the positioning for an adult. The headrest may be lowered to the upper edge of the backrest to accommodate the small child. The child will often sit in a more erect position if the knees are bent and the ankles crossed with the feet placed on the chair seat. Again application of good body mechanics is important to the provision of comfort and accessibility of the mouth.

Operator Position for Oral Prophylaxis Techniques. Application of the principles of good body mechanics is more important to the operator's position than to that of the patient because of the potential for fatigue during the working day. Standing or sitting in an erect position enhances blood circulation and respiration and prevents muscle and nerve fatigue. Placement of the patient in correct relationship to the operator prevents strain on the operator's neck, back, arms and shoulders. When the operator's arm is held at a point one half the distance between the waist and shoulder, it should be at approximately the same level as the patient's mouth. The stature of the patient or operator and the specific area of operation may require adjustment of this basic position.

Equal distribution of weight is essential to either a standing or a sitting operating position. When standing, the operator's weight should be distributed equally on both feet. The rheostat is activated by sliding the foot along the floor rather than placing it on the pedal. Good posture is maintained when working beside or behind the dental chair.

Adjustment of the operating stool is critical to the maintenance of optimum posture while working from a sitting position. The stool is adjusted to the height that will allow the operator to sit with the feet on the floor and the thighs and lower legs forming an angle of approximately 90 degrees. The angle formed by the thigh and leg may vary. Prevention of excessive pressure on the back of the thigh is the important factor in leg position. If, after the optimum sitting position is attained, the patient's mouth is too high or low for visibility and accessibility, adjustments of the dental chair should be made before resorting to adaptations of the operator's position. If the patient is too high, the dental chair is lowered, then tilted back if necessary. Tilting the chair back will require minor readjustment of the patient's head to bring the opened mouth back to a correct operating position. For the very tall patient or short operator, the additional adaptation of raising the operating stool will be required. The operator's feet then must be placed on the top of the rheostat and the engine activated by applying a forward pressure to the upper edge of the pedal.

Effective use of the operating light influences the posture of the operator. Throughout oral prophylaxis procedures the light is readjusted to provide maximum illumination. For highest intensity the source of light is positioned as close to the field of operation as possible, while allowing free movement of the operator's head and the engine arm of the unit. Maximum illumination of the mandibular arch generally is achieved by raising the light and directing the beam at a downward angle into the mouth. The maxillary arch usually is illuminated best by lowering the light and directing the beam at an upward angle onto the teeth. For increased illumination, the light is turned to one side or another at an angle to the area of operation. Whenever operations cease, the light beam is directed toward the floor to prevent patient discomfort.

A request to the patient to raise, lower or turn the head will result in increased illumination and accessibility of an area. Application of the principles of light reflection and instrumentation will indicate the direction of the head readjustment. The principles of sterile technique and courtesy require verbal instructions to the patient for readjustment of the head rather than physical contact.

Accessibility of posterior buccal areas of the mouth is often greater if the patient's mouth is partially closed. The resultant relaxation of the muscles of the cheeks provides easier manipulation of instruments. The lingual surfaces of the teeth and adjacent tissue are more visible and accessible when the patient's mouth is fully opened.

GENERAL PRINCIPLES OF ORAL PROPHYLAXIS INSTRUMENTATION

Instrument Grasp

Correct instrument grasp is of primary importance in all instrumentation techniques. It has a direct bearing upon the operator's ability to manipulate instruments and consequently upon the efficiency and comfort with which operations are performed. Incorrect instrument grasp is frequently the source of instrumentation difficulty. Investigation of technique problems should begin with an evaluation of the operator's grasp and hand position.

Two instrument grasps are employed in dental hygiene clinical techniques: the modified pen grasp and the palm grasp. The modified pen grasp, usually referred to as the pen grasp, is the most versatile and widely used of the two.

Pen Grasp. With the pen grasp (Fig. 4–2) the instrument is held in basically the same manner as the pen or pencil in writing. The thumb, index and middle fingers hold the instrument. Placement of the pad of the middle finger on the instrument rather than resting the instrument against the side of the finger constitutes the greatest modification of the conventional pen grasp. The thumb and index finger are placed opposite each other and beyond the middle finger away from the working end of the instrument. The joint between the second and third phalange of the index finger is only slightly flexed. Care must be taken to maintain the instrument handle in a position superior to the second phalange of the index finger. If the instrument handle moves beyond this point toward the fingertip, the thumb and fingers are forced into incorrect positions thus inhibiting manipulation of the instrument. The thumb assumes a perpendicular relationship to the index finger, the joints of the index and middle finger are severely flexed and the side of the middle finger rests against the instrument. Novice operators frequently assume this incorrect pen grasp in an attempt to position an instrument correctly on a tooth surface. The error can be avoided by adjustment of the hand and wrist position in preference to an alteration of instrument grasp. The instrument handle may rest against the hand at any point between the joint of the first and second phalange and the angle formed by the thumb and index finger. The point of rest will vary with the instrument, area of the mouth and tooth surface to which the instrument is being applied.

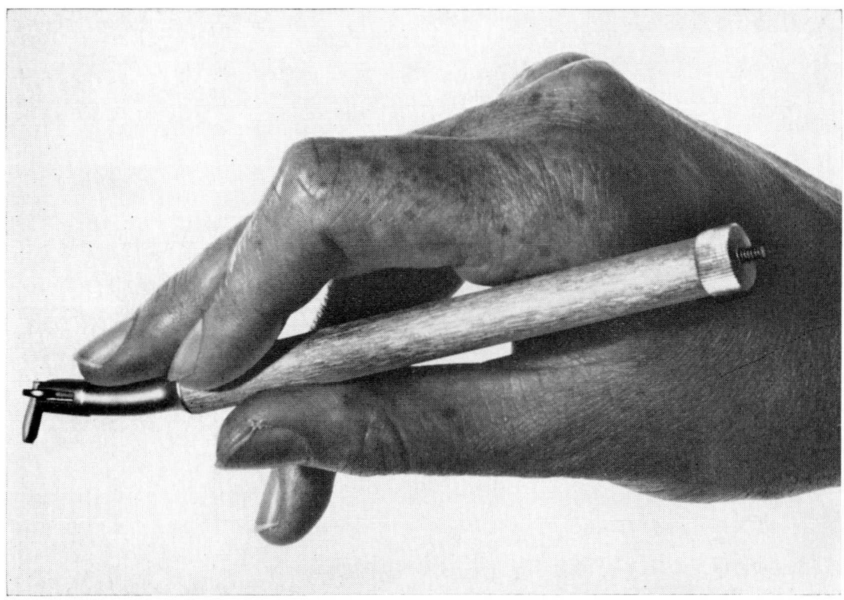

FIG. 4–2. *Modified Pen Grasp.* The thumb and index finger are placed opposite each other. The pad of the middle finger is placed on the instrument shank near the working end.

Palm Grasp. In the palm grasp (Fig. 4–3) the instrument is placed across the first phalange of the fingers which are then flexed over the handle into the palm of the hand. The thumb is free. Use of the palm grasp is usually confined to the polishing of the labial surfaces of the maxillary anteriors with the porte polisher, adaptations of scaling instruments when exceptional force is required and manipulation of the air syringe. There is a tendency to use finger motion in activation of the instrument grasped in this manner, which causes rapid fatigue.

Instruments are grasped close to the working end, near or at the union of the shank and handle. When it is necessary to extend the working end far beyond the fingertips, instrument control is lessened.

Force and Direction of Instrument Stroke

The force of instrumentation is transmitted from the musculature of the shoulder, upper arm and forearm through the wrist, hand and fingers to the instrument. Instruments are positioned and directed but not activated by the fingers. During instrumentation finger movement is confined to maintenance of the proper relationship of the instrument with the tooth. The thumb, index and middle fingers direct

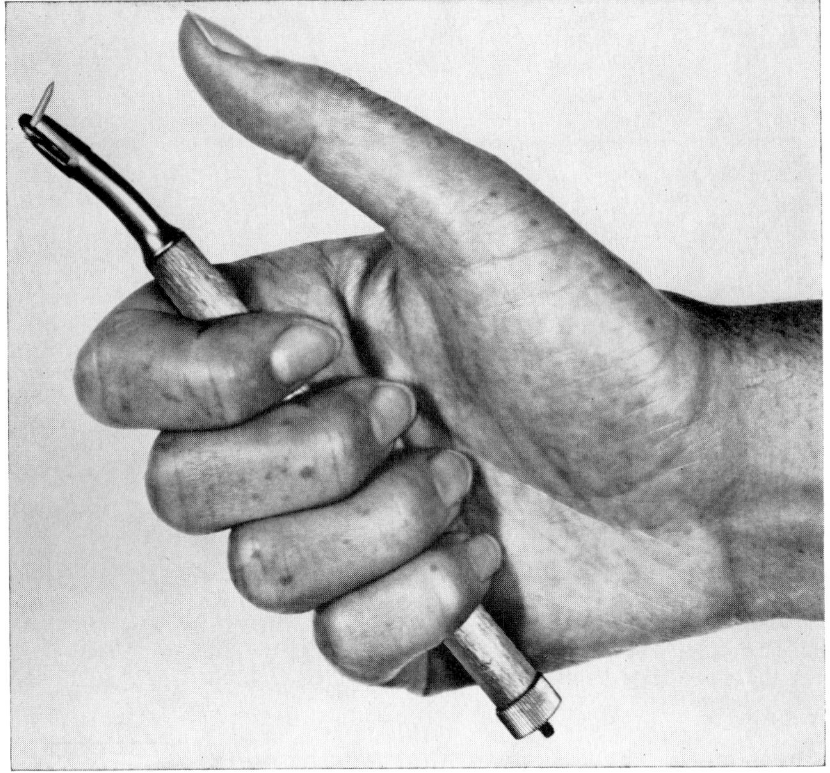

FIG. 4–3. *Palm Grasp*. The instrument is placed across the first phalange of the fingers which are flexed over the handle into the palm of the hand.

instruments as they are activated on the tooth surface, when the pen grasp is used, while the entire hand guides the direction of the instrument when the palm grasp is employed. In both grasps, the hand turns and the wrist pivots to maintain correct instrument position during its activation. In general, the elbow is raised and the wrist held straight or arched upward and turned to either side for manipulation of instruments on mandibular teeth. For instrumentation on the maxillary teeth the elbow is lowered, the wrist held straight or arched downward and turned to either side. A mere turn of the wrist will often provide the desired instrument position.

Use of a Fulcrum[60]

To assure control, a fulcrum or finger rest is always used in instrumentation. A fulcrum is the support or point of rest on which a lever turns in moving a body. In instrumentation, the point of rest or fulcrum is the tooth. The lever is the hand and the moving body the instrument. Use of a fulcrum serves to control the instrument and prevent injury by limiting the scope of its travel and by steadying the hand. The third finger is designated as the fulcrum finger in the pen grasp. The thumb acts as the fulcrum finger in the palm grasp. For maximum security, the fulcrum finger is placed upon the tooth structure. Because of mobility, the lips, chin and adjacent parts of the face provide inadequate finger rests. Since pressure is applied to the fulcrum finger during some procedures, pontics and mobile or sensitive teeth are not used for finger rests. The use of anterior teeth should be avoided whenever possible. Greater control and direction of force is achieved by placing the fulcrum finger as close as possible to the area of instrumentation. Ideally, maxillary fulcrums are used for the maxillary arch and mandibular fulcrums for the mandibular arch. However, optimum instrument placement and manipulation takes precedence over the position of the fulcrum finger.

THE ORAL INSPECTION[22,26,32,58,66]

The intraoral procedures of the oral prophylaxis appointment are initiated with an appraisal of the condition of the patient's mouth. Just as an architect studies the topography of the building site before designing a structure, the dentist and dental hygienist survey the oral cavity before formulating and executing a plan of operation. The oral inspection determines the needs of the patient, the sequence in which the needs should be met, and the patient education required for acceptance and maintenance of services.

Sequence

A functional sequence of inspection has two phases: observation of the entire oral mucosa, and examination of the teeth and the gingival sulci. The first phase begins with an inspection of the patient's lips, then moves intraorally to the labial, buccal and vestibular mucosa with attention to the fornices. The oral pharnyx, retromolar area, maxillary tuberosity and soft palate are examined. From the soft palate, it is logical to proceed with inspecting the hard palate and gingiva on the lingual aspect of the maxillary arch. Particular attention is given to the tongue, its dorsal, lateral and ventral surfaces, and the sublingual mucosa. The first part of the oral inspection is completed with the observation of the alveolar mucosa, attached and free gingiva. In the second phase of the oral inspection, the gingival sulci are examined to determine their depth and to detect the presence and extent of stains, soft and hard deposits, defects and dental caries.

The hygienist does not make a diagnosis from inspection of the soft and hard tissues of the mouth, but recognizes deviations from normal and relates them to oral prophylaxis techniques. The first phase of the oral inspection should reveal the presence of any deviation from normal which might prohibit continuation of the appointment, such as lesions which may be malignant or manifestations of virus infections. Conditions that may cause patient discomfort during instrumentation are also considered. Cheilosis or herpes labialis will indicate the need for periodic lubrication of the involved area with petroleum jelly. The presence of intra-oral ulcerations will require care in the manipulation of tissue in the involved area. Instrumentation in areas of gingival inflammation may cause patient discomfort. Severity of the inflammation and the pain threshold of the patient will determine the need for topical anesthesia.

In the second phase of the oral inspection the condition of the gingiva is related to the patient's dental history, home care practices and presence of stains and deposits, all of which influence the hygienist's approach to dental health education. Knowledge of the type, location and amount of stains and deposits also facilitates the planning of the oral prophylaxis appointment. If the inspection of the teeth reveals extensive decay with possible pulp exposure, techniques will necessarily be altered. For example, topical application of fluoride compounds is contraindicated because of pulpal reaction to fluorides. Areas of extensive decay also may interfere with scaling and polishing procedures. During this second phase of the oral inspection, the presence of fixed and removable appliances is noted and consideration is given to the selection and adaptation of oral prophylaxis procedures. Removable appliances must be taken from the mouth before a complete assessment of the adjacent teeth and oral mucosa can be made. The patient's occlusion is classified and related to instrumentation and patient education. Severely malpositioned teeth require ingenuity in instrument selection and manipulation, along with adaptation of home care techniques.

Instruments

The instruments of the oral inspection are few but essential. The mouth mirror is used for vision, illumination and retraction. The explorer is employed for the detection of deposits, defects and decay. The periodontal probe is indispensable in determination of the depth of the gingival sulci and existence of pockets. The air syringe and compressed air also renders assistance (Fig. 4–4).

Mouth Mirror. The mouth mirror is one of the instruments most frequently used by the hygienist. It provides visibility of tooth surfaces in areas of the mouth that are beyond the range of direct vision. In addition to providing increased illumination, the mouth mirror is also a useful retractor of the patient's cheeks and tongue.

In the oral inspection and all other procedures in which it is used, the mouth mirror is held with a modified pen grasp. The mirror is stabilized by use of a fulcrum except during the appraisal of the entire oral mucosa. Then the scope of the inspection requires the continuous and rapid repositioning of the mirror, making the use of a fulcrum impractical.

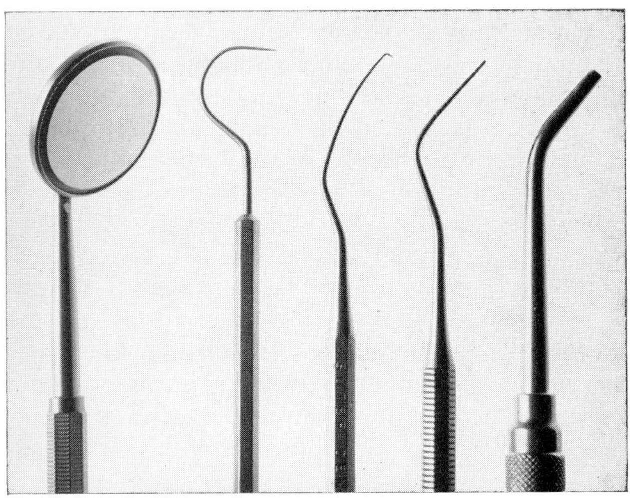

FIG. 4–4. Oral inspection instruments: mouth mirror, S.C. 23 explorer, G-2 explorer, Williams periodontal probe and air syringe tip.

The reflecting surfaces or lens of mouth mirrors are of three types: plane, front surface and magnifying. Because the image is formed on the front rather than the back of the lens, the front surface mirror provides a clearer image. The magnifying lens presents the problem of distorting the image when the mirror-object distance is altered. The differences in the size, shape and length of handles should be considered in their selection. The handle should allow an easy and secure grasp and extension of the working end beyond the grasp. If the mirror handle is short, the operator will not be able to extend the working end freely while maintaining correct instrument grasp.

Adept use of the mouth mirror provides immeasurable assistance in detecting the presence of stains and deposits on the teeth. Ingenuity in positioning the mirror will determine the degree of visibility of the surface being examined. Areas of the tooth covered by free gingiva can often be seen by effective positioning of the mouth mirror, while the soft tissue is being deflected with compressed air. When the mirror face is turned to catch the beam from the operating light, and reflects it back onto the tooth surface, greater illumination and visibility result.

Care should be taken in manipulation of the mouth mirror to avoid patient discomfort. Pressure of the mirror shank or handle on the angle of the lips and pressure by the edge of the mirror itself on the gingiva will cause considerable discomfort. The patient's lip can inadvertently become pinched between the shank or handle of the mirror and the fulcrum finger during procedures. Teeth are often sensitive to the contact of metal, therefore the mirror should be inserted into, and removed from the mouth in a manner which will avoid its contact with the dentition. Insertion of the mirror into the vestibular area of the mouth is facilitated by holding the instrument with the mirror face in a vertical plane. The mirror can be moved easily between the two dental arches when it is held with the face in a horizontal plane. If the temperature of the mirror is lower than that of the patient's mouth, the mirror face will fog. Defogging is accomplished easily by turning the mirror face against the patient's buccal mucosa.

Air Syringe. Compressed air is directed onto the teeth and oral mucosa by means of the air syringe for purposes of drying and deflecting tissue, thereby assisting in the recognition of soft and hard tissue lesions, the detection of deposits and stains and determination of the extent and condition of dental restorations. If the tip of the air syringe is adjustable, the direction of the air stream can be controlled more easily. To permit adequate sterilization or disinfection, the syringe tip should be removable.

It is important to realize that precautions must be taken in the use of compressed air. Patients with hypersensitive teeth and open carious lesions will experience discomfort from the indiscriminate use of air. Short intermittent activation of the air syringe can often be tolerated in areas of hypersensitivity when a continuous stream of air cannot. Synthetic restorations will be dried out and thus damaged through prolonged use of compressed air on their surfaces. Therefore, caution is indicated when applying air to teeth that have been restored with synthetic materials.

The air syringe handle is held with a palm grasp. Air is released from the air tip by applying pressure with the thumb to the syringe lever. The air stream is directed on the surface to be dried or cleared of debris or saliva. When the air stream is directed into the gingival sulcus, the free gingiva is deflected and the tooth surface dried, exposing submarginal calculus. The white chalklike supramarginal calculus that is frequently found on the mandibular anterior and maxillary molar teeth is elusive and can remain undetected without the application of compressed air. Calculus is more apparent to the observer when it is dehydrated. As the dehydration is not achieved immediately, it is important to observe the area in question for several seconds after drying before making a decision regarding the presence of calculus. Drying the tooth surface assists in detection through increasing the potential for tactile as well as visual recognition of the presence of defects, deposits and stains. Instruments easily slip over slight irregularities in or on tooth surfaces that are lubricated by saliva and blood. Therefore, a dry, clear field of operation is necessary for accurate determination of the presence of calculus and the completeness of its removal.

Periodontal Probe. Because periodontal disease is insidious, cautious examination of the periodontal tissues for signs of disease is imperative. Gingival stippling is not always a sign of health. Its absence indicates disease; its presence can mean nothing. Radiographs are helpful but unreliable aids in recognizing periodontal disease and detecting calculus. However, radiographs may indicate the presence of calculus and will provide an index of bone level which justifies their use in oral prophylaxis procedures. The only accurate means of determining the presence, form and depth of periodontal pockets is by using the periodontal probe. Probing is necessary to determine how far toward the apex of the tooth instruments should travel. If the operator fails to recognize the depth of the sulcus or pocket, all calculus will not be removed and in essence nothing of any importance will have been accomplished toward improving the patient's periodontal health.

The hygienist employs the periodontal probe for periodontal charting procedures, as an adjunct to calculus detection and for evaluating the effectiveness of routine oral prophylaxis procedures. Recording pocket depths, determined through use of the probe, provides the only means by which an objective evaluation can be obtained of the periodontal condition for patients on recall appointments.

Probes are rectangular, oval or round in cross section. They are of a thickness which allows for their insertion into the gingival sulcus or pocket. The shank of the instrument forms an angle between the working end and handle. The working end of the probe is scored at millimeter intervals for use in measurement. Some probes are scored every millimeter from 1 through 10, while others have millimeter markings from 1 through 3, 2 millimeter markings from 3 through 7 and 1 millimeter markings again from 7 through 10. The 2 millimeter interval allows for easy identification of the midline reading of 5. In reading the probe measurement, the operator counts back from 10 when the depth of the pocket is over 5 millimeters (Fig. 4–5).

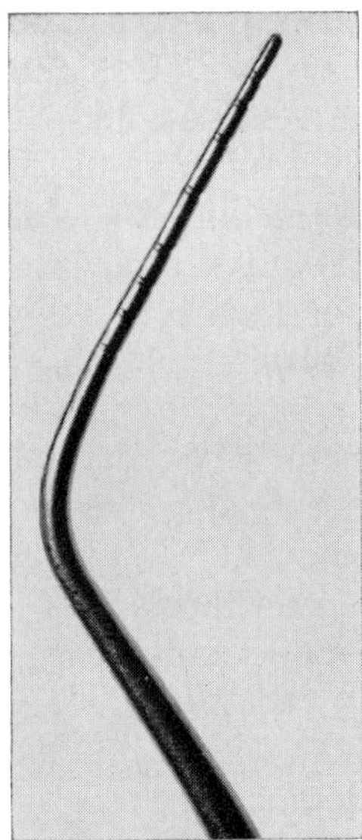

FIG. 4–5. Periodontal probe with 1 and 2 millimeter markings.

The probe is held with a modified pen grasp and secured with a fulcrum. It is manipulated gently to determine the level of the attachment apparatus. Force will destroy the integrity of this apparatus, cause discomfort and render an inaccurate reading. The probe is initially inserted into the sulcus in an area where the tissue is flexible. While maintaining contact with the tooth, the probe is gently pushed into the sulcus. When the instrument tip first meets resistance, the probe is moved horizontally against the crevicular epithelium, then gently pushed in a vertical direction toward the apex of the tooth. If the obstruction is calculus, it will then be bypassed; if it is the attachment apparatus, the resistance will give easily and the vertical force of the probe should cease. Once the probe has been inserted and an initial depth recognized, the remainder of the sulcus can be easily probed by drawing the instrument up and down along the tooth surface; this has been called "walking" along the floor of the sulcus. The instrument tip remains in the sulcus during the probing of an area. For accuracy of measurement, the working end of the instrument is kept in a relationship as nearly parallel with the long axis of the tooth as is possible (Fig. 4–6). Tooth contours prevent a strict parallel relationship between the tooth and the probe. Greater deviation from the ideal position is necessary when probing proximal areas, because the contact point of adjacent teeth cause interference. Unfortunately, periodontal involvement frequently occurs in this area.

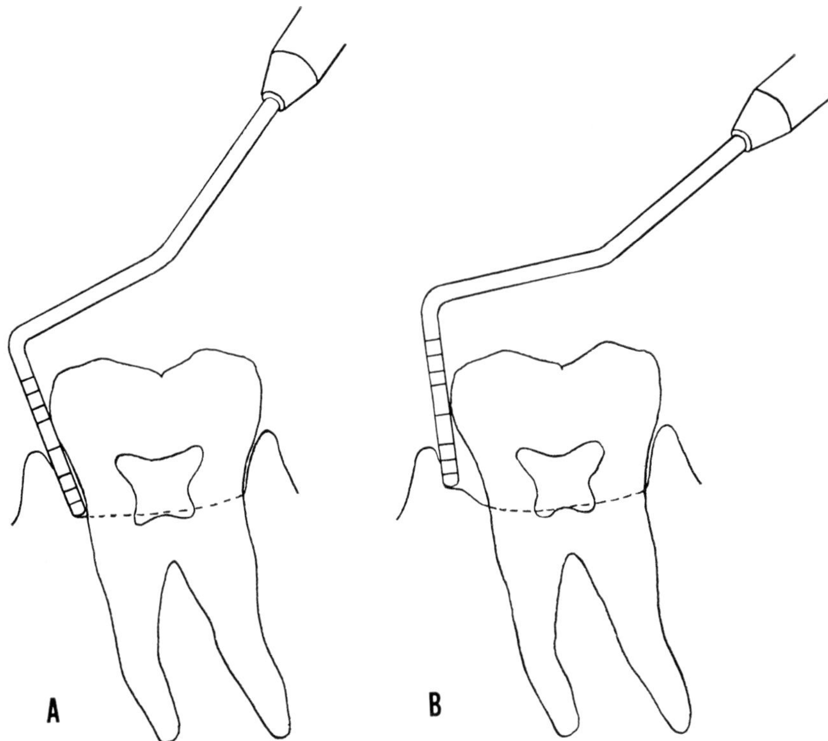

FIG. 4–6. *A*, Periodontal probe correctly positioned for accurate measurement. *B*, Periodontal probe incorrectly positioned, giving an inaccurate measurement.

Periodontal charting is a relatively simple procedure. Sulcus or pocket depths are measured and recorded on a form selected by the dentist. Usually six measurements are recorded. For example, the following measurements of the sulcus or pocket depth are recorded for a posterior tooth: disto-buccal, buccal, mesio-buccal, disto-lingual, lingual and mesio-lingual. Corresponding measurements are taken in the anterior area of the mouth.

Explorers. Explorers used in the oral inspection and other oral prophylaxis procedures are selected for their versatility and sensitivity. A fine working end accompanied by a relatively small and light handle will provide a sensitive explorer. Explorers with piano wire working ends are particularly sensitive to irregularities in or on the tooth surface. The curvature or angle of the working end and shank determine the versatility of the instrument. Although two explorer designs have been selected for illustration, the fact that there are other equally effective instruments is recognized. The specific selection of an explorer depends upon the purpose for which it is to be used and the preference of the operator. Of the two explorers pictured (Fig. 4–4) the S.C. 23 or crook-like explorer is most useful for application to posterior teeth. Anterior teeth and the readily accessible surfaces of posterior teeth are effectively explored with the G-2 instrument. The high degree of sensitivity of the G-2 makes it an invaluable instrument for detection of submarginal calculus, particularly on anterior teeth.

The explorer is held with a secure, but light grasp. If the instrument is held with pressure, the operator's tactile sense will be impaired and the movement of the instrument will be inhibited. The explorer tip is held against the tooth at all times. If allowed to wander into the gingiva, crevicular epithelium or attachment apparatus, the explorer tip will cause tissue trauma and patient discomfort. As much of the working end as possible is applied to the tooth for greater efficiency in searching out calculus deposits. Transitions across line angles are made with caution to insure adherence of the explorer tip to the tooth surface and to follow the attachment contour. The tip of the instrument is drawn from the attachment toward the exposed surface of the tooth when exploring the depths of the gingival sulcus. A stroke in a horizontal, oblique or vertical direction is employed in the exploring technique. The stroke used is determined by the type of explorer and the specific tooth surface being examined. The explorer is more likely to catch on calculus deposits if the working end is gently pushed or pulled against the tooth. Concentration is required during exploring and all other oral prophylaxis procedures to make them meaningful. Knowledge of tooth anatomy and the anatomy and histology of periodontal tissues is extremely important, if the operator is to use the explorer effectively and differentiate between the tooth surface, its irregularities, deposits and dental caries. In exploring, the tactile sensation received from calculus varies with its hardness and form. The presence of calculus should be suspected whenever the velvet-like texture of the root surface or hard smooth texture of the crown changes.

While calculus represents an excess on the tooth surface, a carious lesion represents a deficiency. The degree of destruction of tooth structure resulting from dental decay will vary with the advancement of the lesion. Initial decalcification which appears as a white area on the tooth surface is smooth to the touch. As decalcification advances the surface becomes roughened. Decalcification at this stage may be misinterpreted as calculus. Drying the surface with compressed air will often provide enough improvement of visibility to make the differentiation between the two. With moderate pressure, the explorer will drop into and catch in the decalcification. The detection of decay in proximal surfaces challenges the operator's technical ability. Again, tooth anatomy should be considered as well as the tactile sensation from the projection of the explorer tip into the questionable area. The sensation of placing the instrument into a decayed area has been compared to that of sticking a pin in a cork.

In addition to recognizing the presence of carious lesions for purposes of selection and performance of oral prophylaxis techniques, the hygienist employs this skill in charting procedures. Selection of the form and the method of recording or charting existing conditions in the mouth is the prerogative of the dentist employer. It is the hygienist's responsibility to become acquainted with the particular office procedure and execute it with accuracy. The degree of tooth destruction that is recorded will vary from the slightest decalcification to unquestionable decay. Existing restorations and the condition of their margins are often recorded in the initial charting. The hygienist should be able to recognize a deficient or overhanging margin not only for charting procedures, but also for calculus removal techniques. Differentiation between the unseen margin of a restoration and calculus is facilitated by becoming acquainted with the texture of the restoration on an exposed surface before moving to the submarginal area in question. As the explorer moves in an apical direction in the gingival sulcus, the transition from the identified texture of the restoration to the texture of the adjacent tooth or calculus is recognized. Further verification is made by extending the explorer to the depth of the sulcus and drawing it coronally. Knowledge of tooth morphology should be applied to differentiate between tooth structure, calculus and the margin of the restoration as the instrument is pulled in a coronal direction.

A notation of missing and extracted teeth and removable appliances is usually made on the chart. Again the exact information and form for recording differs. A systematic procedure of charting, which will prevent omission of information is essential to all methods. When instructed by the dentist to do so, the hygienist records observations of defective margins and caries appearing in the patient's radiographs.

Throughout the charting and all other oral inspection procedures, the hygienist must avoid any comment that may be interpreted as diagnosis by either the patient or dentist. Application of information secured from the oral inspection relevant to oral prophylaxis techniques is not considered diagnosing. Patient questions requiring a diagnostic answer are referred to the dentist.

INSTRUMENTS AND TECHNIQUES OF SCALING AND ROOT PLANING[11,19]

The terms scaling and root planing refer to those techniques which are used to remove calculus from the clinical crowns of teeth. Scaling techniques are used to remove supramarginal calculus and submarginal calculus that is attached to the tooth surface. Root planing techniques are frequently employed to remove the remaining pieces of submarginal calculus that are tenaciously attached to the tooth and to smooth root surfaces. Root planing is sometimes referred to as root curettage. The term gingival or soft tissue curettage refers to the technique of debriding the gingival wall of a pocket with a curet. Although dental practice acts do not always define the extent of calculus removal that is within the purview of the dental hygienist, it is generally accepted that all calculus must be removed to complete the oral prophylaxis. Calculus occurs at the depth of the sulcus or pocket and often penetrates the root surface, thus, submarginal scaling and root planing are required for its complete removal.[48] However, directed soft tissue curettage which is essential to complete periodontal treatment is not within the realm of dental hygiene practice.

General Principles of Scaling and Root Planing[27]

A variety of opinions have been expressed regarding instrument selection and methods of their application. Certain basic principles apply to all methods, and once these principles are understood proficiency can be attained with any instrument. Knowledge of anatomic, histologic and physiologic characteristics of the teeth and periodontium, as well as theories of calculus formation and attachment is essential to understanding principles of instrument design and to developing operative skills. Because much of the area of operation is beyond visual perception, the operator must recall anatomical features of root surfaces and utilize tactile sensitivity to limit instrumentation on hidden tooth surfaces. A tooth has no flat surfaces, but is a continuum of convexities and concavities. Therefore, constant adaptation of the instrument blade and its cutting edges is required.

The width of the tooth surface must be considered in instrumentation. Some instruments have blades that are longer than the width of the root surface, particularly apical to the cervical one-third. Therefore, care must be taken to avoid overextension of the blade and its projection into the gingiva. Mesio-distal, labio-lingual and bucco-lingual dimensions of teeth vary with each tooth and individual, as well as with the area of the tooth surface. For example, the blade may be extended further from buccal to lingual on the proximal surface of a bicuspid at the cemento-enamel junction, than midway on its root surface. A longer blade or greater projection of the blade can be used on proximal surfaces of posterior teeth than on proximal surfaces of anterior teeth at a given level.

Knowledge of the contour of the cemento-enamel junction of a tooth assists the operator in determining the relative position of the epithelial attachment, particularly on proximal surfaces. However, the contour of the attachment apparatus often deviates from that of the cemento-enamel junction.[43] An understanding of the relationship of the instrument blade to the crevicular epithelium is essential to preserve the integrity of the periodontium. The side of the instrument tip must be in constant contact with the tooth during activation of the blade, to avoid lacerating soft tissue.

Use of the periodontal probe, explorer, mouth mirror, compressed air and radiographs in scaling techniques is invaluable in the detection and removal of calculus. Calculus detection is also dependent upon knowledge of where and how it forms. An awareness of methods for calculus attachment guides the operator in selecting instruments and techniques for its removal.

Instrument Design and Principles of Use[23,27]

Scaling and root planing instruments are designed for specific areas and use. Carefully selected and correctly used instruments will provide effective service. No scaling or root planing instrument can be adapted to all surfaces of all teeth; therefore, a variety of instruments are included. Calculus removal instruments have been variously categorized in the literature. For purposes of this chapter, they will be categorized according to their use in one of the following classifications: chisels, curets, files, hoes and sickles. Instruments in each of these classification can be called scalers as they are all used to remove calculus. Chisels, files, hoes and sickles frequently are grouped under "scalers" in the literature. Curets are often separated from the others because they are used for root planing.

Design. There are innumerable blade and shank designs within the specific instrument categories. Features of design which must be considered are: balance, sensitivity, flexibility, dimensions and angulation of the shank, dimensions of the blade and the number of cutting edges. The blade must be centered along the long axis of the handle in order to give the instrument balance when it is grasped and activated. A large heavy instrument interferes with the sense of touch or tactile sensation experienced when the blade is moved over irregularities on the tooth surface. The shank and blade need to be slightly flexible to transmit sensations through the handle. If the shank and

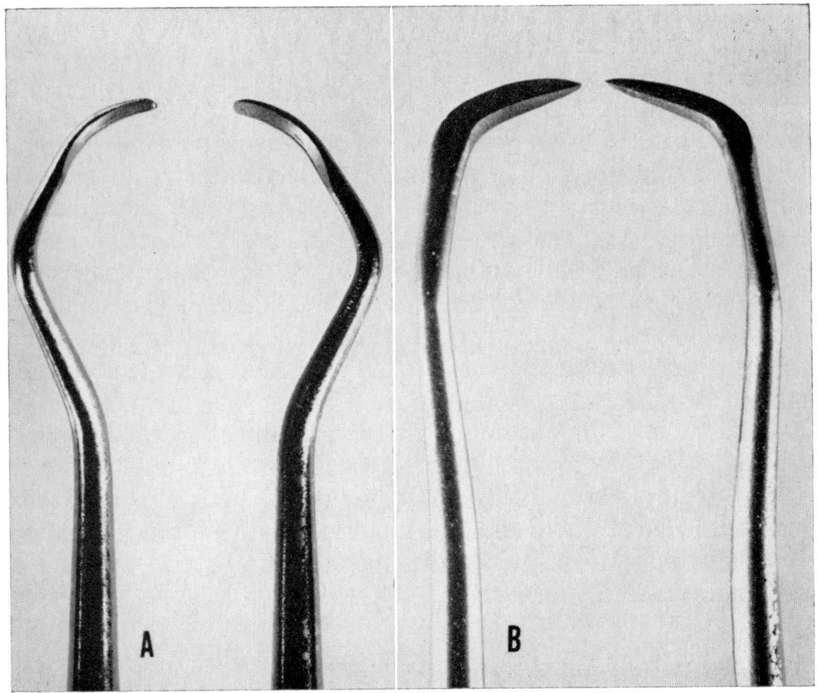

FIG. 4–7. Paired instruments: one blade and shank is a mirror image of the other. *A,* Curets. *B,* Modified sickles.

blade are too flexible, the optimum relationship of the blade and the tooth cannot be maintained when pressure is applied to remove calculus. The blades of instruments used submarginally must be small enough to be inserted into the gingival sulcus without soft tissue traumatization. Instrument shanks are designed to permit access to specific tooth surfaces. Severely angulated and relatively long shanks allow adaptation of blades to surfaces apical to the height of contour and contact areas of posterior teeth. Instruments with slight shank angulation and short blades adapt better to anterior teeth than posterior teeth. Some instruments are designed in pairs, one blade and shank being a mirror image of the other (Fig. 4–7). The two instruments in the pair complement each other in area of use.

Grasp. Scaling and root planing instruments are held with a pen grasp for calculus removal techniques, with few exceptions. The *proficient* operator may, at times, resort to a palm grasp in order to acquire optimum instrument positioning for removal of a tenacious piece of calculus.

Fulcrum. A stable fulcrum is especially critical for scaling and root planing techniques because of the sharpness of the instruments and nature of the deposits to be removed. It is particularly important to place the fulcum finger as close as possible to the tooth to which the instrument is being applied, in order to assure maximum control of the working end.

Angulation. During activation of the instrument designed for calculus removal a specific surface of the blade and the tooth surface should form an angle of more than 45 degrees, but less than 90 degrees. This basic concept, termed *angulation,* is the essence of correct scaling and root planing techniques. "Angulation of the cutting edge" has been used to describe this blade position, but is technically incorrect, as an edge is not a surface, but a line angle formed by the union of two surfaces. An edge or "line angle" cannot form an "angle" with a tooth surface.

Correct blade angulation permits effective use of the cutting edge. When optimum angulation is achieved, with the cutting edge engaged on the tooth, the edge will "bite" the tooth surface; or, rather than slipping, the edge will move along with a slight dragging or shaving

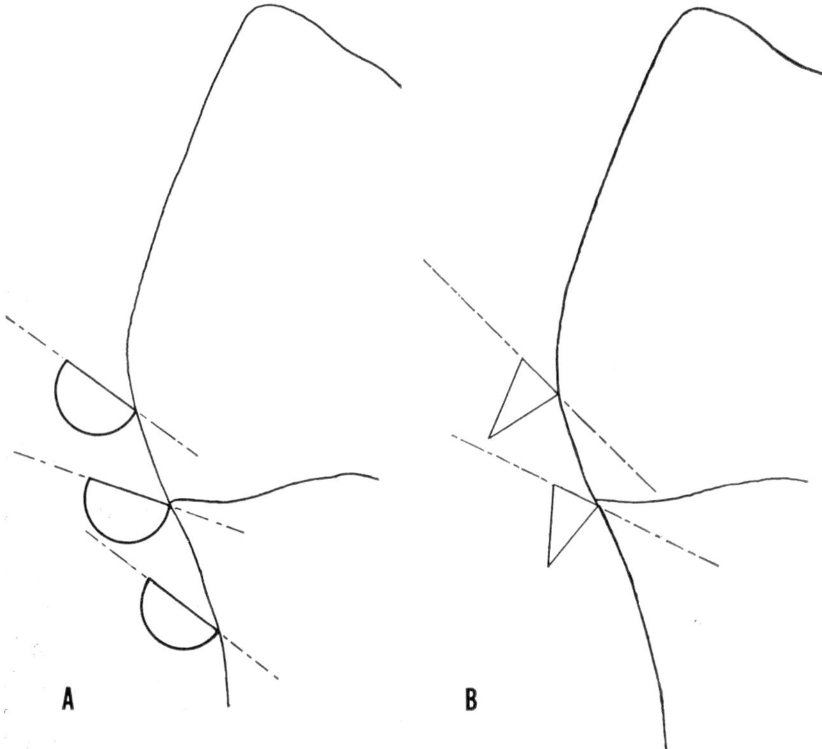

FIG. 4–8. *A,* Cross section views of the curet blade as it is adapted to the curved tooth surface with correct angulation. *B,* Cross section views of the sickle scaler blade as it is adapted to the curved tooth surface with correct angulation.

effect. Because the tooth surface is a continuum of convexities and concavities, the blade must be adjusted constantly in order to maintain correct angulation, thus removing calculus effectively without injuring the adjacent tissue (Fig. 4–8). Ability to achieve correct instrument angulation is directly related to the shank and blade design.

Application and Insertion. The application of an instrument to the exposed surface of a tooth is relatively easy. The instrument is placed against the tooth surface and turned so that the angulation of the blade is correct. The application of an instrument to submarginal areas of the tooth is more difficult since it requires the insertion of the blade and often a portion of the shank into the sulcus or pocket. This insertion is accomplished by turning the blade in the position that requires the least possible displacement of free gingiva, then gently pushing the blade until it rests against the epithelial attachment. After the blade reaches its intended destination, it is adapted to the tooth just beyond the deposit and correctly angulated.

Stroke. Instruments are activated by exerting a pushing or pulling force. Two general types of stroke are used to exert either force: *exploratory stroke* and *working stroke.* The difference between the exploratory and working stroke is merely in the pressure which is applied to the instrument, and the use to which each is put. The exploratory or "searching" stroke, with *light* pressure is used to locate deposits. When the cutting edge of the instrument engages a deposit, pressure is applied to remove the calculus, and the exploratory stroke becomes a working stroke. Both strokes are used interchangeably in scaling and root planing. Greater efficiency is achieved through the utilization of as much of the cutting edge of the instrument as possible during the stroke. In the working stroke, the instrument should be pulled away from the epithelial attachment and gingiva. Pushing the instrument toward the epithelial attachment and gingiva with pressure is hazardous, because fragments of calculus can thus be easily "pushed" into the soft tissue. However, the instrument may be pushed, *without pressure,* to reposition the blade during a series of calculus removal strokes, and in exploratory strokes.

Whenever possible the force of a stroke is directed in the same plane as the long axis of the tooth, because the longitudinal curvatures in tooth contour usually are more gradual than adjacent horizontal convexities and concavities. Therefore, less adaptation of the blade is required during the stroke. However, the direction of the stroke is governed by the instrument, the area of the mouth and the tooth surface to which the instrument is applied. Sometimes the stroke can be in a vertical direction in line with the long axis of the tooth; but sometimes it must be in an oblique direction at an angle to the long axis of the tooth.

Instruments and Their Use

Curet. Of all the instruments used for calculus removal, the curet is the most versatile. It is used for root planing, removal of submarginal deposits and removal of small adherent supramarginal deposits. Because of its design, the curet will adapt well to the curvatures of teeth and to those tooth surfaces that are surrounded by firm, relatively normal gingiva. It is particularly useful for removal of the deposit located deep within the pocket.

Curets are "paired" instruments. One pair of curets with moderately angulated shanks can be adapted to all surfaces of the teeth when occlusion is normal and the periodontium is healthy; thus curets are termed "universal instruments." In practice, however, it is preferable to have at least two pairs of curets of different design. The fact that some instrument designs adapt better than others to particular areas of the mouth makes the use of at least two pairs of curets desirable.

The curet blade has two curved cutting edges (Fig. 4–9). Since the two cutting edges merge to form a rounded tip, the curet blade sometimes is said to have one continuous cutting edge. The rounded tip is a safety feature, providing less possibility of scratching the tooth

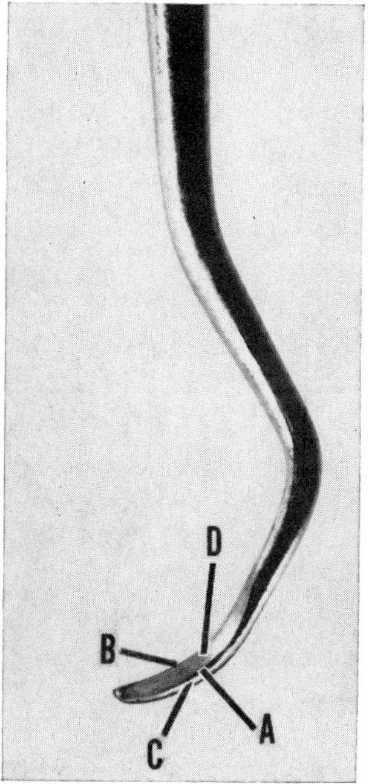

FIG. 4–9. Curet with an angulated shank. The blade has two curved cutting edges: *A* and *B*, which merge to form a rounded tip. The lateral surface: *C*, is convexly curved. The facial surface: *D*, lies between the two cutting edges.

surface or lacerating soft tissue during instrument activation. The *back* surface of the curet blade is convex, which is a decided advantage in submarginal use. This feature enables blade positioning in the sulcus or pocket with less danger of damage to the soft tissue. The sides or *lateral* surfaces of the blade are a continuation of the convex back surface. The surface of the blade that lies between the lateral surfaces and opposite the back of the blade is designated as the *facial* surface. The angles formed by the facial surface and the lateral surfaces form the two cutting edges.

The facial surface is straight in a horizontal plane from one edge of the blade to the other. In the longitudinal plane, from the shank to the tip, the facial surface has the same curvature as the edges of the blade. If a cut is made across the width of the blade at any point between the tip and the shank, the cross section view attained would be a half circle or a half oval, dependent upon the specific curet. An understanding of the cross-section dimension of the width of the blade is essential to establishment of correct angulation when the blade is applied to a tooth. The instrument is placed against the tooth so that the facial surface and the tooth surface form an angle of less than 90 degrees, and the convex back surface is directed toward the crevicular epithelium. The longitudinal contour of the facial surface and the cutting edges allow the instrument to be adapted to curved tooth surfaces.

The shank of a curet may be straight or angulated with respect to the long axis of the handle. The blade is turned away from the long axis of the instrument handle. The degree to which the blade is turned away from the handle, the angulation of the shank and size of the blade determine the areas in which the instrument can be used. Generally, a curet with a long and severely angulated shank and relatively long blade can be adapted readily to proximal surfaces (particularly those of posterior teeth) and to root furcations. A curet with a short, small blade turned at an angle to a straight shank can be used to remove calculus from labial and lingual surfaces of anterior teeth.

Use of the Curet in Scaling. Two basic positions of the curet blade in relation to the tooth surface and epithelial attachment will be discussed: the horizontal position (Fig. 4–10*A*) and the vertical or oblique position (Fig. 4–10*B*). In the horizontal position, the length of the blade is perpendicular to the long axis of the tooth with the length of the curved back surface paralleling the epithelial attachment. This position is used for proximal surfaces. If the design of the instrument permits, the horizontal position can be used on the facial and lingual surfaces of posterior teeth. However, it is rarely possible to achieve correct angulation on these surfaces with the curet blade in a horizontal position. It is much easier to place the blade in a horizontal position on the facial and lingual surfaces of

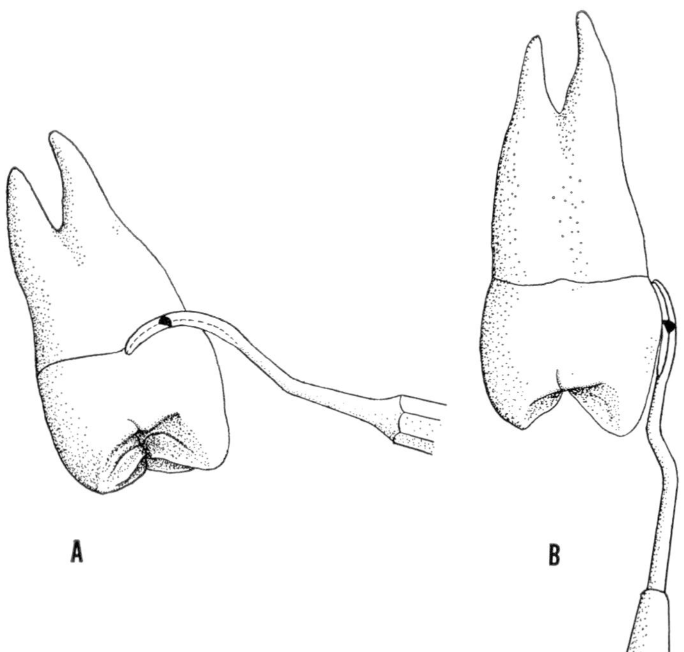

FIG. 4–10. *A,* Curet placed in a horizontal position on the proximal surface of a maxillary molar. The cutting edge indicated by the broken line is correctly positioned. In the cross-section view the facial surface forms an angle of less than 90 degrees with the tooth surface. *B,* Curet placed in a vertical position on the buccal surface of a maxillary molar. The cutting edge adjacent to the tooth is correctly positioned. The facial surface forms an angle of less than 90 degrees with the tooth surface.

anterior teeth, particularly if the instrument is designed specifically for this area.

The curet blade is placed in a vertical position on facial and lingual surfaces with the length of the blade approximately paralleling the long axis of the tooth and the tip directed apically. Whenever possible, this vertical position is modified by placing the length of the blade at an angle to the tooth somewhere between a vertical and horizontal position. The position of the blade is then termed oblique.

Even for the adept operator, it is difficult to make the transition from a vertical position to a horizontal position without removing the instrument from the tooth surface and reapplying it. The instrument should not be drawn across the line angle from one surface to an adjacent surface with a continuous stroke. Strict attention must be paid to the contour of the attachment apparatus and the relationship of the interdental papillae when scaling or planing the line angles of

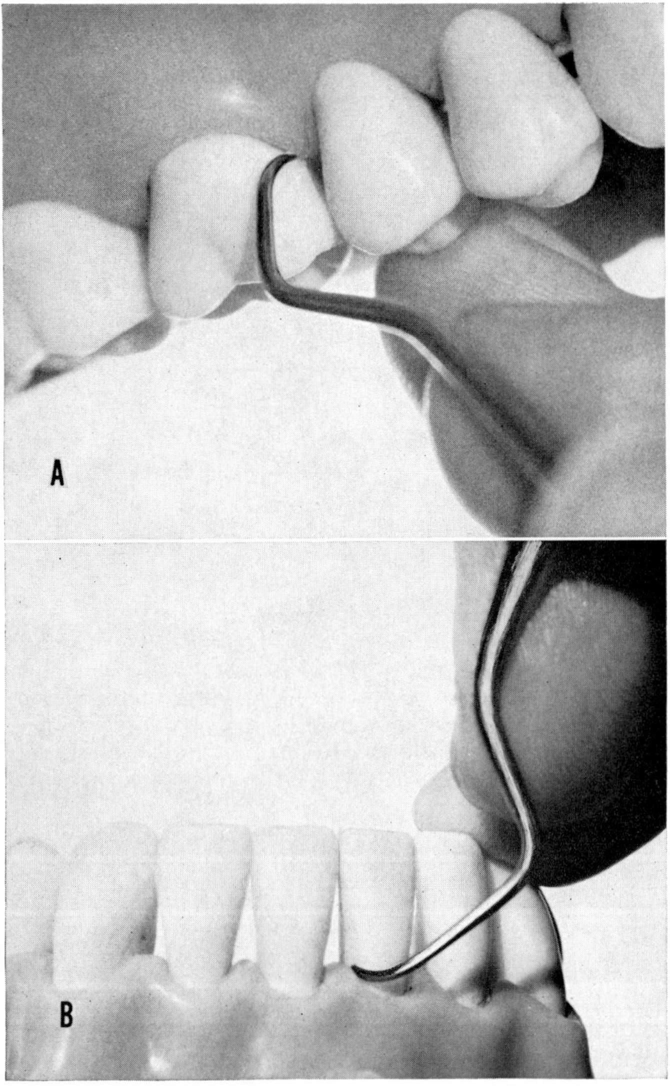

FIG. 4–11. *A,* Curet placed in a horizontal position on the mesiobuccal line-angle of the maxillary right first permanent molar. The blade is pulled toward the occlusal surface in the *working* stroke. *B,* Curet placed in a horizontal position on the mesiolabial line-angle of the mandibular left central incisor. The blade is pulled toward the incisal edge in the *working* stroke.

teeth. The length of the blade is ideally placed in a horizontal position and the tip carefully adapted to the tooth surface when the instrument is applied to the line angle (Fig. 4–11). Calculus frequently is not removed from these surfaces because of failure to extend the blade to the attachment apparatus or correctly adapt the cutting edge to the tooth surface. Laceration of the interdental papilla frequently occurs as a result of failure to maintain proper adaptation of the tip portion of the cutting edge during the scaling or planing stroke.

There are three phases to a scaling stroke: blade application, which includes insertion into the sulcus in submarginal scaling; establishment of angulation, and activation of the instrument. These phases have been described in the section on Instrument Design and Principles of Use. However, further discussion of the activation of the curet is pertinent. During scaling the curet is activated with a *working* pull stroke. The blade is pulled in a coronal direction when it is positioned horizontally. When the blade is used in a vertical or oblique position, it is pulled coronally and obliquely away from the epithelial attachment. In either position, the instrument is pushed with an *exploratory* stroke to reposition the blade for the next working stroke. A series of overlapping working strokes, each consisting of application, angulation and activation, is used to remove a deposit on a single tooth surface. Once the deposit has been removed the instrument is applied to the next surface in the scaling sequence. It is usually preferable to use one curet for all surfaces to which it can be adapted in one quadrant before changing to the other instrument of the pair.

Use of the Curet in Root Planing. The technique of root planing is based upon that of scaling. It is a more exacting technique requiring the well-developed tactile sensitivity and instrument control of the experienced and proficient operator. During root planing the blade may be used in horizontal, oblique and vertical positions on a single tooth surface. The positions that can be used are dependent upon the specific tooth and surface, and the instrument design. A pull *working* stroke with correct blade angulation is recommended for root planing. The instrument is applied repeatedly in one or more positions. Planing strokes are continued until the root surface is free of calculus and completely smooth. This procedure is not recommended for the novice operator and should be performed only after advanced instrumentation instruction. More detailed descriptions of this and other root planing techniques can be found in periodontal texts.

Sickles. The design of the sickle scaler places some limitations upon its use. It is most useful for removing deposits of considerable size that are located supramarginally or submarginally within 1 to 2 mm. of the gingival margin.

Sickle scalers are classified as straight and modified. The term "contra-angle" is sometimes substituted for modified. The two types of sickle are the same except for the relationship of the blade and handle. The straight sickle blade lies in the same longitudinal plane as its handle. The modified sickle blade lies in a longitudinal plane other than that of the handle. Modified sickles are "paired" instruments. They are designed to adapt to the proximal surfaces of posterior teeth. Straight sickles are designed to adapt to facial and lingual surfaces and proximal surfaces of anterior teeth.

The facial surface of the sickle blade is flat in a horizontal plane and either flat or curved in a longitudinal plane. The lateral surfaces are flat or slightly convex, converging toward the back of the blade and meeting to form an angle. The facial surface and two lateral surfaces converge toward the blade tip and terminate in a sharp point. The angles formed by the facial surface and two lateral surfaces constitute the two cutting edges. The cutting edges are straight or curved, dependent upon the contour of the longitudinal plane of the facial surface (Fig. 4–12).

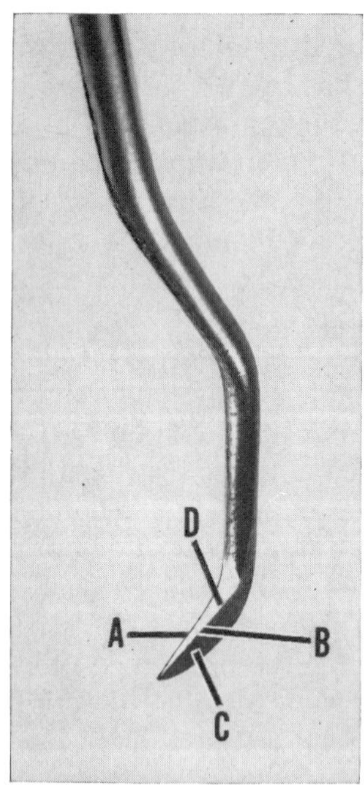

FIG. 4–12. Sickle scaler. The blade has two straight cutting edges: *A* and *B*, which terminate at the tip in a point. The flat or slightly convex lateral surface: *C*, joins the opposing lateral surface at the back of the blade, forming a sharp angle. The facial surface: *D*, lies between the two cutting edges.

If a cut is made across the width of the blade at any point between the tip and the shank, the cross-section view attained would be that of an isosceles triangle, the apex being the angle of the back surface of the blade and the base being the facial surface. As with the curet, an understanding of the cross-section view of the instrument blade is essential to the establishment of correct angulation when it is applied to a tooth. The facial surface of the sickle, or base of the triangle, and the tooth surface form an angle of less than 90 degrees when the blade is correctly placed against the tooth (Fig. 4–13).

Some sickles vary in their blade design. The lateral surfaces do not meet at the back of the blade, but join a flat back surface, forming two angles rather than one. The cross-section view is that of a trapezoid, with the back surface forming the shorter of the two parallel sides.

The straight sickle shank may be straight or angulated. Modified sickle shanks are always angulated. The angulation and length of the shank determine the areas and tooth surfaces to which the sickle can be applied. When the shank is relatively long and angulated the blade can be manipulated more easily without the instrument handle contacting the tooth.

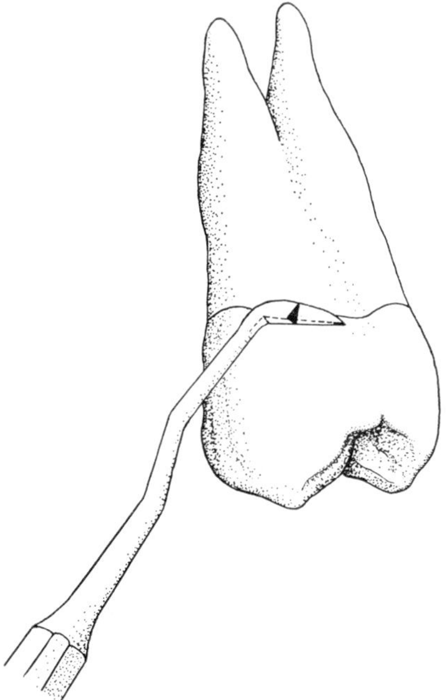

Fig. 4–13.—Modified sickle in a horizontal position on the proximal surface of a maxillary molar. The cutting edge indicated by the broken line is correctly positioned. In the cross-section view, the facial surface forms an angle of less than 90 degrees with the tooth surface.

Use of the Sickle Scaler. Use of the sickle scaler requires considerable caution. The angle or angles of the back surface and the pointed tip of the blade can traumatize the marginal gingiva, crevicular epithelium and epithelial attachment. If directed into the tooth, the tip of the blade will scratch the tooth surface. The sickle is applied to the tooth in the same manner as the curet. Modified sickles are applied to the proximal surfaces of posterior teeth in a horizontal position (Fig. 4–14). Straight sickles are applied to proximal surfaces of anterior teeth in a horizontal position and to facial and lingual surfaces in an oblique position (Fig. 4–15).

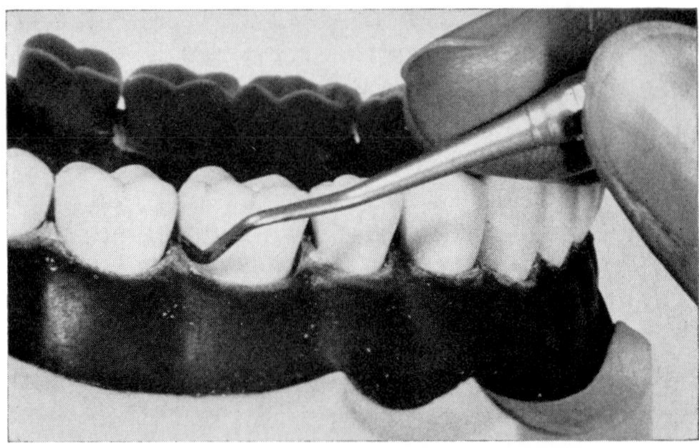

FIG. 4–14. Modified sickle. The blade is placed in a horizontal position on the disto-buccal line-angle of the mandibular right first permanent molar and pulled toward the occlusal surface in the *working* stroke.

During the working stroke the sickle is pulled in a vertical direction away from the epithelial attachment on proximal surfaces and obliquely away from the attachment on facial and lingual surfaces. Throughout the stroke the side of the instrument tip is in constant contact with the tooth surface. If the pointed tip of the blade is allowed to wander, the soft tissue surrounding the tooth will be severely lacerated. Extreme care must be taken when scaling line-angles of teeth to avoid laceration of the interdental papillae. The entire length of the cutting edge of the sickle can be used only when the blade is small and the edges curved. Straight edged and medium or large sized sickle blades do not adapt to the curvatures of the tooth surface, therefore only a part of the cutting edge can be used for scaling.

Sickle scalers are not inserted to the depth of the gingival sulcus because the epithelial attachment will be damaged when the sharp angle or angles on the back surface of the blade are pushed against

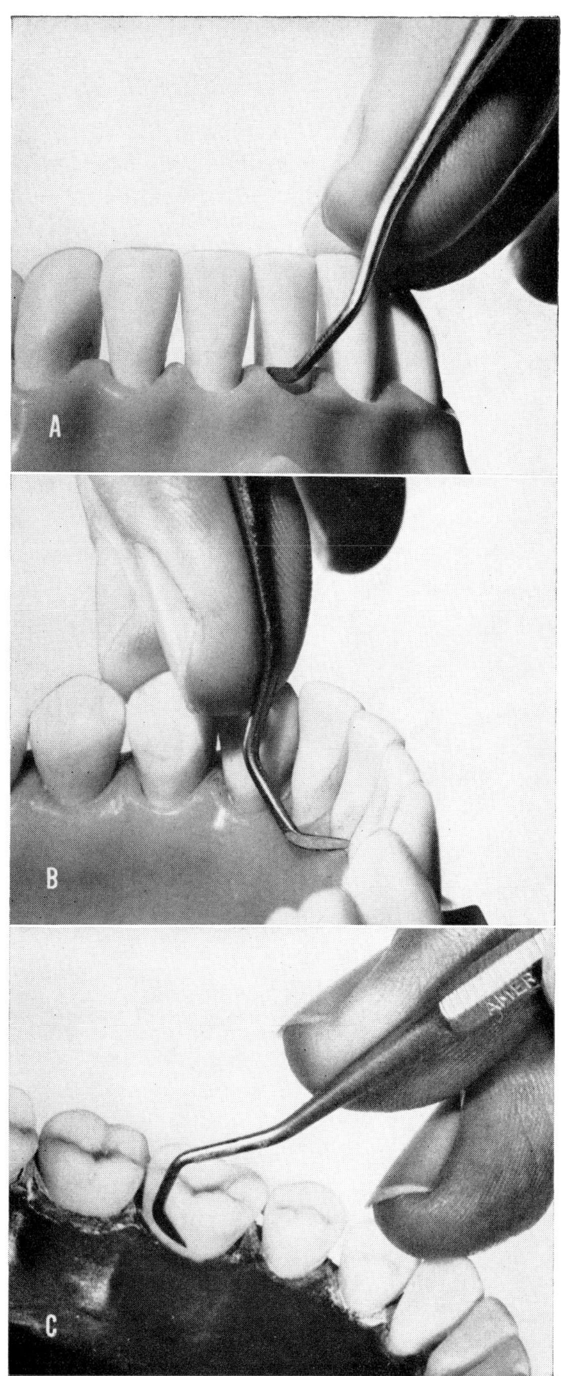

FIG. 4–15. Straight sickle. *A* and *B,* The blade is placed in a horizontal position on the mesial surface of the mandibular left central incisor and pulled toward the incisal edge in the *working* stroke. *C,* The blade is placed in an oblique position on the lingual surface of the mandibular left first permanent molar and pulled forward and away from the epithelial attachment in the *working* stroke.

it. The sickle scaler is carefully inserted into the sulcus with an exploratory stroke and adapted to the tooth surface or apical portion of the calculus. The calculus immediately adjacent to the epithelial attachment is removed with a curet. A series of overlapping working strokes is used with the sickle to remove supramarginal deposits and superficial submarginal deposits. Scaling with the sickle should be followed by scaling and planing with the curet.

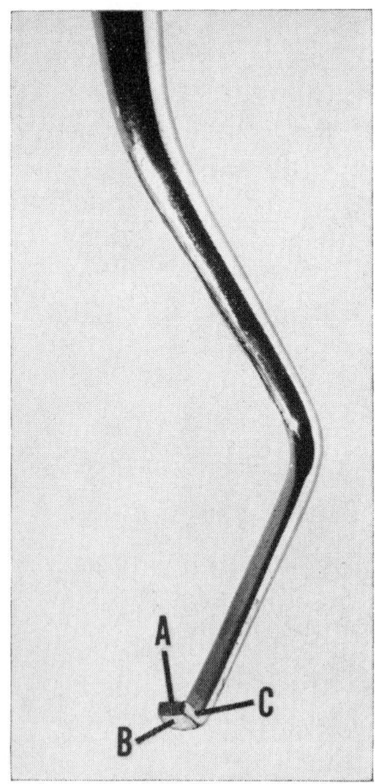

FIG. 4–16. Hoe scaler. The end of the shank is turned at a right angle to form the blade. *A*, Straight cutting edge; *B*, Outer surface bevel; *C*, Lateral surface.

Hoes. Hoes are particularly useful when leverage is needed to dislodge large or tenacious deposits. Their design prohibits their use for final scaling or removal of deep submarginal calculus. Hoes are either paired or single instruments. Access to all tooth surfaces can be gained with a complete set of well-designed hoes. The angulation of the hoe shank determines the area and tooth surfaces to which it may be applied. A hoe may be designed for use on a specific surface, such as the distal of the terminal posterior tooth; or as a pair, designed to adapt to opposite surfaces of the same tooth.

The end of the hoe shank is turned at a right angle to form a blade.

The outer surface of the angle is beveled at the terminal end. A straight cutting edge is formed by the union of the bevel and the inner surface of the blade. The lateral, outer and inner surfaces of the blade converge at each end of the cutting edge to form a sharp point (Fig. 4–16). To lessen the possibility of damaging the tooth surface upon instrumentation, the points or corners of the blade are rounded during sharpening procedures.

Because of its design, the selection of a hoe for calculus removal is a matter of necessity rather than choice. The bulk of the shank impairs the instrument's sensitivity. The sharp corners can easily scratch the tooth surface and the straight cutting edge does not adapt well to the tooth curvatures. If the tooth surface is too narrow or its curvature too great to accommodate the entire cutting edge, the corners of the hoe blade will extend into the adjacent soft tissue.

Use of Hoe. Hoes may be used submarginally or supramarginally on tooth surfaces of sufficient width to accommodate the entire cutting edge. Use of the hoe requires maximum skill and control. The straight cutting edge of the blade must be held against the tooth surface both in positioning against the tooth and in utilizing the working stroke. Should the instrument be pivoted as it is adapted to the tooth, one corner of the blade will gouge the tooth surface. If pivoted when placed submarginally, the tooth surface will be gouged with one corner and the other corner will project into the crevicular epithelium.

The hoe is positioned against the tooth surface with the length of the cutting edge in a perpendicular relationship to the long axis of the tooth. The shank of the hoe parallels the long axis of the tooth. Because of the bulk of the shank and dimensions of the blade, insertion into the sulcus requires deftness. The free gingiva must be flexible to allow initial projection of the blade into the sulcus or pocket. Once inserted the cutting edge is maneuvered cautiously to the apical margin of the deposit. Angulation is established by drawing the shank of the instrument toward the tooth crown. The inner surface of the blade is thus moved toward the tooth so that it forms an angle of less than 90 degrees with the tooth surface (Fig. 4–17).

A pull *working* stroke in a vertical direction is used to activate the instrument. The working stroke is continued for the extent of the deposit. Depending upon the curvature of the tooth surface, the hoe at given positions has a two-point contact with the tooth—one, the cutting edge, and the other, part of the shank. The two-point contact occurs infrequently as the hoe is positioned and activated and the operator need not be concerned if the shank does not contact the tooth. Contact of the entire cutting edge with the tooth surface is of utmost importance.

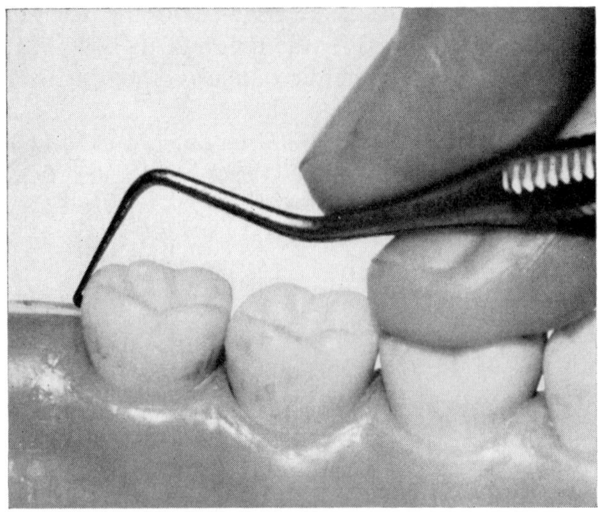

FIG. 4–17. The hoe seated for scaling on the distal surface of the mandibular third permanent molar. The instrument is activated by pulling it vertically toward the occlusal surface.

Files. The periodontal file with its multiple cutting edges is designed to fracture or break off the outer layers of tenacious deposits leaving the remaining pieces of calculus more accessible to other instruments. Because of its design, the file cannot be used for the final planing of root surfaces. Files are either paired or single instruments, which are designed in sets to allow their application to all tooth surfaces. When the working end is small and narrow, the file can be inserted into the confines of the sulcus or pocket and adapted to relatively narrow root surfaces.

File shanks are angulated from the long axis of their handles in the same manner as hoe shanks, providing access to different tooth surfaces. The blade, which is a continuation of the shank, is comprised of a series of blades similar to that of the hoe, but usually shorter in length from shank to edge. The inner surfaces and outer beveled surfaces of each blade form the cutting edges. The two lateral surfaces of the working end join with the inner and outer surfaces of each blade to form corners, which present the same hazards as the corners of the hoe blade (Fig. 4–18).

Use of the File. The file is inserted into the sulcus or pocket in the same manner as the hoe and positioned against the deposit or at its margin. Angulation is established by drawing the instrument handle toward the tooth surface until the cutting edges "bite" the deposit. Initially the file is activated by pressing the blade against the calculus

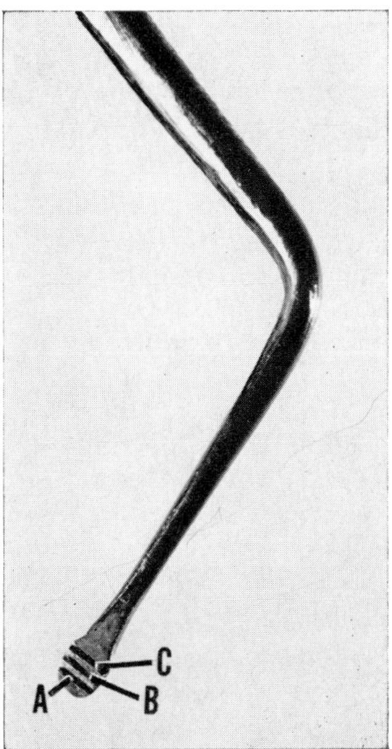

FIG. 4–18. Periodontal file with three cutting edges: *A, B, C.*

deposit. The pressure crushes the deposit between the instrument blades and the tooth. The blade is activated further with a pull working stroke in a vertical, oblique or horizontal direction away from the epithelial attachment. Once the blades are placed, maximum control is required during activation to avoid scratching the tooth surface or traumatizing the sulcular epithelium with the corners. The entire length of each cutting edge is maintained on the tooth surface throughout the working stroke. Working strokes are repeated in one or more directions until the calculus is removed. Final planing of the root surface is accomplished with the curet.

The potential for damaging the tooth surface and injuring the soft tissue, and also the difficulty encountered in sharpening, relegate the file to a secondary position. However, since the file is a decided asset in removing tenacious submarginal calculus, techniques of use and sharpening of the instrument should be mastered.

Chisels. Use of the periodontal chisel in dental hygiene procedures is limited by the instrument design. Although it is not a recommended instrument, the chisel may be used for removal of heavy supramarginal calculus deposits which bridge open interproximal spaces in the anterior part of the mouth. With few exceptions, other instruments can be used as effectively and will be less likely to injure tooth structure or adjacent soft tissue.

The straight cutting edge of the chisel is formed by the beveled terminal end of the shank (Fig. 4–19). Sharp corners are formed at each end of the cutting edge where the beveled surface, its opposing surface and the lateral surfaces of the blade converge. Usually the chisel shank is only slightly curved; the blade, shank and handle are, therefore, in approximately the same longitudinal plane.

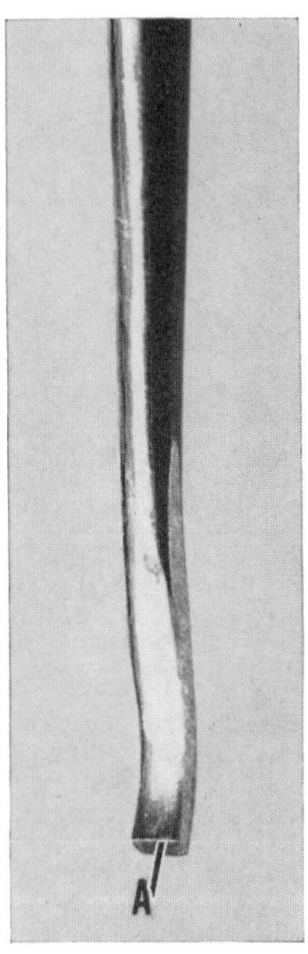

FIG. 4–19. Chisel scaler. The terminal end of the shank is beveled to form the straight cutting edge: *A*.

Use of the Chisel. Use of the relatively straight shanked chisel is limited to the anterior region of the mouth. The blade is placed against the proximal tooth surface from the labial aspect with the length of the cutting edge approximately parallel to the long axis of the tooth. The inner surface of the shank is positioned near the tooth, for if it is moved too far away from the tooth surface the cutting edge will "dig" in when the instrument is activated. When the entire cutting edge has been well positioned, the instrument is activated with a push working stroke in a horizontal direction toward the lingual surface of the tooth. Maximum control is required during the working stroke to maintain the entire cutting edge on the tooth surface and to avoid scratching the tooth with a corner of the blade. The chisel can be activated in a vertical direction, but this method of use is not recommended because of the potential hazard to the soft tissue.

Chisels are designed with curved shanks for application to posterior teeth. However, with the increased difficulty of instrumentation in the posterior part of the mouth there is even less rationale for use of the chisel in this area than in the anterior region.

ULTRASONIC SCALING DEVICES[7,20,28,38,41]

Ultrasonic devices have wide application in dentistry. Various devices are used for periodontal surgery, soft tissue curettage, contouring and polishing of restorations, removal of orthodontic cement and calculus removal. Such devices sometimes are included in the hygienists' scaling instruments. Some authorities regard ultrasonic scaling as a useful adjunct to hand scaling procedures, while others regard the use of ultrasonics with unreserved skepticism. The hygienist should evaluate current research in the field of ultrasonics.

Ultrasonic vibrations are high frequency vibrations ranging from 20,000 cycles per second (cps) to multi-million cps. In periodontal instrumentation, a metal tip is inserted into an ultrasonic handpiece and vibrated at a frequency of approximately 25,000 cps. When the tip is held against the calculus with very light pressure, the vibration fractures the deposit releasing it from the tooth surface. The vibration frequency is related to the size and shape of the tip; a heavy tip may vibrate at 23,000 cps, while a small light tip may reach 26,000 to 28,000 cps. Heat produced by the vibration is dispelled by a continuous flow of water through the handpiece to the instrument tip. The water is dispersed from the tip in a spray of minute droplets which serve to flush out the gingival sulcus or the pocket and remove pieces of calculus. A variety of interchangeable handpiece tips have been designed to provide access to tooth surfaces in all areas of the mouth. In contrast to hand scaling, sharp instruments are unnecessary and undesirable. A dull tip lessens the potential for scratching or overplaning the tooth surface in ultrasonic scaling.

Use of Ultrasonics. Manufacturer's instructions are followed for adjustment of the vibration frequency and water flow of the ultrasonic instrument in preparation for scaling. The handpiece is held with a modified pen grasp. The ring finger is used to establish a stable fulcrum before the instrument tip is applied to the calculus. With the instrument shank parallel, or at less than a 15 degree angle to the tooth, the tip is held lightly against the deposit. Vibrations are transmitted from the ultrasonic unit to the handpiece and tip by applying pressure to the unit foot pedal. The instrument tip is drawn over the calculus deposit with a very light push or pull stroke in a vertical direction. Whether a push or pull stroke is used will be determined by the tip design. Overlapping strokes are used until the calculus has been removed. Upon completion of the vertical strokes, the instrument is moved horizontally across the tooth surface to complete scaling and debridement of the sulcus or pocket. Because tactile and visual detection of deposits is impaired by the instrument vibration and water flow, the smoothness of the tooth surface is evaluated periodically with an explorer. Final scaling and root planing is accomplished with a curet.

The ease and rapidity with which large and tenacious calculus deposits are removed is one of the significant advantages in the use of ultrasonic devices. The disadvantage of the push stroke is overcome to some extent by the cleansing effect of the water spray which flushes out the sulcus or pocket, thereby preventing calculus from becoming imbedded in the soft tissue. However, caution is required during ultrasonic scaling. The operator must watch for overheating of the instrument tip and tooth sensitivity from the vibration. If the patient manifests sensitivity to ultrasonic instrumentation, it should be discontinued and scaling completed with hand instruments. The continuous water flow necessitates the use of an evacuation or efficient suction apparatus during ultrasonic scaling. It is advisable to protect patient's clothing from the water spray.

Current research supports the opinion that the major advantage of ultrasonic scaling techniques is in the removal of gross calculus deposits. To be most effective, ultrasonic scaling must be followed by hand instrumentation. Constant appraisal of new research reports is important in evaluating the usefulness of ultrasonics. Radical changes in instrument design and techniques of use probably will occur with advanced research.

INSTRUMENTS AND TECHNIQUES OF POLISHING

Oral prophylaxis polishing procedures include techniques for removal of all film, plaque and extrinsic stains from the clinical crowns of the teeth, and from fixed and removable appliances. A completely clean and smooth tooth surface inhibits the formation of new deposits and stains, which have etiological significance in the occurrence of dental caries and periodontal disease. Abrasion is the wearing away of a surface, while polishing is the smoothing of a surface until it reflects light uniformly. Both are used in the oral prophylaxis—abrasion for cleansing the tooth surface by removing soft deposits and stains, and polishing for the production of a smooth, glossy tooth surface. Minute scratches can be produced on the tooth or appliance when abrasives or polishing agents are applied with hand and motor driven instruments. Therefore, the hygienist must use discretion in selecting and applying abrasives or polishing agents. The complete polishing materials include abrasives and polishing agents, hand and motor driven instruments and attachments, abrasive strips, dental floss and tape, and disclosing agents.

Abrasives and Polishing Agents[54]

The particle size and shape of abrasives and polishing agents determines the depth of the scratches which they produce. The larger and more irregularly shaped particles of abrasive materials leave relatively deep scratches on the surface to which they are applied; while the smaller and less irregular particles of polishing agents produce shallow scratches, leaving a smooth, glossy surface. The size and irregularity of the particles, and the number that contact the surface per unit of time and the pressure with which they are forced against the surface determines the rate of abrasion or polishing. Particle size or fineness is determined by the mesh size of the finest sieve through which the material will pass. The fineness of commercial abrasives ranges from 6 to 220. A material with a fineness greater than 220 is designated as a powder or flour and graded F, FF, FFF and continued multiples of F as its fineness increases. The coarsest abrasive suitable for use on tooth surfaces is grade FFF flour of pumice. Its use on exposed root surfaces is not recommended, because the relatively soft cementum is easily worn away. When flour of pumice is used on tooth enamel, polishing should be completed with a finer material. The mouth should be rinsed thoroughly and a clean attachment inserted into the polishing instrument when changing from a coarser to a finer polishing agent. It is not possible to attain a highly polished surface if particles of the coarser material contaminate the finer material.

Exposed root surfaces, acrylic, and metallic restorations are polished with fine polishing agents such as tin oxide and precipitated calcium carbonate or chalk, which is sometimes distributed as whiting. Chromium oxide is useful for polishing stainless steel. Jeweler's rouge is a choice agent for polishing gold and precious metal alloys, but is quite dirty to handle. The particle size of commercially prepared polishing compounds used on enamel surfaces should not be greater than that of FFF flour of pumice. Commercially prepared compounds used on acrylic and metallic restorations and appliances should be at least as fine as tin oxide. The National Formulary provides detailed information regarding qualities of abrasives and polishing agents.

Dry powders or flours are mixed with water, mouthwash or some other wetting agent to reduce the frictional heat produced during application. Heat production and the rate of abrasion is then reduced, because fewer particles reach the surface being polished per unit of time. Excessive frictional heat can cause patient discomfort and injury to the pulp tissue.

Polishing Instruments and Their Use[24,29,67,68]

Porte Polisher. The hand polishing instrument used in dental hygiene procedures is called a porte polisher. Although there has been modernization of dental equipment, the porte polisher continues to be a useful supplementary instrument. There are two types of porte polishers, one of which is double ended (Fig. 4–20). A wooden peg or orangewood point inserted into an opening at the end of the instrument shank constitutes the working end. The shank or shanks of the porte polisher are angulated to provide for adaptation to all areas of the dentition. The length of the woodpoint and its placement in the opening will determine the maneuverability of the instrument. A long woodpoint will require greater retraction of the cheeks, lips and tongue during instrument manipulation. The shank of the instrument will contact the tooth surface and interfere with the polishing stroke, should the point be too short. If the point

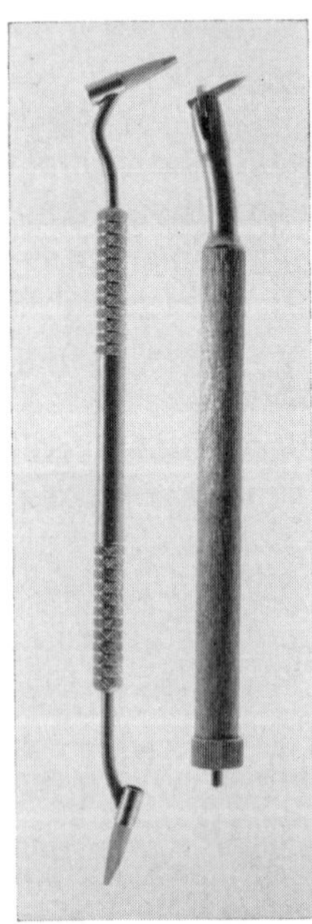

FIG. 4–20. Double-ended and single-ended porte polishers used for hand polishing, with woodpoints inserted correctly.

projects beyond the back surface of the opening or shank, it can contact the oral mucosa during polishing, causing trauma and patient discomfort. A woodpoint length of approximately ½ inch is functional. Commercially prepared points usually need to be cut to a shorter length. Narrow and tapered points are adaptable to proximal and occlusal tooth surfaces. The use of wide points with beveled ends is more efficient for polishing facial and lingual surfaces.

Use of the Porte Polisher. The porte polisher is used as a supplementary instrument in polishing, and for application of some tooth desensitizing agents. The instrument is held with a pen or palm grasp and stabilized by a fulcrum. Use of the palm grasp is confined to the polishing of the labial aspect of the maxillary anterior teeth. The pen grasp may also be employed in this area. The polishing agent is carried to the tooth with the woodpoint, and the end or side of the point applied to the tooth surface with moderate pressure and a circular or longitudinal stroke. Use of a short circular stroke in areas adjacent to the gingival margin lessens the possibility of pushing the instrument point onto the gingiva. A short longitudinal stroke is more easily controlled than a long one. As woodpoints become frayed they should be discarded.

The epithelium of the free gingiva can be abraded during porte polishing, if the woodpoint is allowed to cross over the gingival margin. The slight nudging action of the controlled woodpoint should not cause injury to the soft tissue. Such contact is inevitable in polishing cervical areas and proximal surfaces. If the operator uses ingenuity in adapting one or more surfaces of the woodpoint to tooth contours, successful polishing will be accomplished. As with all instrumentation procedures, a logical sequence of instrumentation should be followed. The patient should be instructed to rinse periodically to remove the excess polishing agent from the mouth and clear the field of operation.

Handpiece. There are three types of handpieces used for polishing procedures: the straight handpiece which is directly attached to the engine arm of the dental unit, the contra-angle and the prophylaxis right-angle handpiece (Fig. 4–21). The contra-angle or the right-angle is attached to the straight handpiece for intra-oral polishing procedures. The straight handpiece is used alone for polishing removable appliances and instrument sharpening.

Rubber cups and bristle brushes are designed for attachment to each type of handpiece. Screw-shank and snap-on polishing attachments are used with the prophylaxis right-angle. Cups and brushes mounted on a metal rod or mandrel are used with the contra-angle and straight handpiece. Rubber cups should be flexible and of a size that can be adapted to tooth surfaces which are narrow or relatively inaccessible. Soft cups are more flexible and have less potential for abrading the marginal gingiva than rigid or hard cups. However,

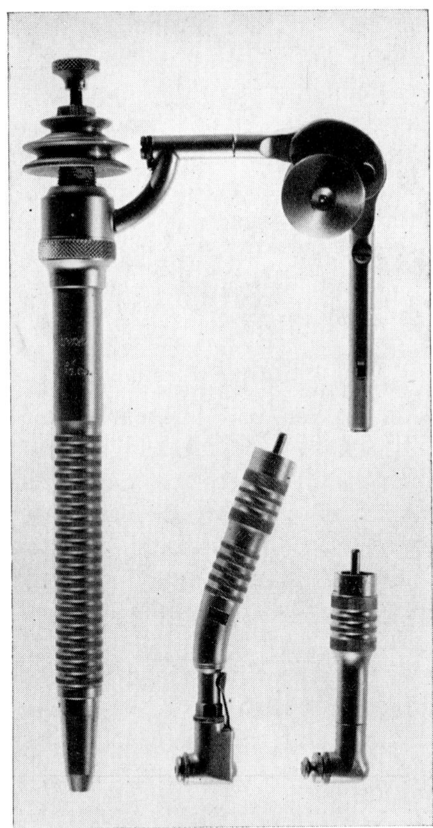

FIG. 4–21. Handpieces used for engine polishing. Left to right: straight handpiece, contra-angle handpiece and prophylaxis right-angle handpiece.

softer cups do not remove stains and soft deposits as efficiently as more rigid cups. The texture of bristle brushes ranges from very soft to extremely hard. Softer bristles will bend and adapt to occlusal surface contours more readily than hard bristles. Hard bristle brushes have greater abrasive action than soft bristle brushes, and must be used with more caution. Polishing cups may be used on all tooth surfaces. Because of their potential for abrading soft tissue, it is recommended that the use of polishing brushes be limited to occlusal surfaces.

Use of the Handpiece and Attachments. The dental engine or rheostat provides the driving force for rotation of handpiece attachments. To minimize the production of frictional heat and the possibility of abrading soft tissue adjacent to the surface being polished, the rheostat is operated at its lowest speed of approximately 1200 rpm.

The handpiece is held as close to the working end as possible with a pen grasp. A firm grasp and secure fulcrum are required to maintain instrument control. Fulcrums which will support the weight of the handpiece, and are in close proximity to the area of instrumentation are selected. To lessen operator fatigue, the handpiece should be rested against the hand between the thumb and index finger.

The operator's foot and hand action are coordinated during engine polishing. After the cup or brush containing the polishing agent has been placed against the tooth surface, the foot engages the rheostat foot pedal. When the polishing attachment is moved away from the tooth, its rotation is stopped by releasing the foot pedal.

The edge of the cup is held against the tooth with light pressure. As the cup is moved over the tooth surface with a circular wiping stroke, it is lifted away from the tooth periodically. The slight lifting of the cup minimizes frictional heat by allowing air to pass between it and the tooth. The cup should be continually moved from one area of the tooth to another during polishing to prevent discomfort and injury from overheating.

The polishing cup is adapted to tooth contours by turning the instrument hand and wrist. It is important to position the cup so that its edge will travel into the gingival sulcus, rather than onto the marginal gingiva, for complete polishing of the cervical portion of the tooth and prevention of gingival abrasion (Fig. 4–22).

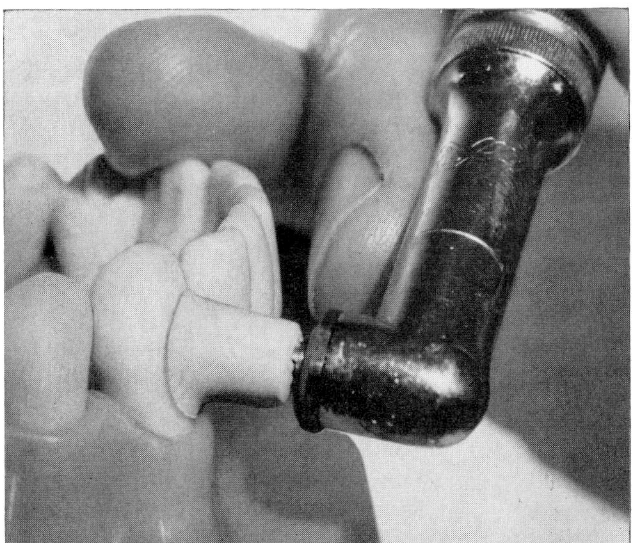

FIG. 4–22. Rubber polishing cup correctly applied to the cervical area of the tooth. The edge will project into the gingival sulcus.

The bristle brush is applied with light pressure to occlusal surfaces. The polishing stroke follows the contour of the occlusal anatomy, moving from the pits and fissures toward the ridges. Occlusal anatomy of restorations will be distorted if high speed or excessive pressure is used when applying the brush.

The hygienist should be familiar with the mechanism of the handpieces she uses and follow the manufacturer's instructions for their cleaning and lubrication. Daily maintenance is necessary for the proper operation and continued service of engine polishing instruments.

Abrasive strips.[69] When small pieces of supramarginal calculus and extrinsic stains on proximal tooth surfaces are inaccessible to scaling and polishing instruments, abrasive strips may be used for their removal. The flat and narrow linen strips which are used for this purpose have very fine abrasive particles attached to one side. Only the *extra fine* grade of cuttle or abrasive strip is appropriate for dental hygiene techniques.

Because the edges of the abrasive strips can lacerate the soft tissue, their use is limited to the proximal surface coronal to the interdental papillae. The strip is held with the thumb and index finger of each hand. Approximately 1 inch of the strip lies between the two hands. The thumb or index finger of one hand supplements the conventional third finger fulcrum. The hand used to establish the fulcrum is dependent upon the position of the tooth and surface to which the strip is being applied. The strip is placed diagonally across the incisal or occlusal embrasure and drawn apically over the contact area with a sawing motion in a labio-lingual direction. The abrasive side of the strip is adapted to the tooth surface. When the stain or calculus has been removed, the strip is pulled carefully in a coronal and facial direction from the contact area. Because the abrasive particles are removed during its use, a new section of the strip is selected for the next application. Dental floss is used to remove the abrasive particles left on the tooth surface.

Dental floss and tape.[64] Dental tape is used to polish proximal tooth surfaces and the saddles of fixed partial dentures after hand and engine polishing procedures have been completed. Dental floss is used after scaling and polishing to remove debris from the gingival sulcus. Tape and floss are made of silk or nylon fibers. Dental tape which is coated with wax is flatter and wider than dental floss, which may or may not be wax coated. The fibers of unwaxed floss fan out when it is adapted to the tooth, increasing its ability to pick up debris. The use of waxed tape and floss is contraindicated prior to the application of topical fluoride compounds since wax adheres to the tooth's surface.

The technique for application of dental tape and floss is basically the same as that for the use of abrasive strips. However, tape and floss are moved into the gingival sulcus. The piece of dental tape or floss should be of a length that will enable the operator to grasp it securely as new sections are used for each application. For the most efficient service, the tape or floss is pulled or pushed against the tooth surface to which it is being applied. If the tape or floss is "snapped" past the contact point of adjacent teeth onto the interdental papilla or pulled across the marginal gingiva with pressure, the soft tissue will be traumatized.

Dental tape is inserted between the soft tissue and saddle of the fixed partial denture for the purpose of polishing the proximal surfaces of the abutment teeth and the gingival surface of the pontic. The end of the tape is inserted between the tissue and the abutment or pontic, where there is an open space, from either the facial or lingual aspect. It is pushed toward the opposite surface until it can be grasped with the fingers or cotton pliers. Insertion of the tape is made easier when the last half inch of the tape is stiffened by turning it back and twisting the two pieces together. After the tape has been inserted, it is pulled back and forth in a facio-lingual direction across all the proximal and gingival surfaces of the fixed partial denture. The tape is removed from the area by releasing the grasp of one end and slowly pulling. Dental floss is used in the same manner, without the polishing agent, to debride the area after polishing with tape. If the tissue adheres so closely to the fixed partial denture that the insertion of tape is impossible, dental floss is used for polishing.

The end of dental floss can be stiffened in the same manner as dental tape. Flat plastic needles designed for inserting dental floss between the soft tissue and fixed partial denture are particularly useful when there is little space between them.

Disclosing agents.[6,14,30,70] Disclosing agents are applied to the teeth during the oral prophylaxis to reveal the presence of deposits and stains. They may be used in the oral inspection to assist in patient education techniques, or during scaling and polishing procedures for detection and evaluation purposes. Disclosing agents impart color to the deposit or stain, but not to clean tooth surfaces.

Solutions of iodine, mercurochrome, bismarck brown and basic fuchsin are commonly used. Iodine preparations include the popular Skinner's solution. An erythrosin dye is the coloring agent used in disclosing tablets. There are some limitations in the use of these agents. With the exception of basic fuchsin solution and the erythrosin dye tablets, disclosing agents will discolor synthetic restorations and stain clothing. Mercurochrome is not used when the patient has an allergy to mercury or its compounds. Tissue sloughing and retarded healing can result from the use of iodine solutions in the mouths of diabetic patients.

Use of Disclosing Agents. The application of disclosing solution is a simple procedure. The teeth are dried with compressed air, and the solution applied with a cotton applicator or cotton pellet and cotton pliers. The patient is instructed to rinse thoroughly. Inspection with the mouth mirror and compressed air will reveal deposits and stains. The tongue, lip and cheeks are retracted during disclosing solution application to provide access to the teeth, and to avoid staining the oral mucosa. A small cotton pellet between ⅛th and ¼th inch in diameter will cover the cotton plier tips and allow control of the solution. The solution should not be applied in close proximity to synthetic restorations.

Use of disclosing tablets is convenient. The patient is instructed to chew the tablet, then rinse thoroughly. The teeth are then inspected with compressed air and the mouth mirror.

CLEANING THE REMOVABLE DENTURE[9,15,71]

The complete oral prophylaxis for the partially edentulous patient includes cleaning and polishing the denture. During the oral inspection the denture is removed by the patient and immersed in water, sodium hypochlorite solution or acetic acid solution. A solution of one tablespoon of sodium hypochlorite (Chlorox or Purex) in one cup of water will promote easier stain removal. Calculus attachment will be weakened if the denture is left standing in a solution of one tablespoon of acetic acid (white vinegar) and one cup of water.

If calculus is attached to the denture surface, it is removed before polishing procedures are begun. When the intra-oral techniques have been completed the denture is removed from its solution, dried with compressed air, and inspected for residual deposits and stains with illumination from the operating light. Either a sickle scaler or curet may be adapted for calculus removal. Extreme caution is necessary to avoid scratching the denture surface. The instrument is held in the operating hand with a pen grasp and stabilized with a third finger fulcrum on the denture, which is grasped in the other hand.

Various cleaning and polishing techniques may be employed to remove soft deposits and stains from dentures. The dental engine and attachments, hand polishing instruments, the dental lathe and ultrasonic cleaning devices may all be used. In any procedure, the denture must be handled carefully to prevent it from being broken or distorted. The denture will break easily if it is dropped. Distortion will occur if the denture comes in contact with extremely hot water, is overheated in mechanical polishing, or grasped too firmly. Abrasives and polishing agents are used only on the outer surfaces of the denture which do not come in contact with the palate and/or ridges. To avoid overheating, polishing devices are applied with light pressure and moved constantly from one area of the denture to another. Resin teeth, characterized dentures with stippling and partial denture clasps should not be polished with the dental lathe. High shine polishing agents are not used on acrylic surfaces of esthetic dentures which have a low-gloss finish.

Cleaning and Polishing With a Handpiece and Attachments

Because the abrasive and polishing agent will spatter, the denture is held over the cuspidor when it is cleaned and polished with the straight handpiece and soft wheel brush. A brush such as the Dixon C wheel is recommended for this procedure. The cuspidor water flow is turned off and the bowl cushioned with paper towels. A palm grasp is used to hold the handpiece. The thumb of the operating hand establishes a fulcrum on the denture, which is grasped securely with the thumb and fingers of the other hand. The brush is revolved at slow speed and constantly repositioned on the denture. Moist flour of pumice may be used on all outer acrylic surfaces. A finer polishing agent is applied with a clean brush to give the acrylic surfaces a higher gloss and to polish the metal parts. Clasps should be polished cautiously since they can be easily bent.

The contra-angle or right-angle handpiece with a rubber cup or soft bristle brush, or porte polisher and woodpoint may be used for denture cleaning and polishing, applying the technique used with the straight handpiece. The one deviation in technique is the use of a pen grasp and third finger fulcrum rather than a palm grasp and thumb fulcrum.

Cleaning and Polishing With the Dental Lathe and Attachments

When the denture is cleaned with the dental lathe and flour of pumice the muslin wheel is saturated with water. Before the wheel is placed on the lathe spindle, the excess water is squeezed out. With a towel held in front of the revolving wheel, the lathe is operated at *high* speed to complete the removal of excess moisture. Water is continually added to the pumice during the cleaning procedure.

After pumice has been applied to the denture, it is placed against the edge of the wheel with the lathe operating at *low* speed. The denture is moved against the wheel with short intermittent strokes. The surface which is applied to the wheel is changed constantly. Pumice is reapplied to the denture at frequent intervals. To remove tenacious stains, the bristle wheel and pumice are used in the same manner. After the denture has been rinsed and dried, it is polished with a clean, dry muslin wheel and fine polishing agent. Water is not used, and the lathe is operated at high speed. Denture clasps are then polished with the handpiece and rubber cup.

When the outer surfaces have been cleaned and polished, the inner surfaces of the denture are scrubbed with a denture brush, warm water and soap. During scrubbing, the denture is held over a sink partially filled with water to act as a cushion. Before returning the denture to the patient, it is rinsed thoroughly in warm water to remove cleaning and polishing materials.

TOPICAL ANESTHETICS[3,48]

Topical agents are used to anesthetize the terminal nerve endings of the gingiva when the patient experiences discomfort during an oral prophylaxis. Because anesthetic agents can produce toxic reactions, their application must be carefully controlled. Anesthetic agents are applied in gel, liquid, ointment or spray form. Use of the spray form is discouraged because of the accompanying hazards. It is difficult to confine the spray to a specific area and control the amount of the anesthetic agent dispensed to the tissue. When used in the area of the oral pharynx, sufficient quantity of the anesthetic may be inhaled to produce a toxic reaction. The long spray nozzles and metered valves on some dispensers partially eliminate this hatard. Agents containing the potent tetracaine should be avoided. High concentrations of alcohol in the anesthetic vehicle may irritate the oral mucosa when application is prolonged or repeated. Topical anesthetics dispensed in other than aqueous solutions have a slower absorption rate and are, therefore, safer than more water-soluble agents. *Accepted Dental Remedies* should be consulted to determine the effectiveness and safety of a particular preparation.

Liquids, gels and ointments are applied to the free gingiva with a cotton applicator or cotton pellet and cotton pliers. Greater absorption, and subsequent anesthesia will result if the tissue is dried prior to applying the anesthetic agent. Isolation of the area should be maintained for a few minutes after application to allow the agent to act, undiluted by the saliva. It is advisable to apply the anesthetic a few minutes before instrumentation in a specific area, because the preparations are short acting. Reapplication may be necessary, if scaling or root planing is extensive.

A hypodermic syringe with a blunted and angulated 30 gauge needle can be employed for ointment and gel application. When the needle aperture is directed toward the gingival sulcus, the agent will flow into the sulcus and over the marginal gingiva.

POSTOPERATIVE PROCEDURES TO PROMOTE HEALING[4,31]

Discretion should be used in the application of antiseptic solutions to gingival tissue, upon completing the oral prophylaxis. Contents of the antiseptic solution must be investigated before use. Toxic qualities of iodine, mercury and phenol compounds limit their usefulness. Because antiseptics are non-specific in their attack upon microorganisms, they are fairly unsuccessful in reducing the oral flora. When used, antiseptics are applied with a cotton applicator or cotton pellet and cotton pliers.

Rinsing with a hypertonic sodium chloride solution (½ teaspoon sodium chloride and 1 cup of water) following the oral prophylaxis will promote healing and retard swelling. Because sodium chloride has a low molecular weight and high solubility, it cannot lower surface tension. As a result it does not penetrate tissues, but draws water from them and stimulates capillary action. Blood circulation is increased, promoting tissue metabolism. The patient is instructed to rinse with the solution every two hours until postoperative discomfort subsides.

DESENSITIZATION OF HYPERSENSITIVE DENTIN[12,35,52]

The hygienist may apply topical agents to teeth which reduce sensitivity caused by one or more of the following stimuli: mechanical action of the toothbrush or instruments, chemical action of acids ingested or produced in the mouth, and thermal changes from liquid or air. Research indicates that these stimuli cause changes in the protoplasmic processes (Tomes' fibers) of the dentinal tubules, producing pain. Precautions are taken during the oral prophylaxis to avoid stimulating sensitive areas. Compressed air is not directed onto sensitive tooth surfaces. Warm water is used for patient rinsing. When possible, instruments are not applied directly to sensitive areas.

Usually, desensitizing agents are applied after the oral prophylaxis has been completed. However, if the patient cannot tolerate instrument application in areas of exposed dentin, desensitization procedures may be performed prior to scaling and root planing.

Of the several types of desensitizing agents, those which are used most frequently by the hygienist will be discussed. Fluoride preparations used for desensitization include solutions of 2 and 4 per cent sodium fluoride and 0.9 per cent sodium silicofluoride. Sodium fluoride paste, composed of equal parts of sodium fluoride, kaolin and glycerin, is a widely accepted desensitizing agent. Glycerin gives the paste an extended shelf-life. Sodium fluoride solutions are stored in pyrex or polyethylene containers, because they hydrolyze readily in glass. Sodium silicofluoride is stored in powder form and mixed with distilled water before use.

Before desensitizing agents are applied, the tooth surface is isolated with cotton rolls and cleaned with a cotton applicator or cotton pellet saturated with 4 per cent sodium fluoride solution. The surface is then dried with a fresh applicator or pellet.

Application of Sodium Fluoride Desensitizing Paste

Sodium fluoride desensitizing paste is applied with a porte polisher and woodpoint. The tooth surface is burnished with short circular strokes of the woodpoint until sensitivity disappears, which usually takes from one to five minutes. The rubber cup may then be used for further burnishing. If the patient experiences acute pain at the onset of the desensitization procedure, the paste should be removed with warm water, the surface dried and the application begun again. From 3 to 6 applications, given at intervals, may be required to achieve desensitization.

Application of Fluoride Solutions

Sodiumsilico fluoride solution is applied to the clean and isolated tooth surface with a cotton applicator or cotton pellet. The solution is applied continuously for five minutes, keeping the tooth surface moist, but not wet. If the procedure is going to be effective, desensitization will occur after 2 or 3 applications have been given at intervals.

Sodium fluoride solutions of 2 or 4 per cent are applied in the same manner for desensitization and caries prevention. The procedure is described in the section: *Application of Topical Fluoride Preparations.*

Iontophoresis[50,53]

When a small electric current is used in the topical application of medicaments the procedure is called iontophoresis. Synonyms for iontophoresis are: electrophoresis, ionization, cataphoresis, anaphoresis and electrolytic medication. The concentration and speed of ion penetration of hard tissue is increased by the electric current. Devices are manufactured for the application of desensitizing agents with iontophoresis. An electrode which is held by the patient transmits a positive charge to the tooth. When sodiumsilico fluoride solution is applied to the sensitive area with a small negatively charged brush, fluoride ions are drawn into the tooth. The current voltage, which is indicated by a meter is adjusted according to the patient's tolerance. Manufacturer's instructions for the care and use of iontophoretic devices should be followed.

The principle of iontophoresis is applied to a toothbrush which is used by the patient with a fluoride dentifrice. A battery produces a positive charge in the handle, and a negative charge in the head of the brush.[37]

Desensitizing dentifrices are available also, but research of their effectiveness has been limited. Benefits have resulted from use of a strontium chloride preparation.[55,56]

APPLICATION OF TOPICAL FLUORIDE PREPARATIONS[5,13,16,42,44,49,51,61,72]

One of the major preventive techniques performed by the dental hygienist is the topical application of fluoride preparations. The degree of benefit to the patient from this procedure is, in part, determined by the exactness with which it is performed.

There are a variety of fluoride compounds, vehicles and methods for topical application. Solutions of 2 per cent sodium fluoride and acidulated sodium fluoride may be used. Acidulated sodium fluoride can also be purchased in gel form. Because of its instability, stannous fluoride is distributed as a powder and mixed with distilled water just before use. Acidulated sodium fluoride and stannous fluoride are given in one application, while 2 per cent sodium fluoride is given in a series of four applications two to seven days apart. Stannous fluoride may be incorporated in a polishing agent and applied during polishing procedures.

General Principles

To attain maximum benefit from topical application of fluoride compounds, the teeth must be completely clean and free of saliva. Stains and deposits on the tooth surface will interfere with the fluoride compound contacting the enamel. Saliva will dilute the fluoride preparation and lessen its potency. Before the initial topical application of each sodium fluoride series, the teeth are scaled and polished. Since the benefit of a sodium fluoride series is cumulative, a prophylaxis preceding the remaining three applications would reduce the effectiveness by removing the surface layer of fluoride impregnated enamel. Prior to each of the last three applications of a sodium fluoride series the teeth are inspected for cleanliness and debris is removed with scalers, unwaxed dental floss and a 3 per cent solution of hydrogen peroxide. Waxed dental tape and floss are not used before a topical fluoride application, because the wax may adhere to the tooth surface.

The mouth is not rinsed and nothing is ingested for one-half hour following the application of acidulated sodium fluoride or stannous fluoride compounds. This rule may be followed after sodium fluoride applications. During the fluoride compound application, a suction apparatus is used to remove excess solution or gel from the mouth and to maintain a dry field of operation.

Fluoride compounds are usually applied to one-half of the mouth at a time, either one side, or one arch, dependent upon the device used for isolation. It may be necessary to apply the compound separately to each of the four quadrants of the dentition if the child is uncooperative, or the mouth is too small to accommodate the isolation apparatus.

A Method for Applying Topical Fluoride Compounds

In the oldest and most generally accepted method of topical fluoride application, cotton rolls are used to isolate the teeth from the buccal mucosa, tongue and saliva. The cotton rolls are held in position by metal holders which fit into the mouth and clamp under the chin. The holders are paired for the right and left side of the mouth.

All materials are prepared for the complete procedure before the fluoride application is begun. These include: cotton rolls, cotton applicators or large cotton pellets (approximately ¼ inch in diameter), cotton pliers, saliva ejector, air syringe, prepared fluoride solution and a timer.

Cotton rolls of different length and diameter are available. Because larger diameter cotton rolls are more absorbent, they are used when the patient's mouth will accommodate them. Six-inch cotton rolls can be cut in optimum lengths for the individual patient to assure continued isolation during the fluoride application. If the cotton rolls are too long, they will be forced onto the terminal teeth by the mucobuccal fold or tongue. Should the mandibular lingual cotton roll extend too far beyond the distal buccal surface of the most posterior tooth, the gag reflex will be stimulated.

Either two or three lengths of cotton roll are required for each side of the mouth. The lingual surfaces of the mandibular quadrant are isolated with one cotton roll cut to extend from the midline to the retromolar area, just distal to the terminal tooth. The facial surfaces of the mandibular and maxillary quadrants may be isolated with one cotton roll, if the second permanent molar has not erupted or the dental arch is short. The 6-inch cotton roll is cut to extend from the mandibular labial frenum to the maxillary labial frenum. The fold of the cotton roll must not be in contact with the posterior teeth. When the dental arch is long two cotton rolls are used to isolate the facial tooth surfaces—one for the mandibular quadrant, and one for the maxillary quadrant. If the ends of the cotton rolls are cut at a 45 degree angle, they will adapt more readily to the oral mucosa. The cotton rolls are cut and attached to the holders so that the beveled surface will rest against the attached gingiva and alveolar mucosa (Fig. 4–23). Should the cotton roll holder tilt toward the tongue, the cotton roll on the mandibular facial surface will move up onto the teeth. This problem can be alleviated by placing a short cotton roll next to the tongue before inserting the cotton roll holder.

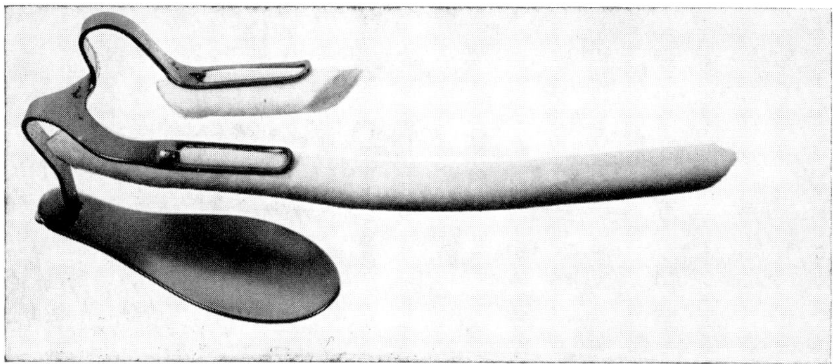

FIG. 4–23. Left cotton roll holder prepared for insertion into the mouth. The long facial cotton roll is turned back for insertion.

Application Procedure

After the cotton rolls have been inserted into the mouth and the holder secured with the chin clamp, a final inspection for complete isolation is made. The cotton roll holder and cotton rolls should not be in contact with the oral mucosa, or teeth (Fig. 4–24). Cotton pliers may be used to adjust the position of the cotton rolls. The maxillary cotton roll is held in place by the thumb, index and middle fingers of the non-operating hand. The saliva ejector is inserted in the anterior lingual area on the opposite side of the mouth. The teeth are dried completely with compressed air. With the cotton applicator or cotton pellet, the fluoride solution is applied to all surfaces of the isolated teeth. Then timing of the application is begun. When either acidulated sodium fluoride or stannous fluoride is used the solution is applied continuously for four minutes. The cotton applicator or pellet is repeatedly saturated with the solution. Two or three applicators or pellets will be needed for each side of the mouth. Sodium fluoride solution may be applied with a single or continuous application.

Upon completion of the application the cotton roll holder clamp is released and the cotton rolls carefully removed. Cotton pliers are

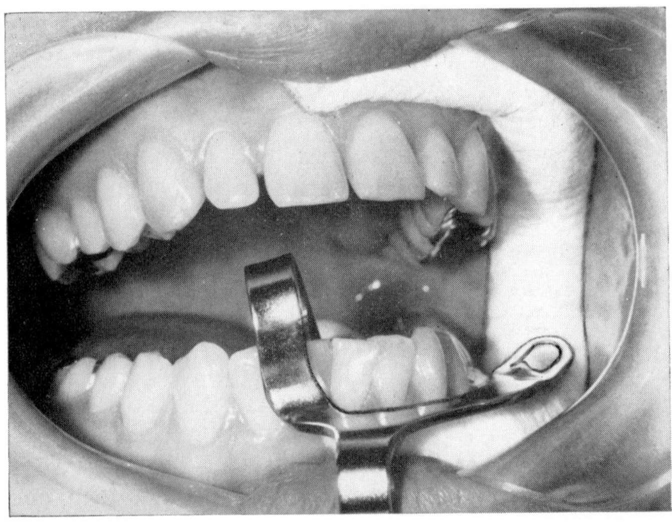

FIG. 4–24. Left cotton roll holder in place. When the clamp is secured under the chin the cervical areas of the anterior teeth will be exposed.

used to remove cotton rolls which are retained in the mouth. The patient is not allowed to rinse, but may eliminate excess solution before application to the second side of the mouth is begun. Swallowing the solution can cause nausea. The procedure is then repeated on the opposite side of the mouth.

New devices have been developed for topical fluoride application. Before using these devices the hygienist should be assured that the teeth will be completely isolated throughout the application procedure, and that an adequate amount of the fluoride preparation will be in contact with the teeth for the optimum length of time. The hygienist must be aware of and evaluate current research being conducted in the area of preventive dentistry.

INSTRUMENT SHARPENING[25,57,73]

Correctly sharpened instruments are essential to successful calculus detection, scaling and root planing. Sharp scaling and root planing instruments significantly minimize the number of strokes and the pressure required to remove calculus, thus preventing soft tissue trauma, patient discomfort and operator fatigue. For maximum instrumentation efficiency and wear, instruments should be sharpened at the first sign of dullness.

Tests for Sharpness

Two tests for instrument sharpness can be used. In the easiest and often most reliable test for sharpness, the instrument blade is adapted to the fingernail and angulated as in scaling. The blade is then drawn across the fingernail with light pressure. If the cutting edge of the blade is sharp, it will "bite" or shave the nail surface. Visual inspection of the blade also may be used to test sharpness. The cutting edge or angle of a dull blade is rounded and reflects light. The lateral and facial surfaces of the instrument blade should be examined for deviations from their original contour which require correction.

Sharpening Devices

Natural and artificial stones or a metal instrument may be used for instrument sharpening. The fine Arkansas oilstone is a natural stone. The coarser aloxite, diamond, india and ruby stones are artificial. The texture of the sharpening stone affects the rate of sharpening, fineness of the cutting edge and smoothness of the instrument surface that is ground during the sharpening procedure. Coarse stones cut more rapidly and produce a roughened instrument surface and burred cutting edge, which will leave microscopic scratches on the tooth. Fine stones produce a smooth instrument surface and a fine cutting edge. Coarse stones are used most effectively for sharpening very dull instruments and recontouring blades. A fine stone should be used after the surfaces of the instrument blade have been ground with a coarse stone. The Neivert Whittler sharpening instrument is made of a metal alloy which is harder than that of scaling and root planing instruments. When used correctly the Neivert Whittler produces a relatively fine cutting edge and smooth instrument surface.

Stones which are attached to mandrels for use with a dental handpiece are called *mounted* stones. Stones which are held in the hand or placed on a flat surface during use are called *unmounted hand* or *unmounted flat* stones.

Sharpening stones are manufactured in many shapes and sizes. Mounted stones are cylindrical or cone shaped. Unmounted stones are rectangular, cylindrical, cone or wedge shaped. The stone that is selected for sharpening is determined by the specific instrument design. In general, unmounted stones are preferred to motor driven mounted stones, because they wear away less of the instrument surface during use.

Manufacturer's instructions for care and sterilization of sharpening devices should be followed. Dirt particles on a stone will interfere with sharpening procedures. Stones are handled carefully because they can be broken or scratched easily. To avoid the formation of a groove in a stone, different areas are used for sharpening. Some stones are lubricated with oil or water during use. The Arkansas, aloxite and india stones are coated with a light film of oil for sharpening procedures. The ruby stone is lubricated periodically with water during sharpening. Artificial stones may be autoclaved or chemically disinfected. Arkansas stones may be sterilized in the autoclave or hot oil sterilizer. All surfaces of the Arkansas stone should be covered with a light film of oil when it is not in use.

Instrument Sharpening Procedures

Instruments are sharpened by grinding one, or both of the surfaces which form the angles or cutting edges of the blade. The original blade proportions will be maintained if all surfaces are ground. When the blade is sharpened at the first sign of dullness, little grinding will be required to attain a fine cutting edge. The instrument should be tested for sharpness after every two or three strokes to prevent unnecessary grinding. The surface of the blade will be ground uniformly if it is maintained in an optimum relationship with the sharpening device during the procedure. The operator's arms are rested against the body or a table, and fulcrums are used to provide stability. Good illumination is necessary for inspecting the instrument blade and for establishing the correct relationship between the blade surface and the sharpening stone or instrument.

The variety of scaling and root planing instrument designs makes the use of more than one sharpening device desirable. The flat surfaces of the sickle, hoe and chisel blades adapt well to hand stones with flat surfaces. Cylindrical or conical mounted and unmounted stones adapt to the curved surfaces of the curet blade. The Neivert Whittler may be adapted to either sickle scalers or curets. The Jeweler's Tang File, which is a hardware item, is used for sharpening periodontal files.

Grasps and Fulcrums

The instrument and sharpening device are held with either a modified pen or a palm grasp. The grasp that is comfortable and convenient for the particular sharpening device and instrument is used. The operating hand fulcrum is established on the stone, table or the other hand.

Sharpening Curets

The same basic technique is used for sharpening curets with cylindrical or conical mounted and unmounted stones and the Neivert Whittler. The two cutting edges of the curet blade may be sharpened

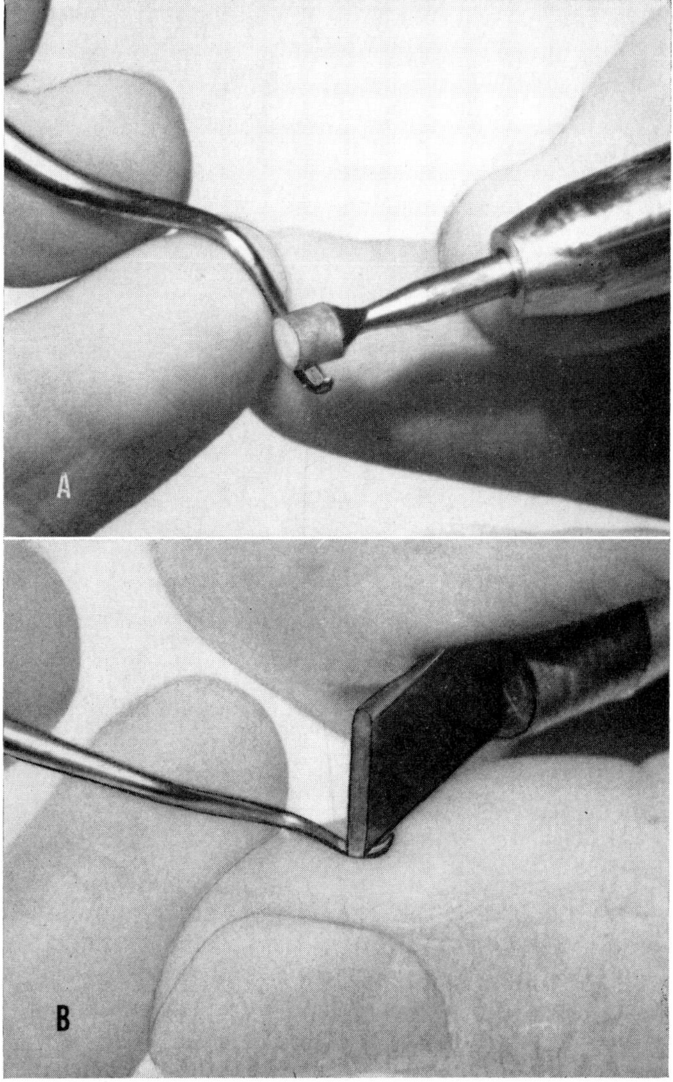

FIG. 4–25. *A,* A mounted stone adapted to the facial surface of a curet. The handpiece is held with a pen grasp. The third finger is used to establish a fulcrum on the finger which is stabilizing the curet.

B, The Neivert Whittler adapted to the facial surface of a curet. The sharpening instrument is held with a palm grasp. The thumb is used to establish a fulcrum on the finger which is stabilizing the curet.

simultaneously by grinding the facial surface. The curet is held with an appropriate grasp and stabilized by holding the shank against the edge of a table, a block of wood, or the thumb or third finger of the hand in which it is held. The tip of the blade is directed toward the operator. The sharpening device is held in the operating hand and stabilized with a convenient fulcrum. The side of the stone or the flat sharpening surface of the Neivert Whittler is placed on the facial surface of the blade near the instrument shank so that it is in contact with both cutting edges (Fig. 4–25*A* and *B*). The surface is ground by pulling the stone or sharpening instrument from the shank to the tip

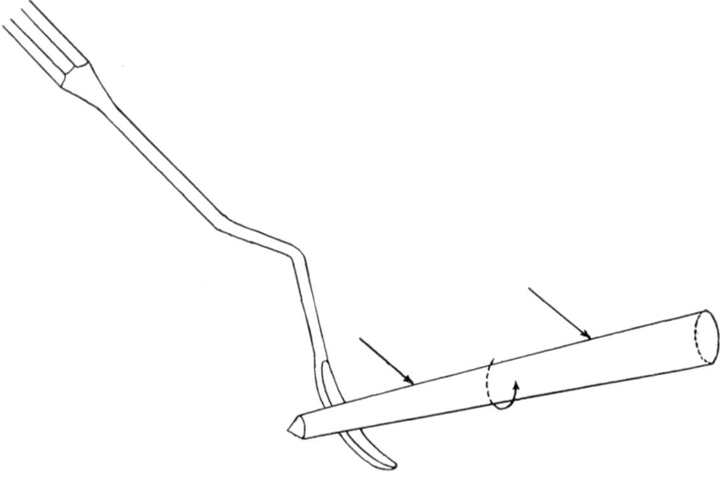

FIG. 4–26. A conical hand sharpening stone adapted to the facial surface of a curet. The instrument is rotated in a counterclockwise direction during the sharpening stroke.

of the blade with moderate and even pressure. Hand and mounted stones are rotated in a counterclockwise direction as they are pulled toward the tip of the blade. Hand stones are rotated with the fingers (Fig. 4–26). The rheostat is operated at low speed to rotate the mounted stone. The rheostat pedal is not engaged until the stone has been adapted to the facial surface of the blade.

To retain the original proportions of the curet, the lateral and facial surfaces and back of the blade are ground during sharpening. If a proportionately narrower blade is desired, only the lateral surfaces are ground. The lateral surfaces and back of the blade are ground with overlapping strokes of the sharpening stone from the shank of the instrument to the tip. If the stone is allowed to move onto the cutting edge during this procedure, the edge will be rounded and dulled.

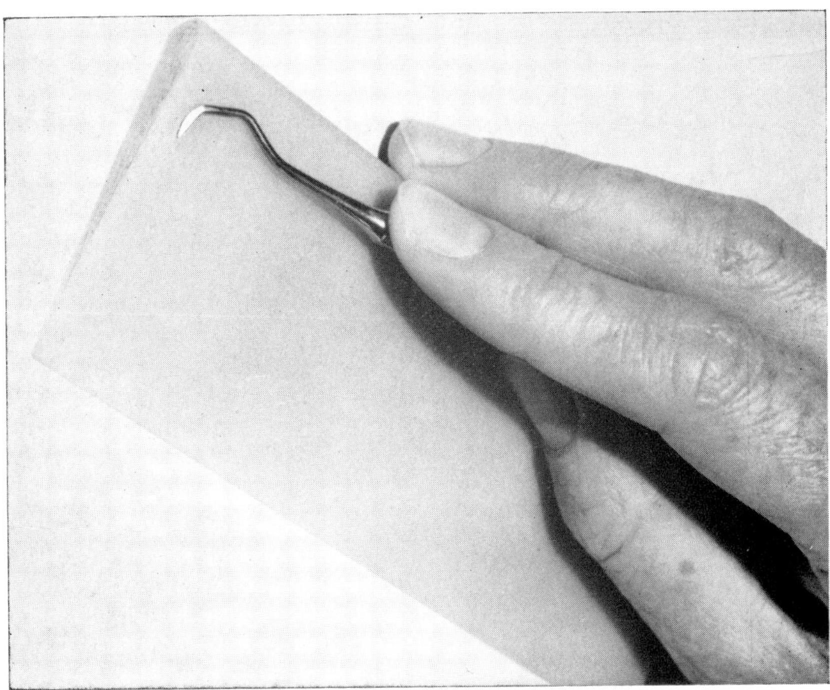

FIG. 4–27. Lateral surface of a straight sickle scaler adapted to a flat stone. A modification of the palm grasp is used to hold the instrument.

Sharpening Sickle Scalers

The cutting edges of the sickle scaler are sharpened by grinding the lateral surfaces and/or the facial surface of the blade. The lateral surface is ground by placing it on the surface of the flat stone and pulling the instrument against the cutting edge with moderate pressure. The pressure is then released and the instrument blade repositioned for the next sharpening stroke. It is not necessary to lift the blade from the stone for repositioning. If the entire lateral surface is not held against the stone during the procedure, the blade will be beveled.

For easier adaptation of the lateral surface to the sharpening stone, the straight sickle may be held with a slightly modified palm grasp. The thumb, index, third and fourth fingers are used to hold the instrument; and the middle finger is used to establish a fulcrum. The fulcrum finger moves with the instrument during the sharpening and repositioning strokes (Fig. 4–27).

Different surfaces of the flat stone are used for grinding each of the lateral surfaces of the modified sickle (Fig. 4–28*A* and *B*). The straight or modified sickle blade is positioned on the side or end of

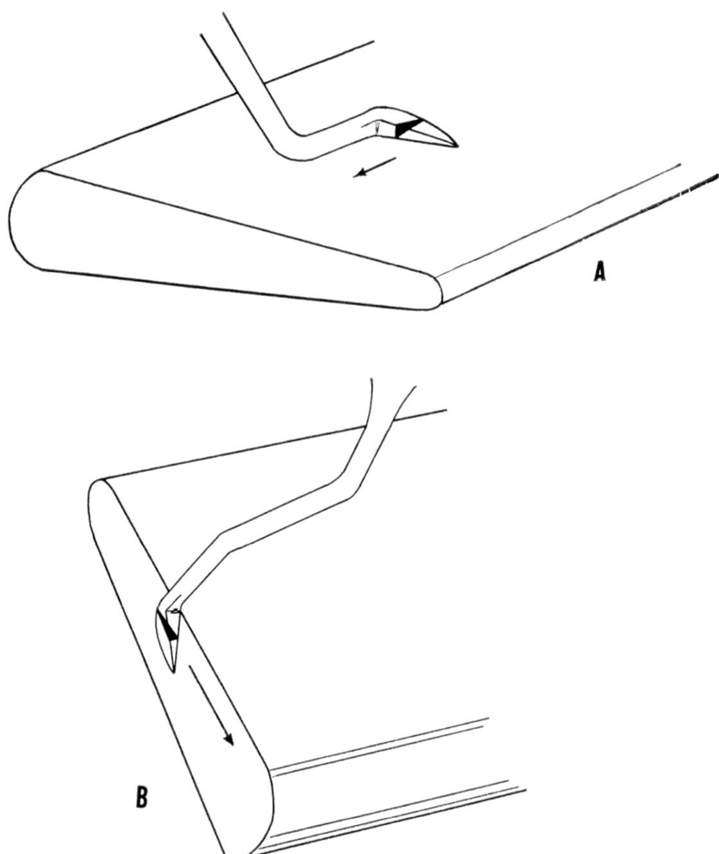

FIG. 4–28 *A* and *B*. Lateral surfaces of a modified sickle scaler adapted to a flat stone. The instrument is held with a pen grasp.

the flat stone with the tip down to grind the facial surface. With moderate pressure, the blade is pulled in a vertical direction (Fig. 4–29). The pressure is released to reposition the instrument for the next sharpening stroke. If the instrument is rocked laterally during the sharpening stroke, the cutting edge will be rounded. A horizontal stroke may be used also to grind the facial surface. However, it is more difficult to maintain the correct blade and stone relationship when a horizontal stroke is used.

After the cutting edge has been sharpened, the angle at the back of the blade and the tip are rounded. This is done by either drawing the stone over the back of the blade and tip with a brushing stroke, or by moving the angle and tip back and forth across the stone. Mounted stones and the Neivert Whittler may be used for sharpening sickle scalers with the technique used for sharpening curets.

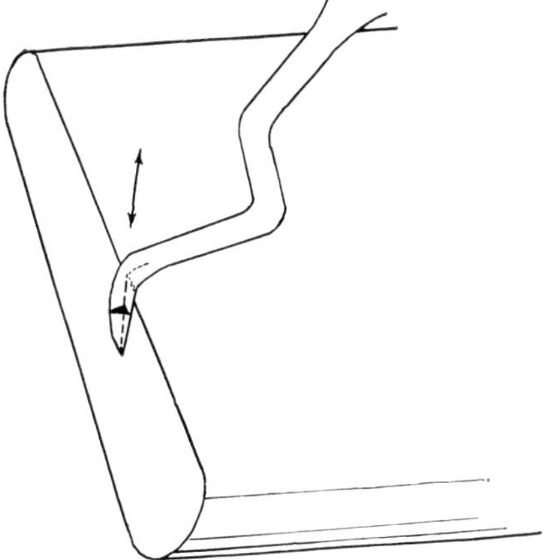

FIG. 4–29. Facial surface of modified sickle scaler adapted to a flat stone. The instrument is held with a pen grasp.

Sharpening Hoes and Chisels

Hoes and chisels are easily sharpened. The beveled surface of the blade is placed on the surface of the flat stone and the instrument is pulled against the cutting edge with moderate pressure. The pressure is released for the repositioning stroke. The modification of the palm grasp which is used for grinding the lateral surfaces of the straight sickle can be used for sharpening the hoe and chisel. If the beveled surface is not seated on the stone throughout the sharpening procedure, the blade will be damaged. The sharp corners of the hoe and chisel blade are rounded by drawing them across the stone two or three times.

Sharpening Periodontal Files

Each cutting edge of the periodontal file is sharpened separately. The tang file is placed in a horizontal position against the inner surface of the individual file blade and pulled back and forth across the blade surface until the cutting edge is sharp. The procedure is repeated for each blade (Fig. 4–30). The tang file is then used with a back and forth motion to round the blade corners. Because periodontal files have small blades, particular care must be taken when seating and activating the tang file to avoid damaging the cutting edge.

Explorers

Explorer tips become rounded with use. The flat stone may be used to restore the sharp point at the explorer tip. The working end of the explorer is placed on the stone and the instrument raised so

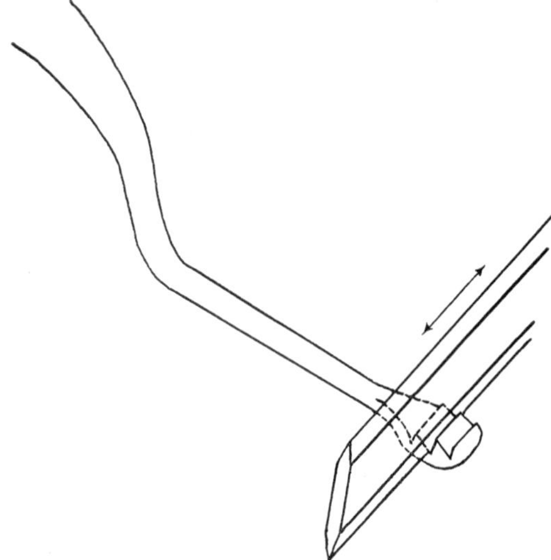

FIG. 4–30. The Jeweler's Tang File adapted to a periodontal file blade for sharpening.

that the side of the tip and the stone form an angle of approximately 15 degrees. As the instrument is drawn across the stone in an arc, the handle is rotated by the fingers to assure even grinding of the working end. If the instrument is raised too far from the stone, the tip will be rounded rather than sharpened.

ACKNOWLEDGMENTS: I wish to express appreciation to Mr. Clifford L. Freehe and Mr. Dean Auve for all the photographs, and to Mr. Michael Thrall for the line drawings which appear in this chapter.

BIBLIOGRAPHY

1. American Dental Association, Council on Dental Therapeutics: *Accepted Dental Remedies,* 30th ed., Chicago, American Dental Association, pp. 31-32, 1965.
2. ———: Ibid., pp. 34-40.
3. ———: Ibid., pp. 67-68.
4. ———: Ibid., pp. 130-143.
5. ———: Ibid., pp. 157-159.
6. ARNIM, SUMTER S.: The Use of Disclosing Agents for Measuring Tooth Cleanliness. J. Periodont., *34,* 227, 1963.
7. BANDT, C. L., KORN, N. A., and SCHAFFER, E. M.: Bacteremias from Ultrasonic and Hand Instrumentation. J. Periodont., *35,* 214, 1964.
8. BARNHART, C. L. and STEIN, JESS: *The American College Dictionary.* New York, Random House, p. 971, 1962.
9. BOLENDER, CHARLES: Personal communication.

10. BOYD, WILLIAM: *An Introduction to Medical Science,* 4th ed., Philadelphia, Lea & Febiger, Ch. 9, 10, 14, 16; pp. 69-70, 1952.
11. BRADEN, B. E.: Personal communication.
12. BRÄANSTRÖM, MARTIN: Dentin Sensitivity and Aspiration of Odontoblasts. J.A.D.A., *66,* 366,1963.
13. BRUDEVOLD, F., SAVORY, A., GARDNER, D. E., SPINELLI, M., and SPEIRS, R.: A Study of Acidulated Fluoride Solutions—I. In Vitro Effects on Enamel. Arch. Oral Biol., *8,* 167, 1963.
14. BUNTING, RUSSELL W.: *Oral Hygiene,* 3rd ed., Philadelphia, Lea & Febiger, p. 275, 1957.
15. *Dental Hygiene Clinic Handbook.* Seattle, Department of Dental Hygiene, University of Washington, 1965, p. 49.
16. ————: Ibid., p. 45.
17. DILLE, J. M.: *Drug Therapy for Dentists,* 1st ed., Chicago, Year Book Medical Publishers Inc., 1963, Ch. 18.
18. ————: Ibid., pp. 75-77.
19. DRENNAN, G. A.: Personal communication.
20. EWEN, SOL J. and SORRIN, SYDNEY: Ultrasonics and Periodontal Therapy. Dent. Clin. North America, pp. 145-164, March, 1964.
21. GEHRIG, JOHN D.: Personal communication.
22. GLICKMAN, IRVING: Clinical Periodontology, 3rd ed., Philadelphia, W. B. Saunders Co., 1964, pp. 460-462.
23. ————: Ibid., pp. 462-471.
24. ————: Ibid., pp. 478-482.
25. ————: Ibid., Ch. 39.
26. GOLDMAN, H. M., SCHLUGER, S., FOX, L., and COHEN, D. W.: *Periodontal Therapy,* 3rd ed., St. Louis, C. V. Mosby Co., 1964, Ch. 7.
27. ————: Ibid., Ch. 11, 12
28. ————: Ibid., p. 329.
29. ————: Ibid., p. 344.
30. ————: Ibid., p. 640.
31. ————: Ibid., p. 638.
32. HALL, WALTER: Personal communication.
33. HOOLEY, JAMES R.: Personal communication.
34. *How the Dentist Can Protect His Patients from Bacterial Endocarditis,* American Heart Association publication, 4-55-25M.
35. HOYT, W. H. and BIBBY, B. G.: Use of Sodium Fluoride for Desensitizing Dentin. J.A.D.A., *30,* 1372, 1943.
36. JAWETZ, ERNEST: Virus Infections of Interest to the Dentist. In a Bibliography: Transmission of Serum Hepatitis by Needles and Syringes and Preventive Technique, Wilmot Castle Co. n.d.
37. JENSEN, ARTHUR L.: Hypersensitivity Controlled by Iontophoresis. J.A.D.A., *68,* 216, 1964.
38. JOHNSON, W. N. and WILSON, J. R.: The Application of the Ultrasonic Dental Unit to Scaling Procedures. J. Periodont., *28,* 264, 1957.
39. KUTSCHER, A. H., ZEGARELLI, E. V., and HYMAN, G. A.: *Pharmacotherapeutics of Oral Disease,* New York, McGraw-Hill Book Co. Inc., 1964, p. 79.
40. ————: Ibid., p. 357.
41. MOSKOW, B. S. and BRESSMAN, EDWARD: Cemental Response to Ultrasonic and Hand Instrumentation. J.A.D.A., *68,* 698, 1964.
42. MUHLER, J. C., STOOKEY, G. K., and BIXLER, DAVID: Evaluation of the Anticariogenic Effect of Mixtures of Stannous Fluoride and Soluble Phosphates. J. Dent. Child., *32,* 154, 1965.

43. ORBAN, BALINT: *Oral Histology and Embryology,* 3rd ed., St. Louis, C. V. Mosby Co., 1953, p. 239.
44. PAMEIJER, J. H. N., BRUDEVOLD, F., and HUNT, E. E.: A Study of Acidulated Fluoride Solutions—III. The Cariostatic Effect of Repeated Topical Sodium Fluoride Applications With and Without Phosphate: a Pilot Study. Arch. Oral Biol., *8,* 183, 1963.
45. REDDISH, GEORGE F.: *Antiseptics, Disinfectants, Fungicides, and Chemical and Physical Sterilization,* 2nd ed., Philadelphia, Lea & Febiger, 1957, Ch. 2, 31.
46. ———: Ibid., Ch. 24; pp. 26, 636-639.
47. ———: Ibid., Ch. 17; pp. 24, 27.
48. SCHAFFER, E. M.: Histological Results of Root Curettage of Human Teeth. J. Periodont., *27,* 296, 1956.
49. SCOTT, D. B.: Electron Microscopic Evidence of Fluoride Enamel Reaction. J. Dent. Res., *39,* 117, 1960.
50. SCOTT, HAROLD M.: Reduction of Sensitivity by Electrophoresis. J. Dent. Child., *29,* 225, 1962.
51. SEGRETO, V. A., HARRIS, N. O., and HESTER, W. R.: A Stannous Fluoride-Silex-Silicone Dental Prophylaxis Paste With Anticariogenic Potentialities. Texas, School of Aviation Medicine, United States Air Force, 60-11, November, 1959.
52. SICHER, HARRY: *Orban's Oral Histology and Embryology.* St. Louis, C. V. Mosby Co., 1962, pp. 174-175.
53. SIEMON, W. HARRY: Observations on the Value of Iontophoretic Procedures in Dentistry, Dental Digest, *68,* 172, 1962.
54. SKINNER, E. W.: The Science of Dental Materials. 4th ed., Philadelphia, W. B. Saunders Co., 1954, Ch. 33.
55. SKURNIK, HARRY: Control of Dental Hypersensitivity—Preliminary Report on a Strontium-Containing Dentifrice, J. Periodont., *34,* 183, 1963.
56. SMITH, B. A. and ASH, M. M.: Evaluation of a desensitizing Dentifrice, J.A.D.A., *68,* 639, 1964.
57. WAGNER, PATRICIA MCCULLOUGH: Personal communication.
58. WAINBERG, A. S.: A Modified Periodontal Probe, J. Canad. D.A., *30,* 419, 1964.
59. *Webster's New World Dictionary of the American Language.* College Edition, Cleveland, The World Publishing Company, 1956, p. 1168.
60. ———: Ibid., p. 585.
61. WELLOCK, W. D. and BRUDEVOLD, F.: A Study of Acidulated Fluoride Solutions—II. The Caries Inhibiting Effect of Single Annual Topical Applications of a Phosphate Fluoride Solution. A Two Year Experience, Arch. Oral Biol., *8,* 179, 1963.
62. WILKINS, E. M. and MCCULLOUGH, P. A.: *Clinical Practice of the Dental Hygienist.* 2nd ed., Philadelphia, Lea & Febiger, 1964, p. 101.
63. ———: Ibid., Ch. 5.
64. ———: Ibid., Ch. 35.
65. ———: Ibid., Ch. 6.
66. ———: Ibid., Ch. 8.
67. ———: Ibid., Ch. 17.
68. ———: Ibid., pp. 178-181.
69. ———: Ibid., Ch. 19.
70. ———: Ibid., pp. 190-192.
71. ———: Ibid., pp. 181-183.
72. ———: Ibid., Ch. 21.
73. ———: Ibid., Ch. 4.

5

Dental Caries: Etiological Factors, Pathological Characteristics, Therapeutic Measures

Harold R. Englander

and Paul H. Keyes

DENTAL caries is an infection that attacks and destroys the crowns of teeth in younger persons, and may affect root surfaces in older adults with gingival recession.

In the United States, fewer than five persons in a hundred escape the disease. The National Health Survey, U. S. Public Health Service, reported that dental caries is the most common physical defect of children. Statistics on the incidence of dental decay, extractions of carious teeth, and costs of restorations are staggering, and in most communities the increment of new lesions is many times the rate of repair. Indeed, it has been estimated that Americans have accumulated at least 700 million untreated cavities. Although a restoration or filling will stop the progression of an active cavity, it does little to prevent new lesions from developing. The prospect is dim that in the foreseeable future there will be enough dentists to handle the rapidly accumulating restorative needs of the population. As it is, only about 40 per cent of the population visits a dentist during any calendar year. Because of the ever widening gap between need and care, it has become increasingly apparent that methods need to be found for controlling and preventing this infection. If new lesion formation could be substantially prevented, moderate increases in dental manpower would permit the oral health needs of the nation to be met more effectively.

The literature dealing with dental caries is voluminous, *e.g.*, between 1940 and 1960 approximately 3800 papers were published on the subject. There are many differences of opinion and controversial points in regard to etiological factors, partly because some investigators have not considered the multifactorial nature of the disease. Nevertheless, sufficient knowledge does exist to form the basis of practical and highly effective programs of control and prevention.

It is the primary purpose of this chapter to discuss the salient etiological factors associated with dental caries, the rationale for therapeutic measures, and several procedures for control which can be used in the home, and supervised in schools and offices by dentists and dental hygienists.

ETIOLOGICAL MECHANISMS

Dental caries results from biological interactions between microorganisms in the mouth, certain dietary ingredients (carbohydrates), and various anatomical, physiological, biochemical, and behavioral characteristics of the host. In Figure 5–1, overlapping circles depict

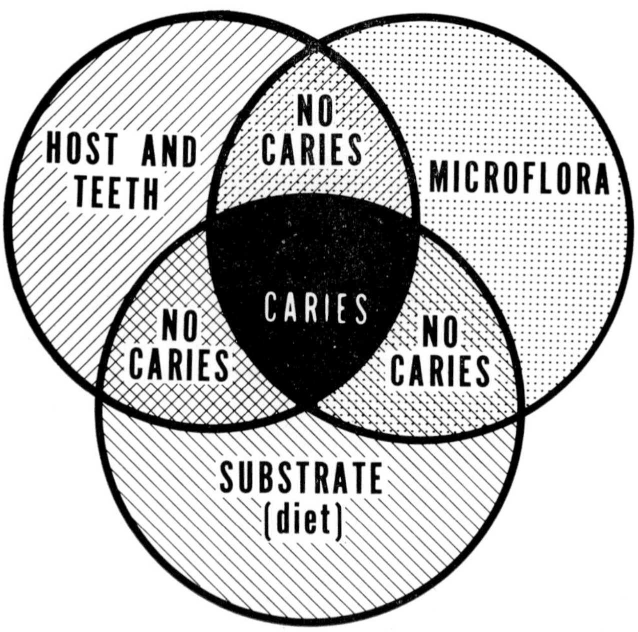

FIG. 5–1. Three overlapping circles depict several possible relationships between the factorial components associated with dental caries. Since there are numerous variables in each of the three groupings, the intensity of the contribution from any single one is always difficult to assess. For the infection to be active, conditions in each area must be conducive; however, when the infection is inactive, it is often exceedingly difficult to know whether one contributory group or more is responsible for the result. (From Keyes, Int. Dent. J., *12,* 443-464, 1962.)

several interrelationships in the factorial triad which contribute to this morbid process. Activity of the infection is affected by conditions which can vary widely in each of the etiological groups indicated. From numerous laboratory studies with experimental animals, researchers have found that rather exact conditions must prevail before the disease will develop and progress. There is no reason to presume that conditions are less complex in human beings.

Flora and Bacterial Factors

It has been well established that microorganisms must be present in order for dental caries to occur. Lesions will not form unless bacteria are in contact with surfaces of the teeth. Although microbes were implicated in the carious process by several investigators in the latter half of the nineteenth century, it remained for W. D. Miller, whose investigations have had a profound influence on caries research, to formulate the "Chemico-Parasitic Theory" of tooth decay. He explained lesion formation in terms of two properties of bacteria, namely, acid production (acidogenesis) and the breakdown of proteins (proteolysis). Miller believed that dental caries was a nonspecific bacterial disease; hence, any acidogenic microbe which could ferment carbohydrate might decalcify the teeth. Although it has been established that acidogenic bacteria are necessary for the formation of carious lesions, there have been several opinions since Miller concerning the relative importance of the various types of acid-producing microorganisms found in the mouth. Experiments with germ-free rats, observations in hamsters, and *in vitro* studies on extracted teeth have shown that not all oral acidogenic bacteria are associated with caries, not all carbohydrates are caries-conducive, and proteolytic bacteria are not necessarily involved.

Some investigators have maintained that the bacterial factor in dental caries is nonspecific and that lesions can be caused by numerous species of acidogenic microorganisms; other workers have implicated one genus of acidogenic bacteria more than others; accordingly, considerable attention has been focused either on the lactobacillus or the acidogenic streptococcus. For example, Bunting and co-workers stated that "dental caries has been definitely proved to be a truly infective disease and that B. acidophilus may be considered to be the specific etiologic factor responsible for the initial stage of the disease." Emphasis has been placed on lactobacilli because they are both highly acidogenic and aciduric; they tend to increase in dental plaques before the clinical appearance of caries develops, and they can usually be isolated from all stages of the carious lesion. Indeed, so much importance has been attached to the role of lactobacilli that caries activity tests have been based upon their enumeration in spittle. Although the role of lactobacilli in caries is still not fully understood, it seems unlikely that they are completely innocent bystanders in the carious process. As Burnett and Scherp have pointed out, these bacteria must glycolyze to live, and glycolysis inevitably produces lactic and other harmful organic acids.

The succeeding summarizes the more important research findings which have implicated the lactobacillus in dental caries:

1) Lactobacilli have been found abundantly in plaque covering carious lesions and in deep dentinal caries, but not often in tooth scrapings from persons who remain caries-free.

2) Results from several studies have shown a strong relationship between caries activity and the number of lactobacilli isolated from spittle (salivary lactobacillus count). In general, large numbers of lactobacilli can be isolated from individuals with rampant caries, whereas few are apt to be obtained from caries-inactive persons. But this relation has been by no means consistent; often persons with few lesions manifest high counts and those with many lesions may have low counts.

3) Rats reared in germ-free tanks have developed "fissure" caries following an inoculation with certain single strains of lactobacilli.

Attempts have been made to use the salivary lactobacillus count to predict the clinical onset of carious lesions. For large groups of people, lactobacillus counts from persons who become caries-active tend to be higher than counts from persons remaining caries-inactive, but there is considerable overlapping of counts for individuals between the two groups. The salivary count of lactobacilli is subject to wide momentary and daily variations. The number of these bacteria which can be plated out on appropriate culture media (Rogosa or tomato juice agar) depends largely on what can be displaced from the more accessible plaque deposits on the teeth during the processes of chewing a stick of paraffin wax and expectoration. Therefore, the so-called "salivary lactobacillus count" is probably an imprecise reflection of the total number of microorganisms on less accessible tooth surfaces, in crevices, and in cavities.

The role of lactobacilli as primary or as secondary agents in caries needs further clarification. Although they can produce greater terminal acidities than streptococci and continue to metabolize and multiply in an acidic environment (pH below 5.6), they are only about one-thousandth as numerous in the dental plaque as the streptococci. However, the fact remains that the oral cavity must contain a high concentration of carbohydrate residues in order to support large numbers of lactobacilli. Therefore, it is reasonable to assume that, when these bacteria can be repeatedly recovered in high numbers, the oral environment favors caries activity, and from this viewpoint the "lactobacillus count" may be of value as an indicator of unfavorable eating habits and poor oral hygiene.

Evidence has been growing steadily that streptococci play an important etiologic role in dental caries. Many investigators have implicated these bacteria because: (1) These organisms are found in the vanguard of the advancing lesion; furthermore, they have been isolated from inflamed pulpal tissue beneath caries in the dentin. (2) They have been the predominant forms in early stages of dentin invasion, *i.e.*, lesions in which enamel has been penetrated but before gross cavitation has developed. (3) Gram-positive cocci have been found invading carious enamel in histological sections of human teeth. (4) It has been demonstrated that "caries-like" lesions can be produced in extracted teeth which have been incubated in liquid media containing carbohydrates and inoculated with streptococci.

Additional evidence incriminating streptococci in dental caries has been derived from experiments with rats and hamsters. Orland reported that certain types of streptococci could produce carious lesions in gnotobiotic rats (*i.e.*, previously germ-free animals infected with known strains of microorganisms). Fitzgerald, Jordan, and Stanley also were able to induce extensive dental caries in gnotobiotic rats that had been infected with an acidogenic, but non-proteolytic streptococcus (Fig. 5–2). In Syrian hamsters maintained under ordinary laboratory conditions, dental caries rapidly develops on coronal surfaces of molars when the animals are infected with certain strains of hamster streptococci, and a high carbohydrate diet containing over 50 per cent sucrose is also eaten. Moreover, human streptococcal isolates have been pathogenic to the teeth of hamsters (Fig. 5–3).

For several years researchers have been trying to determine whether streptococci isolated from human carious lesions could produce the disease in rats. Results from some of these studies in monoinfected, gnotobiotic rats have been promising, and dental caries has followed inoculations of some human streptococcal strains. All things considered, it is reasonable to assume that streptococci are important contributors to dental caries activity in humans. Generally speaking, if an infection in man is associated with a specific microbe, a comparable situation usually exists in experimental animals susceptible to the disease. However, the organisms that cause the disease in man may be less virulent when inoculated into an animal.

Recent work in hamsters by Jordan and Keyes has implicated acidogenic filament-forming microorganisms as the agent involved in the development of root surface lesions initiating in cementum (Fig.

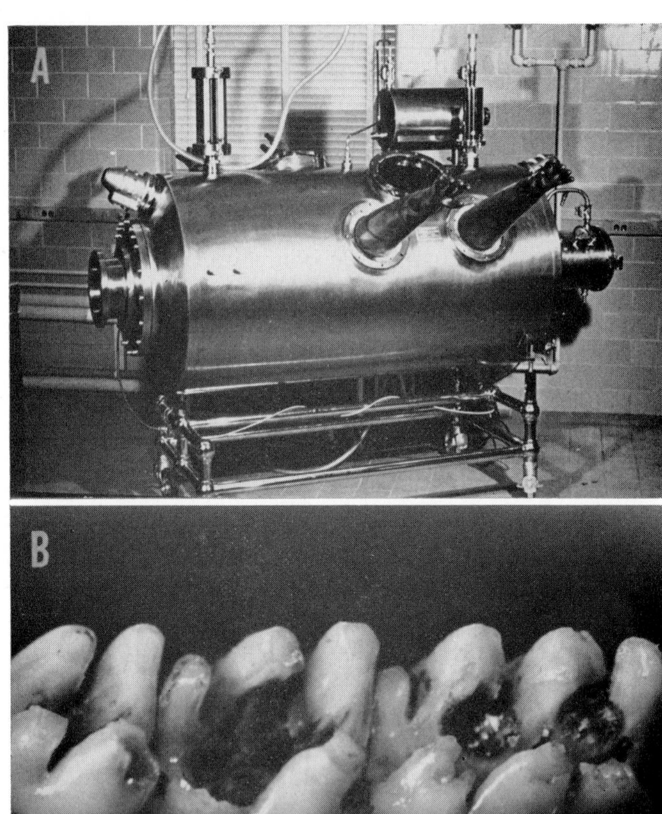

FIG. 5–2. *A,* Isolator tank for keeping animals either germ-free or mono-infected with a single bacterial strain. The caries conducive potential of various microorganisms can be assessed by inoculating germ-free rats with bacteria and feeding them an appropriate diet high in carbohydrate. *B,* Carious lesions in mandibular teeth of a rat which had been inoculated with a streptococcus previously obtained from a caries active rat. The jaw has been hemi-sectioned to show lesions in the sulci or "fissures" of the teeth. Similar lesions have followed inoculations of streptococci isolated from hamsters and humans. Some strains of lactobacilli have also induced caries activity in mono-infected rats. (Photographs courtesy, R. J. Fitzgerald. Nat. Inst. Dent. Res., Bethesda, Md.)

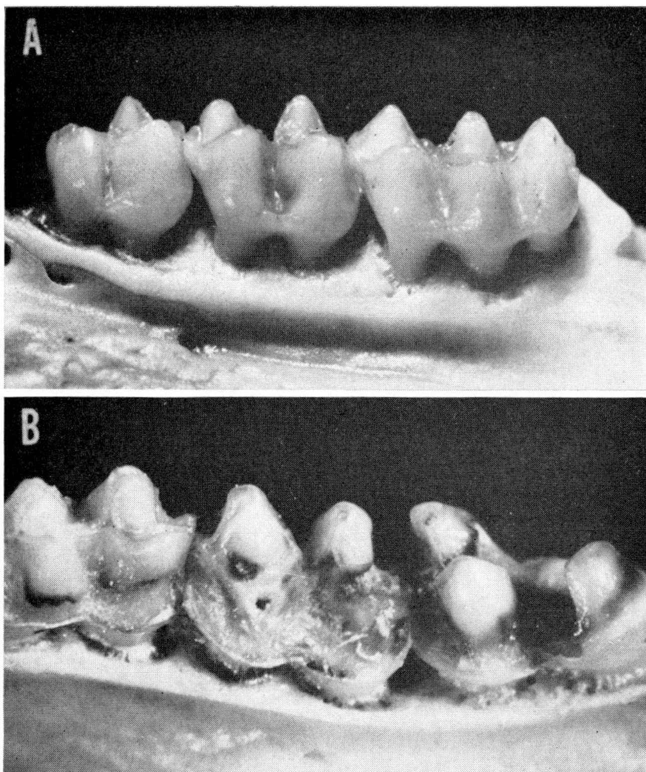

FIG. 5–3. *A,* Normal, caries-free, molar teeth from a conventionally caged but non-infected hamster fed a high-carbohydrate low-fat diet containing 56 per cent sucrose. *B,* Extensive carious lesions in molar teeth of a hamster fed the same diet but also inoculated with a caries-conducive streptococcus. Streptococci from both hamsters and human beings have been tested. Some strains are pathogenic to hamster teeth, but others are not. (From: Fitzgerald, R. J. and Keyes, P. H. J. Am. Dent. Assoc., *61,* 9-19, 1960.)

5–4). They form dense tenacious plaques at gingival margins and on root surfaces, when animals consume fine particle diets high in certain sugars and starches.

Although considerable emphasis has been placed on the acidogenic properties of bacteria and dental caries, this is only part of the story. Recent work has disclosed that dental caries does not always occur in experimental animals although they harbor many types of acid producing bacteria, including streptococci, and eat a diet high in sucrose. The question might be asked, why are some acidogenic bacteria pathogenic while others are not? The answer seems to be found in the potential of microorganisms to colonize on tooth surfaces and

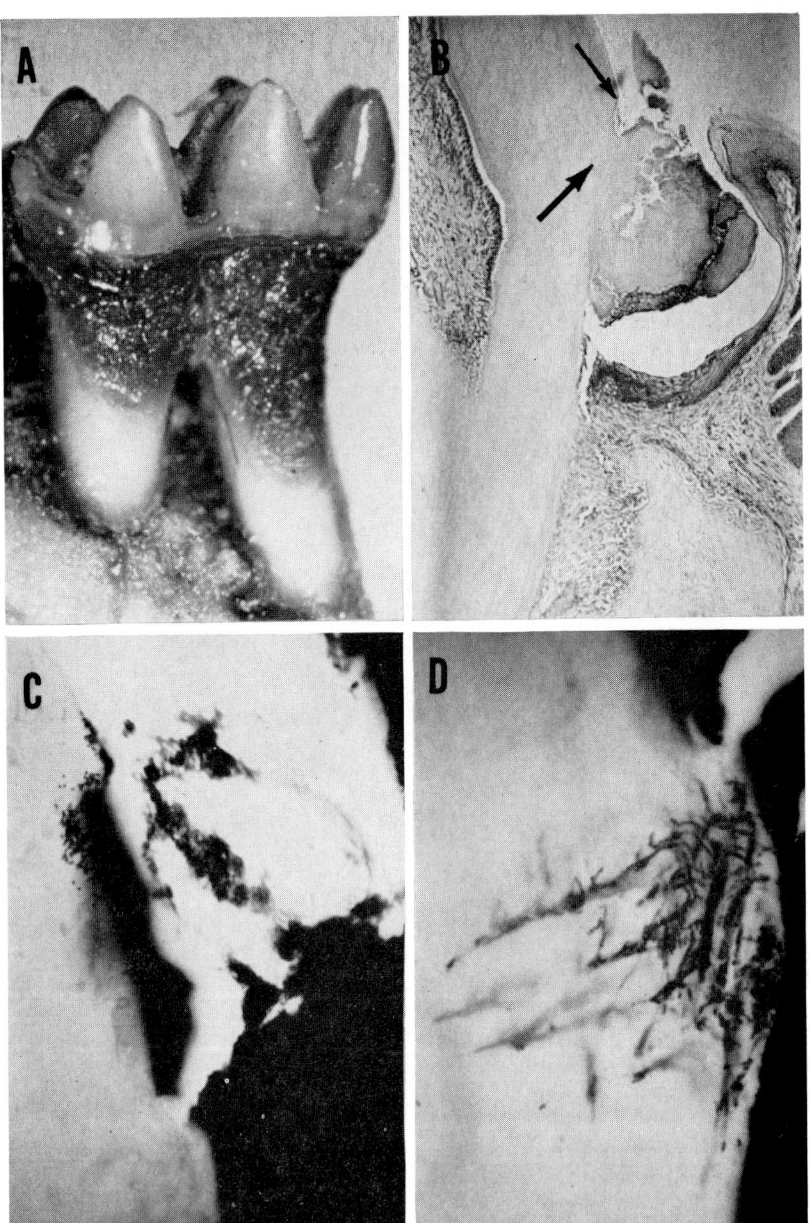

FIG. 5–4. *A,* Root surface caries developed in this mandibular first molar, when the hamster harbored filament forming bacteria in its mouth and consumed a high carbohydrate diet. *B,* Histological section of a hamster molar shows a small carious lesion which had penetrated cervical enamel (small arrow) and an area where filaments have invaded root surface (large arrow). A massive accumulation of plaque is attached to the root surface causing a gingival pocket, inflammation, and bone loss. *C,* Under an oil immersion lens, cocci can be detected in the carious lesion initiated in enamel (Gram stained section). *D,* Below the invasion of the cocci, filament forming microorganisms can be found invading the root surface. (From Keyes, P. H. and Jordan, H. V. Arch. Oral Biol., *9,* 377-440, 1964.)

form plaques. The acid by-products of organisms which do not colonize and form adhesive masses are probably relatively harmless to the teeth because they are dispersed and neutralized in the saliva; whereas, high concentrations of acid can be damaging in adherent plaques or in confined areas.

Dental plaque consists principally of mucoid microbial masses which are loosely adherent to tooth surfaces, and varies in color from white to yellowish gray. It has been called materia alba, dentobacterial plaque, gelatinous plaque, microcosm, oral debris, and sordes; but all these designations refer essentially to the same microbial mass. Because of its sticky mucilaginous consistency and its many living microorganisms, Arnim has called it zooglea, meaning living glue. Although it harbors numerous microorganisms capable of producing acids, it also contains salivary mucin, other constituents derived from saliva and the oral environment, and food residues which have dissolved and diffused into it. Greater quantities of plaque material tend to accumulate on the less accessible and more sheltered areas of the smooth surfaces of teeth, and rinsing with water alone usually will not dislodge it. It may also develop in pits and fissures from which it is particularly difficult or impossible to remove by mechanical or other means. As the bacteria grow and multiply, the mass of the plaque increases in size becoming thicker and more viscous due to the increased number of microorganisms, many of which produce a polysaccharide slime in addition to acids.

It has been generally accepted that carious lesions are initiated when the concentration of lactic and other acids, produced by the acidogenic microorganisms in adherent bacterial deposits, become sufficient to demineralize the tooth surfaces. The enzyme systems of many acid-producing microorganisms living in dental plaques are capable of producing large quantities of lactic and other organic acids by the fermentation of certain types of residual carbohydrates of dietary origin. However, lactic acid is the predominant acid produced by the metabolic activity (anaerobic) of "cariogenic" microorganisms, and repeated acid attacks on tooth substance lead to disintegration of the inorganic elements of the tooth and eventual cavitation.

The acid concentration of plaque on tooth surfaces can be estimated by means of chemical indicators which exhibit definite color changes at different acidities, or it can be measured more precisely by electrometric means with a potentiometer (pH meter) and appropriate electrodes. These acid concentrations are expressed conventionally in terms of pH units, lower pH values indicating greater acidities.

Normally, before eating, the pH of plaque on tooth surfaces exposed to saliva is close to neutrality (pH 7.0), but soon after foods containing high concentrations of glucose, sucrose, or other readily fermentable carbohydrates are eaten, acid is formed in plaque with the greatest acid concentration occurring about five to fifteen minutes afterwards (Fig. 5–25). The rate of acid production depends upon the characteristics and number of microorganisms present in the plaque and the concentration, chemical structure, and physical form of the carbohydrate ingested.

Acidities which produce hydrogen ion concentrations in the vicinity of pH 5.5 or below are considered harmful to teeth, because experiments have shown that enamel and dentin begin to decalcify when this degree of acidity is reached.

Although the acid produced may be dissipated by the buffering and washing action of saliva, frequently this does not occur before damage to the tooth surface has taken place. If sufficient plaque acidities develop, the tooth will be affected because the acids combine with its crystalline mineral structure (hydroxyapatite) and form soluble salts resulting in demineralization and cavitation. The fact that tooth mineral, instead of the saliva, reacts with the acids contributes to the decomposition of enamel and dentin and seems to be an essential part of the carious process.

Dietary Substrates, Nutrition, and Dental Caries

For many years there has been convincing evidence that dental caries cannot be initiated unless carbohydrate residues are available for metabolism by acidogenic microorganisms on the teeth. The relationship between consumption of refined carbohydrates and caries activity is no longer seriously questioned.

Coronal caries, which develops on the enamel surfaces of teeth, is largely a disease of modern man. Indeed, highly active lesions have seldom been found in ancient man, in persons living under primitive conditions, or in those ingesting natural unrefined foodstuffs. Root surface caries, however, has been observed in primitive persons subsisting on diets high in certain types of starchy foods. These lesions are associated with gingival recession and destructive periodontal disease. An increase in coronal caries has been frequently observed in persons who have changed from diets of meat, fish, milk, fruits, and coarser cereals to ones which also contain substantial amounts of highly refined cereals, sugars, and other processed foods containing high concentrations of readily fermentable carbohydrates.

Dental caries differs from other infectious diseases. The severity of most infections is increased by starvation or malnutrition, because systemic resistance to disease is reduced (Fig. 5–5). However, dental caries tends to be less active in such instances, probably because the cariogenic microorganisms are deprived of sufficient caries-conducive

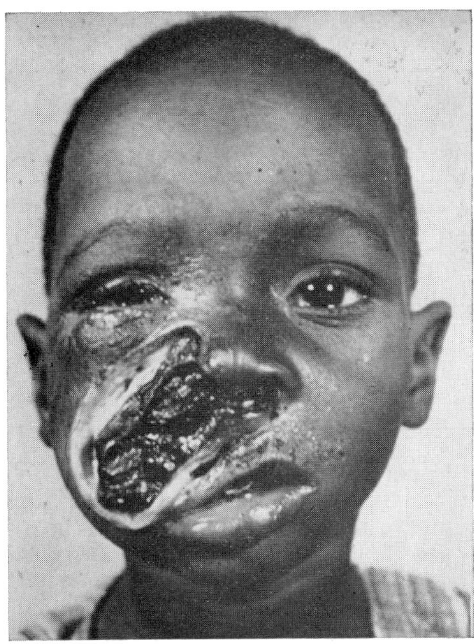

FIG. 5–5. A case of cancrum oris, noma, or gangrenous stomatitis in a Nigerian child. This type of facial gangrene occurs largely in children who are malnourished and who may also suffer debilitation from other infections. Spirochetes and fusiform bacilli have been implicated as agents of etiological importance. The disease responds dramatically to penicillin therapy. Carious lesions may not be found in the teeth of children with this infection, although bacterial deposits are found on their teeth and the principal foodstuff is carbohydrate (yam). (Photograph courtesy Dr. C. O. Enwonwu, Nigeria.)

substrates (Fig. 5–6). Resistive factors, especially immunologic blood responses, operative in combatting most infectious processes, are apparently unimportant in dental caries. In general, individuals consuming inadequate or near starvation diets are not attacked by this disease. A recent example of this was seen in western Europe and in prisoners of war during World War II. For example, the caries activity of children in war-torn or occupied countries dropped steadily during and shortly after the war. Some of the diets consumed were deficient in proteins and vitamins and consisted mostly of less soluble and slowly fermentable starches. Little or no sugar was available. A low incidence of dental caries has been observed also in famine areas of India, in protein deficient natives of Nigeria, and in other underdeveloped countries where malnutrition is commonly found. Thus, dental caries may be considered as a disease of the better fed, at least in the sense that malnutrition in the host is not necessary.

INGESTA-SALIVA SUBSTRATE

COMPOSITION and/or QUANTITY	
(Chemical Physical)	(Proportion Duration)
HOST	PARASITE(S)
1. Adequate	Inadequate
2. Inadequate	Adequate
3. Inadequate	Inadequate
4. Adequate	Adequate

FIG. 5–6. Correlations between dietary ingredients, nutrition, and dental caries are exceedingly difficult, because it is necessary to distinguish between the nutritional requirements of the host animal and those of the pathogenic microorganisms involved in the carious process. The requirements for the host and for the microflora may differ widely. An eating pattern which is adequate or satisfactory for one may or may not be favorable for the other. (From Keyes, P. H. and Jordan, H. V. Mechanisms of Hard Tissue Destruction, Am. Assoc. Advance Science, Wash. D.C., 1963.)

Since 1900 the per capita consumption of sugar (sucrose) in many countries of the world has steadily risen and there has been a concomitant increase in tooth decay. In some of the Scandinavian countries, for example, dental caries is not only highly prevalent but often very severe. Several comprehensive reports have implicated the ingestion of large quantities of sugar in this elevated caries rate. This is not to imply that the intake of sucrose is the only dietary ingredient which contributes to caries activity, but there are abundant data which indicate that this carbohydrate in particular has a high caries-conducive potential.

While there is little disagreement about the importance of refined carbohydrates, the relative caries conduciveness of different types of carbohydrates needs further clarification. As previously mentioned, lesions are occasionally found in the pits and fissures of teeth from persons who consume diets containing cereal products but little refined carbohydrate-containing food. The intake of refined, processed foods and "sweets" is associated with an increase in caries attack on all coronal surfaces especially on the buccal, proximal, and labial smooth surfaces. On root surfaces, carious lesions do not appear to be closely related to sucrose intake.

Experimental work with the rat and hamster is helping to clarify the role of carbohydrates and caries. The following points seem to be emerging: (1) Animals can eat a diet containing adequate amounts of nutrients essential for normal growth, development, systemic health, and satisfactory reproduction and yet experience dental cavities. (2) Diets differ widely in their "cariogenic" potential. Some favor lesions in pits and fissures, others favor smooth surface activity, and still others, root surface changes, but there can be overlapping of activity with certain diets. (3) The quantity of food eaten, its texture and physical consistency, the concentration of carbohydrate in the diet, and the frequency of eating, all affect the activity of the disease. (4) Negligible caries develops if watery diets are consumed or are intubated directly into the stomach. (5) The chemical structure of the carbohydrate consumed is also important. Caries is less active when starches, and monosaccharides (dextrose and fructose) are substituted for sucrose. Thus, in the experimental animal, activity of the disease may be altered at will by appropriate changes in any of the aforementioned dietary and feeding conditions.

Recent work has disclosed that the streptococci which are responsible for caries in hamsters produce not only acid from sucrose but also a watery, slimy polysaccharide substance. Certain strains of streptococci found in humans also produce this substance and form gummy colonies on culture plates (Fig. 5–7). This substance may be partly responsible for plaque formation. The tendency for organisms to form plaque depends to a degree on the type of carbohydrate

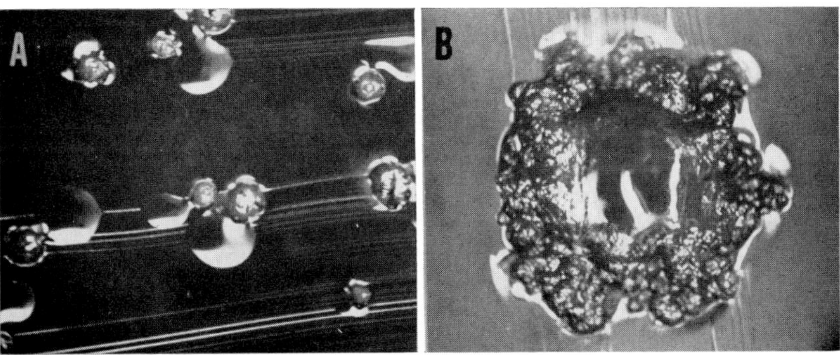

FIG. 5–7. *A,* When caries-conducive streptococci from the hamster grow on a culture plate containing sucrose, they produce lactic acid and a watery polysaccharide slime which can be seen as droplets of liquid flowing away from sides of the colonies. *B,* A large colony of human streptococci (*Streptococcus salivarius*) forms viscous slime and acid in the presence of sucrose. This extracellular slime may favor the formation of plaque on tooth surfaces. (Courtesy, H. V. Jordan, National Institute for Dental Research, Bethesda, Md.)

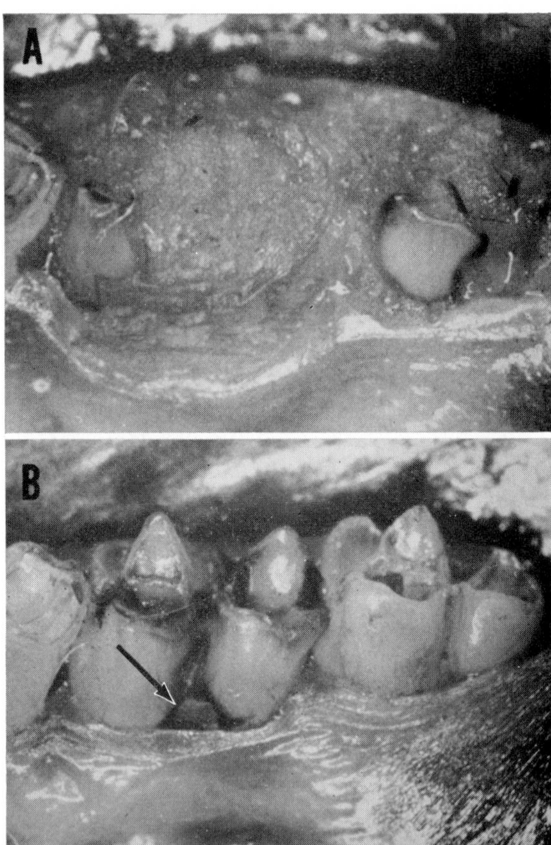

FIG. 5–8. The control of dental caries activity by alteration of conditions in one of the factorial groups. *A,* Extensive plaque and caries destroyed the teeth of an animal continuously fed a diet containing 56 per cent sucrose for 39 days. *B,* Teeth of an animal which was fed the diet containing sucrose for 8 days and then placed on a diet containing 56 per cent hydrogenated potato starch in place of sucrose for 31 days. Most of the bacterial plaque disappeared and the lesion which started while the animal was on sucrose (arrow) progressed at a very slow rate. Far less active caries also occurred when glucose and fructose were substituted for the sucrose. Similarly appearing arrest of caries has been found when infected animals have been topically treated with fluoride solutions or gels or with various antibiotics such as penicillin, erythromycin, or vancomycin. (Photographs courtesy, Prof. Göran Frostell, National Institute of Dental Research, Bethesda, Md. and Royal Dental School, Stockholm, Sweden.)

fed to the hamster. Abundant plaque forms when animals, which harbor caries-conducive streptococci, eat a diet containing sucrose, but when fructose, glucose, and certain hydrogenated starches are substituted for sucrose, the amount of plaque which develops is strikingly less, and the disease becomes less active (Fig. 5–8). Although acid production by the bacterial cells may not be appreciably changed, there is less tendency for the organisms to form plaque. As a result the acid produced from these monosaccharides and starches is not concentrated on tooth surfaces but is rapidly dispersed in the oral cavity, swallowed, or neutralized. In Sweden today, some candies are being manufactured from hydrogenated potato starch sweetened with sugar substitutes, because bacterial fermentation of these products occurs slowly and the high terminal acidities associated with sucrose are not produced. If the human situation turns out to be somewhat comparable to the animal, less slime should be formed when the oral microflora metabolizes such products, and conditions conducive to the formation of plaque might be less favorable. The animal findings do not suggest that simple sugars and all starches are "harmless," but they do suggest that these substances may be less caries-conducive than sucrose, particularly for certain types of lesions. Indeed, if this turns out to be the case in man, less hazardous sugar substitutes can be recommended in dietary programs for caries control.

Human experimentation has also shown that the frequent consumption of sugar, especially between meals is associated with increased dental caries. The Vipeholm Dental Caries Study was conducted in institutionalized persons in Sweden by allowing selected patients additional amounts of sugar either during or between meals. After several years of observation, it was found that caries activity increased when sugar was consumed in a sticky form which tended to remain on or in the vicinity of the teeth for prolonged periods of time. The disease became more active when patients consumed sugar in the form of sticky taffy or caramels. However, if the sugar was ingested in a form that was more rapidly cleared from the oral cavity, lesion formation did not increase rapidly. Sugar ingested in solutions with meals in quantities up to twice that usually consumed did not "distinctly" increase caries activity. The disease became less active after withdrawal of sugar supplements from the diet.

A direct and consistent relationship between dental caries experience in the deciduous dentition and the frequency of eating items of high sugar content between meals has been demonstrated by Weiss and Trithart. As the frequency of between meal snacking for preschool children increased, there was a corresponding increase in dental caries activity (Fig. 5–9). Studies in experimental animals have also shown that caries activity decreases if the frequency of eating is restricted.

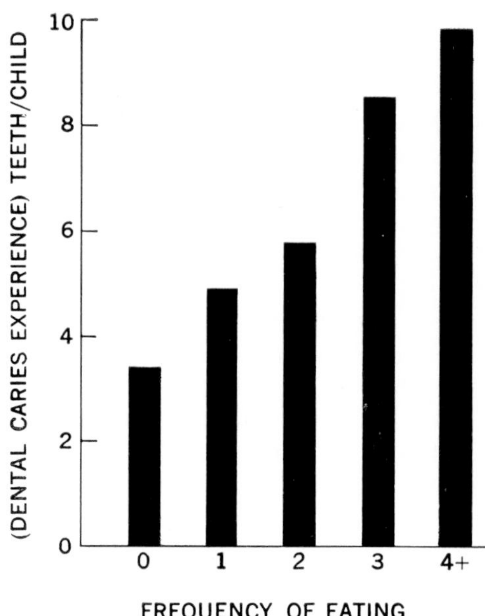

FIG. 5–9. Dental caries experience in the deciduous teeth of children according to frequency of between meal eating. Children who snack more frequently tend to have greater caries activity. (Adapted from Weiss and Trithart. Am. J. Pub. Health, *50,* 1103, 1960.)

Becks, Jensen, and Millar were able to control dental caries effectively in a large number of patients by the virtual elimination of fermentable sugars, and in some cases starches. They recommended the substitution of high protein diets containing meat, eggs, fish, milk, and milk products. It has been also well established that dental caries activity is negligible in diabetic children who are carefully maintained on their prescribed low carbohydrate diets.

Severe cases of dental caries can be effectively controlled for prolonged periods of time by the periodic restriction of carbohydrate foods for six week periods. Jay has offered dietary recommendations that many patients accept more willingly than those which advocate continuous restriction of these foods. The dietary program consists essentially of three, two-week diet plans which start by limiting the daily intake of carbohydrates to 100 grams with no free sugar allowed. This is followed by a two-week regimen in which most carbohydrates, but no sugar, can be consumed. In the last period, sugar is allowed at one meal per day. Patients are then put on a maintenance program which is not highly restrictive, but they are cautioned to refrain from the intake of snacks containing sugar between meals.

Severe curtailment of carbohydrate consumption is generally difficult for economical and psychological reasons. Carbohydrates are inexpensive, and they furnish a readily available source of energy. Candies, confectionery products, carbonated beverages containing sugar, and other "sweets" occupy a fairly well established place in contemporary civilized diets. Many persons derive pleasure and satisfaction from them; therefore, it is difficult to change their eating habits drastically. As a practical alternative it would seem important to prescribe forms of carbohydrate that have the least caries-conducive potential, to recommend sugar substitutes, and to eliminate the most hazardous eating patterns.

From the foregoing remarks, it should be apparent that the process of dental caries is related to eating patterns as well as to dietary ingredients. Evidence to support the contention that the disease is dependent upon nutritional deficiencies (malnutrition) in man is not convincing. This lack of dependence has been abundantly confirmed in laboratory animals. Rats, hamsters, and occasionally higher primates, have been fed a wide variety of diets in which essential nutrients have been deleted or added to excess. The effect of vitamins, minerals, proteins, and fats have been studied in various ways. However, there are no data which show that any of these substances are of basic etiological importance. When animals eat more than normal amounts of certain salts and fats, caries activity may diminish somewhat, probably because the food additive has a minor local effect on either the bacteria themselves or on their acidic by-products. Furthermore, laboratory experiments designed to investigate the relationship between dental caries and nutrition are often difficult to evaluate, because the experimental conditions (challenges) imposed may affect not only the host but also his eating patterns. Therefore, when both oral and systemic conditions are altered, the results of two variables must be interpreted. Consequently, it may be impossible to elucidate the mechanisms responsible for any given observed anti-caries effect.

Factors in the Host and Teeth

It has not been possible to identify a large group of factors in the host which affect caries activity. An inadequate flow of saliva has been associated with increased caries susceptibility, probably because of the resultant loss of buffering capacity and poor oral clearance of food residues. Some workers have reported the isolation of caries-inhibitory substances (thiocyanates and anti-lactobacillus factors) from the saliva of caries inactive persons, but the significance of these findings is not fully understood. The shape and arrangement of the teeth may have a slight influence on the distribution of lesions if a person has acquired the infection. Crowded and malaligned teeth may favor food and bacterial retention. The dental hygienist should be aware of the fact that calcium cannot be withdrawn from the enamel of fully formed erupted teeth via the bloodstream. Endocrine disturbances, diseases affecting blood and bone metabolism, vitamin D deficiency, and pregnancy cannot directly mobilize mineral from erupted teeth and cause an increase in decay. Any increase in dental caries that may occur during pregnancy results from a change to undesirable eating patterns rather than absorption of calcium from the teeth by the dental pulp or saliva.

Effects of Fluorides

Enamel deficient in the fluoride ion is more vulnerable to demineralization and cavitation than enamel which contains a high fluoride concentration. The anti-caries effect of fluoride in enamel is one host factor which is not only impressive but also widely recognized. The discovery of the relationship between fluoride salts in drinking water and resistance to dental caries constitutes an exceedingly important advance in the field of preventive dentistry. Enamel surfaces which contain "adequate" concentrations of the fluoride ion are less susceptible to caries attack. Persons who continuously consume from birth water containing approximately one part per million (1 ppm) of fluoride develop, on the average, far fewer cavities than persons not fortunate enough to consume such water throughout life.

The studies which disclosed the benefits of fluoride began with surveys in communities where an enamel defect (mottled enamel) was endemic. It was observed that, although mottled teeth were discolored and sometimes structurally defective, they were far less susceptible to tooth decay. However, mottling of the teeth generally did not occur unless the water contained above 2 ppm of fluoride, and it did not occur in persons who consumed such water after their teeth had been completely formed. Many studies have shown that enamel fluorosis is not caused by the posteruptive effect of fluoride, but rather by its effect on the cells (ameloblasts) which produce the enamel during tooth formation.

Observations on children by Dean and his associates in a total of 21 American cities showed that dental caries experience, *i.e.*, numbers of decayed, missing and filled (DMF) teeth, was consistently less when the natural fluoride concentration of water approximated 1 ppm, and that mottled enamel was not a problem at this low level. Although natural fluorides in water had been associated with less dental caries, it was necessary to determine whether the addition of controlled amounts of fluoride salts to fluoride-deficient water would result in similar protection against decay. Accordingly, starting in 1944, the dental caries experience of children was determined in Grand Rapids, Michigan; Newburgh, New York; Evanston, Illinois; Brantford, Ontario, and other cities which had a negligible amount of fluoride in their water supplies. Then in each of these cities the water was "fluoridated" to a level of 1 ppm. In every instance, dental caries has been reduced approximately 60 per cent (Fig. 5–10). Comparable children living in nearby non-fluoridated cities have not experienced reductions. That this protection against dental caries persists throughout adulthood in persons continuously imbibing fluoridated water was demonstrated in Colorado Springs, Colorado, and in Aurora, Illinois. It was later demonstrated that mean annual tempera-

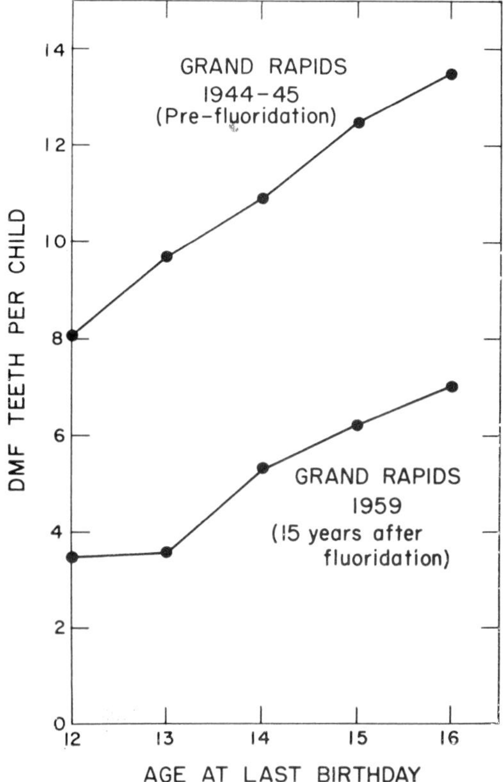

FIG. 5–10. Effect of controlled fluoridation on dental caries experience of children, aged 12-16 years, in Grand Rapids, Michigan. The children were examined, and in 1945 the fluoride concentration of the water was adjusted to 1.0 ppm. Fifteen years later children of the same ages who had consumed fluoridated water continuously had significantly less caries activity. (Adapted from data of Arnold, F. A., Jr., Likins, R. C., Russell, A. L., and Scott, D. B. J. Am. Dent. Assn., *54,* 780, 1962.)

ture affected amounts of fluoride ingested by influencing the volume of water consumed. Persons living in warmer climates may drink more water and receive maximum protection from dental caries at fluoride concentrations as little as 0.7 ppm. Additional field, clinical and laboratory studies have shown that continuous consumption of water containing approximately 1 ppm of fluoride, and even higher concentrations are non-toxic. Other findings have suggested that persons who consume fluoridated water are likely to experience less periodontal disease than those who do not.

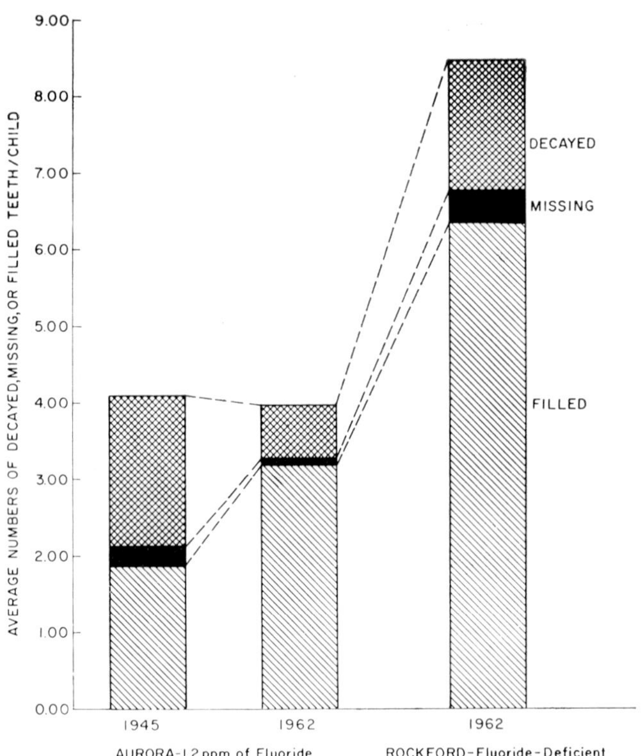

FIG. 5–11. Comparison of average dental caries experience for lifetime residents, aged 13–16 years, of Aurora, Ill. and nearby Rockford, Ill. Aurora has had an optimum concentration of naturally fluoridated water (approximately 1.2 ppm of fluoride) for over 50 years, while Rockford water is flouride-deficient. Adolescents in Aurora were examined in 1945 and their counterparts of the same ages were examined 17 years later in 1962. The Rockfordians, 13-16 years old, were examined in 1962. Little change occurred in the overall dental caries experience of the Aurorans in 17 years, but a greater proportion of decayed teeth were found to be filled in 1962 than in 1945. The dental caries attack for Rockfordians has been more than twice that for Aurorans. (Adapted from data of Englander, H. R. Int. Den. J., *14,* 497, 1964.)

The communal water of Aurora, Illinois, contains approximately 1.2 ppm of naturally occurring fluoride, and the water of nearby Rockford, Illinois, is fluoride-deficient (0.1 ppm). While it has been found that the dental caries experience of natives of Aurora, aged thirteen to sixteen years, is less than half that of similar natives of Rockford, there seems to have been little overall change in the low dental caries experience for Aurorans in seventeen years (Fig. 5–11). However, dental care in Auroran children has improved, because there has been an increase in the proportion of carious teeth being filled. Apparently, dental caries rates in Aurora have remained essentially unchanged, and although they are low it would be helpful to reduce them even further. To achieve this objective, some dentists are advocating a therapeutic program which includes in addition to water fluoridation: topical applications of fluorides, less frequent between-meal eating, and proper oral hygiene measures.

Mechanism of Fluoride Action

The manner in which fluoride "suppresses" dental caries is not fully understood. Numerous studies indicate that it probably exerts its effect in several ways: (1) by making the enamel more resistant to acid demineralization; (2) by inhibiting the bacterial intracellular enzyme systems which convert sugars into acids; (3) possibly by preventing microorganisms from deriving benefit from the breakdown and invasion of enamel and dentin.

Numerous studies have shown that dental enamel is less soluble in acids when its crystalline structure contains fluoride. No other chemical agent has been found which has this effect on enamel solubility. All of the reasons which account for this reduction in solubility are not known. If the apatite crystals in bone contain fluoride, they appear to be larger and more perfectly formed, a property which is believed to reduce solubility of crystalline materials. Enamel which contains optimum amounts of fluoride appears white and glassy, perhaps because its crystal structure is also better.

Fluoride can also limit acid production and affect growth of bacterial cultures. It has been reported that fluoride concentrations as low as 1 ppm can inhibit acid production, but concentrations in excess of 250 ppm are needed to affect the growth of streptococci and lactobacilli. It is not known whether the concentrations of *free* F ions in plaque of persons drinking fluoridated water ever reach a sufficiently high level to suppress the microorganisms or affect bacterial metabolism. It is conceivable that high concentrations of fluoride in topically applied medications—for example, as gels or pastes applied in mouth applicators—can have a direct antibacterial effect, indeed one approaching lethal levels.

Observations in hamsters have disclosed that enamel surfaces of molars treated with fluoride do not decay even when they have plaques of caries-conducive streptococci growing on them. However, the color of the plaques appears white instead of yellow and the amount of the deposit is less than on untreated teeth. The suggestion has been made that the enamel surface containing fluoride may affect bacterial activity adversely, because the acids produced by the fermentation of sugars cannot be neutralized by the enamel surface; moreover, other substances (carbonate and phosphate) which the bacteria use are not released and made available by the demineralization process.

It is generally believed that the optimal benefit from ingestion of fluoride occurs if some can be acquired during the process of tooth formation. Additional amounts are acquired topically from the ingestion of foods and liquids containing fluoride after eruption, and fluoride concentration continues to build up on the outer surfaces of the enamel throughout life. When contact with the fluoride ion is essentially derived from low concentrations (1 ppm) in drinking water, the systemic effect may be more important. When more concentrated solutions of fluoride are applied to the molars of hamsters (5000 ppm), very beneficial post-eruptive effects can be demonstrated, but pre-eruptive effects are not impressive. Indeed, under the experimental conditions used no protection against new lesion formation results when fluoride is intubated, injected, or fed only during the period of tooth formation. The *post-eruptive* effect is undoubtedly important no matter what the source may be. Recent studies suggest that in persons consuming fluoridated water even greater protection against caries can be derived by topical applications of fluoride in solution, in a prophylactic paste, and in a dentifrice. In the laboratory, it is necessary to apply very high concentrations of fluoride frequently to retard lesions which have already formed and are active. The possibility that similar results can be duplicated in human beings needs exploration.

PATHOLOGICAL CHARACTERISTICS

The general term caries (derived from the Latin word for "rottenness") refers to the molecular decay or disintegration of mineralized tissue. The word caries is always plural; a single carious lesion is not a "carie." Caries of the bone, usually caused by tuberculosis, may be referred to in medical texts as caries fungosa or caries sicca. When dental caries affects the crowns of the teeth, it causes dissolution and disintegration of the enamel and dentin. When it affects root surfaces, the cementum and dentin are destroyed.

Since the dental hygienist may play an important auxiliary role in the prevention of dental caries, it is important for her to recognize the different types of lesions, to appreciate the difficulties often associated with their diagnosis, and to understand some of their gross and microscopic characteristics.

An excellent technic of learning about various types of carious lesions is by direct visual examination of the defects in extracted teeth. Since it is not difficult to obtain extracted teeth with carious lesions, students are urged to obtain specimens and to examine them under a low-power binocular microscope or some other type of magnifying instrument which will enlarge the field 10 to 15 times. Teeth should be preserved in 10 per cent neutral formalin (10 cc. of Formaldehyde Solution per 90 cc. of water plus enough calcium carbonate to give a neutral test with litmus paper). The lesions should be examined while wet, after the teeth have been rinsed in water. The full extent and pattern of bacterial plaque formation on the various tooth surfaces can best be appreciated by an application of a few drops of basic fuchsin, F.D. and C. No. 3 (green), erythrosine, or other disclosing solutions.

After the gross lesions have been examined, representative types should be x-rayed and sectioned. Several kinds of sections can be prepared, depending upon the facilities available. Simple grinding on a stone wheel with water or a single cut through the center of lesions with a steel or carborundum disc will reveal many interesting details. In more ambitious projects the teeth can be imbedded in clear plastic* and then cut in half or sliced serially. This makes an excellent permanent preparation showing both the outside and inside of lesions, which can be used for teaching purposes. Most of the specimens illustrated in this text have been treated in this manner.

Carious lesions may be classified into three principal types according to their anatomical locus of initiation on the tooth surface as follows:

Pit and Fissure Caries

The most prevalent lesions originate in the crevices on coronal surfaces. With the exception of buccal pits on molars and lingual pits on incisors, most of the crevicular lesions start in the "pits and fissures" on the occlusal surfaces of the molars and premolars.

Smooth Surface Coronal Cavitation

Lesions which begin on the proximal and facial (smooth buccal and labial) surfaces are referred to as smooth surface types. Lingual surfaces may be affected in cases of rampant disease.

*Ward's Bio-Plastic, Ward's Natural Science Establishment, Inc., Rochester New York and Monterey, California.

Root Surface Caries

In older persons with gingival recession, lesions often develop in the cementum and spread into the underlying dentin. Such lesions are occasionally seen in primitive persons who have had severe periodontal disease, but in such cases carious lesions on coronal surfaces may be exceedingly rare.

Pit and Fissure Lesions

These lesions may not be easily recognized until they have reached a fairly advanced stage of development because the crevices in which food residues impact and bacteria grow may be exceedingly small. Often there is only a thin covering of enamel over the dentin at the bottom of deep pits and fissures. Consequently, if the carious process starts in the depths of these crevices it can readily penetrate through the enamel and invade the dentin (Fig. 5–12). Once invasion of the dentino-enamel junction has occurred, conditions in the lesion tend to favor highly active demineralization of dentin. Food residues, especially fermentable carbohydrates, may continue to become impacted or seep into the lesions and provide excellent substrates for caries-conducive bacteria. In such instances there is little opportunity for sufficient amounts of saliva to penetrate and neutralize the acid produced before demineralization occurs (Figs. 5–12, 13, 17).

From a study of pit and fissure lesions, it is easy to understand why some investigators have believed that dental decay begins within the tooth itself. Indeed, the origin of carious lesions was a controversial matter for many centuries. Galen (130-210 A.D.) held that abnormal conditions in the blood affected teeth internally (pulpally), causing lesions, and even John Hunter (1728-1793) reasoned that caries originated internally. However, during the 19th century most writers on the subject recognized that caries started on the external surfaces of the teeth, that it was associated in some way with food residues, and that acid demineralization was involved. No one who has carefully studied the lesions of dental caries doubts that the defects start on the external surfaces.

The portal of entry through a pit may be so minute that even the fine point of an explorer may not "catch" in it. However, as illustrated in Figures 5–12 and 13, after the carious process has channelled into the dentin, there may be extensive undermining beneath "normal" enamel. If conditions favor progression of caries activity, undermining may affect all cusps coalescing with lesions which have had their origin on other surfaces (Fig. 5–17). Biting pressure will eventually crack off the enamel of a severely undermined crown, exposing a large plug of denuded carious dentin.

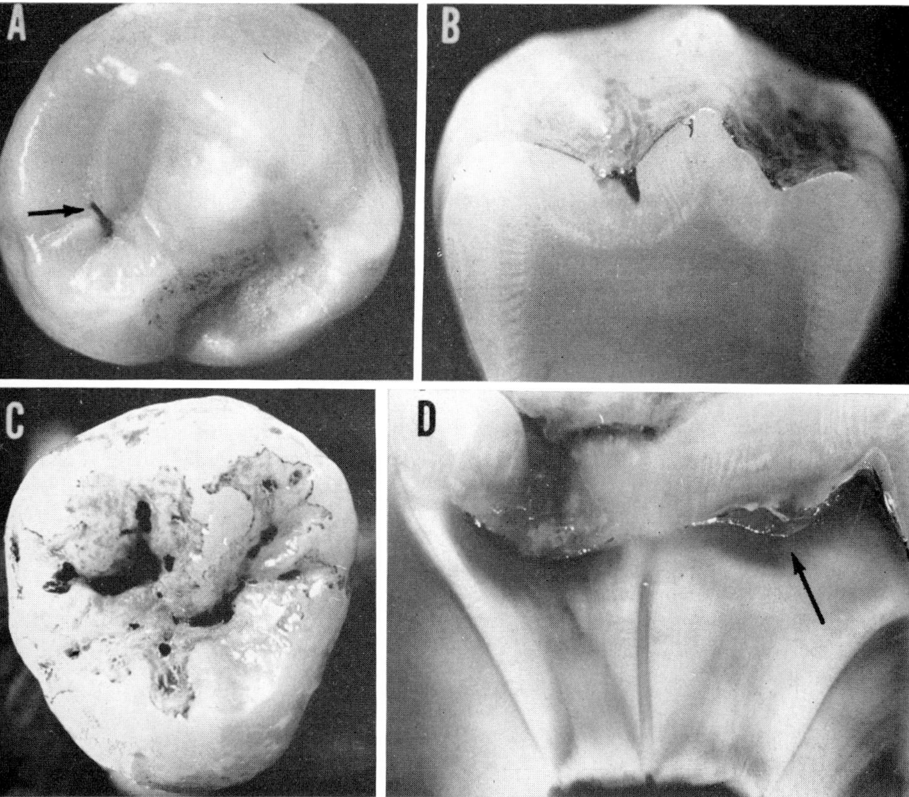

FIG. 5–12. Carious lesions in occlusal pits and fissures. *A,* Occlusal view of a mandibular right first premolar extracted from a young person. The small dark spot at the bottom of the mesial fossa (arrow) is a minute developmental defect (pit) which would favor impaction and retention of food residues and the colonization of acidogenic bacteria. *B,* The lingual surface of this premolar was ground away to show the depth and shape of the pit. A dye has been used to reveal bacterial plaque and debris in this vulnerable area. *C,* The occlusal surface of a maxillary third molar has been stained to disclose bacterial deposits on the surface and in two "pit and fissure" areas. Because such areas are filled with plaque and can be probed with an explorer, one would anticipate dentin involvement at the bottom of the openings, but the amount of subcuspal demineralization is often more than expected. *D,* Cross section of lesion seen in the more central fossa shows path of entry and spread of decay along the amelo-dentinal junction. The decayed dentin beneath the cusp (arrow) was caused by an expanding lesion which originated in the other fissure. The portal of entry is not shown.

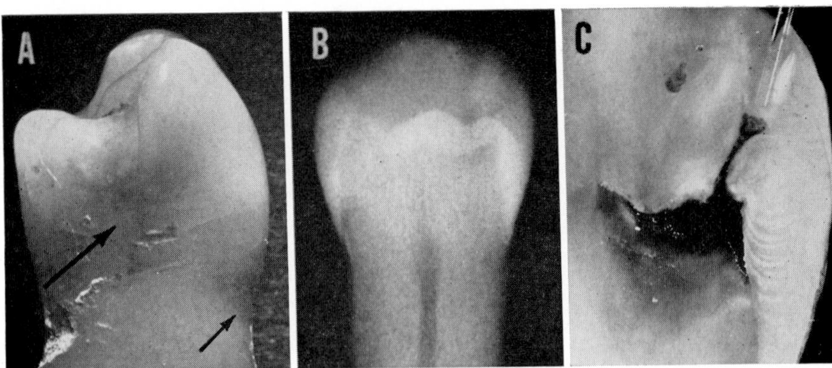

FIG. 5–13. *A,* This lower left premolar extracted from an older patient showed only minor changes indicative of caries. The occlusal pit was filled with hard, dark brown material and there was no visible opening or defect. Beneath the enamel slight discoloration and changes in translucency could be seen by transmitted light (large arrow). Root surface caries (small arrow). *B,* Radiograph showed only minor radiolucency beneath occlusal enamel. *C,* Mesio-distal ground section through the occlusal lesion reveals former portal of entry and sub-enamel cavitation. Very little evidence of enamel demineralization is apparent. The occlusal pit became occluded, and activity in the lesion diminished markedly or stopped. A single nylon bristle from a toothbrush has been placed over the opening to the lesion to show that it could not be possible to dislodge food residues and bacterial deposits in such areas by brushing the teeth.

Obviously, caries activity does not occur in all occlusal crevices (Fig. 5–19). Among the several possible reasons for this is that impacted food residues of persons subsisting on diets of coarse and unrefined carbohydrates are only slowly fermentable. Furthermore, gritty foods, frequently eaten by more primitive peoples, cause abrasion of the cuspal surfaces and result in a dentition that is less conducive to retention of food deposits. In other cases, pits and fissures become occluded with organic or mineralized deposits which prevent further ingress of bacteria and food residues.

Smooth Surface Caries

In the more active cases of dental caries, which occur in the deciduous and permanent teeth of children, an increasing number of lesions tend to form on the proximal and facial surfaces (Fig. 5–14). Clinical impressions and laboratory findings suggest that the very frequent ingestion of foods containing sucrose by small children and young adults is especially conducive to rampant caries on smooth surfaces. It seems reasonable that the bacteriological and dietary factors associated with smooth surface lesions differ from those which produce pit and fissure activity. This difference has been discussed from time to time over the past sixty-five years, and is well illustrated by the divergent opinions between Miller, and Williams and Black.

Miller did not believe that bacterial plaques were important in the etiology of caries, because he felt that food deposits established a nidus for bacterial growth and acid production. He was able to

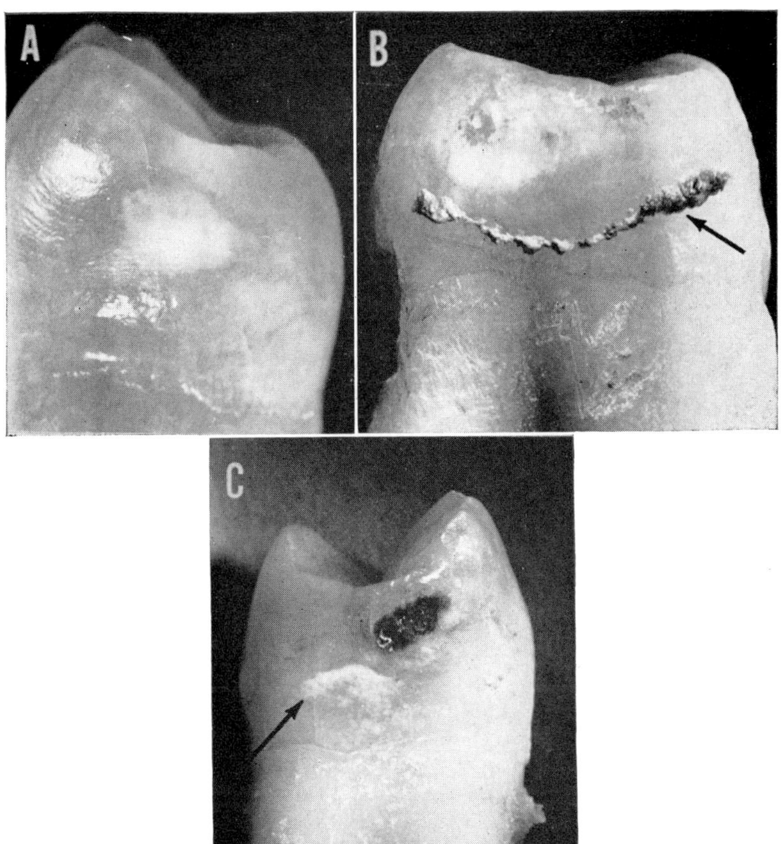

FIG. 5–14. Incipient lesions on proximal surfaces. The so-called "white spots" opacities are caused by subsurface demineralization. There is no loss of contour and surface gloss in the earliest stages of such lesions which are not detectable in radiographs. *A,* Opaque change in the distal surface of the mandibular premolar whose occlusal surface is shown in Figure 5–12*A*. *B,* White spot on mesial surface of maxillary third molar shown in Figure 5–12*C*. Arrow points to deposit of calculus. Caries and periodontal disease may occur simultaneously, contrary to some prevalent opinions. *C,* Area of demineralization (arrow) on proximal surface of maxillary premolar has developed below an oval discolored lesion. This may represent new caries activity, because highly pigmented areas generally are believed to be relatively inactive.

demonstrate that teeth were demineralized after they were incubated with substrates containing fermentable carbohydrates and acidogenic bacteria. From the results of his *in vitro* tests, performed under highly artificial conditions, he postulated that retained carbohydrate residues in "pits and fissures" and in interproximal spaces were conducive to bacterial activity which produced acid and coincidental demineralization of the teeth. Other microorganisms which would attack protein were believed to be responsible for the lysis of the dentin after it had been demineralized. No single species of microorganism was thought to be involved. Because this appears to be a logical sequence of events not many persons have questioned it. However, recent evidence indicates that this sequence of events does not occur in the same order on smooth surfaces. Indeed, the streptococcal strains which are odontopathic and cause severe destruction of dentin in gnotobiotic rats and in conventionally reared hamsters are not proteolytic when tested by common laboratory methods. Moreover, bacterial plaque, responsible for coronal caries, will not develop in hamsters fed a high sucrose diet unless specific strains of acidogenic streptococci are present (Figs. 5–3 and 8).

The initiation of lesions in *non-retentive* areas (smooth surfaces) was first explained by observations of Williams (1897) and Black (1898). They observed tenacious accumulations of bacteria, "gelatinous microbic plaques," on these surfaces. Substances produced by the organism in plaques were thought to be responsible for caries activity. These observations have been well substantiated in both man and experimental animals. When factors in the oral environment are favorable, tenacious bacterial plaques form on the tooth surfaces. These microbial mats absorb many of their essential nutrients (sugars) from foods which dissolve in the mouth during the process of ingestion.

Bacterial plaques on smooth surfaces can be readily disclosed by the application of the various dyes to teeth in the mouth as well as to those which have been extracted. If factors in the plaques have been conducive to dental caries, changes in the underlying enamel can be detected after such deposits have been removed. The incipient changes in enamel, occurring before obvious softening and cavitation occurs, appear as superficial white opaque areas (Fig. 5–14). The "white spots" usually become more distinct as they dry out in moistened teeth, or when specimens are illuminated by transmitted light (Fig. 5–22).

Although incipient smooth surface lesions can be detected on the labial and buccal surfaces of the teeth, the earliest stages of interproximal lesions are impossible to diagnose clinically, because contact of one tooth with another obscures direct observation of the surfaces, and radiographs are not sensitive enough to register the earliest stages of demineralization. Some of the difficulties related to diagnosis of incipient lesions can be appreciated by a study of the photographs in this chapter; however, greater insight can be gained by comparing lesions in extracted teeth with their radiographic appearance.

When smooth surface caries is active, the acid by-products in the bacterial plaque penetrate into the enamel causing a conical or wedge-shaped pattern of demineralization pointing towards the

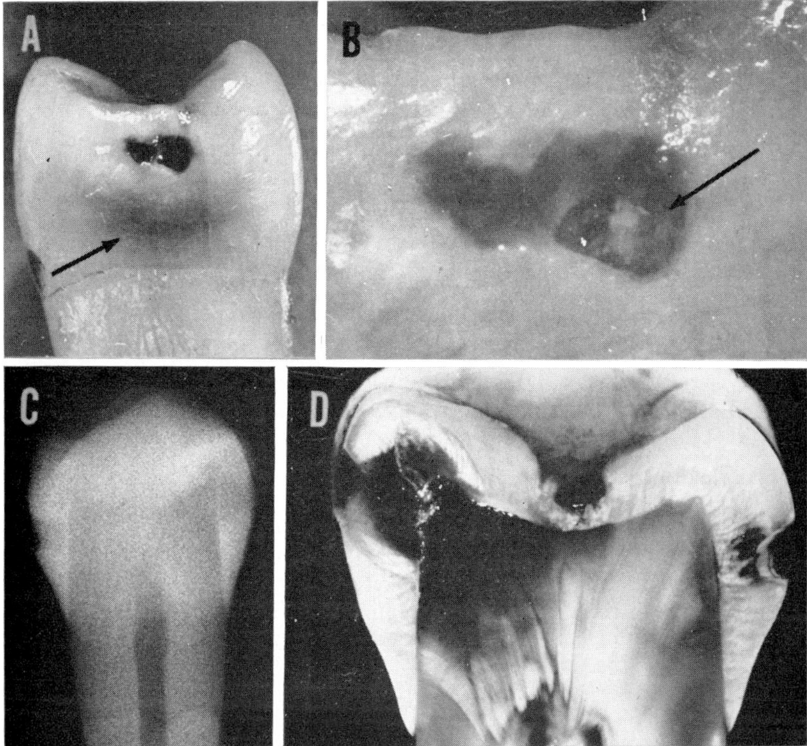

FIG. 5–15. Maxillary second premolar which had active carious lesions on mesial, occlusal and distal (MOD) surfaces. *A,* The carious lesion on the distal surface had penetrated the enamel and caused considerable sub-surface decay. The discolored dentin beneath the enamel appears as a shadow in the photograph (arrow). *B,* This lesion has been enlarged to show the actual bacterial plaque on the surface of the partly decomposed dentin (arrow). *C,* Radiograph shows radiolucent changes on both mesial and distal surfaces. *D,* Sectioned specimen. Cavitation of the distal surface was associated with appreciable sub-surface spread of decalcification in the enamel of the marginal ridge as well as extensive demineralization of dentin. This lesion has almost reached the pulp horn. In the occlusal groove, the carious process penetrated the enamel and partly coalesced with the larger proximal lesion. Early cavitation on mesial surface had just penetrated the dentin.

dentino-enamel junction. The physico-chemical and biological processes which account for the surface changes and the pattern of invasion are not completely understood despite extensive study of this phenomenon. After the dentino-enamel junction has been reached the dentin is rapidly destroyed by the acid and other by-products of bacterial metabolism. The enamel continues to become demineralized and softened so that eventually its structural form is lost, resulting in frank cavitation (Figs. 5–15 and 17). Simultaneously bacteria from the plaque invade the enamel and dentin through microscopic open-

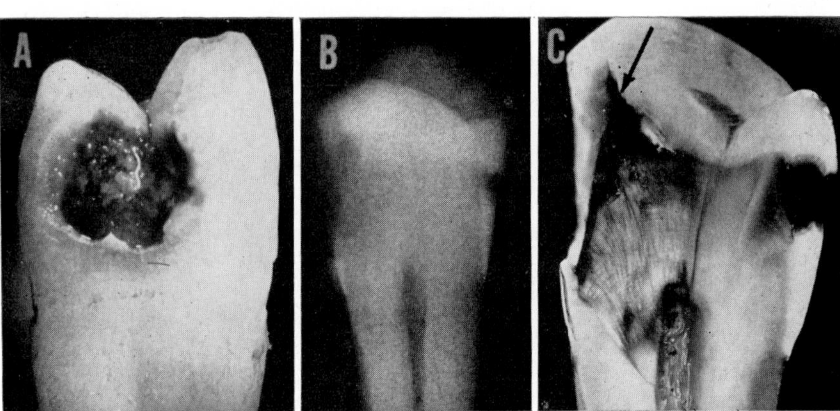

FIG. 5–16. *A,* Maxillary premolar with an extensive proximal lesion. The marginal ridge had been undermined and crumbled away under the forces of mastication. Note bacterial colonies on surface of decaying dentin. *B,* Radiograph reveals discrete lesions on the mesial and distal surfaces. *C,* Although this lesion appears considerably larger than that shown in Figure 5–15, highly demineralized dentin, seen as a homogeneous dark area (arrow), was not more extensive. Beneath the demineralized dentin, there are opaque changes in the dentinal tubule that extend to the pulp. This is associated with degeneration of the odontoblastic processes.

ings and channels which form after disruption of the crystalline structure of the enamel. It is probable that the invading bacteria benefit from the carious lesion because they find the environment of the cavity favorable for reproduction and survival. Inasmuch as bacteria do not grow as well in a highly acidic environment, their growth and activity may be improved if the acid they produce is buffered by its reaction with the tooth mineral (hydroxyapatite). In the process of being neutralized, the acids also release small amounts of carbon dioxide, phosphate, and other substances derived from the tooth which the bacteria can use in their metabolic processes. Moreover, the lesion offers the highly anaerobic conditions which many of the microorganisms require.

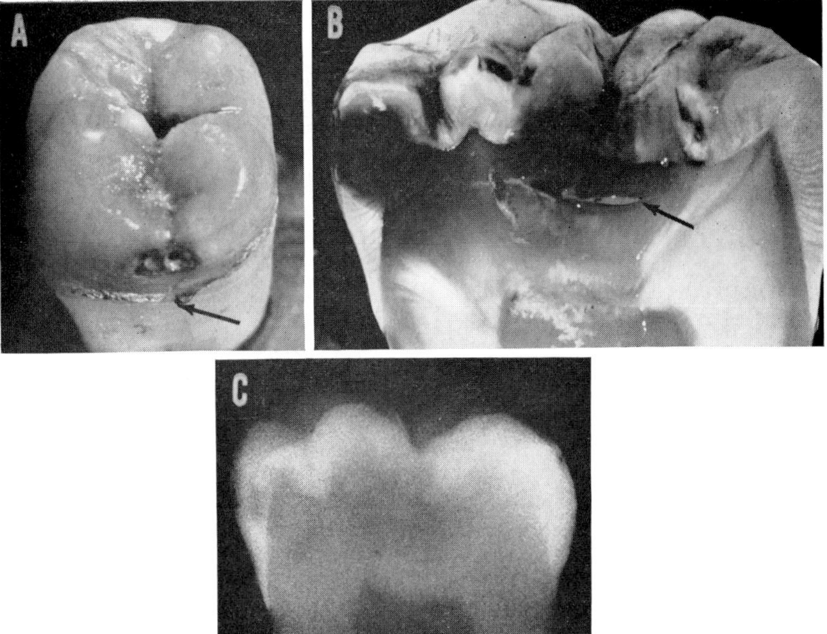

FIG. 5–17. *A,* Mandibular second molar with coalesced carious lesions. On the occlusal surface an obvious "pit" lesion can be seen in the central fossa and bacterial plaque and debris has accumulated in the mesial groove and fossa. On the mesial surface there is a proximal lesion with a calcareous deposit below it (arrow). *B,* Sectioned specimen shows coalescence of occlusal and proximal lesions with extensive demineralization and relatively few opaque dentinal tubules. The process had reached the pulpal horn and little secondary dentin had formed. The highly demineralized dentin was not completely infiltrated with the plastic embedding material. As a result a shrinkage artefact (arrow) appeared when the softened dentin was exposed to the air. *C,* Radiograph of tooth indicates coalescence of demineralized dentin beneath marginal ridge and occlusal enamel.

Coalesced Lesions

Carious lesions often start on several areas of the teeth simultaneously and coalesce beneath the marginal ridges and cusps (Figs. 5–15 and 17). Since the outward appearance of the tooth may not be markedly changed, an untrained person may overlook the not-too-obvious signs of the disease. Patients with severe caries are often unaware of their problems, because lesions may not be painful until the pulp has become infected, and even then there may be little discomfort. Occasionally it is possible for the dentin of molar teeth to be almost totally demineralized beneath the overlying enamel. Since

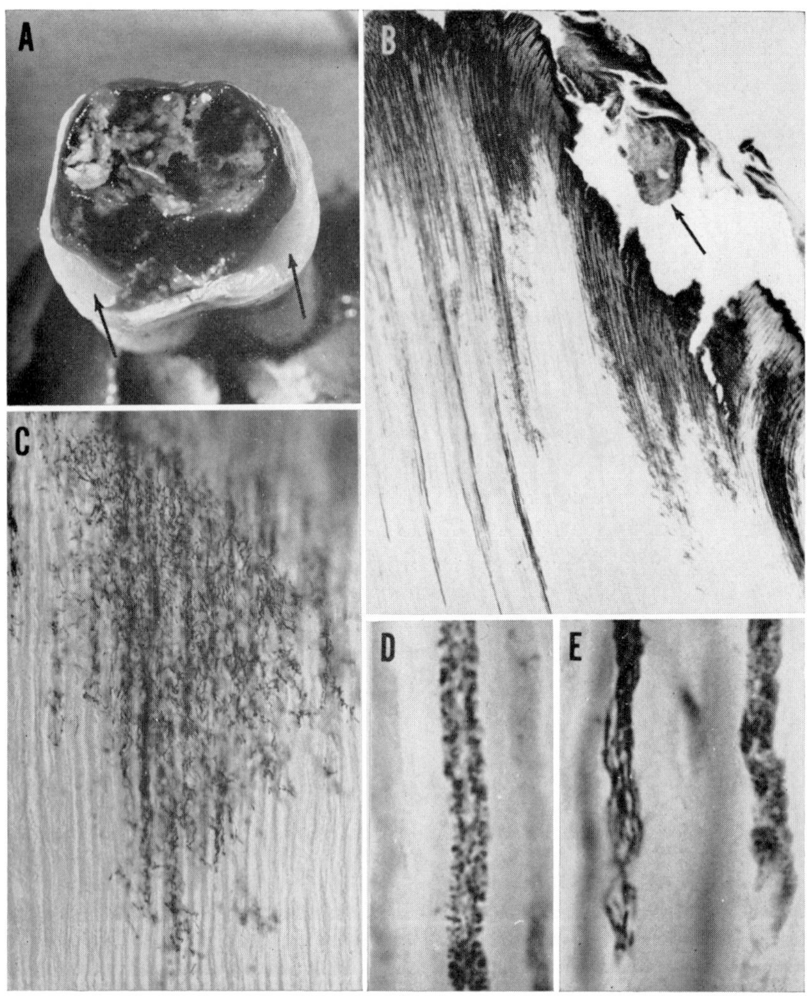

FIG. 5–18. *A,* Mandibular second molar almost totally devoid of enamel. The enamel covering this crown crumbled away at the time of extraction and only remnants remained near the cervical line. Although almost all of the coronal dentin had been demineralized, it retained its original shape remarkably well. The dark demineralized dentin stands out in marked contrast to the small amounts of normal dentin (arrows). Colonies of microorganisms have spread across the dentinal surface and are grossly visible as white plaques. *B,* Histological section of this dentin shows bacterial deposits on the surface (arrow) and bacteria invading some of the dentinal tubules. It is apparent that decalcification has spread far in advance of bacterial invasion. *C,* Masses of filament forming microorganisms have spread in a random pattern in one zone. *D,* Coccoidal shaped bacteria in a dentinal tubule. *E,* Cocci and filaments in nearby tubules. The cocci tend to invade more rapidly and deeper than the filaments. All sections stained by the Gram's method.

the dentin retains its structural form, proteolytic mechanisms could not have been highly active. When the enamel shell crumbles away, as sometimes happens during the process of extraction, the entire dentinal portion of the crown may be found in its original form with discrete colonies of bacteria growing on the outer surface (Fig. 5–18). Histological sections made of such material show masses of bacteria on the surface of the dentin and zones in which microorganisms have invaded the tubules and softened dentin. Gram-positive spherical forms, filaments, and rods can usually be found within the dentinal tubules (Fig. 5–18). However, it is apparent from histological studies and assays of demineralized dentin that demineralization antecedes bacterial penetration. Presently, opinions differ on whether or not all dentin altered by demineralization should be excavated before insertion of a filling, particularly when there is risk of pulp exposure. Some clinicians feel that it is better to remove only the highly softened dentin and to leave the partly softened layer undisturbed so that the vital pulp can recede and deposit secondary dentin. This will usually occur if the lesion is properly sealed off from the oral environment. Non-irritating antibacterial agents may be temporarily sealed in such cavities before permanent restorations are placed.

Root Surface Caries and Erosion

Patients with periodontal disease often experience recession of the gingival tissues. When this happens, microbial plaques on the root surfaces may cause destructive changes in cementum and dentin. The conditions which favor these changes apparently differ somewhat from those which cause caries on the enamel. The cemental surface may be softened along the cervical line and the enamel directly coronal to it may not be appreciably affected (Figs. 5–19 and 21). As previously mentioned, root surface lesions in the hamster are associated with filament forming microorganisms which colonize on the root surfaces, especially when the diet contains considerable amounts of carbohydrate (Fig. 5–4). It is quite probable that some human root surface lesions are induced by similar filaments and dietary substrates. The etiological agents involved in root surface caries appear to differ from those of coronal lesions.

Defects from mechanical abrasion or chemical erosion may be found on crowns and root surfaces, but these are not usually considered the primary result of bacterial action. A hard, clean defect may result from improper toothbrushing, the sucking of lemons, or the frequent intake of highly acidic juices (Fig. 5–21). The effects of mechanical abrasion may be superimposed on root surface caries.

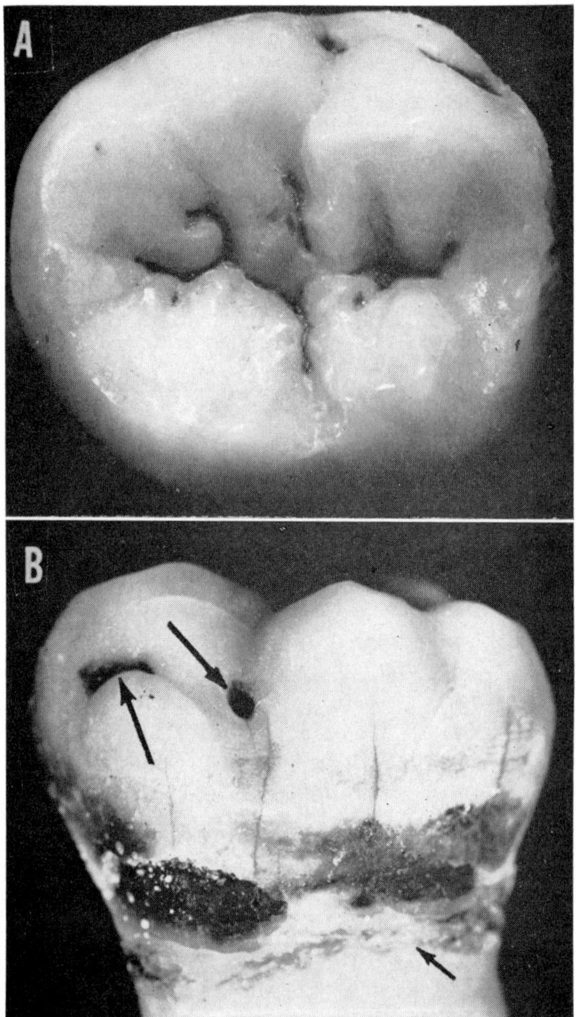

FIG. 5–19. Mandibular first molar extracted from an older person with periodontal disease. *A*, The pits and fissures on the occlusal surface, filled with dark brown material, showed no gross evidence of caries and no apparent activity in ground sections. *B*, Buccal surface shows two buccal pits which were not carious (large arrows). Caries activity had involved the cervical area and destroyed some of the enamel, cementum, and dentin. Small arrow points to calcified deposit. The fact that these three conditions: caries-free pits, cervical caries, and calculus, can occur so close to one another, indicates that the intensity of disease conducive factors can vary widely within a very short distance on the tooth surface. See Figure 5–4 as another example.

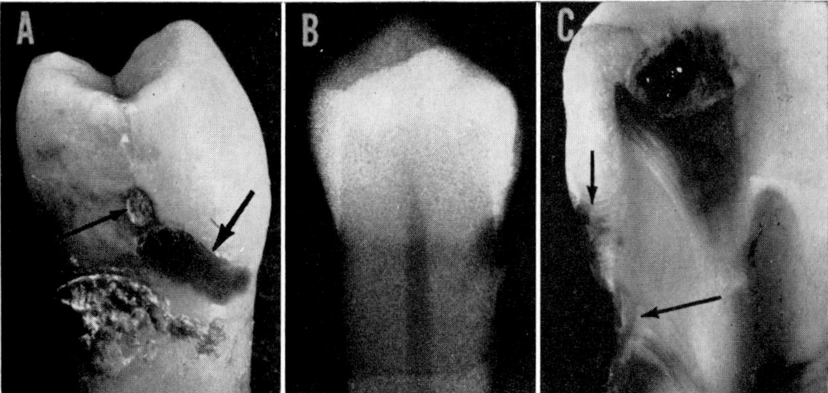

FIG. 5–20. Mandibular premolar with several types of carious lesions. *A,* Proximal surface shows: (1) superficial etching of the cervical enamel (small arrow); (2) dental caries which has affected the root surface (large arrow); (3) an inactive occlusal "pit" lesion; (4) a large calcified deposit. *B,* Radiograph shows the root surface demineralization and calcified deposit. The occlusal surface lesion cannot be detected. *C,* Sectioned specimen. The occlusal surface lesion appears larger than outward changes in enamel would suggest. However, this lesion was not highly active. Sub-surface decalcification was slight and the coronal pulp cavity was filled with secondary dentin. The superficial etching in the cervical enamel (short arrow) was probably related to the plaque which induced the root surface lesion (long arrow).

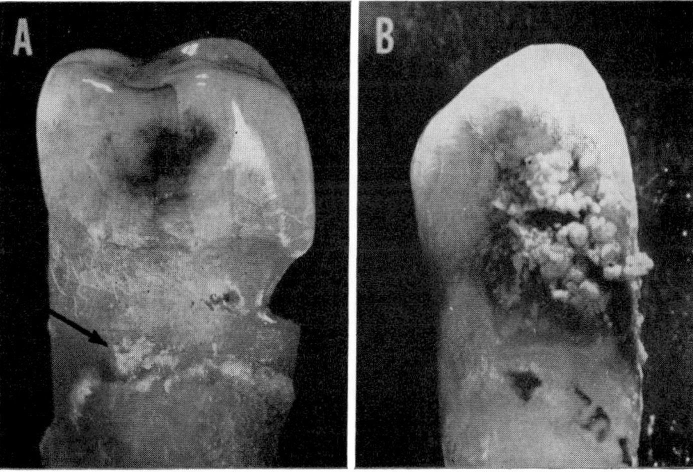

FIG. 5–21. *A,* Mandibular second premolar from an older person shows occlusal wear, an arrested proximal lesion, and a wedge-shaped area of abrasion in the cervical area of the buccal surface. Arrow points to remnants of periodontal tissue. *B,* A mandibular first premolar with large deposit of bacterial plaque. Although the enamel surface has not been appreciably affected, considerable root surface demineralization has occurred.

Arrested Carious Lesions

Theoretically dental caries will stop if contributing factors in any one of the etiological groups are sufficiently changed. In laboratory animals, this can be demonstrated by changing the diet, by altering the frequency and duration of ingestion, by fortifying the teeth with sufficient fluoride, and by suppressing or eliminating bacteria. In man, changes in diet and eating habits probably account for the arrest of most lesions. Obviously, many persons never alter their eating regimen sufficiently to affect their disease picture. Caries activity then

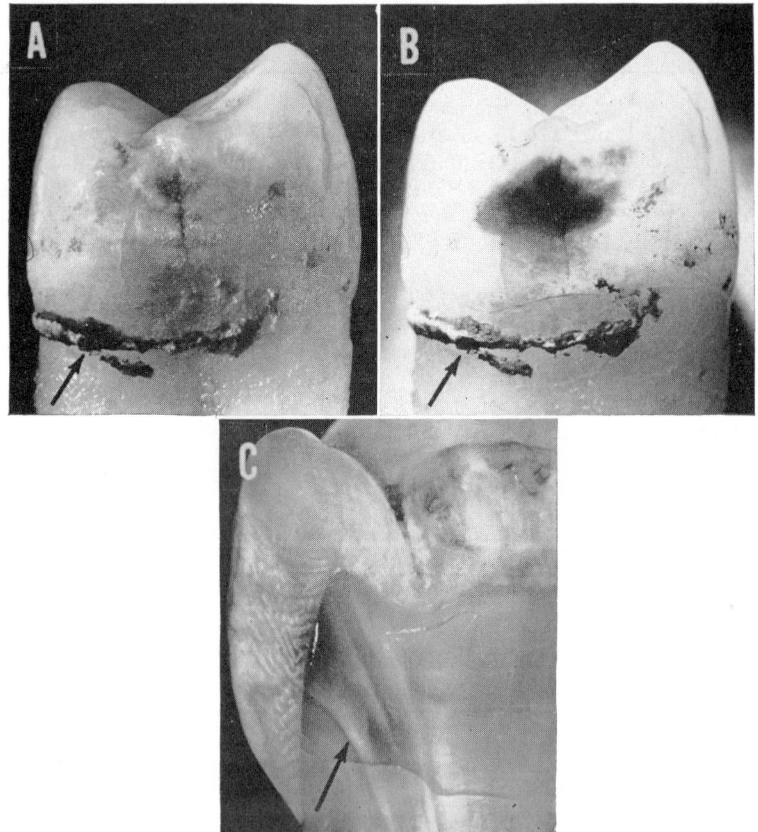

FIG. 5–22. Arrested carious lesion in a maxillary premolar extracted from a patient with periodontal disease. *A,* Proximal surface shows variable discoloration and negligible opacity under reflected light. *B,* Same area viewed by transmitted light reveals actual zone of enamel which had been demineralized and partially invaded. Arrow points to deposit of calculus. *C,* Section through lesion shows wide wedge-shaped zone of enamel penetration. In the underlying dentin which was only slightly demineralized along the amelodentinal junction, an opaque tract of tubules (arrow) extends about halfway to the pulp chamber. Caries activity did not affect the occlusal fissure.

progresses until almost all vulnerable surfaces are affected. Some persons, knowingly or unknowingly, may reduce their frequency of carbohydrate intake or otherwise change their eating habits enough to arrest the disease. Consequently, the lesions may not progress further because the pathogenic bacteria may disappear or greatly diminish in number. Arrested lesions generally discolor, becoming dark brown or black (Fig. 5–22 and 23). If the original cavity was fairly large and the overlying enamel breaks away exposing the

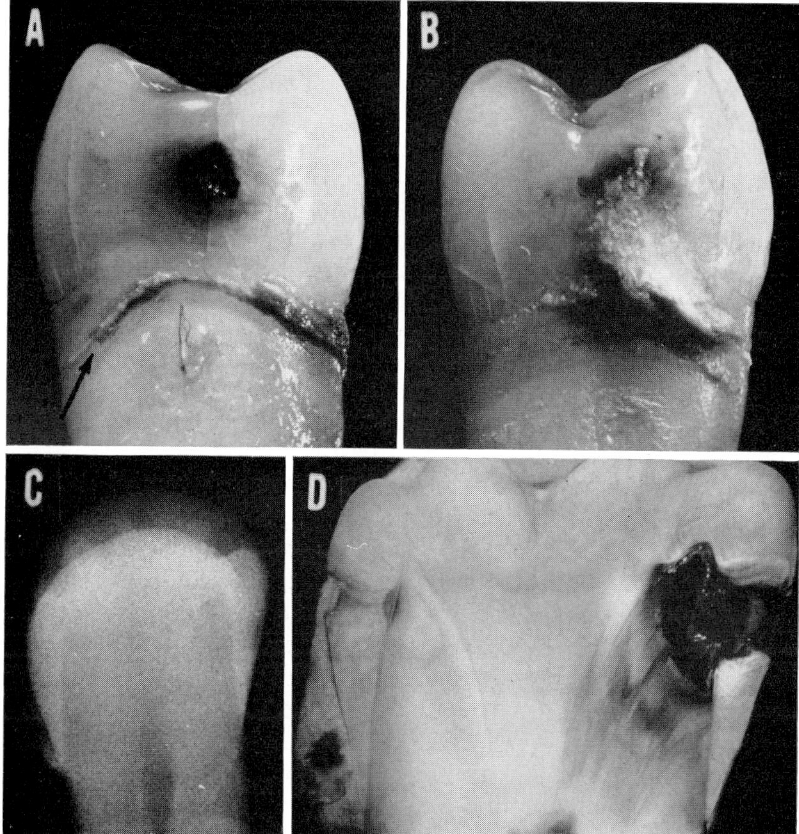

FIG. 5–23. Arrested proximal caries in a maxillary premolar. *A,* Mesial surface shows a highly pigmented (black) carious defect which did not appear to be active. Arrow points to calculus. *B,* Large mass of calculus covers cervical line and smaller carious defect on distal surface. *C,* Radiograph reveals mesial lesion but not the distal one. D, Section through tooth confirms impression that lesions were not active. In the larger lesions, the demineralized dentin had turned black and the underlying tubules were both highly pigmented and opaque. The degenerative changes in the odontoblastic processes had not reached the pulp chamber. Only minor changes affected the dentin under the lesion filled with calculus.

carious defect to the washing, neutralizing, and mineralizing action of saliva; the carious dentin may become eburnated as well as discolored. The reasons for the discoloration of carious dental tissues are not fully understood, but apparently chemical changes in protein components are partly responsible.

Findings in the laboratory suggest that enamel, and possibly dentin may remineralize. From time to time, powders or pastes have been proposed for inducing remineralization in enamel slightly "decalcified" by caries activity. Such formulae, however, have not been extensively used. More recently there has been renewed interest in the possibility of mineralizing partially demineralized enamel. The work of Pigman indicates that solutions containing phosphate and fluoride can remineralize enamel that has been partially demineralized, *i.e.,* without destruction of the enamel matrix. It is conceivable that solutions or gels will be formulated which will favor remineralization of incipient carious lesions before development of cavitation and that such agents can be applied in mouth applicators under the supervision of dental hygienists.

CONTROL AND PREVENTION OF DENTAL CARIES

Highly effective control of dental caries depends partly upon measures which either reduce or eliminate the bacteria responsible, mitigate against the injurious acidic by-products, or prevent demineralization of the teeth. In laboratory animals, excellent control can be attained by changing conditions in each of the factorial groups illustrated in Figure 5–1. Beneficial results can be demonstrated: (1) by reducing the frequency of eating and limiting intake of readily fermentable carbohydrates, (2) by enhancing resistance of the tooth surfaces with agents such as fluoride, and (3) by suppressing cariogenic bacteria with antibiotics or other antibacterial agents. In man comparable results have been found, although it is more difficult to regulate conditions in humans than in animals. In order to achieve highly effective control of human dental caries it will probably be necessary to use several therapeutic measures which simultaneously influence diet, bacteria, and tooth resistance. Cases of rampant caries may require that all factors be controlled for a while.

Dietary Recommendations

The rationale for dietary regulation has been previously discussed. In practice, this means one should caution against the frequent intake of all foodstuffs which contain sucrose and readily fermentable carbohydrates. An optimal eating program for caries prevention reduces food intake to three times a day, eliminates nibbling between meals, particularly before bedtime. This, however is a rather difficult program for many parents and children to follow. Whereas in previous years dietary recommendations advocated drastic restrictions of most refined carbohydrates and "sweets," the current, more practical, trend is to recommend that intake of sweets be limited to once a day, preferably at meal time.

Acid production is related inversely to the rate at which certain carbohydrate substrates are cleared from tooth surfaces; accordingly, more rapid clearance is associated with less acid formation. The physical consistency and solubility of food is important, because the bacteria quickly use very soluble foods which can diffuse into the plaque masses and through the cell walls. Sucrose and other sugars penetrate rapidly and some are converted to acid within minutes after they are absorbed by the bacterial cell. The rate of diffusion of sugar into dental plaque also depends upon its concentration. Some microorganisms store sugars as intracellular polysaccharides and then continue to metabolize them, producing acids for long periods of time.

It should be re-emphasized that in patients with a serious dental caries problem there is great need for changes in dietary and eating habits (Fig. 5–24). An ounce of sugar eaten at one time will favor far

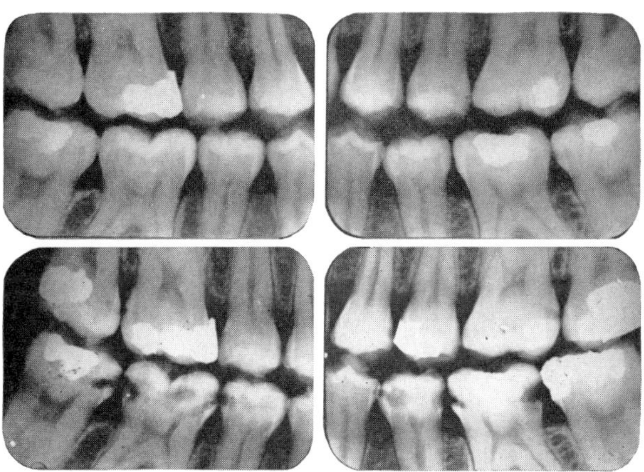

FIG. 5–24. Bitewing radiographs of an eighteen-year-old woman. Above, two films made in December, and below, comparable films made the following July. Note the apparent initiation of new lesions, and the remarkable progress of established lesions. Meanwhile, dental restorations had been placed in the upper right second premolar, upper right second molar, lower right second molar, and the upper left first and second molars. During the year prior to the July films this woman had moved from her home to an apartment and had changed many of her former eating habits. (Courtesy, David F. Mitchell, Indiana University School of Dentistry.)

less activity than the same total amount sucked in the form of hard candy several times during the day. Hence, the latter type of between meal eating pattern should be strongly advised against. Parents and patients may be instructed in the preparation of a simple diet history of food intake, which should be kept for five to seven days. A simple record of foodstuffs eaten at breakfast, mid-morning, lunch, afternoon, dinner, and before bedtime can enable the dentist or dental hygienist to identify those foods containing sugar and the frequency with which they have been eaten.

If between meal snacks cannot be eliminated, one should recommend such non-cariogenic foods as carrot sticks, celery strips, fruits, hard boiled eggs, cheeses, cold meats, unsweetened popcorn, nuts, and unsweetened milk, as substitutes for cookies, candies, and other sweets. Many of the snack items can be attractively arranged on a foil covered dish or tray and kept in the refrigerator. Jay and his group at the University of Michigan have published several recipes for the preparation of palatable non-cariogenic treats. Sugar-free soft

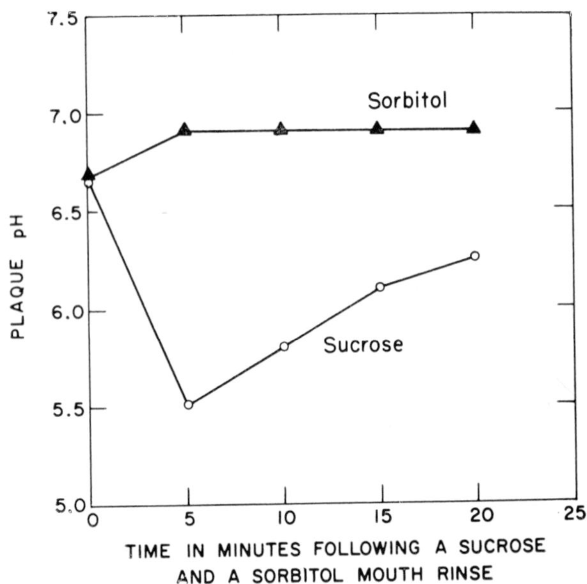

FIG. 5–25. Plaque acidity (pH) in a typical caries-active person given a one-minute sucrose and later a sorbitol mouth rinse. The pH values were measured before and at 5, 10, 15, and 20 minutes after the mouth had been rinsed for one minute. There was a precipitous drop in plaque pH after sucrose; whereas, no acid was produced when the mouth had been rinsed with the non-fermentable sugar substitute, sorbitol. If anything, the pH increased slightly after sorbitol because the sweet taste stimulated salivary flow and buffering action. (Adapted from data of Fosdick, Englander, Hoerman, and Kesel.)

drinks should be advised for persons who tend to develop carious lesions. Sugarless chewing gums or candies, sweetened with sorbitol, saccharin, or other sugar substitutes are confections which are not followed by a drop in plaque pH after ingestion (Fig. 5–25).

Oral Hygiene

In experimental animals, dental caries do not occur if the teeth remain free of bacterial deposits (plaque) regardless of the diet consumed. Theoretically, if it were possible to keep human teeth free of bacterial deposits, dental caries would not occur and periodontal disease would be minimal. Much can be achieved in plaque control by its mechanical removal with proper oral hygiene technics. This involves recognition of plaque, and as much removal as possible with brushes, effective dentifrices, dental floss, and rinsing. A disclosing solution may be a valuable aid in recognizing residual plaque. To be most effective oral hygiene measures need to be rigorously practiced at appropriate times. Many persons do not know the proper techniques for thorough removal of plaque and food debris nor do they understand the need for frequent and effective cleansing.

The dental hygienist occupies a unique position for teaching the principles of proper oral hygiene, and for providing information that will enable patients to receive maximum benefits from cleansing procedures. Instruction in oral hygiene should stress the proper technique and the appropriate timing of mechanical cleansing. The choice of a dentifrice should be a secondary consideration.

Arnim and Sandell have discussed a number of helpful measures for teaching oral hygiene to school children. They have suggested that acid production in bacterial plaques on the teeth may be demonstrated by using 0.02 per cent aqueous solution of methyl red.* In order to illustrate how the acid indicator dye reacts to changes in pH, a drop of the methyl red is placed on a clean glass slide or petri dish over a white background, and a few drops of water containing soap, or ammonia water, or other basic salt is added. This will cause an increase in the yellow color of the indicator, signifying an alkaline reaction. If another drop of indicator is placed on the slab together with a drop of acetic acid solution (white vinegar), the color of the indicator will change to deep red.

*Stock solution formula: In 100 cc. of distilled water dissolve 0.216 grams of Methyl Red, *water soluble pH indicator* (Harleco®). Store the solution in a Pyrex® glass bottle with a pipette dropper stopper. The working solution is made by adding 12 drops of stock solution to 4 cc. of distilled water, just prior to performing the experiment. Harleco is produced by Hartman-Leddon Co., Philadelphia, Pennsylvania.

In order to demonstrate in a convincing way the acidogenic potential of bacteria on the teeth, plaque can be scraped from tooth surfaces and placed on a slide. Two or three drops of the methyl red solution should be used to cover the material and a few drops of a sugar solution should then be added. If the plaque material has been obtained from persons who form acid quickly, the indicator will turn red within a matter of seconds. It may be necessary to add a few more drops of the indicator to the deposit and solution and mix them together with a small instrument in order to intensify the color.

Deposits on the teeth can be more readily observed by rinsing the mouth with a weak solution of basic fuchsin or by dissolving a tablet containing erythrosine (F.D. and C #3, red) in the mouth and swishing the colored saliva over the tooth surfaces. Methods for mechanical removal of the stained deposits can then be used to best advantage. Dental floss should always be used in conjunction with toothbrushing. Probably the best time to use dental floss is *before brushing,* as this will clear plaque from inter-dental spaces and allow better interproximal penetration of the dentifrice and any other agents that may be applied.

In order to remove plaque before dangerous acidities occur, some dentists advise that the teeth be brushed before meals as well as immediately afterwards. However, this is not always possible. Benefit will result from a careful brushing after breakfast, a mouth rinse after lunch if brushing is not possible, and another brushing after the evening meal. An especially careful cleansing is recommended before retiring.

Conscientious and skillful persons can achieve equally good cleansing of buccal, lingual, and occlusal surfaces with manual brushing as with electro-mechanical or automatic toothbrushing. However, the automatic tooth brush can clean faster, permits better cleansing by physically handicapped persons who have difficulty coordinating hand movements, and can be an incentive to children. It is doubtful whether tooth brushing, *per se,* can ever be totally effective in controlling cases of severe caries. Even in conscientious persons, it is not always technically possible to remove all accumulations of plaque and food residues from the depths of pits and fissures and from inaccessible proximal surfaces (Figs. 5–12 and 13).

In previous years dentifrices were considered primarily as toiletries and cosmetic agents designed to "whiten" teeth and "sweeten" the breath, but today many brands are being recommended as therapeutic agents in anticaries programs. Certain products have been "accepted" and highly advertised for such purposes. However, if oral hygiene is optimum, one dentifrice is likely to be almost as good as another. When oral hygiene is sub-optimal, some type of anti-caries agent incorporated into a dentifrice could be of value provided it diminishes plaque or delivers enough fluoride to tooth surfaces. However, better methods must be used for distributing the therapeutic dentifrice into pits and fissures, into interproximal spaces, and over other surfaces. Furthermore, it is also necessary to keep the active ingredients in a high enough concentration and for a long enough time to exert their effect. It is difficult to see how these objectives can be attained by *conventional methods of application* by means of a toothbrush or even a mouthwash.

Many compounds have been incorporated into the formulae of dentifrices in order to help eliminate plaque, render it harmless, and also to increase tooth resistance. The mode of action or rationale for the use of these substances has been as follows: (1) to reduce the numbers of acidogenic bacteria by germicidal action: hexachlorophene, penicillin, and other antibacterial agents; (2) to dissolve or denature plaque: urea, proteolytic enzymes, and oxidizing agents; (3) to prevent or retard acid development by various enzyme inhibitors: sodium N-lauroyl sarcosinate (SLS); (4) to neutralize acids in plaque: milk of magnesia and alkalizing agents; and (5) to increase tooth resistance: fluorides.

Fluoride Therapy

Fluoridation of community water supplies is an excellent public health measure since it is safe, effective, economical, and requires no additional individual effort. Presently about 70 million persons in over 5000 American communities enjoy the benefits of natural or controlled fluoridation, and the measure is being widely adopted in other countries of the world.

One might expect to find the following dental health benefits in a typical fluoridated city for persons consuming the fluoridated water continuously from birth: (1) The average person has about two-thirds fewer decayed, missing, or filled (DMF) permanent teeth, and the deciduous dentition of children is similarly protected. Protection of the permanent teeth persists throughout adulthood. (2) There is a striking reduction in lesions affecting the approximal surfaces of posterior teeth; therefore, fewer complicated multisurface fillings are required. (3) A very high percentage of the anterior teeth remain caries-free. (4) Caries-free persons are commonly found. (5) There is less tooth loss and, consequently, fewer adults are edentulous.

In recent years, tablets containing 1 mg. of fluoride have been prescribed for use by children not consuming fluoridated water. Daily use of one tablet appears to confer protection similar to that obtained from fluoridated water and provides about the amount of daily fluoride intake as would be obtained from fluoridated water. Probably greater benefit can be obtained from tablets, if they are slowly dissolved in the mouth at bedtime or used so that the fluoride is present in all the liquid consumed by the child. Adoption of either of these procedures favors the topical effect also. If tablets or other fluoride medications are quickly swallowed each day, the fluoride has little opportunity to combine with the surface enamel of the erupted teeth. The cost of fluoride tablets as a public health measure in the mass control of dental caries is greater than water fluoridation.

The value of topically applied (post-eruptive) fluorides against dental caries has been supported by numerous studies with enamel from extracted human teeth and in experimental animals. Indeed, there has been increasing evidence that enhanced protection occurs if the teeth are exposed to fluoride shortly after they erupt into the mouth. Apparently, the enamel surface is very reactive at this time and can absorb additional fluoride rapidly.

The affinity of enamel for fluoride has been the basis for the topical application of fluoride solutions in dental caries prevention. Since 1942, there have been numerous clinical trials testing the effectiveness of different solutions of fluoride salts on human dental caries, and

FIG. 5–26

this prophylactic measure is now widely used by dentists and hygienists, especially for treatment of children not consuming fluoridated water. In the early studies by Knutson and associates, a four-minute application of a 2 per cent solution of neutral sodium fluoride was made 4 times within a two week period to the dried teeth of children, aged three, seven, ten, and thirteen years. It has been found that children receiving the latter series of treatments develop about 40 per cent fewer cavities.

FIG. 5–27

FIGS. 5–26 and 27. Use of mouthpieces or applicators for applying drugs to the teeth. The school children in these pictures are applying a water-soluble gel containing 0.5 per cent fluoride to their teeth in custom-fitted vinyl mouthpieces. A thin film of gel is painted into each applicator which is then worn for six minutes each day. Applications are supervised by dental hygienists. It is possible for several hundred children to be treated in less than an hour. (Photographs provided through the courtesy of the Buffalo Evening News.)

A number of fluoride salts have been assessed *in vitro* and *in vivo* in order to find more effective or desirable compounds. Tin, lead, zirconium, and vanadium fluorides have been tested as well as fluorophosphates and organic fluorides. Opinion is presently divided on whether any of these compounds is definitely superior to the sodium salt, which has the advantage of being inexpensive, readily available, stable, and not unpleasant to taste. Furthermore, it does not stain the teeth. There appears to be merit in almost all topical fluoride formulations and techniques of application; for example: acidulated solutions with phosphate, mouthwashes, water soluble gels, and iontophoretic methods. At least one study with chewing gum has shown that fluoride can be picked up by enamel while the gum has been chewed.

From time to time various types of trays and mouthpieces have been advocated for the application of fluorides and other drugs to the teeth and gingivae. The purpose of these devices is to bring the medicament into intimate contact with the tissues, to prevent its dilution with saliva, and to keep it in place long enough to achieve a satisfactory therapeutic action. A miniature thermoplastic vinyl mouthpiece has been used to apply gels and powders containing fluoride to the molar teeth of hamsters. Two minute applications, 5 times a week, have produced beneficial results in the control of the dento-bacterial plaque associated with dental caries and periodontal disease. In a recent study with the hamster, dental caries has been prevented and periodontal disease minimized by repeated daily topical applications of gels containing 0.5 per cent fluoride ion. This has been accomplished by coating the gels on the teeth with a small camel's hair brush. Also, there is increasing evidence from human clinical studies that additional benefit can be attained by frequent applications of fluoride. We feel that it might be possible to use plastic mouthpieces in an oral hygiene program for human beings. The potential of this measure is now being assessed in school children who have been wearing custom-fitted vinyl mouthpieces (mouthguards like those used by athletes) which are coated with a water soluble gel containing 0.5 per cent fluoride. The applications are made daily by the children themselves under the supervision of dental hygienists (Figs. 5–26 and 27).

It seems more than likely that beneficial results in oral hygiene and plaque control could result from a formulation which contained: (1) a fluoride compound; (2) an antibacterial agent; (3) a stain for disclosing bacterial plaque; and (4) a mild abrasive agent and detergent. Such a formulation could be applied to the teeth and gingivae in an applicator, which could be worn for five to ten minutes. Persons with a serious caries problem might even continue the application for prolonged periods. Biting on the applicators would tend to force the paste or gel into pits, fissures, and other inaccessible areas. Since bacterial plaques and debris would be stained, the patient would be obliged to brush and floss his teeth immediately afterwards in order to remove these deposits. An even better result might be realized if, as a preliminary measure, the inderdental spaces were flossed and the teeth brushed and rinsed before application of the gel or paste.

The use of dentifrices containing fluoride is now an accepted procedure in a caries control program. Although toothbrushing has its limitations, theoretically such a measure would tend to replenish the fluoride ion on the enamel surface where the highest, and probably most important, concentration occurs. In view of the fact that some studies suggest that this layer can be removed by heavy polishing with strong abrasives, it would seem advisable to incorporate a fluoride compound in polishing agents which might tend to disrupt the surface layers. As a general policy, some form of topical fluoride application is indicated following plaque removal, scaling, and polishing of teeth.

Antibacterial Measures

All of the preceding measures for treating caries have depended upon indirect methods for controlling caries-conducive bacteria. Methods for sterilizing microbial plaques have not been extensively tested, although attempts along these lines can be traced back to Bunting and co-workers who applied Metaphen and aniline dyes to tooth surfaces in order to check bacterial overgrowths. It is well recognized that the bacterial ecology of the mouth is difficult to change, partly because it is highly dependent upon eating habits. Although various components of the oral microflora can be reduced by adequate local contact with antibacterial drugs, these bacteria tend to re-establish themselves rapidly, when the drug is discontinued.

Since an important infectious component is involved in the process of dental caries, it would seem reasonable to employ chemotherapy in the control of microbial factors, as is done customarily in the treatment of other infections. It is important to explore the potential of various antibacterial agents and to find methods for applying them effectively. The scope of professional responsibility for good oral health is rapidly widening. Today there is an increased concern for the mentally and physically handicapped child and adult, many of whom are unable to use conventional oral hygiene measures. Persons who suffer from inadequate salivary gland function (because of irradiation or surgery for facial tumors or primary degeneration of the glands) have serious problems with plaque control and caries activity. Comparable oral hygiene problems may be found in persons incapacitated with serious heart disease and strokes.

The proper administration of antibiotics or other antibacterial agents could be beneficial in the control of pathogenic plaque and its sequelae. In cases of rampant caries, it would seem desirable to suppress the microbial components while other anti-caries measures are brought to bear. Results from animal studies support these recommendations. In the animal a wide variety of antibiotics, which suppress gram-positive bacteria, have been applied in ways which assure an adequate concentration in the mouth, particularly on tooth surfaces and carious lesions. Beneficial agents have been effective in dispersion of plaque, in the arrest of existing lesions, and in the prevention of new lesion formation.

In anti-plaque therapy and caries control no one would suggest the haphazard, indiscriminate, or unsupervised use of powerful broad spectrum antibacterial agents. Comprehensive chemotherapeutic measures require: (1) selection of drugs which have a minimal tendency for inducing allergic reactions, and are non-irritating and non-toxic; (2) development of agents which will be selective against the pathogenic gram-positive bacteria, particularly those that form plaque, while having little effect on the normal flora; (3) drugs that should be inactivated and not absorbed in the lower part of the alimentary canal; (4) administration of the drugs which should not produce imbalances in the normal oral ecology and the overgrowth of other pathogens, *e.g.*, Candida albicans; and (5) methods of application which should assure sufficient concentration for an adequate time.

Although there are few published reports on the use of antibiotics to control caries, some dentists have prescribed troches containing antibiotics (penicillin), to control caries in persons who have lost function of their salivary glands and have dryness of the mouth from lack of normal secretion (xerostomia). Littleton and White found somewhat less active caries in children taking tablets of penicillin for the prophylactic control of rheumatic heart disease. More effective results might have been found if the tablets had been dissolved in the mouth before swallowing so that effective concentrations of penicillin would occur in saliva, since only about 1/100 of the antibiotic level in the blood is reached in salivary secretions.

Soon after penicillin became generally available, it was tested in dentifrice powders as an anticaries agent. The results of these trials have been inconclusive because one of the penicillin salts used was not readily soluble, and there was no way of assuring that an adequate concentration of the drug was maintained for a sufficient time by the method of application used—in this case toothbrushing. After persons realized that some individuals could develop a sensitivity to this antibiotic, further testing was discontinued.

Today, the use of antibacterial agents for suppression of plaque forming bacteria needs further exploration. At present, the number of antibacterial agents available is steadily increasing, and it should be possible to find or to develop some which are suitable for topical use in the mouth. Laboratory studies with hamsters have shown that dento-bacterial plaque and caries can be controlled by the oral administration (topical application) of vancomycin, an antibiotic effective against certain gram-positive bacteria. Mitchell and Holmes have assessed the plaque reducing potential of this drug in mentally retarded patients with poor oral hygiene and gingivitis. Very effective results were obtained by an application once daily for eight days of an adhesive paste containing approximately 3 mg. of vancomycin to the anterior vestibule of the mouth. Clinical improvements in oral hygiene have also followed sustained therapy with the antibiotics: chlortetracycline and spiramycin. There is little doubt that antibacterial adjuvants can be beneficial in oral hygiene programs. Not only are there many possible drugs but also there are numerous methods for administration, including adhesive pastes, adhesive powders which can be insufflated into the mouth, pastilles, troches, chewing gums, medicated gels which can be applied in plastic applicators, mouthwashes, and dentifrices.

Although the possibility of developing an anticaries vaccine has received attention from time to time, work toward this end has not been promising to date. Firstly, the bacteria implicated in the disease do not induce high levels of antibody in the circulating blood when repeatedly injected into animals (or human beings), and even if reasonable titers could be attained in blood, only small amounts would be secreted in the saliva. Perhaps one should consider dental caries as a superficial ectodermal disease, somewhat analogous to acne. Generally speaking, infections of this type are not effectively controlled by vaccines, but often respond favorably to chemotherapy.

EPILOGUE

With the knowledge available today, it is possible to develop a program which will effectively control dental caries, but in order to do so requires effort by the patient, the dentist, and the dental hygienist. It appears unlikely that there will be a simple panacea which will eradicate this infection. It should be re-emphasized that the best possible results will follow the simultaneous application of the principles described herein, and no one factor should be employed to the exclusion of others. Realizing that it is generally difficult to attain the maximum benefit from a single measure, one should strive to achieve as much as one can from diet regulation, oral hygiene, fluoridation, topical fluorides, and anti-bacterial measures.

To some extent in the development of measures for the control of dental caries, especial emphasis has been placed on the control of acids. Although few doubt that the control of bacterial acids would be of value, this measure by itself would still leave the patient with a potentially dangerous oral health problem unless the formation of plaque could be simultaneously controlled. One does not need to look far to find the serious consequences that occur when plaque continues to form in the *absence* of dental caries. The poor oral health, especially the severe periodontal disease, seen in many caries-free persons living under primitive conditions and in persons suffering from mental retardation or illness illustrates well what can happen. In this chapter, several photographs of teeth extracted from both young and older patients have shown calcified deposits a short distance from or even in carious lesions.

It is difficult to consider the treatment of caries without including the control of plaque forming microorganisms: either the rapid acidogens such as streptococci, the less rapid acidogens such as actinomycetes, or others. Regardless of the specific bacteria involved oral health is in great measure related to plaque control. In theory, if plaque can be controlled, the acidogenic reaction becomes relatively unimportant. As new therapeutic measures are advanced for the control and prevention of oral infection, the dental hygienist can play an increasingly important auxiliary role in the management of cases.

BIBLIOGRAPHY

ANDRESEN, V.: The physiological and artificial mineralization of the enamel. Oslow. Statens Tandlaegeinstitute. p. 93, 1926.

ARNIM, S. S., and SANDELL, P. J.: How to educate high school students in oral hygiene. JOPHERS, 1960.

ARNOLD, F. A., JR., LIKINS, R. C., RUSSELL, A. L., and SCOTT, D. B.: Fifteenth year of the Grand Rapids fluoridation study. J.A.D.A., *65,* 780-785, 1962.

ARNOLD, F. A., JR., and MCCLURE, F. J.: Observations on induced dental caries in rats. The effect of subcutaneous injections of fluorides. J. Dent. Res., *20,* 457-463, 1941.

ARNOLD, F. A., JR., MCCLURE, F. J., and WHITE, C. L.: Sodium fluoride tablets for children. Dent. Progr., *1,* 8-12, 1960.

AST, D. B., and FITZGERALD, B.: Effectiveness of water fluoridation. J.A.D.A., *65,* 581-587, 1962.

BECKS, H., JENSEN, A. L., and MILLAR, C. B.: Rampant dental caries: Prevention and prognosis; a five-year study. J.A.D.A., *31,* 1189-2000, 1944.

BIBBY, B. G.: Use of fluorine in the prevention of dental caries. I. Rationale and approach. J.A.D.A., *31,* 228-236, 1944.

BIBBY, B. G., and VAN KESTEREN, M.: The effect of fluorine on mouth bacteria. J. Dent. Res., *19,* 391-402, 1940.

BLACK, G. V.: Dr. Black's conclusions reviewed again. Dent. Cosmos, *40,* 440-451, 1898.

BLAYNEY, J. R.: A report on thirteen years of water fluoridation in Evanston, Illinois. J.A.D.A., *61,* 76-79, 1960.

BRISLIN, J. F., and COX, G. J.: Survey of the literature of dental caries 1948-1960. University of Pittsburgh Press, 1964.

BROWN, H. K., MCLAREN, H. R., and POPLOVE, M.: The Brantford-Sarnia-Stratford fluoridation caries study—1959 report. J. Canad. Dent. Assoc., *26,* 131-142, 1960.

BRUDEVOLD, F.: Fluorides in prevention of dental caries. Dent. Clin. North America, p. 397, 1962.

BRUDEVOLD, F., HEIN, J. W., BONNER, J. F., NEVIN, R. B., BIBBY, B. G., and HODGE, H. C.: Reaction of tooth surfaces with one ppm of fluoride as sodium fluoride. J. Dent. Res., *36,* 771-779, 1957.

BUNTING, F. W., NICKERSON, G., and HARD, D. G.: Further studies of the relation of bacillus acidophilus to dental caries. Dent. Cosmos, *68,* 931-942, 1926.

BUNTING, R. W., and PALMERLEE, F.: The role of bacillus acidophilus in dental caries. J.A.D.A, *12,* 381-413, 1925.

BURNETT, G. W., and SCHERP, H. W.: *Oral Microbiology and Infectious Disease.* 2nd ed., Baltimore, The Williams & Wilkins Co., 1962.

DEAN, H. T., JAY, P., ARNOLD, F. A., JR., and ELVOVE, E.: Domestic water and dental caries. II. A study of 2,832 white children aged 12-14 years, of eight suburban Chicago communities including L. acidophilus studies of 1,761 children. Publ. Health Rep., *56,* 761-792, 1941.

DEAN, H. T., ARNOLD, F. A., JR., and ELVOVE, E.: Domestic water and dental caries. V. Additional studies of the relation of fluoride domestic waters to dental caries experience in 4,425 white children aged 12-14 years, of 13 cities in 4 states. Publ. Health Rep., *57,* 1155-1179, 1942.

EMSLIE, R. D.: Cancrum oris. Dent. Prac., *13,* 481-495, 1963.

ENGLANDER, H. R.: Dental caries experience of teen-aged children who consumed fluoridated or fluoride-deficient water continuously from birth. Int. Dent. J., *14,* 497-504, 1964.

ENGLANDER, H. R., KESEL, R. G., and GUPTA, OM P.: The Aurora-Rockford, Ill. study II. Effects of natural fluoride on the periodontal health of adults. Amer. J. Pub. Health, *53,* 1233-1242, 1963.

ENGLANDER, H. R., and KEYES, P. H.: The prevention of dental caries in the Syrian hamster following repeated topical applications of fluoride-gels. J.A.D.A. (accepted for 1966 publication).

ENGLANDER, H. R., REUSS, R. C., and KESEL, R. G.: Roentgenographic and clinical evaluation of dental caries in adults who consume fluoridated versus fluoride-deficient water. J.A.D.A., *68,* 14-19, 1964.

ENGLANDER, H. R., SHKLAIR, I. L., and FOSDICK, L. S.: The effects of saliva on the pH and lactate concentration in dental plaques. J. Dent. Res., *38,* 848-853, 1959.

FITZGERALD, R. J., JORDAN, H. V., and STANLEY, H. R.: Experimental caries and gingival pathologic changes in the gnotobiotic rat. J. Dent. Res., *39,* 923-935, 1960.

FITZGERALD, R. J., and KEYES, P. H.: Demonstration of the etiologic role of streptococci in experimental caries in the hamster. J.A.D.A., *61,* 9-19, 1960.

FOSDICK, L. S.: The role of sugar in dental caries. J. Calif. St. Dent. Assoc., *26,* 1-8, 1950.

FOSDICK, L. S., ENGLANDER, H. R., HOERMAN, K. C., and KESEL, R. G.: A comparison of pH values of *in vivo* dental plaque after sucrose and sorbitol mouth rinses. J.A.D.A., *55,* 191-195, 1957.

FROSTELL, G.: Ny typ av s. k. tandvanliga sotsaker (A new type of presumably low-cariogenic sweets). Sv. Tandlak.forb. Tidning, *18,* 1-14, 1963.

GALAGAN, D. J.: Climate and controlled fluoridation. J.A.D.A., *47,* 159-170, 1953.

GIBBONS, R. J., and SOCRANSKY, S. S.: Intracellular polysaccharide storage by organisms in dental plaques. Its relation to dental caries and microbial ecology of the oral cavity. Arch. Oral Biol., *7,* 73, 1962.

GISH, C., and MUHLER, J.: Effect of dental caries in children in a natural fluoride area of combined use of three agents containing stannous fluoride: a prophylactic paste, a solution, and a dentifrice. J.A.D.A., *70,* 914-920, 1965.

GUSTAFSSON, B. E., QUENSEL, C. E., LANKE, L. S., LUNDQUIST, C., GRAHNEN, H., BONOW, B. E., and KRASSE, B.: The effect of different levels of carbohydrate intake on caries activity in 436 individuals observed for five years. Acta Odont. Scandinav, *16,* 232-364, 1954.

HARDWICK, J. L.: The incidence and distribution of caries throughout the ages in relation to the Englishman's diet. Brit. Dent. J., *108,* 1-9, 1960.

HARRISON, R. W.: Lactobacilli versus streptococci in the etiology of dental caries. J.A.D.A., *37,* 391-403, 1948.

HARVEY, R. F.: Clinical impression of a new antibiotic in periodontics; Spiramycine. J. Canad. Dent. Assoc., *27,* 576-585, 1961.

HILL, T. J.: Fluoride dentifrices. J.A.D.A., *59,* 1121-1127 (Dec.).

HILL, T. J., SIMS, J., and NEWMAN, M.: The effect of penicillin dentifrice on the control of dental caries. J. Dent. Res., *32,* 448-452, 1953.

HOLLINSHEAD, B. S.: Commission on the survey of dentistry in the U. S. The Survey of Dentistry, The Final Report, Washington, D.C. The Amer. Coun. on Education, 1961.

HOLLOWAY, P. J., JAMES, P. M. C., and SLACK, G. L.: Dental disease in Tristan da Cunha. Brit. Dent. J., *115,* 19-25, 1963.

HOPPERT, C. A., WEBBER, P. A., and CANNIFF, T. L.: The production of caries in rats fed an adequate diet. J. Dent. Res., *12,* 161, 1932.

ISSAC, S., BRUDEVOLD, F., SMITH, F. A., and GARDNER, D. E.: Solubility rate and natural fluoride content of surface and subsurface enamel. J. Dent. Res., *37,* 254-262, 1958.

JAY, P.: The reduction of oral lactobacillus acidophilus counts by the periodic restriction of carbohydrate. Amer. J. Odont. & Oral Surg., *33,* 162-184, 1947.

JAY, P., BEEUWKES, A. M., and MACDONALD, H. B.: Dietary program for the control of dental caries. The Overbeck Co., Publishers, Ann Arbor, Michigan, 1-28, 1959.

JENKINS, G. N.: The effect of pH on the fluoride inhibition of salivary acid production. Arch. Oral Biol., *1,* 33-41, 1959.

JOHANSSON, B.: Remineralization of slightly etched enamel. J. Dent. Res., *44,* 64-70, 1965.

KEYES, P. H.: Recent advances in dental caries research. Bacteriology. Internat. Dent. J., *12,* 443-464, 1962 (Dec.).

————: The infectious and transmissible nature of experimental dental caries. Arch. Oral Biol., *1,* 304-320, 1960.

KEYES, P. H., FITZGERALD, R. L. JORDAN, H. V., and WHITE, C. L.: The effect of various drugs on caries and periodontal disease in albino hamster. Arch. Oral Biol. Suppl., *7,* 159-177, 1962.

KEYES, P. H., and JORDAN, H. V.: Factors influencing the initiation, transmission, and inhibition of dental caries. Mechanisms of Hard Tissue destruction. R. F. Sognnaes, editor. Publication No. 75. Amer. Assoc. Advance. Sci. Washington, D.C., 1963.

KITE, O. W., SHAW, J. H., and SOGNNAES, R. F.: The prevention of experimental tooth decay by tube-feeding. J. Nutrition, *42,* 89-105, 1950.

KNUTSON, J. W.: Sodium fluoride solutions: Technic for application to the teeth. J.A.D.A., *36,* 37-39, 1948 (Jan.).

KOULOURIDES, T.: Remineralization of enamel and dentin. Dent. Clinic North America, 485-497, 1962.

KRASSE, B. O.: The effect of caries inducing streptococci in hamsters fed diets with sucrose or glucose. Arch. Oral Biol., *10,* 223-226, 1965.

LARSON, R. H., RUBIN, M., and ZIPKIN, I.: Frequency of eating as a factor in experimental caries. Arch. Oral Biol., *7,* 463-468, 1962.

LIND, V., STELLING, E., and NYSTROM, S.: Test of fluoride-containing chewing gum (in 229 children aged 11). Odont. Revy, *12,* 341-347, 1961.

LITTLETON, N. W.: Dental caries and periodontal diseases among Ethiopian civilians. Publ. Health Rep., *78,* 631-640, 1963.

LITTLETON, N. W., and WHITE, C. L.: Dental findings from a preliminary study of children receiving extended antibiotic therapy. J.A.D.A., *68,* 520-526, 1964.

MCCLURE, F. J.: Fluoride drinking waters. Washington, D.C. Superintendent of documents, U.S. Government Printing Office, PHS, Publication No. 826, 1962.

MCKAY, F. S.: The establishment of a definite relation between enamel that is defective in its structure, as mottled enamel, and the liability to decay. Dent. Cosmos, *71,* 747-755, 1929.

MARSHALL-DAY, C. D.: Nutritional deficiencies and dental caries in Northern India. Brit. Dent. J., *76,* 115-122, 1944.

MILLER, W. D.: *The Micro-organisms of the Human Mouth.* Philadelphia, S. S. White Dental Manufacturing Co., 1890.

MITCHELL, D. F., and HOLMES, L. A.: Topical antibiotic control of dentogingival plaque. J. Periodont., *36,* 202-208, 1965.

MUHLEMANN, H. R., MEYER, R., KONIG, K. G., and MARTHALER, T. M.: The cariostatic effect of some antibacterial inhibitors. J. Dent. Res., *40,* 697, 1961.

ORLAND, F. J., BLAYNEY, J. R., HARRISON, R. W., REYNIERS, J. A., TREXLER, P. C., ERVIN, R. F., GORDON, H. A., and WAGNER, M.: Experimental caries in germ-free rats inoculated with enterococci. J.A.D.A., *50,* 259-272, 1955.

PAMEIJER, J. H. N., BRUDEVOLD, F., and HUNT, E. E., JR.: A study of acidulated fluoride solutions. III. The cariostatic effect of repeated topical sodium fluoride applications with and without phosphate: A pilot study. Arch. Oral Biol., *8,* 183-185, 1963.

PIGMAN, W., GILMAN, E., POWELL, R., and MUNTZ, L.: The action of individual bacterial strains on human teeth under *in vitro* conditions. J. Dent. Res., *36,* 314-324, 1957.

PIGMAN, W., KOULOURIDES, T., and CUETO, H.: Rehardening of softened tooth enamel. Arch. Oral Biol. Suppl., 133-134, 1962.

ROGOSA, M., MITCHELL, J. A., and WISEMAN, R. F.: A selective medium for the isolation and enumeration of oral and fecal lactobacilli. J. Dent. Res., *30,* 682-689, 1951.

ROSEBURY, T.: The parasitic lactobacilli. Arch. Path., *38,* 413-437, 1944.

ROTH, L. H.: A report of long sustained therapy with chlortetracycline. Antibiot. Med., *1,* 13-19, 1955.

RUSSELL, A. L., and ELVOVE, E.: Domestic water and dental caries. VII. A study of the fluoride dental caries relationship in an adult population. Publ. Health Rep., *66,* 1389-1401, 1951.

RUSSELL, A. L., LEATHERWOOD, E. C., LE VAN HIEN, and VAN REEN, R.: Dental caries and nutrition in South Vietnam. J. Dent. Res., *44,* 102-111, 1965.

SCHIFFER, C. G., and HUNT, E. P.: Illness among children. (Data from U.S. Natl. Health Survey). U.S.P.H.S., Children's bureau. U.S. Govt. Printing Office. 20402, Washington, D.C., 1963.

SCHLESINGER, E. R., OVERTON, D. E., CHASE, H. C., and CANTRELL, K. T.: Newburgh-Kingston Caries-Fluorine Study XIII. Pediatric findings after ten years. J.A.D.A., *152,* 296-306, 1956.

SHAW, J. H.: Caries-producing factors: A decade of dental research—project No. 3 of the sugar research foundation. J.A.D.A., *55,* 785-789, 1957.

SNYDER, M. L., PORTER, D. R., CLAYCOMB, C. K., and SIMS, W.: Evaluation of laboratory tests for estimation of caries activity. J.A.D.A., *65,* 30-45, 1962.

SOGNNAES, R. F.: *Chemistry and Prevention of Dental Caries.* Springfield, Charles C Thomas, 1962.

————: Advances in experimental caries research. Amer. Assoc. Advance. Sci., Washington, D.C., 1955.

STEPHAN, R. M.: Intra-oral hydrogen ion concentrations associated with dental caries activity. J. Dent. Res., *23,* 257-266, 1944.

STRALFORS, A.: Disinfection of dental plaques in man. Odont. Tidskr., *70,* 183-203, 1962.

TOVERUD, G., RUBAL, L., and WIEHL, D. G. The influence of war and post-war conditions on the teeth of Norwegian school children. The Milbank Memorial Fund Quarterly, XXXIX: No. *3,* 489-539, New York, 1961.

TUNNICLIFF, R., and HAMMOND, C.: Smooth and rough greening streptococci in pulps of intact and carious teeth and in carious dentin. J.A.D.A., *25,* 1046, 1938.

VOLKER, J. F.: Prevention of dental caries: General principles. Dental Clin. North America, 1962.

WEISS, R. L., and TRITHART, A. H.: Between meal eating habits and dental caries experience on pre-school children. Amer. J. Publ. Health, *50,* 1097-1104, 1960.

WEISZ, W. S.: Sodium fluoride mouthwash—can it help? J. Dent. Children, 4th Quarter, 267-272, 1960.

WILLIAMS, J. L.: A contribution to the bacteriology of the human mouth. Dent. Cosmos, *41,* 317-349, 1899.

ZINNER, D. D., ARAN, A. P., JABLON, J. J., BRUST, B., and SASLAW, M. S.: Experimental caries induced in animals by streptococci of human origin. Proc. Soc. Exptl. Biol. & Med., *118,* 766-770, 1965.

6

The Histology and Embryology of the Face and Oral Structures

James K. Avery

INTRODUCTION

IN THE PREVIOUS chapters you became familiar with the shape and structure of the teeth, tongue, salivary glands and other tissues of the oral and facial areas. With the anatomy of these areas in mind, we can now direct your attention to the growth, development and histologic structure of these tissues. It is important to analyze the structural framework of the body using the aid of a microscope. The microscope enables us to discern that the tissues of the human body are made up of cells, intercellular substances and fluids. *Cells* are the smallest units of living structure capable of independent existence. They carry out functions of absorption, assimilation, respiration, irritability, conductivity, growth, reproduction, excretion and secretion. The shape of a cell may be related to the function it will perform. A cell on the surface of the skin, for example, functions best as a thin flat cell, whereas a red blood cell functions best as a round biconcave disk. The substance surrounding each cell is the *intercellular* material. This is the substance that gives the body form and it may be soft in consistency as in loose connective tissue or hard as in bone, cartilage or teeth. The third component of the body is *fluid* such as blood and lymph which travels throughout the body in vessels and the tissue fluid which bathes each cell and fiber in the body.

The body is derived embryologically from three primary germ layers: the *ectodermal* tissue, which forms the outer epithelium and nervous system; the *mesodermal* components, from which the skeleton, blood and muscles are derived, and the *endoderm* cell layer, which gives rise to the lungs, gastrointestinal epithelium and its derivatives. The outer epithelial tissue is designed to cover the external surfaces of the body, while the nervous tissue comprises the central and peripheral nervous system and functions to characterize the irritability and individuality of the person. Connective tissue is the supporting tissue of the body, such as the skeleton, tendons, cartilage and fibers which support various organs. Some connective tissues give rise to the blood elements and others conduct the blood. The muscular tissue is made up of skeletal, smooth and cardiac type muscle cells. These tissues are designed to function in contraction, producing the vital involuntary and voluntary movements of the body. The inner epithelial tissue provides the lining of the intestine and the glands connected with it such as the liver, gall bladder and pancreas, the tubes of the respiratory and the urinary systems. These tissues thus function in absorption and secretion and carry this latter function best as cells that have differentiated into the glands associated with the lining of these tubes. With an understanding of the intricate structure of each of these tissues, it is possible to comprehend how they are capable of carrying out specific yet interrelated functions. Thus with a knowledge of the embryology, gross and microscopic anatomy of oral tissues, a solid foundation is established for discussions in succeeding chapters concerning the morphology and pathology of oral structures.

DEVELOPMENT OF THE HUMAN FACE

Tissues covering the region anterior and ventral to the brain begin organizing to form the human face early in prenatal development. About five weeks after the fertilized ovum implants itself in the uterine wall, the embryo has become approximately one-quarter of an inch long. At this time a dimple appears just below the bulging forebrain area and immediately surrounding the dimple are several lumps of tissue. This dimple is the future mouth and it is bounded above by the rapidly growing forebrain and below by a series of bar-like tissue masses, *the branchial arches* (Fig. 6–1). Each branchial arch is separated from its neighbor by a cleft or groove, termed a *branchial groove*. There are six of these arches, though only four are visible on the surface of the embryo. The tissue above the mouth will form the forehead and the nose. It is thus termed the *fronto-nasal process*. On either side of the developing oral cavity appear wedge-shaped masses of tissue. These small wedges at the corners of the mouth will expand to circumscribe the superior border of the mouth and give rise to most of the upper lip and the cheeks. Deep in the face these tissues will help form the upper jaw and are thus termed the *maxillary processes*. The bar of tissue immediately below the mouth will form the lower lip and mandible and is termed the *mandibular* or *first branchial arch*. The adjacent arch below the mandibular is the *hyoid* or the *second branchial arch*. It will contribute structures developing within the neck and part of the external ear. The relationship of these

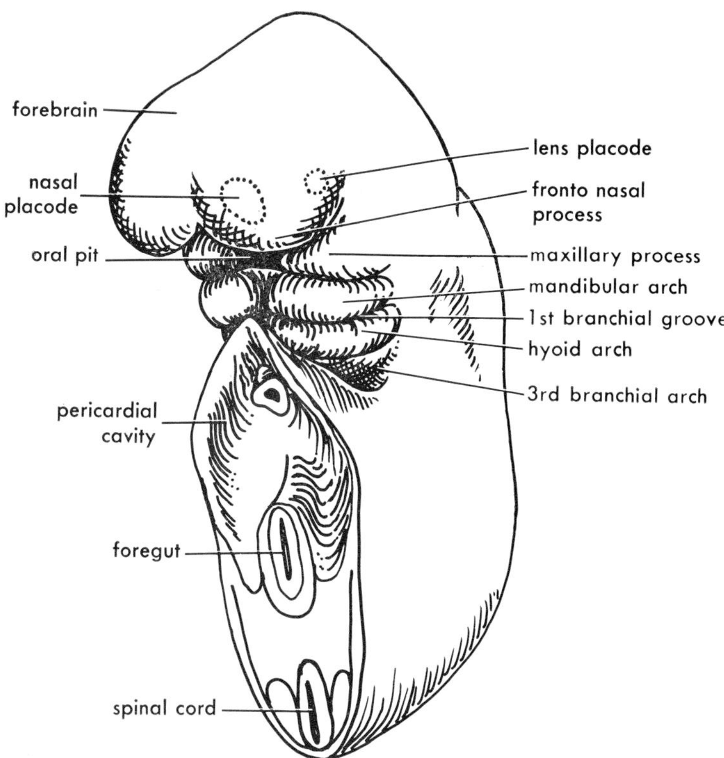

FIG. 6–1. A five-week-old embryo with the lower part of the body removed to more clearly show the craniofacial region. The branchial arches segment the area of the future face. Locate the oral pit below the forebrain and observe the location of all structures that will contribute to the face, such as the eye, nose, cheeks and lower jaw primordia. Follow the development of the face further in Figures 6–2 and 6–3.

developing facial tissues to each other at five weeks is shown in Figure 6–2*A*.

The embryo rapidly increases in size; at the end of the sixth week it is twice the size it was at five weeks. Above the corners of the mouth epithelial lined pockets, or nasal pits, have appeared. The maxillary tissue wedges and the mandibular area have increased in size, and the forming eyes are now visible on the sides of the head (Figs. 6–2*B* and *C*). All of the branchial grooves will gradually disappear except the one between the mandibular and hyoid arch. It will persist and form the future external auditory canal. Six small hillocks of tissue are grouped along this groove. Three arise from the hyoid and three from the mandibular arch. They will later fuse together around the canal to form the external ear or auricle.

By the end of the sixth week cranial expansion posterior to the eyes has broadened the head, causing the eyes and nasal pits to appear nearer the center of the face. The tissue lateral to the nasal pits is termed the *lateral nasal processes,* and that tissue medial to the pits, the *medial nasal process.* The angles of the mouth are more medially located due to fusion of the maxillary and mandibular tissues. At this time, the fusion lines of the face show clearly the location of possible future developmental abnormalities of the face (Fig. 6–2*D*).

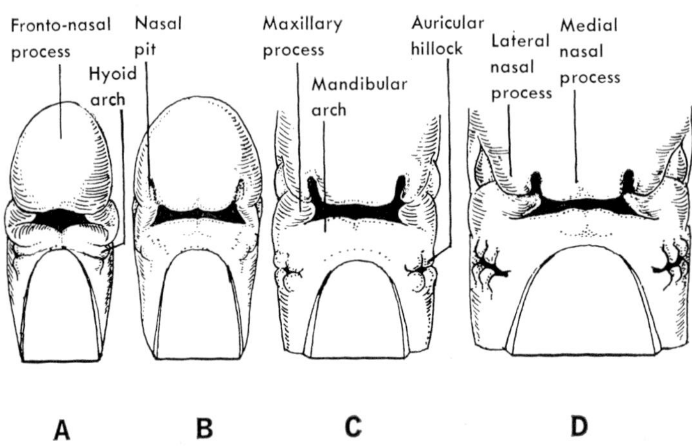

FIG. 6–2. Developing human face during the period of migration and fusion of facial processes. The development of the upper and lower lips, nostrils, and the anterior positioning of the eyes occur during this time period. *A,* fifth prenatal week; *B,* early sixth week; *C,* middle sixth week; *D,* early seventh week.

By the beginning of the seventh week the embryo is three-quarters of an inch long. The face is now recognizably human. The lateral and medial nasal processes have fused with the maxillary processes to form the upper lip and the floor of the external nares or nostrils. Due to further lateral growth of the head the eyes are located nearer the front of the face. The nose and eyes are on the same horizontal plane due to the lack of vertical growth of the face. The three auricular hillocks from the mandibular arch and three from the hyoid arch surround the external auditory meatus to form the external ear (Fig. 6–3*E*).

By the ninth week the embryo face is broad and flat due to lateral cranial growth (Fig. 6–3*F*). The eyes are now at a level above the nose and the bridge of the nose has become evident due to growth in vertical dimension of the face. The corners of the mouth are more medially located due to further fusion of the maxillary and mandibular

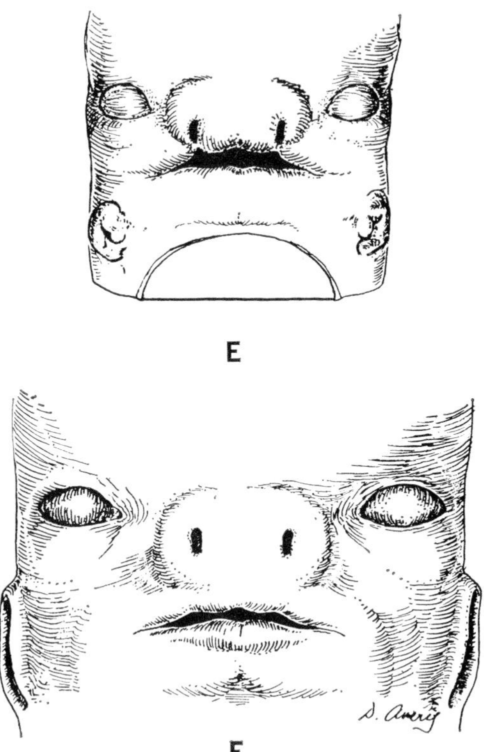

FIG. 6–3. Developing human face. *E*, early eighth week; *F*, ninth week.

tissues and the cheeks have become apparent. The upper and lower eyelids have appeared and will close over the eyes until birth. The six auricular hillocks have now fused to form the auricle of the ear. At birth an over-all increase in size of the face is notable, but general proportions are not appreciably altered. The cheeks are more fully developed, giving the face a fat, chubby appearance. The eyes and ears are proportionately large and the nostrils are still evident from the front of the face. From birth to maturity, the face increases greatly in vertical dimension due to facial skeletal growth. The nose increases in size and the nostrils are directed downward. Since the cranium increases in size proportionately more than the face during the prenatal period, the cranium is 8 times the size of the face at birth. At two years, however, it is only 5 times, at six years only 3 times, and in the adult only 2 times larger than the face. The cranium thus has completed most of its size increase by the second year, whereas the face increases greatly through the sixth year and continues to a lesser extent through the twenty-fifth year.

DEVELOPMENT OF THE JAWS

At about the sixth week of prenatal life, when the maxillary processes are fusing with the fronto-nasal process, the internal structures of the upper and lower jaw regions appear as solid masses of mesoderm. The first sign of alveolar ridge differentiation occurs as the oral epithelium forms a furrow which separates the lips from the developing maxilla and mandible. This is accomplished by proliferation of the oral mucosal cells pushing a wedge of epithelium down into the

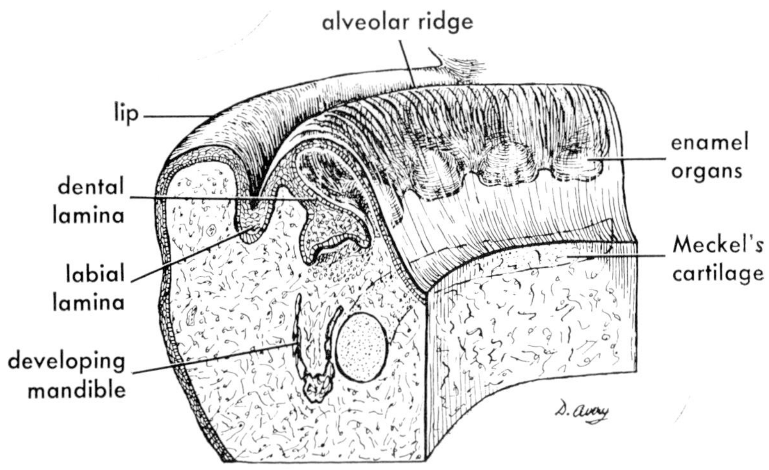

FIG. 6–4. Developing right side of mandibular arch illustrating division of the tissue of the lip and jaw by the developing labial lamina. The dental lamina and attached tooth germs are indicated. Meckel's cartilage extends from the middle ear region anteriorly to the midline of the developing jaw giving support to the soft tissue until the bone of the mandible is developed.

underlying mesoderm. A cleft forms later as the central mucosal cells of the wedge degenerate. The resultant cleft separates the lip from the developing jaw tissues (Fig. 6–4). In the developing soft tissue of the mandible, a slender bar of cartilage differentiates to lend support. This is termed *Meckel's cartilage* and it extends from either side from the chin or symphysis anteriorly to the middle ear region posteriorly. In the hyoid or second branchial arch, a similar bar of cartilage extends from the anterior aspect of this arch posteriorly to the region of the ear. This relationship is not difficult to visualize at this time since the developing ear region is on the same plane as the first and second branchial arches, being situated just behind and below the posterior aspects of the developing mouth. The first branchial groove which separates these two arches will form the external auditory meatus. As growth proceeds more rigid support is needed in the developing jaws; thus bone growth begins. Islands of bone, surrounded by embryonic connective tissue appear located within future bone areas in the developing jaws during the seventh and eighth weeks. The bone appears at first as minute areas of ossification with bony fingers or trabeculae radiating out from the center much as spokes from the hub of a wheel. These areas of bone initiation are termed ossification centers and all facial bones are formed by two or more of these centers. Those in the upper jaw appear in the anterior region of the face or premaxilla, throughout the maxilla and in the palate. Bone spreads upward in the maxilla into the tissues underlying the face, the orbit and toward the midline in the palatine processes. Increase in size of the prenatal face is due to the rapid growth of embryonic connective tissue and differentiation of muscle masses. Bone growth in the face keeps pace because of the simultaneous expansion of each of the many ossification centers. In later prenatal life, the trabeculae of adjacent ossification centers come in contact and fuse to form the individual bones of the face. Bands of connective tissue persist between the facial bones. They supply the fibers and cells for continued bone apposition along these areas which are termed sutures. Further facial bone growth occurs along these sutures and also by deposition on the external aspects and resorption of the internal aspects of each bone. Sutures act as connective tissue hinges which hold the bones of the face together but allow each of them some freedom of movement. In the mandible, an ossification center appears in the area of each lateral incisor enamel organ and replaces Meckel's cartilage in this area. Growth of bone from these bilateral centers spreads posteriorly, surrounding the cartilage bar and the developing tooth organs. Meckel's cartilage thus remains until the bony mandible is rigid, from the central incisor region posterior to the temporal fossa (Fig. 6–5*A*). At twelve weeks the mandible appears as a curved bar of bone inclined slightly at the posterior aspect where pronounced coronoid processes and short stubby condyles appear (Fig. 6–5*B*). Growth of the ramus upward into the temporal fossa is slow so that during the early months of prenatal development the mandible lags behind the forward growth of the upper face. The cartilages of the first and second arches soon separate posteriorly from the mandible and hyoid skeletons and the most posterior aspects of Meckel's bar contribute to the later ossifying malleus and incus bones (Fig. 6–5*A*). The stapes bone arises from the hyoid cartilage. These middle ear bones are then encased by the ossifying temporal bone. As the mandible establishes contact with the temporal fossae, cartilage develops from the fibrous tissue covering the condyles. As this cartilage is replaced by bone, further cartilage forms continuously on the head of the rami, causing them to grow in length similar to long bone growth.

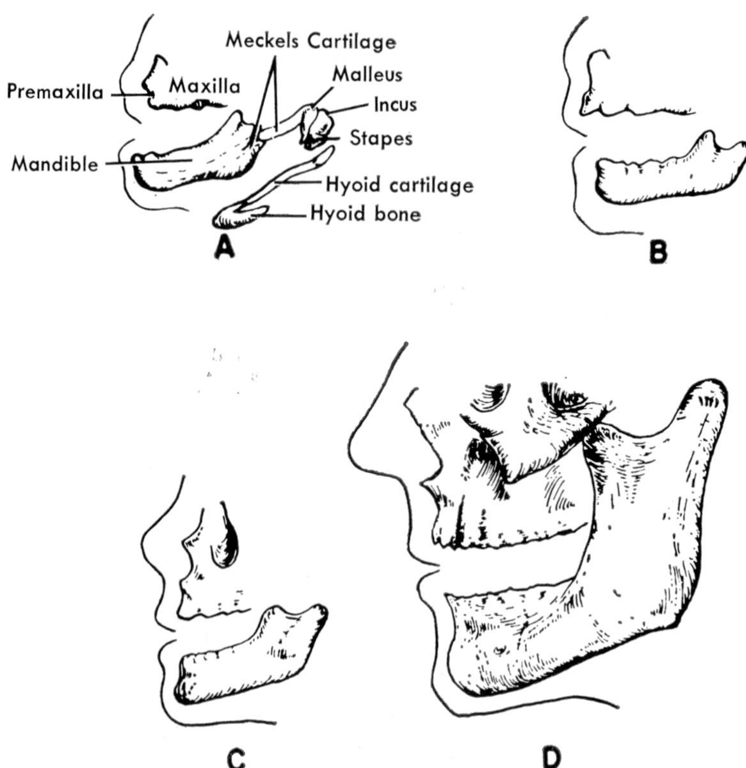

FIG. 6–5. Morphology of the developing jaw skeleton from the eighth week to the adult. The early continuity of Meckel's and hyoid cartilages to the middle ear region is illustrated. *A,* eight prenatal weeks; *B,* 12 weeks; *C,* birth; *D,* adult.

With the condyles in contact at the base of the skull, further condylar growth results in the lower jaw overtaking the upper in anterior position during the later prenatal months (Fig. 6–5*C*). Increase in length of the lower face also results from this growth. For example, the ears previously located behind the body of the mandible are at birth far above it. The facial skeleton increases greatly in size from birth to maturity. Some of the contributing factors are condylar and sutural growth; external bone deposition; enlargement of the ethmoidal and maxillary sinuses; increase in the size of the nose and development of the alveolar processes. As the mandible grows downward and forward from the ramus, space is created for the downward and forward growth of the upper face and development of the alveolar processes of both jaws. The mandible increases in width at the symphysis until the second year and in length by the deposition of bone on the posterior border of the ramus while at the same time resorbing it on the anterior border. The mandibular body grows in height by apposition of bone along the free borders of the alveolar processes (Fig. 6–5*D*). The upper face completes its growth by the eighteenth year, but growth continues in the mandible to a slight degree until the twenty-fifth year of life.

DEVELOPMENT OF THE PALATE

As tissue masses undergo organization to form the face, other deeper tissues develop the future nasal and oral areas. The nasal pits or developing nostrils first appeared as epithelial lined shallow pits on the front of the face. These pits deepen until they open into the roof of the anterior part of the mouth. Between the nasal pits is an area of tissue which is continuous from their anterior to their posterior openongs. On the front of the face this tissue is termed the *medial nasal process* and it forms the future philtrum of the lip. The deeper aspect of this tissue is termed the *medial palatine process* and from it develops the premaxilla. The *premaxilla* is the triangular shaped anterior segment of the palate in which the four maxillary incisor teeth develop (Fig. 6–6*A*). Immediately posterior and lateral to the premaxilla, tissue masses develop from the maxillary processes. These tissue masses enlarge and move towards the midline where they fuse to form the palate. As the horizontal palatine processes meet at the midline, the oral cavity and the overlying nasal cavities are separated. The fusion of the parts of the palate begins in the anterior region of the palate just posterior to the premaxilla at about the seventh to the ninth week and extends posteriorly to the soft palate. It will be noted in Figure 6–8 that the palate shelves must move above the tongue in

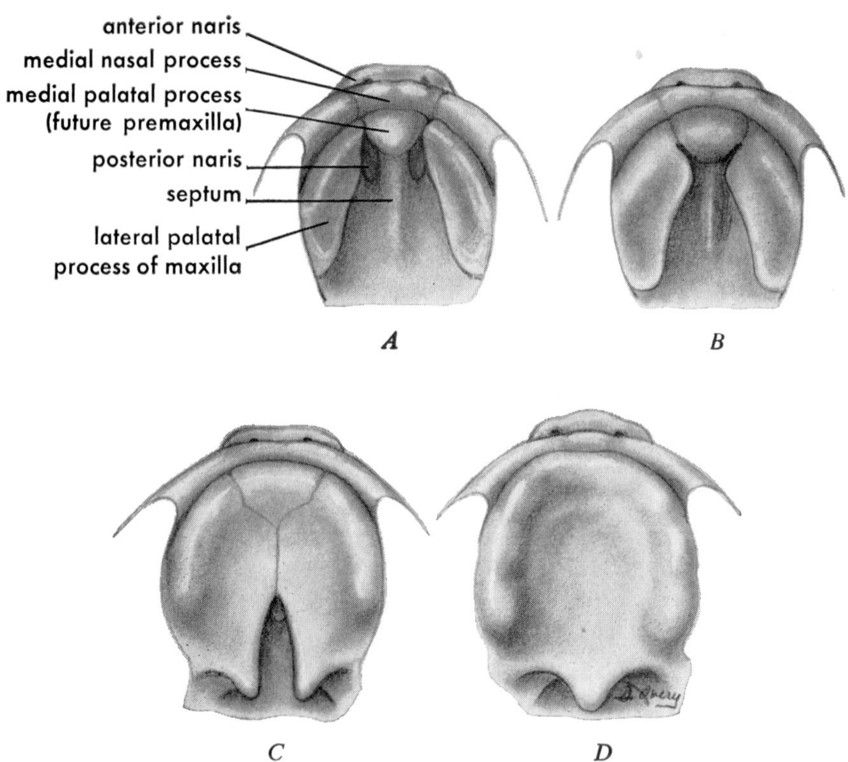

FIG. 6–6. The development of the human palate, viewed from below, illustrating the fusion of the lateral palatine shelves with the premaxilla.

closing. If they do not, a cleft-palate will result. Meanwhile, in the nasal cavity, the nasal septum grows downward to fuse with the upper surface of the midline of the palate (Fig. 6–6*A* and *B*). In doing so, it separates the right and left nasal cavities. Bone quickly forms in the palate to give it rigidity (Fig. 6–8*C* and *D*). Three ossification centers contribute to the bony framework of the palate: the premaxillary, maxillary and palatine. Growth in width of the palate occurs along the midline where a suture forms, termed the median intermaxillary suture (Fig. 6–8*D*). Increase in length of the palate occurs by growth of the premaxillo-maxillary suture, palatomaxillary suture and along the posterior border of the palate. As the teeth grow and erupt, alveolar bone is formed in the ridges bordering the palate. In early childhood the palatal sutures fuse and further size increase is by surface apposition of bone. The palate has reached eighty per cent of its final size by the fourth year and attains its maximum width by the tenth year.

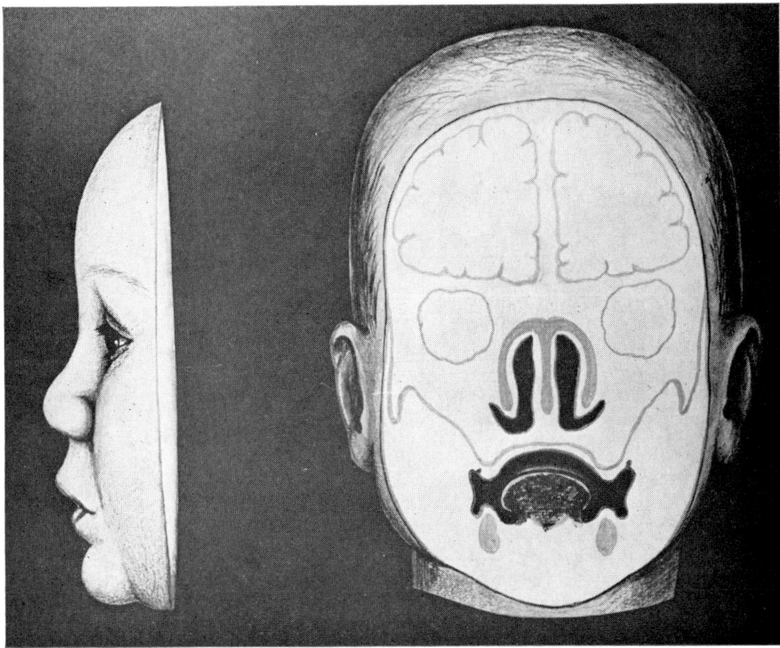

FIG. 6–7. The palate or roof of the mouth is situated just behind the face. This figure illustrates where the tissue sections in Fig. 6–8 are taken.

DEVELOPMENT OF THE TONGUE

As the palate is forming the roof of the mouth, the tongue is developing in the posterior floor of the mouth. Late in the fifth week the body of the tongue arises from two lateral swellings and a centrally located tubercle, the *tuberculum impar*. The root of the tongue is arising from a median ventral elevation of the hyoid arch which is termed the *copula*. Posterior to the forming base of the tongue, the epiglottis is developing from contributions of the third and fourth branchial arches (Fig. 6–9). The enlarging lateral lingual swellings are limited from expanding laterally by the developing lower jaws. The bilaterally originating masses thus push toward each other along the midline filling in the median depression except at the posterior central area of the body of the tongue, which is formed by the enlarging tuberculum impar (Fig. 6–9*A*). During the seventh week the tongue grows rapidly in size, filling the oral cavity and extending upward between the palatal shelves into the overlying nasal cavity (Fig. 6–8*B*). The rapid expansion of the tongue at this time is due to the growth and differentiation of its voluntary muscle. The lateral swellings and the

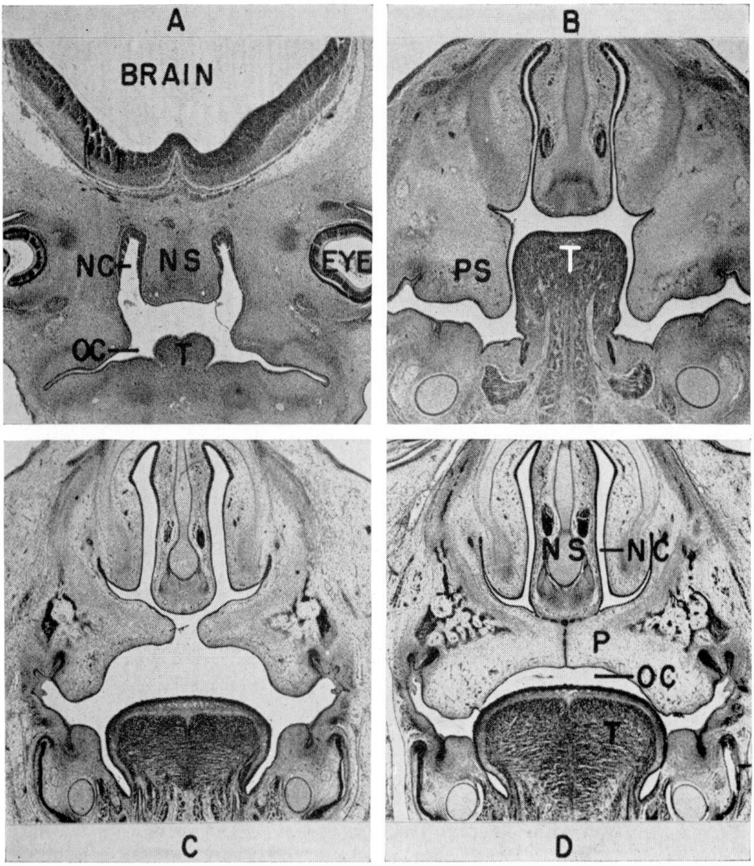

FIG. 6–8. Transverse sections through developing face illustrating the closure of the palatal folds in the separation of the nasal and oral cavities. *A,* six-and-a-half weeks; *B,* seven-and-a-half weeks; *C,* eight-and-a-half weeks; *D,* nine-and-a-half weeks. *NC,* nasal cavity; *NS,* nasal septum; *OC,* oral cavity; *T,* tongue; *PS,* palatal shelves; *P,* palate.

tuberculum impar have now completely grown together to form the body of the tongue. During the eighth week the face broadens and space is created for the tongue to expand laterally. As it does this the tongue flattens and recedes down from the nasal cavity into the floor of the mouth (Fig. 6–8*C*). The tongue then appears wider laterally and with a flat dorsal surface. The filiform, fungiform and vallate papillae begin to differentiate at this time on the dorsum of the body of the tongue. With no tongue obstructing the contact of the palatine shelves in the midline, they close in a short period of time (Fig. 6–8*C* and *D*).

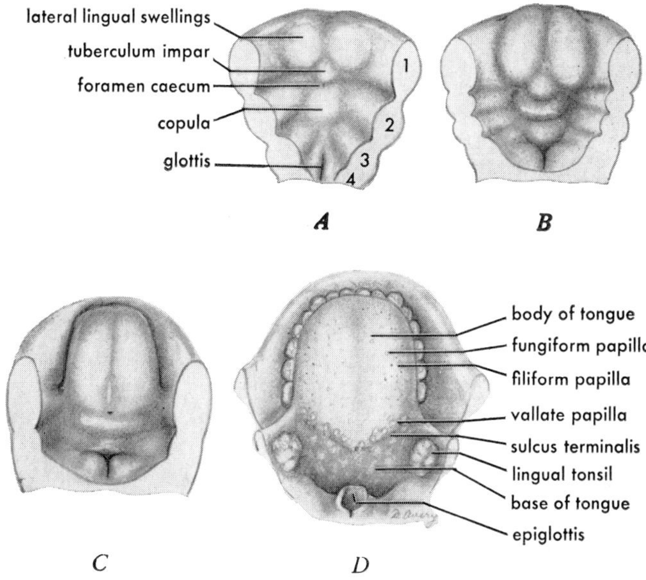

FIG. 6–9. Development of the human tongue, viewed from above. The body of the tongue is formed by the fusion of the lateral lingual swellings and the tuberculum impar. The base of the tongue develops from the coupla. (*A*, *B* and *C* are prenatal weeks; *D* is young adult. Numbers 1, 2, 3 and 4 are arches.)

HISTOGENESIS OF SALIVARY GLANDS

Human beings and other food chewing mammals develop oral glands, whose secretions aid in chewing and swallowing. All of these glands develop initially as bud-like growths of oral epithelium which invade the underlying mesodermal tissue. The bud grows quickly into a cord of epithelial cells which remains attached to the oral mucosa. It then increases in length until it reaches the area of future gland location where it branches into many secondary cords or twigs. These numerous twigs of epithelial tissue cells multiply and differentiate into secretory cells. The branching epithelial cords continue to grow in size and the center of the cords become hollow which will later function as the duct system of the gland. A nest of these secretory cells grouped around a duct make up an alveolus, the functioning unit of the gland. A larger gland is composed of thousands of cell groups or alveoli, whereas only a few make up the smaller accessory glands of the oral cavity. The cells of the alveoli gradually differentiate into either mucous or serous secreting cells and the surrounding mesodermal connective tissue grows between groups of alveoli to divide the gland into lobules and finally enclosed the entire gland in a capsule.

The parotid gland begins development during the fourth week, the submandibular at the end of the sixth and the sublingual during the eighth week. The glands begin to function shortly after birth.

HISTOGENESIS OF THE TEETH

Early Tooth Development

During the sixth prenatal week, as the developing lip and jaw tissue become differentiated, the first signs of tooth formation begin. This is observed as a thickening of the oral mucosa covering the developing gingiva. The basal layer of the mucosa proliferates, causing a sheet of epithelial cells to push into the underlying mesodermal tissues of the gingiva. This sheet of epithelial penetration is a continuous band within the gingival tissue completely circling each jaw. It is termed the *dental lamina* (Fig. 6–4). At intervals around each jaw the free border of the lamina develops cup-like enlargements. These are termed *enamel organs* and from them the enamel of the twenty deciduous teeth will develop. The enamel organs gradually enlarge and the cells within them differentiate. The layer of epithelial cells covering the outer surface of each organ is termed the *outer enamel epithelium,* (Fig. 6–10*B*). This layer of epithelial cells continues into the concave part of each cup-shaped organ and is termed the *inner enamel epithelium.* The inner enamel epithelial cells will later differentiate into enamel forming cells. These cuboidal-shaped cells elongate into columnar cells as they begin enamel production. They are then termed ameloblasts. The interior of the enamel organ is filled with a network of star-shaped cells connected by thin processes. This meshwork is termed the *stellate reticulum* (Fig. 6–10*D*). Since the enamel organ is essentially non-vascular, this tissue meshwork may function in passing elements from the vascularized outer enamel epithelium to the enamel forming cells. Within the enamel organ adjacent to the inner enamel epithelial cell row is a layer of spindle-shaped cells termed the stratum intermedium cells (Fig. 6–12). These cells possibly function in enamel formation also. Mesodermal tissue has filled the concavity of each enamel organ. These connective tissue elements, termed the *dental papillae* at this stage of development, will form the future pulp of the tooth from which differentiate the dentin forming cells, the blood vessels, and collagenous fibers. As the enamel organ and the associated dental papillae form, the dental lamina has performed its function of enamel organ formation and begins to disintegrate, so that connection of the enamel organ to the oral epithelium is lost (Fig. 6–10*E*). The free end of the lamina continues to develop, however, pushing behind the deciduous tooth organ further into the gingival tissue to form the enamel organs of the later developing permanent teeth (Fig. 6–10*C*).

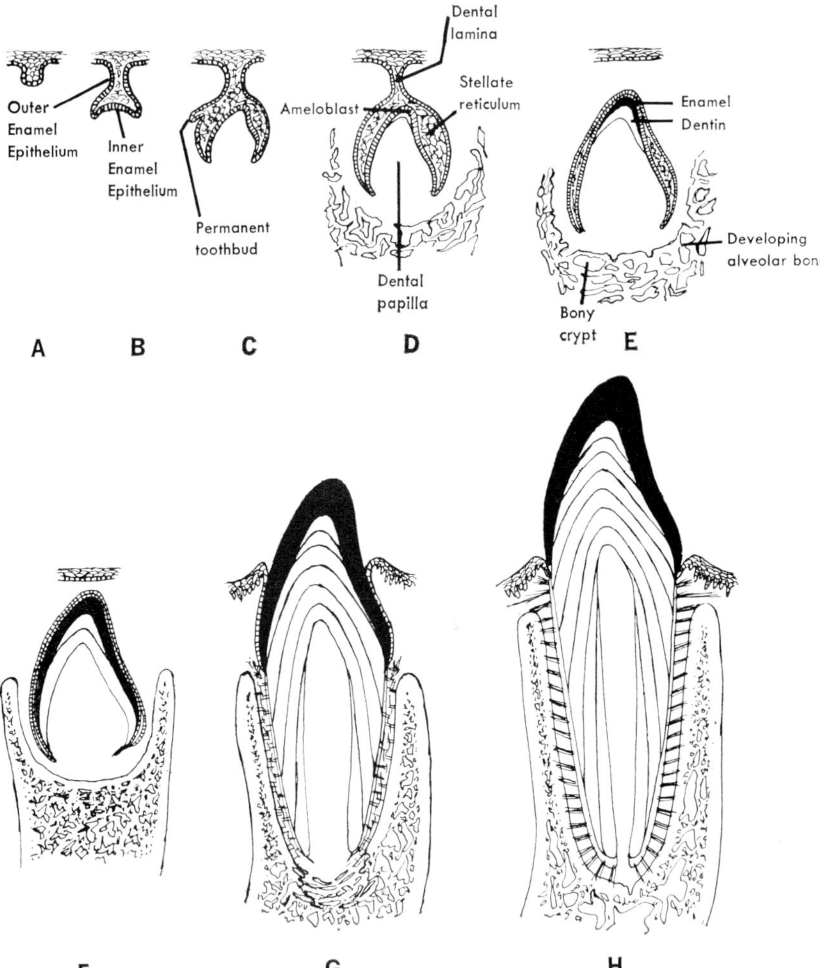

FIG. 6–10. Developmental stages in tooth formation. *A,* bud stage, initiation of anlage; *B,* cap stage, proliferation of anlage; *C,* bell stage, histodifferentiation of anlage; *D,* dentinogenesis, beginning dentin formation; *E,* amelogenesis, beginning enamel formation; *F,* incremental deposition, appositional growth and calcification of crown; *G,* clinical eruption and root formation; *H,* occlusion and function.

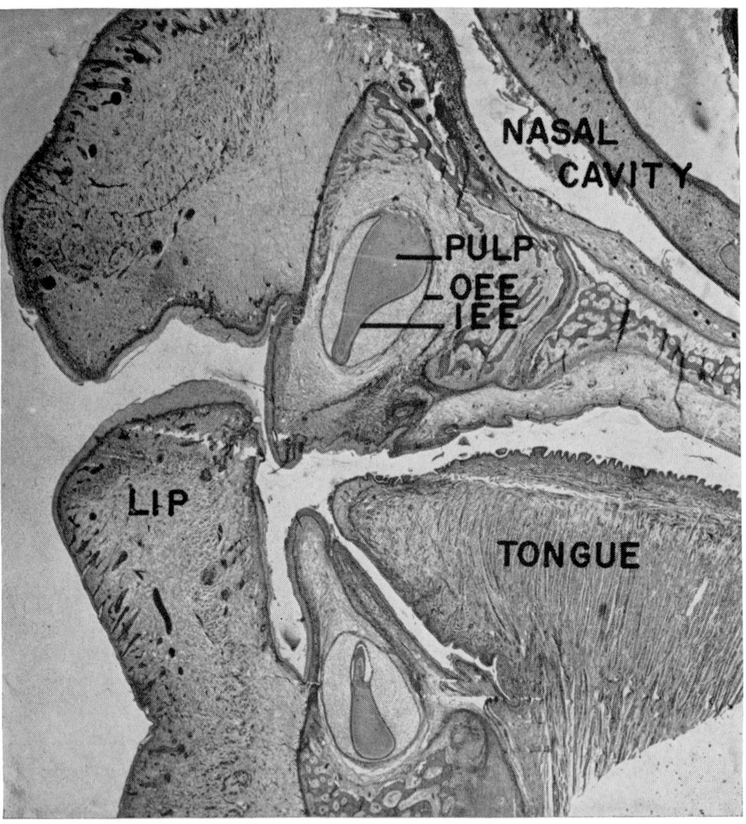

FIG. 6–11. Lateral view of a four-month fetal oral cavity illustrating the positional relationship of the lips, alveolar processes, tooth germs, tongue, palate, and nasal cavity. *OEE,* outer enamel epithelium; *IEE* inner enamel epithelium.

As each enamel organ increases in size it begins to resemble the shape of the future tooth that it will form (Fig. 6–10*E*). The inner enamel organ cells gradually alter their shape from cuboidal-shaped cells, elongating into a columnar form with the nucleus located at the non-secreting end of the cell (Figs. 6–12 and 6–13). As soon as these cells differentiate into a columnar form they are termed *ameloblasts.* The ameloblasts appear as closely packed cells lining the concave surface of the enamel organ (Fig. 6–13). The connective tissue cells of the dental papilla adjacent to the ameloblasts then elongate into a columnar form and are termed *odontoblasts.* The odontoblasts thus cover the surface of that portion of the dental papilla in contact with the enamel organ, and lie in a position adjacent to the ameloblast row (Fig. 6–13). As both types of cells differentiate, the ameloblastic and odontoblastic cell rows take a position which outlines the shape of the future crown tip (Fig. 6–11). The formative cells of the prospective dentin and enamel are thus oriented and are ready for production of enamel and dentin.

Dentinogenesis and Amelogenesis

All the ameloblasts and odontoblasts do not differentiate and begin secretion at the same time. The cells at the tips of the cusps mature and begin secretion first, forming the site of the first enamel and dentin deposition and the cells nearer the base of the cusp mature and begin secretion later.

The enamel organ increases in size by growth at the base or rim of the cone-shaped organ. The epithelial cells of this area undergo division and differentiation into enamel epithelial cells and increase the dimension of the enamel organ or the future crown.

The odontoblasts begin to function slightly before the ameloblasts and they form a thin layer of *predentin* between themselves and the ameloblasts (Figs. 6–12 and 6–13). After a layer of predentin the thickness of a fingernail has been deposited, the ameloblasts begin depositing enamel matrix. Meanwhile the predentin mineralizes and is then termed dentin and a new layer of predentin is deposited along the border of the pulp. Since both cell rows were originally positioned end to end they must move away from each other to make room during deposition of enamel and dentin (Fig. 6–13). The odontoblasts thus move pulpward, leaving a deposition of dentin between them and the ameloblasts. The ameloblasts meanwhile move peripherally away from the pulp with enamel matrix deposited behind them. The enamel and dentin are thus deposited in contact with each other forming the *dentino-enamel junction.* Each ameloblast deposits a single rod of enamel matrix which has its beginning at the dentino-enamel junction and extends to the outer surface of the enamel (Fig. 6–13). At intervals along the length of the rod there are cross striations caused by a hesitation in the deposition process. These are lines indicating deposition of enamel increments and are thus termed *incremental lines* (Figs. 6–18 and 6–22). Since a large number of ameloblasts deposit enamel at the same time, the lines are not limited to single rods, but extend the entire circumference of the forming enamel. The enamel matrix of a tooth crown can be visualized as a number of cups or cones which have been stacked one upon the other. If one were to cut through the stack of cones from apex to base, we would see alternating cones and spaces. This is an exaggerated example of the incremental deposition of enamel. In the forming enamel matrix there

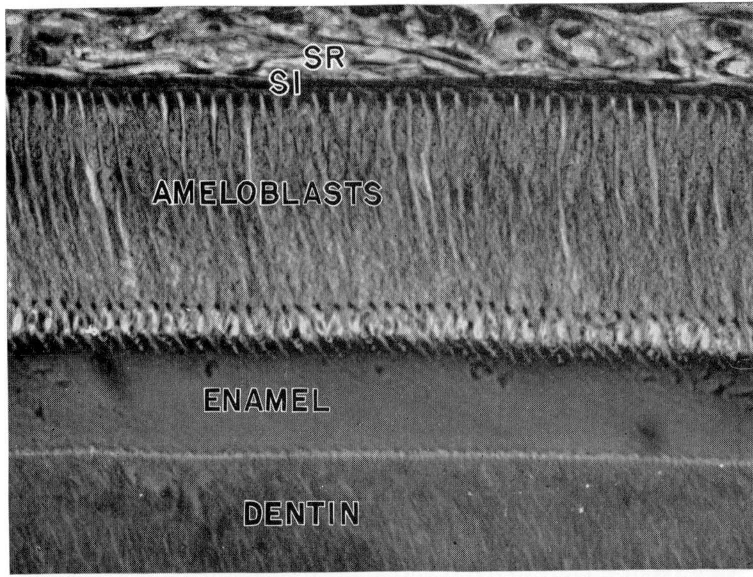

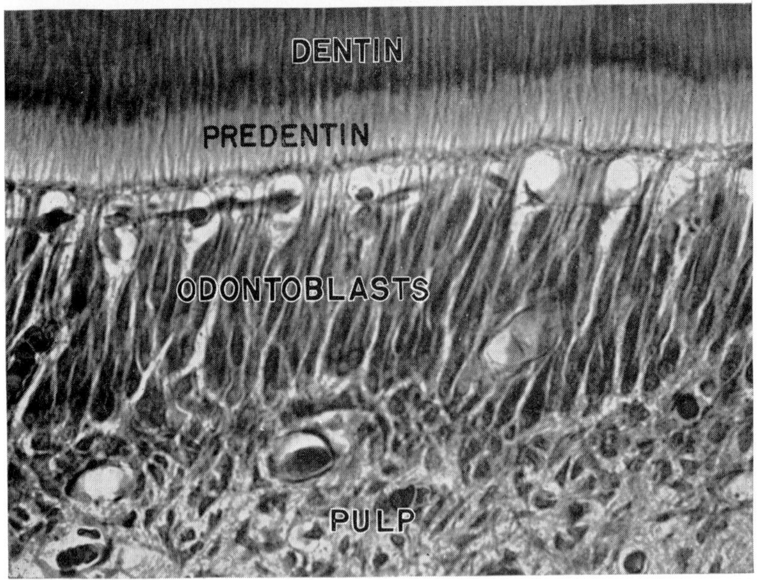

FIG. 6–12. Photomicrograph of enamel and dentin formation. Top picture illustrates relationship of stellate reticulum, stratum intermedium, ameloblasts, and enamel matrix. *SR,* stellate reticulum; *SI,* stratum intermedium. Bottom picture shows relationship of dentin, predentin, odontoblasts, and pulp.

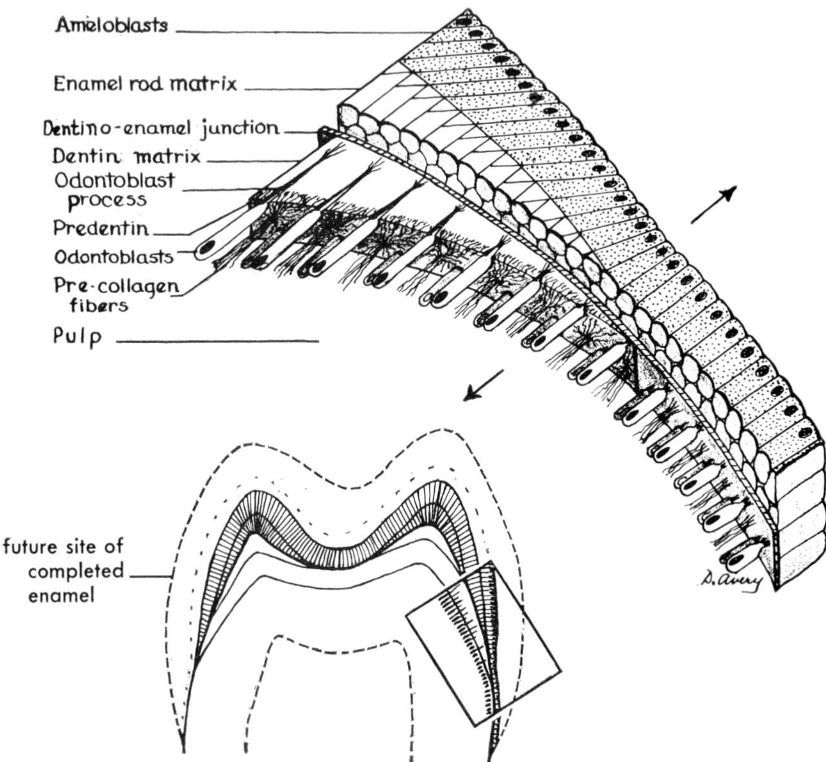

FIG. 6–13. Diagram of early dentinogenesis and amelogenesis. The relationship of the formative cells before and after hard tissue formation is shown. In the lower right area, the ameloblasts and odontoblasts are in near contact. Upper left, the cells gradually move apart as enamel and dentin are deposited. The small figure in the lower left indicates where this section is located in the developing crown. Note that when each increment of enamel and dentin is deposited more ameloblasts and odontoblasts are activated to function in its deposition. The lower diagram illustrates the area of the crown from where the detailed diagram is taken.

are no breaks in the rod but lines of pigmentation representing the rhythmic recurrent deposition of enamel matrix. When first deposited, the enamel rod is not the characteristically hard enamel with which dentists are familiar when examining teeth in the mouth. Thus, it is termed pre-enamel or non-calcified enamel matrix. As the enamel rod matrix is being deposited from the dentino-enamel junction peripherally, salts begin diffusing into this soft matrix. This primary calcification proceeds from the dentino-enamel junction end of the rods to the surface of the enamel, following closely the incremental pattern of matrix deposition.[2] After the final increment of matrix has been deposited over the tooth cusps, there is a further influx of mineral into the enamel. The tissue fluid within the matrix is displaced as the solidification process occurs. The deposition of the enamel matrix as well as the mineralization of the enamel begins in the cusps and then moving down over the sides of the teeth, finally reaches the cervical region of the crowns.[3] The resulting mature enamel is very hard as it consists of 96 per cent inorganic salts.

The *dentin* is not deposited in the form of rods, but initially as a meshwork of connective tissue fibers termed pre-dentin and is located adjacent to the pulp (Fig. 6–12). A short time after deposition, inorganic crystals begin appearing in and on these fibers at the pre-dentin-dentin junction. Thus, the dentin calcifies along the predentin-dentin junction and the initial matrix deposited is termed predentin and after mineralization the final product is called dentin. Similar to ameloblasts, a number of odontoblasts function simultaneously to deposit increments of matrix and in this instance at the expense of the pulp. The result is the same as placing a series of cups or cones inside each other until the length of the entire root of the tooth is formed.

Each odontoblast begins its journey at the dentino-enamel junction. At this junction, each of these cells attaches a process which lengthens as the dentin becomes thicker and the odontoblast moves farther away from its initial position. As the dentin deposition proceeds, a tubule remains which contains the process of the odontoblast (Fig. 6–13). In the completely formed tooth the odontoblast is in the pulp and its process extends from the pulp through the dentin to the dentino-enamel junction.

Root Development

After the enamel is formed, the enamel organ functions in root development. Continued proliferation of the base of the enamel organ results in an epithelial sheath which defines the shape of the developing root (Fig. 6–14). The inner and outer enamel epithelia fuse to form a two cell thick tube which grows as a continuance of the base of the enamel organ of the crown. As growth of this epithelial tube proceeds, more connective tissue is enclosed within the tube which then becomes *pulp tissue.* This tube is called *Hertwig's epithelial root sheath.* The presence of the epithelial sheath cells induces some of the pulpal connective tissue cells to differentiate into odontoblasts which, in turn, begin depositing dentin along the inner surface of the root sheath. As increments of dentin are deposited the size of the newly incorporated pulp tissue is decreased and the root is increased in length. The epithelial root sheath continues to proliferate at its free end. Odontoblasts differentiate and dentin deposits until the root is complete.

Cementum and Periodontal Ligament Formation

As the root dentin is deposited, a reorientation of the connective tissue fibers surrounding the developing root occurs. These fibers begin to group themselves into three layers or zones. The fibers near the root surface and those at the surface of the surrounding bony crypt become partially embedded in them and are oriented at right angles to these structures. The area of fibers in the center of the ligament are termed the *intermediate zone fibers* and during eruption some of them are oriented in the direction of the long axis of the tooth (Fig. 6–23). The tooth crypt or follicle fibers are thus developing into the *perio-*

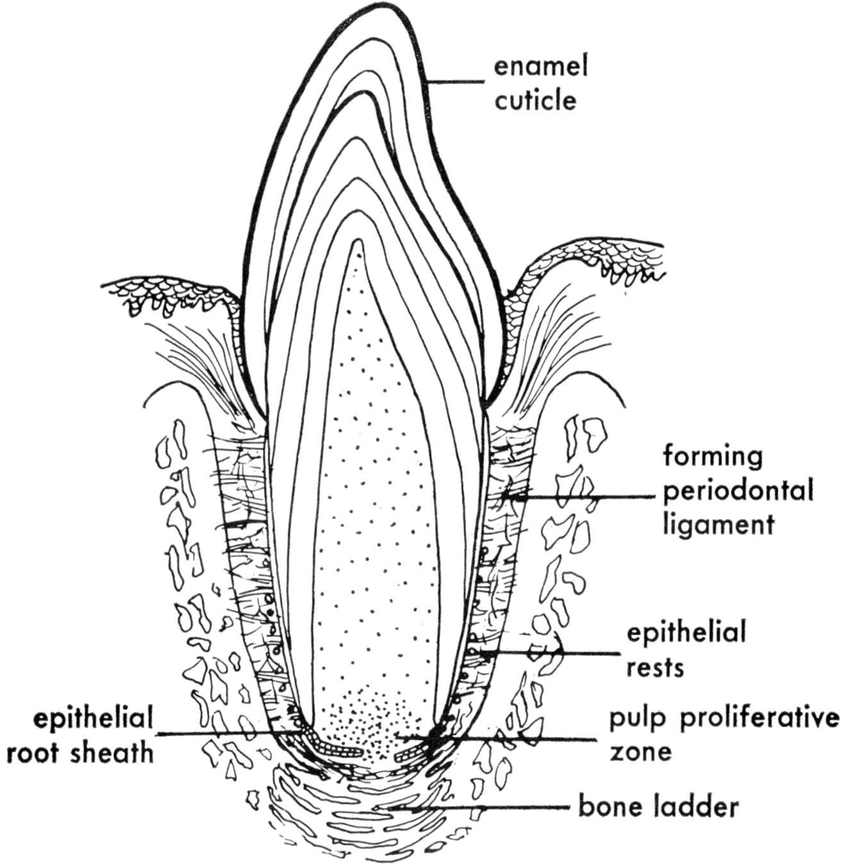

FIG. 6–14. Erupting tooth. Bone trabeculae forming below the apex of erupting root.

dontal ligament. In an area where the root dentin has just been deposited, its surface remains temporarily covered with the epithelial root sheath. With the formation of dentin, the root sheath has completed its function in that area. It then breaks up into small cell groups, losing its continuity as a sheet of cells. These cell islands are then termed *epithelial rests* (Fig. 6–14). The neighboring connective tissue cells then migrate between the epithelial cell islands to come in contact with the root surface. As these cells line up along the surface of the root they change into a cuboidal shape and can be termed *cementoblasts.* The periodontal membrane fibers lying at right angles to the root surface then pass between the epithelial rests and cementoblasts and form a fiber meshwork on the root surface. A secretion of the cementoblasts causes this meshwork to become a homogenous appearing matrix. This substance is termed *precementum.* Minerals then diffuse into this feltwork and when the precementum is calcified, it is then termed cementum. *Cementum* will gradually cover the entire root surface of the tooth and serve as an attachment of the periodontal fibers to the tooth (Fig. 6–18). It is not quite so hard a substance as dentin. As the cementoblasts move away from the surface of the dentin, successive layers of cementum are deposited. On the surface of the cementum there is constantly being formed a precementum layer in which the periodontal fibers are embedded. The epithelial rests meanwhile are pushed farther out into the periodontal membrane. Fibers of the peripheral portion of the periodontal membrane are also at right angles to the surface of the alveolar bone. In this area connective tissue cells align themselves along the bone and become bone forming cells, the *osteoblasts.* As bone deposition occurs the peripheral fibers of the periodontal membrane are attached to the bone. The inner fibers of the periodontal membrane are thus attached to the surface of the root and the outer one to the adjacent bone. The center of the membrane is composed of loosely arranged fibers, which allows for the eruption of the tooth (Figs. 6–14 and 6–23).

Eruption Process

The last function of the ameloblasts after the enamel is completely formed is the deposition of an organic secretion on the surface of the tooth. This thin structureless membrane is termed the *primary cuticle.* Meanwhile the outer enamel epithelium, stellate reticulum and stratum intermedium become compressed against the ameloblasts, forming a thick epithelial membrane over the surface of the unerupted crown. With the completion of the crown, active eruption begins. As the crown was developing, bone grew around and over the tooth so that the tooth lay in a protective bony crypt. As the tooth begins to erupt, bone is resorbed over the roof of the crypt while other bone is deposited on its floor. Simultaneously the root is growing in length. Although all the factors associated with tooth eruption are not yet known, it is thought that growth of the jaws and elongation of the root are important factors. During eruption, bone trabeculae develop in the form of a ladder under the apex of the root (Fig. 6–14). These bony plates probably aid the tooth in eruption. There is rapid growth and expansion of the pulp at this time and it may exert some pressure against the bone underlying the tooth. As the crown of the tooth moves toward the oral cavity, there is a resulting fusion of the oral epithelium with the reduced enamel epithelium (Figs. 6–15 and 6–16).

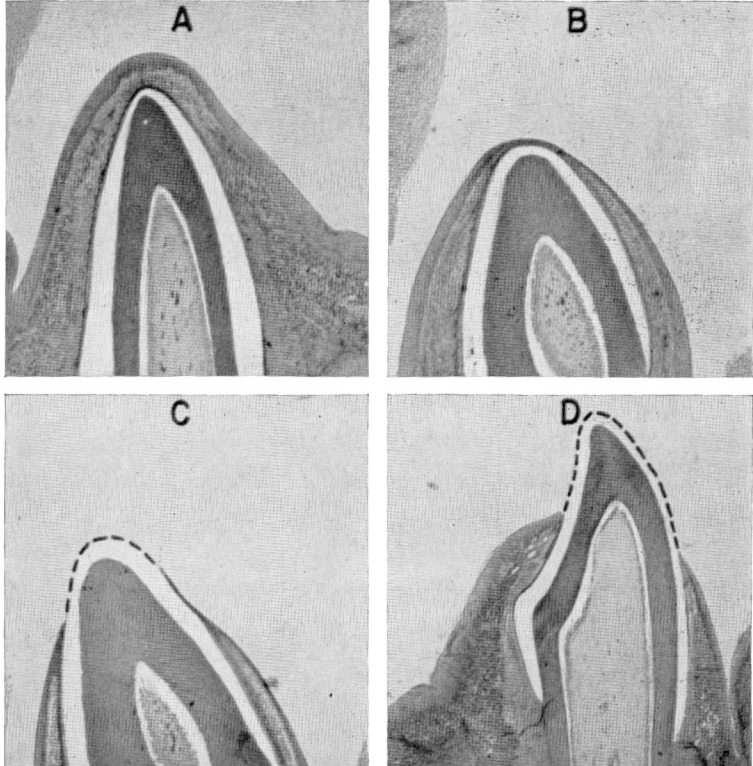

FIG. 6–15. Stages of eruption of crown tip into the oral cavity. *A*, reduced enamel epithelium overlying enamel space (acid-soluble enamel is decalcified away), is in near contact with overlying oral mucosa; *B*, fusion of enamel and oral epithelia; *C*, rupture of composite epithelium and emergence of cusp tip into the oral cavity; *D*, further eruption. The enamel epithelium is still in contact with the enamel of the cervical half of the crown.

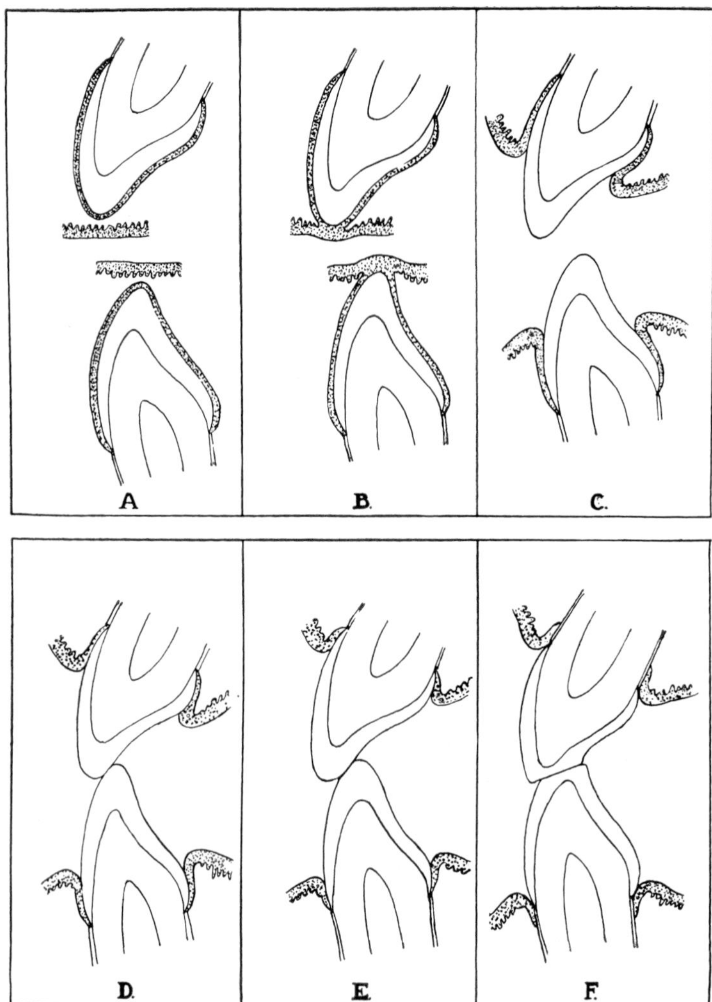

FIG. 6–16. Eruption of the teeth and attachment of the gingiva. *A,* approximation of the reduced enamel epithelium of the teeth and the oral epithelium; *B,* fusion of the reduced enamel epithelium and the oral epithelium; *C,* emergence of the crown into the mouth at which time the oral epithelium is continuous with the reduced enamel epithelium. The epithelial attachment, which is the reduced enamel epithelium, extends from the oral epithelium to the cemento-enamel junction. The gingival crevice extends from the face margin of the gingiva to the epithelial attachment. *D,* as the teeth erupt into occlusal contact, the length of the attachment decreases and the clinical crown increases; *E,* after the teeth are in occlusal contact, there is relatively less change in the length and position of the epithelial attachment in the absence of occlusal wear and periodontal disease; *F,* when the crowns become worn down as in attrition, the teeth may compensate by further eruption. The epithelial attachment may then be located on the cementum. *A* through *D,* eruption rate relatively fast; *E* and *F,* slow.

Due to the pressure exerted by the erupting tooth, this composite epithelium over the tip of the crown then atrophies and a perforation results. The tip of the crown then emerges through this perforation into the oral cavity (Figs. 6–15 and 6–16). The reduced enamel epithelium which remains attached to the unerupted part of the crown is termed the *epithelial attachment*. Only the primary cuticle (Nasmyth's membrane) remains on the surface of the erupted crown tip. The oral epithelium immediately surrounding the crown in combination with the reduced enamel epithelium forms the gingiva. As eruption proceeds, the epithelial attachment, cervical to the erupted portion of the crown, separates from the enamel surface. A crevice thus develops between the enamel surface and the gingiva which is termed the *gingival sulcus*. At the bottom of the sulcus the gingiva is attached to the enamel by means of the reduced enamel epithelium (epithelial attachment) (Fig. 6–16). The eruption of the crown and the resulting formation of the gingival sulcus is more rapid before the teeth reach occlusal contact. Then, the rate of eruption decreases and may extend over a period of years. During this latter period of eruption the epithelial attachment develops into a thicker layer of cells, probably by proliferation of the adjacent mucosal epithelial cells. As further eruption of the crown occurs, it is accompanied by a further separation of the epithelial attachment from the tooth. This occurs either by a pulling away from each other of the epithelial cells forming the base of the gingival sulcus (intra-epithelial split), or by their pulling away from the enamel surface. The separation results in a cervical shift in the position of the sulcus on the enamel surface (Fig. 6–16*C, D* and *E*). The epithelial cells which now form the attachment to the enamel surface at the base of the gingival sulcus multiply and strengthen the new attachment site. The normal site of the adult epithelial attachment is on the enamel at the enamel-cementum junction (Fig. 6–16*E*). After the teeth have undergone wearing off of the incisal edges (attrition), as in old age, further eruption and migration of the epithelial attachment may occur. The epithelial attachment in this instance will be on the cementum of the root (Fig. 6–16*F*).

During active eruption the fibers of the central zone of the periodontal membrane undergo reorientation. This zone of loosely arranged fibers appears more distinct as the fibers orient themselves in the direction of the long axis of the tooth (Fig. 6–23). When the erupting teeth have reached occlusion the intermediate or central zone of the periodontal membrane becomes indistinct; fiber bundles then can be seen passing from the surface of the root to the alveolar bone (Fig. 6–24). The periodontal membrane thus becomes a strong attachment apparatus which will be further strengthened as mastication begins.

Eruption Chronology

The chronology and sequence of mineralization, eruption and root formation of the human teeth is subject to much variation. As a rule, the sequence of deciduous tooth formation proceeds from the anterior part of the mouth to the posterior, the central incisors thus preceding the molars in development. The eruptive pattern does not entirely reflect this developmental pattern, however.

YEARS AND ORDER OF ERUPTION OF THE DECIDUOUS TEETH

	CI.	*LI.*	*CU.*	*1M.*	*2M.*
Maxillary	2	3	7–8	5–6	10
Mandibular	1	4	7–8	5–6	9

The cuspids erupt and root formation is complete at a later time than the first molars. This condition is due partially to the longer, curved path of eruption that they follow through the maxilla and because growth of the long roots of the cuspid takes a longer period of time to complete than the shorter molar roots. The eruption of the deciduous male teeth slightly precedes that of the female. The sequence of eruption of the permanent teeth is somewhat more complicated.

YEARS AND ORDER OF ERUPTION OF THE PERMANENT TEETH

	CI.	*LI.*	*CU.*	*1PM.*	*2PM.*	*1M.*	*2M.*	*3M.*
Maxillary	4	6	12	7–8	10	2	14	15
Mandibular	3	5	7–8	9	11	1	13	16

The first permanent teeth to erupt are the first permanent molars. They do not replace a deciduous tooth as the anterior permanent teeth do, but erupt posteriorly to the deciduous molar teeth. During the period of development of the first permanent molars, the jaws have lengthened to create this space in the posterior arch for them. The permanent incisors, cuspids and premolars erupt into the space created by the shedding of the deciduous incisors, cuspids and molars. The second and third permanent molars erupt later as space is made available for them by further growth in length of the jaws. The eruption of the permanent teeth of females and males follows the same general sequence except that in boys the first maxillary premolars precede the eruption of the mandibular canines. The reverse is true in girls. In general, the permanent teeth of girls erupt slightly earlier than those of boys. The following table on crown and root completion and eruption is based on radiographic analysis.

Deciduous Dentition

	Crown Completed[9]		*Eruption*[11]		*Root Completed*[9]	
	Maxilla	*Mandible*	*Maxilla*	*Mandible*	*Maxilla*	*Mandible*
Central	1½ mo.	2½ mo.	9⅓ mo.	7½ mo.	1½ yr.	1½ yr.
Lateral	2½ mo.	3 mo.	11 mo.	13¼ mo.	2 yr.	1½ yr.
Cuspid	9 mo.	9 mo.	19½ mo.	19⅔ mo.	3¼ yr.	3¼ yr.
1st Molar	6 mo.	5½ mo.	15⅔ mo.	16 mo.	2½ yr.	2¼ yr.
2nd Molar	11 mo.	10 mo.	28 mo.	26½ mo.	3 yr.	3 yr.

Permanent Dentition

	Crown Completed[8]		*Eruption*[6]		*Root Completed*[8]	
	Maxilla	*Mandible*	*Maxilla*	*Mandible*	*Maxilla*	*Mandible*
Central Inc.	4½ yr.	3½ yr.	7–7½ yr.	6–6½ yr.	10–11 yr.	8½–10 yr.
Lateral Inc.	5½ yr.	4–4½ yr.	8–8½ yr.	7¼–7¾ yr.	10–12 yr.	9½–10½ yr.
Cuspid	5½–6½ yr.	5½–6 yr.	11–11⅔ yr.	9¾–10¼ yr.	12½–15 yr.	12–13½ yr.
1st Premolar	6½–7½ yr.	6½–7 yr.	10–10⅓ yr.	10–10¾ yr.	12½–14½ yr.	12½–14 yr.
2nd Premolar	7–8½ yr.	7–8 yr.	10¾–11¼ yr.	10¾–11½ yr.	14–15½ yr.	14½–15 yr.
1st Molar	4–4½ yr.	3½–4 yr.	6–6⅓ yr.	6–6¼ yr.	9½–11½ yr.	10–11½ yr.
2nd Molar	7½–8 yr.	7–8 yr.	12¼–12¾ yr.	11¾–12 yr.	15–16½ yr.	15½–16½ yr.
3rd Molar	12–16 yr.	12–16 yr.	20½ yr.	20–20½ yr.	18–25 yr.	18–25 yr.

Shedding of Deciduous Teeth

The roots of the deciduous teeth are not completely formed until a year or more after eruption. During this time, the permanent tooth crowns are forming lingually and apically to the deciduous teeth. A short time after the roots are completed the crowns of the permanent teeth begin to stimulate root resorption. At this time, the developing crowns of the permanent teeth are in a position lingual to the roots of the anterior deciduous teeth and between the roots of the posterior deciduous molar teeth. The resorption is not a rapid process as it begins approximately a year after eruption of the deciduous teeth and continues until they are shed, the time at which the permanent teeth erupt. The process of resorption is a progressive but intermittent destruction of the root dentin and cementum (Fig. 6–17). It does not affect the entire root surface simultaneously so that some attachment fibers are present to hold the tooth in place. Thus, as one area of the root undergoes dissolution, another previously attacked area undergoes repair of its attachment fibers. After a short period of time, the repaired area is further attacked and the other area is repaired. During repair, cementum is deposited on the area of resorbed root surface and periodontal fibers become embedded in it and reattach the root to the socket. Finally only a hollow crown remains, attached only by fibers of the gingival region. As the deciduous teeth are shed the permanent teeth erupt.

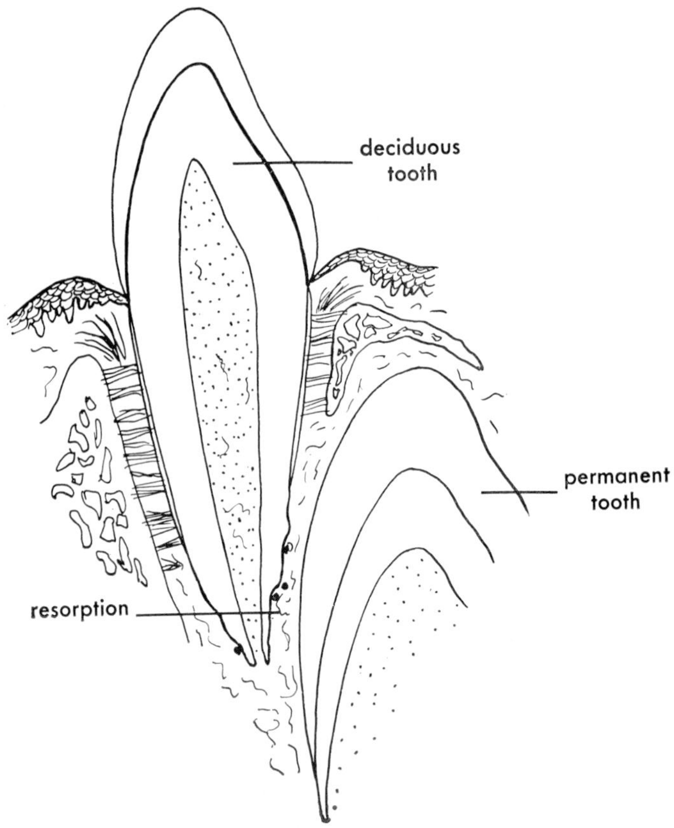

Fig. 6–17. Shedding tooth. Deciduous incisor root undergoing early stages of resorption. Calcifying permanent incisor crown at lower right.

HISTOLOGY OF THE ORAL MUCOSA

The lining of the mouth is similar to skin in that it is stratified squamous epithelium growing from a basal germinating layer while simultaneously shedding its surface cells. It differs from skin in that it is a more delicate membrane lacking a tough external layer and in general having a more fragile attachment to underlying structures. Unlike skin, the mucosa is kept constantly moist by the many mucous and serous glands which it contains. The mucosa consists of two recognizable layers, a basal germinating layer or *stratum germinativum* and a granular layer, the *stratum granulosum.* With adequate attrition a superficial layer of cornified cells, termed the *stratum corneum,* can be seen on the mucosa of the hard palate and gingiva. The mucosa varies thus throughout the mouth in regard to its thickness and its attachment to underlying structures. On this basis it is divided into regions. The epithelium covering the gingiva and hard palate is called the *masticatory mucosa* since it functions in the mastication of foods. The epithelium covering the inner surface of the cheeks, lips, soft palate, floor of the mouth and under surface of the tongue is termed *lining oral mucosa.* The epithelial covering of the dorsum of the tongue is designated as *specialized mucosa.*

Masticatory Mucosa

The gingiva and hard palate have a thick, firm, hornified epithelium which has an immovable attachment to the underlying bone. The gingiva exhibits no glandular or fatty tissue (submucosa) underlying the mucosa, whereas most of the hard palate does. The gingiva is composed of the attached gingiva and free gingiva. The free gingiva is that area of epithelium and underlying connective tissue immediately surrounding the necks of the teeth (Fig. 6–18). It has two free

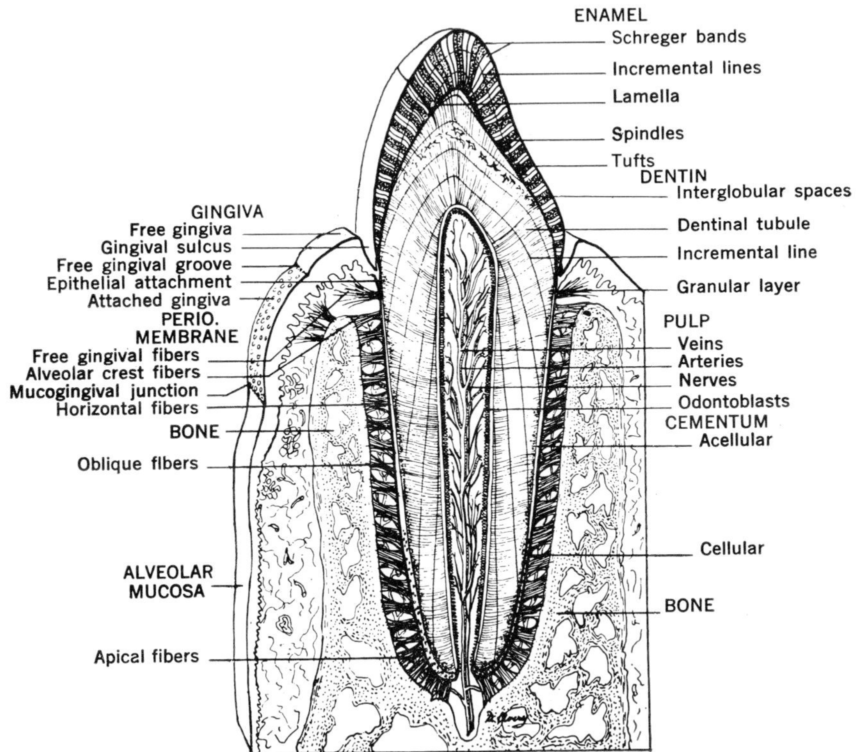

FIG. 6–18. Diagram of a tooth *in situ*. Relationship of enamel, dentin, pulp, cementum, periodontal membrane, bone, and gingiva illustrated.

surfaces. It is bounded internally by the gingival sulcus and externally by the oral cavity. The free gingiva is slightly movable and is compressed against the adjacent attached gingiva during mastication. A shallow groove in the epithelium, termed the *free gingival groove,* runs parallel to the gingival margin and divides the area of the free from the attached gingiva (Fig. 6–18). This groove is situated at the level of, or slightly below, the bottom of the gingival sulcus. The area below this groove is known as the attached gingiva, whereas that above it is the free gingiva. The attached gingiva is bounded internally by its attachment to the tooth's surface and externally by the oral cavity. In contrast to the free gingiva, the attached gingiva appears normally stippled, although the degree of stippling varies among individuals. An absence of stippling is usually due to an excess of tissue fluid (edema) beneath the epithelium. Both the free and attached gingiva contain many nerve fibers. Numerous branching nerve fibers are present in the deeper layers of the mucosa and the underlying connective tissue. The gingiva is continuous around the necks of all teeth. The gingival tissue located between the necks of adjacent teeth is known as the *interdental papilla.* The attached gingiva blends with the alveolar mucosa, along a scalloped line termed the *mucogingival junction* (Fig. 6–18). The alveolar mucosa covers the remainder of the alveolar process and is continuous with the lining mucosa of the lips and cheeks. There is a noticeable difference between the structure of the alveolar mucosa and the attached gingiva. On examination it is observed that the alveolar mucosa is thin, pink and loosely attached, whereas the gingiva is thick, hornified, stippled and with an immovable attachment to the underlying bone.

Lining Mucosa

The mucosa covering the remainder of the oral cavity, except for the dorsal surface of the tongue is known as lining mucosa. In contrast to the masticatory mucosa, the lining mucosa of the cheeks, lips, soft palate and floor of the mouth is movable and elastic and exhibits no hornification of its surface cells. The capillaries in the underlying connective tissue are quite close to the surface, causing the mucosa to appear deep pink or red. The lining mucosa varies in its firmness of attachment. The epithelium of the lips and cheeks has limited mobility, whereas that of the inferior aspect of the tongue, the soft palate and especially the floor of the mouth is relatively loosely attached. The lining mucosa of the lips and cheeks must follow the movement of the muscles underlying these areas. A firm connection between the mucosa and underlying muscles is necessary to prevent folding of the lining mucosa resulting in trauma and interference of function.

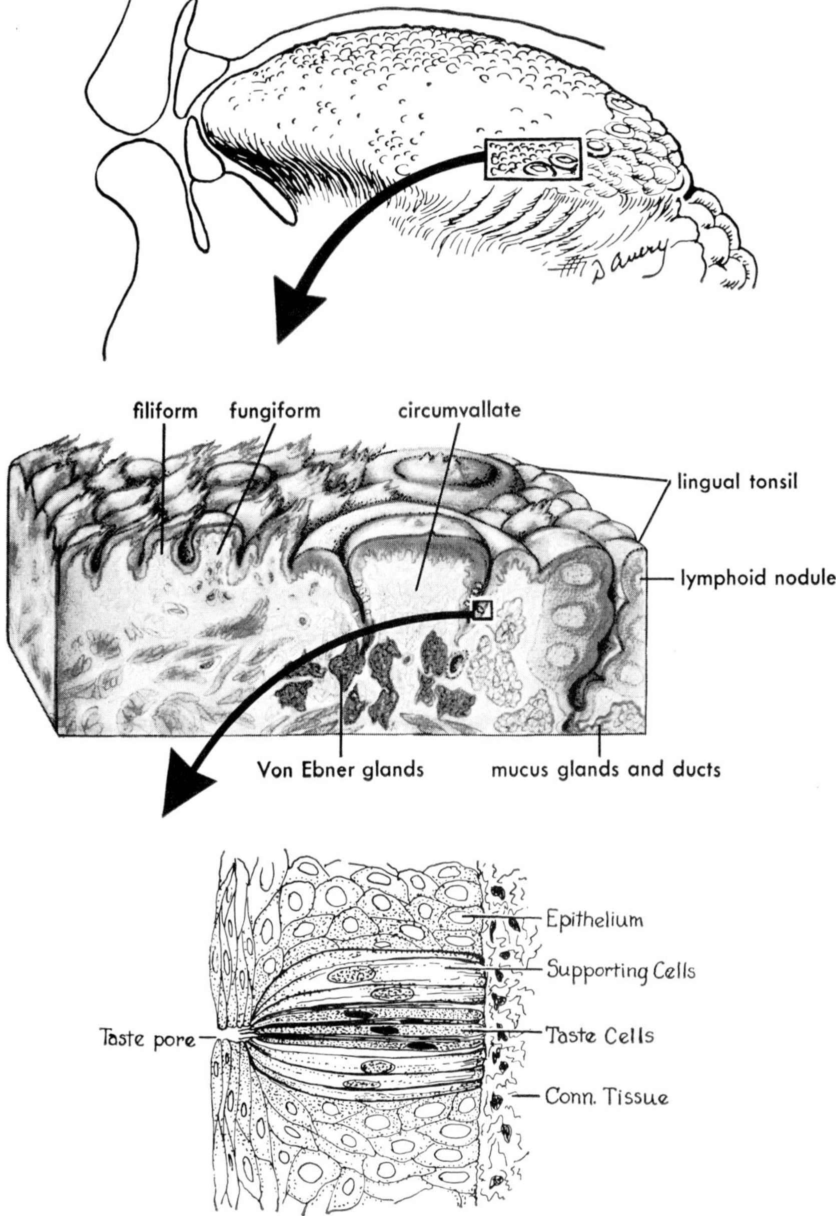

FIG. 6–19. Above, diagram of the body and base of the tongue. Center, a diagram showing the microscopic anatomy of the tongue. Below, a taste bud with a taste pore opening on the surface of the epithelium.

Specialized Mucosa

The third type of oral mucosa, known as specialized mucosa, is limited to the dorsal surface of the body and base of the tongue. The dorsum of the body or anterior two-thirds of the tongue differs from that of the base. The body of the tongue is covered with small papillae. These papillae are of four different types. The *filiform papillae,* numbering thousands, cover most of the dorsal surface on the tongue along with a scattering of *fungiform papillae* (Fig. 6–19). Along the lateral borders of the tongue are located the parallel furrows or *foliate papillae* and along the boundary between the body and base of the tongue are the *circumvallate papillae.* The base of the tongue is covered with oval hillocks of lymphoid tissue which constitute the lingual tonsil. Each of the hillocks is known as a lingual follicle and is composed of one or more lymph nodules containing lymphocytes. The follicles are covered with squamous epithelium which lines a centrally located pit in each follicle termed the lingual crypt. At the junction of the base and body of the tongue are a row of eight to twelve vallate or circumvallate papillae (Fig. 6–19). Although fewest in number, they are the largest of the papillae of the tongue. They are cylindrical with a flat top which is sunken below the surface of the epithelium (Fig. 6–19). Surrounding each papilla is a trench into which food in a fluid state may flow. On the sides of each papillae and occasionally on the adjacent walls of the circular trench there are an average of two hundred and fifty taste buds. These are small barrel-shaped organs containing taste receptor cells which are stimulated when food contacts them (Fig. 6–19). At the bottom of these trenches are excretory ducts of serous glands (*Glands of Von Ebner*). It is thought that these glands function to cleanse the area of the taste buds after tasting is effected. On the lateral borders of the posterior part of the body of the tongue are numerous parallel furrows in the epithelium. These are the foliate papillae and they also contain taste buds. The surface of the anterior two-thirds of the tongue is covered with thousands of filiform papillae and a sparse scattering of fungiform papillae. The filiform papillae are the smallest, yet most numerous of the lingual papillae. They appear on the surface of the tongue as slender folds of hornified epithelium with pointed tips curved towards the back of the tongue (Fig. 6–19). They have a thin connective tissue core containing blood vessels. These papillae account for the rough surface of the tongue and afford traction necessary to lick a semi-solid food such as an ice cream cone. (In many of the lower animals they are more highly developed, as in a cat combing loose hair from its coat.) The fungiform papillae are several times larger than the filiform papillae and appear as small, round, pink elevations on the dorsum of the tongue (Fig. 6–19). The connective tissue cores of these papillae contain many blood vessels which underlie the thin epithelial covering and account for the pink color. On the lateral sides of many of these papillae are found taste buds. The taste buds of various areas of the mouth all appear structurally similar (Fig. 6–19), although the sensations effected are quite different. The four primary taste sensations are sour, bitter, salty and sweet. Bitter taste perception is mediated on the posterior center of the tongue by the taste buds of the circumvallate papillae. The sour taste sensation is effected along the posterior lateral area by taste buds of the foliate papillae. The sweet taste is perceived at the tip of the tongue and salty along the sides, by taste buds of the fungiform papillae.

HISTOLOGY OF THE TEETH

The Enamel

Enamel is the hardest and most highly calcified tissue in the body. This is attributed to its high content of inorganic salts, to the structural arrangement of the enamel rods and the minute crystallites making up the rods. Mature enamel is composed of ninety-six per cent inorganic salts and only four per cent organic material and water. Although the enamel rods are oriented at right angles to the surface of the dentin at the dentino-enamel junction they do not travel a straight course to the enamel surface. Groups of adjacent rods, ten to twenty in number, spiral in a clockwise-counter clockwise relationship to each other as they direct themselves to the periphery of the enamel. This characteristic of enamel rod orientation is termed *Hunter-Schreger bands* (Figs. 6–18 and 6–20). In the cusps of molar crowns, twisting of groups of enamel rods is more extreme. In these areas, bundles of enamel rods appear to intertwine. This condition is known as *gnarled enamel.* Bending or intertwining of enamel rods probably strengthens the enamel to withstand occlusal stresses. It is believed that planes of tension arise in the enamel during formation and calcification. This tension results in defects appearing as thin sheet-like spaces which result from inadequate development of some enamel rods. Hypocalcified clefts extending from the outer surface of the enamel to the dentino-enamel junction are termed *lamellae* (Fig. 6–22). These enamel lamellae sometimes extend into the peripheral dentin, and are filled with organic material. Tension created from the twisting of groups of enamel rods may be responsible for another defect seen in enamel, *enamel tufts* (Fig. 6–22). Tufts are curved ribbon-like hypocalcified zones appearing at the dentino-enamel junction. They extend from the dentino-enamel junction into the enamel one-fifth to one-third

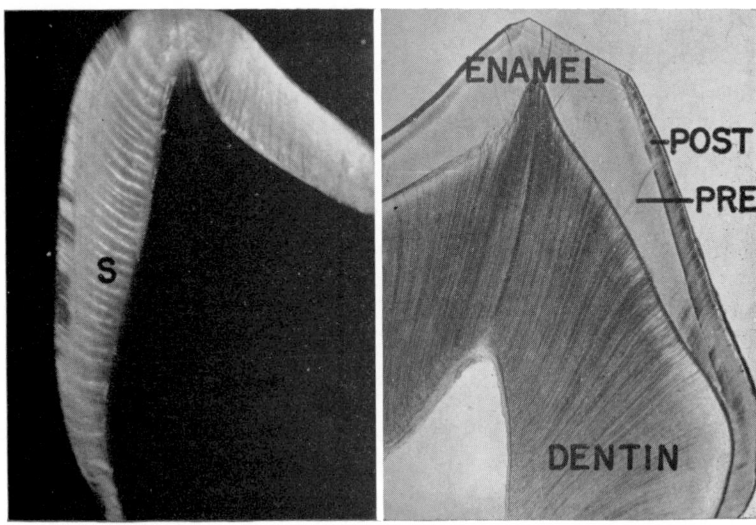

FIG. 6–20 FIG. 6–21

FIG. 6–20. A photomicrograph of enamel taken by reflected light to illustrate the alternating light and dark bands of Schreger. *S*, Hunter-Schreger bands.

FIG. 6–21. A photomicrograph of enamel and dentin taken by transmitted light to illustrate neonatal line. *Pre*-enamel is that portion of the enamel formed before birth, and *post*-enamel is that formed after birth.

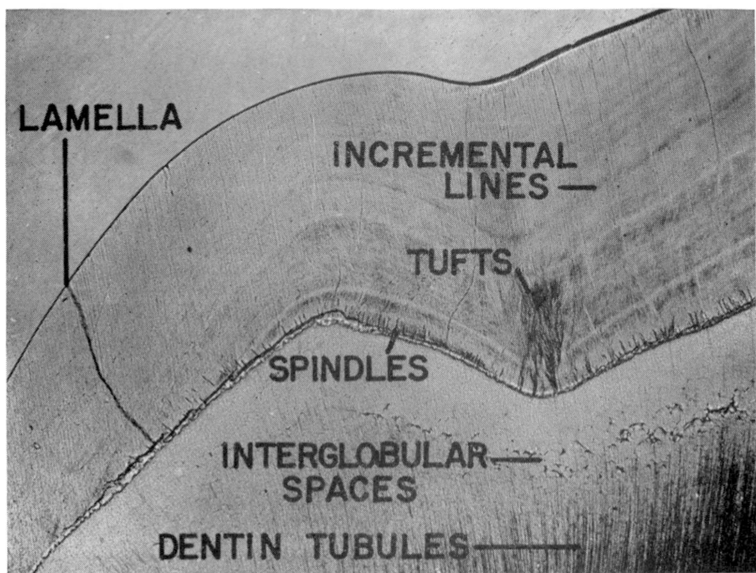

FIG. 6–22. Photomicrograph of tooth section by transmitted light illustrating structures found in enamel and dentin.

of its thickness. The area of the outer surface of enamel is greater than that at the dentino-enamel junction. Thus, the rods become slightly larger in diameter as they near the periphery of the crown. The enamel rods are all held together by means of a cement termed *interprismatic substance.* This substance was formed at the time the rods were developed covering all surfaces of the square or hexagonal shaped rods. Since many ameloblasts simultaneously deposited enamel rods, there are hypocalcified lines appearing where the ameloblast hesitated during the process of enamel production. The resultant lines established each successive contour of enamel matrix during its deposition. These incremental lines are termed *lines of Retzius* (Fig. 6–22). Part of the enamel of deciduous teeth is formed before and part after birth. This abrupt change in environment and nutrition is recorded in the enamel as a more pronounced incremental line termed the *neonatal line* (Fig. 6–21). The enamel matrix internal to this line represents the enamel formed before birth and the enamel external to it is enamel formed after birth. Covering the surface of the crown is an organic cuticle termed enamel cuticle or *Nasmyth's membrane.* It is a product of secretion of the ameloblasts and reduced enamel organ epithelium and persists on the crown only in areas not subject to attrition or mechanical abrasion.

The Dentin

Dentin, in contrast to enamel, is a living tissue, which under normal conditions is laid down throughout the life of the tooth. It consists of seventy per cent inorganic salts and the remainder is organic matter and water. The inorganic crystallites have similar properties to those of enamel and bone since they all chemically have an hydroxyapatite-like crystal structure. The organic material of dentin, as in bone, is collagen; but it is unlike that of enamel, which is a keratin-like substance. This condition is logical, since enamel is derived from epithelium which produces keratin, whereas bone and dentin form from connective tissue cells which produce collagen. Dentin does not contain cells within its matrix as bone does, but it does contain the processes or protoplasmic extensions of odontoblasts, the cells that aid in its formation. The odontoblastic processes, known as *Tome's fibers,* are situated within tubules in the dentin (Fig. 6–13). These processes extend from the odontoblast in the pulp through the entire thickness of the dentin and terminate at the dentino-enamel and dentino-cemental junctions. Near the termination of the process they branch and anastomose with adjacent processes. These branches are termed *secondary Tome's fibers.* The dentinal tubules are positioned at right angles to the pulpal surface of the dentin. They do not pass in a straight line through the dentin, but describe an S curve

(Fig. 6–18). The wall of the dentinal tubule is described as having a structure different from surrounding dentin. The tubule wall is termed the *sheath of Neumann.*

The dentin is formed by apposition of layers or increments of matrix. Along the border of the pulp a layer of *predentin* is deposited (Fig. 6–12). This layer is later calcified as another adjacent layer of predentin is being formed pulpally to it. The incremental lines in the dentin indicate this pattern of predentin-dentin formation and suggest that it is not a continuous process, but one of recurrent periods of deposition and hesitation (Fig. 6–13). The incremental lines in dentin are termed *contour lines of Owen* and appear at right angles to the direction of the dentinal tubules. A pronounced incremental line separates the prenatally from the postnatally deposited dentin.

In the dentin, near the dentino-enamel and dentino-cemental junctions, small hypocalcified zones sometimes appear. The irregularly shaped spaces near the dentino-enamel junction are termed *inter-globular spaces* (Figs. 6–18 and 6–22). Underlying the cementum is a narrow zone of granular appearing dentin, termed the *granular layer of Tomes* (Fig. 6–18). The reason for the appearance of these hypocalcified zones is not yet known.

External stimuli cause changes within the dentin as well as deposition of additional dentin. Pulpally, in the dentin underlying an area of attrition or a carious lesion, inorganic salts are sometimes deposited in the dentinal tubules. The tubules are gradually filled, isolating the pulp from the area of stimulation. These areas are termed *transparent dentin.* In other areas subject to stimuli, the odontoblasts may die and disintegrate, producing what are termed *dead tracts* in the dentin. Deposition of increased amounts of dentin occurs pulpally underlying such areas. This dentin usually appears morphologically different from the surrounding earlier formed dentin. The tubules may be fewer in number and bend sharply where they contact the area of earlier formed dentin. The earlier formed dentin is known as *primary dentin;* the secondary deposition is termed *secondary dentin.* If the stimuli is more severe than that causing the formation of primary or secondary dentin, a deposit of more rapidly formed dentin appears. This dentin appears more irregular with tubules twisted or lacking. This substance is termed *irregular dentin.* It seems evident that the blocking of dentinal tubules and addition of dentin pulpally are defense reactions of the pulp to preserve its vitality.

The Pulp

The pulp is made up of specialized loose connective tissue consisting mainly of fibroblasts and collagenous fibers. In contrast to connective tissue found elsewhere in the body, there are no elastic fibers in the dental pulp except in the walls of arteries. The matrix of dentin is composed of collagenous fibers derived from the pulp. Thus, there appear numerous young collagen fibers near the periphery of the pulp which are gradually incorporated in the forming predentin. These young fibers have the affinity for silver stain (argyrophillic) and are termed pre-collagen or *Korff's fibers.* As they are incorporated in the forming dentin they become mature collagen fibers and lose the silver staining affinity (Fig. 6–13).

The odontoblasts which have differentiated from the pulpal fibroblasts are situated adjacent to the predentin border along the periphery of the pulp (Figs. 6–12, 6–13, 6–18). They are columnar-shaped cells with an oval nucleus which is situated at the end of the cell farthest from the predentin. The protoplasmic extensions of the odontoblasts pass peripherally into the dentinal tubules. Small arteries and veins and numerous capillaries are present in the pulp. Nerve bundles enter the pulp and divide into many fine fibers (Fig. 6–18). Many of them are associated with walls of the blood vessels, regulating their dilation and contraction. Other nerves branch and terminate among the odontoblasts near the predentin. These are all pain reception fibers, and stimuli such as heat, cold and pressure that the tooth may experience are interpreted only as pain.

HISTOLOGY OF SUPPORTING STRUCTURES

The Cementum

Cementum is the bone-like substance deposited on the surface of the root of the tooth. Cementum is first deposited on the root at its junction with the crown, and later, as the root develops in length, along the entire root surface. Like bone, cementum is composed of 46 per cent inorganic substance, 32 per cent water and 22 per cent organic material. It functions as an attachment of the tooth to the socket by means of the periodontal fibers; it compensates for the continuous eruption of the tooth by apical deposition, and by the attachment of new periodontal fibers it makes possible their rearrangement during the eruption process.

Cementum may or may not contain cells within its matrix. Cellular cementum is usually limited to the apical third of the tooth while acellular cementum covers the remainder of the root surface (Fig. 6–18). Cellular and acellular cementum may be found deposited in alternating layers on areas of the root surface. The cells incorporated in cementum are termed *cementocytes.* They have numerous long processes radiating from the cell cytoplasm. They exist in spaces in the cementum termed *lacunae* (Fig. 6–25).

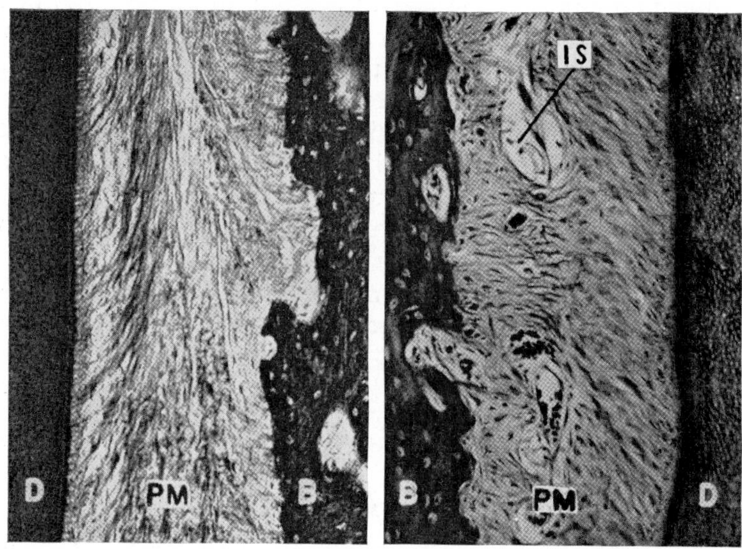

FIG. 6–23 FIG. 6–24

FIG. 6–23. Supporting structures of an erupting tooth. The central fibers of the periodontal membrane are aligned in the direction of the long axis of the tooth. *D,* dentin; *PM,* periodontal membrane; *B,* bone.

FIG. 6–24. Supporting structures of a tooth in occlusion. The periodontal fibers extend from bone to cementum. *B,* bone; *PM,* periodontal membrane; *D,* dentin; *IS,* interstitial space.

The Periodontal Membrane

The fibrous ligament attaching the tooth to the surrounding alveolar bone is termed the *periodontal membrane.* It is composed entirely of collagenous connective tissue fibers with no elastic fibers present. The fibers are grouped in bundles which are separated by areas of loose connective tissue, termed *interstitial spaces.* In these spaces are the nerves and blood vessels of the periodontal membrane. The epithelial rests appear scattered along the fibrous membrane near the cemental border. Although the ends of the periodontal fiber bundles are embedded in the bone and cementum, the direction and wavy course of the fibers allow the tooth limited movement. The fiber bundles of the periodontal membrane are termed *principal fibers* and are divided into three groups according to their position in relation to the tooth and surrounding structures. The *gingival group* fibers are attached to the cementum and traverse laterally into the free and attached gingiva (Fig. 6–18). The *transseptal group* fibers are attached in the cementum of two adjacent teeth. The fibers connect the teeth over the crest

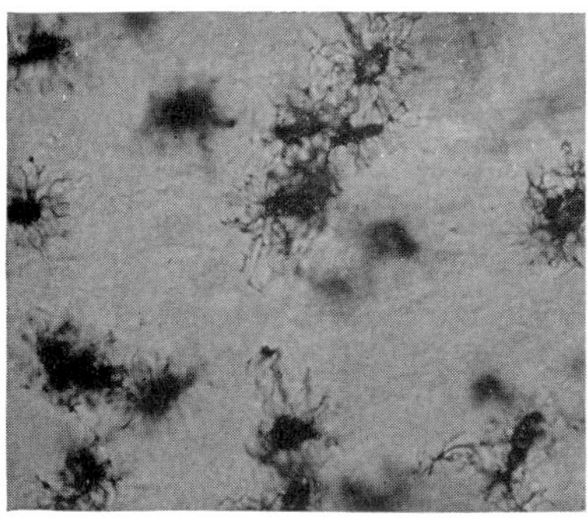

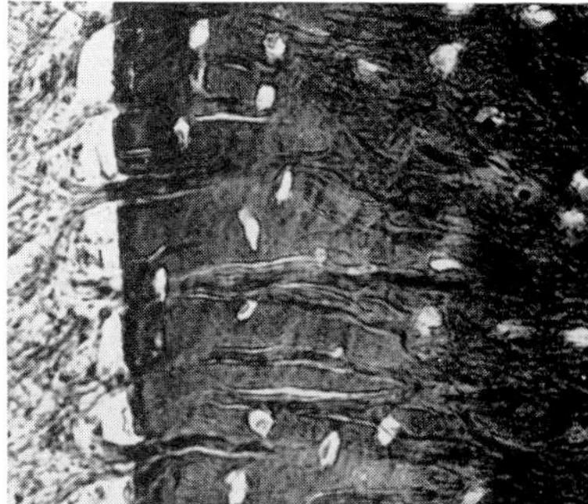

FIG. 6–25 FIG. 6–26

FIG. 6–25. Cellular cementum from the surface of the apical third of the root, illustrating lacunae with radiating canaliculi. Cementocytes normally occupy the lacunae with their processes filling the canaliculi.

FIG. 6–26. Perforating fiber bundles in bone. The principal fibers of the periodontal membrane penetrate the surface and are embedded in the cementum and alveolar bone.

of the alveolar process. The third group are the *alveolar fibers* which attach the tooth to the surrounding alveolar bone (Fig. 6–18). This group is subdivided into five groups according to the position of the alveolar fiber bundles. Proceeding from crown to root apex, the first group is the *alveolar crest fibers,* extending between the cementum and the tip or crest of the alveolar process. The next is the *horizontal group,* whose fiber direction runs horizontally from the cementum to the bone. The next group is the *oblique fiber group,* which traverses at an angle upward from the surface of the tooth to the adjacent bone. Near the apex of the root is the *apical group* of fibers which run at right angles to the root surfaces across to the alveolar bone. The *interradicular group* fibers attach the tooth root to the crest of the alveolar bone between the roots of the multi-rooted teeth.

The Alveolar Bone

The bone of the maxilla and mandible which surrounds and supports the teeth is known as alveolar bone or the alveolar process. This bone is similar to spongy and compact bone found elsewhere in the body, although its architectural design is suited to function in the attachment and the support of the roots of the teeth. The alveolar process may be anatomically divided into *alveolar bone proper* and *supporting bone*. The alveolar bone proper is the thin plate of compact bone immediately surrounding the roots forming the inner wall of the sockets of the teeth (Fig. 6–18). The principal fibers of the periodontal membrane are embedded in this bone. These small tufts of collagen fibers are termed *perforating* or Sharpey's fibers (Fig. 6–26). The dense alveolar bone proper is described radiographically as the *lamina dura,* since it appears in radiographs as a continuous white (radiopaque) line around the roots of teeth. The bone surrounding the alveolar bone proper is known as *supporting alveolar bone* and is composed of the compact bone of the outer cortical plates of the maxilla and mandible and the spongy marrow bone positioned between these plates and the alveolar bone proper. Microscopically, the outer cortical bone and the lamina dura consist of dense compact bone plates or lamellae. The interior of the alveolar processes is composed of numerous interconnecting bone trabeculae with blood vessels and nerves interposed (Fig. 6–18). In the anterior jaw areas these marrow spaces have been decreased in size by further deposition of bone in the form of numerous Haversian systems. These systems consist of series of bone lamellae laid down in concentric rings which encircle a nutrient canal. This bone is compact and dense in contrast to the spongy bone located in the interior of the alveolar processes around the molar teeth.

HISTOLOGY OF THE SALIVARY GLANDS

The salivary glands are classified according to their secretion as either serous or mucous. The parotid glands and glands of the vallate papillae are serous glands; the submandibular gland is predominantly serous with a few mucous cells; and the sublingual, the labial, small buccal, and anterior lingual glands are primarily mucous and contain a few serous cells. The glands of the glossopalatine, the base and border of the tongue and palatine glands are pure mucus secreting glands. The names of most of the salivary glands are in accordance with their location in the oral cavity. Approximately 1,500 ml. (quart and a half) of saliva is secreted daily and most of it by the three major salivary glands—the parotid, submandibular and to a lesser extent by the sublingual.

The largest salivary glands are the *parotid glands,* located bilaterally in front of the ears. Each is composed of a number of lobes which are individually sheathed in connective tissue and the entire gland is enclosed in a tough fibrous capsule. Each lobe of the gland is made up of numerous ball-like cell masses which are termed alveoli. These alveoli are composed of serous cells grouped around a narrow terminal portion of a duct which collects the watery secretion and carries it to larger ducts (Fig. 6–27). They join the parotid (Stenson's) duct which discharges the secretion into the oral cavity. The opening of the duct is located on the inner surface of the cheek opposite the second maxillary molar teeth. The pyramidal-shaped serous (albuminous) cells also secrete zymogen granules which are precursors of the enzyme amylase (Fig. 6–27).

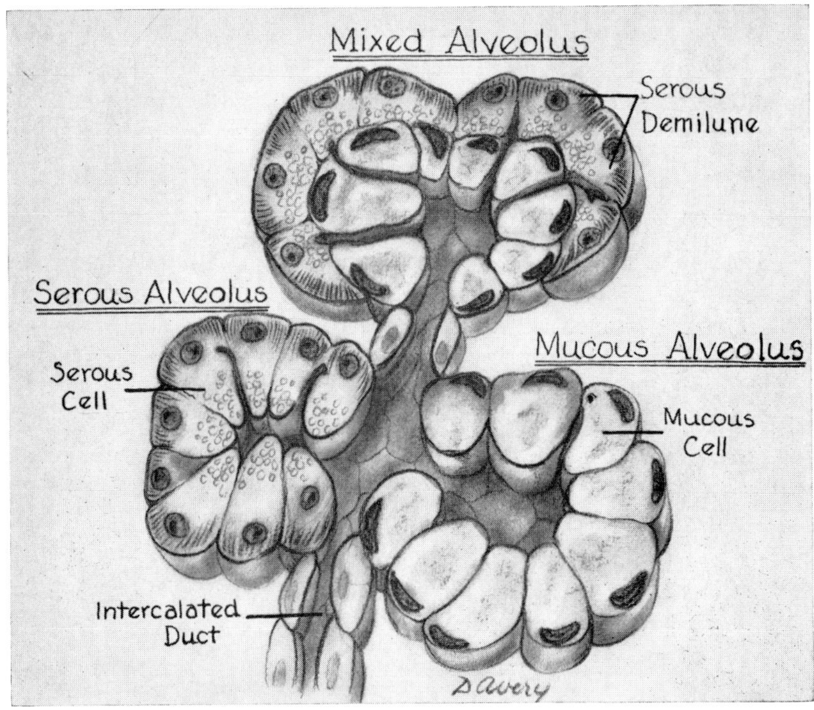

FIG. 6–27. Diagram of the alveoli of the salivary glands. The characteristics of a mucous, serous, and mixed alveolus are shown.

The two *submandibular glands* are loosely encapsulated in connective tissue. Each is about the size of a walnut and is located below and inside the angle of the mandible. It is a mixed gland containing both mucous and serous cells, but predominantly serous cells. The serous cells are similar to those of the parotid gland. The cuboidal-shaped mucous cells are grouped in lobular masses around the tubule into which the cells secrete mucin (Fig. 6–27). Mucin is accumulated in the duct system of the gland and is emptied into the submandibular (Wharton's) duct which, in turn, drains into the oral cavity behind the lower incisors on either side of the frenum of the tongue. The mucin, when mixed with the watery oral fluids, becomes mucus, causing the saliva to be thick and viscous.

The bilateral *sublingual* (under tongue) glands are composed of one larger and several smaller glands which do not have a connective tissue capsule. It is a mixed gland, made up primarily of mucus secreting cells. The serous cells are found generally in this gland as crescent-shaped masses of cells termed demilunes which overlie or cap the mucous cells of the alveoli (Fig. 6–27). The resulting serous and mucous secretion is transported by the sublingual (Bartholin's) duct to its orifice which is either in common with or adjacent to the submandibular duct opening, lingual to the mandibular incisor teeth.

HISTOLOGY OF THE TEMPOROMANDIBULAR JOINT

The temporomandibular joint is composed of the condyles of the mandible and the fossa and articular eminence of the temporal bone. The joint is enclosed in a loose but strong fibrous connective tissue capsule which is lined with a thin layer of synovial tissue. Positioned between the condyles and temporal bone is the dense fibrous articular disk (Fig. 6–28). It is composed mainly of collagenous connective tissue with a few scattered elastic fibers. Lining the bony articular fossa and covering the tubercle and the condyles is a layer of fibrous

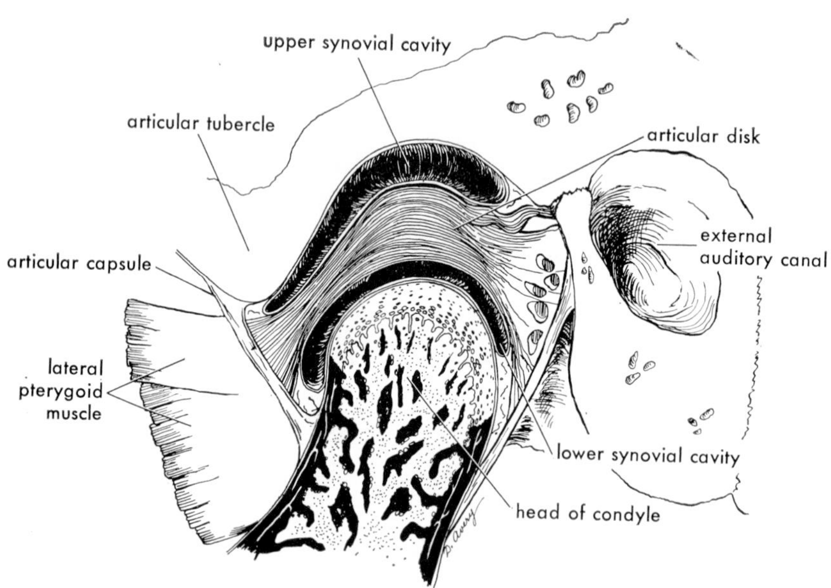

FIG. 6–28. A section through the temporomandibular joint, illustrating the dense fibrous articular disk with the adjacent superior and inferior articular spaces. Underlying the dark stained fibrous covering of the condyle is a band of hyalin cartilage. Below the cartilage is the cancellous bone of the growing condyle.

connective tissue. In the less superficial layers of this fibrous tissue overlying the condyles, cartilage cells originate. The chondroblasts deposit cartilage on the head of the ramus underlying the fibrous covering. As the cartilage layer becomes thicker, the earliest deposited cartilage deep in the head of the ramus is utilized in the formation of bony trabeculae within the ramus (Fig. 6–28). These bony trabeculae increase in size by further deposition of layers of bone on their surfaces. As they enlarge they contact other trabeculae, fusing together to form a network of bone with marrow spaces between them. This network comprises the cancellous bone of the interior of the growing ramus. On the surface of the ramus, a layer of compact bone persists and is remodeled by deposition externally and resorption internally to compensate for the increase in size during growth. In older individuals the cartilage of the condyles is replaced by bone and the marrow spaces are decreased in size.

BIBLIOGRAPHY

1. Arey, L. B.: *Developmental Anatomy*. 7th Ed. Philadelphia, W. B. Saunders Co., 1965.
2. Avery, J. K., Visser, R. L., and Knapp, D. E.: The Pattern of the Mineralization of Enamel. J. Dent. Res. *40,* 1004–1019, 1961.
3. Diamond, M., and Weinmann, J. P.: *The Enamel of Human Teeth*. New York, Columbia University Press, 1940.
4. Ham, A. W., and Leeson, T. S.: *Histology*. 4th Ed. Philadelphia, J. B. Lippincott Co., 1961.
5. Hamilton, W. J., Boyd, J. D., and Mossman, H. W.: *Human Embryology*. Baltimore, The Williams & Wilkins Co., 1952.
6. Hurme, V. O.: Ranges of Normalcy in the Eruption of Permanent Teeth. J. Dent. for Children, *16,* 11–15, 1949.
7. Bloom, W., and Fawcett, D.: *Textbook of Histology*. 8th Ed. Philadelphia, W. B. Saunders Co., 1962.
8. Nolla, C. M.: The Development of the Permanent Teeth. Thesis and Unpublished Data, University of Michigan, Ann Arbor, 1952.
9. Sicher, H.: *Orban's Oral Histology and Embryology*. 5th Ed. St. Louis, C. V. Mosby Co., 1962.
10. Patten, B. M.: *Human Embryology*. 2nd Ed. New York, Blakiston Division, McGraw-Hill Book Co., Inc., 1953.
11. Robinow, M., Richards, T. W., and Anderson, M.: The Eruption of Deciduous Teeth. Growth, *6,* 127–133, 1942.
12. Schour, I.: Early Human Tooth Development, with Special Reference to the Relationship Between the Dental Lamina and the Lip-Furrow Band. J. Dent. Res., *6,* 699–717, 1929.
13. ———*Noyes' Oral Histology and Embryology*. 8th Ed. Philadelphia, Lea & Febiger, 1960.

7

Oral Pathology

Elmer E. Kelln

ORAL DEVELOPMENTAL DISTURBANCES

Disturbances of the Oral Cavity and Its Related Structures

Clefts of the oral cavity and its related structures are among the most dramatic of the oral anomalies. They are a congenital defect resulting from a failure in development or approximation of embryonal processes during embryogenesis. Such defects vary widely in degrees of severity. Some occur rarely; these include cleft tongue, cleft mandible, and oblique facial clefts. Two defects of this sort, however, are relatively common; these are the cleft lip and cleft palate.

A cleft lip results when the soft tissues of the maxillary process and the globular process fail to fuse. Should the maxillary process of both sides fail to unite with the globular process, the consequence is a bilateral cleft lip . A similar but more compound defect results when the globular process is absent or underdeveloped whereby the central part of the upper lip is involved (Fig. 7–1).

A cleft palate results from a failure of approximation and fusion of embryonal processes of the upper jaw (Fig. 7–2). The cleft may extend posteriorly-anteriorly or anteriorly-posteriorly to any degree. When an anterior-posterior cleft is present, the failure is in bony fusion between the maxillary and globular processes; thus, this type of cleft palate is frequently associated with a cleft lip.

While the various kinds of clefts are of great clinical concern, the most common of oral anomalies are not. One anomaly, known as Fordyce's spots, is manifested as yellowish granules under the oral mucosa, primarily that of the cheeks. Fordyce's spots are deep-seated ectopic sebaceous skin glands and therefore readily seen from the opposite or mucosal surface of the cheek (Fig. 7–3). Another common anomaly is the bony enlargement known as a torus (Fig. 7–4). If it is located on the midline of the palate, it is called torus palatinus;

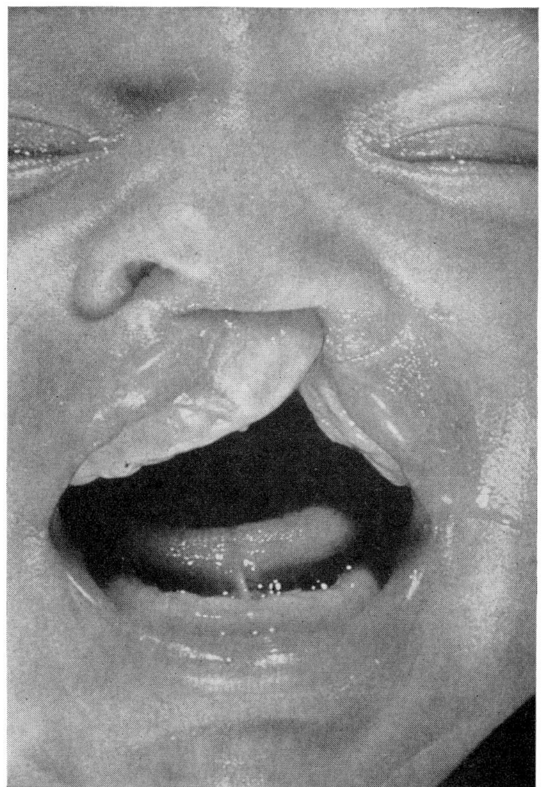

FIG. 7–1. The anastamosis between the left maxillary and globular processes has failed, resulting in a unilateral cleft lip. Note that the bony tissue of this fissural line has also failed to unite; thus this infant has an associated unilateral cleft of the anterior palate.

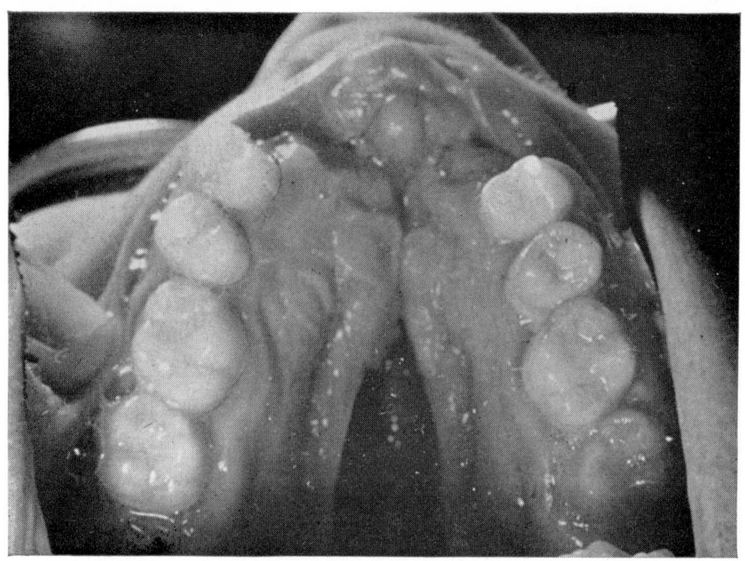

Fig. 7–2. This palatal view reveals a posterior-anterior cleft as well as an anterior cleft caused by the underdevelopment of the globular process. The rudimentary globular process is seen as a nodular growth in place of the premaxilla.

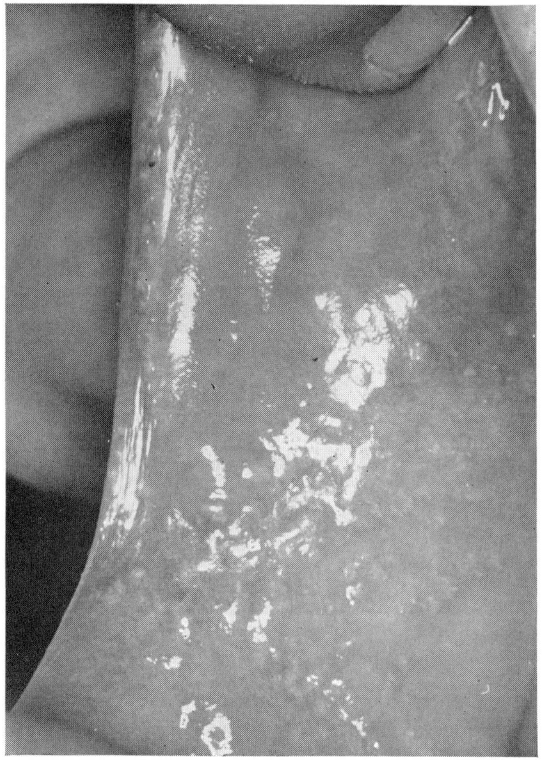

Fig. 7–3. Note the whitish granules on the inner side of the cheek mucosa. Since sebum yellows as the individual ages, Fordyce's granules become more conspicuous as age progresses.

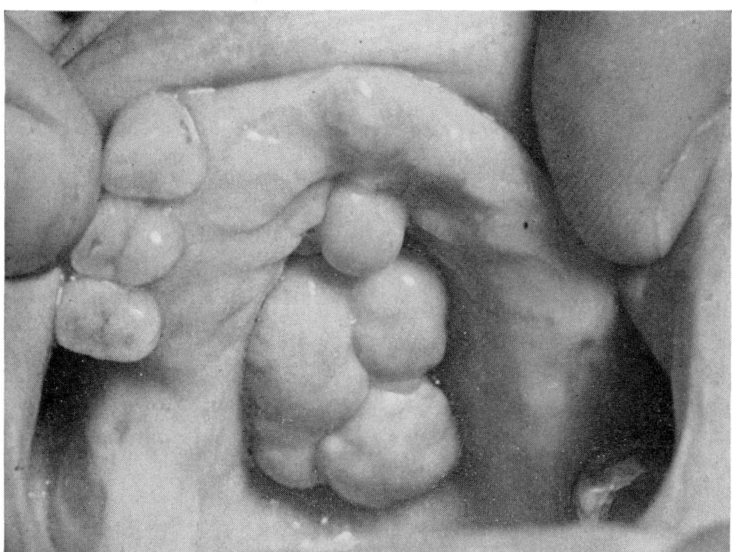

FIG. 7–4. This near edentulous person has a large bony tumor on the arch of the palate. Only if these are excessive or interfere with the fabrication of a denture, is there indication for removal. Such lesions are a common clinical finding.

if on the lingual aspect of the mandible, it is called torus mandibularis. Mandibular tori usually are adjacent to the cuspids and bicuspids. Tori are true bony tumors and will be discussed in greater detail in the section on neoplasias.

As was mentioned before, the tongue is rarely found cleft. It is, however, subject to specific developmental anomalies which may be classed as clinically significant or clinically nonsignificant. There are three nonsignificant anomalies which require recognition. Fissured tongue is a congenital alteration in which the dorsal surface of the tongue is furrowed and rugated. It is readily demonstrated by spreading the mucosa (Fig. 7–5). A condition known as rhomboid glossitis appears as a diamond-shaped area just anterior to the foramen caecum and denuded of normal lingual epithelium (Fig. 7–6). It occurs when the tuberculum impar, which normally is submerged when the copula fuses with the two lateral anterior portions of the tongue, fails to become covered. Frequently one sees a tongue which has a map-like dorsal surface. This mosaic pattern, termed geographic tongue, is the result of alterations in the regularity of the lingual epithelium. Causative factors are thought to be nutritional, familial and/or neurogenic, but since this issue is not settled and it appears to be of little clinical significance, it would be well not to consider it in detail here.

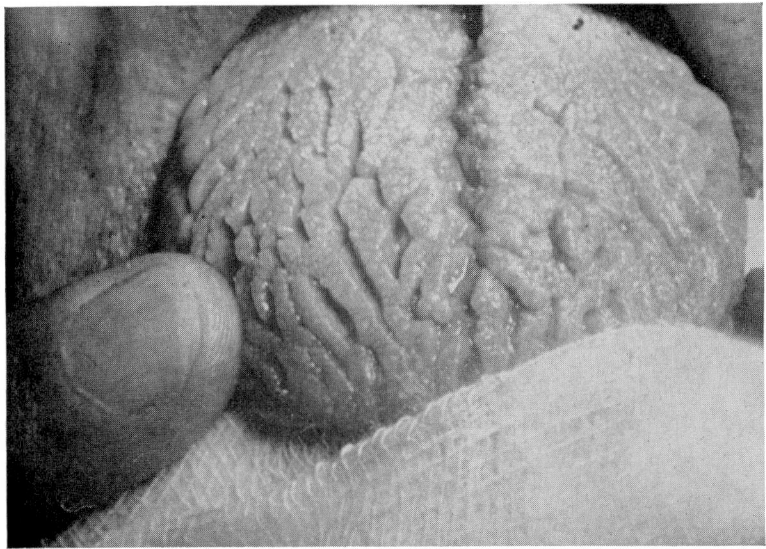

FIG. 7–5. Note the deep fissures on the surface of this tongue. Unless the mucosa is spread as shown, the fissures may be collapsed and the surface epithelium appear typical. It is obvious that a fissured tongue presents grooves in which microorganisms could flourish should an individual become debilitated.

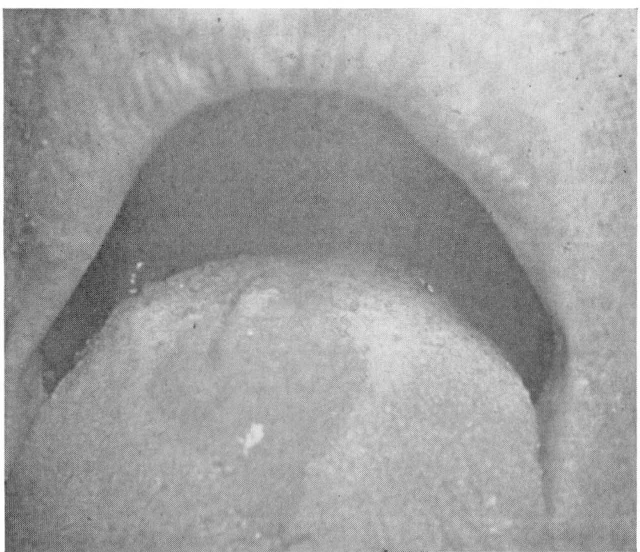

FIG. 7–6. The dark diamond-shaped area is termed rhomboid glossitis. The name only describes an early erroneous impression that this was an inflammatory lesion. Other than proper recognition, this lesion has no further clinical significance.

An anomaly of the tongue which is of clinical significance is familiarly known as tongue-tie (Fig. 7–7). Termed ankyloglossis, the condition is the result of a persistent and anteriorly attached lingual frenulum. It may interfere with the freedom of tongue movements and cause speech defects. The embryonal cells destined to form the thyroid gland originate as an epithelial invagination at the area of the foramen caecum at the base of the tongue. Should these cells fail to travel to the proper thyroid level, thyroid tissue may form in the base of the

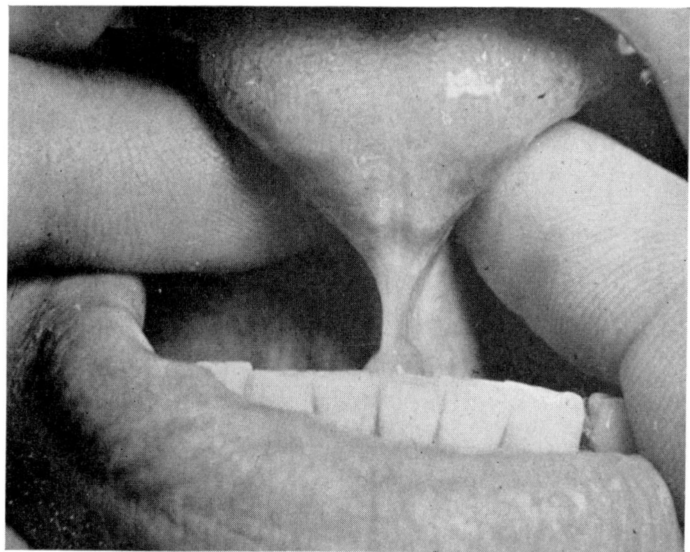

FIG. 7–7. Ankyloglossia. Note that the lingual frenulum is prominent and follows along the ventral surface of the tongue, thus attaching the anterior tongue to the floor of the mouth. Such an attachment may interfere with speech and prevent the individual from protruding the tongue to any extent.

tongue.[2] Should the channel formed by the invagination (thyroglossal duct) fail to involute, it may undergo subsequent pathological degeneration. This channel may extend from the base of the tongue to the proper thyroid level. The degeneration is usually cystic, resulting in a thyroglossal duct cyst. The final developmental disturbance of the tongue to be considered is that of the excessively large tongue, or macroglossia. The most common childhood etiology is a vascular tumor such as a hemangioma or lymphangioma[7] (Fig. 7–8). In the adult, the most common causes of macroglossia are amyloidosis and cancer. The lingual myxedema seen in a hypothyroid condition also causes macroglossia and associated speech problems.

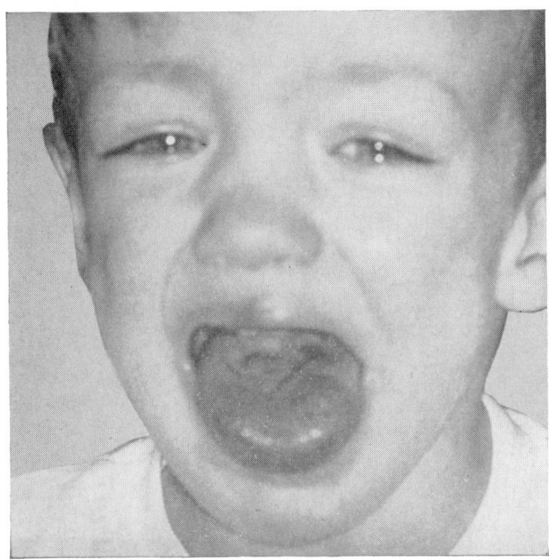

FIG. 7–8. A mixed angiomatous lesion in this tongue made it impossible for this child to retain the tongue inside the mouth. Thus it frequently dried and cracked causing much pain and predisposing it to infection.

Disturbances in Dentition

The first disturbance to be regarded here is based on the number of teeth. The absence of teeth is referred to as anodontia (Fig. 7–9). This may be partial anodontia, should a few teeth be missing, or total, should all the teeth be missing. If the teeth are congenitally missing, it is best to refer to this as true anodontia and the term false anodontia should be used if the missing teeth are unerupted. Should an individual have total extractions, the term "edentulous mouth" is preferred. The teeth most frequently found to be congenitally missing are second bicuspids, third molars, and maxillary lateral incisors.

An extra tooth or teeth are termed supernumerary; like congenitally missing teeth their occurrence is not unusual. Supernumerary teeth result from extra tooth-forming organs over and beyond the proper number.[4] These teeth are usually of a malformed and dwarfy nature. The most frequent site of supernumerary teeth is posterior to a third molar or between the maxillary central incisors. The latter is referred to as mesiodens.

Certain disease complexes exist where the above disturbances are part of the symptom complex. In ectodermal dysplasia, many or all the teeth may fail to form and this would be an example of a true partial or total anodontia, depending on the number of teeth that are present.

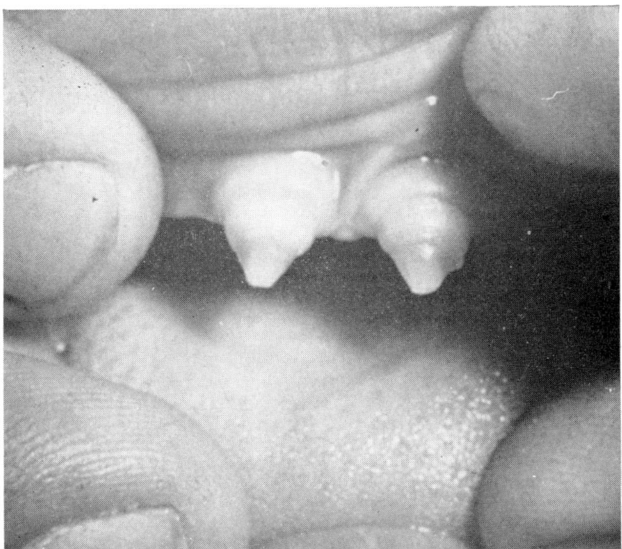

FIG. 7–9. Ectodermal dysplasia with almost true total anodontia. The two conical teeth seen constitute this child's entire dentition. Due to a lack of expression on the part of ectodermal genes, this child also had sparse light hair, blue eyes, and atrophic appearing skin which lacked adnexal structures.

In cleidocranial dysostosis, it may clinically appear that the teeth are missing. On roentgenograms, however, it may be apparent that teeth had developed but never erupted. This would be an example of false anodontia.

The second disturbance in dentition to be regarded is based on tooth formation and structure. During the tooth development many anomalies can occur which actually represent embryonal accidents or laxities. The most common are various forms of hypocalcifications of enamel and dentin. In this condition, the normal formation of the calcium hydroxy apatite crystal is disturbed. These disturbances may be caused by defective tooth germs, dietary defects, and disease, thus influencing tooth calcification. A common structural defect is an under-sized tooth or microdontia. Should only one or a few teeth be so affected, the condition would be known as localized microdontia. Should the entire dentition be affected, the condition would be generalized microdontia. The most common teeth displaying microdontia are third molars and maxillary lateral incisors. The common so-called peg-shaped lateral is an appropriate example.

Many lesser occurring structural defects should be considered. Dens in dente is the result of an invagination of the enamel-forming organ giving the roentgenographic picture of a tooth within a tooth. The splitting of the enamel forming organ resulting in what appears to be a siamese crown on one root is termed gemination (Fig. 7–10). A similar clinical picture may be seen in fusion; however, here two teeth

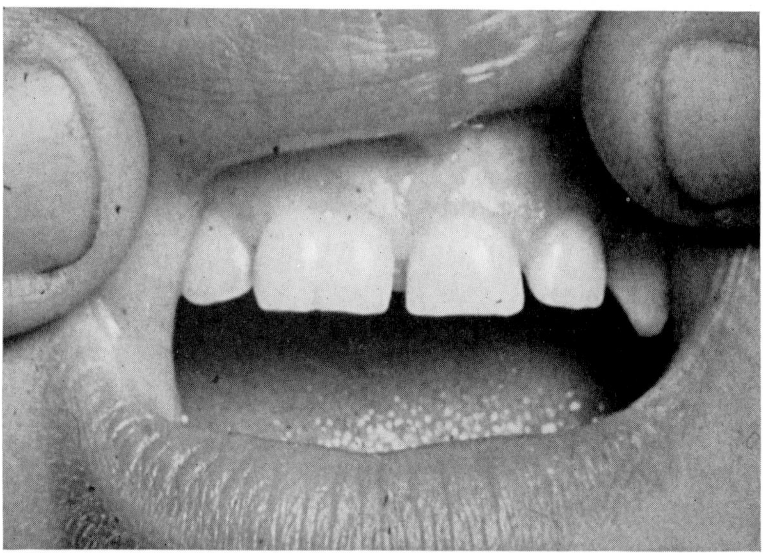

FIG. 7–10. Gemination. During crown formation the enamel-forming organ duplicated itself thus forming a twin crown on a single root. A roentgenogram is often required in differentiating such an anomaly from fusion.

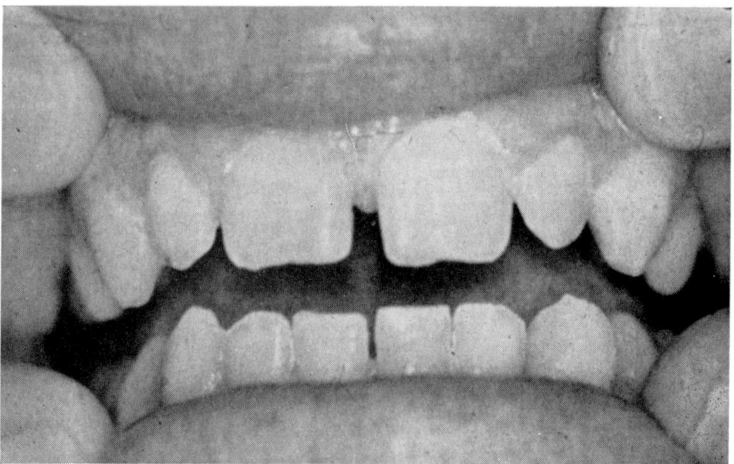

FIG. 7–11. Note the massive size of the maxillary central incisors in relation to the other teeth. This is an example of relative localized macrodontia. This would have been generalized or total macrodontia if all teeth were larger than that anticipated by the overall size of the individual.

are fused during formation and the union is by dentin and enamel. Fusion in turn should not be confused with concrescence, for this indicates that two adjacent teeth are attached to each other by cementum only.

There is no limit to examples of structural defects; a few additional ones are dwarfed teeth, shovel teeth, abnormally large teeth (macrodontia), hypercementosis, dilacerations, enamelomas, and odontomas (Fig. 7–11). The last two will be discussed under odontogenic tumors.

Anomalies Related to Specific Disease Conditions

Two specific diseased conditions which contribute to the malformation of the overall dentition have been mentioned in the examples of ectodermal dysplasia and cleidocranial dysostosis. Other important ones remain to be discussed.

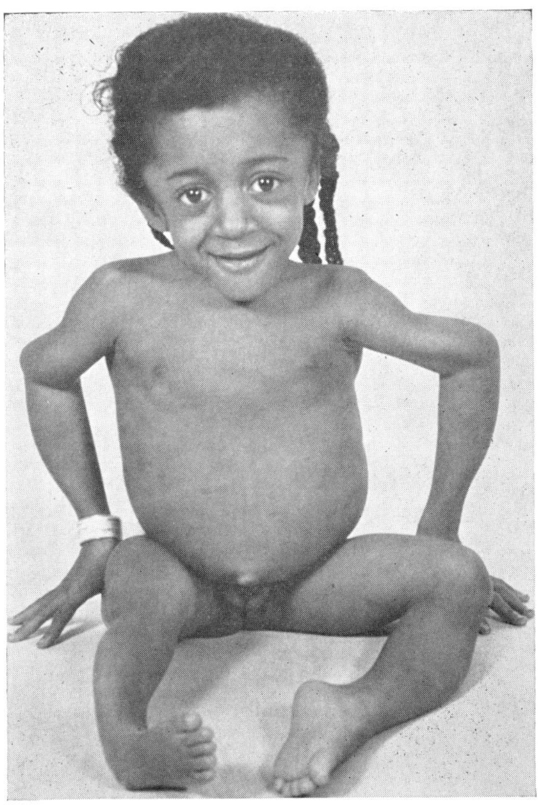

Fig. 7–12. This child has experienced numerous fractures since birth. In osteogenesis imperfecta the cortical shaft of the bone is poorly developed, thus the name. The subsequent illustration (Fig. 7–13) shows associated tooth anomalies in an older individual.

Osteogenesis imperfecta is an overall skeletal disease where it would appear that the mesenchymal genes lack expression (Fig. 7–12). This results in poor bone and dentin formation subjecting the survivor to frequent bone fractures and tooth root pathology. The root is usually shortened and spindle shaped, lacking a pulp canal. The hypoplastic dentin formation renders disturbance in crown color, giving a blue hue to the teeth; it is referred to as opalescent dentin or dentinogenesis imperfecta. It must be remembered that the enamel is normal and only reflects the underlying poorly developed dentin (Fig. 7–13).

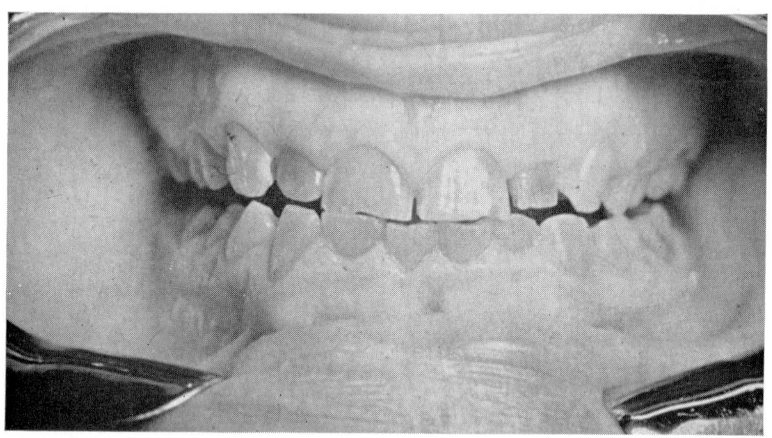

FIG. 7–13. Dentinogenesis imperfecta. While it is typical for this tooth anomaly to accompany osteogenesis imperfecta, forme frustes occur and possibly only the teeth are affected. The teeth have a blue tone and the enamel fractures readily due to poorly developed supporting dentin.

Another classic disease affecting tooth formation is congenital syphilis. Should the fetus become infected with the treponema palidum, the spirochetes interfere with maturation of the teeth undergoing development at the time. The spirochete paralyzes the middle mamelon of the tooth-forming organ, resulting in a notched defect if the lateral sides of the crown are already firm. If the lateral sides are still malleable when the middle mamelon is paralyzed, they will collapse to cover the defect and result in a peg-shaped or barrel-shaped tooth.

In molars the organism interferes with cusp formation and the end product is a pebble or mulberry-like occlusal surface; therefore these teeth are referred to as mulberry molars. The tooth defect seen in congenital syphilis is one part of Hutchinson's triad, a hallmark of congenital syphilis.

ORAL AND RELATED CYSTS

A cyst is an epithelial lined cavity containing a fluid. Variations occur in which an epithelium lining may never form or be destroyed. This latter group is best referred to as pseudo-cysts. The histogenesis and formation of a cyst is based upon degeneration of epithelial cell aggregates which have been entrapped into deeper tissues[3]. This inclusion of epithelial cells may be the result of two embryonal processes meeting and the epithelium covering the converging edges is retained and embedded when the processes become autonomous. A cyst may develop along these embryonal cleavage lines; the histogenesis of these cysts is therefore developmental. The class includes globulo-maxillary cysts, median palatine cysts, and nasopalatine cysts (Fig. 7–14).

Another source of epithelial inclusions in deeper structures are the epithelial cells of the enamel-forming organ which remain behind in

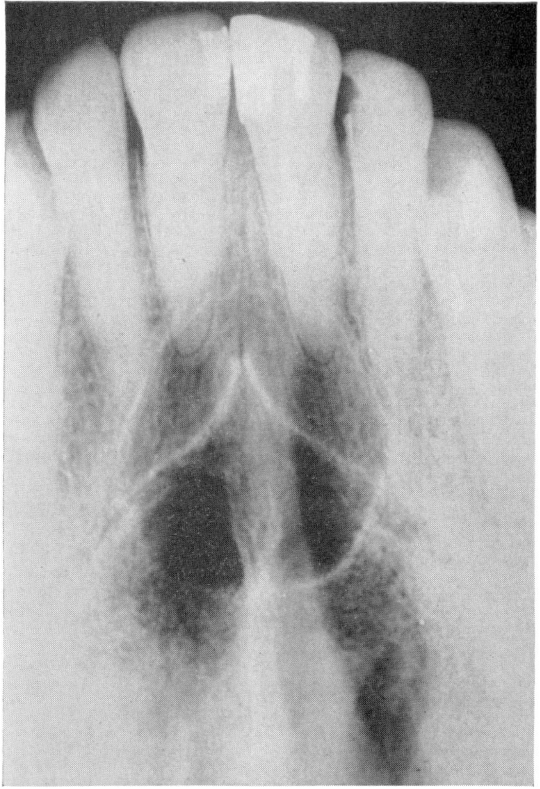

FIG. 7–14. Median palatal cyst. The epithelial cells lining this cyst were entrapped when the two opposing primitive palatine shelves converged to form the hard palate. Therefore this is an example of a nonodontogenic fissural cyst.

the periodontal ligament and are referred to as epithelial rests of Malassez, which are normally dormant. The cysts which become lined by the rest of Malassez or any part of the tooth-forming organ are also developmental but odontogenic in this case. This group consists of the radicular cysts, residual cysts, dentigerous cysts, primordial cysts, lateral periodontal cysts, and eruption cysts (Fig. 7–15).

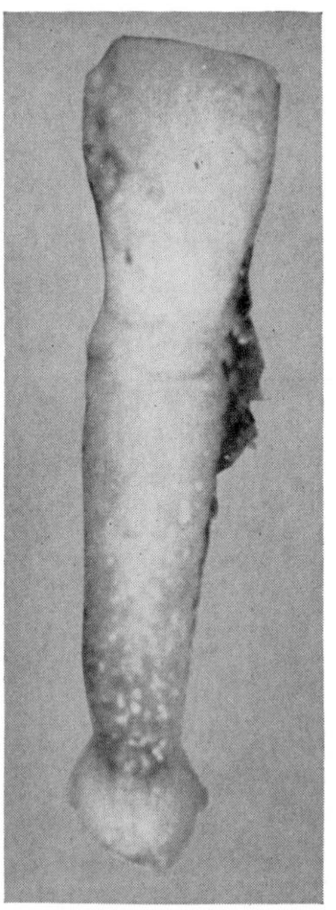

FIG. 7–15. Radicular or apical cyst. This cyst was small enough and attached firmly to the tooth root thereby enabling its removal with the tooth. On a roentgenogram one would have noted a radiolucent area at the tooth apex.

Retention cysts are a group of cysts best referred to as pseudocysts. Should the normal opening of a saliva-secreting gland become obstructed, the continuous secretion of the gland would cause a bleb. Blebs occurring from one of the minor salivary glands are mucoceles; however, should the obstruction occur in a duct, a large dilatation or retention cyst may form. A ranula is such a retention cyst occuring on the floor of the mouth (Fig. 7–16*A*). Wharton's duct is the most frequent salivary duct in which a ranula forms, and is usually the result of a salivary stone (sialolith) blocking its long tortuous duct (Fig. 7–16*B*).

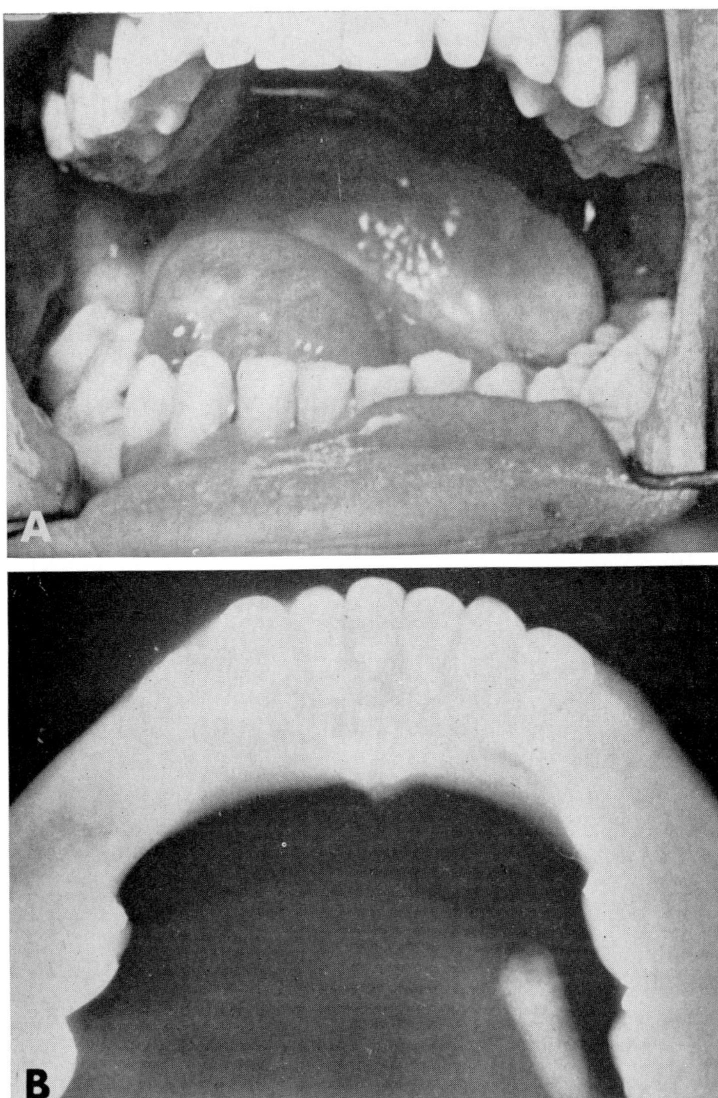

FIG. 7–16. *A* shows a large retention cyst on the floor of the mouth. This cyst is boggy to palpation and has a blue dome over it. Its similarity to a frog's belly gave rise to the name "ranula" and this term is still used today. *B* shows a stone (sialolith) in one of the ducts of the floor of the mouth. This was taken from an occlusal roentgenogram.

DISEASES OF THE ORAL MUCOSA AND JAWBONES

The oral cavity is subject to many diseases unto itself, in addition to becoming involved when other diseases are present. Frequently the initial signs of systemic diseases are in the oral cavity. The life of an oral epithelial cell is about thirty days in contrast to the life of a skin epithelial cell, which is about one hundred days. So it stands to reason that when a systemic disease affects cellular physiology, it can manifest itself orally before manifesting itself cutaneously. For the benefit of better correlation, diseases of the oral mucosa will be discussed under separate heading of infections, relation to skin diseases, signs of endocrine disturbances, and oral changes which accompany blood dyscrasias.

Oral Infections

The most common oral infection is herpetic gingivo-stomatitis. This is caused by the Herpes simplex virus which creates a mucosal vesicle when the virus is activated.[5] On the skin or lip surface the vesicle remains for several days and is commonly referred to as a cold sore; but on the oral surfaces the roof of the vesicle is rapidly shed and an ulcer is the final lesion and is commonly known as a canker sore. This type of infection is usually self-limiting and has a tendency to recur should the patient have a high fever or overexposure of the lips to the wind and sun. The ulcerated oral lesions are painful in contrast to the exterior lip lesions (Fig. 7–17).

Candidiasis (monoliasis) is a fungal infection which usually occurs on skin and mucosa; however, the oral and vaginal mucosa are infected by Candida albicans more frequently than other areas. This infection is usually seen in infants and elderly females, especially if the latter is a diabetic. The most confusing complication in diagnosing the condition in the infant is the similarity of the white patches of candidia to curdled milk. The white patches of candidiasis do not rub off as milk curds would and if you should succeed in rubbing one off, an erythematous base would remain.[16]

Actinomycosis is an uncommon oral infection usually occurring as osteomyelitis following a long chronic course after a mandibular tooth extraction. It superficially appears that this organism enters the extraction socket and incubates. Here it invades slowly in the direction of gravity, migrating through the bone and to the soft tissues near the angle of the mandible resulting in cervicofacial actinomycosis. At this point abscess-like enlargements occur at the angle of the mandible and cervicofacial area. These eventually rupture and exfoliate a yellowish granule. The diagnosis is clinically based on a lumpy-like jaw, chronic course, presence of sulfur granules, and demonstration of the organism (Fig. 7–18).

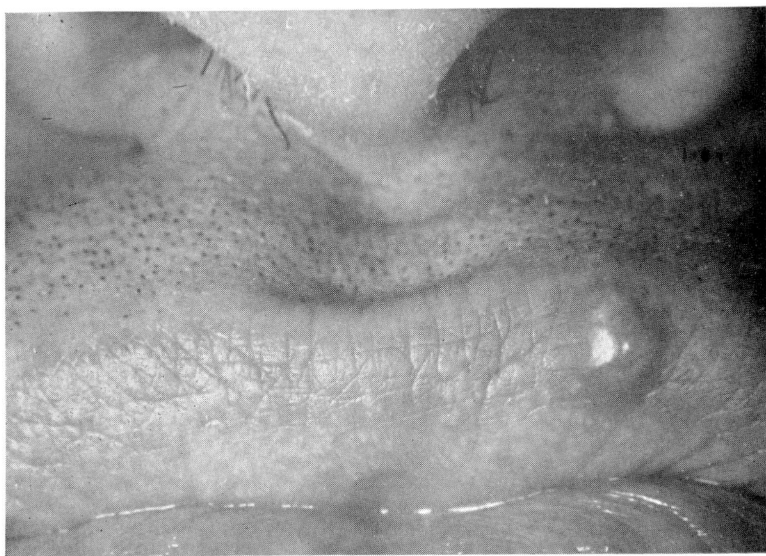

Fig. 7–17. Herpes labialis. Note the intact vesicle on the upper lip. This is commonly known as a cold sore or fever blister. The vesicle usually remains intact on the lip or skin until it resolves. In the mouth, it forms a painful ulcer commonly referred to as a canker sore.

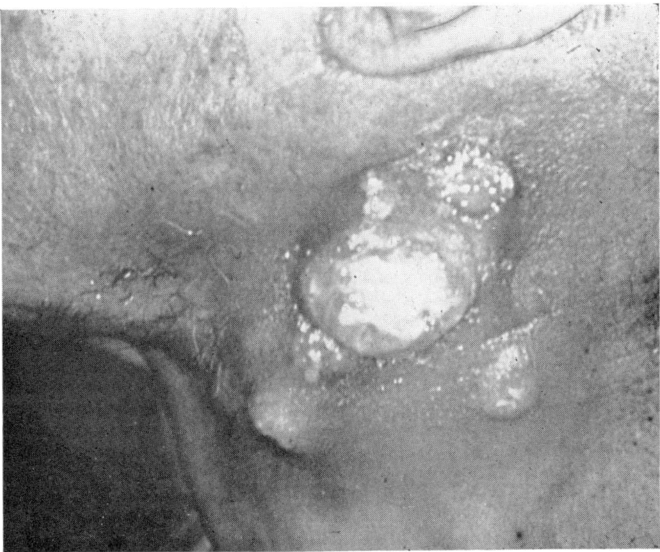

Fig. 7–18. Cervical-facial actinomycosis. This was a chronic ulcerous lesion which followed a large swelling of the left mandible. Yellow sulfur-like granules drained from the lesions and a culture for actinomycosis was positive.

The most dramatic of oral mucosal disease is acute necrotizing ulcerative gingivitis. The causative factors include infection and disturbed constitutional states. The condition is painful, and produces a necrotic ulcer on the intradental papillae which may extend over large areas of gingiva and adjacent soft tissue (Fig. 7–19). Frequently a foul, musty odor is a tell-tale sign of the patient's infection. Vincent's infection and trench mouth fever are well-known synonyms for this disease.

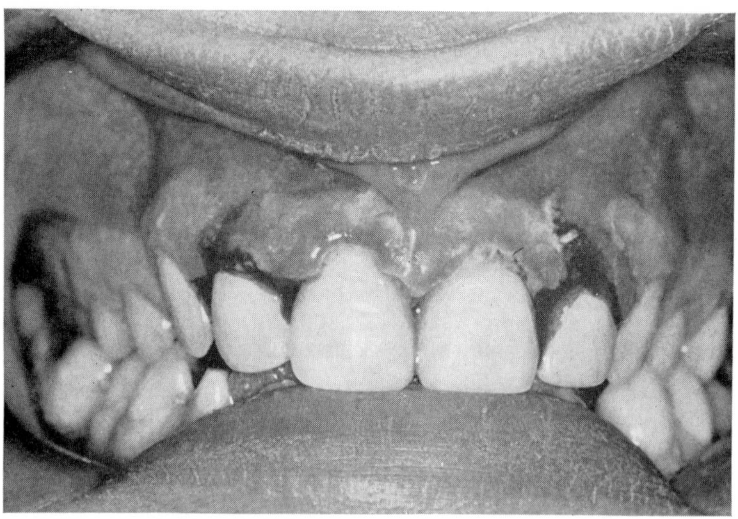

FIG. 7–19. Acute ulcerative necrotizing gingivitis. Note the sloughing of the apex of the interdental papilla leaving a crater-like ulcer. The rest of the gingiva is congested, bleeds readily, and has a musty odor.

While all bone infections constitute an osteomyelitis in the broad sense, dentistry is most often exposed to it in an acute form. The source of most jawbone infections is an infected pulp canal which releases its toxin centrally into bone through the tooth apex. A desirable course of events is in controlling the infection and its source by establishing drainage.

Frequently this infection is progressive and the pressures and enzymes associated with the accompanying inflammatory response forces the lesion to spread. This spread usually takes the path of least resistance, perforating bone, and draining into the oral cavity by forming a fistula. A common gum boil is such a manifestation. Rarely, the infection follows other courses resulting in a fistula to the external facial surface, maxillary sinus, or blood stream.

General infectious diseases may also have oral manifestations and should be considered under oral infections. A large group are the infectious skin diseases seen in childhood. Koplik's spots are oral forerunners to the skin lesions in measles. Chickenpox may produce spots in the mouth as well as on the skin. Since mucosa is an epithelial covering like skin, most skin diseases have oral manifestations.

Oral Manifestations of Non-infectious Skin Diseases

Non-infectious skin diseases also affect or alter the oral mucosa. Lichen planus is a skin disease which may have only oral symptoms (Fig. 7–20). The lesion is of unknown etiology but has close relationship to older individuals and those who are under emotional stress. The oral lesions are whitish lace-like lines forming a mosaic pattern. When these lines cross each other, they form a little nodule. These are referred to as striae of Wickham and nodules of Wickham. An advanced form of oral lesion occurs when the mucosa is sloughed off leaving desquamated areas; this is known as bullous or erosive licen planus. The latter phase can involve all oral areas, while the earlier lace-like lesions are usually limited to the buccal mucosa.

Erythema multiforme is an allergic disease in which epithelium becomes inflamed and vesiculated. Frequently the mouth is the only anatomical part affected. Oral lesions have a red inflamed base when

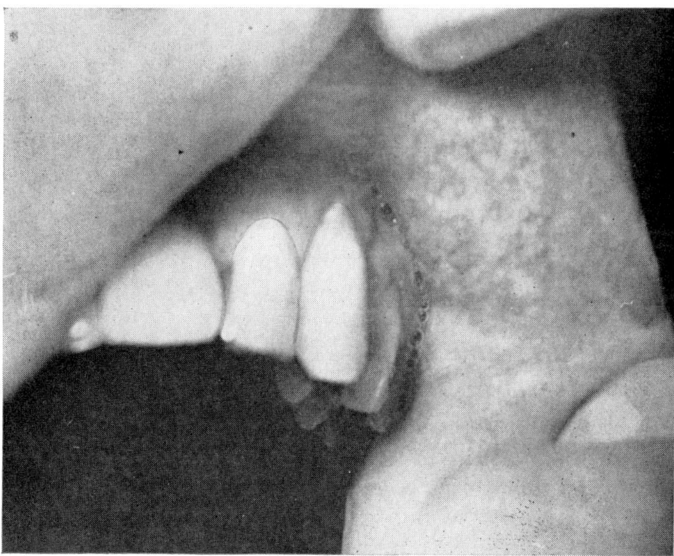

FIG. 7–20. Note the mosaic striae formation. This case has a more dense than usual pattern. This patient was totally unaware that she has lichen planus. A careful search revealed additional skin lesions.

the vesicle ruptures and the epithelium is sloughed. The sloughed epithelium may remain loosely attached becoming a white pseudomembrane inside the mouth, but on lip surfaces it dries and becomes a crusty layer (Fig. 7–21). There is usually a spring and fall seasonal occurrence and a careful search frequently reveals it to be a reaction to medication.

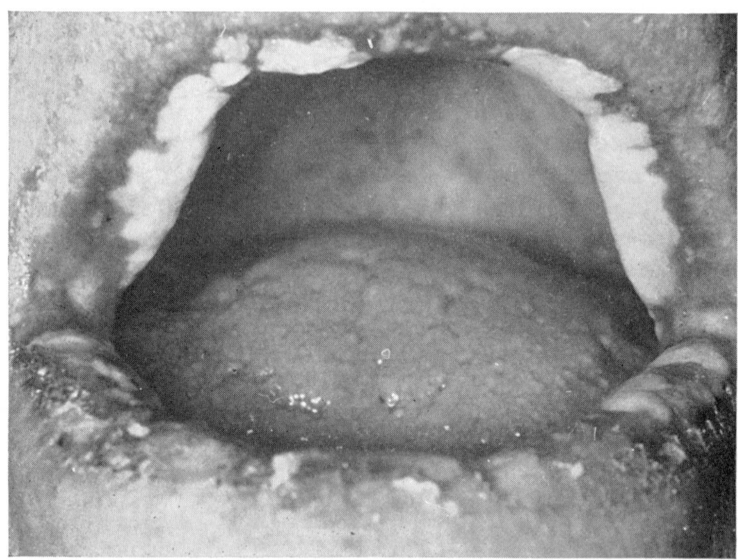

FIG. 7–21. Erythema multiforme. This patient developed oral and cutaneous lesions subsequent to drug intake. Much of the lip mucosa has formed a dry crust while the larger white plaques are still in the moist pseudomembranous stage.

The pemphigus family makes a group of vesicular diseases which range from a benign to a serious form capable of causing death. Although a racial implication exists for people of sub-mediterranean extraction, the cause is unknown. It appears that the inflammatory mechanism is triggered off for no apparent reason and spontaneous vesiculation begins. The most common oral variant is benign mucous membrane pemphigus, but the name is deceiving as the disease can also occur on skin and conjuctiva, and be disabling. The most serious form is pemphigus vulgaris in which the repeated idiopathic bullous formation results in loss of fluid proteins, thereby reducing the normal body defenses. Before the advent of anti-inflammatory drugs, this form of pemphigus usually terminated in infectious death.

Oral Manifestations of Endocrine Disturbances

The endocrine system is vital to normal development and metabolism; therefore it is obvious that these would influence oral health. The pituitary gland regulates growth and size. Hypopituitarism, before normal growth and development is achieved, causes dwarfism and hyperpituitarism at the same developmental plane causes gigantism. Should the pituitary develop an adenoma (anterior portion of gland) after growth centers are closed, the overall body does not increase in size; however, growth in certain bones take place and this disease is called acromegaly (Fig. 7–22 *A* and *B*). Bones persistently enlarging in acromegaly are the mandible, frontal bone, and bones of the hands and feet. The enlargement of the mandible causes spacing between teeth and loss of normal occlusion so that the lower arch is larger than the maxillary arch resulting in a true prognathism and cross bite. Such a patient would admit that glove and shoe size have required increases over the period since disease initiation.

Hypothyroidism also affects growth and maturation. In addition to the usual broad facies there is a delay in tooth development and subsequent eruption. Such a patient could have a chronological age of twelve and an eruption table of age six (Fig. 7–23). On roentgenogram, the developing roots would be flared at the apex, showing delayed root maturity. The myxedema which develops in this disease was discussed previously under macroglossia.

Hyperthyroidism primarily has the opposite effect of hypothyroidism along with a facial expression of surprise. Orally, one would be pressed to diagnose such a case; however, early tooth eruption and precocious puberty appear to be associated.

The effect of parathyroid dysfunction is primarily linked with mineral metabolism. It is probable that most hypocalcification of teeth result from a hypoparathyroid-like influence; if not direct, it may affect calcification secondarily such as focal hypocalcification of enamel resulting from high fever diseases during tooth formation. In hyperparathyroidism, definite oral lesions present themselves. On x-ray film there is a loss of the lamina dura lining tooth sockets, and punched-out central bone lesions may appear. The latter is actually a lesion of bone removal and subsequent replacement with giant cells. This lesion is known as the "brown tumor of hyperparathyroidism" and occurs most frequently in the jaw bones. Some forms of idiopathic root resorption may be linked with hyperparathyroidism.

The influence of the pancreas upon oral health is seen when the patient is a poorly controlled diabetic. In diabetic stomatitis, one sees a sloughing of the mucosa leaving an erythematous base along with

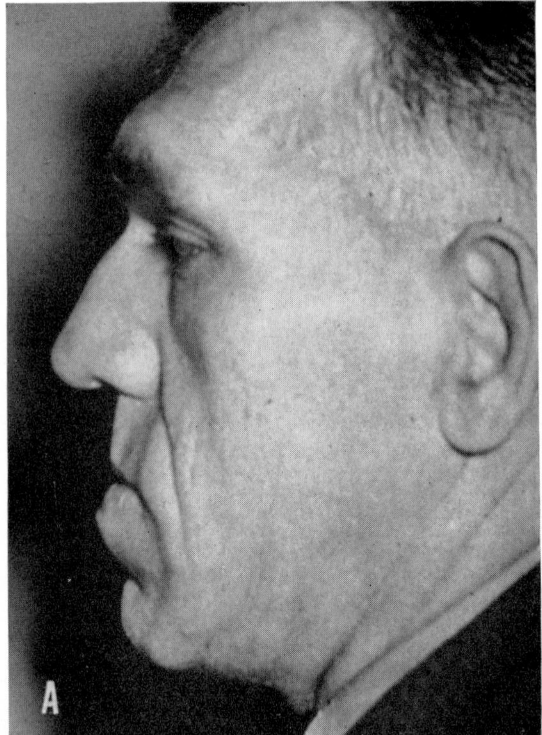

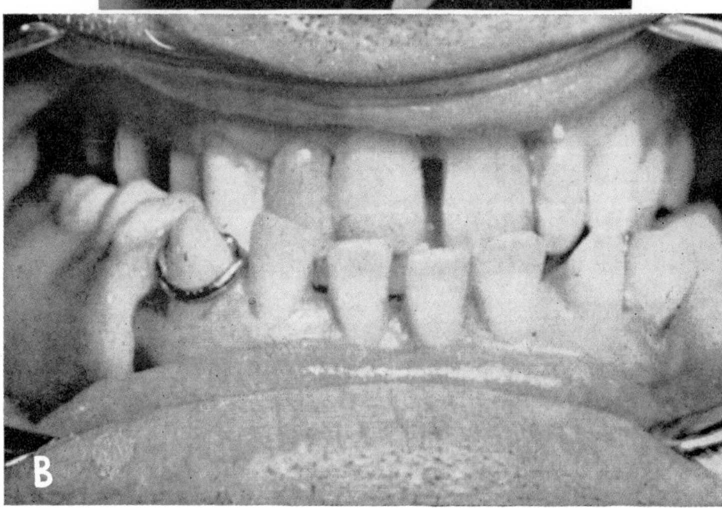

FIG. 7–22. *A* shows acromegaly resulting in elongation and overgrowth of the frontal bone and mandible. As a result of the excessive mandibular enlargement, tooth spacing and a crossbite formed as seen in *B*.

complaints of a burning tongue and dry mouth. The reason for mucosal ulcerations in diabetes include a general susceptibility to infections caused by tissue sugars which enhances bacterial growth, restricted metabolic exchange across thickened blood vessels, and changes in body fluid pH which produce an acidosis. Polymorphonuclear neutrophils, the most important cells in inflammation, are not effective in an acidotic milieu.

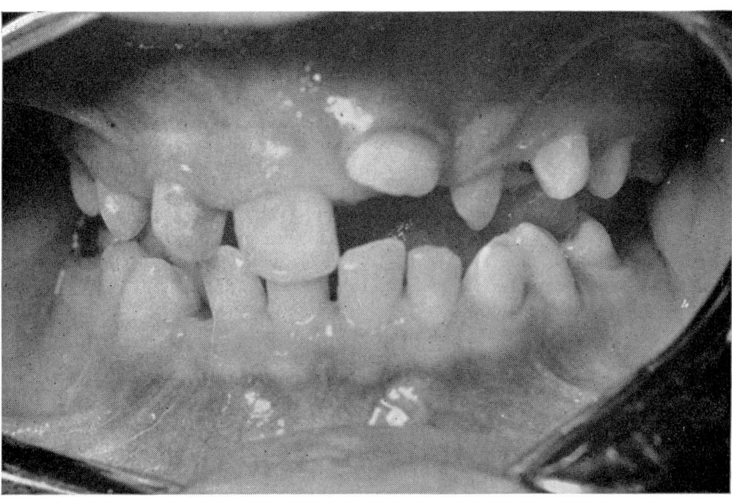

FIG. 7–23. Dentition in a twelve-year-old individual. The late eruption age was indicative of hypothyroidism. This proved to be true. After proper treatment a sound occlusion and eruption table were seen.

The ill effect of the adrenal gland in growth and maturation is referred to as the adrenogenital syndrome. The clinical findings are basically precocious puberty. The infant has an alarmingly early tooth eruption pattern, broad mature face and accelerated genital development. Should this occur in an infant female, breast development and broadening of the pelvis is seen. The adrenal glands also influence metabolism. A destruction of the adrenal cortex is termed Addison's disease. In it, enzymes which control melanin activity in the body are altered. In Addison's disease, any area of surface epithelium which is under pressure (such as watch bands, garter lines, belt lines, brassiere straps, and oral mucosa) will darken. This darkening agent is melanin and the deposit is termed melanosis. Orally, melanosis is seen primarily over the prominent portions of the gingiva, on the tongue, buccal mucosa and lips (Fig. 7–24).

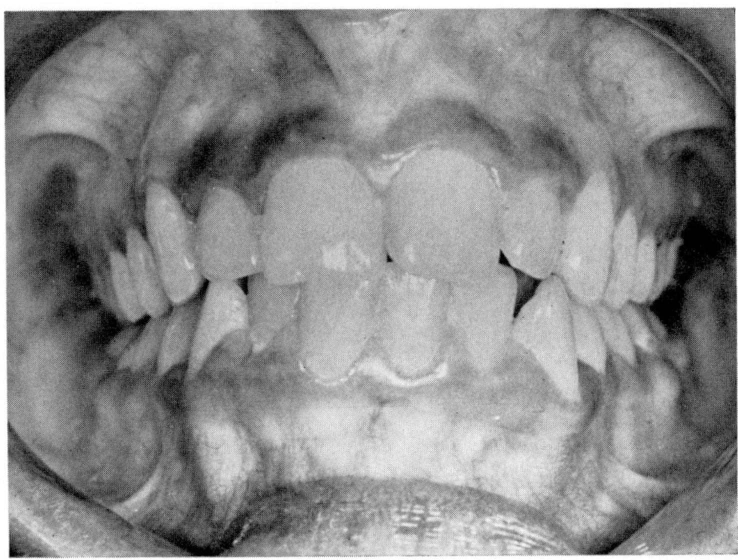

FIG. 7–24. Oral melanosis in Addison's disease. The attached gingiva receives most of the pressure given to soft tissue during mastication; therefore the attached gingiva over the prominent bony areas is pigmented. Note that the free gingiva, which is normally protected by the cervical tooth convexity, is pigment free.

Oral Disturbances Seen in Blood Dyscrasias

All blood diseases will affect the oral cavity on final analysis by virtue of accompanying anemia and malnutrition. There are, however, three blood dyscrasias that have a dramatic oral effect; these are anemia, leukopenia, and leukemia.[8] Pallor, bleeding, and delayed clotting time are the consequences of all severe anemias and should be borne in mind when examining and treating the oral cavity. In pernicious anemia, there are definite oral symptoms over and beyond these. The tongue becomes swollen, atrophic, and beefy red in color (Fig. 7–25). It frequently becomes painful (glossodynia) and has a burning sensation (glossopyrosis). Such a condition of the tongue is called Hunter's glossitis. Another anemia to be considered is sickle cell anemia. It is limited to the colored race and the disease is active in 5 per cent of the colored people. The demand for hemopoietic space in the marrow changes the roentgenographic picture resulting in a verticle hair-on-end pattern of bone trabeculation in the skull roentgenogram. In some anemias, should the demand for hemopoietic space be increased over a long period, the jaw bones will increase in size, specifically the premaxilla in children. This is seen in sickle cell anemia and thalassemia (Fig. 7–26).

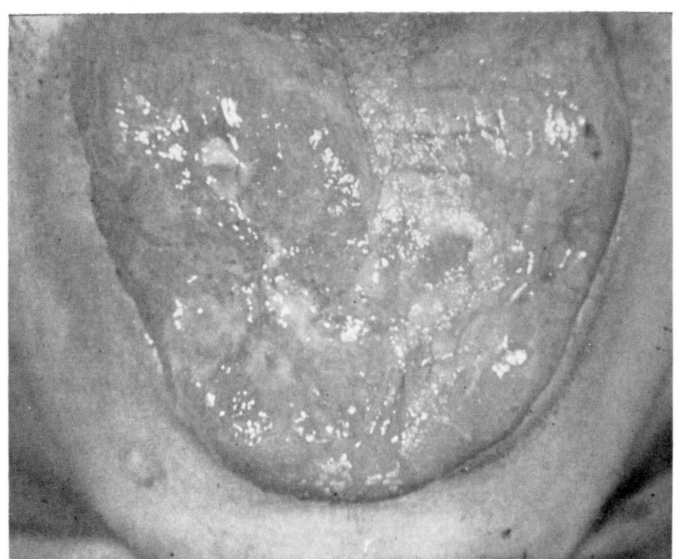

FIG. 7–25. Tongue in pernicious anemia. Sections of this tongue show an atrophic mucosa while another section has the typical "beefy red" appearance. This person experienced both glossodynia and glossopyria.

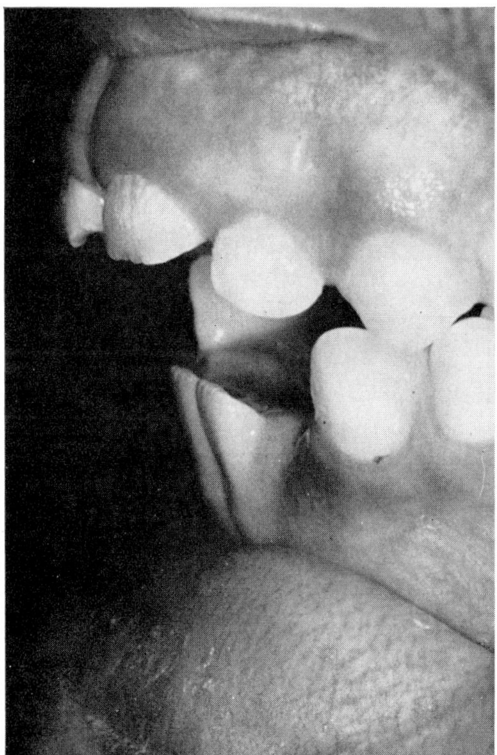

FIG. 7–26. Premaxillary enlargement in Mediterranean anemia. The clinical picture was similar to that one might see in a thumb-sucking habit.

Leukopenia decreases the body defensive mechanism as a result of a depleted white cell population in the circulating blood. The phenomenon of oral ulceration during leukopenia is not fully understood. These ulcers are the largest, deepest, and most painful of the oral aphthae complex (Fig. 7–27). After healing, they usually leave a scar. The leukopenias usually associated with these ulcers are agranulocytosis and periodic cyclic neutropenia. The latter identifies the neutrophils as being the depleted cell and the condition as a cycle. These ulcers occur primarily on the tongue, labial mucosa, and floor of the mouth.

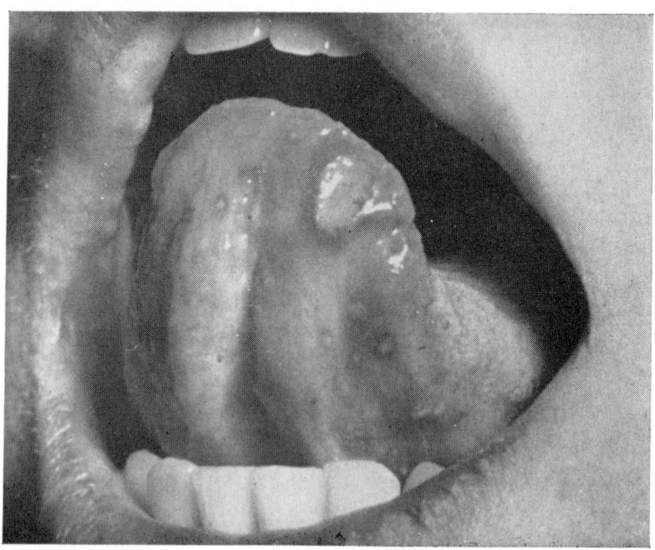

FIG. 7–27. The large ulcer near the tip of the tongue is the sequela of bone marrow suppression by a medication. The total white count in this person was down to 2,000 cells per ml. with a relative agranulocytosis. Soon after the use of the drug was discontinued, the ulcers healed.

Oral ulcerations and susceptibility to infection appear to be on the increase as many modern drugs suppress the bone marrow, thereby creating a transitory leukopenia. Other deep ulcerous oral lesions of identical appearance occur in periadenitis mucosa necrotica recurrens, a disease of unknown etiology.

Leukemia is the most common blood disease which is diagnosed from the oral cavity picture. All leukemias can have oral lesions; however, they are most consistent with acute leukemias. Since the bone marrow in leukemia is possessed with forming of the leukemic white cells, there is a crowding out of red cell forming tissues resulting in anemia. Platelets that are so vital in the blood-clotting mechanism fail to form normally from the megakaryocytes and therefore persistent hemorrhage is seen on the gingiva of the leukemia patient. During many illnesses, patients tend to neglect their oral health and readily develop gingivitis. This excites the bleeding tendency and when the irritation is sufficient to invoke the inflammatory response, the exudation of white cells from the blood vessels is solicited to the irritated area as in the usual inflammatory response. In the leukemic person, the vascular bed contains abnormal white cells and these are attracted to the irritated gingiva. This results in a cellular infiltrate which causes gingival enlargement (Fig. 7–28).

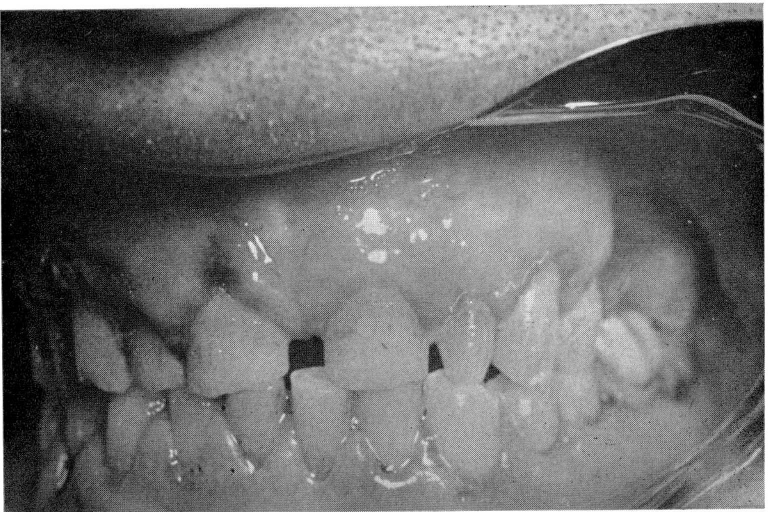

FIG. 7–28. Leukemic gingivitis. The fatal outcome of the disease was rapid in this individual. This, along with the rapid gingival enlargement were compatible with an acute process.

DISTURBANCES OF THE SALIVARY GLANDS

All major and minor salivary glands secrete a serous, mucinous, or mixed fluid depending on the cell type which makes up the gland. The purpose of this secretion is to initiate digestive breakdown of food and to keep the oral mucosa moist and cleansed.

Salivary gland disturbances will be discussed under four major areas: abnormal gland secretion, ductal obstruction, infections, and neoplasia.

Abnormal Gland Secretion

The chief disturbance seen in gland secretion is xerostomia. It can range from a short-term dry mouth to a prolonged period resulting in swallowing difficulty and erosion of mucosa from lack of salivary lubrication. The simplest cause of xerostomia is from fluid loss either by lack of fluid intake or dehydration from vomiting, diarrhea, or hemorrhage. Xerostomia accompanies systemic diseases such as vitamin A deficiency and diabetes. The first is probably based at the cellular level and the latter on an anti-diuretic hormone behavior. Sjögren's syndrome is an infrequent condition usually seen in middle aged and elderly females where total glandular secretion is reduced; dry eyes, nose, throat, etc. is experienced. This condition is believed to be hormonal in etiology.

Ductal Obstruction

Disturbances in the outflow tract of a salivary gland are caused by an inflammatory reaction or obstruction by a foreign body. Inflammation by virtue of its range from edema to healing and subsequent scar formation can cause stenosis of glandular openings. This is commonly seen in children wearing orthodontic appliances when irritation results

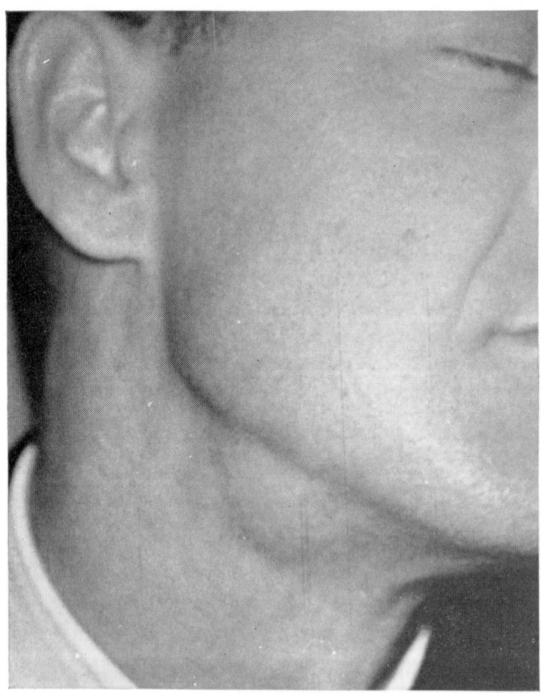

FIG. 7–29. Enlargement of the submandibular salivary gland caused by a sialolith. The chief discomfort this person had was pain and size increase during mealtime. The stone was in Wharton's duct and readily seen on a roentgenogram.

in constriction of the orifice of a mucosal gland and a mucocele forms. Duct obstruction is frequently seen as a mineral salt aggregation in the glands having a long ductal system. A salivary gland calculus is such an aggregation forming a salivary stone with subsequent duct blockage (Fig. 7–29). The longer and more tortuous the path of the duct the higher the incidence of obstruction by this means. The term given to mineral salt deposition and subsequent salivary gland pathology is sialolithiasis. Whenever there is an obstruction in flow of saliva, the back pressure produced ductal dilatation, cellular atrophy, and predisposes the gland to infection. A ranula is a dilated duct in the floor of the mouth. This lesion may become extensive, to the point where it interferes with normal tongue movements. Some salivary gland pathology was also discussed in the paragraph on pseudocysts.

Salivary Gland Infections

Inflammation and infection of a gland is known as adenitis; therefore such involvement in a salivary gland is called sialadenitis. As just mentioned in the previous paragraph, one cause of sialadenitis is obstruction to outflow. The most common form of sialadenitis is endemic parotitis (mumps). This usually occurs in the parotid gland. Other lesser forms of infectious salivary gland diseases are uveoparotid fever, Mikulicz's disease, cat scratch disease, and sarcoidosis. Inflammatory lesions of salivary glands result in transient loss of secretion.

Salivary Gland Tumors

Tumors of the salivary glands vary greatly in histogenesis. There is a direct proportion of tumor site to gland size. The parotid glands are about 10 times larger than the submandibular glands, which in turn are about 10 times larger than the sublingual glands. Therefore the incidence of a tumor in the parotid is about 10 times greater than that of the submandibular gland and 100 times greater than that of a sublingual gland. One must always be mindful of the 400 to 500 mucous glands of the oral cavity which are subjected to the same tumors as the major salivary glands. The benign tumors may be either mesenchymal or epithelial. Mesenchymal tumors are rare in comparison to epithelial tumors. However, the most common parotid tumor of infancy is the hemangioma, which is mesenchymal in origin.

The most frequent salivary gland tumor is the pleomorphic adenoma (or mixed tumor). Other are the oncocytoma, cystadenoma, and papillary cystadenoma. These benign epithelial tumors are well encapsulated, give little or no clinical discomfort, and frequently are present for many months or years.

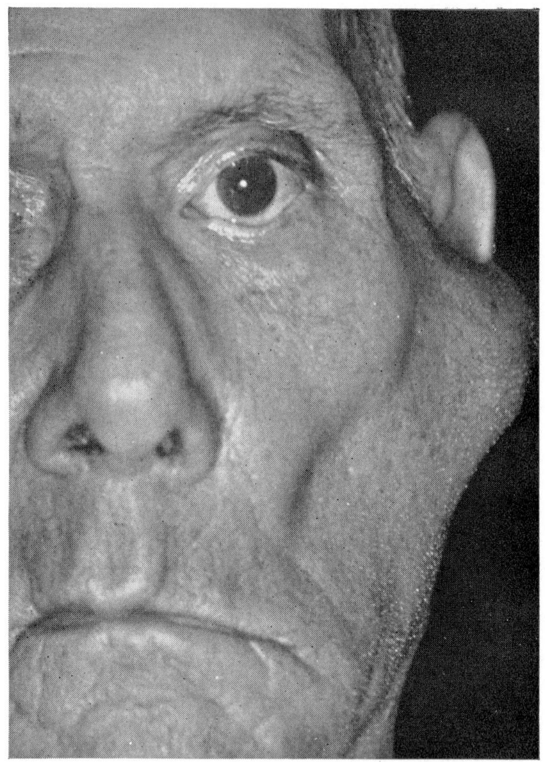

FIG. 7–30. Rapid growing parotid tumor causing paralysis of the same side of the face. Note the lack of facial expression, drop of lower eyelid, and of the side of upper lip. This proved to be a mucoepidermoid carcinoma of the parotid gland.

In contrast to the benign group, the malignant group usually grow rapidly, cause pain, and metastasize (Fig. 7–30). The most common malignant tumor is the malignant variant of the pleomorphic adenoma. The second most common in incidence is the cylindroma, and the third the mucoepidermoid carcinoma. Other malignant salivary gland tumors are squamous cell carcinoma, acinic cell carcinoma, and malignant lymphoepithelial tumors. Malignant mesenchymal salivary gland tumors are rare and depend on cell type such as vessels and nerves.

ORAL NEOPLASIA

Three terms—neoplasia, tumor, and cancer—are variously used in reference to new and abnormal growths in the body. Neoplasia is the general word, while tumor connotes tissue enlargement. Tumors have no established growth patterns, appear to have a one-way enzyme system, have no regard for the physiology of the host, and are not reversible. Should a tumor have the ability to kill its host by any of a number of means, it is known as a malignant tumor. Conversely, a tumor which is either self-limiting (that is, does not metastasize), or does not endanger the life of its host is known as a benign tumor. No such differentiation of benignancy or malignancy is made in the use of the word cancer; it invariably refers to a malignant neoplasm.

Cancer is now a leading killer in the United States, being second only to cardiovascular diseases. It is of particular concern to the dental profession because 14 per cent of all cancer occurs around the head and neck and 8 per cent of all cancer (over half of the head and neck cancer) occurs in the oral cavity. While on final analysis the cause of cancer in man is unknown, there is a definite cause and effect relationship. We know that people who spend much time in the sun have a higher incidence of skin cancer. Also, certain irritants have produced cancer experimentally. A geographic distribution of oral cancer varies with the cause-and-effect relationship. Countries where betel nut chewing is common have a high rate of oral cancer. In Cuba, where reverse smoking is common, there is also a high incidence of oral cancer. In the United States, the cause-and-effect relationship for oral cancer includes hot spicy foods, tobacco habits, syphilis, and alcoholism; however, this is not to say that whoever has oral cancer can be placed in one of these groups. In many oral cancer cases we are at a loss to find a cause-and-effect relationship.

Like all other benign and malignant tumors, oral tumors may be epithelial or mesenchymal. Because the oral cavity is unique from all other anatomical areas in that during one lifetime 52 teeth undergo embryogenesis ranging from early fetal life to late youth, we have to consider a third group of tumors which arise from the tooth-forming organs. These are known as odontogenic tumors. The subsequent discussion of oral tumors is therefore divided into three major groups: neoplasms of epithelial, mesenchymal, and odontogenic origin.

Epithelial Neoplasms

The oral cavity has two major types of epithelium: covering epithelium (stratified squamous cell epithelium) and glandular epithelium (which makes up the salivary glands). All oral epithelial tumors arise from either of these cell types. The benign epithelial tumors arising from stratified squamous cells occur in the form of papillomas. A papilloma may have a broad (sessile) or narrow (pedunculated) base. These may arise on any oral site but are most frequent on the soft palate. Tumors that arise from gland cells are adenomas and therefore would be located wherever salivary glands are located. The reader is referred back to the section on salivary gland diseases for further information.

A malignant lesion arising from covering epithelium is called epidermoid carcinoma. Ninety per cent of all oral cancer is made up of this type. The tongue is most frequently involved with cancer of this type making up about half of all oral cancers. Other sites, the palate, floor of mouth, buccal mucosa, and gingiva, are almost equal in incidence. Epidermoid carcinoma of the oral cavity has a grave

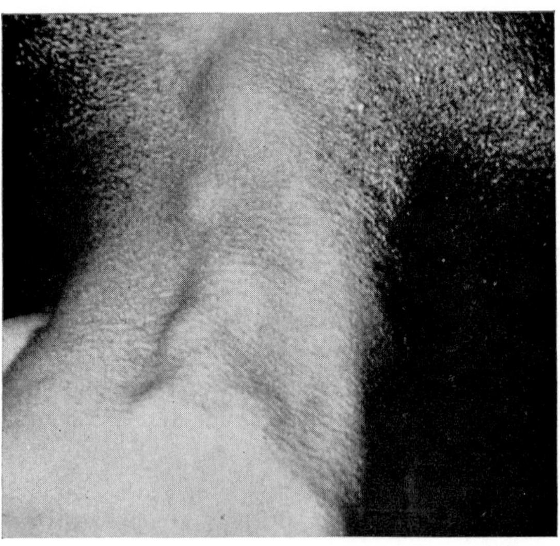

FIG. 7–31. A chain of neck lymph nodes which contain metastatic cancer cells. These nodes were hard and painless. The primary lesion was an epidermoid carcinoma of the base of the tongue.

prognosis; this is enlarged due to latent detection, anatomic problems hindering adequate surgery, and a complex lymphatic pattern which readily allows cancer cells to metastasize (Fig. 7–31). The overall five-year survival rate for oral cancer is about 30 per cent. Oral malignant lesions arising from gland cells are adenocarcinoma. As in the case with adenomas, these also occur where salivary glands are located and are also discussed in greater detail under the section of salivary gland diseases.

There exists a group of epithelial lesions which are considered premalignant. These are carcinoma in situ, Bowen's disease, erythroplasia of Queyrat, and leukoplakia. Of these, leukoplakia is of the greatest interest to the hygienist and will be the only one discussed. Leukoplakia can occur on any mucosal surface, usually the result of some long-standing irritant. It commonly appears as a white opalescent plaque (Fig. 7–32). On palpation it is leather-like. Although these lesions are not a cancer, microscopically they reveal cells which are disturbing and suggestive of cancer and the lesions are therefore referred to as pre-malignant lesions. Should these be ignored, about 25 per cent would turn into frank epidermoid carcinomas. It is the attention given to this lesion that constitutes the best example of preventing oral cancer by early recognition.

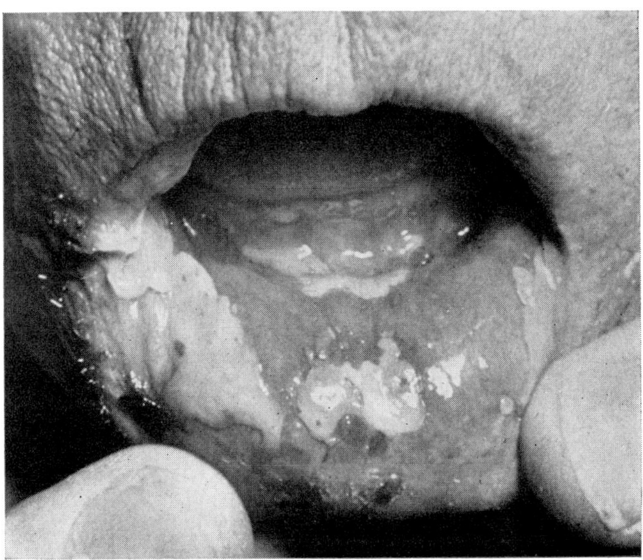

FIG. 7–32. This elderly woman held snuff in the vestibule of her lower lip. This habit began while she was a child. Clinically this appeared as a firm hyperkeratotic area. Microscopically there was enough pleomorphism in the cells to make a diagnosis of severe leukoplakia. Subsequent to a mucosal shave, there has been no recurrence.

Mesenchymal Neoplasms

The benign mesenchymal tumors may arise from fibrous connective tissue, vessels, bone, muscle, and nerves. The most common of all benign oral tumors is the fibroma which arises from connective tissue (Fig. 7–33). It usually is attached by a broad base and has a normal mucosal covering. Most fibromas occur on the tongue. Another common oral tumor arises from blood and lymph vessels (Fig. 7–34). These are best termed angiomas. Those of blood vessel origin are hemangiomas and those made up of lymph vessels are lymphangiomas.

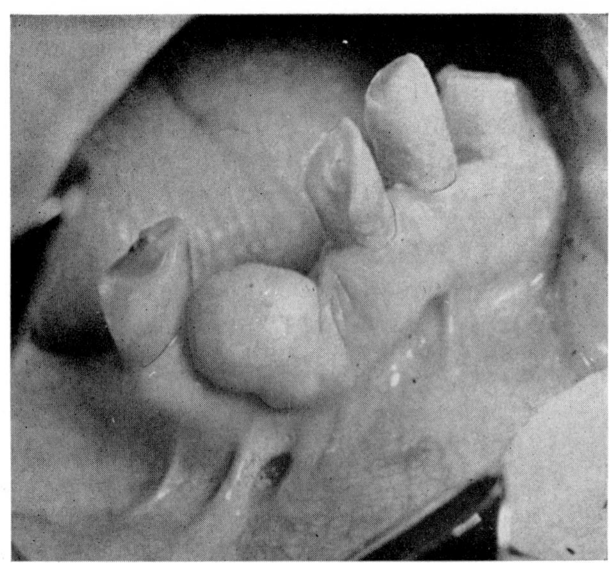

Fig. 7–33. Fibroma of the alveolar ridge. The covering mucosa appeared normal. Microscopically the mass was made up of mature collagen bundles and vascularity was sparse. This fibroma was attached by a narrow base.

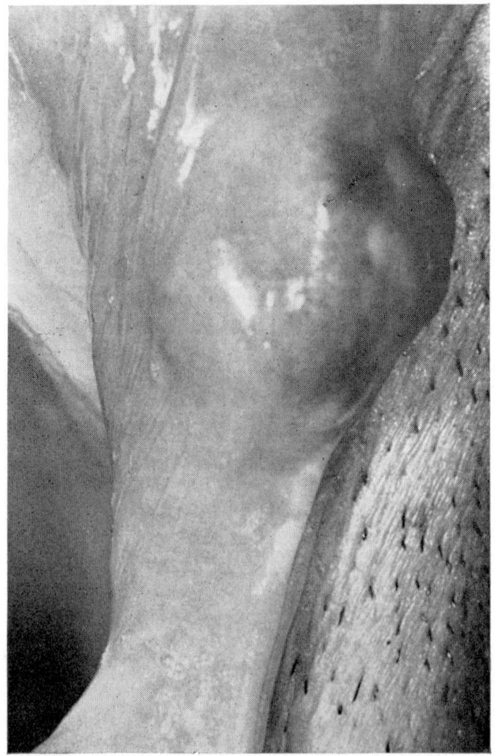

Fig. 7–34. This cavernous hemangioma of the lip was purple in color. It was made up of large spaces containing red blood cells and was removed for cosmetic reasons.

Quite frequently both elements are present at one time. These tumors are purplish in color if they are pure hemangiomas but this color can lighten depending upon the degree of lymph vessel presence. These vascular tumors are the most common cause of macroglossia and macrocheilia in infants.

Another common mesenchymal tumor is the osteoma. Osteomas are tumors made up of cortical bone and usually are attached to the flat surface of other bones. Orally these exist on the midline of the hard

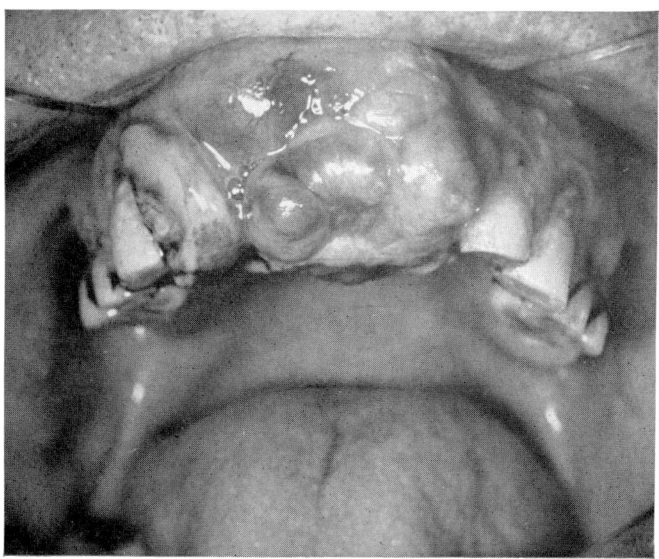

FIG. 7–35. This seventy-year-old male had a painless but rapidly enlarging tumor in the premaxilla area. It turned out to be a chondrosarcoma and a radical resection was done. Six months later the patient died of a brain metastasis.

palate or lingual aspect of the mandible in the bicuspid area. The former is referred to as a torus palatinus and the latter as lingual tori. These were also discussed earlier under developmental disturbances. Other benign mesenchymal tumors such as myomas, lipomas and neuromas, are actually rare.

Oral malignant mesenchymal tumors (sarcomas) occur infrequently in the form of osteogenic and chondrogenic sarcomas of jawbones: or fibrosarcomas and myosarcomas of the tongue and soft tissues (Fig. 7–35). However, in spite of the rarity of oral sarcomas it must be remembered that the oral cavity has all mesenchymal cell types present and therefore any sarcomas may arise.

Odontogenic Tumors

The tooth-forming organ is made up of epithelial and mesenchymal cells. Therefore on final analysis odontogenic tumors are actually epithelial, mesenchymal or a mixture of the two, and are best approached by this division.[6] The terminology used in other tumors is almost forsaken when discussing tumors of odontogenic origin.

Epithelial Odontogenic Tumors. The ameloblastoma is an epithelial odontogenic tumor and is so named because microscopically it has characteristics of ameloblasts. It can occur in any tooth-bearing area but is most frequently seen in the body of the mandible and occurs primarily in the thirty-year-old age group. Although it is a benign tumor, it is aggressive and must be treated accordingly.

Another odontogenic tumor of epithelial origin is the enamaloma (enamel pearl). This is the result of sporadic enamel formation on the part of a few ectopic ameloblasts on the root surface. These hard enamel-like tumors seldom exceed 4 mm. in diameter and are most frequently seen near root bifurcations. On final analysis this lesion does not constitute a true neoplasm but its recognition is important.

Mesenchymal Odontogenic Tumors. Among those of mesenchymal origin are the cementoma, dentinoma, odontogenic fibroma and odontogenic myxoma. The name identifies the predominate hard or soft tissue which makes up each lesion and as one would expect, these are usually closely associated to the dental apparatus. The tumors mentioned above may occur at any age and behave less aggressively than their epithelial counterpart.

Mixed Odontogenic Tumors. In each case of the mixed odontogenic tumors, the name identifies the mesenchymal cell type which makes up the lesion. The group of mixed odontogenic tumors are made up of the odontomas, ameloblastic fibromas, hemangioameloblastomas, ameloblastic neurinomas and ameloblastic odontomas. As is apparent from the nomenclature, some of these actually represent a collision of two cell types and this accounts for calling them mixed odontogenic tumors. The hemangioameloblastomas, ameloblastic neuroma, and ameloblastic odontoma are more like the true ameloblastoma in their clinical behavior; having a tendency to recur, while the ameloblastic fibroma and odontomas require only conservative treatment. Odontomas are the most common of these and are divided into two groups—a compound and complex. The compound odontoma is a tumor made up of aggregates of underdeveloped teeth in a cystic covering (Fig. 7–36). Although these teeth are underdeveloped a distinct resemblance to crown, root, pulp, and cementum is still retained. In the complex group the aforementioned architecture is lost and all the tooth-forming tissues are amalgamated in a complex mass.

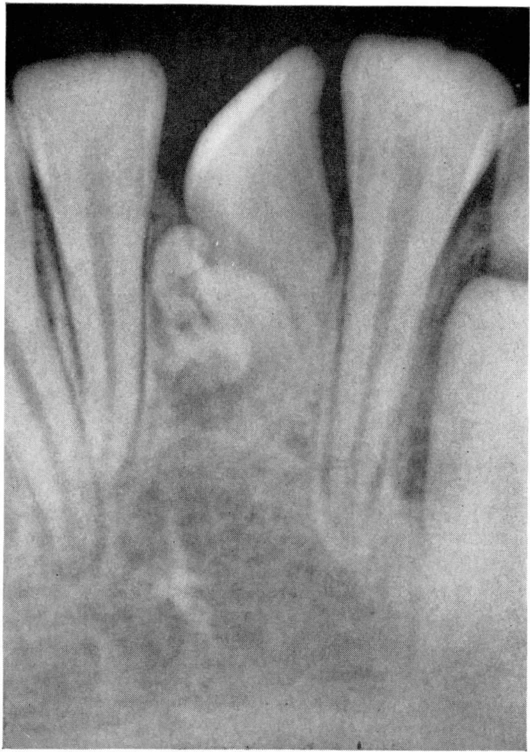

FIG. 7–36. Note the displacement of the anterior teeth. The cause of this is the presence of a compound composite odontoma. In this roentgenogram print, note the similarity of these rudimentary teeth to the normal teeth in their density.

BIBLIOGRAPHY

1. LEHNER, T.: Oral thrush, or acute pseudomembranous candidiasis, Oral Surg., Oral Med. & Oral Path., *18,* 27–37, 1964.
2. MCCORMACK, K. R.: Lingual thyroid, Oral Surg., Oral Med. & Oral Path., *18,* 38–41, 1964.
3. MOLYNEUX, G. S.: Observations on the structure and growth of periodontal and residual cysts, Oral Surg., Oral Med. & Oral Path., *18,* 80–89, 1964.
4. NAGAI, I., FUJIKI, Y., FUCHIHATA, H. and YOSHOMOTO, T.: Supernumerary tooth associated with cleft lip and cleft palate, J.A.D.A., *70,* 642–647, 1965.
5. RIZZO, A. and ASHE, W. K.: Experimental herpetic ulcer in rabbit oral mucosa, Arch. Oral Biol., *9,* 713–724, 1964.
6. SHEAR, M.: The unity of tumours of odontogenic epithelium, Brit. J. Oral Surg., *2,* 212–221, 1965.
7. SHKLAR, G. and MEYER, I.: Vascular tumors of mouth and jaws, Oral Surg., Oral Med. & Oral Path., *19,* 335–358, 1965.
8. WALKER, R. O. and ROSE, M.: Oral manifestations of hematologic disorders, Brit. Dent. J., *118,* 286–289, 1965.

8

Dental Deposits

Richard E. Stallard

THE problem associated with the accumulation of, and the removal of, dental deposits dates back in history before the time of Christ. Ancient records recognize the need for cleaning the teeth and keeping them free of foreign material. Instruments for the removal of calculus also evolved during this period of history and by the middle ages it was accepted that the accumulation of calculus on the teeth contributed to the early loss of teeth.[8]

The exact mechanism of calculus formation is even today incompletely understood; however, the relationship between good oral hygiene and the rate of dental deposit formation is obvious. Accumulation of debris around the teeth is influenced not only by the patient's personal oral hygiene habits, but also by the environment presented. Crowded, tipped or irregular teeth coupled with rough tooth surfaces, the concentration of saliva and the oral bacterial flora all contribute to the accumulation of the original soft deposit (dental plaque) upon the teeth.

Depending on the exact composition or components present within the dental plaque various sequelae are observed. A discoloration or staining of the tooth surface will result if certain pigment producing bacteria are present, while other microorganisms produce acids as a by-product of their metabolism which may cause demineralization of the enamel and eventual dental caries. Still other dental plaques are composed in such a way as to favor the deposition of calcium salts in the formation of dental calculus. In addition, the importance of the presence of a constant flow of saliva in calculus formation can be appreciated by the tremendous calculus deposits often seen opposite the ductal openings of the major salivary glands; the buccal surfaces of the maxillary molars and the lingual surfaces of the mandibular anterior teeth.

A patient's diet can also influence the accumulation rate of dental deposits. The soft sticky foods so often consumed today may adhere to the teeth during mastication. Hard or coarse foods, on the other hand, actually function in the removal of soft deposits from the teeth in addition to providing a mechanical stimulation for the gingival tissues.

DENTAL PLAQUE

The accumulation of soft debris made up of bacteria, salivary components, epithelial cells, food debris within a mucoprotein matrix occurs in all areas of the mouth which are not self-cleansing. This material constitutes what is termed a dental plaque.

Initially these deposits are colorless, but readily pick up extrinsic colored substances taken into the mouth. In the early literature, a distinction was made between bacterial film and dental plaque. However, since bacteria have been shown to be a constituent of all dental plaques, there no longer exists any distinction between a film and plaque. The importance of the bacterial fraction in dental plaque has been demonstrated by the control of the formation of plaque through use of topical antibiotics.[15] Not only was the amount of plaque formation reduced, but a decrease in the occurrence of gingivitis was observed.

Formation

Plaque is retained on surfaces of the teeth which are not self-cleansing (Fig. 8–1) and can be removed from these areas only by effective toothbrushing. In the case of malaligned or tipped teeth

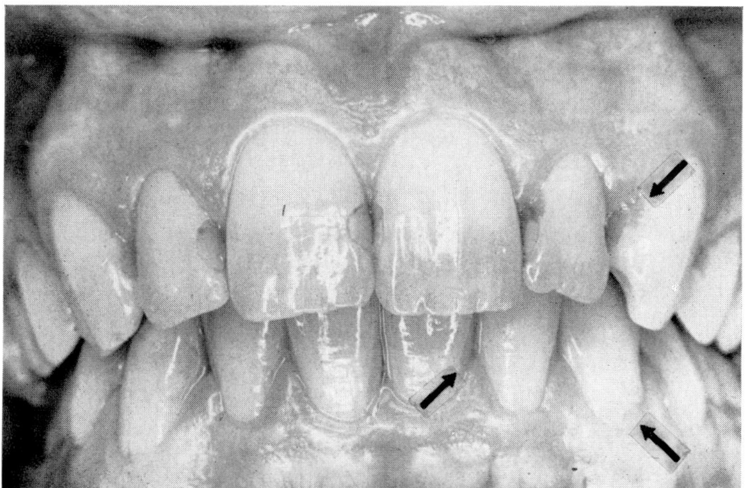

FIG. 8–1. Dental plaque stained with disclosing solution retained in areas which are not self cleansing, in a patient with good oral hygiene.

the removal of dental plaque, even by toothbrushing, is difficult. Therefore, accumulations of plaque are frequently observed in these areas. The rate of dental deposit accumulations is influenced by the contour of the tooth and the roughness of the tooth surface presented in the oral cavity.

In patients with extremely poor oral hygiene and exhibiting malpositioned teeth, exaggerated deposits of a soft white material often occur, which is termed materia alba. Teeth not subjected to occlusal function may be entirely covered by materia alba and exhibit rapid decalcification with dental caries beneath the soft white deposits. This type of plaque can, however, be easily removed by proper home care with a toothbrush.

Clinical Significance

It is not the mere fact that debris has accumulated on the teeth that is important, but rather the bacterial component of the plaque. The products of bacterial metabolism, such as toxins and enzymes, are retained in the matrix of the plaque thereby exerting a direct influence on the tooth structures and the gingiva. For example, acids produced by bacterial action on carbohydrates will lower the pH in the plaque for up to three and one-half hours after eating. Regional differences in the pH levels of dental plaque exist and can be related to the localized incidence of dental caries and periodontal disease. Teeth, such as the mandibular posterior and maxillary anterior, on which the dental plaque has a consistently lower pH than the other teeth exhibit a greater incidence of dental decay. Plaque on teeth bathed by a rapid rate of salivary flow tends to have a higher pH, lingual of mandibular incisor and buccal maxillary molars, and it is in these areas that the greatest deposits of calculus are seen.[10]

Depending on the bacterial flora present within the plaque, different reactions are observed. Certain bacteria produced pigments (chromogenic) and if organisms are present within the plaque a staining or discoloration is observed. Since the plaque is seen most often in non-self-cleansing areas, such as the cervical third of the tooth, it is not surprising that it is this area which is most often stained.

In children characteristic green and orange stains occur. The orange stain, which is the product of pigment producing bacteria within the dental plaque, is easily removed with the plaque during prophylaxis. Its recurrence can be prevented by proper toothbrushing. The green stain, however, is more difficult to remove since the enamel surface in these areas is often roughened. If these rough areas are not polished smooth during prophylaxis, recurrence of the green staining plaque is common. The green stain may also possibly be associated with the remnants of the reduced enamel epithelium.

A black stain resulting from pigment producing bacteria in the dental plaque occurs both in children and adults, especially in the female. This stain is again seen in the cervical areas usually as a thin black line at the margin of the gingiva. Like the green stain it is difficult to remove due to roughness of the enamel surface beneath the stained plaque.

If the bacterial organisms within the plaque produce enzymes which result in the fermentation of carbohydrates to acid, the acids produced

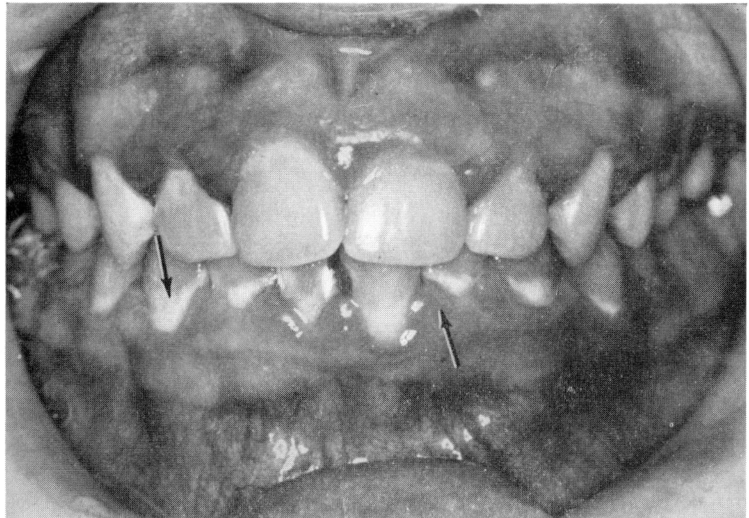

FIG. 8–2. Enamel decalcification due to retention of dental plaque. Also evident are gingival changes (gingivitis) around the teeth with areas of decalcification.

are retained in the plaque and decalcification of the underlying enamel occurs (Fig. 8–2) with eventual tooth decay taking place if the oral hygiene is not improved.[16]

Other bacterial enzymes are also released besides those capable of fermenting carbohydrates, such as hyaluronidase and collagenase. Again as in the case of dental caries the toxic materials are retained in the plaque and produce a direct effect on the gingiva resulting in inflammation and epithelial breakdown. A direct correlation has been made not only between the presence of dental plaque and the occurrence of gingivitis, but also the length of time the plaque was present and the occurrence of gingivitis.[1] Following thorough dental prophylaxis and the institution of proper oral hygiene, the gingivitis usually disappears.

If one examines the gingiva histologically, in addition to a typical picture of chronic inflammation with the appearance of inflammatory cells, the presence of a high number of plasma cells is noted. It is well established that plasma cells function in the production of antibodies. Therefore, their presence in the gingiva suggests that an antigen-antibody reaction is also taking place, initiated by antigens produced by the bacteria and retained within the plaque resulting in an altered local environment.

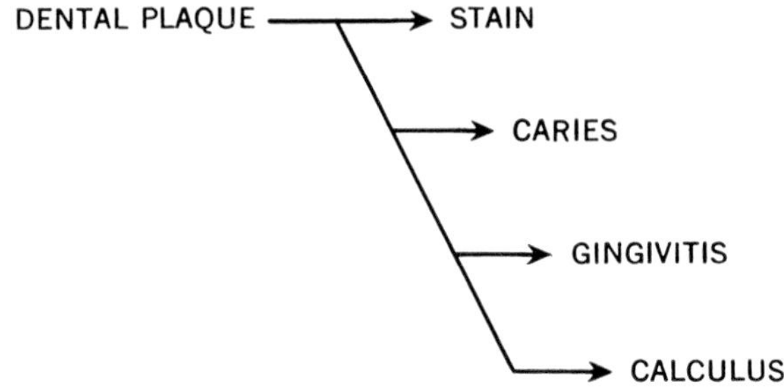

FIG. 8–3. The constituents of dental plaque vary from patient to patient and even between teeth in the same mouth. The importance of the local environment created by the constituents of the plaque can be visualized by the spectrum of sequella depicted in the above scheme. Any or all of these clinical entities may be present in the patient.

Under certain conditions the mucinous matrix of the plaque becomes altered, permitting the precipitation of calcium salts with resultant calculus formation. The exact mechanism involved in this change is unknown but may be related to certain bacterial products since specific bacteria (Actinomyces and Leptothrix) have been demonstrated in naturally occurring calculus and appear essential for experimental calculus formation.

The various reactions or complications resulting from the accumulation of dental plaque on teeth is summarized in Figure 8–3.

DENTAL CALCULUS

Dental calculus has been defined as a calcified or calcifying mass which forms on a tooth surface and adheres to it.[7] On chemical analysis it is found to be very similar to other mineralized tissues in the body, such as bone, dentin, or cementum. It consists of an organic matrix, which represents approximately 20 per cent, containing carbohydrates, proteins, bacteria, cellular debris, and lipids. The inorganic, or major fraction, contains the basic elements calcium, phosphorus, and magnesium plus trace amounts of other minerals. These elements are bound with phosphate or carbonate in a crystalline structure, the most common of which is hydroxyapatite.

Calculus is found clinically in different relationships to the gingival tissue and is often classified by this relationship as: (1) supragingival calculus, that which occurs above the gingiva, and (2) subgingival, that which is present below the gingival margin. The mechanism of formation may differ between the two resulting in the differences observed in the chemical composition. The calcium phosphorus ratio, for a corresponding mineral content, is higher in the deep subgingival than the supragingival calculus. Weight loss on drying is greater for supragingival calculus than subgingival[12,13] providing evidence that deep subgingival calculus is more mineralized than the supragingival calculus. The sodium content of the deep subgingival calculus was also found to be higher than that of the supragingival calculus. The greater degree of mineralization, lower water and higher sodium content of subgingival calculus further suggests that either the mechanism of formation or source of raw materials differs between supra and subgingival calculus.

The morphology of the calcareous deposits varies from relatively smooth, flat accumulations to large, heavy, nodular projections (Fig. 8–4). The external morphology of calculus is also reflected in the internal structure. Thin layers of calculus are normally highly mineralized while gross deposits often exhibit areas of nonmineralized soft debris within the hard structure (Fig. 8–5).

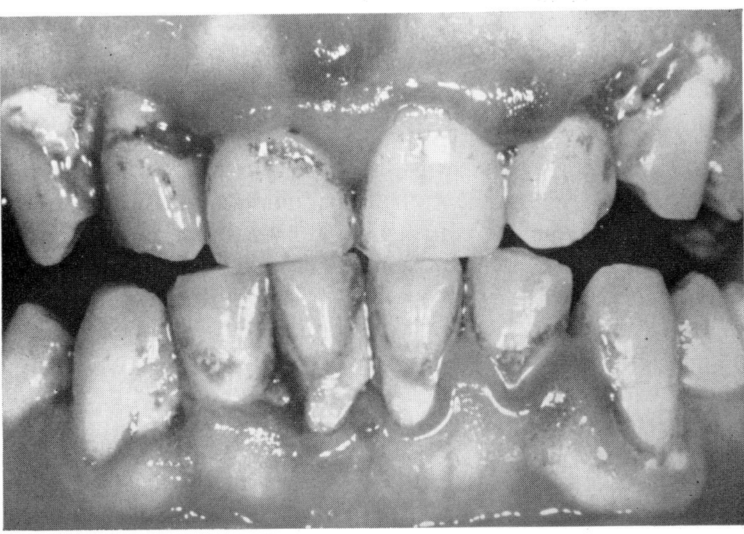

FIG. 8–4. Patient exhibiting heavy deposits of calculus and stain plus alterations in the gingival morphology.

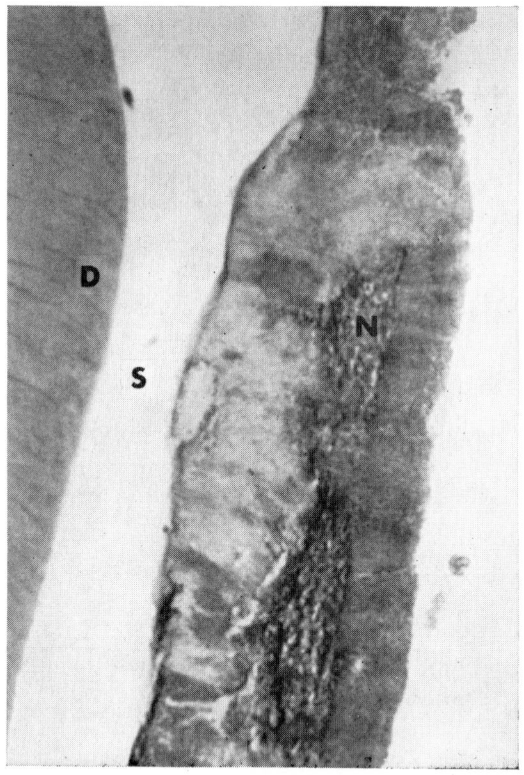

FIG. 8–5. Photomicrograph of a gross calcareous deposit demonstrating areas of varying degrees of mineralization plus a central core of soft debris. (*D*) dentin, (*S*) enamel space, (*N*) non-mineralized central core.

Formation

Calculus formation appears to take place in two steps. The first is the deposition of the organic matrix or mucinous bacterial containing plaque upon the enamel or cementum. It is at this stage when meticulous oral hygiene is extremely beneficial since these deposits can be removed from the teeth by proper home care prior to the beginning of mineralization, thereby effectively reducing the amount of calculus formed. If the plaque is not removed, attachment between itself and the tooth surface occurs. In areas of roughened enamel or cementum a direct attachment of the bacteria to the tooth appears to take place, while upon hard polished surfaces a cuticle-like attachment structure (Fig. 8–6) must be formed prior to calculus formation.[18] The exact mechanism of the alternations within the plaque which initiate mineralization is unknown and many different theories of calculus formation

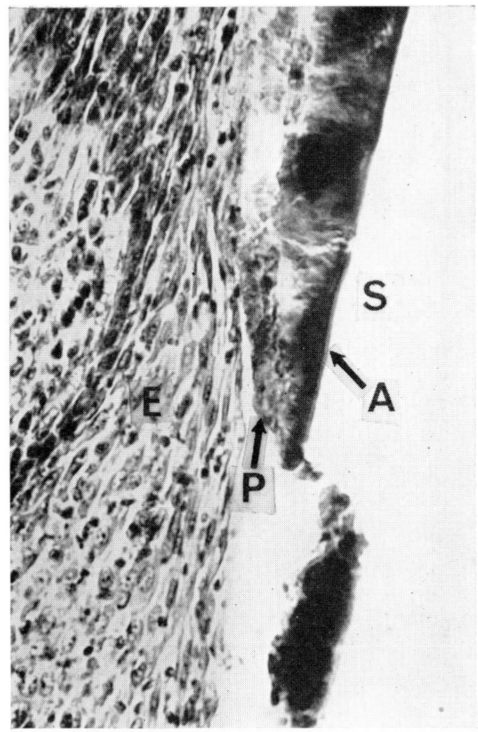

FIG. 8–6. Photomicrograph demonstrating the attachment cuticle between enamel and calculus, plus a layer of plaque between the calculus and the epithelium. (*S*) enamel space, (*A*) attachment cuticle, (*P*) plaque, (*E*) epithelium.

appear in the literature.[6] One of the earliest and simplest theories involves the direct precipitation of mineral salts on the teeth from the saliva due to an increase in the pH of the saliva with the loss of carbon dioxide. Experimental evidence suggesting the feasibility of this method has been presented.[9] Other mechanisms of precipitation of calculus from saliva have also been proposed. The high number of bacteria present within the dental plaque has led to a second theory, that it is the activity of the microorganisms themselves which leads directly to dental calculus formation. Of the bacteria present, the Leptothrix and the Actinomyces appear to be the most directly involved with mineralization both of an intra- and extra-cellular nature.

The most generally accepted theory concerning calculus formation today is that under certain conditions the mucinous matrix of the dental plaque is altered. This alteration of the matrix occurs in much the same way as that observed in the mineralization process of bone or dentin. The possible role of the bacteria in this regard cannot be ignored since mineralization appears to start near them and bacteria are able to manufacture products which can initiate the precipitation of calcium salts. Investigations with germ-free animals,[2,3] however, have demonstrated the formation of calculus without the presence of bacteria, which points up the multiplicity of factors involved in calculus formation.

The first calcific deposits to occur are those above the gingiva and are, therefore, called supragingival calculus. These may occur on any surface of any tooth; however, the greatest quantity appears on the lingual of the mandibular anterior teeth and on the buccal of the maxillary molars opposite the openings of the ducts from the major salivary glands. Initially these deposits are whitish, but often become stained by tobacco or other materials taken into the mouth. The hardness of supragingival calculus varies and it is usually easily removed during a dental prophylaxis. In patients with periodontal disease where gingival recession has taken place, supragingival calculus may be located on rough cemental surfaces where difficulty in its removal is often encountered (Fig. 8–4).

Often as a result of long term gingivitis the epithelial attachment on the tooth migrates apically, allowing for the formation of calculus below the gingiva, termed subgingival calculus. These deposits are usually harder in nature and more difficult to remove than supragingival calculus. The color varies from white to dark brown. The pigments causing the staining often result from the breakdown of red blood cells within the inflamed gingival sulcus. Normally these deposits are found by the use of an explorer, but, in the case of large, highly mineralized deposits they are visible on the dental x-ray (Fig. 8–7).

The state of health of the gingival tissues may be extremely important in the initial formation of subgingival calculus. When inflammation is present, an increase in the rate of gingival cervicular fluid flow is observed providing an abundant source for both the organic and inorganic components of subgingival calculus. The increase in fluid flow coupled with the down growth of the epithelial attachment along the cementum, therefore, provides an ideal environment for subgingival calculus formation. In the normal healthy gingiva, the base of the epithelial attachment is at the cementoenamel junction and an absence of gingival crevicular fluid flow is observed.[14]

The physical and chemical differences between supra- and subgingival calculus have led to the belief that the supragingival calculus is formed from saliva, while the subgingival calculus arises from the tissue fluid found in the gingival crevice. In a recent investigation, salivary mucoproteins were labeled with a radioactive material whereby

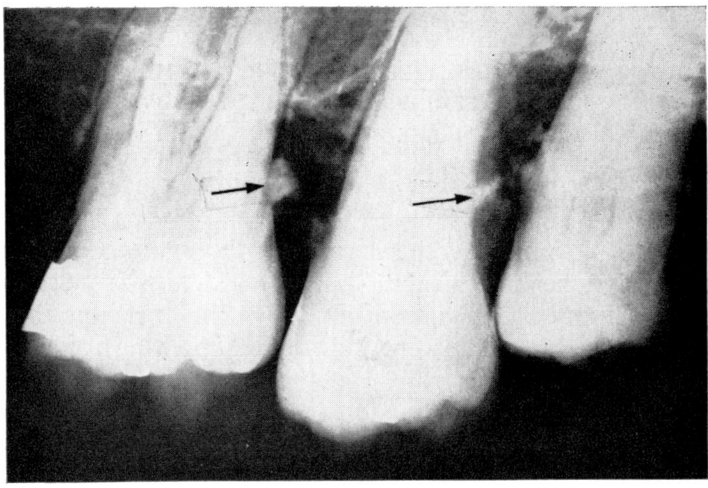

FIG. 8–7. Dental radiograph demonstrating the occurrence of subgingival calculus on maxillary molars.

they could be followed from formation within the salivary glands, secretion into the oral cavity and finally into the dental deposits. The labeled mucoproteins were observed to contribute only to the organic matrix of plaque and supragingival calculus and not subgingival calculus lending further support to the concept that supra- and subgingival calculus have different origins.[4]

Clinical Significance

The association between dental calculus formations and the occurrence of periodontal disease has long been noted. Today, however, the clinical significance of the dental calculus *per se* in the initiation of periodontal disease is being questioned. The mineralized calculus along with food impaction and faulty dental restorations certainly act as mechanical irritants, but interposed between the calculus and the gingiva is plaque containing cellular debris plus bacteria and their toxins (Fig. 8–6). It has been demonstrated that a direct correlation can be made between the appearance of plaque and gingivitis even without the presence of calculus.[1] On the other hand, in the germfree studies periodontal disease did occur in animals where no bacteria were present and the primary local factor was mechanical irritation from food impaction and dental calculus.[2,3]

Evidence presented in epidemiological surveys demonstrates the relationship between periodontal disease and dental deposits containing bacteria. The concentration of bacteria in the dental plaque is probably 1000 times greater than in the saliva and intestinal tract, and their damaging enzymatic products are retained in contact with the teeth and gingiva.[17] Of clinical importance, then, is the prevention of plaque formation, resulting in less gingival inflammation and a decrease in calculus formation.

Calculus Prevention

Numerous attempts have been made at the removal or inhibition of calculus by chemical means. Agents which dissolve the mineral phase of calculus unfortunately have a similar effect on the teeth. The utilization of mucolytic enzymes for the removal of plaques has been tried in chewing gums with only limited success. Therefore, at present the prevention of periodontal disease by removal of dental plaque and calculus is still the most important role of the dental hygienist. In addition to creating a smooth, hard tooth surface on which calculus formation is retarded, the hygienist must act as a teacher since proper oral hygiene can remove much of the dental plaque, with the resultant improvement in gingival health. Instruction in oral hygiene technique is the responsibility of the dental hygienist.

DENTAL STAINS

In spite of the fact that the teeth appear to present a hard impervious surface, the teeth often become colored or stained either on their outer surface or internally through the pulp. The outer surface of the teeth, in certain instances, may become stained by taking into the oral cavity various pigmented substances. The degree to which staining occurs is dependent on the state of oral hygiene and the surface texture of the teeth, as well as the contour of the teeth. Any surface of the tooth which is rough, under the height of contour and improperly cleaned will become stained much more rapidly than a clean smooth surface. Certain bacteria within the dental plaque may produce pigments which could also stain the tooth surface. Stains of this nature are of a non-metallic nature as contrasted with the staining produced by inhalation of metallic dust by industrial workers. Even in the case of the metallic stains it is the rough, unclean, unprotected tooth surface which stains first.

Under specific circumstances the ingestion of metallic ions will lead to a staining or discoloration of the tooth from within. The administration of certain drugs, especially antibiotics of the tetracycline group, will produce both developmental alternations and discolorations of the teeth. Staining of the dentin also occurs from the presence of other pigmented substances within the dental pulp, pulpal pathology, or through developmental defects. Staining of the teeth can, therefore, be classified into two groups, external or internal, regardless of the etiological factor.

External Stains

Continued or repeated contact between certain pigmented substances taken into the oral cavity and the surface of the teeth, combined with poor oral hygiene, often results in staining of the teeth.

Metallic Stains. Such stains are sometimes observed on the teeth of industrial workers who are continually exposed to metallic particles. As noted above, these particles tend to collect on roughened tooth surfaces. The color observed depends on the particular type of metal involved, from a greenish color with copper to brown with iron. The black silver stain commonly observed is most often a result of the application of silver nitrate by the dentist. The degree of penetration of any metallic substance into the tooth surface, determines whether it can be removed during dental prophylaxis. In the case of silver nitrate where deep penetration of the dentin and cementum occur, removal is impossible.

Non-metallic Stains. A black to brown stain on the surface of the teeth can also occur in mouths of heavy smokers (Fig. 8–8). It is, again, heaviest in areas which are not self-cleansing and when poor oral hygiene exists indicating that the stain is not tobacco products alone but probably a combination with other debris. This type of stain may be removed during dental prophylaxis; however, with this group of patients recurrence is rapid.

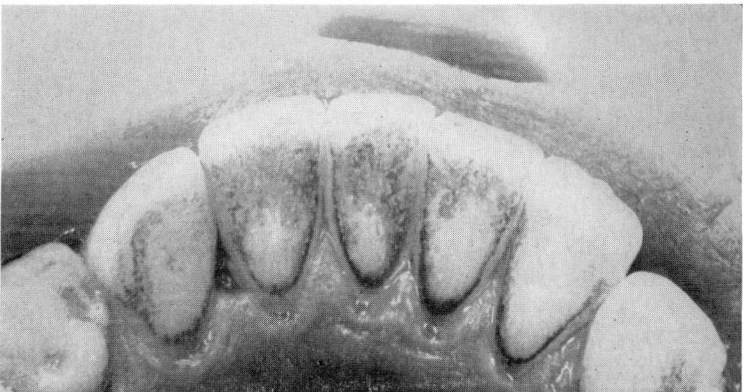

FIG. 8–8. Dark stain on lingual surface of mandibular anterior teeth due to tobacco products.

Stain of various colors within debris, or dental plaque, on the teeth often results from the action of pigment-producing bacteria found in the oral cavity. A complete discussion of these stains is found in the section on Dental Plaque.

Clinical Significance

The mere fact that a tooth surface becomes discolored on its outer surface is, in itself, of no great clinical significance; however, a stained tooth surface is indicative of local areas of poor oral hygiene. It is not uncommon, then, to observe gingival alterations adjacent to the stained areas on teeth.

Internal Stains

During the period of active tooth formation the formative cells of the tooth, odontoblasts and ameloblasts, are sensitive to foreign substances in the circulating blood. Pigmented materials may actually be incorporated directly into the newly forming dentin or enamel while other more toxic substances may alter the metabolism of the formative cells resulting in developmental defects within the teeth. The ingestion of fluorine results in a change in the forming apatite lattice structure with the replacement of hydroxyl groups by the fluorine. In small doses (1 ppm or less) the fluorapatite crystal formed appears normal and is resistant to dental decay. However, fluorine in an excess will interfere with both matrix formation and its subsequent mineralization. The mottled or hypoplastic enamel in a mild form results in white spots, while high concentrations of fluorine in drinking water produce pitted areas in the enamel and a color varying from white to brown or black[5] (Fig. 8–9).

High dosages of the tetracycline antibiotics during tooth formation often result in a yellow discoloration of the enamel which fluoresces under ultraviolet light. With age, these discolorations become darker and may eventually turn brown. As with ingestion of fluorine an excessive dose of tetracycline results in enamel hypoplasia.[11] Alterations in enamel formation may also result from hereditary disturbances where both the morphology and color of the crown are altered. A yellow-brown color of the crown is often associated with amelogenesis imperfecta. Defects in dentin formation related to genetics also occur which are termed dentinogenesis imperfecta. The teeth in these patients tend to appear translucent with a dark hue.

Physical trauma to a tooth of such force that death of the pulp occurs may result in a gray discoloration of the tooth (Fig. 8–10).

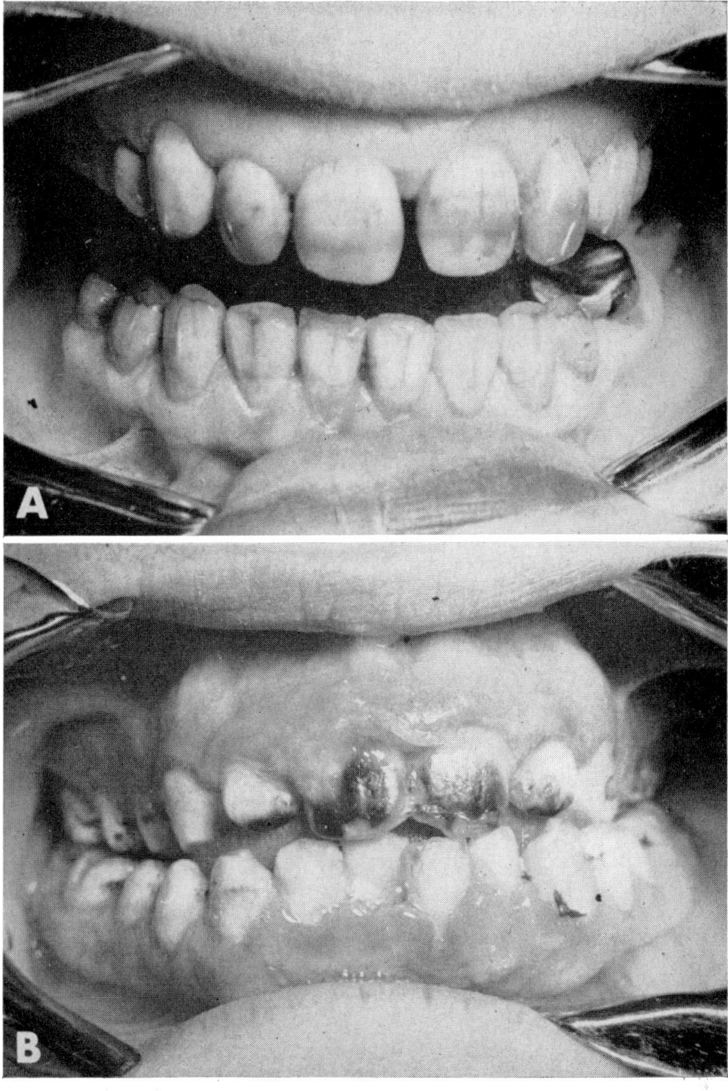

FIG. 8–9. Mottled enamel as a result of a high percentage of fluorine in the drinking water. (*A*), Moderate fluorosis. (*B*), Severe mottling. (Courtesy of R. J. Gorlin, University of Minnesota.)

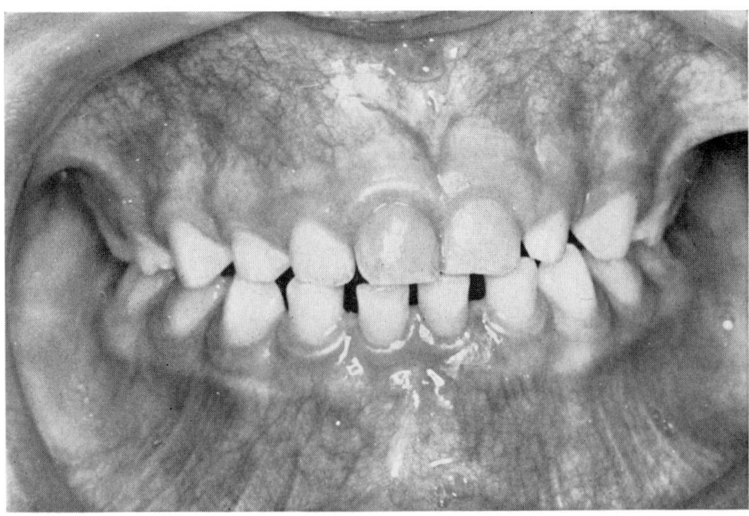

FIG. 8–10. The two maxillary central incisors exhibit a dark color as a result of pulpal death following a traumatic injury.

The trauma in these cases is severe enough to damage the pulpal blood vessels in the apical region resulting in a stasis of blood in the pulp. With the degeneration of the blood elements following injury, especially the red blood cells, pigments are released which enter the dentin producing the discoloration. Under certain conditions internal dentinal resorption takes place. As the pulp chamber enlarges and gets closer to the enamel surface a pink color can be observed in the tooth. The etiology of this particular lesion is unknown and the only treatment is removal of the pulp tissue followed by root canal filling.

Clinical Significance

Staining of the teeth from within may be of considerable importance as it often reveals an underlying local or systemic metabolic disturbance. In the majority of cases, treatment of such conditions is not directly a dental hygiene problem but recognition of the condition is of importance.

BIBLIOGRAPHY

1. ASH, M. M., GITLIN, B. M. and SMITH, W. A.: Correlation between plaque and gingivitis. J. Periodont., *35*, 424, 1964.
2. BAER, P. N. and NEWTON, W. L.: The occurrence of periodontal disease in germ free mice. J. Dent. Res., *38*, 1238, 1959.

3. BAER, P. N., NEWTON, W. L. and WHITE, C. L.: Studies on periodontal disease in the mouse. J. Periodont., *35,* 388, 1964.
4. BAUMHAMMERS, A. and STALLARD, R. E.: Salivary mucoprotein contribution to dental plaque and calculus. Periodont. In press 1965.
5. CLARKE, J. H. C. and MANN, J. E.: Natural fluoridation and mottling of teeth in Lincolnshire. Brit. Dent. J., *108,* 181, 1960.
6. DAWES, C. and JENKINS, G. N.: Some inorganic constituents of dental plaque and their relationship to early calculus formation and caries. Arch. Oral Biol., *7,* 161, 1962.
7. GLICKMAN, I.: *Clinical Periodontology,* Philadelphia, W. B. Saunders Company, 1964.
8. GUERINI, V.: *History of Dentistry,* Philadelphia, Lea & Febiger, 1909.
9. HODGE, H. C. and LEUNG, S. W.: Calculus formation. J. Periodont., *21,* 211, 1950.
10. KLEINBERG, I. and JENKINS, G.: The pH of dental plaques in different areas of the mouth. Arch. Oral Biol., *9,* 493, 1964.
11. KLINE, A. H., BLATTNER, R. J. and LUNIN, M.: Transplacental effect of tetracyclines on teeth. J.A.M.A., *188,* 170, 1964.
12. LITTLE, M. F., CASCIANI, C. A. and ROWLEY, J.: Dental calculus composition: 1. Supragingival calculus. J. Dent. Res., *42,* 78, 1963.
13. LITTLE, M. F. and HAZEN, S. P.: Dental calculus composition: 2. Subgingival calculus. J. Dent. Res., *43,* 645, 1964.
14. LOE, H. and HOLM-PEDERSEN, P.: Absence and presence of fluid from normal and inflamed gingivae. Periodont., *3,* 171, 1965.
15. MITCHELL, D. F. and HOLMES, L. A.: Topical antibiotic control of dentogingival plaque. J. Periodont., *36,* 202, 1965.
16. PAMEIJER, J. H. N. and MANLY, R. S.: Enamel decalcification by natural dental plaque in sugar solutions. Arch. Oral Biol., *7,* 735, 1962.
17. WAERHAUG, J.: Clinic epidemiology and the problems of basic research in periodontology. Int. Dent. J., *14,* 424, 1964.
18. ZANDER, H. A.: The attachment of calculus to root surfaces. J. Periodont., *24,* 16, 1953.

9

Periodontics

Perry A. Ratcliff
and Gilbert V. Oliver

It is imperative that the dental hygienist be knowledgeable about the diseases of the periodontium. In clinical practice, much effort will be devoted to either preventing or treating gingival inflammation. The hygienist must be able to recognize various periodontal diseases when they occur, must understand the etiology and pathogenesis to play an effective role in prevention, and must also have knowledge of therapeutic procedures to be a part of the dental office team providing dental health care for patients.

There are many periodontal diseases. However, disease characterized by inflammation of the periodontium probably occurs in at least 95 per cent of all the cases observed clinically.

The World Health Organization[15] suggests inflammatory periodontal disease as the malady most frequently occurring in man throughout the various countries of the world. It has been observed that 75 to 90 per cent of the population is in need of some form of periodontal treatment by age forty-five.[1,10] Massler, Schour and Chopra[12] report a rapid rise in the incidence of gingivitis in children beginning at age four to five and progressing to 80 to 90 per cent by age fourteen years. In a clinical investigation confirmed by roentgenographic examination, Marshall-Day *et al.*[11] observed the presence of periodontal destruction in all age groups. Approximately one-fourth of the population demonstrated bone loss at age nineteen with the prevalence increasing to 69 per cent at age twenty-six. By age forty-five almost 100 per cent were affected.

While some investigators have reported a lower incidence, all are in agreement that the vast majority of the population has some degree of disease of the periodontal structures. The most disquieting information from all of these investigations was the report by Marshall-Day *et al.*[11] that only 9 per cent of all subjects examined were aware of the presence of their periodontal diseases. However, the interest of the patient was demonstrated by his findings that 7 of every 9 such people had elected to have some treatment.

Realization of the endemic character of periodontal diseases led the Commission on the Survey of Dentistry[18] in 1959 to recommend marked changes in the dental curriculum. In the report the Commission stated, "The graduate of 1970 should possess many abilities similar to those of the best-trained periodontists of today. . . . The dental school should seek to develop curricula by 1970, at least, which will educate dentists who are much more periodontally and biologically oriented than today's graduate."

Philosophy of Patient Care

A patient who comes to the dentist for care should not be half treated by stopgap or first aid measures. When a carious lesion occurs in a tooth, it is necessary that a filling be placed. However, the dentist's philosophy of patient care may dictate the character of the filling. Treatment may be determined by whether one is trying just to treat the tooth or whether one is treating the tooth as a part of the entire mouth. Significant questions must be asked and answered. What will be the impact of the filling on the supporting structures? Will the form of the embrasure space be such that the patient can keep it clean? Is the filling material going to be placed below the free margin of the gingiva, and if so are the tissues capable of tolerating this material? Are primary and secondary grooves placed in the restoration to provide for the normal escape of food or will the contour of the filling predispose to interproximal food impaction? The success of a filling cannot be measured by the tendency for recurrent decay alone. The prevention or acceleration of breakdown of the periodontal tissues must be considered.

Treating any disease is done by removal of the cause and control of the developed lesion. When one treats a disease that is idiopathic, the necessity for empirical therapy dictates a guarded prognosis. For example, we know that by surgical intervention we may cure cancer. However, since we do not know the cause we can state only that if the patient has no recurrence in a given number of years, it can be assumed that there has been a cure. The intelligent management of *oral health depends upon the rationale of understanding cause-and-effect relationships between irritation and inflammation.* By identification and removal of the irritants periodontal health can be preserved.

Healthy Gingiva

Before the consideration of any disease one must first learn the characteristics of normal. However, it must be understood that the use of the word normal in this context is not that condition which is found in most patients, for most patients have gingival diseases,

"Normal" is a descriptive term relating only to those few patients where the tissues are healthy. Ideal gingiva is one which is not only healthy, but the form and architecture are conducive to the maintenance of health.

Ideal gingiva should have a color that is of *uniform pinkness* throughout the attached gingiva, at the margins and the papilla. The color of the tissue is determined primarily by the character of the underlying circulation. Normal blood circulation provides an adequate supply of oxygenated hemoglobin showing through the tissue as a coral or salmon pink color. This is modified by the amount of melanotic pigmentation present. Since there is a wide variation, depending upon the ethnic and racial background of the patient, it is necessary to compare the tissues from one location on the gingiva to another. Comparisons must be made within the same mouth rather than compare color from one patient to the next.

The most common color variation from normal is created by the venous stasis that is a part of gingival inflammation. The color from unoxygenated hemoglobin shows through the surface of the gingival tissue with a bluish or magenta hue. To identify normal pink vs. discoloration from inflammation the best procedure is to find an uninflamed area of the attached gingiva and let one's eye trace from this spot to the margins and onto the papilla. Since inflammation usually occurs first in the interproximal area and least frequently in the attached gingiva, it is best to start looking at the attached gingiva and then let the eye move onto the papilla.

The accepted concept of gingival architecture is a theoretical ideal providing optimum natural self-cleansing capacity of the mouth. This would be characterized by *conical papilla, knife-like edge buccal and lingual margins, adequate width of attached gingiva,* and an *adequate vestibular space* (Fig. 9–1).

In contrast to a blunted or cratered papilla, a conical form is conducive to the escape of food into the vestibule. Ideally, the crest of the papilla should be located immediately underneath the contact point. A knife-like edge margin reduces the deposit of debris at the dento-gingival margin and provides greater accessibility for cleansing with a brush. In adult life the margin of the gingiva should be positioned just coronal to the cemento-enamel junction, following the outline of the junction as it surrounds the tooth.

The band of attached gingiva between the alveolar mucosa and the free gingiva prevents the development of tensions from the oral muscles pulling against the marginal gingival tissue. Such muscle pulls have been observed to initiate gingival recession. Another function of the attached gingiva is that it provides a surface with sufficient keratinization for protection during eating and brushing. The labial and buccal

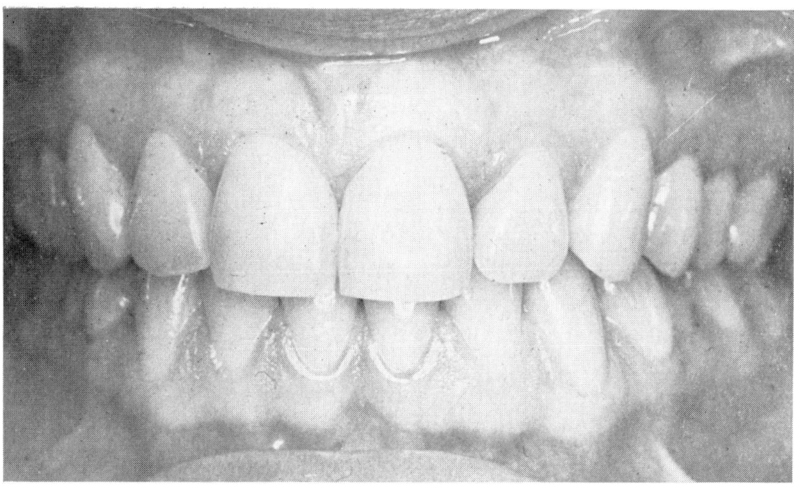

FIG. 9–1. A healthy mouth of a twenty-one-year-old girl. There is uniform color throughout the papilla, marginal gingiva and attached gingiva. Note the architectural form with conical papilla, knife-edged marginal tissue together with a wide band of attached gingiva in both maxillary and mandibular jaws.

mucosa never keratinizes, but the attached gingiva develops some keratinization which makes it possible to eat fibrous foods and brush the mouth with comfort. Just how much attached gingiva is really necessary has never been determined. It is much easier to determine when it has not been adequate rather than to know when there is more than enough.

Another characteristic of normal gingiva is a shallow sulcular depth. Ideally this would be a zero crevice but such is not found nor if created can it be maintained. Fortunately, a gingival *sulcus not in excess of 2 to 3 mm.* in depth can be maintained relatively free from inflammation for most patients who maintain adequate oral hygiene. Biopsies of gingival tissue with varying crevicular depths indicate that there is relatively little inflammatory cellular infiltrate or degenerative process when the sulcular depth does not exceed 2 to 3 mm. However, one rarely finds the absence of significant inflammatory breakdown when the crevicular depth is 4 mm. or greater.

Healthy gingiva should have no purulent or hemorrhagic exudate. Hemorrhage can occur only when there is a break in the continuity of the epithelium. This continuity break can be created only by ulceration or laceration. Within the gingival sulcus, laceration rarely occurs except by instrumentation during scaling procedures. Gingival bleeding observed by the patient at home usually is an indication that *ulceration has occurred in the crevicular epithelium.*

The formation of pus, or a purulent exudate, occurs in a relatively acute inflammatory response. It forms from phagocytic action of white blood cells removing bacterial and cellular debris. Healthy gingiva should have only a serous-like fluid which normally escapes from the interstitial tissues, passes through the intact sulcular epithelium, and acts as a washing device to help clean the sulcular area. Brushing and massage increases the flow of this fluid.

In a healthy periodontium, there should be *no mobility* of the teeth beyond that of normal physiologic movement. A mobile tooth causes open contacts and food impaction. Also, a mobile tooth may not be an effective masticatory device and the patient may avoid the use of this area of the dentition. The avoidance of use complicates the natural detergent effect created by the chewing process. All of this leads to gingival inflammation.

Another criterion of periodontal health is the *absence of pain.* Pain may occur in a tooth as a result of excessive occlusal forces bringing about a pulpitis. This may set off a chain reaction with the patient avoiding the area in mastication. The result is eventual gingival inflammation from the inadequate oral hygiene concomitant with reduced detergent action of food flow.

Pain might occur in the gingiva as a result of inadequate keratinization of the attached gingiva or an inadequate amount of attached gingiva. It is not uncommon for women in the postmenopausal age to have a relatively poor epithelial covering of the gingiva and find it is uncomfortable to brush the mouth, particularly with a stiffer brush. Since the buccal mucosa has no keratinized surface, the absence of a band of attached gingiva presents a similar problem.

Histology of Clinically Healthy Gingiva

In the microscopic examination of healthy connective tissue, taken from a site other than the gingiva, the histologist expects there to be neither infiltrate of plasma cells and lymphocytes nor edema between the connective tissue fibrils. However, gingival tissues that appear healthy clinically do not show the same degree of health in the microscopic specimen (Fig. 9–2). The corium of clinically healthy gingiva always contains a few round cells, mostly plasma cells and lymphocytes. This round cell infiltrate is found in the tissues immediately adjacent to the sulcus. Usually some spaces exist between the connective tissue fibrils indicating the presence of edema. Although the gingiva is amply supplied with blood vessels, specimens taken from clinically healthy tissue show little evidence of engorgement or dilatation. The epithelium usually has some keratinization of the attached gingival surface, and if no keratinization exists the surface will be at least parakeratotic.

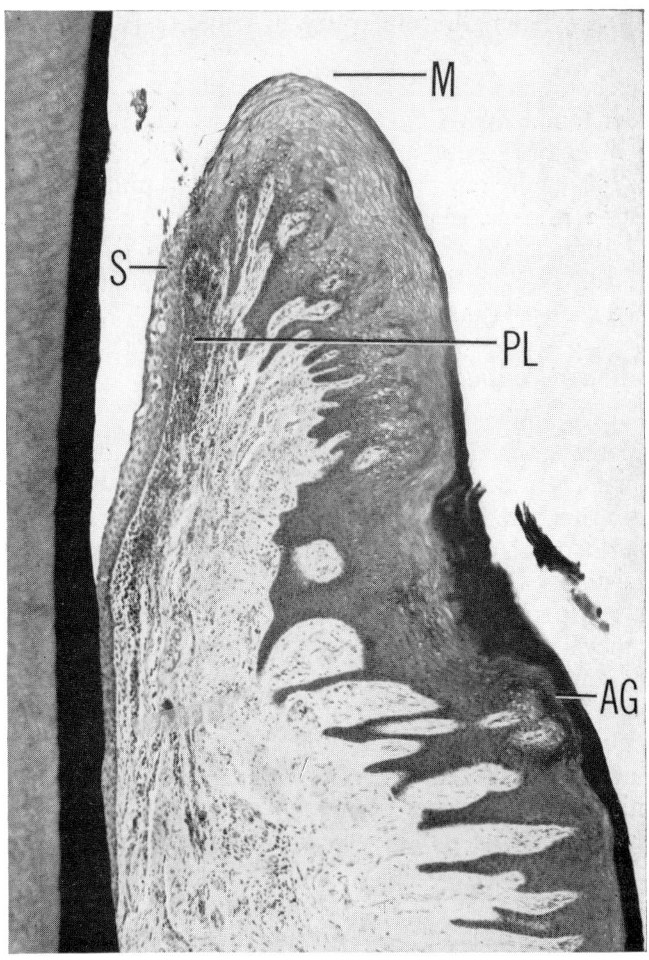

FIG. 9–2. Section from buccal of mandibular bicuspid with clinically healthy gingiva of forty-year-old male. Epithelial keratinization is marked in the attached gingival area (*AG*), becoming reduced as it approaches the margin (*M*) with no keratinization in the sulcular epithelium (*S*). The connective tissue is normal except for some evidences of edema adjacent to the sulcular area. There has been no epithelial invasion of the connective tissue. Plasma cells and lymphocytes (*PL*) are present in some quantity in the area of the sulcus with extension of the inflammatory process into the deep tissue of the attached gingiva. (H. & E. ×50.)

The sulcular epithelium usually is about 3 or 4 cells in thickness and apparently all cells have mitotic capacities. The epithelial attachment may vary in length from 1 mm. to sometimes as much as 8 mm. long.

The mechanism of adhesion of epithelium to the tooth surface is not fully understood. Work by Stern[17] suggests that the epithelium is attached to enamel by a mucopolysaccharide bonding between the interfaces of the reduced enamel organ and epithelial cells. The adhesion of epithelium to cementum also seems to be with a mucopolysaccharide bonding matrix.[21] The distance from the bottom of the epithelial adhesion to the crest of the alveolar bone is consistently maintained at approximately 1 mm.[5]

Classification of Periodontal Diseases

There are a number of periodontal diseases. These are classified as either inflammatory or dystrophic. The inflammatory diseases are gingivitis and periodontitis characterized by similarity in etiology and pathology. Since inflammatory disease is so common, it has been called "periodontal disease." This is wrong, for it implies that the dystrophic diseases do not exist or are not periodontal diseases. Because gingivitis and periodontitis are so prevalent and are a public health problem, they have been the primary object of research in epidemiology, pathology and treatment. Therefore, they are comparatively well understood.

Dystrophic diseases are a group characterized by degenerative changes or excessive cell proliferation. In contrast to gingivitis and periodontitis, gingivosis and periodontosis are *not similar in clinical character, etiology or pathology*. Other dystrophic conditions are atrophy, hyperplasia and trauma.

The chart in Figure 9–3 will provide a brief resume for organization of the classification used in the various periodontal diseases.

Inflammatory	*Dystrophic*
Gingivitis	Gingivosis
Periodontitis	Periodontosis
	Atrophy
	Hyperplasia
	Periodontal traumatism

Fig. 9–3.

Gingivitis and Periodontitis. Gingivitis and periodontitis are essentially the same disease, both characterized by inflammation of the periodontium. The only difference between the two is a reference to the anatomical parts involved. In gingivitis, only the marginal and papillary tissues are inflamed. Generally, the transeptal fibers are considered as a line of demarcation to determine whether the case is called gingivitis or periodontitis. If the involvement is deeper than the transeptal fibers, then the term periodontitis is deemed applicable. Often it is difficult to make a clinical distinction between the two.

Gingivitis and periodontitis may be described by adjectives which provide a better picture of the problem. Modifying terms relate to (1) inflammatory response, (2) anatomical location, (3) etiologic factors, (4) tissue response and (5) severity. From each of these categories, specific terms are selected to accurately describe the pathologic condition observed. The chart in Figure 9–4 lists these terms which may be used singly or in combination.

(1) Inflammatory Response
- Acute
- Chronic

(2) Anatomical location
- Papillary
- Marginal
- Generalized
- Localized

(3) Etiologic factors
- Microbial
- Mechanical
- Allergic
- Traumatic
- Thermal
- Radiation

(4) Tissue Response
- Edematous
- Hyperplastic
- Ulcerative
- Necrotic or necrotizing
- Erosive
- Desquamative

(5) Severity
- Mild
- Moderate
- Severe

FIG. 9–4. Modifying adjectives for gingivitis and periodontitis.

The character of the inflammatory response may be either acute or chronic. The anatomical location may be indicated in more detail stating that the gingivitis is either marginal, papillary, localized or generalized. Etiologic factors may enter into the description indicating that the inflammation is caused by microbial, mechanical, allergic, traumatic or thermal irritants. The response of the tissues may be used as a means of describing the clinical characteristics of the histopathology of the problem. These terms are usually hyperplastic, edematous, necrotic or ulcerative. The severity of the disease may be described as mild, moderate or severe. For example, a full descriptive diagnosis may read, "Chronic generalized marginal gingivitis."

When periodontitis is the more descriptive term, usually the modifying adjectives are limited to the anatomical location as being either localized or generalized, or described by the severity of the problem. Thus, mild, moderate or severe are commonly used terms.

When the patient has a systemic complication which may accelerate progress of the disease this may be indicated by stating that the case is complicated by diabetes, pregnancy, anemia, etc. Thus, a case is described as being a "Generalized severe periodontitis complicated by diabetes." Other examples of a descriptive diagnosis would be, "Severe generalized periodontitis complicated by pregnancy" or "Moderate localized hyperplastic periodontitis."

Gingivosis. The dystrophic problems of the periodontium are gingivosis, periodontosis, atrophy, trauma and hyperplastic changes. Gingivosis, also known as chronic desquamative gingivitis, is a relatively uncommon gingival disturbance of the connective tissue characterized by the inadequacy of the attachment of the epithelium to the underlying connective tissue. Air bubbles are formed underneath the epithelium by the pressure from an air syringe. The tissues appear irritated because of an inadequate epithelial protective mechanism. Both the attached gingiva as well as the marginal and papillary tissues are inflamed. The etiology is unknown but it is believed that the background lies in a hormonal disturbance affecting collagen metabolism.

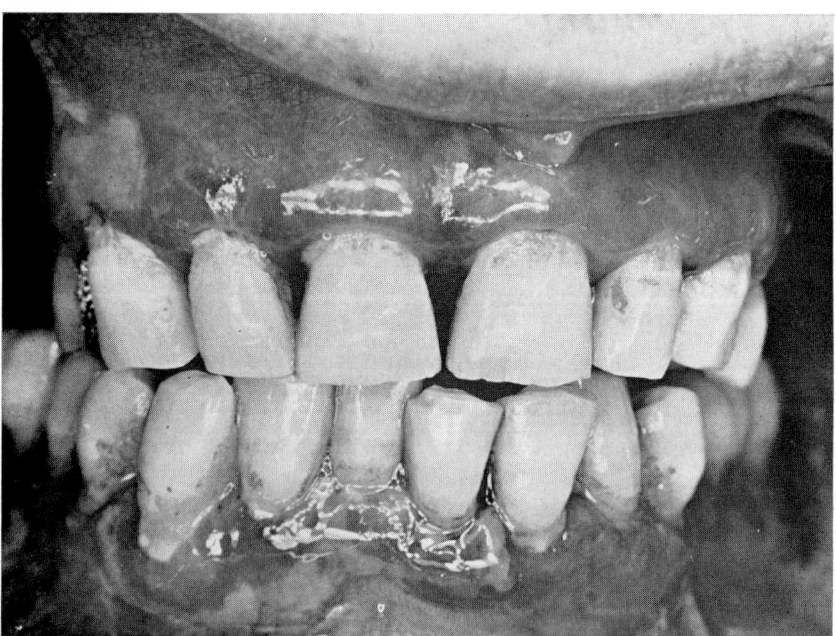

FIG. 9–5. Fifty-two-year-old post-menopausal female with generalized gingivosis. The epithelium is thin and fragile, particularly in the area of the mandibular incisors. The attached gingiva has a glossy appearance. The soft tissues are easily damaged by routine oral hygiene procedures.

Periodontosis. Uncomplicated periodontosis rarely is seen clinically. In the pure state it is a non-inflammatory degeneration of the supporting periodontal tissues, which after pocket formation is complicated by inflammation. The etiology of periodontosis is unknown. The systemic origin of the disease most suspected is a defect in collagen metabolism and an inherited inferiority of the dental organ.

Periodontosis is characterized and diagnosed more from the nature of the developing lesions and the roentgenographic interpretation rather than from the presence of pockets free from inflammation. Usually, this is a so-called vertical bone loss pattern with involvement of the first molars and incisor teeth and the balance of the dentition uninvolved, at least in the earlier stages. It occurs more frequently in the fifteen to twenty-five age population in the United States and there is a higher incidence in the Negro race. It is a major public health problem in India (Figs. 9–6, 9–7 and 9–8).

Periodontal Atrophy. Periodontal atrophy is seen clinically as a reduction in the height of the alveolar bone with a simultaneous recession of the gingiva thereby maintaining a normal dento-gingival alveolar relationship. This has been described as a normal process of aging.[2] However, it has been considered by some to be pathologic, particularly when there has been marked recession.[20] Whether or not it is considered to be a disease process, it is of little clinical significance.

Another form is *disuse atrophy* wherein the pathologic changes occur in the periodontal ligament and bone with no apparent changes in the superficial soft tissues. The changes result when functional stimulation is inadequate to maintain health. The periodontal ligament becomes thinner, the fibers are reduced in number and the fibrocytes lose their normal polarity. Lack of functional stimulation necessary for osteoblastic activity results in failure to replace bone as it is normally resorbed with ultimate reduction in the number and thickness of the bone trabeculae.

Gingival Hyperplasia. Hyperplastic gingiva is characterized by a dense *overgrowth of the connective tissue elements* of the gingiva. As in all hyperplastic responses, there is an increase in the number of cellular elements present. In gingival hyperplasia, the fibrous connective tissue increases in cellular density as well as number of fiber bundles. This creates gingival ledges on the buccals and linguals of teeth, loss of interdental grooves, and blunting or cratering of the interproximal papilla. The etiologic background may be either inflammatory or non-inflammatory.

Inflammatory Hyperplasia. With a low-grade inflammatory response to irritation there is an increase in the number of fiberblasts that proliferate, developing a *scar-like tissue.* A low-grade irritant such as mouth breathing will dry the tissues initiating sufficient inflammatory

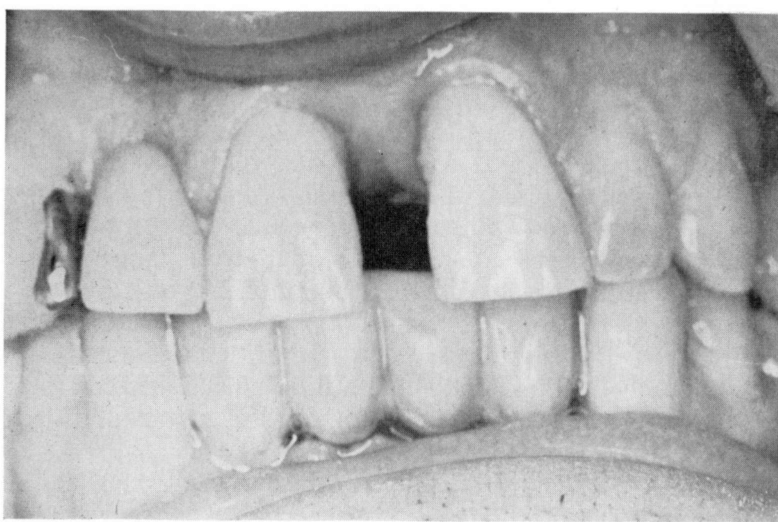

FIG. 9–6. Periodontosis in a twenty-five-year-old male. Note the characteristic diastema between the maxillary central incisors. The four mandibular incisors and the maxillary right lateral incisor have been lost previously and replaced with fixed bridgework.

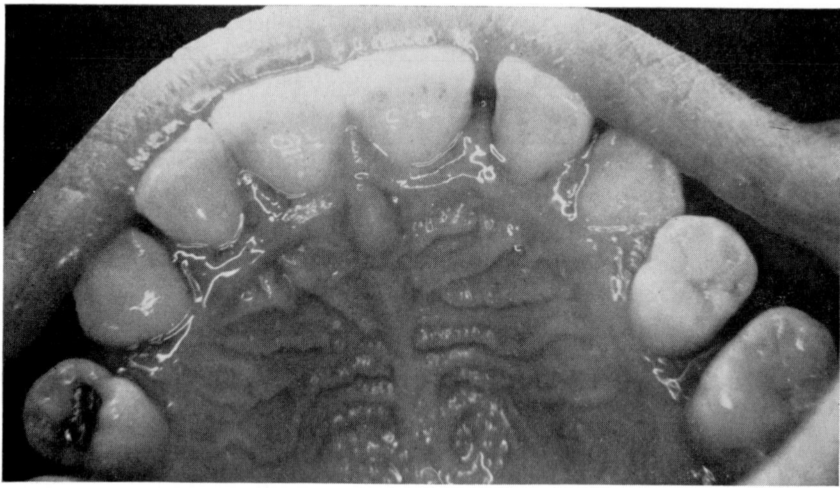

FIG. 9–7. Advanced periodontosis in a nineteen-year-old girl. Clinical manifestations became apparent after initiation of orthodontics. Note the glossy appearance of the gingiva adjacent to the teeth. Deep interproximal pockets are present wherever a diastema exists.

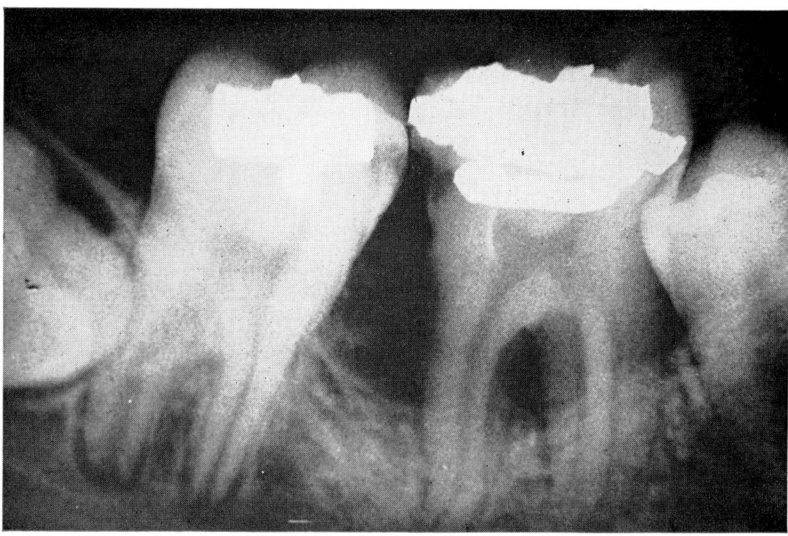

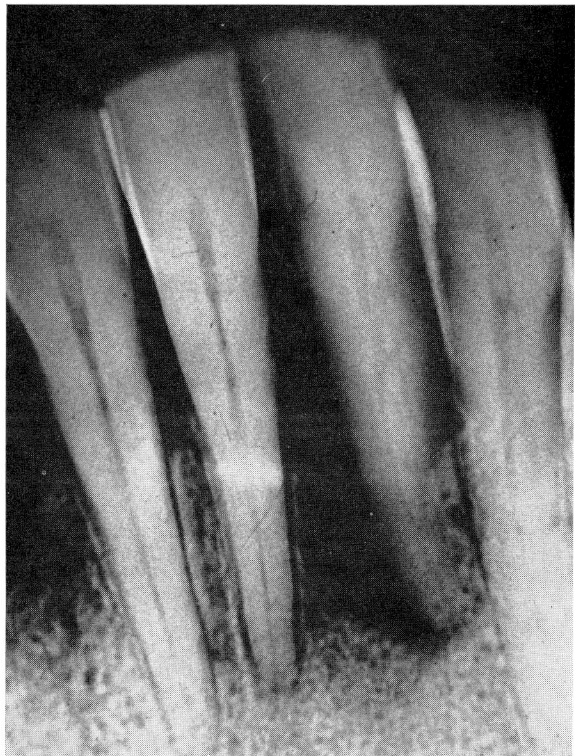

FIG. 9–8. Mandibular incisor and mandibular first molar with characteristic "vertical" bone loss of periodontosis. The involved teeth have extensive loss of support while adjacent teeth have little or no involvement.

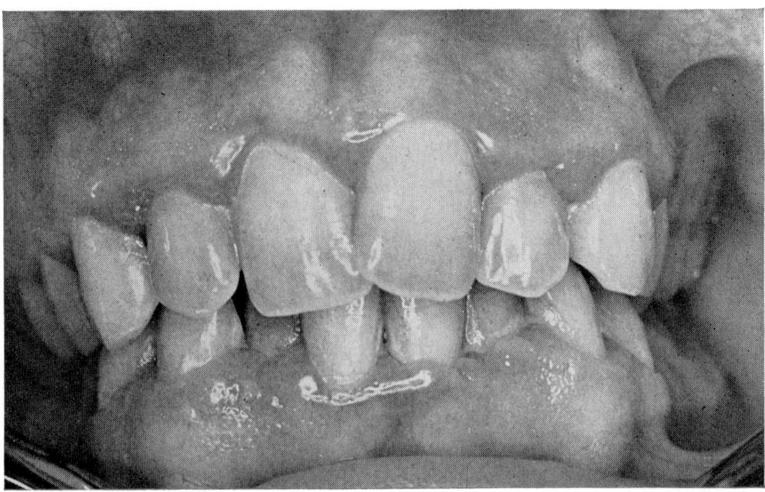

FIG. 9–9. Twenty-one-year-old girl with moderately severe periodontitis primarily caused by mouth breathing. Her adenoids were chronically infected and enlarged, obstructing the nasal air passages. The anterior is inflamed and hyperplastic. The lingual position of the mandibular incisors has complicated oral hygiene and aggravated the mandibular problem.

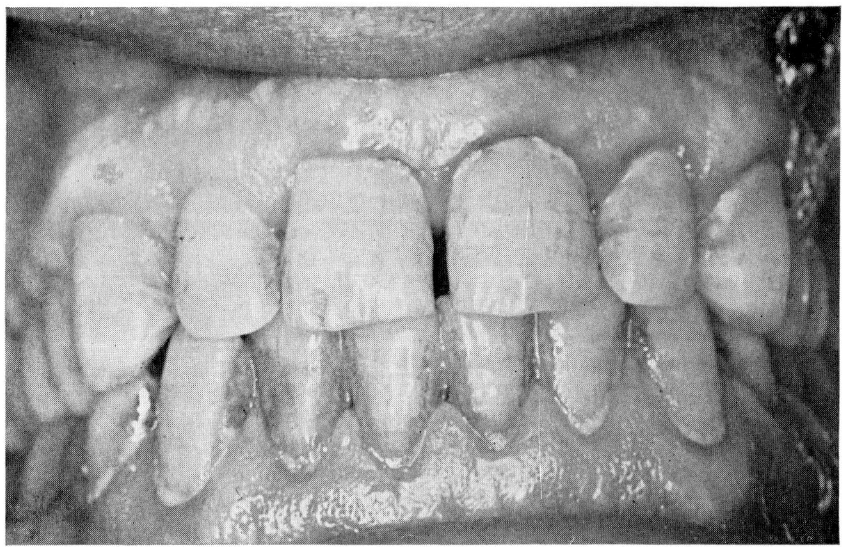

FIG. 9–10. Fifty-year-old male with generalized severe periodontitis. Pocket depth scores ranged from 5 to 7 mm. deep throughout. Hyperplasia has caused generalized gingival enlargement with blunted papilla, marginal ledges and loss of interdental grooves. Note the heavy deposit of plaque and calculus at the gingival margins and interproximals. Patient brushed horizontally with a stiff brush.

reaction to bring about gingival hyperplasia. This is a commonly observed clinical problem (Fig. 9–9). Frequently, when a patient brushes vigorously with a stiff brush, the vascular blockade which is a part of the inflammatory reaction may break down, thereby supplying a relatively higher level of blood and nutrients to the irritated gingival tissues. As a result, the attempt at repair may develop extensive scarring and a large clinically observable hyperplastic defect (Fig. 9–10).

Non-inflammatory Gingival Hyperplasia. The most effective drug for the control of epilepsy is sodium diphenylhydantoinate, commonly called Dilantin. The metabolites of this drug have an apparent capacity to stimulate fiberblastic activity in the gingiva of some patients who use this drug routinely to control the grand mal convulsions of epilepsy. Extensive hyperplastic tissue changes may occur in a relatively short period of time. The extent of overgrowth may be so great that it acts as an orthodontic appliance and moves teeth. It may cover the occlusal surfaces of the teeth involved (Fig. 9–11). Treatment is by surgical excision, discontinuance of the drug and good oral hygiene. Sometimes no other drug can be substituted making it necessary to subject the patient to repeated gingivoplasties.

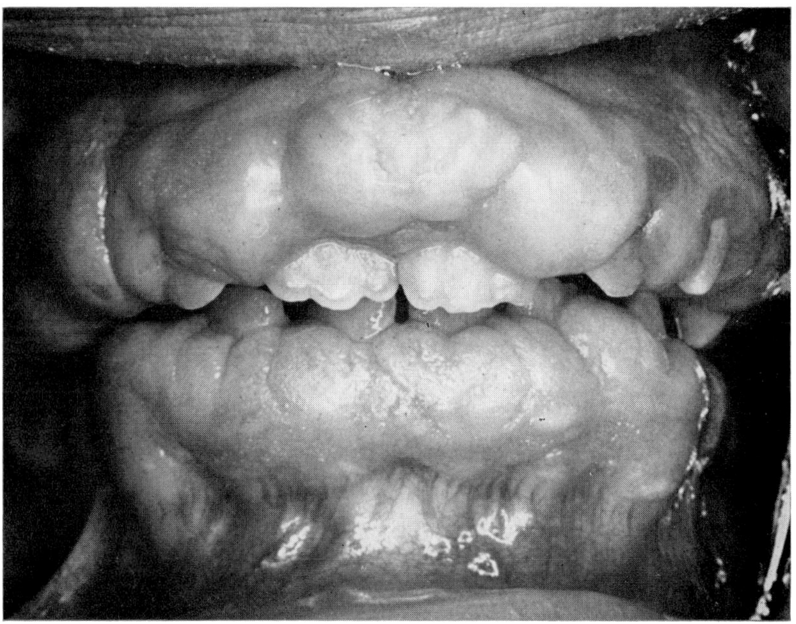

FIG. 9–11. Thirteen-year-old male receiving 1.2 gm. Dilantin sodium for six years in treatment of grand mal epilepsy. Hyperplastic fibrous tissue has nearly covered all teeth. This tissue is very dense. The absence of edema means that no shrinkage can be expected by the removal of any local irritants.

A similar appearing problem with apparent hereditary familial characteristics is an idiopathic hyperplastic enlargement. This has been most commonly known as hereditary fibromatosis, gingival elephantiasis, or idiopathic fibromatosis. Again, the treatment is by surgical excision with a prognosis of non-recurrence after pubertal age.

Periodontal Traumatism. Periodontal traumatism is the injury to periodontal tissues caused by occlusal forces that are greater than the adaptive capacity of the tissues. The emphasis here must be placed upon the tissue rather than the force (Fig. 9–12). Varying amounts of force can be applied safely to tissues without trauma depending on the

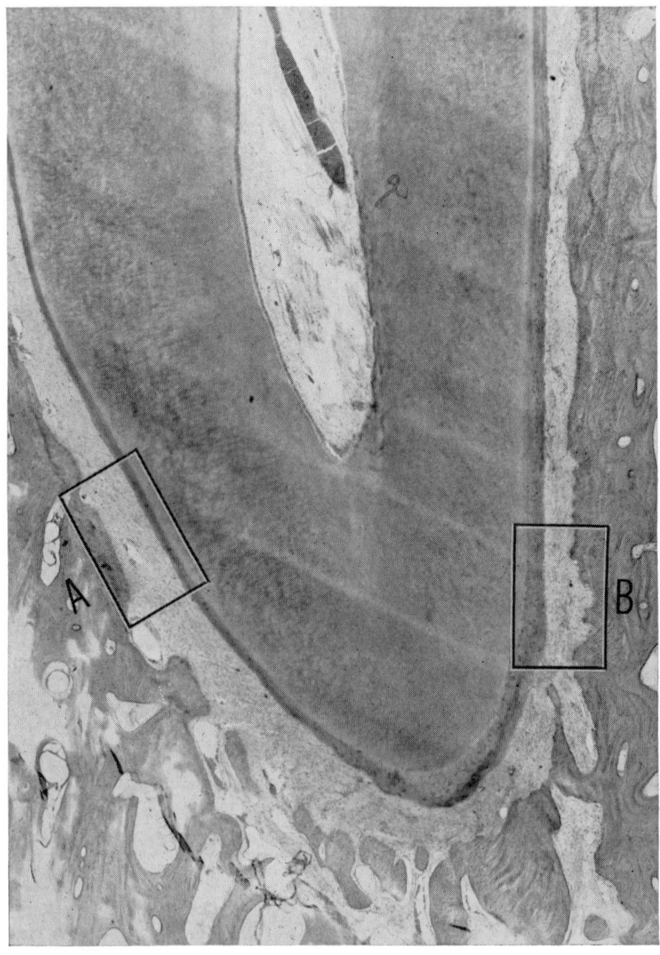

FIG. 9–12. (*Continued on opposite page*)

adaptive capacity of that tissue to withstand the force. Variables concerning pressures are the character of the force, its direction, its frequency and its amplitude.

Periodontal traumatism may be primary or secondary. Primary traumatism occurs when the support of the tooth is normal but the occlusal forces are excessive thereby bringing about traumatic changes in the underlying tissues. An example of this is found in an otherwise healthy mouth with a high inlay. Secondary traumatism exists when the forces are normal, but the support to the teeth is inadequate to withstand normal mastication. This occurs in advanced periodontitis with severe bone loss.

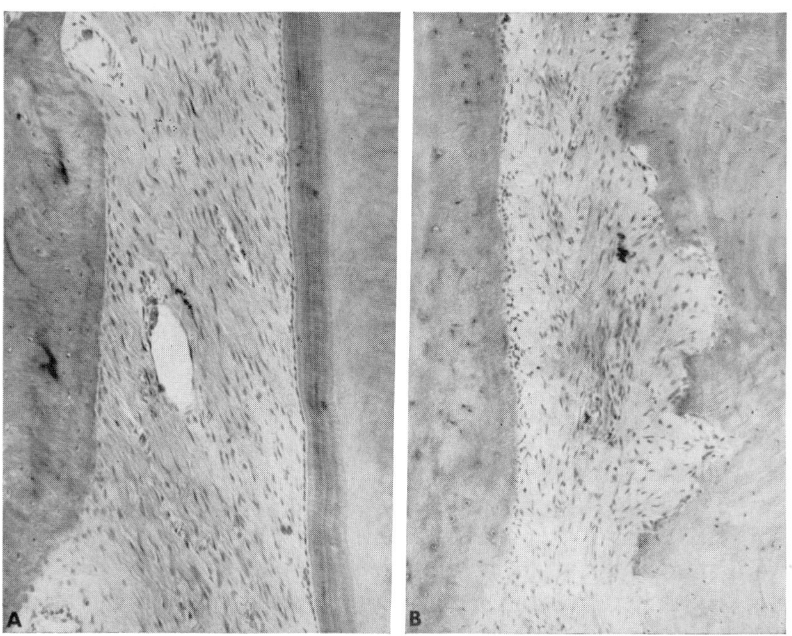

FIG. 9–12. Root tip of tooth demonstrating periodontal traumatism. The side *A* is subject to tension resulting in both bone apposition and a wider periodontal ligament space. Side *B* is subject to pressure with both bone resorption and reduced periodontal ligament space.

A, High magnification from tension side. Note the distinct arrangement of the connective tissue fibers and cell polarity. Incremental lines in the bone indicate different areas of bone apposition. (H. & E. ×125.)

B, High magnification from pressure side. Note the absence of distinct arrangement of the connective tissue fibers with variable cell polarity. Hyaline degeneration marks loss of cell structure. Characteristic Howship's lacunae indicate areas of osteoclastic activity and bone resorption. (H. & E. ×125.)

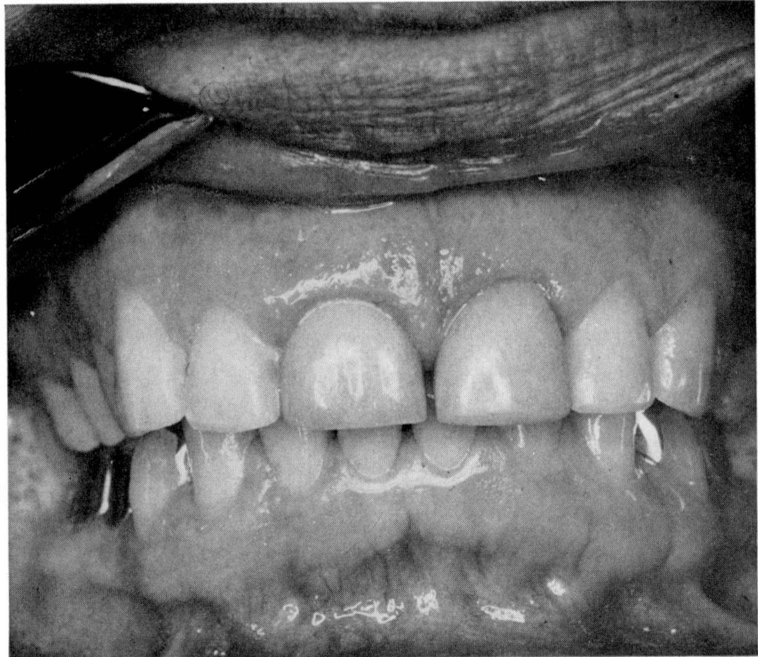

FIG. 9–13. Mild localized periodontitis involving only the maxillary central incisors. Low grade chronic irritation from the margins of the jacket crowns has initiated gingival inflammation, fibrosis and 4 mm. pockets.

Very slight stimulating pressures on the confined periodontal ligament will induce osteoclastic activity. With progressive increase in pressure there is a beginning thrombosis and hemorrhage with hyalinization and ultimate necrosis. The physiologic adaptive capacity of the periodontium is great and will allow for changes even with excessive force. By undermining resorption the cortical plate of the alveolar process is removed and replaced with a new and wider periodontal ligament.

Gingival Inflammation. If one understands the processes of inflammation, one will understand the process of gingival or periodontal disease in the majority of the clinical patients found in the usual dental practice. It is axiomatic that *inflammation is preceded by irritation.* Thus, clinical periodontal practice is founded on a knowledge of the processes of inflammation and the nature and intensity of irritants. Identification of the irritants is essential for good clinical management. Irritants may very in severity, duration and character. However, all irritants can be considered as a group, as the common denominator of the initiation of gingival inflammation.

Gingival tissues respond in either of two ways to irritation. When the tissue response is such that the destructive phase is predominant, the response is characterized by edema. When the tissue response is such that the repair phase is predominant, the response is primarily fibrous with characteristic scarring and hyperplasia of the gingival tissue. In the microscopic slide, one can observe that both processes usually go on at the same time in nearby locations in the same tissue. Next to the tooth the process may be acute and edematous, whereas on the external surface the process may be quite chronic and fibrous (Figs. 9–13 and 9–14). Clinically one may observe that the interproximal may be more acute whereas the buccal and lingual may be far more chronic in character of inflammatory reaction.

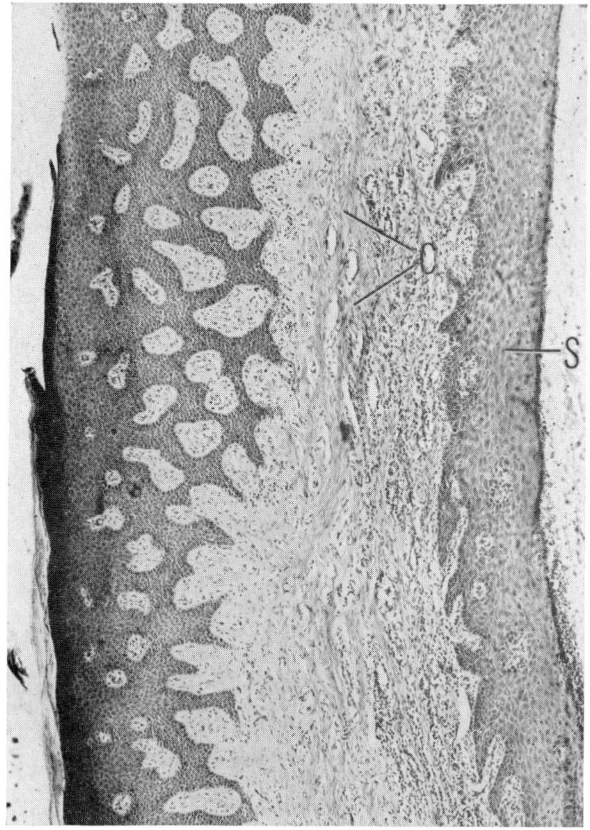

FIG. 9–14. Biopsy from labial of maxillary right central incisor from Figure 9–13. Tissue was cut horizontally, parallel to the occlusal plane. The circular ligament fibers (*C*) act as a barrier largely confining the cellular infiltrate, edema and dilated capillaries to the sulcular side (*S*), next to the tooth. The sulcular epithelium is thickened with some invasion of the connective tissue space. Note the minimal inflammation on the labial side which was seen clinically. (H. & E. ×65.)

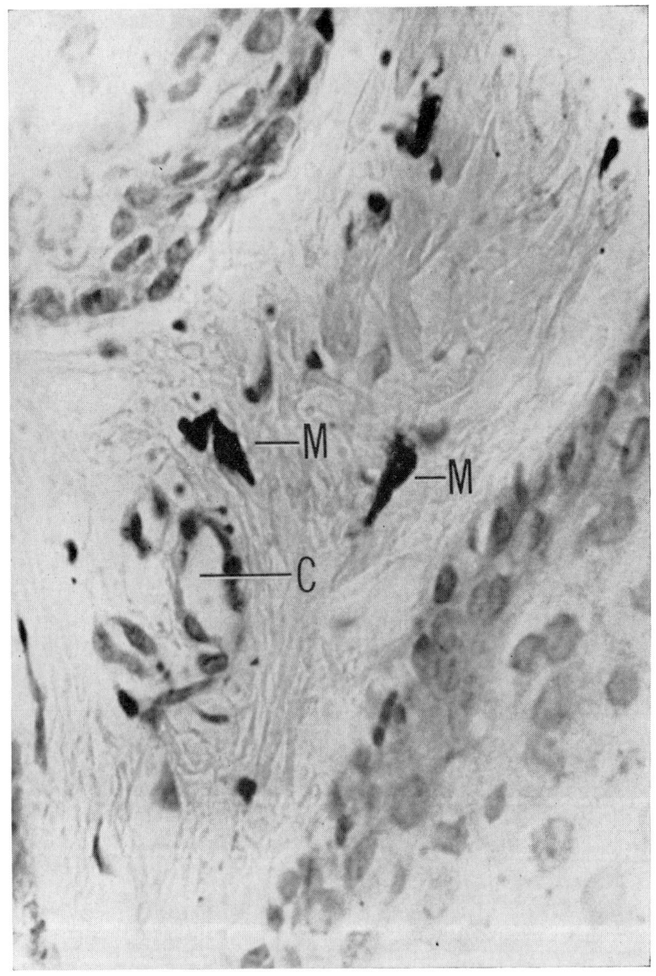

FIG. 9–15. Gingival biopsy taken from gingival margin in a case of gingivitis. Specimen shows capillary (*C*) located between two epithelial rete pegs. Note mast cells (*M*). (Wrights-carbol fuschin ×600.)

Edematous Response. A thorough knowledge of the role and cause of edema is essential in management of early periodontal lesions. Reduction of pocket depth by shrinkage of tissues, with its concomitant improvement in architectural form, is a fundamental objective in the treatment of gingivitis.

Most of the development of edema results from alterations in osmotic balance in the intercellular spaces. The inflammatory response begins with vascular changes which include the opening between the attachment plaques of endothelial cells in capillaries. Histamine and 5-hydroxytryptamine released from mast cells open the attachment plaques (Fig. 9–15) allowing an escape of white blood cells, fibrin, globulins and other particulate matter between the adhesion plaques and through the basement membrane of the capillary into the intercellular space. Passing with these cells, there is an escape of fluids from the lumen of the vessel. Heparin granules discharged from mast cells join the fibrin and globulins in the intercellular spaces. In addition, the disturbance of inflammation brings about a disaggregation of the intercellular ground substance, changing it from a solid to a liquid gel by breaking up the molecular chain into a greater number of shorter chain molecules. *The increased cellular and molecular contents in the intercellular spaces alter the osmotic balance and retain fluid* within the tissue area. This edema causes the gingiva to appear boggy. Often it will pit on pressure by the explorer (Figs. 9–16 and 9–17).

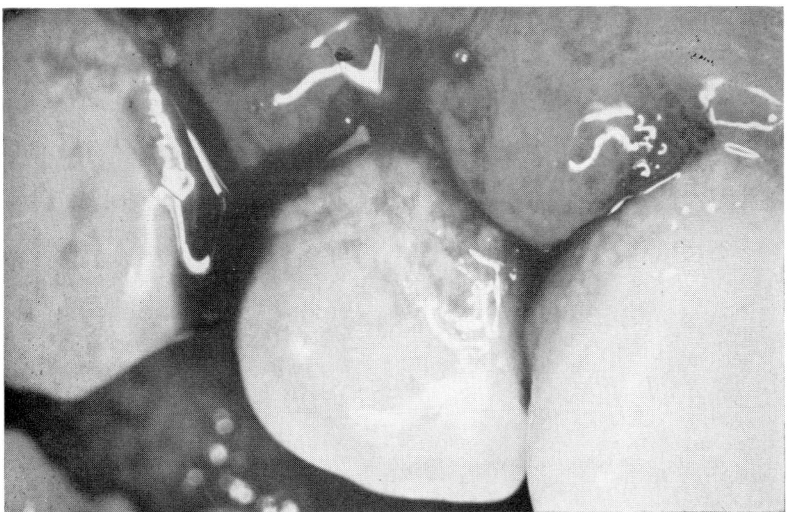

FIG. 9–16. Gingival papilla and margins of highly edematous response in case of periodontitis in a twenty-eight-year-old female. Note the glossy appearance and apparent swelling of the gingiva.

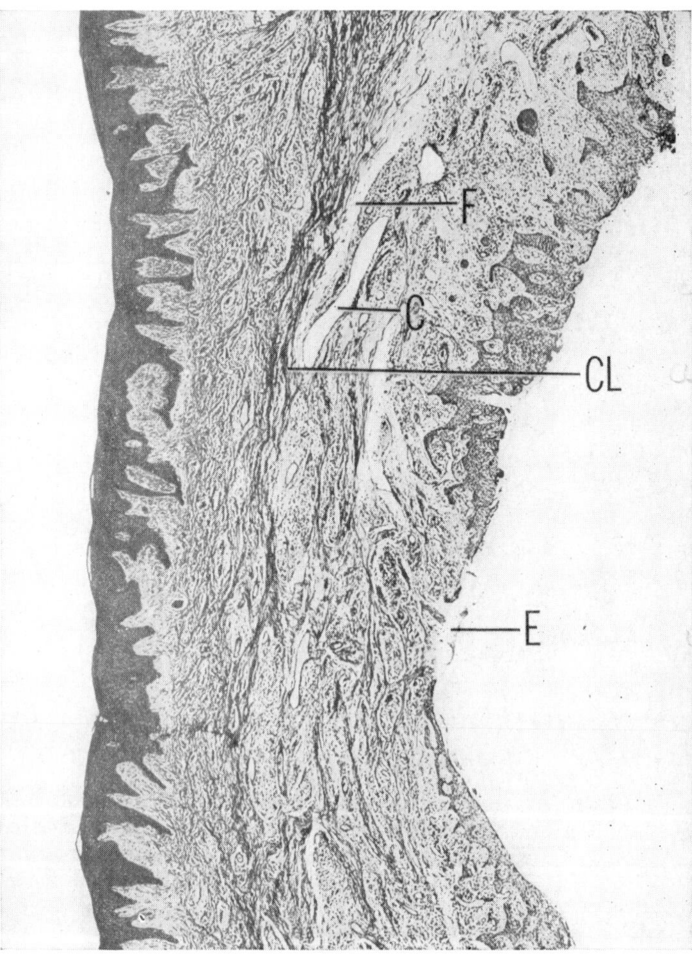

Fig. 9–17. Horizontally cut specimen of case of generalized moderate edematous periodontitis. There is extensive enlargement of the capillaries (*C*) between the circular ligament and the gingival sulcus. Connective tissue fibrils and ground substance have been replaced by fluid (*F*). The sulcular epithelium is ulcerated (*E*) and has invaded the connective tissue space in other areas. Circular ligament fibers (*CL*) are not continuous. (Meth. blue ×40.)

The Fibrous Response. Inflammation is a two phase process that encompasses both breakdown and repair. Edema is developed as a part of the breakdown phase. The fibrous response is developed as a part of the *repair phase.*

In repair, granulation tissue is the body's bonding mechanism to heal cuts and wounds. Originating from undifferentiated mysenchymal cells it is composed primarily of young connective tissue cells or fibroblasts and of endothelial cells. The fibroblasts mature into adult connective tissue and ultimately into a scar. The endothelial cells create a rich capillary bed to supply nutrients to the repairing tissue.

Starting with granulation tissue this same repair or scarring process occurs in the gingiva when the vascular walling off process of inflammation is incomplete. If the irritant level is sufficiently low grade, or if vigorous massage is effected with a stiff toothbrush, vascular thrombi may not develop completely or may be broken up after they are formed. Thus a supply of nutrients are delivered to the inflamed area encouraging the development of granulation tissue. These nutrients supply the differentiating and young repair cells with a greater growth potential. Since repair cannot be effective as long as the irritants remain, numbers of fibroblasts continue to develop until an excess of fibrous tissue is seen clinically (Fig. 9–18).

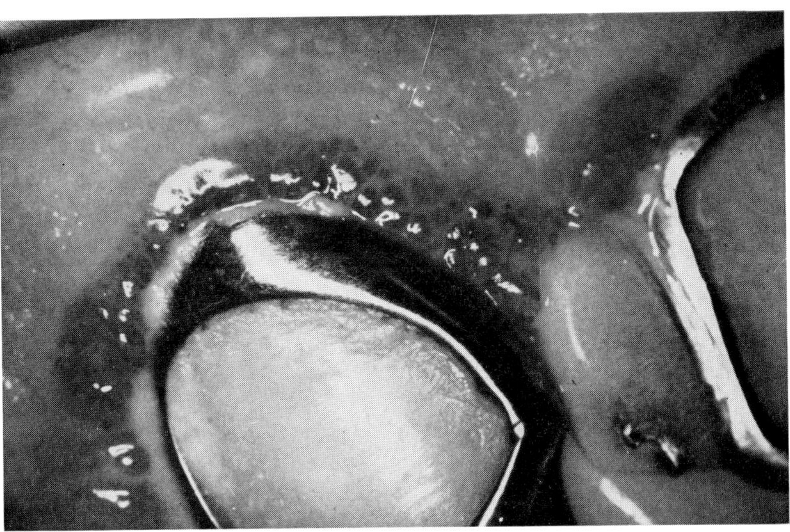

FIG. 9–18. Exuding granulation tissue from the margin of gingiva. The ill fitting crown and plaque have acted as a continuous irritant. There is no color differentiation as a definite line to mark the walling off of the inflamed tissue suggesting unrestricted blood supply to the affected tissues.

A thorough knowledge of the fibrous response is essential in management of periodontal lesions. Since the fluids of edema are absent, shrinkage of tissue cannot be expected. The hyperplastic process may have created gingival ledges, loss of interdental grooves or other architectural defects to complicate the oral hygiene efforts of the patient. These must be treated by a gingivoplasty type procedure (Fig. 9–19).

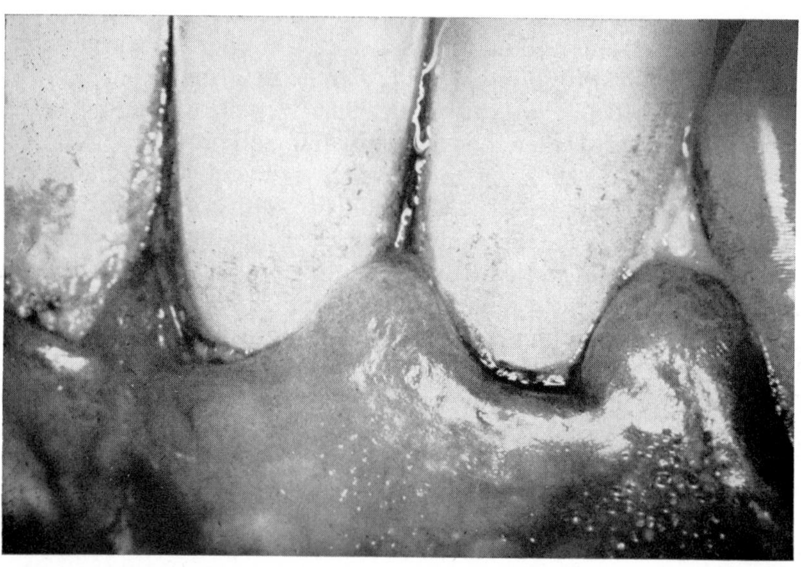

FIG. 9–19. Mandibular incisor area from case of severe generalized hyperplastic periodontitis. Tissues are stippled but grossly enlarged with wide gingival ledges at the labial of the teeth. The interproximal papilla are cratered. The interdental grooves have been eliminated by hyperplasia. Accumulation of plaque and calculus is encouraged by the tissue contours.

The Periodontal Pocket

A sulcus is a crevice occurring between a tooth and an area of detached clinically healthy gingiva. A pocket is a crevice between a tooth and an area of detached diseased gingiva. Usually a crevice that is under 2 to 3 mm. in detachment is free of clinical inflammation. When the detachment is over 3 mm. inflammation usually can be observed in the microscopic specimen if not clinically.

Pocket scores in clinical practice are of great value because they indicate the amount of probable inflammatory involvement of the tissues. Usually as the pocket deepens, it becomes an ever increasing harbinger of irritants with resultant increasing tissue inflammation.

However, it is important to remember that the difference between a healthy sulcus and a pocket is not determined by the depth alone, but rather by the presence or absence of a pathologic process. When the crevice is shallow but inflammation exists, this is characterized as a pocket. Variations in tissue response and presence or absence of systemic disease may alter the individual patient's reaction to irritation. With a constant intensity of irritation, these individual variations may determine whether or not a given crevicular depth would be a sulcus or a pocket.

Types of Pockets. Pockets are of three types. The first, commonly called a *gingival pocket* but also known as a relative pocket or pseudo pocket, occurs as a result of tissue proliferation in a coronal direction. The epithelial attachment remains located in the area of the cemento-enamel junction and there is no involvement of the deeper periodontal tissues. Only because of the coronal migration of the marginal gingiva is there a deepened crevicular space. The migration of the marginal gingiva in a coronal direction may be the result of swelling from edema or by connective tissue hyperplasia.

The second kind of pocket is the *periodontal pocket,* sometimes spoken of as the soft tissue pocket. In the periodontal pocket there is an apical migration of the epithelial attachment with concomitant loss of supporting alveolar bone. When the epithelium detaches from the root of the tooth, there is an increased crevicular space from the top of the epithelial attachment to the marginal gingiva. This deepened space, with gingival inflammation present, creates retractable soft tissue.

The difference between the periodontal pocket and the gingival pocket is both its method of formation as well as its location on the tooth. Whereas the gingival pocket occurs as a result of tissue prolifera-tion with a stationary epithelial attachment, the periodontal pocket occurs as a result of apical migration of the epithelial attachment with sloughing of the more coronally attached epithelial cells. Thus, a gingival pocket is found on the crown of the tooth and a periodontal pocket is found on the root of a tooth. Occasionally both processes go on simultaneously (Figs. 9–20 and 9–21).

The third type of periodontal pocket is the *infrabony pocket* (Fig. 9–22). In this form there is loss of alveolar supporting bone, but the loss is of uneven height. The result is that the bottom of the pocket is located apically to the crest of the remaining alveolar process. The infrabony pocket forms in the same manner as the periodontal pocket, except that it is complicated by periodontal traumatism or by wide bony ledges at the focus of inflammation. Resorption of bone is more exten-sive adjacent to the tooth than it is at the buccal or lingual plate or there is uneven resorption of the interdental bone of the alveolar process.

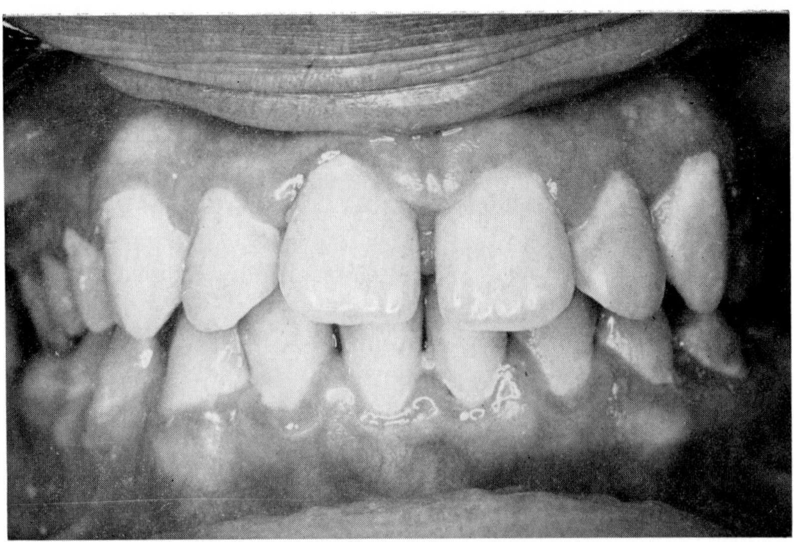

FIG. 9–20. Anterior area of thirty-six-year-old female with generalized moderate periodontitis. Tissue response has been largely edematous although gingival fibrous hyperplasia has occurred between the maxillary central incisors. Loss of interproximal bone support has allowed collapse and blunting of the interproximal papilla. Swollen tissues together with apical migration of the epithelial attachment have created pockets of 4 to 5 mm. in depth.

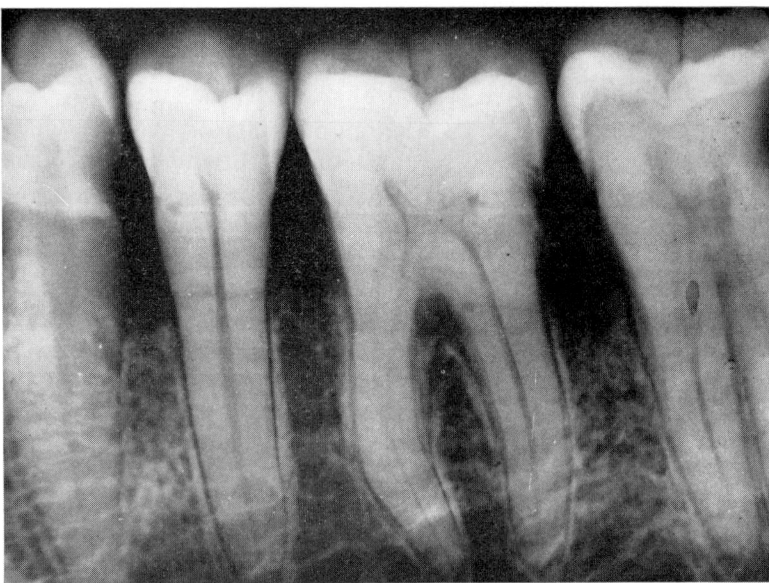

FIG. 9–21. Mandibular posterior roentgenogram from same patient in Figure 9–20. Note the loss of interdental bone height which originally was located about 1 mm. apical to the cemento-enamel junction. Cratering is observed between the two molars. Destruction of the interradicular bone has begun in the root bifurcation of the first molar.

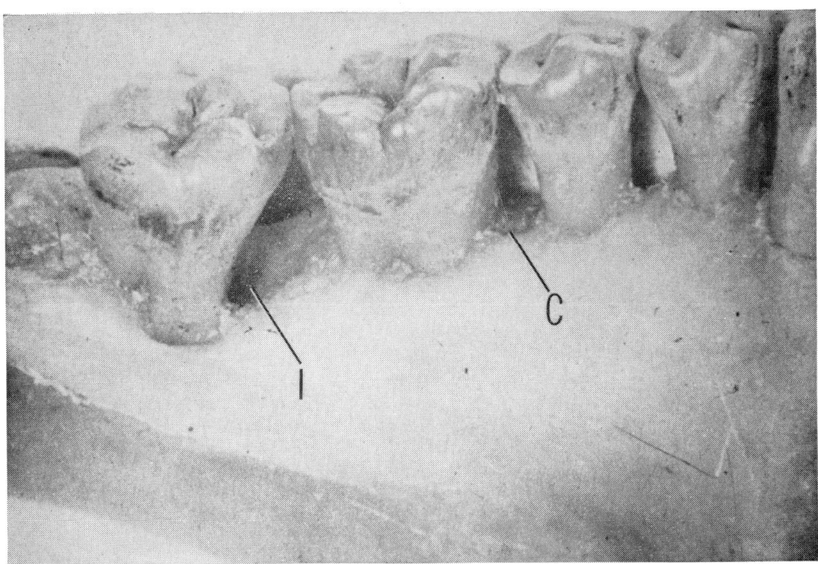

FIG. 9–22. Dry skull specimen of mandible showing resorption from an infrabony pocket on the mesial of the second molar (*I*). The bottom of the pocket was apical to the bone crest. The walls of the defect are created on the distal by the tooth root and on buccal, mesial and lingual by bone. A shallow crater (*C*), another form of an infrabony pocket, can be seen between the first molar and second bicuspid. The bone between the two bicuspids is normal.

Contents of the Pocket. The presence of a fluid exudate from the gingival sulcus and the pathologic pocket has been demonstrated by Brill.[3] Later, Mann and Stoffer[9] showed by paper electrophoresis and micro-double-diffusion that the protein elements were virtually identical in gingival fluid and serum. This can be interpreted to mean that the fluid is an exudate from the low grade gingival inflammation that always is present even though the gingiva appears to be healthy clinically. The fluid has a capacity to wash the pocket continuously. The amount of flow is increased by gingival massage and brushing[4] and the rate of flow is increased in the presence of clinical inflammation.[3]

Other consistent findings in the gingival pocket are bacteria, cellular debris, materia alba, plaque and calculus, which is plaque that has become calcified (Fig. 9–23). As gingival inflammation increases and pocket depth increases the bacterial count seems to increase. Among the products formed by these bacteria are collagenase, proteases, ammonia, fibrinolysin, ribonuclease and desoxyribonuclease and allergenic substances.

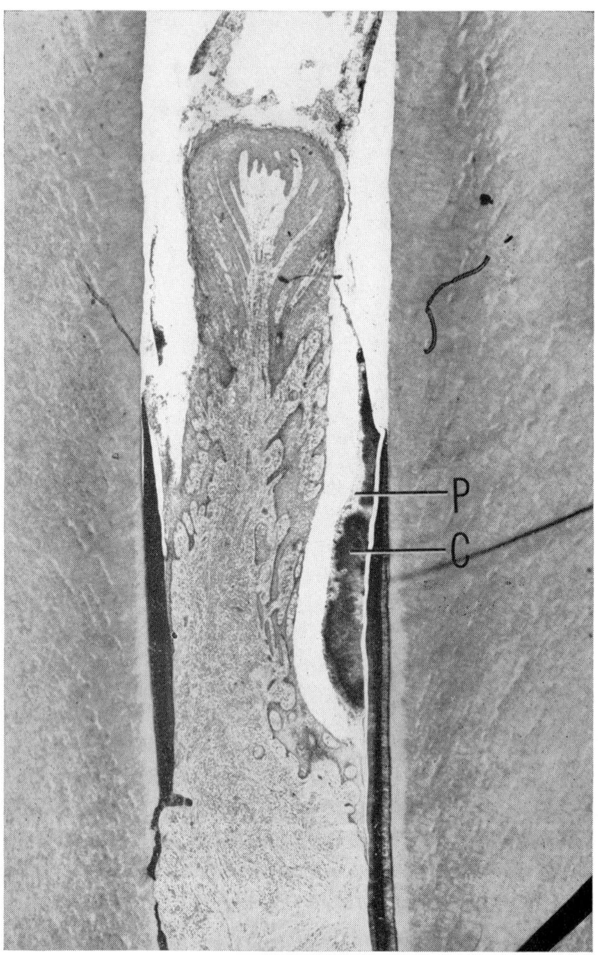

FIG. 9–23. Block section of interproximal area between mandibular bicuspids of case of mild to moderate generalized periodontitis. Note the contents of the pockets with the deeper pocket having the greater accumulations. The darker staining calculus (*C*) is covered with a layer of lighter staining plaque (*P*). Both plaque and calculus penetrated to the bottom of the pocket on the right. Accumulated plaque and debris can be seen above the crest of the papilla. Epithelium has invaded extensively into the connective tissue spaces. (H. & E. ×25.)

With the presence of bacteria, there is a beginning accumulation of leukocytes as a part of the host resistance. When this accumulates in quantity, one can discern it clinically by the presence of pus. This is most easily demonstrated by placing the finger on the gingiva and with a milking action push the exudate out of the gingival crevice. The presence of a purulent exudate is no indication of the depth of the pocket, but rather is a demonstration of the host response to the contents of the pocket.

Pathogenesis of a Pocket. There are several theories regarding the details of the pathogenesis of a periodontal pocket. For example, it is known that an irritant stimulates epithelial mitosis. Thus the irritation may stimulate migration of the epithelium causing it to invade the connective tissue, or it may be that the connective tissue, broken down by inflammation, allows the epithelium to migrate as it seeks a better nutrient base. Perhaps both processes may be going on simultaneously. Regardless of the triggering mechanism, certain events are known to occur. Some of these are occurring sequentially; others are going on simultaneously.

Since all inflammation is preceded by *irritation* this is the first event. The kind of irritant is not so significant as its intensity and its duration. The more intense the irritation, the greater the inflammatory response. However, a low grade irritation of long duration will perpetuate gingival inflammation leading to pocket formation. If the duration of time is of equal length, a lesion will be progressively more severe as the intensity of the irritant is increased.

Understanding the origin-intensity-duration principle is the basis for examination and diagnosis. When lesion development is greater in one area as compared to another of the same mouth, the diagnosis of etiology is dependent on identification of the differences of irritation in the two areas. The differences are understood by an analysis of (1) the kind of irritant present (2) the intensity of the irritant, and (3) the duration of time that the irritant has been present.

Inflammation is both a vascular and cellular response to an irritant. After initial vasocontraction there is vasodilatation, beginning thrombosis and leakage of the contents of the vessels between the endothelial cells into the space between the endothelium and the basement membrane of the capillaries. With a rupture of the basement membrane white blood cells, red blood cells, fibrin, albumin and globulin molecules escape into the tissue spaces. Fibrin in the intercellular spaces and the partial thrombosis of the capillaries creates a walling off process which localizes the area of inflammation.

Cellular changes occurring in beginning inflammation are an initial migration of leukocytes to the area followed a few hours later by lymphocytes. The leukocytes attempt to phagocytize invading bacteria and cellular debris. The role of the lymphocytes and plasma cells is not completely understood. Evidences indicate that lymphocytes play a significant part in the development of antibodies. It is also possible that they may be precursors to fibroblasts. However, at present there seems little doubt that the primary source of fibroblasts is from the undifferentiated mesenchymal cells that are located perivascularly throughout all tissues.

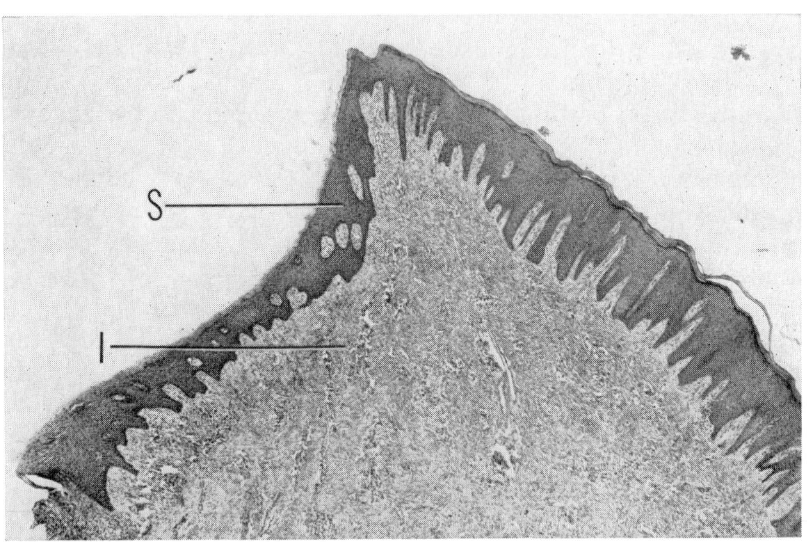

FIG. 9–24. Mild gingivitis. Note the presence of a mild inflammatory reaction characterized by the presence of inflammatory cells (*I*), edema and hyperemia. Sulcular epithelium (*S*) has begun to invade the underlying connective tissue.

The accumulation within the tissues of large quantities of cellular elements, large molecules that have come from the blood stream, and heparin from mast cells alters the osmotic balance. This attracts and holds a higher level of plasma than ordinarily would be present. In addition, during inflammation the intercellular ground substance disaggregates, altering its morphologic form, dividing into an increased number but shorter chain molecules. This adds to the retention of fluids in the part by further altering the osmotic gradient. Disintegrative by-products of cellular breakdown increase the amount of particulate matter in the interstitial spaces to further alter osmotic balance and to accentuate the clinical manifestations of edema (Figs. 9–24, 9–25 and 9–26).

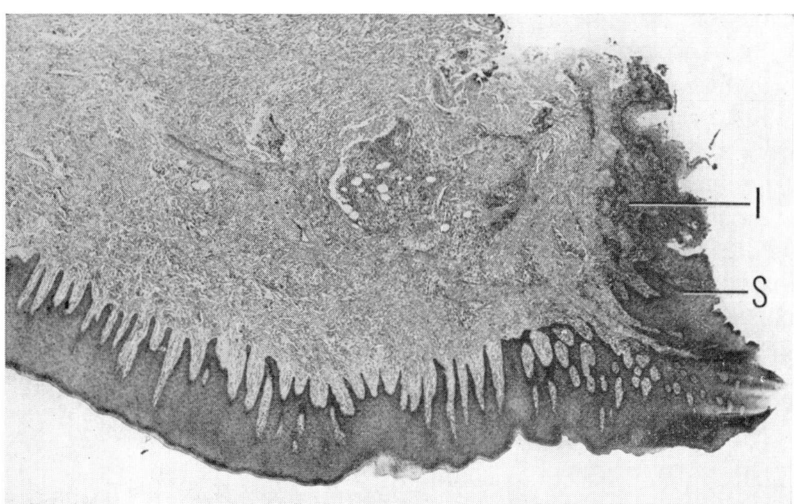

FIG. 9–25. Moderate gingivitis. Sulcular epithelium (*S*) has invaded the underlying connective tissue more than in Figure 9–24. Inflammatory cells (*I*) are present in greater numbers in the sub-epithelial areas. Note increased vascularity and edema.

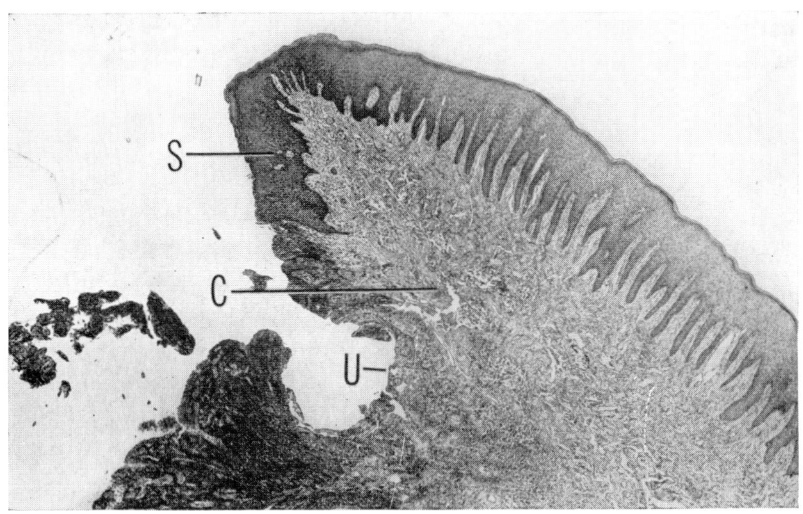

FIG. 9–26. Severe gingivitis. In this biopsy section the same pathologic characteristics are present as seen in Figure 9–25, but the degree of severity is greater. Sulcular epithelium (*S*) is thickened at the margin with ulceration (*U*) and breakdown deeper in the pocket. Larger spaces are present in the connective tissue (*C*) demonstrating severe edema.

The nutrition of the individual cell depends on a very complex transport process. A metabolite must leave the blood stream, pass through the capillary wall and basement membrane, through ground substance into cellular cytoplasm of the nearest cell and in a sequential fashion through ground substance and cellular cytoplasm of subsequent cells repeatedly until it arrives at the given cell which uses the metabolite. The biochemical interchange mechanism must be maintained as an intact chain of events, if the metabolite is to arrive at its ultimate destination. However, disruption of one link of the chain, such as disaggregation of the intercellular ground substance from edema, interferes with normal transport with ultimate deprivation of nutrition to cells. Without nutrition a cell degenerates and ultimately dies.

In an attempt to repair, the body brings into use standby capillaries to replace those that are occluded by thrombosis. Thus, at least some nutrients are transported to the involved tissues. If this were not so, the frank necrosis of an infarct would occur. Polymorphonuclear leukocytes phagocytize cellular debris accumulating during tissue breakdown. Lymphocytes produce antibodies. The undifferentiated mesenchymal cells convert into fibroblasts and endothelial cells to produce granulation tissue, the foundation of all repair. The extent of fibroblastic differentiation is determined in part by the amount of nutrients being delivered to the area. The degree of venostasis varies with the completeness of the walling off process. Thus, the breakdown of a thrombosis by gingival massage or use of a stiff toothbrush may increase the differentiation of fibroblasts to form larger amounts of granulation tissue which are seen clinically as scarring or as fibrous hyperplasia.

If the breakdown phase of inflammation were to go unchecked by attempted repair, frank necrosis of the tissues would be seen. If the repair phase far exceeded that of the breakdown phase, no pathologic pocket would develop, although some architectural defects might be created through fibrous hyperplasia. Usually, however, both processes go on simultaneously with the breakdown phase gradually predominating to an ever increasing extent. With a lower host/tissue response, a given irritant may induce an apparent diffuse response with little repair which is observed clinically as edematous tissue. With a more active host/tissue response, the same given irritant may induce increased fibroblastic proliferation and hyperplastic gingival tissue development simultaneously with slowly progressive pocket formation (Fig. 9–27).

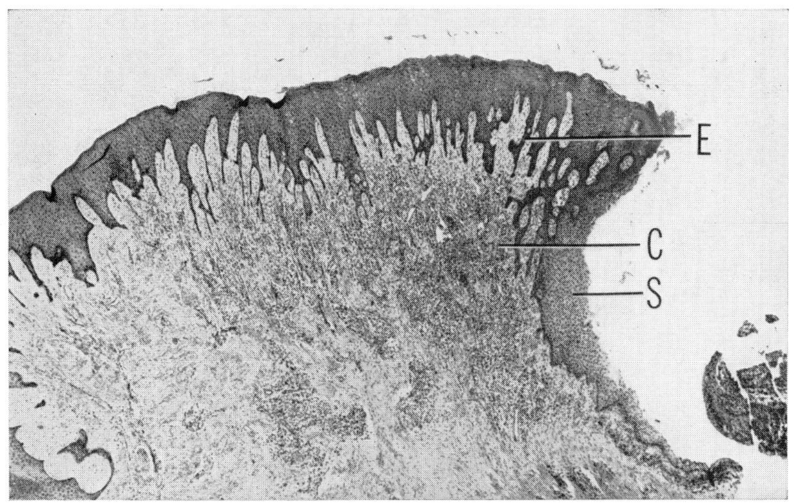

FIG. 9–27. Gingival hyperplasia. This biopsy section exhibits many of the features seen in Figures 9–24, 25 and 26 as chronic inflammation has been present for some time. In addition, evidence of a great deal of inflamed, but dense hyperplastic connective tissue (*C*) is present. Epithelial ridges (*E*) are narrow due to the connective tissue proliferation. The sulcular epithelium (*S*) is thickened and sloughing.

Epithelium Migration. Epithelial migration is essential for the development of periodontal pockets. It is believed that in a healthy normal adult one should find the epithelial attachment at the cemento-enamel junction or just slightly below this point on the root surface. In order for a periodontal pocket to form, the epithelial attachment migrates apically. Even in a very deep lesion one always finds some epithelial adhesion to the tooth.

The migration of the epthelium may be caused by either the stimulation of epithelial proliferation by the irritant or by the breakdown of the underlying connective tissue with the epithelial cells seeking a better nutrient support. It is possible that both things may be occurring simultaneously (Fig. 9–28).

Connective Tissue Breakdown. The mechanism of connective tissue breakdown has been described in the discussion of inflammation. Normal epithelium has no capacity elsewhere in the body to invade healthy connective tissue. The breakdown of gingival connective tissue destroys its capacity to confine the epithelium of the sulcus and epithelial attachment. It is a consistent finding in inflamed gingiva that bizarre penetration of the epithelium into the connective tissue spaces has occurred.

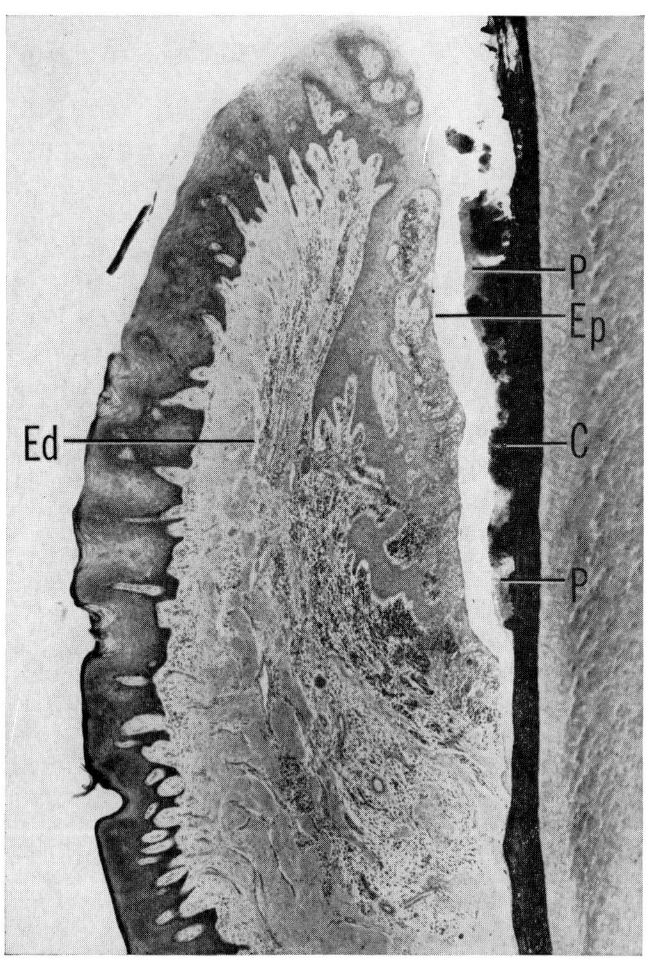

FIG. 9–28. Section showing a periodontal pocket taken from lingual surface of bicuspid shown in Figure 9–2, demonstrating that one side of a tooth may be diseased while the opposite may be clinically healthy. The sulcular epithelium (*Ep*) has invaded the connective tissue spaces. There is edema (*Ed*) in all connective tissue areas except immediately below the buccal epithelium. A heavy round cell infiltrate is present. A coating of plaque (*P*) covers the adhering calculus and extends to the bottom of the pocket. Calculus stains similar to cementum (*C*) but can be differentiated by surface irregularity. (H. & E. ×25.)

Epithelial Sloughing. Sloughing at the bottom of the pocket deepens the pocket (Fig. 9–29). Epithelium is dependent upon the underlying connective tissues for the maintenance of a nutrient supply. There are no capillaries in epithelium. When the underlying connective tissue has a restricted blood supply plus an impaired transport capacity, it is impossible for the epithelium to have normal nutrition. As a result, epithelial cell maturation is incomplete and extensive sloughing of surface cells are a consistent histologic finding (Fig. 9–30 and 9–31).

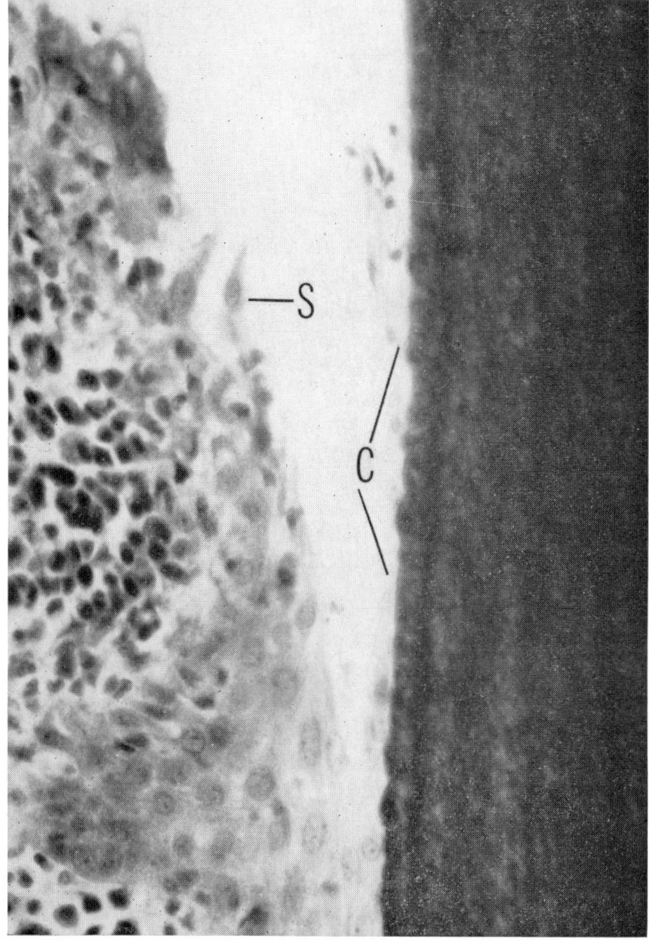

FIG. 9–29. High magnification of bottom of pocket in Figure 9–28. Note the sloughing epithelial cells (*S*). The cells (*C*) remaining on the root surface have been described as demonstrating a greater adhesion of cells to tooth than between cells. (H. & E. ×500.)

Many ulcers are seen in gingival biopsies, particularly opposite an area where plaque is attached to the tooth. It is possible that the microbial component, such as bacteroides melenanogenicus which is a producer of ammonia, may accelerate epithelial degradation. The epithelial sloughing occurs not only in the wall of the pocket, but also at the bottom of the pocket (top of the epithelial attachment). This increases the crevicular depth, providing for increased pocket formation.

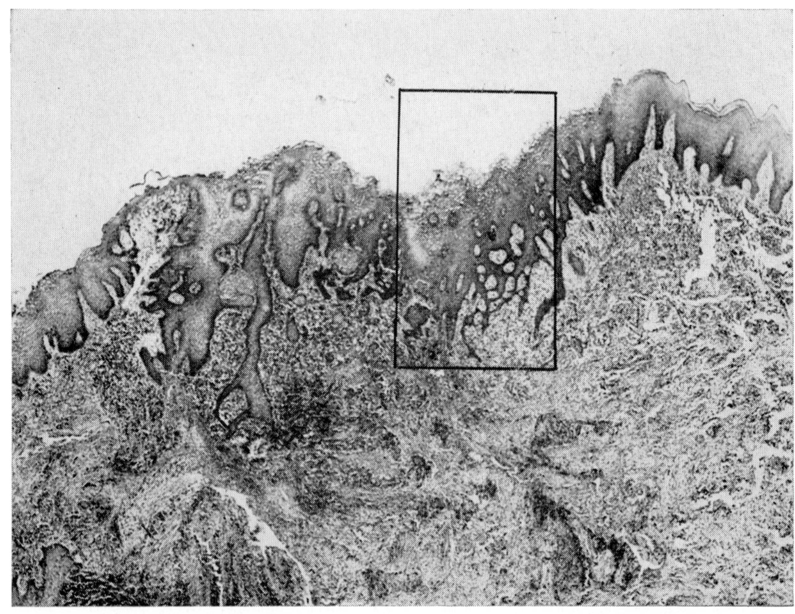

FIG. 9–30. Lining epithelium with edema and hyaline degeneration taken from wall of 7 mm. pocket. Deep penetrations of epithelium into the connective tissue spaces exists in some areas yet only a thin covering exists in others. The corium is edematous and contains a marked round cell infiltrate indicating a reduced nutrient supply to the epithelial layer. (H. & E. ×25.)

Extension of Inflammation. Since the circulation blockade in gingival inflammation is not complete, there is some continual turnover of fluids through standby capillaries and lymphatics. Since fluid from intercellular spaces moves in the pathway of least resistance, as described by Weinmann,[19] the inflammatory exudate primarily travels along the loose connective tissue of the perivascular area into the underlying alveolar bone (Fig. 9–32). With this there is a transport of bacteria from the periodontal pocket into the tissue and ultimately into the blood stream, even though biopsies have not shown accumu-

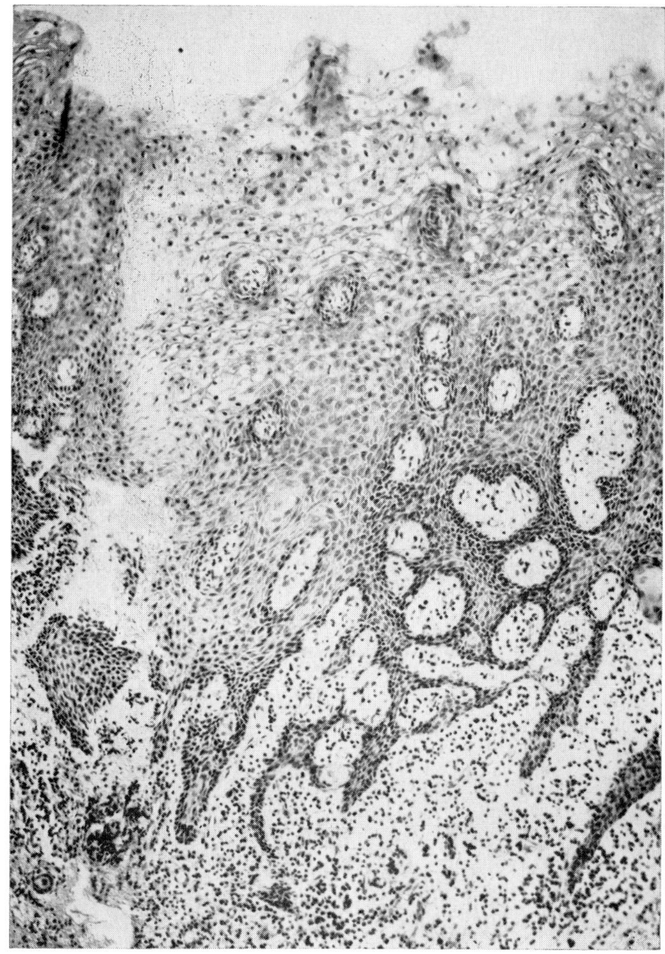

FIG. 9–31. High magnification of area in Figure 9–30. Note the degenerative changes in the epithelial cells with intercellular edema. The surface cells are sloughing. (H. & E. ×100.)

lated bacteria. Transitory bacteremia has been demonstrated by blood studies following tissue instrumentation or mastication of fibrous foods. The introduction of toxic products from bacteria will initiate osteoclastic action. *Bone resorption* is observed roentgenographically as cupping of the interdental process at the exit of the nutrient artery.

Inflammation can pass down through the periodontal ligament when there is an alteration of the integrity of the connective tissue next to the tooth as a result of periodontal traumatism. On the tension side a

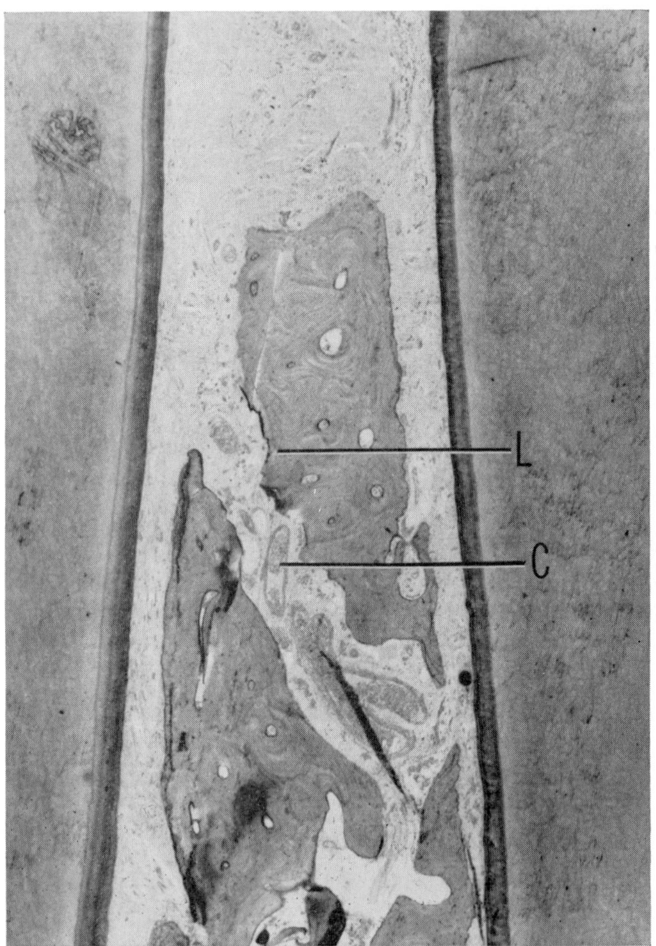

FIG. 9–32. Interproximal section showing typical Howships lacunae (*L*) indicating bone resorption within the interdental bone along the pathway of circulation (*C*). The chronicity of the lesion is demonstrated by the fibrous tissue in the narrow spaces whereas more apically they contain fat cells. (H. & E. ×25.)

stretching of the ligament fibers creates spaces between the fiber elements, altering the normal barrier provided by connective tissue that is intact[7] (Fig. 9–33). On the pressure side, the hyalinization and ultimate necrosis of the connective tissue fibers weakens the resistance of these tissues, again to provide a pathway of lowered resistance for the extension of inflammation.[6] As a result, the bone resorption and extension of the pocket adjacent to the tooth may provide a morphologic defect characterized by uneven bone loss. When the pocket base

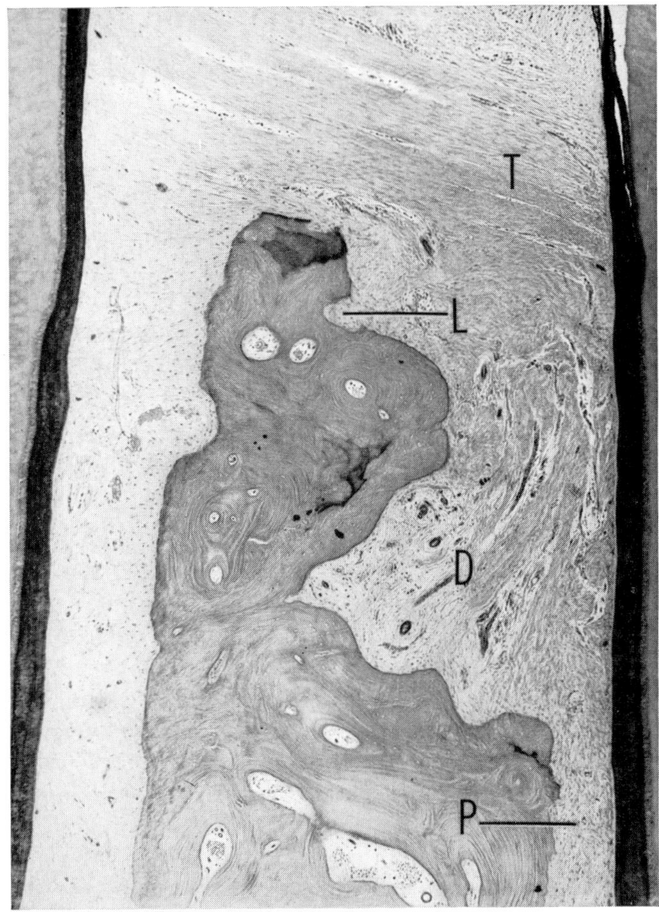

FIG. 9–33. Interdental bone crest showing effects of trauma between bone and tooth on right. Increased vascularity and inflammatory cells are in the large bony defect (*D*) and along the root just below the transeptal fibers (*T*). Note the lack of fiber orientation and cell polarity in the confined periodontal ligament (*P*). Howships lacunae indicative of bone resorption are present (*L*); however, resorption seems to be stabilized in the area of the large defect. (H. & E. ×25.)

next to the tooth arrives at a point apical to the nearby but less involved alveolar process, an intrabony pocket is thus formed.

To state it succinctly, the steps in pocket formation are as follows:

(1) Irritation
(2) Inflammation
(3) Connective tissue breakdown
(4) Epithelial attachment migration
(5) Epithelial sloughing at top of epithelial attachment
(6) Extension of inflammation
(7) Bone resorption

The disease may not advance far enough that the tissues are involved in the entire sequence. When not more than the first three steps occur, only the marginal tissues are affected. This would be diagnosed as a gingivitis. When at least the first six steps occur with inflammation going deeper than the transseptal fibers, the disease would be diagnosed as periodontitis. This is often demonstrated roentgenographically by bone loss which is step seven.

To equate the character of the disease, one must identify the irritant and evaluate the intensity and duration of the irritant against the response of the host tissue. This will provide a better understanding of the pathologic process. It will become the basis of a prognosis when evaluating probable tissue response from the removal of the etiologic irritants.

Etiology of Inflammatory Periodontal Disease

Local Factors. Recurrence of a disease is prevented by the elimination of its cause. When the disease is inflammation, its control is based upon the removal of related irritants. Unless the irritants are identified, a rational therapeutic regimen cannot be established. Sometimes in dental practice this has been done unknowingly or by accident. For example, irritants are reduced when teeth are restored because of carious lesions. Another example is that a patient may start to maintain good oral hygiene after investing a consequential amount of money in new fillings and bridgework. However, the rational therapist does not depend upon accident or luck but attempts to identify every irritant that exists and plans for its removal.

An important clue for identification of irritants is the record of depth of periodontal pockets as scored on all four surfaces of every tooth in the mouth. Since it is logical to assume that the health of the patient would be the same on all four sides of the same tooth, one can use a differential pocket score count as a clue that the environment must be different on the respective sides of that tooth. Thus when one finds a 3 mm. score on the mesial and a 6 mm. pocket score on the distal of the same tooth it is logical to assume that the environment on the distal of the tooth was different from that of the mesial. While irritations may have been present on both sides, the side with the deeper score must have had irritants either longer or of greater intensity. A careful clinical evaluation usually will disclose the intensity and probable longevity of the irritants. These local factors will be either microbial, mechanical or traumatic in nature.

Microbial Factors. Some clinicians and investigators in the field of periodontics think of the microbial flora, materia alba, plaque and calculus as separate etiologic entities. However, it is extremely difficult to separate one from another. Calculus is the calcified end product that started with materia alba and became plaque. A study by Mandel[8] on the histochemistry of calculus formation indicated that plaque is a mucopolysaccharide containing large numbers of bacteria. In the early part of plaque formation, coccus forms of bacteria predominate. Later, by the seventh day the coccoid bacteria are still present but the surface and central portions contain large masses of filamentous organisms. By the twelfth day the mucopolysaccharide is composed almost entirely of both gram-positive and gram-negative filamentous organisms, which in human plaque always contains actinomyces.

Some clinicians have been concerned about the roughness of calculus as a source of mechanical irritation. This is possible, but there seems little doubt that the microbial component is by far the greater problem in the etiology of the inflammation. Apatite crystal structures occurring within the gingiva or elsewhere in the body, but free from microbial content, do not initiate inflammation.

Mineralization, to become calculus, occurs next to the tooth in the older part of the plaque. Any roughness from the mineralized portion of growing dental calculus would be compensated for, at least partially, by the superificial covering of new plaque formation. Thus, the microbial content of plaque and materia alba probably are much more irritating than the calcified part. Food flow patterns may be undesirable and encourage the development of materia alba and plaque. A malposed tooth can create areas for trapping debris or interfering with the natural hygiene potential of the lips, cheeks and tongue. A tooth that is rotated creates problems on both buccal and the lingual surfaces. The interproximal becomes a ramp for food to slide beneath the marginal gingiva (Fig. 9–34).

Teeth that are placed lingual or buccal to the center of the bony ridge will leave a gingival ledge on the opposite side. The excursion of food passing over the tooth may impinge debris in the sulcular area as in a tilted tooth. Even with a vibratory brushing technique it may be impossible for the patient to maintain these areas hygienically (Fig. 9–35).

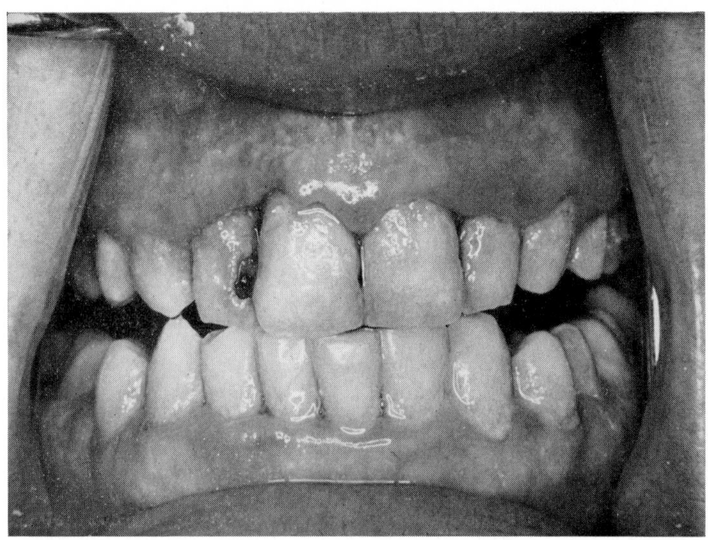

FIG. 9–34. Moderate generalized periodontitis with severe lesions localized between the maxillary lateral and central incisors. Note that greater defects exist where the central incisors overlap the lateral incisors. In spite of the heavy materia alba and plaque the tissues look better where the teeth are in better alignment.

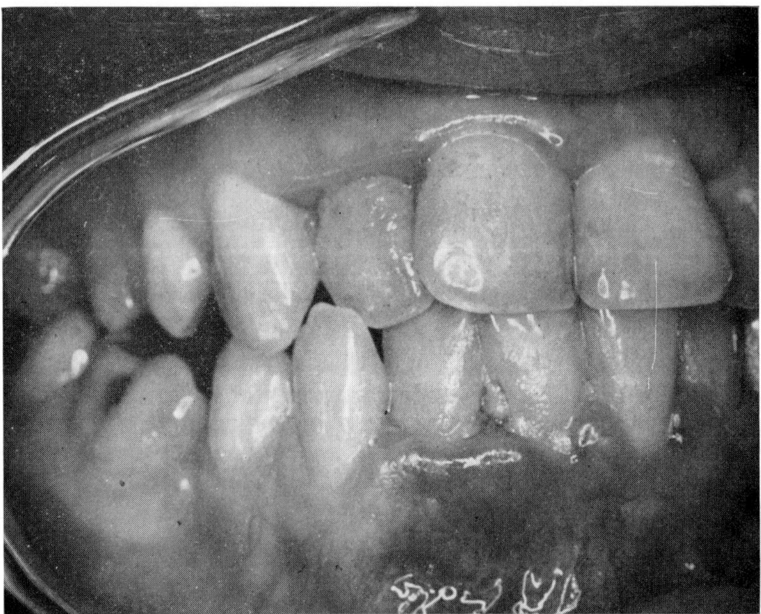

FIG. 9–35. Severe localized periodontitis complicated by the malposition of the maxillary and mandibular lateral incisors. Note the gingival ledges and poor hygiene on the labial of these two teeth as compared to the labial of the adjacent cuspids. The crowding and the uneven axial alignment of the teeth creates long contact surfaces with reduction in size of the embrasure spaces. The problem is further complicated by the locked occlusion restricting chewing movements.

The contour of an interproximal papilla is determined by the position of the two teeth and the character of the contact point. A papilla that is *conical* seems to be one most desirable from a self-cleansing standpoint. A blunted papilla is less self-cleansing, but a cratered papilla is difficult if not impossible for the patient to maintain. A rotated or tilted tooth may reduce the size of the embrasure where the teeth touch each other and a surface rather than contact point is created. This places the contact location sufficiently apical that it forces the development of an interproximal gingival crater (Fig. 9–36).

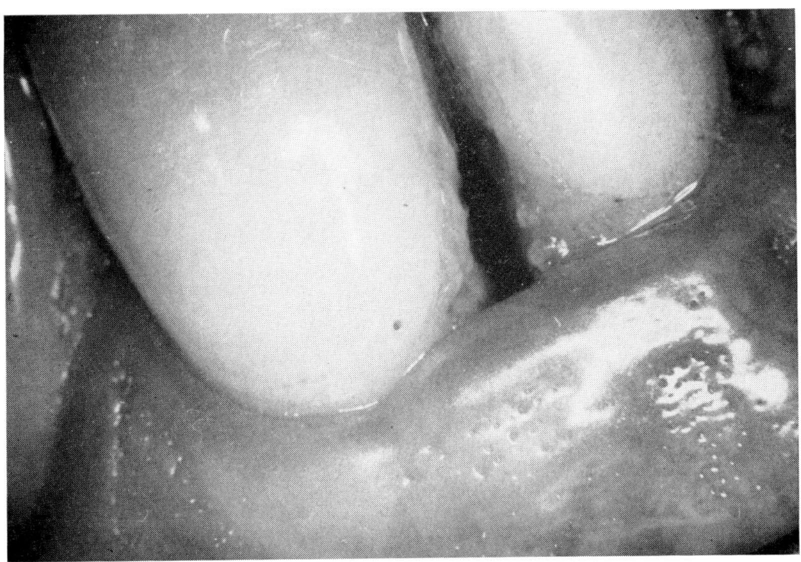

FIG. 9–36. Interproximal tissue has been lost resulting in a deep crater. Large accumulations of plaque and debris adhere to the teeth within the crater. Note that the marginal tissue is edematous while the labial attached gingiva is fibrotic.

Interproximal embrasure morphology and morphology of marginal ridges plays a significant role in the maintenance of good oral hygiene. Both abnormal tooth position and faulty restorative dentistry may change the shape of the embrasure space. A space that is too small does not permit ease of home cleansing. One that is too large may predispose to food impaction. Approximating tooth contacts that cover too much tooth surface alter the amount of embrasure space and complicate hygiene (Fig. 9–37).

A contact that is too loose permits food impaction resulting in subsequent mechanical and microbial irritation. Also, food impaction occurs with wear of marginal ridges and with loss of natural secondary grooves and sluiceways preventing the escape of food out of the embrasure area. Food accumulating in inaccessible areas develops a high microbial content and becomes a source of gingival inflammation.

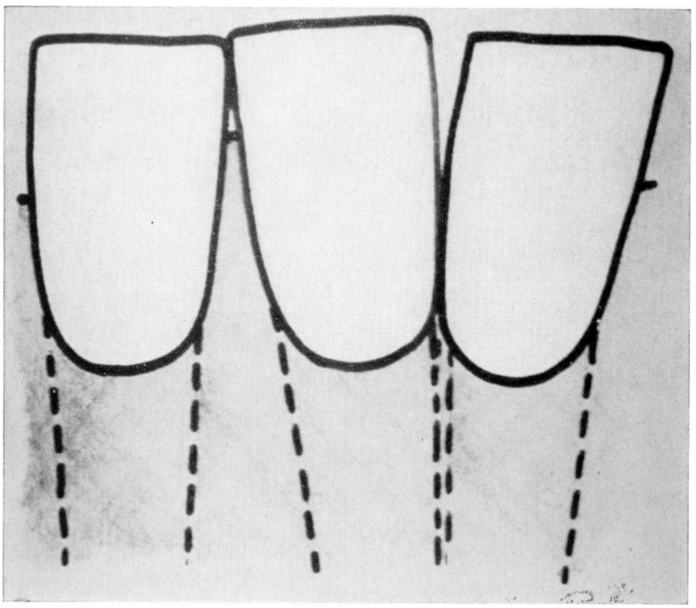

FIG. 9–37. Diagram showing the effects of abnormal axial alignment of teeth. The reduced embrasure space may be too small to maintain good hygiene with ease.

Many interproximal papilla become inflamed due to the presence of faulty dentistry. It is sometimes difficult to maintain good tooth anatomy throughout the years using silver amalgam as a filling material. The amalgam often changes shape as it ages, altering the form of the marginal ridge, contact point and embrasure shape. Improperly contoured or trimmed cervical margins may leave overhangs that are reservoirs for trapping debris with plaque formation and its attendant microbial masses (Fig. 9–38). Rough filling material such as zinc oxyphosphate or silicate cement or unpolished amalgam facilitate the attachment of microbial masses to act as irritants to the gingival tissues. Highly polished gold is not as much a problem in this regard.

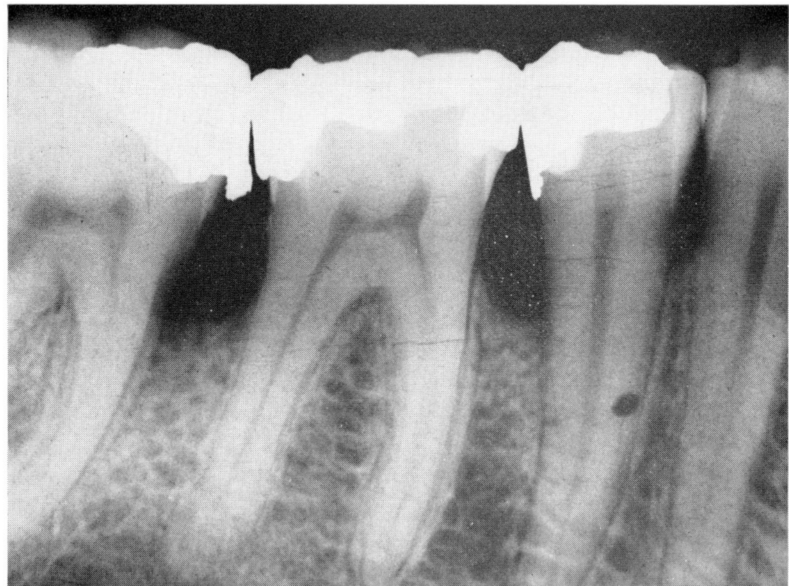

FIG. 9–38. Proximal overhangs on silver amalgam fillings. Note that the bone resorption pattern between the molars and bicuspid is correlated to the location of the overhangs. Also, alveolar crest height is higher on the mesial of the second bicuspid than on the distal.

Mechanical Irritants. Mechanical irritants are not a major factor in either the cause or control of inflamed gingiva. However, trauma from mastication or trauma from improper oral hygiene sometimes is observed as a source of irritation. Toothbrush trauma is observed most frequently on the buccal aspects of the upper cuspids and first premolars. Trauma from mastication of such foods as crisp toast or English muffins may induce trauma, but the wound soon heals and is seldom repeated.

Faulty dentistry, such as an overhanging filling, can be a source of irritation when it is first placed. This ceases to be a source of mechanical irritation following the necrosis and slough of tissue in the area of impingement. However, the area remains one with unhygienic conditions to perpetuate the inflammation. Rough calculus with arrested plaque formation could be a source of mechanical irritation as the gingiva would rub against the mineralized deposit.

Periodontal Traumatism. Periodontal traumatism is a *dystrophic* disease that may occur simultaneously with inflammatory periodontal disease. Trauma occurs when the forces of occlusion are greater than the adaptive capacity of the tissues in the supporting periodontium. It is characterized in its early stages by increased vascularity and hyalinization of the confined periodontal ligament. Subsequently, with increased forces there is crushing necrosis of the ligament and undermining resorption of the alveolar plate adjacent to the tooth.

Periodontal traumatism may be primary when the force is excessive and the periodontal support is normal, such as in a newly placed but high inlay in a healthy mouth. Secondary traumatism exists when the forces of mastication are normal but the tissue support is inadequate.

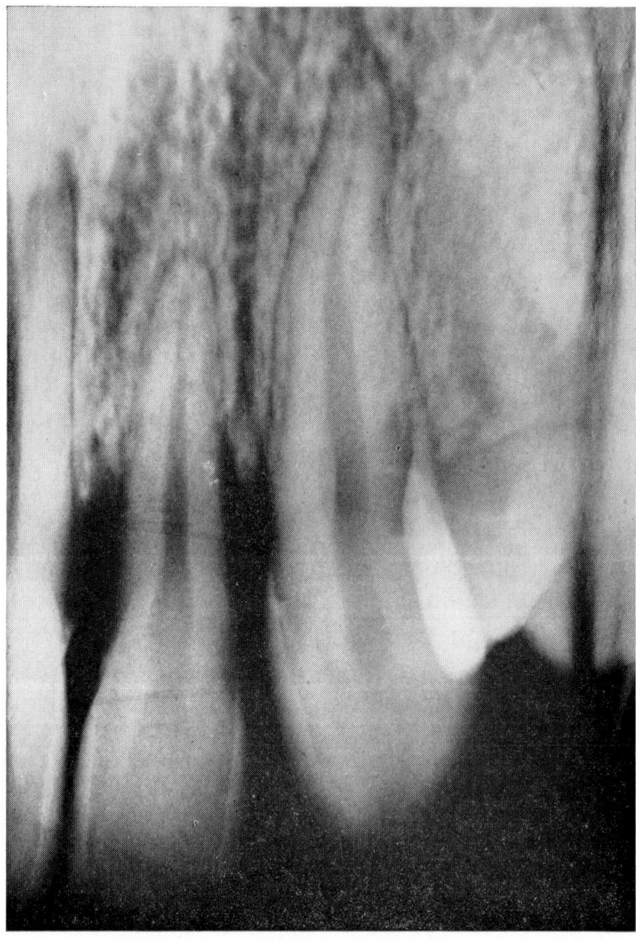

FIG. 9–39. Roentgenogram of maxillary lateral incisor from patient with moderately severe periodontitis complicated by periodontal traumatism. The radiolucent area at the apex of the root created by a thickening of the periodontal ligament. The thickening is part of a functional adaptation to the labial-lingual swinging of the root tip from tooth mobility. The dark streaks in the bone are from resorption initiated by the superficial soft tissue inflammation.

Usually this condition occurs when the diseased periodontium has been so destroyed that it is unable to withstand the pressures of mastication.

Two clinical problems arise as a result of periodontal traumatism. The first, already discussed, is a change in the pathway of the extension of inflammation thereby altering the morphology of the developing lesion. More important is the second change which is the alteration of the oral environment complicating oral hygiene.

When a tooth becomes mobile as a result of periodontal traumatism the most frequently observed movement is in a buccal-lingual direction, although it may move in a mesial-distal or an intrusive direction. When buccal-lingual movement occurs, it tends to open the contact between the mobile tooth and the adjacent teeth (Fig. 9–39). This predisposes to food impaction followed by mechanical and microbial irritation to the underlying interproximal gingival tissues. If the mobility is severe, the assumed angulation of the tooth may provide a natural ramp for sliding food and debris into the sulcus.

Should a mobile tooth become sore the patient will chew on the opposite side of the mouth. With the loss of mastication in an area, there is also the loss of the natural cleansing action effected by the lip and cheek muscles and by the flow of food off the teeth. Any one or a combination of these things will adversely affect oral hygiene, provide irritation and initiate gingival inflammation.

Systemic Factors. Clinicians carefully evaluate the health of the patient to equate the repair potential of the tissues to be treated. Unfortunately, too little is known about the specific mechanisms wherein variations in systemic health effect variations in gingival health. Some clinicians place great emphasis on evaluation of diet. Others are concerned with glucose metabolism or pre-diabetic states. There is little question that the resistance of the host plays a major part in the development and character of the periodontal lesion. Host resistance may determine whether or not one observes a diffuse or localized tissue reaction or one observes either edema or fibrous hyperplasia. However, the therapist must always remember that the patient who is either nutritionally deficient or diabetic will be equally so on all four sides of a tooth. Consequently, the variations in pocket depth in different areas of the mouth reflect variations in the local environment.

There are some systemic complicating factors that have been demonstrated by experimental pathology and observed clinically. The uncontrolled diabetic is known to have a lowered resistance to microbial invasion. Patients with altered glucose metabolism seem more prone to periodontal pockets for a given amount of irritation. Some clinicians have observed an increased frequency of periodontal abscesses in patients in hypothyroid states.

Metabolism of the connective tissue is changed during pregnancy by the altered endocrine balance of the female. Often the pregnant woman has edema throughout all tissues including that of the gingiva. The inflammatory reaction of gingival tissues is markedly accentuated when a woman becomes pregnant. Later, after she comes to term, the inflammation is reduced. Edema alters the density of the confined periodontal ligament and increased tooth mobility is a common finding with pregnancy. The increased mobility will predispose to interproximal food impaction with greater irritation of the gingiva. The edema can alter nutrition of the fibrous connective tissue cells and may facilitate invasiveness of the superficial epithelium.

Vitamin deficiencies are not a clinical problem in most areas of the United States. Although mobility of the teeth originally brought attention to the problem of ascorbic acid deficiency in the diet, apparently a scorbutic individual will not develop periodontal pockets when local irritations are absent. However, if local irritations are present to induce gingival inflammation the extension and progress of the disease is at an increased rate should a vitamin C or any other nutritional deficiency exist.

Diagnosis. Diagnosis is the identification of disease. Diagnosis is achieved by recognition of tissue deviation from normal and identifying the character of the deviation. Of course, this must be based on a prior knowledge of normal. Differential diagnosis is a selection between two or more diseases having some manifestations in common but having other signs that are unique to the individual disease.

To achieve an accurate diagnosis, observations must be made in a manner that consistently will provide an adequate supply of data. Thus a systematized examination procedure must be used for each patient. Areas that must be studied for each individual case are the following:

1. Dental and medical history
2. Color of gingiva and mucosa
3. Architecture and form of gingiva
4. Location of muco-gingival junction and width of attached gingiva
5. Depth of pocket scores
6. Roentgenographic examination for morphology of bone loss and for periodontal ligament space thickening
7. Tooth mobility, bruxism, and clenching
8. Tooth form, arch form and occlusal function
9. Search to identify etiologic factors

Each of these items have been discussed under the consideration of normal, gingivitis and periodontitis. The clinical sign of color change from pink to that of cyanosis is the earliest finding to be observed. Pocket scores will help develop an understanding of the severity of the disease (Figs. 9–40 and 9–41). Also, pocket scores can be a clue to direct the search for etiologic factors. Wherever pocket scores indicate the presence of lesions one must find a correlating cause of irritation. Observation of deviations in architectural form of the gingiva, width of the band of attached gingiva and tooth mobility help to identify some environmental variations predisposing to irritation.

The most important thing about examination is that it be systematized. Only by developing a discipline wherein a routine is repeated for each patient can one be sure that nothing is missed. Eventually, the subconscious mind covers the list of items and the examiner may not be cognizant of his wide search for data. However, the presence of these factors becomes a conscious consideration whenever they are present.

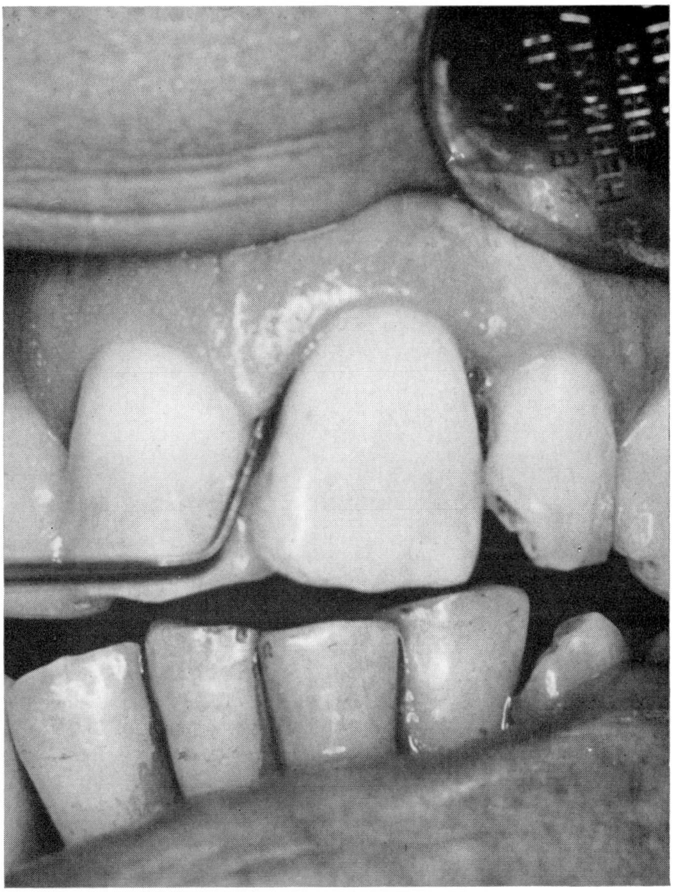

FIG. 9–40. Periodontal probe in pocket on mesial of maxillary incisor. The pocket is between 6 and 7 mm. deep. The gingiva showed no other evidence of disease at this location.

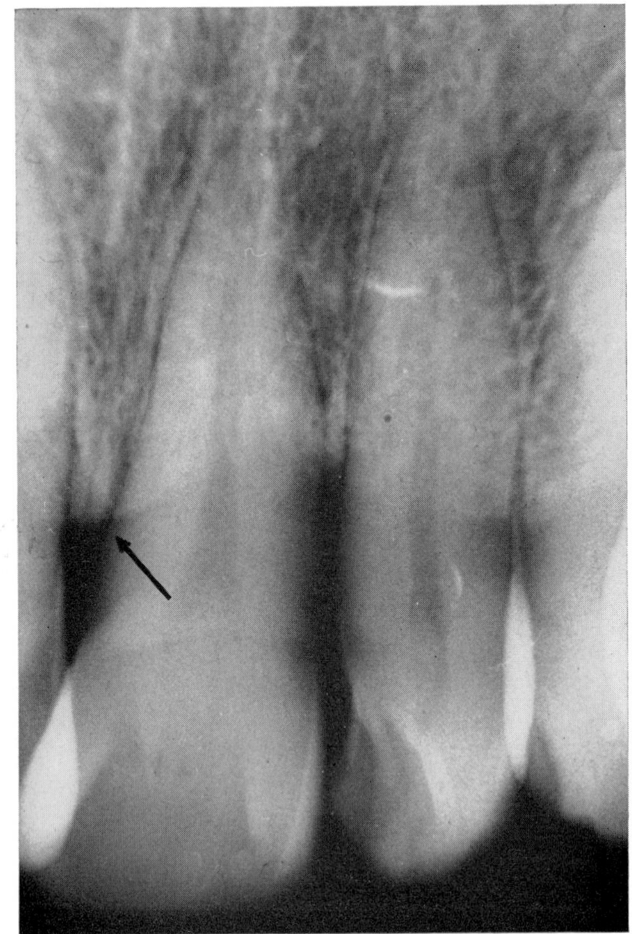

FIG. 9–41. Roentgenogram of maxillary incisors from Figure 9–40. There is no apparent bone loss to suggest a 6 mm. pocket present on the mesial of the maxillary central incisor. This is explained by a crater within the bony septum in which the bottom of the pocket is located. The walls of the crater obscure the internal defect.

Treatment Plan. Treatment planning can be based on either a rational or an empirical approach to therapy. When empirical procedures are used the treatment plan is selected merely because past experience suggests that specific events follow certain procedures. This is based upon previous experience only.

A rational treatment plan is based on a complete understanding of what is present in the oral environment, what etiologic factors must be removed or modified to alter the environment and what lesion therapy should be instituted. When inflammatory periodontal disease is present, the only rational treatment plan is one which identifies the extent and character of the lesion for selection of pocket therapy and identifies the irritants to eliminate inflammation.

The clinician must develop the ability to think in terms of what has transpired in the years previous to the moment the patient is being observed. From this, one can project a probable future path of events, building a hypothesis of what would happen if no changes or therapy were initiated. If irritants are present and they have caused inflammation in the past, one can assume that they will continue to cause inflammation in ever greater severity as they increase through cumulative continued neglect. Then the clinician can devise a second hypothesis establishing a new pattern of events, a new type of oral environment, and the probability of a different future for the health of the patient and his mouth. When this kind of hypothesis is built upon an understading of past oral history with cause and effect relationships, a rational treatment plan is selected. Carried out in all of its phases a rational treatment plan can produce optimum therapeutic benefits for the patient and be a source of great emotional satisfaction for the clinician.

The sequence of treatment should be first, care of emergency problems and then second, rehabilitate the mouth for the maintenance of health throughout the years to come. Thus emergency services such as extraction of hopelessly involved teeth and treatment of deep carious lesions become the first order of business in the treatment plan. Then, rehabilitation treatment can be carried out free from the pressures created by pain or fear of loss of badly diseased teeth.

Treatment begins routinely by establishing a clean mouth. The most frequently observed irritants in the mouth are septic microbial masses accumulating from inadequate oral hygiene. This is an important domain in which the hygienist can become a specialist. It is not enough to scale and polish the teeth every four to six months, but rather there must be created an attitude within the patient to maintain the mouth in a high state of cleanliness between professional visits. Pocket therapy by the dentist is for a similar purpose. Just as fillings are used in teeth for plastic repair to restore physiologic form, so is pocket therapy used to restore physiologic form of the gingiva, making it possible for the patient to maintain a clean sulcus. A deep periodontal pocket is inaccessible to the patient and cannot be maintained by either the toothbrush, dental floss or any other auxiliary aid.

Other than for emergency care, all restorative dentistry should be treated only after the mouth has been made clean and the periodontium has been made healthy. It is impossible to place an ideal filling or bridge when gingival inflammation complicates the restorative procedure. Bleeding contaminates the field and even enters into a chemical reaction with silver amalgam when it is being placed. Silicate fillings become discolored when placed during gingival bleeding. Good restorations must take into consideration the contour of the gingiva. The untreated periodontium may have abnormal swelling or architectural defects that are changed by periodontal therapy. Thus periodontal therapy must precede restorative dentistry.

Treatment. The first step in periodontal therapy is to establish a regimen of home care for the patient. Without adequate home care, the efforts of the dentist will be completely in vain. The etiologic factors would not be removed and soon there would be a recurrence of disease.

Motivation and guidance of the patient in home care are the responsibility of the dental hygienist. In the psychology of patient management, it is important that this be started on the first treatment visit. Only at this time is the patient optimally receptive to beginning a new and usually difficult home care regimen. If started later, the patient seems to adopt a philosophy of let the dentist do all the work.

The hygienist must become skilled in the removal of calculus and in root planing to prevent the rapid return of new deposits. Teeth must be polished not only on the buccal and lingual surfaces, but also on the interproximal to remove all plaque. The hygienist should prepare the mouth so that it is possible for the patient to maintain a state of good oral hygiene.

Following the initial preparation of the mouth the dentist can institute whatever procedures seem indicated for the management of residual pockets. *Curettage* is a surgical procedure wherein the lining epithelium of the sulcus is removed. Some epithelium is removed inadvertently during scaling and root planing by the offset side of the curette blade. During intentional curettage however, the front cutting edge of the blade is used with the specific intent of removal of this epithelial surface (Fig. 9–42).

Gingival curettage is done intentionally to achieve shrinkage by the reduction of edema (Figs. 9–43 and 9–44). Other purposes are to prepare the sulcus with a new epithelial lining to establish a longer area of epithelial adhesion to the tooth or possibly a new attachment with the connective tissue located more coronally than before treatment.

When the curette surgically scrapes away the lining sulcular epithelium, the tissues begin to bleed. Instrumentation breaks down the walling off process that has been established around the area of inflammation. New circulation will return and be maintained if the irritants are removed. As new metabolites are brought to the part, they bring nourishment to individual cells and prepare the tissues for healing. A new lining epithelium develops free from ulceration. This

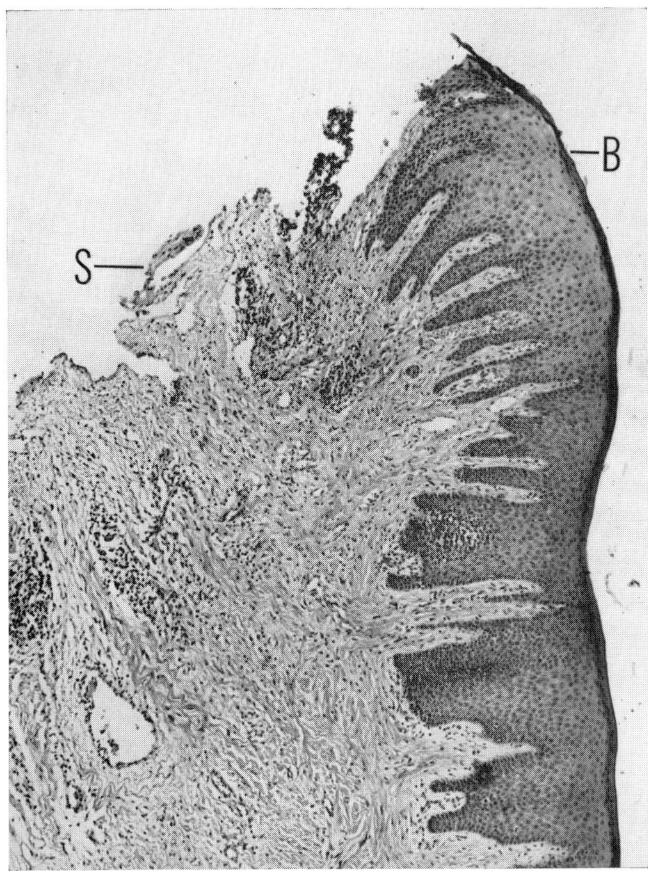

FIG. 9–42. Biopsy of gingiva following curettage. Epithelium remains on the buccal surface (*B*) but has been completely removed from the sulcus (*S*) adjacent to the tooth.

provides the maximum possible protection from the toxic products of the microbial flora living in the sulcular spaces. The embryonic epithelial cells which form in the sulcus have the potential of a new adhesion to the root surface.

After curettage new adhesion or "reattachment" may occur if the root has been planed sufficiently to remove the superficial cementum that has been pathologically exposed during pocket formation. The ends of Sharpey's fibers become calcified after exposure to oral fluids. Root planing exposes collagen in the dentinal tubules as well as removes the superficial cementum that contains the toxic products of the oral environment.

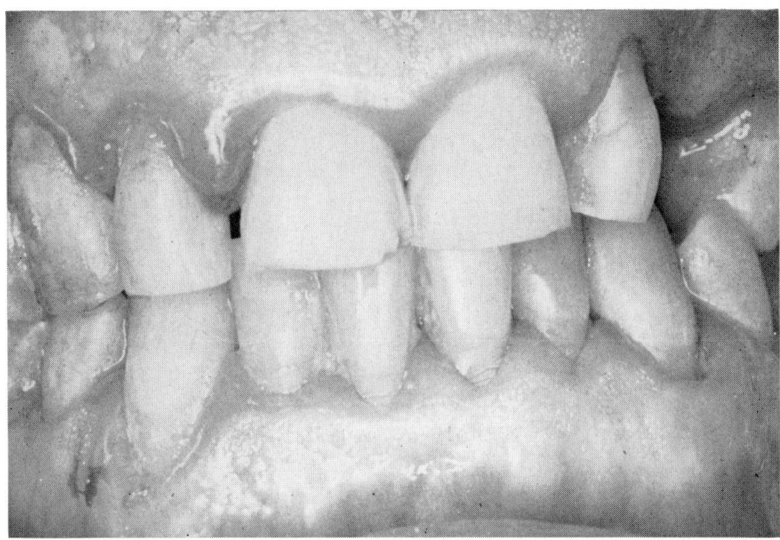

FIG. 9–43. Preoperative photograph of patient with moderate generalized periodontitis.

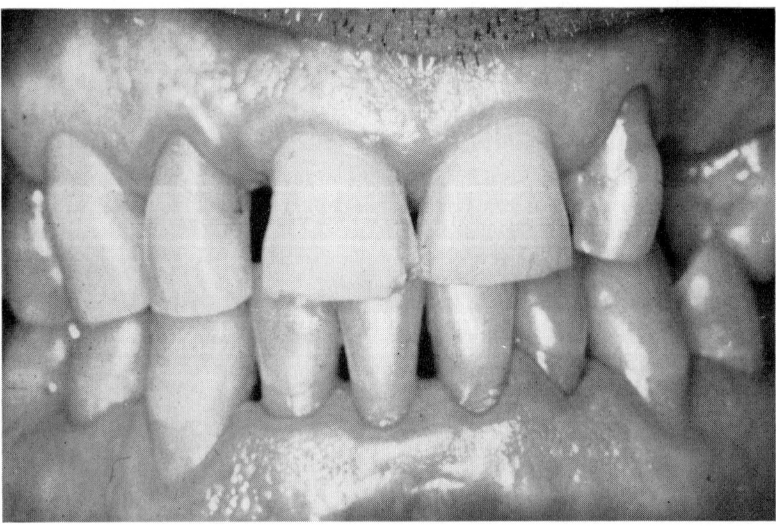

FIG. 9–44. Same patient as in Figure 9–43 demonstrating shrinkage effected by reduction of irritants and gingival curettage.

Some curettement is achieved by the hygienist during scaling, merely because the offset edge of the curette blade is scraping epithelium away. Since this is a surgical procedure, the tissue should be managed with tender care and flushed well following the instrumentation. Gingival biopsies have shown that retained calcific deposits will remain if flushing has been inadequate.

The dentist may be able to rebuild lost alveolar process in intrabony types of lesions. This is known as reattachment or new attachment operation. This has been proven possible when the walls of the pocket are partially supported by bone so that healing may occur similarly to that of an extraction wound. There is general agreement that a pocket

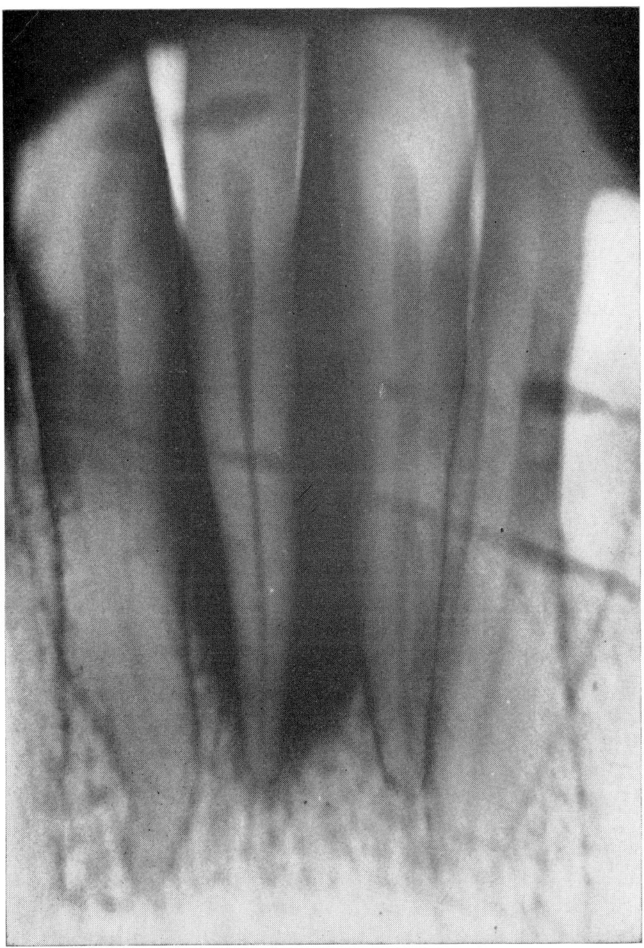

FIG. 9–45. Preoperative roentgenogram of patient with severe localized periodontitis complicated by diabetes.

which has three walls of bone with the tooth root providing the fourth offers the best hope of success. However, the use of bone grafts have brought success when only one pocket wall is formed by bone (Figs. 9–45 and 9–46).

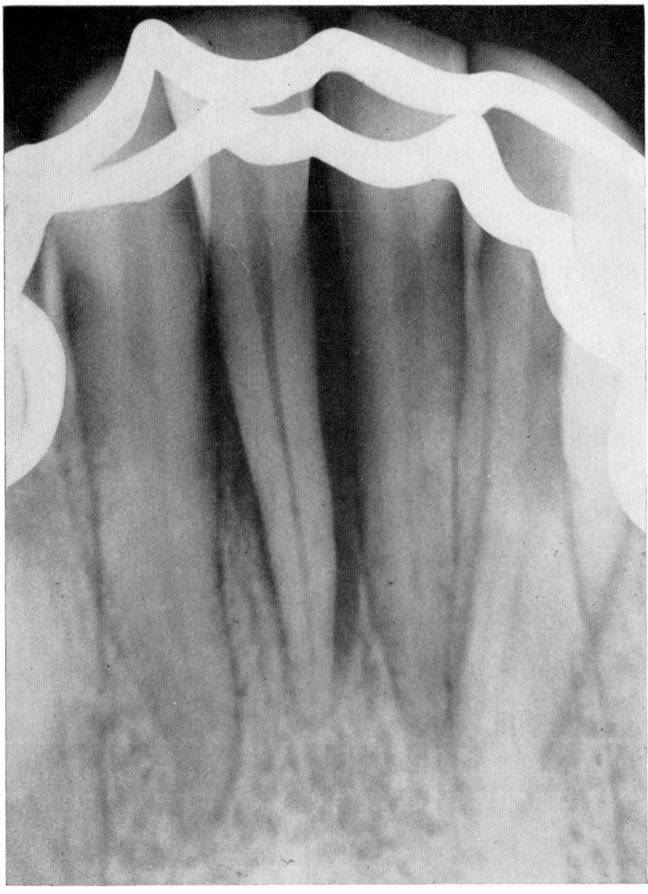

FIG. 9–46. Twelve month postoperative roentgenogram of case shown in Figure 9–45 after removal of granulomatous tissue, scaling, root planing and curettage. The radiopaque lines are created by a removable periodontal splint.

Other surgical procedures may be used by the dentist to eliminate periodontal pockets and improve gingival architectural form. Gingivoplasty is an operation to eliminate soft tissue pockets and provide physiologic gingival architecture (Fig. 9–47). Historically, clinicians spoke of a gingivectomy when the procedure was done with the objective of removing pockets and spoke of gingivoplasty when the objective was to improve gingival architecture. However, pocket removal should not be done without creating good architecture and vice versa. Today, the terms are virtually synonymous, and whether it is called gingivoplasty or gingivectomy the surgical procedure is the same.

Since Nabers[14] first reported the repositioning of attached gingiva many new therapeutic techniques have developed. When the bottom

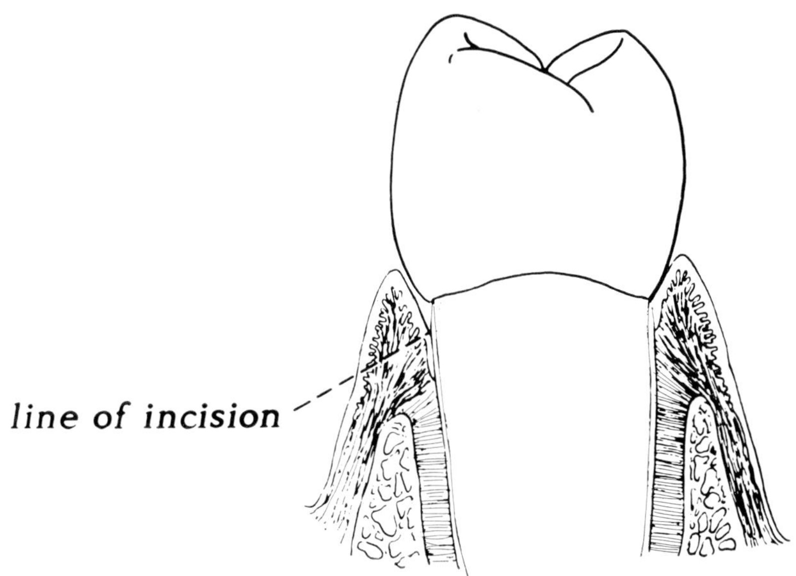

FIG. 9–47. Diagram showing principle of gingivectomy or gingivoplasty. The line of incision indicates the tissues that would be removed and how new architectural form is created.

of the pocket is below the mucogingival junction, the tissues are repositioned apically (Figs. 9–48 and 9–49). This is done in preference to a gingivoplasty that would cut away all the attached gingiva. When the vestibular depth is shallow, it can be extended. When an inadequate zone of attached gingiva exists, it may be increased (Fig. 9–50). When bone resorption has caused bizarre morphologic defects, new contours are created by osseousplasty (Figs. 9–51 and 9–52). The modern periodontal therapist is indeed the plastic surgeon of the mouth. There is almost no limit to the types and severity of lesions that can be treated.

Prognosis. Prognosis is a value judgment made by the clinician to determine the probable outcome of treatment. This is arrived at by a complete knowledge of (1) how the disease entity occurred, (2) how long it took to develop and (3) how well the clinician is able to alter

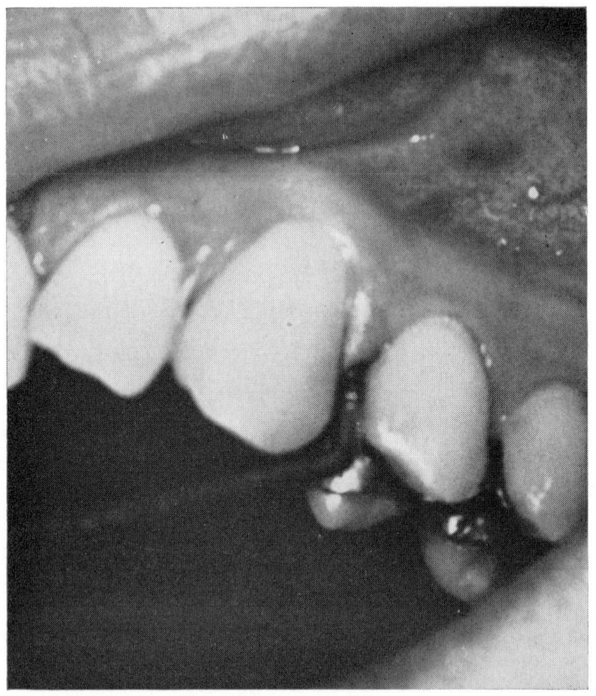

FIG. 9–48. Periodontal probe placed in pocket on distal of maxillary cuspid. Depth is 9 mm.

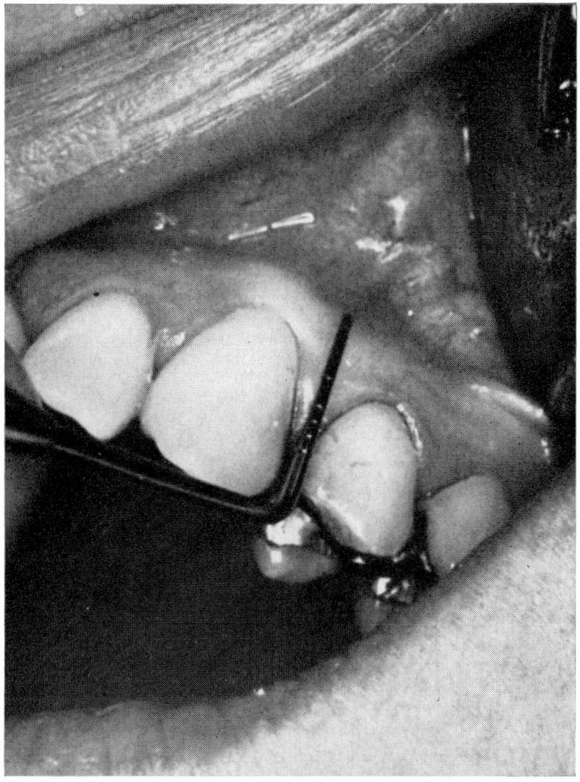

FIG. 9–49. Same case as in Figure 9–48 with periodontal probe on buccal tissue to demonstrate that bottom of pocket is at the muco-gingival junction. If a gingivectomy were used here all of the attached gingiva would be removed.

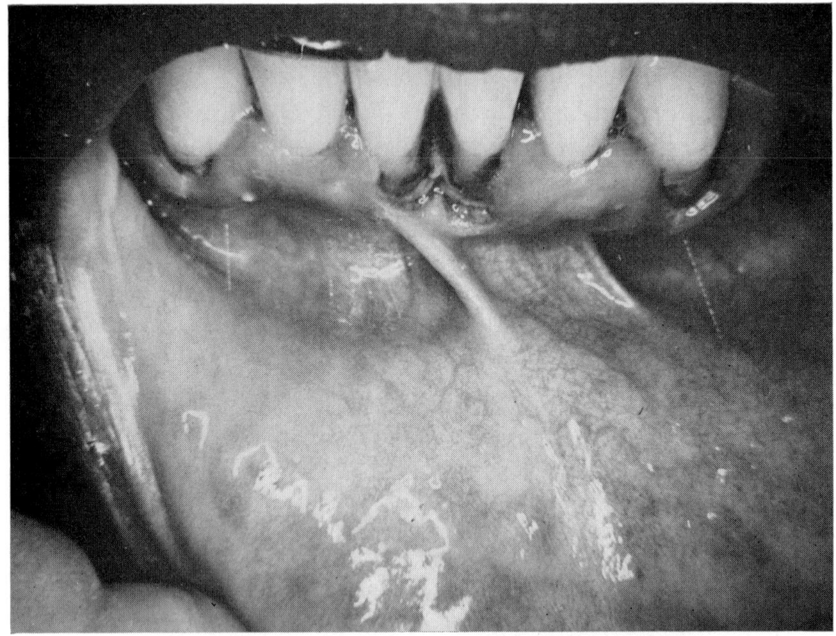

FIG. 9–50. Frenulum attachment into the marginal gingiva pulling the tissue away from the tooth. The muscle action during mastication facilitates the entrance of food into the pocket. No zone of attached gingiva exists at this point.

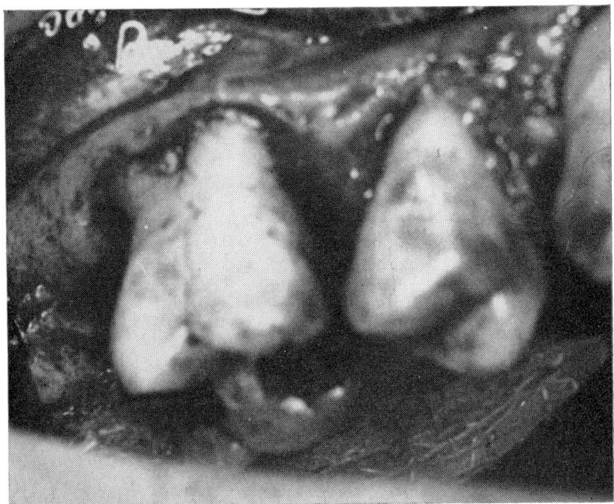

FIG. 9–51. Preoperative view of defect in bone around maxillary first molar. A trough exists on both mesial and distal to create infrabony defects. The buccal trifurcation area contains granulomatous tissue with the bone loss having created a ledge.

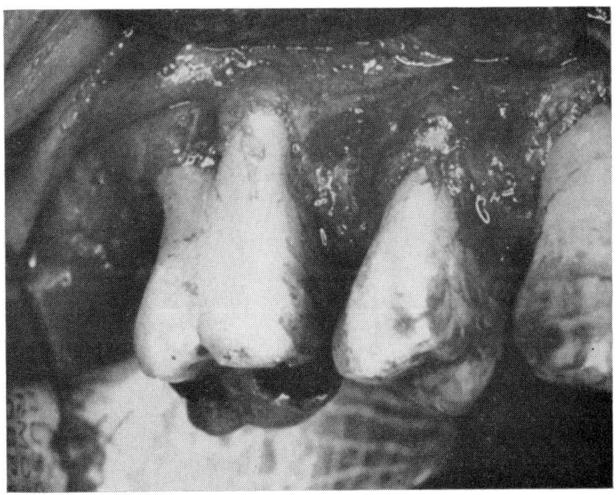

FIG. 9–52. Same area as in Figure 9–51 after the bone has been recontoured. Defects have been eliminated by osseousplasty. The next step is to reposition the gingival flap, carefully suturing so that marginal bone and soft tissue are at the same place. This is a gingival pedicle graft.

the environmental factors which initiated the disease. If the etiologic factors can be removed and the lesions corrected so that the environment is conducive to maintenance of good oral hygiene, the prognosis is extremely good.

When these factors cannot be eliminated in their entirety, a compromise prognosis is developed. The patient should be informed that a compromise prognosis is existent so that embarrassing explanations will not be required later on. Also, this knowledge may help the patient be motivated to a greater extent in maintenance of oral hygiene. This may help compensate for some of the inadequacies of the oral environment. For example, when orthodontic problems are residual and cannot be corrected the patient may compensate for these by improved efforts in home care.

An important factor in determining prognosis is the human equation. What are the attitudes of the patient, the dentist and the hygienist? Is the patient motivated toward adequate home care? If not, can this be achieved? Is the dentist periodontally oriented in his practice methods? Is the hygienist motivated to spend the necessary time with patients to develop their oral hygiene skills? Proper attitudes are the foundation of success—without them, failure.

Necrotizing Ulcerative Gingivitis. Necrotizing ulcerative gingivitis is a disease characterized by necrosis of the crest of the interdental papilla (Figs. 9–53 and 9–54). There are other symptoms and signs that may occur simultaneously, but they are not found as a consistent finding. Because necrosis is active the gingiva and mouth are sore, the fetid odor of necrotic tissue is annoying, and the patient may be sick with fever and malaise. This disease has been called by many names among them Vincent's infection, trench mouth and ulcero-membranous stomatitis.

Studies on the incidence of necrotizing ulcerative gingivitis have indicated that it occurs primarily in the teen age and young adult population. Most frequently the patient will be of high school or college age. On school campuses the disease is found most frequently at the time of final examination periods.

The pathology of the disease is not completely understood. This is not a disease caused by invading microbes. Rather, there is a resistance change in the host that allows a marked increase in the numbers of bacteria present in the mouth. These are the same bacteria that are present in the normal oral flora. It is not a qualitative but rather a quantitative change. During the combination of increased numbers of organisms and reduced resistance of the host, the point of weakest resistance is attacked, the crest of the interdental papilla. This is characterized clinically by a grayish white pseudo-membrane indicating necrosis of the tissues. As the severity of the disease increases, other

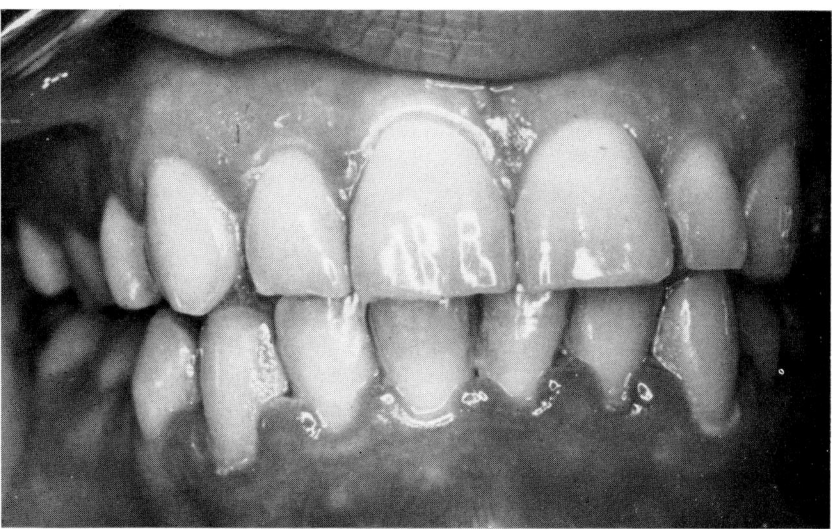

FIG. 9–53. Eighteen-year-old female with necrotizing ulcerative gingivitis. The cardinal sign of necrosis at the crest of the interdental area is marked in the mandibular anterior area. Beginning inflammation is apparent around the maxillary left lateral incisor.

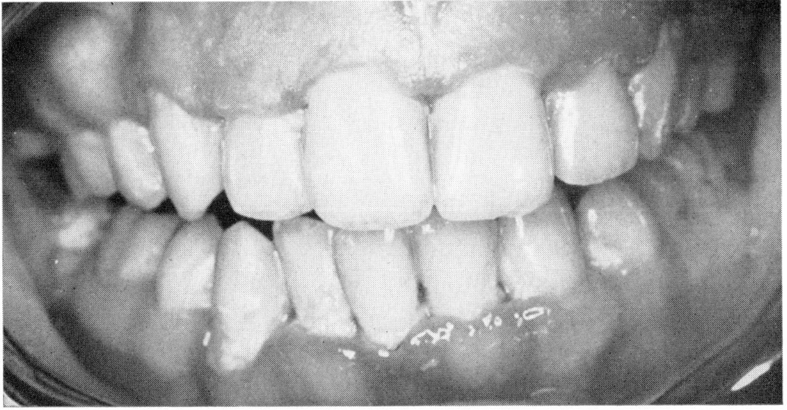

FIG. 9–54. Twenty-year-old male with severe necrotizing ulcerative gingivitis. Extensive necrosis has destroyed the interdental papilla leaving a punched out appearance. Oral hygiene is difficult because the mouth is painful.

areas may subsequently be involved such as the marginal gingiva and even the attached gingiva. Initially the bacteria do not invade the tissues, but live on the superficial surfaces. However, the toxic products of these teeming numbers of organisms may affect the patient and there is a resultant fever and feeling of malaise. In severe cases a cervical lymphadenopathy develops, suggesting drainage of organisms into the deeper tissues.

Etiology. There are four basic causes of the development of necrotizing ulcerative gingivitis. The first is *inadequate oral hygiene.* It rarely develops in a mouth that is completely and meticulously maintained in a state of cleanliness. Prior to the onset of the necrotizing phase inadequate oral hygiene allows a greater number of organisms to accumulate which in turn have initiated a gingivitis with impaired circulation. In the necrotizing phase, there is a rapid increase in number of organisms which can attack a locally lowered tissue substrate.

The second factor, *diet,* seems to be more important in the background of necrotizing ulcerative gingivitis than to other periodontal diseases. The teen age female is frequently involved in crash reducing programs which may leave her in a state of dietary inadequacy. Some clinical investigations have found that vitamin supplementation aids recovery, while other investigations report no benefits. In any event, a good dietary regimen is desirable for all patients regardless of whether or not they are healthy or have necrotizing gingivitis. Therefore, one can never be wrong in recommending good eating habits. The dentist may elect to give vitamin supplementation if this seems indicated.

Fatigue seems to be related to necrotizing gingivitis. Teen age and college age people are involved in a social life that is not conducive to regular sleeping habits. Often, these people get an inadequate amount of sleep and predispose their bodies to lowered resistance and debilitation. As in good dietary practices, so is it desirable for all patients to have good sleeping habits. One cannot go wrong in recommending good sleeping habits, and the necrotizing gingivitis patient may be helped by an adequate amount of sleep.

Emotional problems, the fourth cause, seem to be present in almost every case of necrotizing gingivitis. High school and college age life is one that contains a great opportunity for emotional crises. It is a time in which the young adult must make a sexual adjustment to life. It is a time that a mate is sought, often with great emotional trauma. It is a time complicated by great academic pressures due to the severe demands of academic disciplines. Most young people are aware that they are preparing themselves for a lifetime of adult experiences. Subjectively these adjustments are important, and when difficulties arise they can become a source of deep emotional trauma.

A study of Moulton and Ewing[13] indicated a close relationship between emotional disturbances and the onset of necrotizing ulcerative gingivitis. Schluger[16] observed an increase in the incidence of necrotizing gingivitis in a military population, not when they were in barracks and living in close proximity, but rather when on bivouac under the emotional stress of pseudo-combat conditions. In a college population, the incidence of necrotizing gingivitis increased as the time for examinations neared. After examinations were over, the incidence of necrotizing gingivitis decreased.

Treatment. Again, treatment of any disease is based on an understanding of the etiology as well as the management of the local tissue lesions. The sooner the mouth can be cleaned, the more rapidly the poor hygiene factor can be eliminated. Optimally, this is done at the time the patient is first seen. Sometimes the discomfort may require that a local anesthetic be administered in order that scaling can be completed. Bleeding often is severe, and it is necessary to have suction to maintain a dry field so that calculus can be observed. Always polish the teeth, for the removal of plaque is a major part in the reduction of bacteria and the consequent improvement of blood supply to the gingiva. *Always polish on the first visit.*

Diet can be improved through consultation and prescription of vitamins. Fatigue can be eliminated when the patient acquires an adequate amount of sleep. Emotional problems usually are not treated in the dental office. However, the recognition that these exist may be important, leading to the referral of the patient to a person qualified to deal with the kind of emotional problems present.

When the necrosis is arrested, often there are defects in the architectural form of the gingiva. There are craters where the interdental papillae formerly had been. Since craters are areas inaccessible for patient hygiene, the subsequent irritation initiates inflammation which later develops into periodontitis. Therefore, to prevent periodontitis the therapist must not dismiss the patient after necrosis has been arrested. Rather, complete treatment dictates that the gingiva be restored to an architectural form in which the patient can maintain oral hygiene throughout the years ahead. Often this requires a gingivoplasty or a recontouring of the gingival tissues (Fig. 9–55).

Recurrence. Inasmuch as the patient is the problem, not the microbial population, then recurrence of the disease is a relatively frequent occurrence. The patient who has emotional disturbances at one point in his life may well develop emotional disturbances of equal severity at a later time. A patient who is habituated to poor dietary practices may not continue good eating habits after the mouth is restored to comfort. One that has not been getting enough sleep may

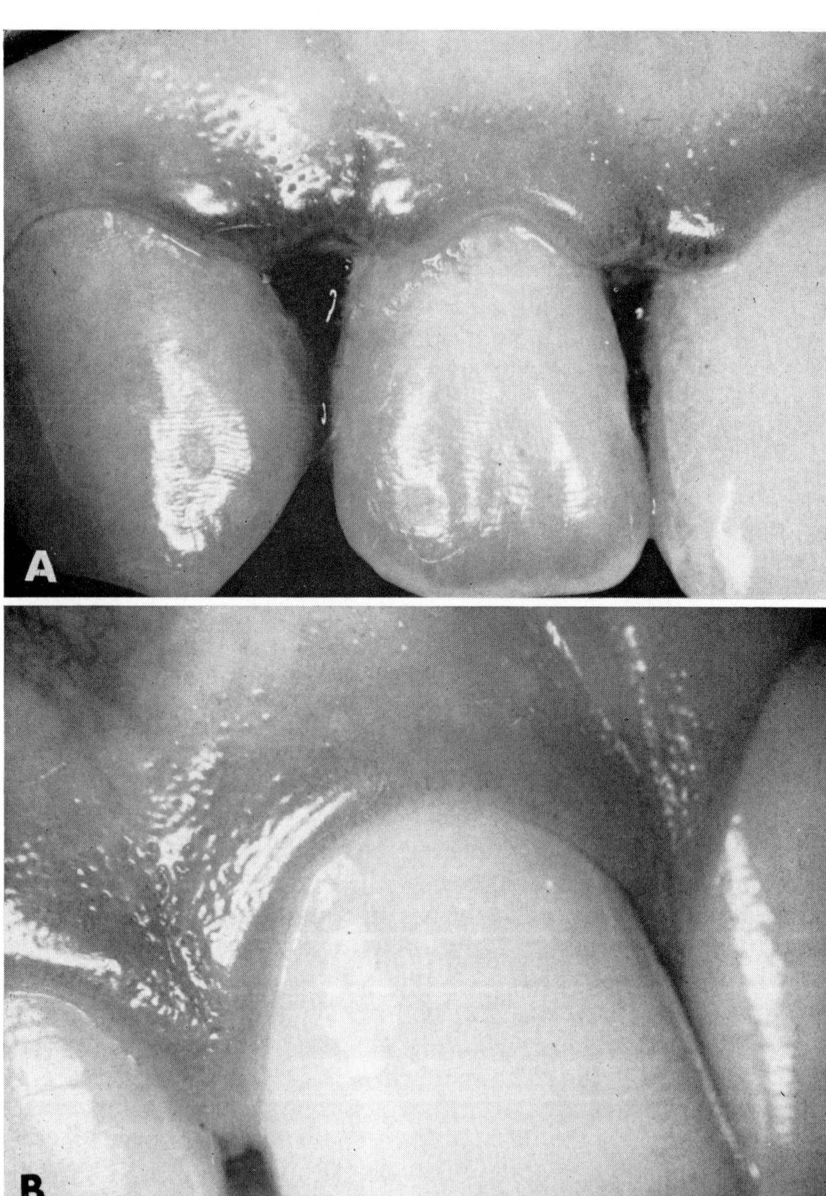

FIG. 9–55. *A,* Arrested necrotizing ulcerative gingivitis leaving deep interproximal craters to make good oral hygiene almost impossible. The case needs to be treated by gingivoplasty to create physiologic gingival form.

B, Same patient as in *A* after contouring by gingivoplasty to provide conical interdental papillae and knife-like edge margins.

relapse into the same kind of living pattern. Patients who are emotionally disturbed may not maintain good oral hygiene regimens. As a result, recurrence of necrotizing gingivitis is observed frequently in those patients having had an initial attack (Fig. 9–56).

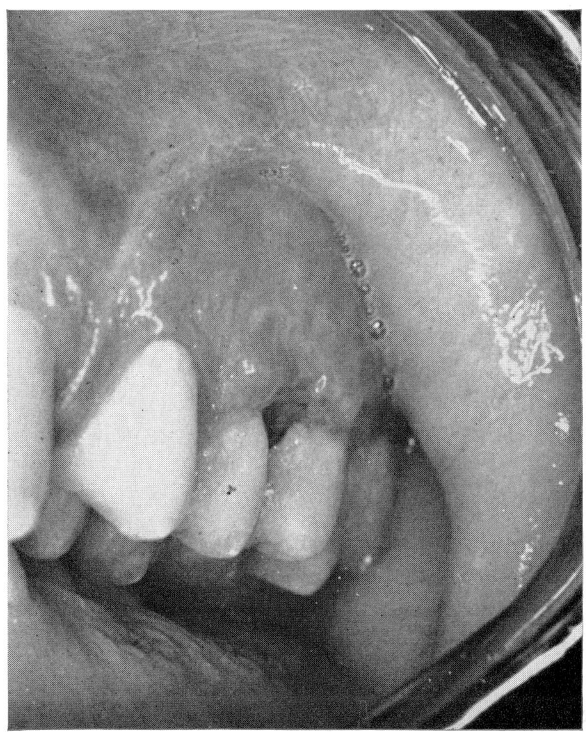

FIG. 9–56. Seventeen-year-old male with recurrent necrotizing ulcerative gingivitis causing loss of interdental tissue between the second bicuspid and the first molar. The onset of disease occurred simultaneously with an emotional crisis between the boy and his mother.

Misconceptions About Necrotizing Ulcerative Gingivitis. There are many misconceptions about necrotizing ulcerative gingivitis. One of the oldest is that it is a "kissing disease." In all experiments attempting to transmit the disease from one patient to another there has been no evidence to show that this is a communicable disease. Since this is not a problem of bacteria but rather one of the host, communicability becomes nearly impossible.

Another misconception about necrotizing gingivitis is that it should be treated with drugs. If drugs are used in the process of therapy, the patient gets the idea that the drugs got them well. They begin to rely upon a pill or mouthwash, thinking that this will solve their problems—not that of good oral hygiene, adequate diet, adequate sleep and preparing their lives so that they are free from emotional crises. It is true that the administration of an antibiotic will suppress the bacteria and perhaps arrest the necrosis. However, since the bacteria are not the primary problem, the basic etiologic factors would not be removed by an antibiotic. Unless the causes of disease have been removed by coincidence, the necrosis of the gingiva would recur when the antibiotic is discontinued.

Another misconception is that the use of oxidizing agents is an efficacious way for treating the disease. This concept developed originally from the belief many years ago that Vincent's infection was caused by anaerobic organisms. Since this was believed to be a communicable infectious problem, it was thought a cure would be established through the use of oxidizing agents to kill off these invading bacteria. It is true that some of the organisms may be anaerobic, but oxygen will not affect the known etiologic problems bringing the onset of disease. Besides, in the event of recurrence the patient will dash to the drug store for the purchase of an oxidizing agent instead of returning to the dental office for correct professional care.

Therapy in Dental Practice

Treatment of periodontal diseases offers one of the most rewarding phases of dental practice. Most patients do not want to lose their teeth but wish to maintain their mouth in health throughout life. Since most patients become edentulous because of an inflammatory breakdown of the periodontium, it is possible to maintain these people in health by utilization of known techniques in treatment and prevention.

Until recently few dental schools provided significant training in periodontics in the undergraduate curriculum. Therefore, many general practitioners rely upon a specialist in periodontics to carry out all therapeutic procedures for them. However, since almost every adult patient needs some form of treatment, there are not enough specialists to care for the public health needs. Only the general practicing dentist can resolve this problem. The dental hygienist can play a significant role in the health team in periodontal therapy.

Since treatment is largely a matter of the removal of irritation to eliminate inflammation, drugs are not a part of the therapeutic regimen. Due to the extensive impact of advertising on public thinking, this may be difficult to explain to the patient. Since most irritation is of microbial origin there is no drug that will remove these organisms for other than an extremely short period of time. The hygienist can play an important role in explaining this problem to the patient.

In a case under treatment, the hygienist can play a significant part in relieving the dentist for other services of patient care. During initial preparation, the patient can be started on a program of home oral hygiene and then complete thorough scaling, root planing, polishing and oral physiotherapy. After pocket therapy has been completed and the environment of the mouth changed, the services of a hygienist can provide the clean-up of post-surgical areas. New instructions in oral hygiene usually are necessary when the oral environment has been changed by gingival surgery.

The dental hygienist has a primary role in prevention of disease before it has occurred and in prevention of disease after it has been treated. This means that hygienists must evaluate patients' oral hygiene problems, must motivate patients to maintain a high level of oral cleanliness and must be responsible for establishing and promoting a recall program for preventive professional care. The frequency of the recall visit is set not just to remove calculus deposits in their early stages of formation, but more important, to see the patient often enough that minor irritants are removed before significant inflammation occurs. Seeing the patient with sufficient frequency acts as a psychological stimulant to maintain the patient on a high level of oral hygiene home care. Repeated motivation of the patient may be the most valuable function that can be performed by the hygienist in a dental office.

The dental hygienist who works in a periodontically oriented practice receives deeply gratifying emotional rewards by being part of the team that helps make periodontically unhealthy mouths become healthy and to maintain them in good condition. Hygienists are rewarded with the knowledge that these patients are not subjected to the emotional and physical trauma which confronts the denture patient.

BIBLIOGRAPHY

1. Belting, C. M., Massler, M. and Schour, I.: Prevalence and Incidence of Alveolar Bone Disease in Men. J.A.D.A. *47,* 190, 1953.
2. Boyle, Paul E.: *Histopathology of the Teeth and Their Surrounding Structure.* 4th ed., Philadelphia, Lea & Febiger, 1955, pp. 376–377.
3. Brill, N. and Bjorn, H. Passage of Tissue Fluid in Human Gingival Pockets. Acta Odont. Scandinavica *17,* 11, 1959.
4. Brill, N. and Krasse, B.: Effect of Mechanical Stimulation on Flow of Tissue Fluid Through Gingival Pocket Epithelium. Acta Odont. Scandinavica *16*, 233, 1958.
5. Gargiulo, A. W., Wentz, F. M. and Orban, B.: Dimensions and Relations of the Dentogingival Junction in Humans. J. Periodont. *32,* 261, 1961.
6. Glickman, I. and Smulow, J. B.: Alterations in the Pathway of Gingival Inflammation into the Underlying Tissues Induced by Excessive Occlusal Forces. J. Periodont. *33*, 7, 1962.

7. MACAPANAN, L. L. and WEINMANN, J. P.: The Influence of Injury to the Periodontal Membrane on the Spread of Gingival Inflammation. J. Dent. Res. *33*, 263, 1954.
8. MANDEL, I. D., LEVY, B. M. and WASSERMAN, B. H.: Histochemistry of Calculus Formation. J. Periodont. *28*, 132, 1957.
9. MANN, W. V. and STOFFER, H. R.: The Identification of Protein Components in Fluid from the Gingival Pockets. Periodontics. *2*, 263, 1964.
10. MARSHALL-DAY, C. D.: The Epidemiology of Periodontal Disease. J. Periodont. *22*, 13, 1951.
11. MARSHALL-DAY, C. D., STEPHENS, R. G. and QUIGLEY, L. F.: Periodontal Disease: Prevalence and Incidence. J. Periodont. *26*, 199, 1955.
12. MASSLER, M., SCHOUR, I. and CHOPRA, B.: Occurrence of Gingivitis in Suburban Chicago School Children. J. Periodont. *21*, 146, 1950.
13. MOULTON, R., EWING, S. and THIEMAN, W.: Emotional Factors in Periodontal Disease. Oral Surg., Oral Med., & Oral Path. *5*, 833, 1952.
14. NABERS, C. L.: Repositioning the Attached Gingiva. J. Periodont. *25*, 38, 1954.
15. RUSSELL, A. L.: The Geographic Distribution and Epidemiology of Periodontal Disease. World Health Organization Expert Committee on Dental Health (Periodontal Disease). WHO/DH *34*, Geneva, 1960.
16. SCHLUGER, S.: Necrotizing Ulcerative Gingivitis in the Army: Incidence, Communicability and Treatment. J.A.D.A. *38*, 174, 1949.
17. STERN, I. B.: The Fine Structure of the Ameloblast-enamel Junction in Rat Incisors; Epithelial Attachment and Cuticular Membrane. Fifth International Congress for Electron Microscopy. *2*, QQ6, New York, Academic Press, 1962.
18. The Survey of Dentistry. American Council on Education, Washington, D. C., p. 420, 1961.
19. WEINMANN, J. P.: Progress of Gingival Inflammation into the Supporting Structures of the Teeth. J. Periodont. *12*, 71, 1941.
20. WILLIAMS, C. H. M.: Present Status of Knowledge Regarding the Etiology of Periodontal Disease. Oral Surg., Oral Path., Oral Med. *2*, 729, 1949.
21. WURTHEIMER, F. W. and FULMER, H. M.: Morphologic and Histochemical Observations on the Human Dental Cuticle. J. Periodont. *33*, 29, 1962.

10

Dental Health Education

Pauline F. Steele

INTEREST in dental health education was initiated with the organization of the Oral Hygiene Movement. This movement was a significant factor in the inception, growth and development of dental health education. The movement originated with those dentists who became interested in the preventive phase of dentistry, rather than adhering strictly to its restorative aspect. Dr. Thaddeus Pomery Hyatt did much to foster the movement and was later to be known as the "Father of Preventive Dentistry." This concept of preventive dentistry created an entirely new division in the field of dentistry; the era of dental health education had come into existence. By the turn of the 20th century, the dental profession began recognizing the paramount importance of dental health education.

One of the first articles treating this new phase of dentistry appeared in 1839 in the *American Journal of Dental Science,* the first dental periodical of this country. As early as 1844 there was an editorial under the title "Dental Hygiene." This editorial deplored the fact that so much attention was being devoted to therapeutics, mechanical dentistry and surgery, while the hygiene of the teeth was being almost completely neglected.

In 1884 Dr. M. L. Rhein of New York City, in an article entitled "Oral Hygiene," described what he termed a prophylactic toothbrush and urged his colleagues to teach their patients the proper methods of toothbrushing. Dr. Rhein became so enthusiastic about the value of oral hygiene therapy that in 1895 he proposed a special committee be organized to petition boards of education to supervise the oral hygiene of children's teeth. The doctor's idea was not implemented by reason of a singular lack of support.

An additional impetus to dental health education was received in 1900 when the National Dental Association appointed the first Committee on Oral Hygiene. However, it was not until after the organization of the Dental Hygiene Council in New York City on January 12, 1909, with Dr. H. L. Wheeler as Chairman, that widespread interest was aroused. Prior to this organized dental health concern, individual dentists were devoting considerable time and effort to searching out the causes of dental decay. During the formative period of dental health education, the dental profession put particular emphasis on children's dentistry. In 1927, Dr. Thaddeus P. Hyatt together with other prominent dentists organized the American Society for the Promotion of Dentistry for Children. This society, which has enjoyed a steady growth since its founding, became the American Society of Dentistry for Children in 1940.

Professor Andrew McLain of the The New Orleans Dental College was one of the eminent early dentists who appreciated the value of dental health education, and stressed mouth hygiene as a personal responsibility of the patient. In the literature of the 1870's, frequent references are found identifying diet as being an important factor in relation to diseases of the gingiva. However, it was considerably later before much attention was given to the significance of dental hygiene. Dr. D. D. Smith of Philadelphia in 1894 began his special preventive practice by requiring his patients to perform oral hygiene procedures at home in the manner in which they had been instructed. Dr. Thaddeus P. Hyatt also was a zealous exponent of education for the public in matters of dental health. However, he was severely criticized by members of his local dental society because they felt he was improperly advertising his services and they threatened charges of unethical conduct. Eventually, the officers were convinced that a dental health lecture could be given in the third person, and that the public could be educated to the value of dental health. In our time these examples of dental health education are commonplace; however, at that time they were daring and unique.

By the later 1890's, the subject of dental hygiene was being discussed in dental literature and in the professional forums. It was during this period that the words *prophylactic* and *prophylaxis* were first utilized to any appreciable extent in dental periodicals. Although the concept of dental prophylaxis progressed slowly, there was a gradually expanding awareness within the dental profession which eventually highlighted the fundamental importance of oral hygiene.

The opening of the 20th century ushered in an era of social movements with a marked interest in various philanthropic pursuits. Until this time, no significant progress was recorded in dental health education endeavors. This new century witnessed the emergence of a broadened enthusiasm for dental health, collectively and individually, among the members of the profession. Special professional committees were created to assist in the dental hygiene movement and, concurrently, privately endowed dental clinics were being established.

One of the most influential professional organizations to promote dental health education has been the American Dental Association which has had a standing dental health education committee since 1900. The American Dental Hygienists' Association, also, has been vitally concerned with dental health education projects, and has an active dental health committee. It was around 1910 that private philanthropic foundations became interested in dental health problems. There were a succession of dental clinics developed in the early years of this century. The earliest one of these clinics was the Forsyth Dental Infirmary of Boston. In subsequent years, the following agencies were established: The Rochester Dental Dispensary, The Guggenheim Foundation, The Children's Fund of Michigan, The Zoller Memorial Clinic, The Hall Foundation and the W. K. Kellogg Foundation. These philanthropic clinics were founded in an effort to provide dental services for underprivileged school age children.

School Dental Health Education Development

In the early 1900's, Mr. Willis A. Sutton, Superintendent of the Atlanta, Georgia, schools, worked diligently to promote interest in the dental health of school children. He was one of the first school administrators to advocate the necessity of schools being concerned with the dental health of children. By virtue of his interest, an experimental school dental health program was initiated.

One of the most notable early school dental health programs was conducted in 1909 at Cleveland, Ohio, under the direction of Dr. W. G. Ebersole. Since Dr. Ebersole was then the chairman of the National Dental Association's Committee on Oral Hygiene, he had considerable influence in promoting this program. The purpose of the study was to show the need for, and the advantage of, dental health education programs in the schools. Through his experiment, Dr. Ebersole demonstrated the value of dental care for the school child. During this investigation, a significant relationship was indicated between dental health and the total well being of the individual. Dr. Ebersole's efforts caused considerable attention to be directed toward the need for improving the dental health of children.

The idea of school dental health programs also occurred to Dr. Alfred C. Fones. This prompted his enthusiasm toward establishing a school for educating dental hygienists to work with children. In 1909, Dr. Fones began a strenuous campaign to obtain dental hygiene services for school children. His purpose was to replace the current relief and repair dental clinics for children with prophylactic and educational facilities. In the fall of 1914, ten dental hygienists began their duties at the Bridgeport, Connecticut, schools. The principal objective of this program was to demonstrate the value of dental health education as a preventive measure in diminishing the incidence of dental disease among school age children.

Before these initial school dental health programs had been implemented, general health programs had been introduced which were principally concerned with communicable diseases and the teaching of physiology and hygiene. The earliest employment of a school dentist was in 1903 at Reading, Pennsylvania, and this event coincided with the development of medical inspection programs within the schools.

The first concerted efforts to retain health education as an integral part of the total school program followed World War I. Health education was being emphasized to the degree that national education groups included the health of the school child as one of the seven major educational objectives. In the beginning, health instruction stressed facts *per se,* but the modern approach emphasizes the adapting of knowledge into action. There has been a renewed interest in health education since the termination of World War II. With this expanded interest (and encouraged by the President's Council on Physical Fitness), there has been an extension and diversification of community agencies participating in school health programs.

Health Concepts

The older philosophy of teaching centered on the impartation of information without any particular interest in its utilization. This method of instruction was designed to enlarge the factual knowledge of the individual irrespective of its practical applications. Such teaching was not effective in putting knowledge into use. Therefore, systems of artificial motivational devices appeared, such as contests in one form or another. It was discovered that competition stimulated temporary performance for the reward received, rather than encouraging favorable permanent health habits. This older philosophy did not take into consideration the capacity of the individual to adopt the recommended practices. This concept prevailed not only in formal instructional groups such as regular school classes, but also in informal presentations that were given to various adult organizations.

A newer philosophy of teaching has evolved which has partially eliminated some of the faults inherent in the older system. Today, it is a recognized concept that for any form of teaching to be meaningful there must be opportunities to put the knowledge into practice. Health education currently seeks to provide experiences that are applicable to the individual. This approach takes into consideration differences of the entire person, including physical, mental, emotional and social aspects. The objective is to improve the status of the individual, but not necessarily to require everyone to conform to a fixed standard. Health education, to be of significance, must be cognizant of the intricacies that become involved.

All instruction should evolve from direct aims or objectives. Specific objectives have been outlined by both health educators and educational organizations. The incorporation of these aims would be most valuable in the preparation of any presentation.

Dr. Delbert Oberteuffer defines the aims of health education as being:[12]

1. To inform the oncoming generations of the vast heritage of science which may contribute to creative development.
2. To modify and direct behavior so that the individual learner will live scientifically.
3. To prevent the onset of disease and disability which may develop from within a technological environment.

The Educational Policies Commission has stated three ways in which a person should be health educated.[9] They are:

1. The educated person understands the basic facts concerning health and disease.
2. The educated person protects his own health and that of his dependents.
3. The educated person works to improve the health of the community.

The American Dental Association has suggested the following dental health objectives:[1]

1. To help every school child appreciate the importance of a healthy mouth.
2. To help every school child appreciate the relationship of dental health to general health and appearance.
3. To encourage the observance of dental health practices, including personal care, professional care, proper diet and oral habits.
4. To enlist the aid of all groups and agencies interested in the promotion of school health.
5. To correlate dental health activities with the total school health program.
6. To stimulate the development of resources for making dental care available to all children and youth.
7. To stimulate dentists to perform adequate health services for children.

Dental Health Knowledge and the Behavioral Sciences

The social science areas are of tremendous importance when considering dental health education. Therefore, it is necessary that those associated with this field have knowledge in both the behavioral and biological sciences. Pertinent and accurate information must be disseminated, but to realize the final goal of changing habits there must be an understanding of the values maintained by the people to whom this information is being presented.

Increased interest in the behavioral studies has provided significant implications for health education which can be transferred specifically to dental health education. One of the greatest changes which has occurred is in the comprehension of the factors that control the responsiveness of the individual. Early efforts were directed in making the person want to accept what was being presented, but eventually it had to be recognized that the stress had to be placed on the real inner needs felt by the individual before an acceptance and change of attitude was possible.

Research studies in the social sciences disclose that the individual is a complex structure who does not easily conform to a prescribed pattern. As educators, hygienists must realize that there are many value concepts, and that they are a major aspect in the promotion of dental health education. That which is valued will be retained, while that which is a contrary value will be denied. Values are acquired from the environment which is comprised of the family, school, neighborhood, church and various other social groups. Each of these forces is involved when considering the factors required in reinforcing dental health education efforts.

The culture of a social group is governed by its acceptable patterns of behavior, and there are wide divergencies of acceptability by the different cultural classes. Frequently, these patterns of behavior are established through the media of small groups such as the family. The recognition of this factor is of extreme importance when working with children, since they are definitely dominated by the family culture. In order to comprehend the health attitudes of individuals and/or communities, there must be an understanding of the total environment in which the person exists. Much remains to be learned about the relationship between culture and health ideals.

Formerly, health education stressed the undesirability of being ill rather than the desirability of being well. This was done by placing fears and anxieties in the minds of people with the hope of forcing them to change their habits. The results of this particular approach were negligible; nothing positive is attained through coercion. However, now the incentive or positive approach is being advocated.

Through this philosophy, the individual becomes involved in wanting to help with the situation. There is a relationship to acceptance and the individual's recognized need. Health education then becomes constructive because it satisfies a learner centered goal.

For health education to be effective, there must be a resultant reaction. Realistically, health education should be concerned in stimulating a desire to improve or implement a regard for good health. The primary purpose of health education is to promote interest in an attitude change. It is a well-known precept that the mere acquisition of knowledge does not automatically initiate a change in health practices. Therefore, the objective of health education should emphasize the importance of modifying behavior and attitudes. By being cognizant of the divergent discrepancies between health knowledge and health habits, dental health education becomes more effective.

Motivation

Now that it is recognized that knowledge without incentive does not produce application, there is the necessity for also understanding the important factor of motivation in dental health education. It is an accepted axiom that change through education is not revolutionary but evolutionary, and is therefore a relatively slow process. However, by this means it is possible to provide beneficial programs for a greater proportion of the population with the least amount of expenditure. For any project to be effective, there must be recognition by the recipient of its usefulness. Having available facilities does not assure their utilization. First, the desire on the part of the individual to improve must be instilled. The challenge for education is in stimulating the recipient to utilize the information received.

Motivational stimulus varies with age, social and cultural groups. For youngsters the satisfaction to be received must be immediate, but for adults it is possible to have a long range goal as the objective. Also, what is considered desirable in one social or cultural environment is not universal. These differences must be realized when preparing educational material. There must be an encouragement to apply that information which is already known as well as instilling a desire to accept further improvements. It is only as objectives are attainable that potential modification of health habits becomes realistic.

Because the effects of dental disease are insidious in nature, there must be created a strong motivational incentive for a response. This very fact complicates educational effectiveness. When results impinge upon the actions of others, there is always a greater possibility for a break in the chain of action. However, when results are not dependent upon individual initiative, there is usually a more immediate possibility for change. To overcome this problem, which definitely is apparent in dental health education, more attention must be devoted to the area of motivation.

A study conducted by the American Dental Association Bureau of Economic Research and Statistics revealed that dental health, to some degree, is of concern to most people, but there are many facets which preclude the proportionate increased interest in dental health care. It was indicated definitely that, to be effective, dental health education must consider the population as being heterogeneous and not homogeneous in structure. Frequently, this fact is ignored and all is approached from a universal concept rather than adapting situationally to existing circumstances. There must be an awareness that each social group possesses its own mannerisms and unique form of attitudes which affect perception and ultimate acceptance of dental health care. Therefore, dental health educators should devote more attention to understanding the significance of both psychological and sociological aspects encountered in modifying established behavioral patterns.

It is a well-established fact that people in the higher income bracket believe that dental care is an integral part of daily life. When the social scale becomes lower, a gradual decline appears in the relative importance accorded to dental care. Although social class is determined to an extent by monetary income, there also are other factors to be evaluated. In essence, "Social class is a concept used by social scientists in helping to explain a variety of differences in behavior, thought and feelings among people. It does not account for his behavior attitudes. Instead, it characterizes a style of life, a body of values and for that matter, a type of personality organization which in large measure determines how a person views himself and the world in which he participates." [2]

To be cognizant of these variations, it is essential that the most differentiating characteristics of each social group be known. In this study by the American Dental Association Bureau of Economic Research and Statistics, it was revealed that the upper middle class envision themselves as being rational thinkers and influenced only by authoritative sources. These people are interested in scientific progress and especially in how it affects their lives. The dentist is held in high esteem and regarded as the authority in dental care. Although the lower middle class attempt to emulate the upper middle class standards, there are entirely different motivational factors in operation. In this class, the drive to perform to proper expectations is highly significant. There is a compulsion to function according to an established or predetermined goal. Again, the dentist is considered to be an authority extremely valuable in maintaining good dental care. Much more motivational exertion must be placed on the upper lower class since they lack a desire for conformity and interest in long range planning. Primarily, they are more self indulgent and permissive in their actions. This general attitude of indifference naturally pervades areas of health concern. There is a resoluteness of accepting whatever occurs. Although these existing attitudes are frequently detrimental, they are pertinent and can not be ignored. The segment of the population known as the lower lower class are the most resistant in applying recognized health habits. As a class, there is much concern for the gratification of present desires with little or any thought for the future. Irrespective of the social level involved, the one common factor prevailing throughout the study indicated a concern for dental health; although the extent of interest varied. From this investigative study, there is definite data of significance for the dental health educator.

Since the health educator works with both individuals and groups, there must be a concern for the responsiveness of each. In considering this facet of education, an attempt should be made to motivate the individual to accept better health practices as well as desiring to provide an improved community environment.

Dental Health Education—Its Necessity

There is no question that the general public has a major need for dental health education. Surveys reveal that less than half of the population will visit the dentist annually. It has been stated that "By the time the average child reaches school age he has 3 carious teeth and 1/5 of these are permanent teeth. At age 12 or 13 the average child has 5 permanent teeth attacked by caries, at 16 six decayed teeth and 18- to 23-year-olds entering the armed forces have 7 decayed teeth in addition to 2.4 missing teeth. One-fifth of 6-year-olds and 3/4 of 18-year-olds have malocclusion, based on a study of 119,000 students. Varying estimates indicate that gingivitis affects about 1/5 of 6-year-olds, 3/5 of 12-year-olds and 4/5 of the groups entering into service."[11] From these statistics, it is quite evident that the dental health problem is extensive and complex. Practically every segment of the population is afflicted with some form of dental deformity.

Dental disease is a problem which can be traced back to antiquity, but it must be concluded that little improvement has been shown when one considers that at least 95 per cent of the total population is presently affected by dental caries. However, only approximately 40 per cent of the entire population obtains dental care. This statement is highly significant because dental problems cannot be solved except by professional services. If this service is not utilized, the problem will become cumulative and will expand to unbelievable magnitude.

Although the prevalence of dental disease is most extensive, the concern of the public about the problem does not rank high according to a health acceptance scale. Evidently, current knowledge is not adequately influencing public opinion regarding this tremendous problem. One reason for the apparent disinterest is the lack of emotional impact which frequently is associated with other crippling diseases. Indifference will have to be dispelled through a more effective educational approach. Perhaps, dental health education has not been used extensively enough. Dr. Bruno Gebhard has stated: "If present knowledge of how dental health can be improved were disseminated, the amount of present dental ills could be reduced by one third. And this could be done by prevention of disease, which must be ranked above cure of disease."[4]

Dental need is far greater than dental demand. Attitudes toward dental care are most instrumental in influencing the demand for treatment or the practicing of good dental health habits. Psychology has proven that attitudes are formed early in life, and that educators must present accurate information to the population as early as possible. This makes it particularly essential that school age children have an opportunity of learning about good health practices. However, it is also imperative that adults have a means of securing accurate health information. It is through guidance that children are encouraged to maintain proper health habits. This principle of reinforcement has been known for centuries; it was Aristotle who wrote, over 2000 years ago: "If you would persuade human beings to act as you wish, you must implant motives that lead to consequent free action. And you must do it again, again and again."[14]

It must be recognized that health attitudes and behavior of people reflect the culture in which they live, and that children in turn imitate the patterns of adults. Modification of such attitudes and behavior depends on more than just knowledge. For change to occur, there is the requirement of a felt appreciation to observe the practice. Education has assisted the public in learning the importance of dental health.

Health Education—Definitions

Health education is the translation of what is known about health into desirable individual and community behavior patterns by means of the educational process.[6]

Health education is the sum of experiences which favorably influence practices, attitudes, and knowledge relating to health.[11]

Health education is concerned with the provision of learning experiences for the purpose of influencing knowledge, attitudes and behavior relating to individual and group health.[7]

Health education can be functionally defined as the process whereby we develop situations in which people can apply what is known scientifically about restoration to health or prevention of disease.[15]

Health education is the media which provides a stimulus for improving existing health conditions.

Fundamental Educational Principles

For any form of instruction to be meaningful, basic educational concepts must be employed. The primary concern of health education teaching is to influence existing attitudes and alter behavior patterns. Certain psychological factors prevail which must be acknowledged if any progress is to be attained. To stimulate action, an element of incentive must be present. Since health promotion is provided through health teaching, it is essential that the basic principles affecting learning be observed. These principles are valuable whether working with an individual patient or speaking before a group. The psychology of teaching health either as an informal discussion or as a formal lecture requires an understanding of the principles of learning.

Educators concur that the following principles should be involved in the teaching process if learning is to be effective.

1. Teaching is most effective when the desire to learn is present.
2. Teaching is most effective when possible attainable goals are presented.
3. Teaching is most effective when individual differences are recognized.
4. Teaching is most effective when participation is feasible.
5. Teaching is most effective when realistic needs are recognized.
6. Teaching is most effective when a positive approach is presented.
7. Teaching is most effective when the information is presented commensurate to the proper age level.
8. Teaching is most effective when the environmental factor is considered.

The following diagram by Dr. Marjorie Young is vividly descriptive in explaining the complexities of the educational process. Two distinct factions are involved; that of the educator and that of the learner must be considered. The desired goals of the educator for the learner are difficult to achieve because the learner also has preconceived goals. The learner is confronted by situational factors that influence the acceptance of the educator's information and which directly affect the learner's decisions. Study of this intricate diagram is most beneficial in comprehending the essentials of the educative process.

A Conceptual Model of the Educational Process as Related to Dental Health[17]

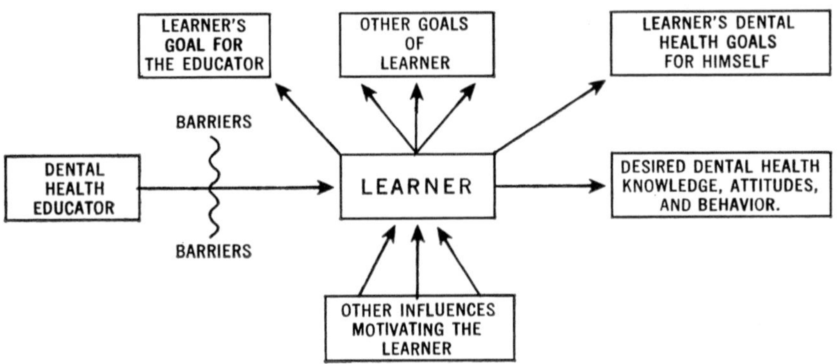

Health Education—Laws of Learning[16]

1. Learning is most effective when the learner is ready for it. If an individual feels a need, or has developed an interest, then he wants to learn a response.
2. A response once made is not fixed. It comes through the continuous process of responding, reacting and adjusting. Satisfaction of some sort must accompany a response if the habit is to be formed and maintained.
3. Repetition of certain elements of training is necessary, and for this reason the gradation of the program in such a way as to provide a fresh approach and new material at each grade level is particularly important.
4. Law of transfer is also important as this law emphasizes the effectiveness of transferring to real situations those patterns of conduct discussed in the classroom as desirable.
5. Specificity is a principle of learning that requires the interpretation of abstract ideas into pictorial patterns that can be understood by young children. As educators we must know that youngsters do not generalize or associate ideas in the manner of adults.

Characteristics of Children

Those who would work with children should be familiar with some of the typical traits which prevail at various stages of development. The knowledge of these common characteristics of children at different chronological ages would be most valuable in the preparation of any teaching material. There are definite standard basic needs of all children which should be acknowledged when instructing them. These needs encompass the desire for affection, security, belonging, achieving, sharing, and the freedom from fear.

Through investigative research, educators have found the following to be characteristic stages of children's emotional, physical and mental development.[3]

Kindergarten children:

1. cease to be completely dependent upon parents
2. activities involve use of large muscles
   a. use large crayons and large pieces of paper
3. have not developed eye or finger muscles ready for reading or writing
4. enjoy hearing favorite stories repeated over and over
5. like much dramatic pretending
6. love to share their experiences with classmates
7. are rapidly expanding their circle of acquaintances
8. play vigorously and actively both in and out of doors

First Graders:

1. find it difficult to control motions voluntarily
2. have better developed large muscles than small muscles
3. are beginning to show improvement in motor skills
4. hold a pencil with difficulty, but enjoy manuscript printing
5. are not ready to do much close work, for their eyes are still immature in size and shape
6. are at the question asking age and WHY is a favorite word
7. learn best from direct experience
8. are in definite need of affection, praise, understanding and encouragement

Second Graders:

1. are losing deciduous teeth and getting permanent teeth
2. can pay attention to any given task for a longer period of time
3. are evidencing improvement in small muscle development
4. are beginning to be safety conscious
5. have expanded their interest to the immediate community
6. have developed attitudes about right and wrong
7. like to gain the approval of adults
8. show rapid improvement in the ability to read and write

Third Graders:

1. enjoy strenuous group games but are not ready to take part in highly organized team play
2. can handle a pencil easily
   a. cursive writing is a new experience
3. have developed the ability to make decisions and judgments from known facts
4. can do work requiring greater manual and visual skills since eyes, hands, and small muscles have become sufficiently mature
5. have grown beyond their immediate community and are intensely interested in how other areas of the world live
6. can assume responsibility for completing many tasks independently
7. extensively use the word HOW
8. have developed an awareness of proper behavior and good manners

Fourth Graders:

1. are able to remain at a task for a longer period of time since their attention span is increasing
2. are anxious to be independent and self-directing
3. enjoy competitive games involving a larger number of friends
4. display greater skill and speed in their activities
5. have acquired a broader interest and perspective of the community
6. are especially sensitive to the criticisms of adults
7. require numerous nonsedentary activities since their skeletal muscles are growing rapidly
8. prefer to associate with members of their respective sex

Fifth Graders:

1. are interested in participating in student group activities
2. have a good sense of rhythm and muscle coordination
3. are capable of outlining academic material
4. receive instruction in fractions
5. have learned how to locate, evaluate and organize information obtained from reference sources
6. enjoy performing simple experiments
7. have matured sufficiently to be approached through appeal and reasoning
8. develop an awareness and respect for the privileges and responsibilities of citizenship

Sixth Graders:

1. often show strong antagonism between boys and girls
2. are now able to read and grasp the main thought as well as specific details contained in a lesson
3. use scientific methods in performing experiments
4. become aware of the value of cooperative community efforts
5. indicate a willingness to accept responsibilities
6. have gained skill in note taking
7. are interested in independent academic research
8. have perfected to a limited degree small muscle coordination

The Dental Hygienist—An Educator

The concept of the dental hygienist's role in the school dental health program is changing. Although it is not considered desirable for a health specialist to perform routine classroom teaching, it still is important to be familiar with teaching procedures to be effective in the program. The most valuable function of the dental hygienist is that of an educator. The dental hygienist can be most effective in the promotion of health education in either private practice or public health. Therefore, knowledge of current health education trends, psychology, social sciences and instructional techniques are of vital concern.

Today, greater emphasis is being placed on the instructional phase of many school dental health programs. This necessitates the dental hygienist to be well prepared to function as an expert resource person for classroom teachers and community organizations. The Council on Dental Health of the American Dental Association recorded the following statement during the January 1954 Conference on Dental Health Education. "The educators agree that dental hygienists as resource people are invaluable in planning and carrying out a dental health program. In the classroom, they should always act as auxiliary to the teacher never in place of her." Very few states have any specific policy or statute defining function of dental hygienists in the schools.

The dental hygienist should be responsible for developing in-service programs for teachers, becoming acquainted with the total school health program, aiding the selection of appropriate teaching materials, suggesting possible resources, participating in program planning, officiating as liaison between school and community and coordinating the dental health program with parent consultations when indicated. It is quite obvious that the role of the dental hygienist is imperative if dental health education is to be effective, but it also should be remembered that the specialist supplements the activities of the regular classroom teacher.

The dental hygienist in private practice, also, has responsibilities in dental health education. These are discharged individually at the dental office as well as by participating in special community programs. The hygienist in private practice has the special opportunity and obligation of educating adult patients who would not otherwise receive dental health information. This particular segment of the population is otherwise seldom available for instruction. Adults do obtain some dental health information from public mass media such as newspapers, television and radio, but there is the hazard of inaccurate information being disseminated. Also, it has been shown that personal influence is much more beneficial in stimulating action. Consequently, individual adult dental health education by the dental hygienist is essential.

Educating the adult not only affects that individual, but also influences others such as the family or the community at large. The statement of Dr. Thomas Parron illuminates this important idea, "Every adult is the hub of the concentric circles of home, work place and community. His and his family's livelihood and comfort, often life, itself, depends on whether he realizes the hazards which confront him in each of these spheres of activity."[13] Adults, non-parents as well as parents, are influential as they control the destinies of communities by determining the health standards that will prevail. Opportunities for educating adults exist either through individual contacts or through organized groups. However, the majority will be by individual contact as only 40 per cent, or a minority, of adults belong to any organization. Therefore, educating the private patient is imperative. Dental hygienists should be cognizant of the unique opportunity in this type of instruction.

Formal Teaching Approaches

Although it has been established that the dental hygienist is required to do only a minimum of actual teaching, it is essential that the various teaching methods be known. With this available information, the hygienist can provide better consultive services to the classroom teacher. There are three recognized methods of instruction which are primarily utilized. Those methods are direct, correlated and integrated teaching. Each has merit. There is no single all inclusive approach.

Since learning is not isolated, the more diversified the presentation the better is the possibility of retention. That which is effective in one instance may need reinforcement at another time. When many experiences are provided, then the student will have an opportunity to adapt the information to the fullest. There is increasing emphasis on incorporating health as a total part of the school program.

The Astoria Study of 1942 conducted by Dr. Dorothy Nyswander disclosed the importance for the planning of well-organized school health curriculums. This study made recommendations that have had extensive repercussions in the area of health education. The team approach was stressed with the classroom teacher being designated the best qualified to work directly with the students; however, cooperation with other members of the school health team were necessary for the teacher to be most effective.

Direct Teaching

The direct teaching method is considered traditional because it has been used to the greatest extent. With this method, a special time is set aside for presenting health information. Although this approach is not looked upon too favorably for the lower elementary grades, it is considered desirable for both the junior and the senior high school level. This form of teaching is particularly effective if the problem-solving technique is utilized. For the elementary age group, teaching the principles of physiology as they apply to healthful living is recommended. In direct health teaching, the subject matter is comprised specifically of health topics.

Correlated Teaching

The correlation pattern of teaching is centered on a particular subject such as biology, social sciences or natural sciences. The discussion of dental health would be studied in relation to an allied or associated course. There would not be a separate health course *per se*, but health would become a part of these other curriculum subjects. Correlation can be easily implemented through the process of a reciprocal arrangement of health with other traditional subject areas. However, the instances used must be realistic and not artificially contrived or the desired results are not obtained. This approach relates health to other subject areas within the established curriculum.

Integrated Teaching

The integrated teaching method utilizes unit areas as the foundation. There is a designated theme or core about which all subjects revolve. Dental health would be just one of several topics that would comprise the total unit being developed. Although this approach has some merit, experience has disclosed that a firmly structured course is frequently more reliable. Principally, this pattern is best adapted to the elementary grades.

Whatever technique is employed, there should be pre-planning to avoid unnecessary repetition in the various grade levels. Thoroughly organizing material with a systematic class presentation will enhance any dental health education endeavor. Within recent years, there has been an extension of health education into the regular school curriculum. This definitely has been beneficial for the promotion of dental health education.

Sample Lesson Plan Outline

I. Statement of topic
II. Listing of aims or objectives
III. Presentation of sub areas
IV. Indication of resource materials
V. Suggestions for audience participation
VI. Conclusions
VII. Evaluation

Criteria For Evaluating A Lesson Plan

1. Definite aim for the lesson
2. Interesting approach
3. Topic discussion based on previous learnings
4. Subject matter on the level of the audience
5. Effective use of teaching aids
6. Lesson length well timed
7. Methods of approach varied
8. Arrange for audience participation

Communication

Adequate communication is vital if teaching and learning are to be effective. To facilitate the educational process, the utilization of audio-visual aids has become extremely popular during the past few years. Therefore, those associated with dental health education should be familiar with this media. Such materials are effective when used in individual patient chairside instruction or when used in group presentations. For any teaching to be effective, there must be a mutual exchange of ideas or thoughts. The use of audio-visual aids can stimulate this process. Since the purpose of communication is to convey a message to another person, various techniques are indicated in transmitting thoughts.

Research has disclosed that learning definitely is facilitated with the utilization of a variety of teaching materials. As with all teaching experiences, audio-visual materials should represent realistic, not fantastic situations. There should be a pertinent relationship between the supplemental material being used and the lesson objective. Frequently, audio-visual aids stimulate learning by creating interest or maintaining interest. Through the incorporation of this form of teaching, there is an opportunity to offer vicariously those experiences which would not otherwise be possible. However, it always should be remembered that audio-visual materials support but do not supplant the teacher.

It is a well founded premise that the use of a variety of teaching techniques is desirable. Investigative studies indicate the following:[8]

Method of Instruction	*Recall Three Hours Later*	*Recall Three Days Later*
1. Telling when used alone	70%	10%
2. Showing when used alone	72%	20%
3. When a blend of telling and showing is used	85%	65%

From this illustration, it is obvious that the spoken word alone is not retained well, but that the use of visual materials produces better results. However, the combination of the spoken word with visual aids provides the best learning atmosphere.

Audio-visual materials have different degrees of acceptance, and this should be considered when they are being selected. The abstract forms are more appropriate for adults, and the direct forms have greater appeal and understanding for children. Dr. Edgar Dale's classification of audio-visual aids explains this principle. His "Cone of Experience" provides a descriptive and concise presentation in the appropriate utilization of audio-visual materials. It will be noted that the form of experience corresponds with the different level at which learning takes place. The proper application of audio-visual aids facilitates communication and, therefore, the following concepts should be observed.[5]

1. Direct experiences 2. Contrived experiences 3. Dramatic participation	involve *Doing* in order of decreasing directness
4. Demonstrations 5. Field trips 6. Exhibits 7. Motion pictures 8. Radio, recordings, still pictures	involve *Observing* in order of decreasing directness
9. Visual symbols 10. Verbal symbols	involve *Symbolizing* in order of increasing abstractness

Summary

This chapter has been developed with the objective of presenting some of the basic principles involved in any form of teaching. Those working in either a formal teaching situation or those teaching in an informal manner should be cognizant of what transpires in the communication of ideas. There, also, has been an attempt to indicate the decided need for emphasizing dental health education as the significant responsibility of all who are associated with the dental profession. Because several topics relating to the area of dental health have been presented, it has not been feasible to develop extensively any one of these subjects.

Dental health education is a relatively new concept when viewed from public acceptance and general professional promotion. It still is developing in the substance of its subject matter, and the professional dental health educator must maintain a current status with the subject matter. In addition, the professional in the field of dental health must be aware of the most effective teaching methods at they exist in other fields and as they are developed and modified within dental hygiene. In substance, concept, and method, dental health education continues to present a formidable professional challenge.

BIBLIOGRAPHY

1. American Dental Association: A Dental Health Program for Schools, 1954, p. 8.
2. American Dental Association: Bureau of Economic Research and Statistics, A Motivational Study of Dental Care, J.A.D.A., *56,* 567, April, 1958.
3. Eibling, Harold: 1956–67 Annual Report of the Superintendent, Columbus Ohio Public Schools, pp. 3–20.
4. Gebhard, Bruno: The Need for Dental Health Education, J.A.D.A., *57,* 784, December, 1958.
5. Grout, Ruth E.: *Health Teaching in Schools,* 3rd. ed., Philadelphia, W. B. Saunders Co., 1958, p. 110.
6. Grout, Ruth E.: *Health Teaching in Schools,* 4th ed., Philadelphia, W. B. Saunders Co., 1963, p. 2.
7. Irwin, Leslie W., Humphrey, James H., Johnson, Warren R.: *Methods and Materials in School Health Education,* St. Louis, C. V. Mosby Co., 1956, p. 153.
8. Jacques, Roger P.: Workshop on Visual Aids, J.A.D.H.A., *33,* 188, October, 1959.
9. Joint Committee on Health Problems in Education: *Health Education,* Charles C. Wilson, ed., 4th ed., Washington, D. C., National Education Association of the United States, 1951, p. 3.
10. Ibid p. 4.
11. Mathewson, Richard L.: Preventive Dental Health in the School, J. School Health, *31,* 262, October, 1961.

12. Oberteuffer, Delbert: An Educator looks at the Dental Health Programs in Schools, J.A.D.A., *60,* 9, January, 1960.
13. Parran, Thomas: Why Adult Education (A Symposium) For Self-Realization-Health Education, Adult Ed. Bull., *6,* 178, August, 1942.
14. Sandell, Perry J.: Effective Methods in Dental Health Education, Dent. Clin. North America, March, 1961, pp. 205–214.
15. Tumelty, Robert E.: A Course in Dental Health Education, J. School Health, *32,* 150, April, 1962.
16. Turner, C. E.: *School Health and Health Education,* 2nd ed., St. Louis, C. V. Mosby Co., 1953, p. 138.
17. Young, Marjorie A. C.: Dental Health Education—Whither? J.A.D.A., *66,* 823, June, 1963.

11

Public Health

Elizabeth M. Warner

THE TERM "public health" has many connotations and implications and it is difficult to describe it either briefly or concisely. Numerous authors have written definitions of public health and each has tried to convey an impression which he felt was especially important to an understanding of the concept of public health. In some instances, the scientific aspects of public health have been stressed; in others, an attempt has been made to define the philosophy of public health, and some authors have felt that the social characteristics of public health best described the term.

One of the most frequently quoted definitions of public health was written by C. E. A. Winslow. He describes public health as "the art and science of preventing disease, prolonging life and promoting physical health and efficiency through organized community effort."[17]

CHARACTERISTICS OF PUBLIC HEALTH PRACTICE

Concern with the group, rather than the individual, is the most important characteristic which distinguishes public health from private practice. In many instances, the technics utilized by the dental public health worker are the same as those used by the private practitioner; it is only the method of application which differs. For example, the technic for applying sodium fluoride topically to children's teeth is the same whether the treatment is provided in a private dental office or in a community public health program. However, while the dentist or dental hygienist in private practice treats one child at a time, public health dental personnel utilize a procedure which makes it possible to treat a group of children simultaneously.

The group, rather than the individual approach, also is significant in public health in terms of securing health services. Although it is customary for the individual to assume responsibility for his own health by obtaining services from a private practitioner, some health services are impossible or difficult for people to obtain through individual effort alone. Fluoridation of the community water supply is an example of such a health service. Only through the cooperation of many different groups of people, can all the children in the community receive the benefits of fluoridation.

This example could be duplicated many times in other community health projects, such as safe water supply systems, sewage disposal plants and vector control programs. Any health problem which can be solved or alleviated more effectively through group endeavor than through individual effort becomes the concern of public health programs.

DENTAL PUBLIC HEALTH PROGRAMS

In describing the activities which comprise dental public health programs, three basic subject areas usually are named: education, prevention and care.

Education includes all those activities which help people develop an appreciation for dental health and an understanding of the steps which are necessary for them to take in order to maintain healthy mouths. Some of the educational technics and tools utilized in dental health education are talks, conferences, workshops, pamphlets, posters, exhibits, films and demonstrations. In most instances, the educational activities of dental public health workers are directed toward groups of people such as school children, mothers, teachers, and almost any other citizen group with an interest in dental health. Some of the most effective dental health education is done by the dental hygienist in chairside discussions with patients, and this opportunity to improve the dental health of the public never should be overlooked.

The preventive aspects of dental health have gained an important place in public health programs with the discovery of the relationship between fluorides and dental health. Fluoridation of community water supplies and topical application of fluorides to children's teeth are the primary preventive measures in dental public health. However, any preventive technic which can be adapted to group methods is a potential public health procedure. Restriction of carbohydrates in the diet to reduce dental caries, for example, might be practiced on a public health basis through school lunch program supervision and elimination of candy sales in schools.

The third component of the dental public health program is dental care. Such service generally is provided to two population groups: (1) those people who are unable, for economic reasons, to assume responsibility for securing dental care; (2) those people living in isolated areas not served by dental practitioners, chronically ill and handicapped persons and others who for special reasons cannot receive dental care through conventional community resources.

There are a number of ways in which dental care may be provided in public health programs. In some instances, dentists and dental hygienists, employed by the health department, provide services in clinics installed in health departments or schools. Local dentists also may make contracts with the health department to provide care, either in clinics or in their own offices. Especially in isolated areas, trailers equipped as dental offices, or portable equipment, are transported to the area so that dental care may be provided for the citizens of the community.

When dental care is a part of the public health program, the amount of service which can be provided is limited by funds and personnel to provide this care. Consistent with the public health philosophy of doing the most good for the most people, priority in care programs usually is given to young children whose mouths can be restored to a healthy state with less expenditure of time and effort than generally is required to rehabilitate the mouths of adults.

THE ROLE OF THE DENTAL HYGIENIST IN PUBLIC HEALTH

There are numerous ways in which dental hygienists can supplement the work of dentists in public health programs. The Committee on Professional Education of the American Public Health Association presented the following summary of the functions of public health dental hygienists:

"The dental hygienist contributes to the public health program by augmenting the services of the dentist in surveys, preventive practices, dental health education and program administration. In accordance with the administrative policies and programs of the agency involved, the dental hygienist working in the field of public health, under the supervision of a licensed dentist, performs one or more of the following functions:

1. Provides dental prophylaxis and other oral hygiene measures, including instruction in home care of the mouth.
2. Applies caries preventive measures such as topical application of fluorides.
3. Demonstrates new dental preventive methods and procedures to other dental hygienists and allied health workers.
4. Participates as a dental health advisor in community health activities, such as well-child conferences, expectant parent classes, pre-natal conferences, and readiness-for-school programs.

5. Assists in community dental surveys, including the examinations, recording, analysis, and interpretation of the data to the community.
6. Assists a community in planning, organizing and conducting a dental health program suitable to the needs and resources of the area.
7. Assists in planning and conducting pre-service and in-service training programs in dental health for:
   a. other public health personnel.
   b. school personnel.
   c. civic groups interested in dental health.
8. Assists in planning and conducting dental public health activities and field experiences for student dental hygienists and student nurses.
9. Assists in planning and conducting school dental health programs by:
   a. Serving as a resource person in dental health to teachers, administrators, and other school personnel.
   b. Performing dental examinations on school children, establishing referral and follow-through systems for dental care.
   c. Maintaining records on the dental status of school children.
   d. Providing dental prophylaxis and topical fluoride treatments for school children on either demonstration or service basis.
   e. Evaluating, developing, and making available effective dental health educational material to interested persons.
10. Assists voluntary health agencies, civic groups, and dental or allied professional groups in carrying out special dental health activities.[2]

Public health dental hygienists are employed for service in public health programs of federal, state, county, and city health agencies. They also are utilized extensively in school health programs. During the past thirty years, the number of dental hygienists working in the public health field has increased steadily. According to data collected in a national survey of dental hygienists in 1960, approximately 900 dental hygienists were employed in official and voluntary health agencies at governmental levels ranging from federal to local.[8] With the increased demand for good dental health among the general population, the expansion of public health programs throughout the country, the greater acceptance by public health dentists of auxiliary personnel, and the growing competence of dental hygienists in the public health field, the potential opportunities for hygienists to serve in this field are exceptional.

Public Health Responsibilities of Dental Hygienists in Private Practice

Dental hygienists in private practice make a sizable and important contribution to the dental health of the public through their role in the maintenance of the oral health of their patients. However, as a member of a health profession, each dental hygienist has responsibilities toward improving the dental health of the community which extend beyond the obligations she has to individual private patients whom she serves. Active participation of dental hygienists in dental health programs staged in the community and cooperation with and support of health department personnel in measures designed to improve dental health are essential to successful public health programs. Community service, especially in the field of health, is a rewarding experience which is the privilege, as well as the responsibility, of every professionally trained dental hygienist.

Public health dentists rely on local dentists and dental hygienists to assist them with numerous aspects of the dental public health program. Participation in dental surveys is one way in which dental hygienists in private practice can serve in public health programs in their communities. This activity will be discussed, in detail, in the following section of this chapter. It is an experience which every dental hygienist is likely to have at some time in her career, regardless of the field of practice chosen.

THE DENTAL SURVEY

Just as the dentist examines the patient's mouth to determine the state of oral health, so the public health dentist examines the teeth of a group of people to determine the extent and nature of the dental health problem in the community. This examination of a large group of people is called a survey.

Four types of dental examinations and inspections are used in making dental surveys:

1. Complete examination, using mouth mirror and explorer, adequate illumination, thorough roentgenographic survey; when indicated, percussion, pulp vitality tests, transillumination, study models, and laboratory tests.
2. Limited examination, using mouth mirror and explorer, adequate illumination, posterior bite-wing roentgenograms; when indicated, periapical roentgenograms.
3. Inspection, using mouth mirror and explorer, adequate illumination.
4. Screening, using tongue depressor, available illumination.

The third type of examination is the one most commonly used in community dental public health programs and is the type to which reference will be made throughout this discussion. Usually, this examination is concerned only with the general status of a particular tooth, such as decayed, filled, or missing, and does not identify the condition of each surface of the tooth.

The survey serves three important purposes in dental public health: it provides information about the occurrence and characteristics of dental disease; it identifies the dental problem in a particular area so that appropriate procedures may be planned for its solution; and it provides data which can be used to evaluate the effectiveness of selected dental program procedures.

The survey in which the dental hygienist engaged in private practice is most likely to participate is the dental survey designed to identify the extent and nature of the dental problem in the community. Usually this survey will be concerned with the dental caries problem, especially among the children in the community. Since schools are the most likely places to find large groups of children, the community schools usually are the sites for dental surveys.

Preparing for the Survey

In most instances, it is not necessary to examine the teeth of all children in the community in order to get the desired information. Only a percentage of the children, referred to as a "sample," need be inspected. The first step in the survey is to select the sample of children which will represent the average characteristics of all children in the community. Since many factors influence sample size and selection, it is wise to seek the assistance of public health statisticians in this phase of the survey.

Many different groups of people may be involved in the community dental survey. The examiners, dentists and dental hygienists are the basic personnel. In addition, volunteer workers will be needed to maintain a steady flow of children into the examining clinic, to record the data collected by the examiners, and to sterilize instruments and maintain neatness and orderliness in the clinic. Parent-teacher groups usually will supply such volunteer workers; they need only a minimum of instruction in order to operate effectively on the survey team. School administrators and teachers should be brought into the survey planning discussions at an early date; their cooperation is essential to efficient examination schedules and adequate clinic quarters.

The equipment needed for the dental survey is not complicated and much of it is available in any community. Each examiner will require approximately 20 mouth mirrors and 20 explorers, cold sterilization facilities, a portable dental chair or a dental headrest, a suitable light, handwashing facilities (running water or a solution such as Zephiran chloride in a wash basin), paper towels for drying hands, and cloth towels for instruments. Adequate tables will need to be provided in the clinic for the examination and sterilization equipment. A desk for the recorder's use and chairs for the convenience of waiting children also will be needed.

Before the survey teams are ready to begin the examinations, all examiners should meet to standardize procedures. For example, it should be agreed upon at the outset of the survey, that a tooth which has a filling in place but shows evidence of additional caries experience is counted as a decayed tooth and not recorded at all as a filled tooth. It also is important for the examiners to establish uniformity in their diagnostic interpretations. In order to accomplish this objective, a small group of children is examined successively by each examiner. Individual findings then are compared and discussed until agreement in diagnosis is reached. This procedure is called "calibration" and it is basic to accurate survey results.

Collecting and Recording the Data

Data collected in dental surveys are recorded on many different types of forms. The form illustrated in Figure 11–1 frequently is used in surveys conducted in schools. In general, data on children of only one age group are recorded on each sheet so that summarization of the data will be simplified.

Under the heading, Permanent Teeth, three different dental conditions are recorded: decayed teeth (represented by the capital letter D); missing teeth (represented by the capital letter M); and filled teeth (represented by the capital letter F). The M component is broken down further into the categories Me (permanent teeth which have been extracted) and Mi (permanent teeth in which decay is so extensive that they are indicated for extraction); a particular tooth is considered missing and noted in one of the "M" columns if either condition is present. The numbers of Me and Mi teeth in each child's mouth are added and the sum is recorded in the column marked Total (Me + Mi = Total M). The numbers in the D, M total and F columns then are added and the sum is recorded in the column headed DMF (D + M + F = DMF).

Similar conditions are denoted in the deciduous dentition by the small case letters, d (decayed deciduous teeth), e (deciduous teeth indicated for extraction), and f (deciduous teeth which have been filled). In the case of deciduous teeth, def denotes the sum of the number of d, e, and f teeth found in a particular child's mouth (d + e + f = def).

Dental Inspection Form

School: *Garfield*									Date: *12/10/55*				Age of Children: *9 Years*
City: *Middletown*									Examiner: *McCarthy*				
Name	Sex	Grade	Permanent Teeth						Deciduous Teeth				Remarks
			D	M			F	DMF	d	e	f	def	
				Me	Mi	Tot.							
A. Ross	*F*	*3*	*7*		*1*	*1*		*8*	*5*			*5*	
K. McCullough	*M*	*3*	*5*		*1*	*1*		*6*	*3*	*4*		*7*	
A. Tolleson	*F*	*3*							*1*		*6*	*7*	
L. Whobrey	*M*	*3*	*3*					*3*	*1*		*6*	*7*	
L. Shiveley	*M*	*3*	*3*					*3*	*5*	*1*	*2*	*8*	
K. Auxier	*M*	*3*							*3*		*5*	*8*	
G. Anderson	*M*	*3*	*5*				*1*	*6*	*4*		*4*	*8*	
J. Klar	*F*	*3*	*3*				*3*	*6*	*2*		*6*	*8*	
T. Fulcher	*F*	*3*	*2*				*2*	*4*	*3*		*4*	*7*	
S. Dolby	*F*	*3*	*2*					*2*	*3*			*3*	
S. Smith	*F*	*3*	*1*					*1*	*3*			*3*	
C. Haugen	*F*	*3*	*5*		*2*	*2*	*2*	*9*			*1*	*1*	
R. Brooks	*M*	*3*	*5*	*1*		*1*		*6*	*2*		*2*	*4*	
J. Johnson	*F*	*3*	*4*	*1*	*1*	*2*		*6*	*4*	*1*		*5*	
TOTALS	Number of Children	*14*	*45*	*2*	*5*	*7*	*8*	*60*	*39*	*6*	*36*	*81*	

FIG. 11–1. Dental inspection form used in community dental survey.

As the examiner inspects each child's mouth, he reports his findings to a volunteer worker who records them on the dental inspection form. The examiner first counts the total number of decayed permanent teeth, then the total number of missing permanent teeth and the number indicated for extraction, then the number of filled permanent teeth. The procedure is repeated for the deciduous teeth. It usually is convenient for the recorder to make the simple computations such as Total M, DMF, and def for each child directly upon completion of the examination.

The summary figures DMF and def provide a numerical picture of the dental health status of the individual. The DMF count and the def count tell how many permanent teeth and how many deciduous teeth, respectively, have been attacked by dental caries. If the components, D, M, F and d, e, f are considered, individually, it is possible to tell how many teeth need dental attention, how many have been lost or should be extracted due to lack of treatment and how many teeth have been filled.

Utilization of the Data

In the same way that the individual's dental status can be determined from a DMF count of his teeth, so the dental status of the community can be described by compiling such data for the total group. For example, the sum of the DMF teeth, divided by the number of children examined, equals the average number of DMF teeth per child or the DMF rate for the group.

$$\frac{\text{Sum of DMF counts for all children examined}}{\text{Number of children examined}} = \text{DMF rate (average number of DMF teeth per child)}$$

The def rate is obtained in the same way, using data collected from examinations of deciduous teeth. It is important to mention here that data for permanent teeth (DMF) and data for deciduous teeth (def) never are considered together, even if they are observed simultaneously in a single mouth. DMF counts cannot be added to def counts because they are not like quantities and their sum does not represent a significant number.

Also, the numbers of DMF teeth for children of different ages never are added for the purpose of computing an average DMF rate for the group. Since the number of DMF teeth rises with age in the average child, it can be seen, readily, that to add the individual DMF counts of a group of children, ages six to sixteen, for example, would result in a DMF count which would be too high for the average six-year-old child, too low for the average sixteen-year-old, and proportionately deceptive for all other ages between those limits. The DMF rate for a group of children has meaning only in terms of one specific age group.

Many other aspects of the community's dental health problem can be described with these same data. For example, the average number of decayed permanent teeth per child (D rate), the average number of missing permanent teeth per child (M rate), and the average number of filled permanent teeth per child (F rate) can be computed with the following formulas:

$$\text{D rate} = \frac{\text{total number of D teeth}}{\text{number of children examined}}$$

$$\text{M rate} = \frac{\text{total number of M teeth}}{\text{number of children examined}}$$

$$\text{F rate} = \frac{\text{total number of F teeth}}{\text{number of children examined}}$$

The percentage of the total caries attack rate (DMF) which each component (D, M, and F) comprises, provides objective information about the amount of dental care needed by the children in the community, the number of teeth which have been lost due to a lack of dental care and the amount of dental care which has been received.

$$\text{\% of decayed permanent teeth} = \frac{\text{D rate for the group}}{\text{DMF rate for the group}}$$

$$\text{\% of missing permanent teeth} = \frac{\text{M rate for the group}}{\text{DMF rate for the group}}$$

$$\text{\% of filled permanent teeth} = \frac{\text{F rate for the group}}{\text{DMF rate for the group}}$$

If the DMF rate for a particular group of eleven-year-old children is 6 and the F rate for that same group is 3, then 50 per cent of the permanent teeth with caries experience have been filled. If the M rate for the group is 1, and the D rate is 2, it is apparent that approximately 17 per cent of the permanent teeth among the group of eleven-year-old children already have been lost or need to be extracted and 33 per cent of the filling needs in the group have not been met.

The data collected in the community survey also describe the situation at the outset of the program and, as such, they are referred to as base line data. Procurement of base line data is essential to program evaluation and thus to effective program operation. As the program proceeds, surveys similar to the initial one are conducted and the collected data are compared with the base line data to measure the effectiveness of program procedures. A striking example of such utilization of data is the evaluations which have been made of the

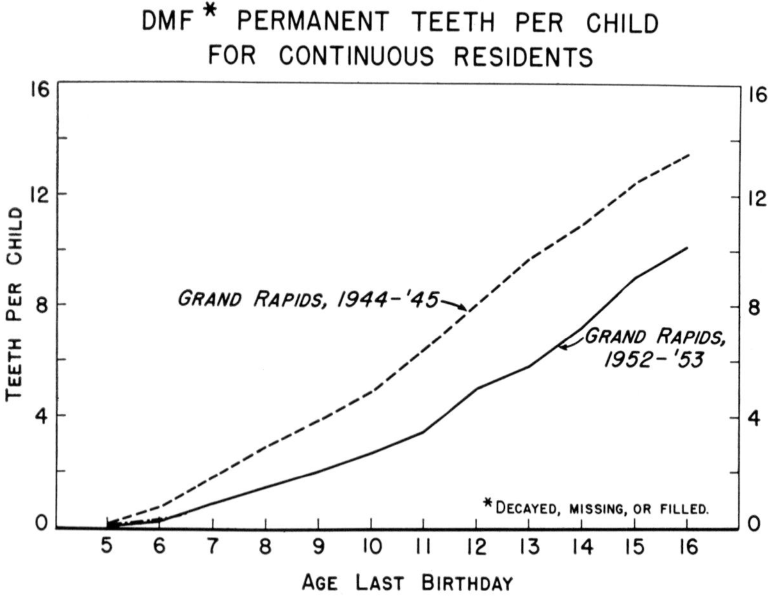

FIG. 11–2. Comparison of DMF rates, Grand Rapids, 1944–45, 1952–53.

effect of fluoridation of the Grand Rapids, Michigan, water supply on the incidence of dental caries among the children in that city (Fig. 11–2).

In addition to the data on the dental health status of the community, the survey designed for program planning purposes will include a review of such characteristics of the community as the dentist/population ratio, clinical facilities available in the community, potential services available for community dental health activities from health and civic organizations, and many other things commonly referred to as community resources. An estimation of these resources is important in planning for the most effective procedures which a community can institute in order to improve its dental health.

MEASUREMENTS OF OTHER DENTAL DISEASES AND CONDITIONS

In the discussion of the dental survey, a system was described for measuring, quantitatively, dental caries experience in population groups. Such a system or method for expressing the relative severity of a disease or condition in a population group, in terms of a numerical value, is known as an index. The indexes most widely used in dental public health programs are measures of dental caries experience, such as the DMF index. However, systems for measuring the occurrence of other types of dental diseases and conditions also have been developed and are in use today.

Several of these indexes will be described, briefly, as an indication of the numerous efforts of researchers to measure the extent and degree of such phenomena as dental fluorosis, malocclusion, and periodontal disease in population groups. Of particular interest to dental hygienists is an index for assessing oral hygiene status in individuals and groups. The bases and methodology of this index will be discussed, in detail, in the following section of this chapter.

Dental Fluorosis Index

An index of dental fluorosis, originated by Dean,[4] has been of significant value in studies of fluorosis (mottled enamel) in population groups living in communities with varying amounts of fluorides in their water supplies. This index is based on a classification of dental fluorosis with numerical weights assigned in relation to various degrees of severity: normal—0, questionable—0.5, very mild—1, mild—2, moderate—3, and severe—4. Each individual examined is classified on the basis of the severest form of dental fluorosis observed in two or more teeth. The individual scores then are added and divided by the number of individuals examined to secure the community fluorosis index. To insure reliability, surveys of dental fluorosis must be conducted by investigators thoroughly familiar with the characteristic signs of fluorosis as distinguished from other enamel opacities.

Malocclusion Indexes

Several indexes have been developed for estimating malocclusion in population groups. The HLD index (handicapping labio-lingual deviations), originated by Draker,[5] is based upon the extent to which the malocclusion constitutes a handicap and consequently requires treatment. To measure factors causing disfigurement, weighted values are assigned to conditions ranging from the extremes of cleft palate and severe traumatic deviations to the more common occlusal defects represented by overjet, overbite, mandibular protrusion, open bite, ectopic eruption, and anterior crowding. The occurrence of cleft palate is such a serious problem that it automatically is designated a handicap. Conditions of less severity are scored according to the extent of deviation from normal, as measured with a Boley gauge. With this system, an individual might be classified as orally handicapped because of a single serious defect or because of a series of lesser defects which, in combination, constitute a handicap.

Another system for measuring malocclusion in population groups is the Malalignment Index developed by Van Kirk and Pennell.[16] This index is based on measurements of the extent of departure of each tooth from its ideal position in the arch. Both rotation and displacement of teeth from their ideal positions are observed.

A small, plastic, gauge-like tool, resembling a ruler, is placed over the teeth and departures from the norm, as indicated on the gauge, are scored and recorded. The Malalignment Index is the sum of the scores recorded in the examination. The index for the group is the average of the indexes of all individuals examined.

These malocclusion indexes are not intended to serve as diagnostic tools nor do they produce data useful for orthodontic treatment planning. Their primary usefulness is in group study and dental public health program planning.

Indexes of Periodontal Disease

Indexes for the assessment of periodontal disease in population groups are based on signs of the disease in the various aspects of the periodontium. Gingivitis, gingival pocket formation, and alveolar bone loss are several of the signs of periodontal disease which, either singly or in combination, form the bases for indexes of periodontal disease.

The P-M-A index,[11,12] developed by Massler and Schour, is a measure of the severity of gingivitis in population groups. Observations are made of the condition of three components of the gingiva: the interdental papilla (P), the marginal gingiva on the labial aspect of the tooth (M), and the attached gingiva under the papillary and marginal gingiva (A). Inflammation is characterized by changes in the color, contour, consistency and texture of the surface of the gingiva and the degree of inflammation is scored as mild—1, moderate—2, or severe—3.

In general, the interdental papilla is the first site affected by inflammatory changes; as the inflammation becomes more severe, the gingivitis tends to spread into adjacent components of the gingiva. Consequently, in surveys of large population groups, it has been found that a simple count of the number of gingival components affected by inflammation, without regard to degree, provides as reliable an index of the severity of gingivitis in the group as the total computed from scoring each affected gingival component on the basis of the degree of inflammation present. For example, a P-M-A score of 10-0-0 (for a total score of 10) indicates that ten gingival papillae are affected, mildly, since neither the marginal or attached gingivae are involved; a P-M-A score of 10-5-0 (for a total score of 15) indicates that ten papillae are mildly inflamed and five are sufficiently involved to spread into the marginal gingivae.

The P-M-A is the best known of the periodontal indexes and has been used extensively as described here as well as in various modified forms.[3,18]

Russell's Periodontal Index (PI)[13] is designed to measure more advanced stages of periodontal disease than the P-M-A index. The effects of periodontal disease on the supporting tissues of the teeth are estimated and scored according to a progressive scale in which relatively little weight is assigned to gingival inflammation and relatively great weight to bone destruction.

Using a mouth mirror and explorer, with adequate light, the supporting tissues of each tooth are examined. If there is no overt inflammation present in the gingiva and no loss of function in the tooth due to destruction of the supporting tissues, a tooth is considered to be negative and assigned a score of zero. Two stages of simple gingivitis are recognized: mild gingivitis, characterized by an overt area of inflammation in the gingiva but not circumscribing the tooth, is assigned a score of 1; gingivitis, characterized by inflammation completely circumscribing the tooth, but without an apparent break in the epithelial attachment, is assigned a score of 2. The presence of a periodontal pocket is assigned a score of 6 and advanced destruction with loss of masticatory function as a score of 8, which is the highest on the scale. (If this index is used in clinical studies, where radiographs are readily available, it sometimes is possible to observe bone resorption before a periodontal pocket has appeared. An intermediate score of 4, not ordinarily used in the field studies, may be assigned to such cases.)

An individual's PI score is the arithmetic average of the scores for the teeth in his mouth. The group PI score is the average of the individual scores for all the persons in the group.

The P-M-A index and the PI are only two of several systems which have been proposed for the study of periodontal disease in population groups. These particular indexes were selected for discussion because they deal with phenomena of periodontal disease familiar to every practicing dental hygienist.

ORAL HYGIENE INDEX

The Oral Hygiene Index, commonly called the OHI, was developed and first reported by Greene and Vermillion in 1960.[6] It is a system for assessing debris and calculus, quantitatively, in a more objective manner than the designations of "good," "fair," and "poor" which frequently have been used to evaluate the oral hygiene status of individuals and groups. In public health this index has been used, in conjunction with other indexes, in studies of periodontal disease. For the dental hygienist engaged either in private practice or a school health or public health program, it can have practical value as a reliable measure of changes in oral hygiene status, particularly as related to the efficiency of toothbrushing.

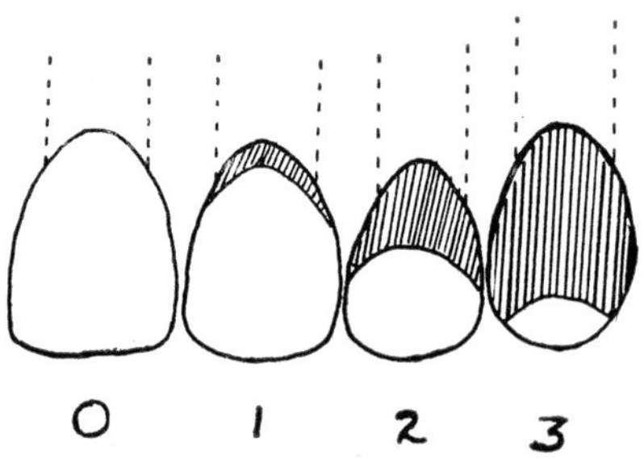

FIG. 11–3. Criteria for scoring oral debris and diagram showing varying amounts of oral debris with corresponding scores. (Greene and Vermillion.[6])

0. No debris or stain present. 1. Soft debris covering not more than one third of the tooth surface, or the presence of extrinsic stains without other debris regardless of surface area covered. 2. Soft debris covering more than one third, but not more than two thirds, of the exposed tooth surface. 3. Soft debris covering more than two thirds of the exposed tooth surface.

Criteria for Classification of Debris and Calculus

Oral debris is defined as the soft deposit on the surfaces of the teeth, consisting of mucin, bacteria and food, usually greyish white in color but sometimes tinged with green or orange. The criteria and corresponding scores for oral debris are outlined and depicted in Figure 11–3.

Dental calculus is defined as a deposit of inorganic salts, primarily calcium carbonate and phosphate, mixed with food debris, bacteria and desquamated epithelial cells. Both supragingival and subgingival calculus are included in this definition. The criteria and corresponding scores for dental calculus are outlined and depicted in Figure 11–4.

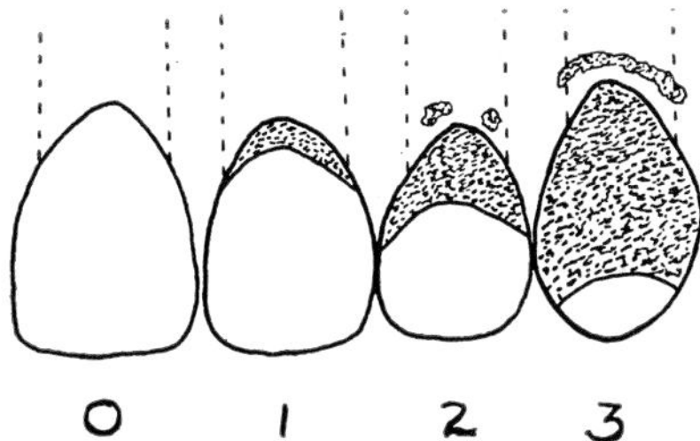

FIG. 11–4. Criteria for scoring dental calculus and diagram showing varying amounts of dental calculus with corresponding scores. (Greene and Vermillion.[6])

0. No calculus present. 1. Supragingival calculus covering not more than one third of the exposed tooth surface. 2. Supragingival calculus covering more than one third but not more than two thirds of the exposed tooth surface or the presence of individual flecks or subgingival calculus around the cervical portion of the tooth or both. 3. Supragingival calculus covering more than two thirds of the exposed tooth surface or a continuous heavy band of subgingival calculus around the cervical portion of the tooth or both.

Since the scores are based on the fraction of tooth surface covered, only fully erupted permanent teeth are scored. To apply the same scoring system to permanent and deciduous teeth, with their clinical crowns of different heights, or to fully erupted and partially erupted permanent teeth, would result in distortion of individual and composite scores. For this reason, third molars also are excluded from the scoring procedure.

Wherever there are one or more permanent teeth present in a segment, scores for both the buccal and the lingual surfaces of that segment are recorded.

Method for Scoring Debris and Calculus

A total of twelve scores, representing a buccal surface and a lingual surface of each of six segments of the mouth, are recorded, first for the amount of debris and then for the amount of calculus present. The areas designated on the chart in Figure 11–5 comprise the twelve areas in which observations are made. The inspection of the several areas of the mouth should proceed in the order in which they are numbered on this chart.

In each area, that tooth surface having the greatest surface area covered by debris is used as the basis for the score for that entire area. Taking into account the frequently observed difference in oral hygiene status between buccal and lingual surfaces of the same tooth or groups

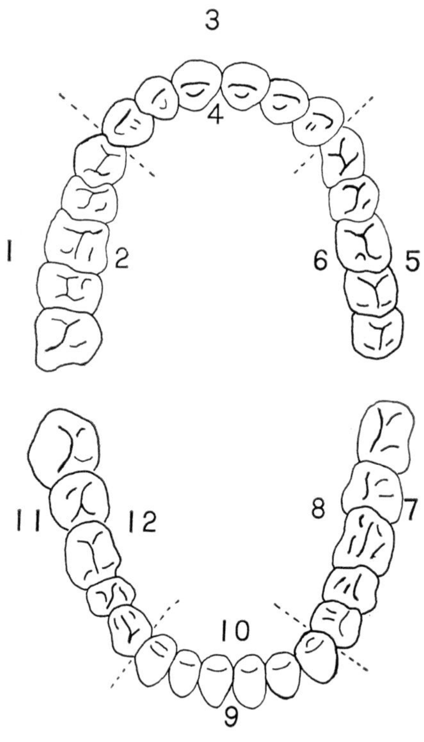

Fig. 11–5. Chart of mouth showing areas included and order of procedure in OHI examination.

of teeth, the debris scores for the buccal surface and the lingual surface of a particular segment of the mouth may be taken from different teeth.

A No. 5 (Shepard's Crook) explorer is used to estimate the amount of tooth surface covered by debris. By running the side of this instrument along the buccal and lingual surfaces of the teeth, the extent of the debris may be noted as it is removed from the tooth surface. Calculus is detected by visual examination and by probing with the same No. 5 (Shepard's Crook) explorer used to estimate the extent of debris. Only definite deposit of hard calculus should be considered in determining calculus scores. As in the case of debris scoring, the tooth surface having the greatest accumulation of calculus determines the score for the area. Again, the buccal score for a particular segment may be recorded from a different tooth than the lingual score for that same segment of the mouth, and only fully erupted, permanent teeth are scored.

Scores for the amount of debris and calculus observed may be recorded on a form similar to the one in Figure 11–6. Note that each score box is divided, by a diagonal line, into two sections: one for the buccal and one for the lingual surfaces of each designated segment of the dental arches. Such information as name, age, sex, date of examination, frequency of toothbrushing and other data pertinent to the particular survey may be added to this basic form.

Debris

	Right	Ant.	Left	Totals
Upper	(B) 3 / 1 (L)	2 / 2	3 / 1	8 / 4
Lower	2 / 2	1 / 1	1 / 2	4 / 5
Totals	5 / 3	3 / 3	4 / 3	12 / 9

Debris Index 21/6=3.5

Calculus

	Right	Ant.	Left	Totals
Upper	(B) 1 / 0 (L)	0 / 0	1 / 0	2 / 0
Lower	0 / 1	0 / 2	0 / 2	0 / 5
Totals	1 / 1	0 / 2	1 / 2	2 / 5

Calculus Index 7/6=1.2

Oral Hygiene Index 3.5+1.2=4.7

FIG. 11–6. Form for recording debris and calculus scores. (Greene and Vermillion.[6])

Computing the Indexes

When there are permanent teeth present in all six segments of the mouth, there will be 12 scores for debris and 12 scores for calculus. The absence of permanent teeth in one or more of the segments would result in a corresponding reduction in the number of debris and calculus scores. Consequently, the possible number of scores for debris or calculus varies from 0 to 12.

Since the individual scores are scaled from 0 to 3, there is a possible range of 0 to 36 in the total score for each debris examination and for each calculus examination.

The Debris Index is determined by adding the debris scores recorded (both buccal and lingual scores for each segment scored) and dividing the total by the number of segments scored. Recalling that the total of the scores may range from 0 to 36 and the number of segments from 0 to 6, the minimum value for the Debris Index would be 0 and the maximum value would be 6.

The procedure described for determining the Debris Index also is used to compute the Calculus Index. The combination of these two indexes comprises the Oral Hygiene Index (Debris Index + Calculus Index = Oral Hygiene Index).

The relative weight of the debris and calculus scores in the Oral Hygiene Index are significantly related to the population and age groups from which the data are gathered. For example, significantly greater values would be expected in the calculus scores for adults than for children. Therefore, the Oral Hygiene Index always should be reported together with the component indexes from which it is derived.

The Oral Hygiene Index for a group is computed by adding the indexes for all the individuals in the group and dividing that sum by the number of persons in the group.

The Simplified Oral Hygiene Index

In numerous trials, by many investigators, the OHI was found to be a reliable method for assessing oral hygiene status, but a somewhat more time consuming procedure than could be used efficiently when dealing with large population groups. Subsequently, the originators of the OHI developed a modified form of the index called the Simplified Oral Hygiene Index (OHI-S).[7]

The simplified index is based on observations of fewer areas of the mouth than are scored in the OHI. Consequently, less time is required to complete individual examinations and surveys of large groups of persons can proceed more rapidly when the OHI-S is utilized.

In large population groups, reliable oral hygiene data may be obtained through use of the simplified index. On an individual basis, however, the OHI is a more sensitive method for assessing oral hygiene. It seems likely that the dental hygienist engaged in private practice will find more use for the original OHI than the OHI-S in securing detailed information about oral cleanliness among patients.

EMERGING PROBLEMS OF PUBLIC HEALTH CONCERN

An important function of public health agencies is to envision future health needs and serve as a pacesetter in working out solutions to emerging health problems in the population. An early example of this role was the involvement of health departments in the development of diagnostic and treatment services for children born with oral clefts. Teams of specialists, skilled in the several problems relating to speech, appearance, and a functioning dentition for the child with an oral cleft, now are providing treatment through crippled children's service programs in all the states.

Consideration for the dental needs of other special groups within the population, previously ignored, has been promoted through public health efforts. Children with handicapping conditions of both mind and body often lacked adequate dental care simply because their handicaps prevented them from receiving dental treatment in the traditional way. Specially equipped dental clinics, in which mentally retarded and cerebral-palsied children can be treated under general anesthesia or with methods for stabilizing them during treatment, have been established in several communities through the efforts of both official and voluntary health agencies. Dentists have been urged to become familiar with these specialized facilities and to promote their development and use in their own communities. The encouraging expansion of facilities and the growing interest in dental care for children with many types of handicaps portends a future in which dental treatment programs for all handicapped children will be as well developed as today's programs for children with oral clefts.

The growing numbers of chronically ill and aged in our society have created a population group of such proportions that its special problems, including those related to dental health, cannot be ignored. Essentially, the problems of providing dental care for this group are similar to those encountered in treating handicapped children. The dental treatment needs of the chronically ill and aged are not unique; it is the management of these patients, including the specialized equipment and facilities required, that complicates providing dental service to them.

Public health agencies have been among the first to mobilize community resources to help meet the dental health needs of the chronically ill and aged. Their efforts have been directed toward fact-finding surveys, experimental studies, demonstration projects, and in-service training programs. Interest has spread to dental societies and other professionally involved groups, as evidenced by workshops and conferences organized and attended by representatives of both public health agencies and organized dentistry.

Providing dental treatment for chronically ill and aged persons who are home-bound has been hampered by the lack of suitable equipment which could be transported to and operated in private homes or nursing home facilities. One of the significant outcomes of experimental and demonstration projects in this field has been the development of portable dental equipment.[15] The requirements of such equipment were identified through experience in these projects and demand for suitable equipment stimulated manufacturers to produce it. In many communities, portable dental equipment is now available for the use of dentists through loan services sponsored by health departments or dental societies.

In surveys of chronically ill and aged persons, the need for prophylactic care and improved oral hygiene has been a universal finding. The implications which this has for the potential contributions of dental hygienists to dental care programs for the chronically ill and aged are expressed well in a report of the Utica Workshop on Geriatric Dentistry. "The number one problem in order of priority appears to be oral hygiene. To remedy this is not a complicated or expensive operation. The potential role of the dental hygienist looms large in this picture."[9]

Relatively minor departures from the traditional mode of operation are required from the dental hygienist in order to provide prophylactic care to home-bound patients. Much of the specialized equipment which the dentist requires to provide treatment services outside his office is not essential for the dental hygienist in the performance of satisfactory prophylactic treatment. If necessary, the entire prophylaxis can be performed with hand instruments. An adequate operating light and a stable, portable headrest, both of which are available, are the primary items of specialized equipment required.

In addition to the direct clinical service which the dental hygienist can provide for the chronically ill and aged, her role in improving these patient's daily oral hygiene care also can be significant. This objective cannot always be accomplished simply by instructing the patient in proper oral hygiene procedures. Frequently these patients are limited in activities, particularly manual skills, by the crippling effects of chronic illnesses or the diminishing motor capabilities of old age. In some instances, patients with disabilities which prevent them from manipulating conventional toothbrushes, can learn to use toothbrushes which have been specially adapted to compensate for their handicaps.

Reports of a dental care program for the chronically ill and aged, conducted in the Kansas City area, describe some of the common disabilities affecting patients' hands and arms and the specially designed toothbrushes which were developed to compensate for these infirmities.[10,14]

Examples cited are: a toothbrush with an elongated handle for the patient who cannot raise his hand to his mouth, a toothbrush with an enlarged handle for the patient whose arthritic hands will not close to grasp a conventional toothbrush handle, or a small hand brush with suction cups screwed to the back for firm attachment to a sink or other flat surface so the patient with the use of only one arm can clean his own denture by moving it briskly across the stabilized brush.

Even with specially designed aids, patients who are totally incapable of self-care will not be able to maintain oral cleanliness for themselves. Either nursing home attendants or family members must be taught and encouraged to perform oral hygiene procedures for them.

Nursing home attendants obviously are key people in the maintenance of oral hygiene among patients. Some patients will be completely dependent upon aides for daily oral hygiene care. All patients' oral hygiene care will be affected, to some degree, by the environment and facilities which the nursing home provides for such care. Impressing nursing home attendants with the importance of a clean mouth to patients' well-being, comfort, and morale, and helping them establish routines for including mouth care in the daily schedule of patient care are important objectives of the dental hygienist's educational program. Instructing attendants in bedside oral hygiene care not only improves their skill in carrying out prescribed procedures, but also extends the influence of the dental hygienist's educational efforts to many more patients than she could reach individually.

There is growing concern, on both health and legislative fronts, for the needs of senior citizens in our society. Health care legislation to benefit this group has been a recurring issue in the Congress for more than a decade. Programs conducted by public health agencies have focused widespread attention on the needs of the chronically ill and aged and projects like the Kansas City dental care program have provided models for other communities to follow. Experience gained in this project demonstrated the contributions which many community groups and agencies make to the solution of complex problems of financing, facilities, and services associated with providing dental care to the chronically ill and aged. In the development of community dental care programs for the chronically ill and aged, as in numerous other projects of public health concern, practicing dentists and dental hygienists will be essential community resources, vital to the programs' success.

BIBLIOGRAPHY

1. American Dental Association, Council on Dental Health: Amer. Dent. A. Tr., *92,* 33, 1951.
2. American Public Health Association, Committee on Professional Education: Educational qualifications of public health dental hygienists. Amer. J. Pub. Health, *46,* 899–905, July, 1956.
3. Cohen, M. M.: The gingiva at puberty. Abstr. J. Dent. Res., *34,* 679, Oct. 1955.
4. Dean, H. T.: The investigation of physiological effects by the epidemiological method. p. 23–31. (In Moulton, F. R., ed. Fluorine and dental health. Washington, Amer. Assoc. Advance. Sci., 1942. 101 pp.)
5. Draker, H. L.: Handicapping labio-lingual deviations: a proposed index for public health purposes. Amer. A. Pub. Health Dent. Bul., *18,* 1–7, Dec. 1958. (Reprinted in Amer. J. Orthodont., *46,* 295–305, Apr. 1960.)
6. Greene, J. C. and Vermillion, J. R.: The oral hygiene index: a method for classifying oral hygiene status. J.A.D.A., *61,* 172–9, Aug. 1960.
7. Greene, J. C., and Vermillion, J. R.: The simplified oral hygiene index. J.A.D.A., *68,* 25–31, Jan. 1964.

8. KESEL, R. G.: Dental practice, pp. 95–238. (p. 198). (In Hollinshead, B. S., dir. The survey of dentistry. Washington, American Council Education, c1961. XXXIV + 603 pp.)
9. LAMAR, HERMAN T. and DRAKER, HARRY L.: The Utica Workshop on Geriatric Dentistry. New York St. Dent. J., *28,* 460–4, Dec. 1962.
10. LAW, F. E.: Dental hygiene for the chronically ill and aged. Amer. Dent. Hygienists' Assoc. J., *37,* 132–4, 3rd Quar. 1963.
11. MASSLER, MAURY, and SCHOUR, ISAAC.: The P-M-A index of gingivitis. J. Dent. Res., *28,* 634, Dec. 1949.
12 MASSLER, MAURY, SCHOUR, ISAAC, and CHOPRA, BALDEV: Occurrence of gingivitis in suburban Chicago school children. J. Periodont., *21,* 146–64, July, 1950.
13. RUSSELL, A. L.: A system of classification and scoring for prevalence surveys of periodontal disease. J. Dent. Res., *35,* 350–9, June, 1956.
14. SHEARY, HELEN C.: The role of the dental hygienist in health care of the chronically ill, handicapped and aged. Amer. Dent. Hygienists' Assoc. J., *37,* 134–40, 3rd Quar. 1963.
15. U.S. DEPT. OF HEALTH, EDUCATION AND WELFARE, PUBLIC HEALTH SERVICE, DIVISION OF DENTAL PUBLIC HEALTH AND RESOURCES: Dental care for the chronically ill and aged, a community experiment. Washington, Government Printing Office, Public Health Service Publication No. 899, 1961, 54 pp.
16. VAN KIRK, L. E. and PENNELL, E. H.: Assessment of malocclusion in population groups. Amer. J. Pub. Health, *49,* 1157–63, Sept. 1959.
17. WINSLOW, C. E. A.: The untilled fields of public health. Mod. Med., *2,* 183–91, Mar. 1920.
18. WOLFE, W. R. JR., and BURRILL, D. Y.: Effect of a penicillin dentifrice on gingivitis. Abstr. J. Dent. Res., *31,* 461, Aug. 1952.

12

History and Organization of Dental Hygiene

Margaret E. Swanson

INTRODUCTION

DENTAL hygiene as a profession provides an opportunity for individuals to serve in an area of health service which is fundamentally preventive in nature. The dental hygienist was formally introduced to the public in the year 1913 as an auxiliary to the dental profession. The intervening years have seen an increase in their status so that now they command national recognition as a profession.

The primary function of the dental hygienist today has not materially changed since the inception of the profession over fifty years ago. They are formally educated at a college level and licensed by law to assist the members of the dental profession in rendering oral health care for the public. They may apply their knowledge and skill in the office of the private practitioner or in formal health educational activities in schools, hospitals, industry and public health programs, either at state or national levels or in the federal services. No matter where they serve, this service must be under the supervision of a licensed dentist. Their service has proven most valuable and important in the field of dental health care.

Even though the basic procedure of operative service has not materially changed since the innovation of this profession, the expansion of the concept of oral health education has materially added to their responsibilities. What the future will hold with respect to further increase in duties can only be a matter of speculation. With the increase in needed dental service for the public, the duties of the dental hygienist may take on added or expanded responsibilities, thus providing for more effective oral health service.

A profession as important as dental hygiene needs a representative organization to support and advance the principles of dental health service. To meet this need, the American Dental Hygienists' Association was organized. This now is the official body responsible to the members of the dental hygiene profession for all facets of the profession and Association.

HISTORICAL BACKGROUND

The idea of dental hygiene is not new. In an editorial which appeared in *The American Journal of Dental Science* as early as 1845, it was stated that "It is much to be regretted, that while dental therapeutics and surgery, as well as mechanical dentistry, are now cultivated in almost every part of the civilized world, with the most commendable and persevering ardor, the hygiene of the teeth is almost wholly neglected."[8] This quotation indicated an early awareness of the need for a preventive rather than a therapeutic approach to dental disease.

In the ensuing years, an increasing number of members of the dental profession came to realize the extreme importance of prophylactic care of the mouth. This concept of prophylactic care as a health measure has become so thoroughly accepted that it is now the basic aim and purpose of dental hygiene service.

One of the earliest advocates of the techniques of prophylaxis was Dr. D. D. Smith of Philadelphia. In 1844 he was so convinced of the necessity of preventive treatment in the "reduction of decay and the general betterment of mouth health" that a prophylactic program was instituted for patients in his own practice. Dr. Alfred C. Fones in his book *Mouth Hygiene* stated "It was the consensus of opinion that Dr. D. D. Smith was truly the father of dental prophylaxis." Dr. Smith's initial offering of a widespread program of preventive care in a private office was the first evidence of the desire on the part of the dental profession to render a more complete service to the patient both from a technical as well as an educational point of view.

In due time, more and more dental practitioners became proponents of Dr. Smith's preventive program by rendering these same services to their own patients. However, it was Dr. M. L. Rhein of New York City who first suggested the use of women, adequately trained and duly licensed, to perform this preventive service. It was found that, while such a regimen of prophylactic care was most beneficial to the maintaining of good oral health, it was also very time-consuming for the dentist. The suggestion of using female personnel for such a preventive program seemed to be the solution to this problem.

In 1906 Dr. Alfred C. Fones, one of Dr. Smith's early followers, undertook the training of his own office assistant, Mrs. Irene Newman, in this preventive service. Through the training of Mrs. Newman, it was demonstrated that by using such auxiliary personnel it was possible to render a vital prophylactic service to patients and simultaneously to conserve operative time for the dentist. In addition, through the services rendered by his hygienist, Dr. Fones was convinced that many dental diseases could be prevented by adhering to his prescribed program of oral cleanliness.

In 1913 in a paper presented before the National Dental Society (the forerunner of the American Dental Association), Dr. Fones stated "the initial purpose of the training of dental hygienists was to show the value of education and preventive treatments when applied to the mouths of school children."[7] Because of the importance of such a training program, Dr. Fones strongly recommended that the training of dental hygienists originate as a formal educational plan. After four years of effort on his part, a grant of $5,000 was appropriated in 1913 by the Board of Education of the City of Bridgeport, Connecticut, for the inauguration of an educational and treatment program within the public schools. In order to have the required personnel to execute this program, it became imperative that some formal plan for educating dental hygienists was necessary.

Therefore, in 1913 Dr. Fones undertook the establishment of the first formal course of instruction for dental hygienists. Lectures were presented and a clinic set up in a building adjacent to his own office at 10 Washington Avenue, Bridgeport, Connecticut. The faculty of this first school consisted of outstanding dental practitioners and teachers from dental and medical schools of eastern universities who were well qualified to present the necessary courses in the basic and allied sciences.

It is of interest to note that the first class of 33 young women included school teachers, trained nurses, experienced dental assistants, and the wives of three practicing dentists. Upon the completion of this initial formal educational course, ten of the graduates were employed by the Board of Education in the City of Bridgeport to carry out the authorized dental health program. This program was established as a five-year endeavor so that individual pupils could be treated and examined periodically and significant statistical findings could be derived. Within this program the dental hygienist gave prophylactic treatments to the children and charted their dental conditions; they gave toothbrush drills and classroom talks; they gave stereoptican lectures to children in the higher grades; and they conducted educational work in the homes by the circulation of special lectures for the parents."[9] This dental hygiene program in the schools of the City of Bridgeport was the first dental hygiene service in the area of dental public health.

DENTAL HYGIENE EDUCATION

The first school for the education of dental hygienists was inaugurated in 1913. Half a century later the existence of 54 schools of dental hygiene is evidence of the growth and development of dental hygiene education.

With the notable success of the initial dental hygiene program in the public school system of Bridgeport, there was an increased demand for educationally qualified dental hygienists for other areas of dental health service to the public. These demands necessitated the offering of two successive courses at the Fones School in 1915 and 1916. It is of interest to note that there were 97 graduates in the three classes from this original school. Because of the increasing interest in this new profession and the passage of licensure laws governing dental hygiene in both New York and Massachusetts, three additional schools were started in those states.

The New York School of Dental Hygiene was organized in 1916 by Dr. Louise C. Ball with a sum of $2,500 secured from the Rockefeller Foundation. This course was started as a summer course by Hunter College, but with the fall session, the course became affiliated with the Vanderbilt Clinic of Columbia University. At a later date, this same course was made a department of the College of Dentistry of Columbia University.[9]

At almost the same time as the founding of this first New York School, an additional school for dental hygienists was organized under the guidance and direction of Dr. Harvey J. Burkhart at the Rochester Dental Dispensary at Rochester, New York. The fourth school for dental hygienists was organized at the Forsyth Dental Dispensary for Children in Boston, Massachusetts, under the direction of Dr. Harold De Witt Cross.

During the ensuing years others in the dental profession, realizing the valuable assistance given by this group of trained auxiliary personnel, urged the establishment of additional dental hygiene schools. Between the years 1913 and 1946, the development of such schools was rather slow. During that period only 14 schools came into existence. However, since 1946 the increase in the number of schools has been rapid. Between 1946 and 1956 the number had increased to 33 and in the next eight years, to 54.

It should be realized that while dental hygiene education has been pursued since 1913, it is only within the past decade and a half that there has been any semblance of similarity in teaching, both as to course content and teaching methods. During the early period the courses within the schools of dental hygiene were established on the basis of requirements of local dental practitioners and licensing boards. Therefore, the school's curricula were composed of a variety of courses with the greater emphasis being placed on those pertaining to the area of private practice. This emphasis on the area of private practice was due to the fact that the dental profession as a whole did not yet recognize or appreciate the merits of utilizing the dental hygienist in other phases of the dental health field.

In 1944, Dr. Charlotte C. Greenhood of California surveyed the course content of dental hygiene schools. This survey revealed a total of 54 different subjects within the curricula, and of these 54 subjects only 5 were found to be common to all schools. Such diversity indicated the need for standardization of the course content as well as the number of hours offered in the individual subjects. In the years immediately following 1944 it was apparent that some standardization had been undertaken, for the total number of offered courses declined from 54 to 20. In addition, the schools also adjusted the clock hours of courses toward a more desirable balance of theory, laboratory, and clinical practice.

Concurrently, in 1944, the American Dental Hygienists' Association established a committee for the "Purpose of Standardizing the Training Requirements of the Dental Hygienist." This committee arranged a conference of dental school deans, the directors of dental hygiene programs, and practicing dentists. This conference showed conclusively that there was a definite need for serious consideration of the entire educational curriculum.

Following two years of joint endeavor with the Secretary of the Council on Dental Education of the American Dental Association, this Committee, in 1946, formulated the "Minimum Standards of a Curriculum for Schools of Dental Hygienists." After approval by the American Dental Hygienists' Association's Board of Trustees and House of Delegates, these "Minimum Standards" were presented to the Council on Dental Education of the American Dental Association. The study by the Council of these "Minimum Standards" resulted in the establishment of the "Requirements for the Accrediting of a School of Dental Hygiene" which were subsequently approved by the House of Delegates of the American Dental Association on August 7, 1947. These same "Requirements" are the basis upon which all programs for the education of dental hygienists must be established. They embody all phases of the educational program and thus form the foundation for standardization.

At present, thought is being given to revising these "Requirements" in order to re-evaluate the role of the dental hygienist in the expanding field of oral health service. Several conferences were held in 1964 and 1965 working toward this revision, and it could be anticipated that within the next decade changes in the curricula will be initiated to make the services of the dental hygienist even more meaningful as an auxiliary to the dental profession.

The Council on Dental Education in its "Requirements" defines a school for dental hygienists as a "non-profit organization affiliated with or conducted by an accredited dental school, or other responsible agency, requiring as a minimum for admission the completion of an accredited four-year college entrance high school course, or the recognized equivalent, and conducting a course for the training of dental hygienists covering two academic years and leading to a certificate."

While graduation from high school still remains the minimum requirement for entrance into an educational program, the majority of schools have raised their individual requirements and now require that the applicant have completed some collegiate work. Clinical operative performance remains at a high level. However, because of increasing demands in other areas of service, it is felt that the added maturity gained from the inclusion of a liberal arts education is desirable and necessary. Most of the educational programs are now so structured that students desiring to obtain a baccalaureate degree in addition to the dental hygiene certificate may do so by meeting the necessary additional collegiate requirements.

By 1957, it became apparent that the reservoir of applicants meeting the basic minimum requirements for entrance to schools of dental hygiene far exceeded the student space available. In an effort to assist the admission officers of the schools in the selection of the best qualified student, the American Dental Hygienists' Association established what is now known as the Dental Hygiene Aptitude Testing Program. This is a battery of tests especially designed for "predicting probable academic success in dental hygiene courses."[11] These tests are given prior to entrance into such schools and although they may not be a requirement for entrance, a majority of schools of dental hygiene now utilize the results of these tests in their determination of the eligibility of applicants.

In order to insure the continuance of the high standards of education which had been established, in 1952 the Council on Dental Education of the American Dental Association undertook an active program of accreditation. The announcement of the program of accreditation was the realization of a goal toward which the American Dental Hygienists' Association had striven for a long time.

The formal accreditation program began in 1952 and periodic visits are made to all schools of dental hygiene to evaluate their curricula.

This evaluation will assure the maintenance of standardized curricula while still allowing the flexibility necessary for a teaching program to meet changing demands. Although basic uniformity is desired within a dental hygiene program, the increasing scope of dental hygiene activity necessitates some variation. The profession of dental hygiene continues to develop, and periodic revision of educational curricula will facilitate adaptation to changing trends.

TABLE 12–1. Dental Hygiene Programs: 1946–1964*

Year	*Students Enrolled*	*Total Graduates*
1946	729	399
1947	720	450
1948	958	455
1949	1091	506
1950	1454	529
1951	1598	575
1952	1705	675
1953	1794	727
1954	1938	774
1955	2009	856
1956	2104	902
1957	2156	945
1958	2131	977
1959	2237	960
1960	2497	992
1961	2752	1023
1962	3005	1219
1963	3276	1257
1964	3390	1429

*Dental Students' Register, Council on Dental Education, American Dental Association. 1950–1964.

DENTAL HYGIENE STUDENT ENROLLMENT

Currently there are 54 dental hygiene schools in the United States. There are 29 schools affiliated with accredited dental schools and 25 schools affiliated with other institutions of higher education.

In the fall of 1963 there were 3276 students enrolled in all dental hygiene schools, and of this figure 51.6 per cent were enrolled in those schools affiliated with dental schools. See Table 12–1 for the increase in the student enrollment.

LICENSURE

Significant evidence of the progress of dental hygiene is reflected in the field of licensure. The practice of dental hygiene in any state is a privilege granted by the state and because it is in the interest of public health and safety, it is subject to regulation and control. The individual state dental practice acts regulate the limits of dental hygiene practice within each state and specify the requirements of eligibility for examination. Following successful completion of such examination, the dental hygiene graduate is licensed to practice within the state where such examination was taken.

The first licensure law was passed by the State of Connecticut in 1916. The following four years saw the inauguration of similar licensure laws in nine additional states. In the following fifteen years the acceptance of the profession was reflected in the adoption of amendments to the dental practice acts, legalizing the practice of dental hygiene in 19 other states, including the District of Columbia. In 1935 a dental hygiene licensure law was adopted by the then Territory of Hawaii and from 1935 to 1951 eighteen additional states adopted licensure laws governing dental hygiene. Since 1950 dental hygiene has become recognized in all remaining states of the United States as well as in the Commonwealth of Puerto Rico. Figure 12–1 shows the progressive establishment of dental hygiene licensure laws over a forty-year period.

Generally, the licensure laws require that the dental hygienist work under the direction and supervision of the dentist. In addition to the usual prophylactic and educational service which all dental hygienists render, many states permit the dental hygienist to perform certain limited operative procedures as defined within the individual state dental hygiene practice act.

NATIONAL BOARD DENTAL HYGIENE EXAMINATION

The National Board Dental Hygiene Examination program was inaugurated in 1962 and is conducted by the Council of National Board of Dental Examiners of the American Dental Association. The purpose of this examination is that of "service to the dental and dental hygiene professions and ultimately to help maintain a high standard of dental care for the public."[2]

As indicated in the section titled LICENSURE, the practice of dental hygiene in all states is subject to the laws of the individual states. Each state licensing board has the responsibility and authority for evaluating the competence and qualification of those candidates

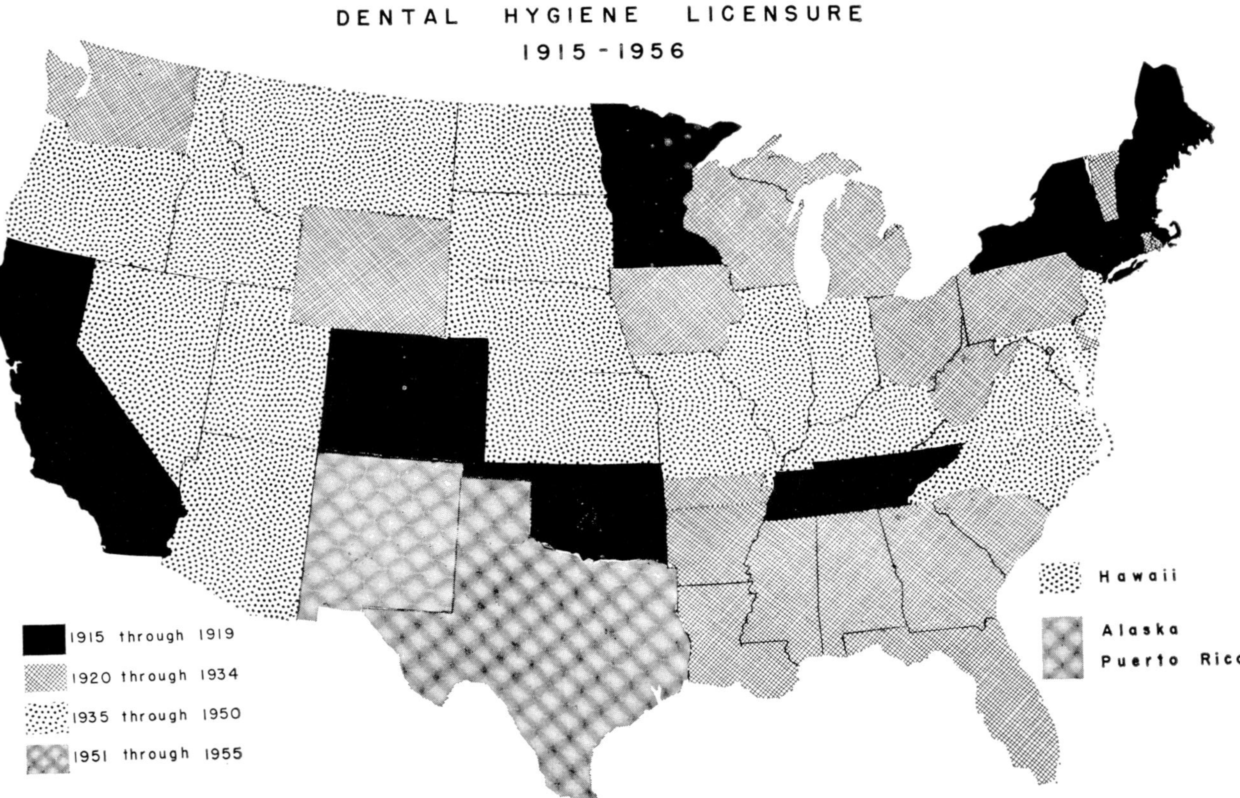

FIG. 12–1. Passage of Dental Licensure Laws. (Courtesy of Marjorie Houston, D.M.D.)

seeking to enter the practice of dental hygiene. To fulfill this responsibility, the licensing boards administer both a clinical examination and a theory examination in which the candidates' knowledge and understanding of the sciences related to dental hygiene are evaluated. It was with a view to assisting in the evaluation of the theory examination that the National Board Dental Hygiene Examination was developed and is currently being conducted.

At present, the following 40 licensing boards recognize this examination in lieu of their own theory examination:

Alabama	Maine	Pennsylvania
Alaska	Maryland	Rhode Island
Arizona	Massachusetts	South Carolina
Colorado	Michigan	South Dakota
Connecticut	Minnesota	Tennessee
District of Columbia	Missouri	Texas
Georgia	Nebraska	Utah
Hawaii	Nevada	Vermont
Idaho	New Hampshire	Virginia
Indiana	New York	Washington
Iowa	North Dakota	West Virginia
Kansas	Ohio	Wisconsin
Kentucky	Oklahoma	
Louisiana	Oregon	

The National Board Examination is divided into four sections, covering the areas of the basic sciences.

Part I—General Anatomy, Dental Anatomy, Physiology
Part II—Histology, Pathology, Roentgenology
Part III—Chemistry, Nutrition, Microbiology
Part IV—Pharmacology, Dental Materials, Preventive Aspects of Dentistry

All sections are developed as objective or multichoice type examinations. It has been demonstrated that this type of examination is more valid for testing purposes than the essay examination, because the latter depends to a great extent on the subjective evaluation by the examiner.

The payment of the initial examination fee provides the candidate with the opportunity of selecting three state boards of examiners to whom the test results are made available. Each additional request requires a further fee payment.

As stated in the policies covering the conduct of the examination, "A dental hygiene student is eligible for examination only when the director or administrator of the dental hygiene school certifies that the student is within four months of graduation. The dental hygiene school must be accredited by the Council on Dental Education of the American Dental Association at the time the application for examination is filed."[2]

"A dental hygienist graduated after 1954 from an accredited dental hygiene school is eligible for examination upon submission of evidence of graduation and ethical conduct. Membership in the American Dental Hygienists' Association at the time the application is filed is adequate evidence of high ethical standards. A non-member must submit evidence of ethical conduct in the form of prescribed letters of recommendation."[2]

A dental hygienist graduated prior to 1951 is no longer eligible for participation in the program as the waiver date for this classification expired in January of 1965.

All examinations are scored on the basis of 100 points, with 75 as a passing score. It is possible for a candidate to be re-examined only in those parts in which the original score was below 75. A candidate may be re-examined twice in any part but should the second re-examination be failed, the candidate will be required to repeat and pass all four parts in order to be eligible for certification.

This National Board Examination has been a most significant step in the progress of dental hygiene education and licensure. This program took several years to develop and was done as a cooperative endeavor by the American Dental Hygienists' Association and the Council of National Board of Dental Examiners of the American Dental Association. While the initial acceptance of this examination by state boards was outstanding, it is to be hoped that in the near future there will be national acceptance by all 50 state licensing boards.

PROFESSIONAL ASSOCIATION

The American Dental Hygienists' Association is the official representative organization of the dental hygiene profession. The history, activities, aims and objectives of this professional organization should be of interest to the student entering the study and practice of dental hygiene. Without the active operation of this organization it is highly probable that many of the advances that have occurred would not have been possible.

The American Dental Hygienists' Association was organized in Cleveland, Ohio on September 12, 1923 by a group of 46 dental hygienists representing 11 states. Actually the basic planning was done three years previously in Boston, Massachusetts, when a meeting of dental hygienists was held to discuss the feasibility of a national organization. No official action was taken on the organizational plans at that time because of the small number of representatives.

In 1922 the dental hygienists of California, under the leadership of Miss Elma Platt, decided that organizational plans should again be considered. In July of the same year Miss Platt appeared before the Board of Trustees of the American Dental Association, then meeting in Los Angeles, and presented a set of resolutions adopted by the California Dental Hygienists' Association. These resolutions requested "the American Dental Association to take steps to promote the organization of an American Dental Hygienists' Association after the plan of organization of the American Dental Association, which shall become closely associated or affiliated with it for the good of humanity."[3]

After considering this request, the Board of Trustees of the American Dental Association recommended to their House of Delegates the adoption of the following resolution "that dental hygienists, dental mechanics, and dental assistants, except associations for profit, be encouraged to establish associations in their respective states, and that they be given conference relations with the American Dental Association, state associations, and subsidiary organizations."[5]

In 1923 Miss Anita Junk, president of the California Dental Hygienists' Association, with Miss Platt as Organization Committee Chairman, began plans for an organizational meeting to be held in Cleveland, Ohio. At a meeting of the Board of Trustees of the American Dental Association held in Cleveland prior to the convention, it was voted that an announcement be made stating that there would be a national organization of dental hygienists proposed at the Cleveland convention. A conference committee was then appointed, with Dr. Anna Hughes as chairman. Other members were Dr. Harris Wilson, director of the Cleveland Mouth Hygiene Association; Dr. Alfred C. Fones, founder of the profession of dental hygiene; Dr. Harold Cross of Massachusetts; Dr. Guy Millberry of California, and President J. P. Buckly and Secretary Otto U. King of the American Dental Association.

The organizational meeting was held on September 12, 1923. This meeting was convened by Dr. W. R. Wright, chairman of the Commission of Mouth Hygiene and Public Instruction of the American Dental Association. Mrs. Hubert Hart of Bridgeport, Connecticut, was appointed temporary chairman and Miss Platt, temporary secretary.

The proposed Constitution and By-laws were provisionally adopted, and the initial officers elected. To those officers, the members of American Dental Hygienists' Association owe their organizational existence. Through their combined endeavors many advantages have been provided for dental hygienists.

From its beginning in 1923, the Association has grown in professional stature. In each succeeding year, new projects were undertaken which brought about the advances necessary for the fulfillment of the aims and objectives of the profession. During the first ten years of the Association, activities were directed toward consolidation of the Association so that it would be acknowledged as the official representative of the profession. Without an official voice, the profession had difficulty in this respect.

The objectives of the Association at that time included "the elevation and sustaining of the professional character and education of dental hygienists, the promotion among them of mutual improvement, the dissemination of knowledge of oral hygiene; and the enlightenment and direction of public opinion in relation to oral hygiene and dental prophylaxis."[5] It was decided in 1927 that the most effective manner in which to accomplish these objectives was to publish a journal to be known as *The Journal of the American Dental Hygienists' Association.* To the *Journal's* first editor, Miss Dorothy Bryant of Maine, and her staff is due all credit for its successful beginning. Credit must also be given to Dr. C. N. Johnson, former editor of the *Journal of the American Dental Association,* for his continuous cooperation during the formative period.

The Association was incorporated under the laws of the State of Michigan in 1927. The American Dental Association had granted the American Dental Hygienists' Association permission to adopt a seal which carried the insignia of the dental profession, and this seal was attached to the Article of Incorporation which is still carried as the official seal of the Association.

Much of the work during this formative period was devoted to the building of a strong foundation through the organization of constituent or state groups. During the years 1923 and 1933, twenty-three constituent associations were organized and formally chartered. The *Constitution and By-laws* of the American Dental Hygienists' Association provided for the election of six trustees to represent the constituent association districts in the official business of the Association.

In the second decade, 1933 and 1943, the Association showed considerable growth both in membership and activity. The substantial increase in number of constituent associations necessitated the amendment of the *By-laws* to increase the number of trustees from six to nine. This move gave a larger governing body and greater recognition to the increased number of constituent associations.

As in all organizational endeavors, *By-laws* cannot become fixed, for with changing trends and circumstances, revisions are constantly required. The upward surge of membership and the formation of additional constituent associations continued in the 1950's. In order to assure proper representation on the governing body of the Association for this increase, the *By-laws* were again amended in 1960 to enlarge the Board of Trustees to twelve district representatives. Today, in 1965, there are 51 constituent associations and 114 component societies. The future for growth of the constituent associations is limited, for only the State of North Dakota remains unorganized; however, the future for component societies is unlimited. In all local areas where there are groups of dental hygienists, serious thought must be given to the formation of societies, as this is one method to insure growth of the professional organization.

As the number of students in the schools of dental hygiene were increasing, it was believed advisable to consider some type of membership for them in order to provide an early indoctrination into the professional organization. In 1938 plans were completed for the establishment of a junior membership. These junior members have the privilege of attending local, state, and national meetings and receiving issues of *The Journal of the American Dental Hygienists' Association.* Today, active chapters for junior members are established in the schools of dental hygiene where professional association activities are carried on. In addition, at the time of the Annual Session of the American Hygienists' Association, a meeting for junior members is held. This activity is under the guidance of the Sub-Committee on Junior Membership and it has become one of the outstanding features of the Annual Session. The students in all chapters are invited to attend this meeting, but since this meeting is held when schools are in session, only selected representatives can be present. Regional meetings for junior chapters have also been inaugurated in various areas of the country. It is anticipated that this movement will expand, and it is hoped that all areas might take advantage of adopting such professional regional meetings.

A further achievement during the second decade was the undertaking of the first survey in the field of dental hygiene. Under the sponsorship of the Education Committee of the Association an extensive survey was made in 1939 covering the duties, salaries, and needs of dental hygienists in the various fields of their performance. The results showed that (1) the majority of dental hygienists were employed in private dental offices; (2) remuneration of school and public health positions averaged higher than private practice; and (3) those surveyed were almost unanimous in stating that their training was lacking in certain subjects. About 40 per cent of the surveyed group were endeavoring to correct this educational deficiency by additional study. *This was true in 1939 when most hygienists had but one year of formal dental hygiene education.*

War intervened during the second decade and many dental hygienists entered various branches of the Armed Forces. A motion was adopted by the House of Delegates in 1940 which provided that the Association contact the Military Affairs Committee of the House of Representatives of the United States asking that dental hygienists be included in a bill then before Congress to commission dietitians and physio-therapy aids. This action was not successful, but because the dental hygienists were convinced that their services were needed, they continued to enter the Armed Forces under civil service status.

This decade brought continued growth of the Association and national recognition. Because of this nation-wide acceptance of dental hygiene as a profession, in 1949, by action of the Board of Trustees of the Association, a central office with a part-time executive secretary was established in Washington, D.C. The existence of a central office not only enhanced the current activities of the Association but made possible the undertaking of additional ones.

By the third decade the Association had grown to such a degree, both in numbers and activities, that it was necessary to employ a full-time executive secretary. Also, because so many of the activities of the Association were correlated with activities of the American Dental Association, the Board of Trustees felt it expedient that the office be transferred to Chicago, Illinois, and this was accomplished in 1958.

Today, all committees of the Association have very active programs which continue to add to the prestige of the profession and the Association. The Committee on Membership and its Sub-Committee on Junior Membership both have active programs for recruitment of members. Manuals have been developed by both to assist constituent and component societies in the development of strong membership programs and for the transition of junior members into active membership. The Committee on Dental Health has prepared several brochures to assist in the development of active dental health programs at both the state and local levels. The dental hygienist, as a member of the health profession should serve actively in community health programs, thus fulfilling her duties as a citizen.

The Committee on Insurance has made available to all members of the Association four programs of group insurance and participation in this area is expanding. The Committee on Aptitude Testing administers and directs the very effective Dental Hygiene Aptitude Testing Program. Special Committees are also functioning in the area of public information and liaison with the Bureau of Dental Health Education of the American Dental Association. In 1965 the Special Committee on Film undertook the production of a sound motion picture depicting the profession of dental hygiene.

Within the past several years, concern has been expressed by many over the need for a complete review and possible re-evaluation of the professional role and responsibility of the dental hygienist as an active member of the dental health team. To assist in the initial re-evaluation, the American Dental Hygienists' Association, through its Committee on Dental Hygiene Education, in cooperation with the Council on Dental Education of the American Dental Association and the American Association of Dental Schools held a profession wide Workshop in 1964. While the results of this Conference do not dictate what their role will be in the future, it nevertheless pointed out some vital areas of dental hygiene that should be considered in the immediate future. Further conferences are being planned by the Committee on Dental Hygiene Education to provide additional study in some of the vital areas being considered toward a revision of the "Requirements" of the Council on Dental Education.

The formal education of the dental hygienist must prepare her for the professional role which is demanded of all those in the health professions. The dental health team of which dental hygienists are members, becomes more important as one realizes that in total health there is no segment that can be neglected. The role of the dental hygienist, under supervision of the dentist, serves to complement his procedures, especially in the area of preventive dentistry but not necessarily limited thereto.

Much work needs to be done in the re-evaluation but with the aid of every member of the profession working in close harmony with the dental profession, we can be confident that the profession of dental hygiene will develop and expand.

STRUCTURE OF THE AMERICAN DENTAL HYGIENISTS' ASSOCIATION[6]

In order that the present and future members of the Association may be better informed concerning their professional Association, a discussion of its structure is important. It is certain that an informed person who becomes a knowledgeable member will be prepared to contribute toward the advancement of the Association.

The objective of the American Dental Hygienists' Association as stated in the *Constitution* should motivate the actions of every member of the Association. The objectives are "to cultivate, promote and sustain the art and science of dental hygiene, to represent and safeguard the common interest of the members of the dental hygiene profession, and to contribute toward the improvement of the health of the public."[3]

The Association, like other professional organizations is regulated by its *Constitution and By-laws* and these serve as the written laws of the Association. Contained within this document can also be found the *Principles of Ethics* which regulate the moral code and personal obligations of each member and are a requisite for membership in the Association.

The mainstay of any organization is its active membership. The progressive thinking and planning of the leaders of the Association, together with the unified efforts of the active membership, have made possible the accomplishments and progress of the Association.

Membership in the American Dental Hygienists' Association is divided into five classifications: (1) active members; (2) life members; (3) affiliate members; (4) junior members; and (5) honorary members.

An active member must be "an ethical dental hygienist who possesses a certificate or degree in dental hygiene granted by a school of dental hygiene accredited by the Council on Dental Education of the American Dental Association, and who is licensed to practice in any one of the states, districts, territories or dependencies of the United States and who is a member in good standing of this Association and a member in good standing of one of its constituent associations and of a component association thereof, if such exists."[3]

Life membership is granted to each president of the American Dental Hygienists' Association at the expiration of her term of office.

Affiliate membership is extended to dental hygienists practicing in any country other than the United States or its possessions.

A junior member is an undergraduate student of a school of dental hygiene accredited or in the process of accreditation by the Council on Dental Education of the American Dental Association who has been recommended by the Dean of the school.

An honorary member is "any individual who has contributed materially to the advancement of the art and science of dental hygiene, and who has been elected by the House of Delegates on the nomination of the Board of Trustees"[3] of the Association.

Within the framework of the Association there are constituent societies or state groups, and these in turn are composed of component, city or district groups. At the present time there are 51 constituent associations and approximately 114 component societies. Active membership in the American Dental Hygienists' Association is predicated on membership in a constituent association, for a member in a constituent association automatically becomes a member of the American Dental Hygienists' Association on payment of appropriate dues.

The American Dental Hygienists' Association has its broad projects on the national level, while the constituent and component groups have their immediate projects on a local level, all of which are in harmony with the projects of the parent organization. In addition there are individual state projects for the advancement of improvement of the professional activities in the local communities.

The American Dental Hygienists' Association was legally incorporated in 1927 under the laws of the State of Michigan as a non-profit organization. This incorporation serves to protect the property of the Association and gives it exclusive right to its name. The Association has also received a ruling from the Internal Revenue Service of the United States as a tax exempt organization by virtue of its structure and function.

While the *Constitution* serves as the mode of organization of the Association, the *By-laws* are an extension of these Articles and establish the organization and administrative pattern of the Association by indicating areas of responsibility for the various facets of the Association, constituent associations, Board of Trustees, officers and committees.

Figure 12–2 represents the organizational pattern of the Association.

The House of Delegates is the supreme authoritative body of the organization. It has all legislative powers and determines the policies which govern the Association in all of its activities and functions. The House of Delegates also has various other duties to perform: it elects the elective officers, it elects the members of the Board of Trustees, and it adopts the annual budget.

The House of Delegates is composed of officially certified delegates elected by each constituent association. Each of the constituent associations has the privilege of representation in the House of Delegates by at least one delegate. In those associations with a membership of more than one hundred, representation is based on one delegate for each additional one hundred members.

The House of Delegates is in official session annually, although special sessions can be called by the President under a specified provision. The Speaker of the House of Delegates, who is elected by that body, serves as the presiding officer; the executive secretary of the Association serves as the secretary.

Since the House of Delegates meets only once each year, and since this body is too large to carry on the day-to-day administration of the Association, a Board of Trustees is established as the "managing body of the Association, vested with full powers to conduct all business of the Association, subject only to the laws of the State of Michigan, the Article of Incorporation, the *Constitution and By-laws* and the mandates of the House of Delegates."[3]

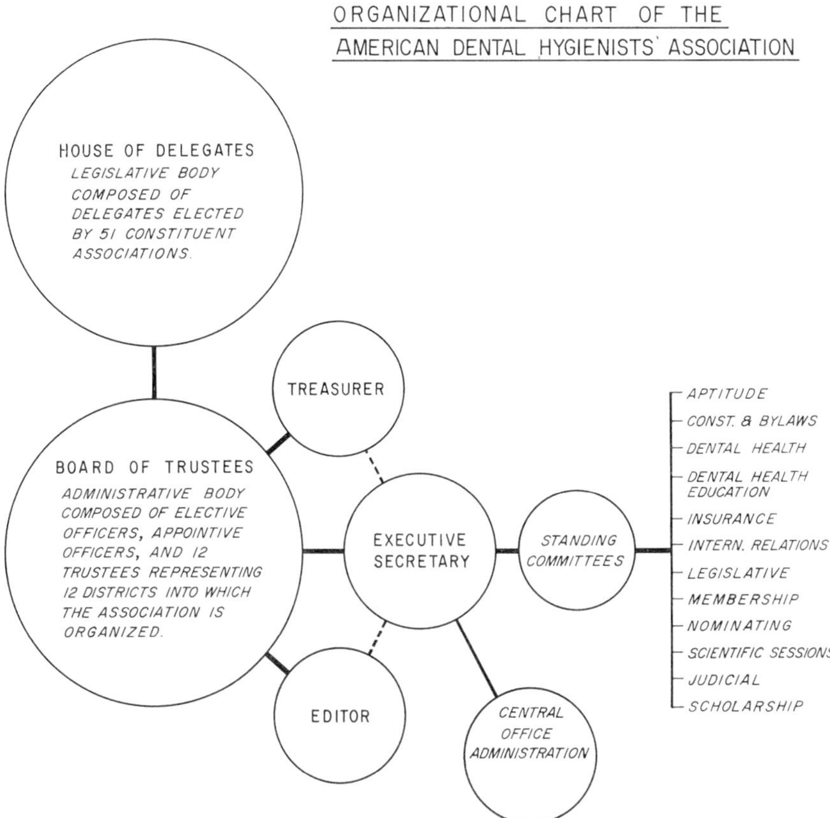

FIG. 12–2. Organizational chart of the American Dental Hygienists' Association.

The Board of Trustees is composed of the elective officers of the Association, with the exception of the Speaker of the House of Delegates, the twelve members elected by the House of Delegates who serve as trustees of the twelve districts into which the Association is divided, and the retiring president. In addition, the appointive officers of the Association are ex-officio members of the Board of Trustees without a right to vote.

The Board of Trustees meets regularly three times a year, but additional meetings may be called when necessary. The president of the Association serves as the presiding officer and the executive secretary of the Association serves as the secretary.

The elective officers of the Association are the president, president-elect, first vice-president, second vice-president, and Speaker of the House of Delegates. These officers are elected by the House of Delegates at each Annual Session and hold offices for one year.

The appointed officers are the executive secretary, treasurer, editor, associate editors, advertising, business and circulation manager of the *Journal* and are appointed by the Board of Trustees. The terms of their appointment and salaries are determined by the Board of Trustees.

The Central Office of the Association is located in Chicago, Illinois and has a full time staff of four individuals. The Central Office is under the general supervision of the Board of Trustees but is directly administered by the executive secretary of the Association.

The major working areas of the Association are the committees which carry on the projects and programs of the Association. As authorized in the *By-laws,* there are currently twelve standing committees: Committee on Aptitude Testing, Committee on Constitution and By-laws, Committee on Dental Health, Committee on Dental Hygiene Education, Committee on Insurance, Committee on International Relations, Judicial Committee, Committee on Legislation, Committee on Membership, Committee on Nominations, Committee on Scholarship and Committee on Scientific Sessions.

Each committee has specific duties and it is their responsibility to keep activities current with the advancing trends of dental hygiene activity that are important to the attainment of the objectives of the Association. Committees of the Association are the policy recommending bodies and they present their recommendations for future activities of the Association to the Board of Trustees and House of Delegates for final adoption.

The official publication of the Association is *The Journal of the American Dental Hygienists' Association.* This was established in 1927 as a monthly publication and continued as such until 1933 when it became a quarterly. The main objective of *The Journal* is to "report, chronicle and evaluate all activities of scientific and profession."[3] The editor of *The Journal* serves as the Editor-In-Chief and she is assisted by two associate editors. The executive secretary of the Association serves as advertising, business and circulation manager.

From time to time, the Association has received sums of money for the purpose of conducting various major programs vital to the profession. In order that the Association might be able to accept these funds, it was necessary to establish an Educational Trust Fund. This Fund was legally executed on February 3, 1957 by the Association and is a fully detached Fund from any other funds of the Association.

The purposes of the Fund are "to advance the art and science of dental hygiene; to promote public welfare through the development of higher standards of practice in the field of dental hygiene; to encourage and engage in professional education and scientific research in dental hygiene and aid in the health education of the public with respect thereto; to conduct and carry on programs of testing students for achievement and prospective students for aptitude to determine their potentials in the field of dental hygiene; to provide financial assistance, at the discretion of the Trustees of the Fund, through scholarships, or otherwise, to needy, worthy and qualified graduate and undergraduate students of dental hygiene. All of these to the extent that the foregoing are exclusively for charitable, scientific, literary or educational purposes."[4] Operating under the terms of the Educational Trust Fund is the scholarship program of the Association. At present, through the Fund, four scholarships in the amount of $800 each are awarded annually. One of these is presented through the American Fund for Dental Education, one from the Weber Dental Manufacturing Company, one from the American Dental Hygienists' Association, and the remaining, the Alfred C. Fones Memorial Scholarship is maintained through contributions from individual members, constituent and component societies and friends. Many of these gifts are contributed as memorials and remembrances to friends and loved ones.

As previously stated, a vital program established by the Association in 1957 was the *Dental Hygiene Aptitude Testing Program.* This was instituted as a service program for the schools of dental hygiene to assist in the selection of highly qualified student applicants, and ultimately to serve as a means of assuring the profession of an adequately educated membership. This is one of the major continuing activities conducted by the Association.

STATUS OF MEMBERSHIP

In 1923, the first year of organization, there were fewer than 100 members. Through the concerted effort of these original members, others were recruited. With each succeeding year, new members have been added to the rolls of the Association. Figure 12–3 shows a consistent increase in membership, both active and junior members. In Figure 12–3, the term "active" includes all classes of members other than junior and honorary members, *i.e.*, life, active, and affiliate.

The Association was organized to serve both the public and the dental profession as well as the dental hygienist. For this service to be continuous, it is the responsibility of each graduate to aid the Association in furthering its objectives by becoming an active member.

Without the untiring work of many individuals over the years, dental hygiene as a profession would never have attained its present status.

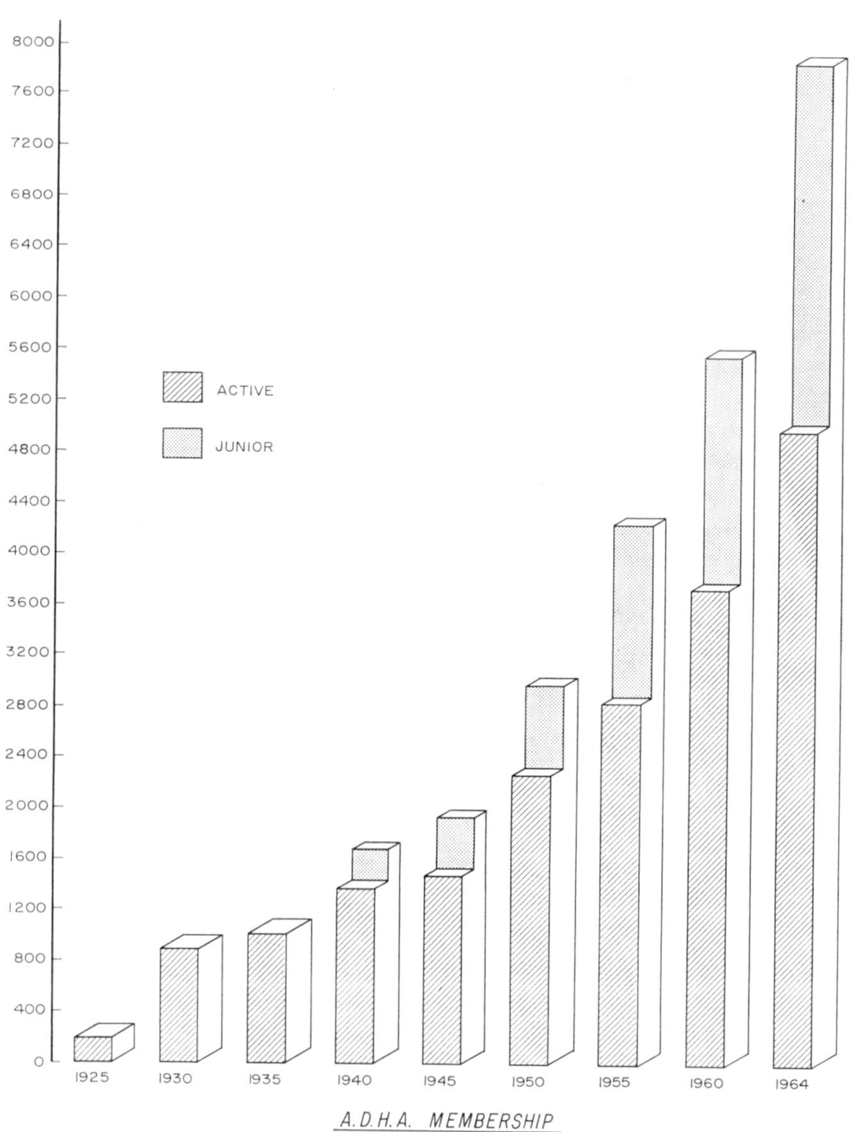

FIG. 12–3. Active and junior membership of the American Dental Hygienists' Association.

To Dr. Alfred Civilion Fones, the founder of the profession, goes our respectful commendation for envisioning the potentialities of this auxiliary dental health group. As a memorial to his endeavors, the American Dental Hygienists' Association has now established The Alfred C. Fones Memorial Scholarship.

To the American Dental Association goes much of the credit for the establishment of the American Dental Hygienists' Association. The guidance of the members of the American Dental Association, both individually and as a group, has aided considerably in the organization and development of the Association.

Lastly, highest respect is due all officers and members—past and present—of the American Dental Hygienists' Association for their untiring efforts to make dental hygiene a recognized profession within the health professions.

BIBLIOGRAPHY

1. American Dental Association: Council on Dental Education, Requirements for the Accreditation of Schools of Dental Hygiene, 1947, 211 East Chicago Avenue, Chicago, Illinois.
2. American Dental Association: National Board Dental Hygiene Examination, 211 East Chicago Avenue, Chicago, Illinois.
3. American Dental Hygienists' Association: Constitution and By-laws, 211 East Chicago Avenue, Chicago, Illinois.
4. American Dental Hygienists' Association: Educational Trust Fund of the American Dental Hygienists' Association, 211 East Chicago Avenue, Chicago, Illinois.
5. American Dental Hygienists' Association: Minutes of the Meetings of the American Dental Hygienists' Association, 1923–1964, 211 East Chicago Avenue, Chicago, Illinois.
6. American Dental Hygienists' Association: Structure and Function of the American Dental Hygienists' Association, 211 East Chicago Avenue, Chicago, Illinois.
7. Bunting, Russell W.: *Oral Hygiene,* Philadelphia, Lea & Febiger, 1954, p. 272.
8. Editorial: Dental Hygiene, Amer. J. Dent. Sci., 1844–1845, pp. 244–245.
9. Fones, Alfred C.: *Mouth Hygiene, A Textbook for Dental Hygienists,* 2nd ed. Philadelphia, Lea & Febiger, 1921.
10. _________ The Necessity for and Training of a Prophylactic Assistant, Dent. Cosmos, *54,* 284–289, 1912.
11. Wallace, Wimburn L.: The Past, Present and Future of the Dental Hygiene Aptitude Test, J.A.D.H.A., *38,* 191–196, 1964.

Index

(*Italic* figures refer to illustrations; numbers with a "*t*" refer to tables.)

A

Abrasion, mechanical, 253
Abrasives and polishing agents, 195, 200
Abscess, periodontal, 415
Accepted Dental Remedies, 204
Acids, bacterial, 356
  demineralization, 230
Acromegaly, 337, *338*
Actinomyces, 358, 361
Actinomycetes, 270, 409
Actinomycosis, 332, *333*
Addison's disease, 339
Adenocarcinoma, 348
Adenoma, malignant, 346, *346*
  pleomorphic, 345
Administrators, school, 441
Adrenogenital syndrome, 339
Aged and chronically ill, 267, 462, 479–481
Agranulocytosis, 342
Air syringe, 168, 208, 209
Alfred C. Fones Memorial Scholarship, 503, 505
Allergies, 154
Alveolar bone, *77*
  fibers, 313
  mucosa, 304
  process, *80*, 313–314
Alveoli, *79*
Ameloblastoma, 352
Ameloblasts, 290, 296
Amelogenesis, 291–294
  imperfecta, 366
American Association of Dental Schools, 498
American Dental Association, 441, 485, 494, 495, 505
  Bureau of Dental Health Education, 497
  Bureau of Economic Research and Statistics, 446
American Dental Association,
  Commission of Mouth Hygiene and Public Instruction, 494
  Council on Dental Education, 487–489, 493, 498, 499
  Council on Dental Health, 453
  Council on Dental Therapeutics, 24, 105, 110, 120–122
  Council of National Board of Dental Examiners, 490, 493
  Dental Health Program for Schools, 443
American Dental Hygienists' Association, 441, 484, 487, 488, 493–505
  annual session, 496
  associations and societies, 495, 496, 499
  Board of Trustees, 500–502
  central office, 497, 502
  committees, 496–498, 501, 502
  constitution and by-laws, 494–496, 498–500, 502
  Dental Hygiene Aptitude Testing Program, 503
  dues, 499
  Educational Trust Fund, 502–503
  ethics, 499
  field surveys, 496
  growth and recognition, 495, 497
  House of Delegates, 500, 501
  incorporation, 495, 500
  Journal, 495, 496, 502
  meetings, 496
  membership, 496, 497, 499, 503–504, *504*
  objectives, 495, 498
  officers, 497, 501, 502
  organization and structure, 493, 498–503, *501*

American Dental Hygienists' Association, projects, 500
scholarships, 503
seal, 495
tax-exempt status, 500
trustees, 495, 496
Workshop, 1964, recommendations, 498
American Fund for Dental Education, 503
American Public Health Association, Committee on Professional Education, 462
Anatomy, circulatory system, 50–55
muscular system, 42–46
nervous system, 46–49
oral and dental, 34–103
oral region and associated structures, 55–70
skeletal system, 35–41
skull, 36, *36*, *41*
teeth, 70–83, *76*, *77*, *81*
nomenclature, 80–83
Anemia, pernicious, 340, *341*
sickle cell, 340
Anemias, oral signs, 340, *341*
Anesthetics, topical, 204
Angulation, 177, *177*
Animal experiments, 223, 225, *226*, 227, 228, 233, 237, 242, 248, 256, 264, 268
Ankyloglossis, 323, *323*
Anodontia, 324, *325*
Antibacterial agents, 253, 268, 269
Antibiotic dentifrices, 268
levels, blood *vs.* saliva, 268
premedication, 155
Antibiotics, topical, plaque control, 355
Anticoagulant therapy, 155
Antiseptics, 151
postoperative, application, 205
Apatite crystals, 241
Apical foramen, 77
Appliances, removal of stains, 194
Apthae, oral, 342
Arteries, 40, 46, 50, 52, *53*, 54, *54*
face and scalp, *52*
principal, *51*
Articulation, maxillopalatine, *37*
Associations, dental hygiene, state, 494
Atrophy, periodontal, 376, 379
Attachments, instrument, hand and motor driven, 195
polishing, 197
screw-shank and snap-on, 197
Audio-visual aids, 456, 457

B

Bacteremia, 406
Bacteria, 223, 241, 258, 269, 354–356, 362, 397, 409
cariogenic, growth conditions, 251
chromogenic, 356
concentration in plaque, 363
Bacterial deposits, correlation with periodontal disease, 363
plaque. *See* Plaque.
stains, 354
Ball, Louise C., 486
Behavioral sciences, 444–445
Benign tumors, 346
Bicuspids, 91–95, *92*, *93*, *94*
Biopsy, detection of neoplasms, 27
Black stain on teeth, 357, 365
Black to brown stain on teeth, 365
Bleeding, gingival, 420, 433
Blood dyscrasias, 156
oral signs, 340–343
Boley gauge, 472
Bone defects, 337
development, acromegaly, 337, 338
loss, periodontal disease, 370
marrow suppression, drugs, 342
resorption, 406, *406*, 407, *407*
Bones, 38, 41, *41*
classification, 35
facial, development, 281
formation, 35
Brown stain on teeth, 365
Brushes, bristle, polishing, 197
denture, 110, *111*
Bryant, Dorothy, 495
Buccae, structure, 58
Buccinator, 39, 44
Buckly, J. P., 494
Burkhart, Harvey J., 486

C

Calcification, 293
Calcium carbonate, precipitated, 195
salts, 362
Calculus, 17, 104, 179, 270, 354, 356, 358–364, *359*, 361, 409, 420
areas of greatest deposit, 354, 362
classification, 474–475
constituents, 358, 474
definition, 358, 474

Calculus, detection, air syringe, 168
explorers, 172
periodontal probe, 169
experimental, *234*, 358, 362
index, 478
photomicrographic structure, *360*
removal, chemicals, 364
scaling and planing, 174
scoring, 475–477, *475*, *476*
subgingival, *363*
etiologic factors, 362
subgingival and supragingival, 359, 362, 475
Cancer, oral, 20, 27, 347
Cancrum oris, *231*
Candidiasis, 332
Canker sore, 332, *333*
Carbohydrates, 230, 244, 258, 461
bacterial acidogenesis, 356
Carcinoma, epidermoid, 348, *348*
salivary glands, 346
Caries, 22–24, 221–270, 356, 357, *357*, 461
arrested, *256*, *257*
coalesced, 251–253, *251*
control, recommendations, 267
studies, 258
definition, 242
detection, 172
diet in, 225, 229, 230–237, 246, 253, 257, 258–261, *259*, 461
epidemiology, 238
etiology, 221–238, *222*, 244, *245*, 247, 269
experimental. *See* Animal experiments.
incipient, 247, 249
ingesta-saliva substrate, host-parasite dietary correlations, *232*
inhibitory substances, 237
lesion progression, 244, 253
lesion types, 243, *254*, *255*
microscopic study of, 243
pathology, 242–258
permanent preparations, 243
pit and fissure, 243, 244–246
prevalence, 22, *23*, 221, 447
Scandinavia, 232
prevention, 24, 30, 104
fluoride dentifrices, 120
levels of, 17, *18*
topical fluorides, 207
therapy, 258–270
toothbrushing limitations, 262
surveys, 470
Cavity outline, 20
preparation, 17
Cells, physiology, 275
structure, 275
Cementum, *77*, 78, 79, 303, 311, *313*
composition, 311
formation, 295–296
physiology, 311
Charting, 165, 166, 169, 171, 173
Chemico-Parasitic Theory, 223
Chemotherapy, 267, 268
Chickenpox, oral signs, 335
Children, age level traits and needs, 450–453
handicapped, 479
kindergarten, 451
underprivileged, 441
Children's Fund of Michigan, 441
Chisel scaler, 191–193, *192*
Chisels, sharpening of, 217
Chlortetracycline, 269
Chromium oxide, 195
Cleft lip, 318, *319*
palate, 318, *320*, 471
Clefts, oral, 27–28, 318, 478
Clinics, dental, privately endowed, 441
public, 462
special, 479
Cold sore, 332, *333*
Collagenase, 357
Commission on the Survey of Dentistry 371
Common carotid artery, 50, 52, 54
Communication, 456
Community dental surveys, 463, 464–478
preventive programs, 29–30
Compressed air, 205
Cone of Experience, 457
Contact points, 411, 412
Contents, Table of, 9–13
Coronal caries, 230, 242
Correlated teaching, 455
Cotton roll holder, 209, *209*, *210*
rolls, 208
Craters, interproximal gingival, 411, *411*
Cross, Harold De Witt, 486
Cross bite, 337, *338*
Crown, *77*, 83, 296
abnormal, hereditary factors, 366
formation, 301
removal of stains, 194
Curet, *179*
root planing, 183
scaling, 180, *181*, *182*

Curets, sharpening of, 212, *213*, *214*
Curettage, 420, 421
Cuspids, 89–91, *90*
eruption, 300
Cuticle, plaque attachment, *361*
primary, 296
Cysts, oral, 329–331, *329*, *330*, *331*
retention, 330
thyroglossal duct, 323

D

Dale, Edgar, 457
Data collecting and recording, survey, 466–468
Debris, oral, 229, 474–477, *474*, *476*
index, 477
Deglutition, 56
Dens in dente, 325
Dental calculus. *See* Calculus.
care, class attitudes, 446
community, measure of need, 469
Kansas City program, 481
psychologic aspects of, 446
public, limitation of funds and personnel, 462
public participation in, 447
caries. *See* Caries.
disease, indexes, 471–473
prevalence, 22
preventive approach, 484
equipment, portable, 479
examinations, 463
public, four types, 464
floss, 110, 112, 195, 200, 261, 262
formula, 73
health, adult education, 454
behavioral sciences in, 444
community survey, 464
increasing demand for, 463
in-service teacher programs, 453
motivation and incentives, 442, 448, 449
objectives, 443
public interest, 447
public, programs, 461–462
Dental health education, 439–458, 461
behavior and attitudes, modification of, 445
communication, 456–457
community service, 20, 30, 31
conceptual model, 450
dental hygienist, 453–454
Dental health education, lesson plans, 456
materials, 463
motivation, 444, 445, 451
need for, 447
positive approach, 444
principles, 449
professional challenge, 458
school, 441–442, 456
teaching approaches, 454–456
Dental health facilities, community, 470
Dental health problem, extent and complexity, 447
Dental health programs, 463
base line data, 471
Bridgeport, Connecticut, 485
dental hygienist in, 464
evaluation, 470
Dental hygiene. *See also* Oral hygiene.
Dental hygiene, aims and purpose, 484
early training emphases, 487
history and organization, 483–505
instruction, 485
malocclusion, 75
motion picture, 497
soft tissue curettage in, 174
Dental Hygiene Aptitude Testing Program, 488, 497
Dental Hygiene Council, 439
Dental hygiene movement, 439, 440
schools, 441, 486–489
accrediting requirements, 487, 488
entrance requirements, 488
standardization of curricula, 487, 488
students, 489, 489*t*
Dental hygienist, 25, 28–31, 145, 242, 261, 270, 364, 370, 419, 420, 436, 437, 444, 453–454, 461–465, 474, 478, 480, 481, 483–485, 490, 497, 498
application of topical fluorides, 207
armamentarium, 146
associations, 493
education and licensing, 483, 486, 490, *491*
increasing need for, 463, 483
private practice, public health responsibilities of, 464
public health, 460, 462–463
scholarships, 503
state licensing boards, 490

Dental plaque. *See* Plaque.
practice, periodontic orientation, 437
therapy in, 436–437
services, public health, 461
use of, 22
surveys. *See* Surveys, dental.
tape, 110, *113*, 200
visits, annual, statistics on, 447
Dentifrices, 24, 119–121, 261, 262
antibiotic, 268
desensitizing, 207
fluoride, 267
ingredients, 263
therapeutic, 263
Dentin, 77, 77, 303
composition, 309
destruction, 250
formation, *292*, 310
histology, 309–310
hypersensitive, desensitization, 205–207
hypocalcification, 325
imperfect, hereditary factors in, 366
malformation, 328, *328*
origin, 288, 291, 294
physiology, 310
primary, secondary and irregular, 310
remineralization, 258
stains, 366
structures in, *308*
Dentino-enamel junction, 291, 307
Dentinogenesis, 291
and amelogenesis, 291–294, *293*
imperfecta, 328, *328*, 366
Dentist population ratio, 470
Dentistry, children's, 440
faulty, traumatic, 412, 413
preventive. *See* Preventive dentistry.
Dentists, need for, 221
Dentition, 71
ages of completion, 301
aspects, 123
malformation, 324–329
osteogenesis imperfecta, *327*, 328
pathology, 324–328
permanent, 87–101
primary, 84–87, *84*, *85*, *86*
Dentobacterial plaque. *See* Plaque.
Denture brushes, 110, *111*
stains, removal, 202
Dentures, cleansing of, 121
gold, polishing of, 195
Dentures, precious metal alloys, polishing of, 195
removable, cleaning of, 202–204
stainless steel, polishing of, 195
Deposits and stains, disclosing of, 201
Deposits, dental, 354–368
Desensitization, iontophoresis in, 206
Desensitizing agents, 205
Development, oral, disturbances of, 318–328
Diabetes, 157, 339, 344
oral pathology in, 337
Diagnosis, 416
Diet, 19, *234*, 354, 433, 440
carious, 461
dental deposits, 354
necrotizing ulcerative gingivitis, 432
Diet recommendations, 31
Digital massage, 119
Direct teaching, 455
Disclosing agents, 123, 195, 201–202, 243, 248, 261, 262
Disclosing solution, fluoridated, 267
Disclosing solutions, use of, 355
Disclosing tablets, 202
Discoloration, arrested carious lesion, 258
gray, 366, *368*
Discomfort, postoperative, treatment, 205
Disinfectants, chemical, 149
DMF index, 469–470
DMF rate, age-related increase of, 468
meaningfulness of, 469
Drugs, 342, 435, 436
Dyes, antibacterial, 267
plaque-disclosing, 31
Dysplasia, ectodermal, 324, *325*
Dystrophic disease, periodontal, 376

E

EBERSOLE, W. G., 441
Edema, gingival, 374, 386, 387, *387*
pregnancy and, 416
osmotic balance in, 389
Education, audio-visual methods, 457
Educational concepts and principles, 449–450
Elephantiasis, gingival, 384
Embryo, five weeks, 276–277, *277*
seven weeks, 279
six weeks, 277–278
Embryogenesis, oral, defects in, 318

Embryology, bone formation, 35
deciduous teeth, 288
face, 275–317
jaws, 280, *282*
mandible, 276
mandibular arch, *280*
maxilla, 276
mouth, 276
roots, 294
teeth, 288
teeth and mouth, positional relationship at four months, *290*
Embryonic germ layers, 275
Emergency treatment, periodontal disease, 419
Enamel, 76, 303
demineralization, 250
fluoride content, 238
fluoride effect on, 241
formation, *292*
gnarled, 307
histology, 307–309
hypocalcification, 325
hypoplastic, 29, 366
mineral content, 307
mottled, 29, 238, 366, 367, 471
origin, 288
remineralization, 258
stains, 366
structures in, *308*
Enamel destruction, *252*
Enamel matrix, formation, 291
Enamel tufts, 307, *308*
Enameloma, 352
Endocrine system, 337
Enzymes, bacterial, 356, 357
mucolytic, 364
Epileptic seizures, 157
Epithelia, gingival, attachment, 376
Epithelial lesions, premalignant, 348
Equipment, portable, 479
positioning and adjustment, 158
Equipment needed, surveys, 465
Eruption, *297*, *298*
chronology, 300–301
deciduous teeth, sequence, 300
premolars, 300
Eruption process, 296–299
Eruption sequence, permanent teeth, 300
Erythema multiforme, oral lesions, 335, *336*
Examination, dental, 463
importance of systematized, 417
Exfoliative cytology, 27
Experience, directness, audio-visual materials classification, 457
Explorers, sharpening of, 217
use of, 171–173, 362, 389, 464, 476
Exploring, 17
differentiation of calculus from caries, 172
differentiation of calculus from margin of restoration, 173
Extraction, 17, 20
Extractions, 324, 419
Exudates, gingival, 395

F

Face, histology and embryology, 275–317
Facial bones, 38
Fibroblasts, proliferation, 391
Fibroma, 349, *350*
Fibromatosis, hereditary, 384
Fibrosis, gingival, 387
Files, periodontal, 190, 191, *191*
Fillings, irritation from, 412, *413*
Film, removal, 194
Fluoridated disclosing solution, 267
Fluoridation, 16, 19, 20, *23*, 24, 30, 239, 263, 366, 461, 471
community studies, 470, *470*
Grand Rapids, 470
Fluoride, sodium, advantages, 266
Fluorides, 16, 19, 22, 238–242, *239*, *240*, 258, 263–267, 461, 463
application, 209–210, *209*, *210*, 264, *264*, *265*, 266
choice of, 264
dentifrices, 120
desensitizing, 205–206
excess of, 366
experiments, 266
mechanism of action, 241
metallic, 266
microorganisms, 241
optimum concentration in drinking water, 29
optimum time of application, 242, 264
organic, 266
tablets, cost of, 264

Fluorides, topical, 463
application, 24, 31, 207–210, 241, 460, 462
Fluorine, tooth stains, internal, 366
Fluoroapatite, 366
Fluorosis, endemic, 29
Fluorosis index, 471
Fones, Alfred C., 16, 441, 484, 485, 494, 505
Memorial Scholarship, 503, 505
Fones School, 485, 486
Food impaction, 363, 411, 412, 415
Foods, dental deposits, 354
non-cariogenic, 260
Fordyce's spots, 318, *320*
Forms, survey, 466, *467*
Forsyth Dental Dispensary for Children, 486
Forsyth Dental Infirmary of Boston, 441
Foundations, private, dental hygiene, 441
Fulcrum, 176, 199, 212, 215

G

GAG reflex, stimulation of, 208
Gauze strips, cleaning of teeth, 114
Gebhard, Bruno, 448
Germination, 326, *326*
Gingiva, 62–64, *77*, 79, 303
attached, 63, 303, 373, 374
repositioning, 425, *426*, *427*, *428*
bleeding, 373
crevice, 63
diseased, appearance, 372
edematous response to irritation, 389–390, *389*
fibrous response, 391–392, *391*
formation, 299
free, 62, 303
healthy, 271, 371–374
appearance, *373*, 374, *375*
characteristics, 372
immobility of teeth, 374
serous-like fluid in, 374
mechanical stimulation, 355
pathologic exudates, 373
Gingival elephantiasis, 384
Gingival epithelia, attachment of, 376
Gingival exudates, 395
Gingival hemorrhage, 343
Gingival hyperplasia, 158, 376, 379, 383, 384, 387, *401*
biopsy section, *401*
dilantin-induced, 158
idiopathic, 384
inflammatory, 379
non-inflammatory, 383–384
dilantin sodium in, 383, *383*
oral hygiene in, 392
toothbrushing in, 383
Gingival inflammation, 386–388
Gingival recession, 372
Gingival response, edematous *vs.* fibrotic, *386*, 387, *387*, *394*
Gingival tissue, origin, 288
Gingival ulcers, 373, 404
Gingivectomy, 424, *425*
Gingivitis, 24–25, 357, 376, 408, 472, 473
antibiotics in, 355
antigen-antibody reaction in, 358
biopsy, *388*, *390*
desquamative, 378
incidence, 370
inflammatory reaction, *398*, *399*
leukemic, 343, *343*
necrotizing ulcerative, 334, *334*, 430–436
recurrence, 433, *435*
plaque in, 363, 364
prevalence of, 447
treatment, objectives, 389
Gingivitis and periodontitis, modifying terms for, 377
Gingivitis severity index, 472
Gingivoplasty, 383, 392, 424, *425*, 433, *434*
Gingivosis, 376, 378, *378*
Gingivostomatitis, herpetic, 332
ulcerative necrotizing, 24–25
Glands, 67–68, *67*
parotid, 314
sublingual, 316
submandibular, 315
Glossitis, 340
rhomboid, 321, *322*
Glossodynia, 340
Glossopharyngeal nerve, 47, 49
Glossopyrosis, 340
Gnarled enamel, 307
Graduates, dental hygiene, number of, 489, 489*t*

Granulation tissue, excess formation from chronic irritation, 391, *391*
Grasps, 212
Gray discoloration, 366, *368*
Green stain on teeth, 356, 365
Greenhood, Charlotte C., 487
Guggenheim Foundation, 441
Gum boil, 334

H

HALL Foundation, 441
Handpieces, 197, *198*
Handwashing technique, 151
Hart, Miss Hubert, 494
Health, oral. *See* Oral hygiene.
Health, public, 460–481
Health attitudes, cultural influence on, 448
Health care legislation, need for, 481
Health concepts, 442–443
Health education, definitions, 448–449
 knowledge *vs.* practice, 442
 laws of learning, 450
 levels of responsibility, 455
 materials, age level of, 451
 methods, 454–456
 objectives, 443
Health instruction, school, 442
Heart and kidney disease, 154
Hemangioma, 345, 349, *350*
Hemophilia, 156
Hemorrhage, gingival, 343
Hepatitis, infectious, 156
Hereditary defects, 29
Herpes simplex virus, 332
Hertwig's epithelial root sheath, 294
Histogenesis, roots, 294
Histology, alveolar, 313–314
 face, 275–317
 gingiva, 374–376
 oral mucosa, 302–307
 periodontal membrane, 312–313
 pulp, 366
 salivary glands, 314–316, *315*
 supporting structures of teeth, 311–314
 teeth, 307–311
 temporomandibular joint, 316–317, *316*
 tongue, 306
History taking and review, 153, 154, 158
Hoe scalers, 188, *188*, 189, *190*
 sharpening of, 217
Home-bound patients, 480
Home care, regimen, 420
Hunter-Schreger bands, *303*, 307, *308*
Hyaluronidase, 357
Hyatt, Thaddeus P., 439, 440
Hydrotherapy, 119
Hydroxyapatite, 250, 309, 325, 359
 reaction with bacterial acids, 250
Hyoid bones, 41
Hyperparathyroidism, 337
Hyperplasia, gingival. *See* Gingival hyperplasia.
Hypocalcification, 325, 337
Hypoglossal nerve, 47, 49
Hypoparathyroidism, 337
Hypothyroidism, 415

I

INCISORS, 87–89, *88*, *89*, 283, 300
Index, calculus, 478
 caries, 464–470
 debris, 477
 DMF, 469–470
 fluorosis, 471
 gingivitis severity, 472
 handicapping labio-lingual deviations, 471
 malalignment, 472
 malocclusion, 471–472
 OHI, 474–478, *476*, *477*
  simplified, 478
 oral hygiene, 474–478
 periodontal disease, 472–473
 PI, 473
 P-M-A, 472, 473
 Russell's Periodontal, 473
Indicators, salivary lactobacillus count, 225
Infection, Vincent's, 334, 430
Infections, jawbone, drainage, 334
 oral, 332–335
 streptococcal, 156
 tuberculosis, 156
Inferior dental artery, 40
Inferior dental vein, 54
Inflammation and irritation, relationship, 386
Inflammation, gingival, 386–388
 periodontal, pocket, 397

Inflammatory disease, periodontal, 376
Inflammatory response, granulation tissue repair in, 400
    malnutrition of cells in, 400
    nature of, 391, 400
    vascular and cellular elements, 397
Inlays, trauma from, 414
Inspection, oral and dental, 165–166, *167*
Instruction methods, 454–456
Instruction, oral hygiene, 261, 462
Instrument attachments, 195
Instrumentation bacteremia, 406
Instrumentation, general principles, 162–165
Instrumentation trauma, 373
Instruments, chemical disinfection of, 149
  force and direction of stroke, 163–165
  fulcrum, 164
  grasp, 162–163, *163*, *164*
  polishing, 194–204
    porte polisher, 196, *196*
  root planing, 174
  scaling and planing, 175, 176, *176*
  sharpening of, 210–218
  sharpness, test of, 211
  sterilization, 147
Integrated teaching, 455
Interdental papillae, 304, 334
Interdental stimulators, 31, 114–117, *116*, *117*
Internal maxillary vein, 54
Iontophoresis, 206
Irritants, 386, 397, 408, 413
  microbial, 409
Irritation, 344, 391
  periodontal pockets in, 392, 397
  reduction by restorations, 408
  removal, 436
  response of gingival tissues, 386
Irritation and inflammation, relationship, 371

J

Jawbone, infections, importance of drainage, 334
Jawbones, pathology, 332–343
Jaws, development, 280–283
Jeweler's rouge, 195
Johnson, C. N., 495
Junk, Anita, 494

K

Keratinization, gingival epithelia, 373, 374
King, Otto U., 494
Knitting yarn, use in cleaning teeth, 114

L

Lacerations, 200
Lactobacilli, 223, 229
  fluorides, 241
Lamellae, 307
Lamina dura, 314
Learning, laws and principles, 449, 450
Leptothrix, 358, 361
Lesson plans, 456
Leukemia, oral lesions, 342
Leukocytes, drug depression, 342
Leukopenia, 342, *342*
Leukoplakia, 348, *349*
Licensure, dental hygiene, 490, *491*
Lichen planus, oral lesions, 335, *335*
Lip, cleft, 28
Lips, structure, 57–58
Lymphangioma, 349
Lymphatic system, 55

M

McLain, Andrew, 440
Macrodontia, *326*, 327
Macroglossia, 323
Malalignment, 238
Malignancies, 346, *346*
Malnutrition and caries, 231
Malocclusion, 28–29, 75, *75*, 471
  prevalence, 28, 447
Malocclusion indexes, 471–472
Malposition, 409, *410*
  prostheses in, 20
Mandible, 38, *39*, *40*
  articulation, *70*
  development, 276
  enlargement in acromegaly, 337, *338*
Mandibular arch, development, *280*
Mandibular teeth, *72*
Marginal ridge, 411, 412
Masseter, 40, 45–46

Mastication, 56, 299
  cleansing action, 415
  detergent effect, 374
  movements of mandible, 69
  muscles of, 40, 45–48, 69
Mastication trauma, 413
Materia alba, 229, 356, 409
Maxilla, *38*
  development, 276
Maxillary artery, 46, 52, *54*
Maxillary teeth, *72*
Measles, oral signs, 335
Melanosis, oral, 339, *340*
Microcosm, 229
Microdontia, 325
Microorganisms, role in oral disease, 122
Microscopic studies, 374, *375*
Migration of teeth, 75
Models, dental, study, 464
Molars, eruption, 300
  mandibular, 98–100, *98*, *99*, *100*
  maxillary, 95–98, *96*, *97*
Moniliasis, 332
Morphology, jaws, 280–283
  mouth, 56–58
  teeth, 83–87
Mottling, teeth, 29
Mouth, dry, 343
  edentulous, 324, 436
  embryonic development, 276
  structure, 56–58
Mouth breathing, 379, *382*
Mouth mirror, 166, 464
Mouthwashes, 121, 122
Mucocele, 345
Mucogingival junction, 304
Mucosa, alveolar, 63
  erosion, 344
  pathology, 332
Mucosal ulcers, 339
Muscles, 39, 40, 42, *43*, 44–46, *45*, 61, *66*

N

NATIONAL Board Examination, 492–493
National Dental Association, Committee on Oral Hygiene, 439, 441
National Education Association, Educational Policies Commission, statement of, 443
National Formulary, 195
National Health Survey findings, 21, 25, *27*
Necrosis, tissue, 400, 433
Necrotizing ulcerative gingivitis. *See* Gingivitis, necrotizing ulcerative.
Neoplasia, 20, 27, 320, 323, *324*, 347
  mesenchymal, 349–351
  odontogenic, 352–353
  oral, 346–353
  pituitary, 337
  salivary glands, 345–346, *346*
Nerves, 47, 48, 49, *49*
  classification of, 46
  inferior dental, 39, 40
  maxillary and mandibular, distribution, *48*
Neutropenia, periodic cyclic, 342
New York School of Dental Hygiene, 486
Newman, Irene, 484
Noma, *231*
"Normal" *vs.* "healthy," 371
Oberteuffer, Delbert, 443
Occlusion, 74, 299
  normal, *74*
Odontoblasts, 290
Odontomas, 352, *353*
Oral cavity, *56*
Oral health. *See* Oral Hygiene.
Oral health care, 15, 16
Oral health problems, 21–29
Oral hygiene, 19, 29, 30, 31, 261–263, 270, 354, 415, 439, 440, 461, 480
  buccal *vs.* lingual surfaces in, 475, 476
  estimates, 474
  instruments and aids, 104
  interproximal embrasure, 411, *412*, 413
  motivation, 430
  nursing home attendants in, 481
Oral Hygiene Index, 25, 474–478, *474*
Oral Hygiene Movement, 439
Oral infections, 332–335
Oral mucosa, 62, 63
  histology, 302–307
  pathology, 332–343
Oral structures, histology and embryology, 275–317
Orthodontic appliances, irritation from, 344
Orthodontics, 28
Osmotic balance, edematous alteration, 389
  inflammatory alteration, 398
Osseousplasty, 425, *429*

Osteoblasts, 296
Osteomas, 351
Oxidizing agents, 436

P

PAIN, 205, 251, 311, 374, 430
Palate, bony, and alveolar arch, *59*
 cleft, 28
 development, 283–285, *284*, *285*, *286*
 hard, 59–60, 303
 soft, 60–61
Papillae, conical, 411
Papillomas, 347
Parathyroids, 337
Pathology, oral, 318–353
  developmental, 318
  systemic, oral signs, 332
Patient care, philosophy, 371
Pedicle graft, gingival, *429*
Pemphigus, oral lesions, 336
Penicillin, 268
 topical application, 121
Periodontal disease, 24–27
  acute *vs.* chronic, 377
  acute gingivitis, 24–25
  anatomical location, 377
  bacterial plaque, 261
  calculus, 363
  chronic destructive, 25, *26*, *27*
  classification, 376–377
  clinical signs, 416
  dental plaque, 270, 363
  diabetes, 157, 415
  diagnosis, 64
  etiologic factors, 377
  etiology, 80, 363
  fluoridated water, 240
  inflammatory, diagnosis, 416–418
   etiology, 408, 416
   prognosis, 425–430
   treatment, 418–425, *421*, *422*, *424*, *425*, *426*, *427*, *428*, *429*
  levels of prevention, 17, *18*
  pH of plaque, 356
  pocket formation, 25
  prevalence, 22, *23*, 25, *27*, 370
  prevention, oral hygiene in, 25, 30
  systemic disorders in, 378, 415
  tissue response, 377
  treatment, 436
Periodontal disease indexes, 472–473
Periodontal files, sharpening of, 217, *218*
Periodontal health, identification and removal of irritants, 371
Periodontal hyperplasia, 376, 379
Periodontal Index, 25
Periodontal lesions, early, management of, 389
Periodontal ligament, formation, 295–296
Periodontal membrane, *77*, 79, 303, 312, 314
  histology, 312–313
Periodontal pockets, 392–408, 473
  irritation from, 392
Periodontal probe, function, 169
  proper use, 169–171, *171*, *417*
  markings, *170*
Periodontal surveys, calculus scoring, 475–477, *475*, *476*
Periodontal traumatism, 376, 384–386, *384*, *385*, 406, 413–415, *414*
Periodontics, 370–437
Periodontitis, 376, *382*, 408, 433
 diabetes, *423*, *424*
 hyperplastic, appearance of, *392*
 local factors, 408
 mild localized, *386*
 mouth breathing, 379, *382*
Periodontosis, 376, 379, *380*, *381*
 incidence, 379
Permanent teeth, 87–101, 451
Personnel, survey, 465
Pharynx, muscles, *66*
 structure, 65–67, *66*
Physiotherapy, 104–144
 recommendations, 136–137, 137*t*
Pituitary, 337
Plaque, 229, 233, 243, 247, 248, 259, 261, 268, 270, 354, 355–358, 360, 409
 animal experiments, 269
 calculus as calcified, 395, *396*
 calculus formation, 360
 demonstration of, 262
 microbial, sterilization of, 267
 periodontal disease, 363
 prevention, 364
 removal, 194, 261, 263
  mucolytic enzymes, 364
 retention after cleansing, 355, *355*
 streptococci in, *233*
 sugars and starches in, 235, *260*
Plaque pH, 260, 356
Platt, Elma, 494
Pocket, periodontal, *vs.* sulcus, 392

Pocket depth, gingival, reduction, 389
Pocket therapy, 419, 424
Pockets, connective tissue breakdown, 401, *402*
contents, 395–397, *396*
depth scoring, 416, *417*, *418*
epithelial migration, 401, *402*, *404*
epithelial sloughing, 403, *403*, *404*, *405*
gingival, 392–408, *394*, 473
infrabony, 393, 395
periodontal, 408
pathogenesis, 397–408
types, 393–395
soft tissue, 393
Polishing, 194, 198, 420, 433
dental floss and tape, 200
engine, handpieces, *198*
instruments and techniques, 194–202
Polishing agents, chromium oxide, 195
fluorides, 267
jeweler's rouge, 195
precipitated calcium carbonate, 195
tin oxide, 195
Polishing brush, bristle, 200
Polishing handpieces, engine, *198*
Positioning, patient and operator, 158
patient's head, *160*
Posterior dental vein, 54
Predentin, 291
Pregnancy, cariogenic effect, 238
Premolar caries, *249*, *250*
Preventive dentistry, 15–33, 238
basic concepts, 17–18
dental hygienist in, 25, 28–31
dentist in, 32
early interest, 439–440
history, 15–17, 439
levels of prevention, 17–21, *18*
need for, *vs.* demand, 21
objectives, 17
office practice, 30–32
Process, alveolar, 38
Prognathism, 337, *338*
Prognosis, 425
Programs, caries control, 269
dental health, school, 441
Prophylaxis, 20, 145–220, 439, 440
accepted sterile procedures, 153*t*
instruction in, 462
Prostheses, 20
ill fitting, 391
Pterygoid plexus, 54
Public Health, 460–481
dental hygiene services, 485
Pulp, *77*, 78, 303
death, 366
histology, 310–311
origin, 288
physiology, 311
polishing trauma, 196
vitality tests, 464
Pulp caries, 251
Pulp tissue, 294
Pulpitis, 374
Pumice, 195
Purpura, 156
Pus, 374, 397

R

Radiography, 17
Rampant caries, 268
Ranula, 330, *331*, 345
Reattachment operation, 423
Recession, gingival, 372
Resorption, bone, 406, *406*, 407, *407*
dentinal, 368
roots, 301
Respiratory diseases, 156
Restoration, compound, contour of, 20
Restorations, 419
acrylic, polishing of, 195
antibacterial adjuvants in, 269
metallic, polishing of, 195
need for, 221
periodontal tissue health, 371
preparation, 253
supporting structures, 371
Rhein, M. L., 439, 484
Rinsing, 205
Rochester Dental Dispensary, 441, 486
Roentgenograms, 337, 362, *394*, 406, 408, 464
Root planing, 179, 420, 421
Root surface caries, 230, 232, 242, 244, 253–256
Root surfaces, polishing of, 195
Roots, *77*, 78, 84
development, 294–295
formation, 301
origin, 294
resorption of, 301
scaling and planing of, 179
Rubber cup polisher and stimulator, 117, *118*
Rubber cups, polishing, 197, 199

S

SALIVA, amount, 314
calculus formation, 354
consistency, 315
Saliva ejector, 208, 209
Salivary flow, 237, 267, 354, 356
Salivary function, loss of, 268
Salivary glands, 39, 67–68, *67*
development, 287–288
disturbances, 343–346
ductal obstruction, 344–345, *344*
histology, 314–316
infections, 345
pathology, 348
tumors, 345–346, *346*
Salt solution, hypertonic, postoperative rinsing, 205
Sample selection, survey, 465
Sanitization, dental chair and equipment, 152
Sarcomas, oral, 351, *351*
Scaling, 433
ultrasonic, 193–194
Scaling and polishing, disclosing agents in, 201
Scholarships, dental hygiene, 503
Schools, dental hygiene. *See* Dental hygiene schools.
Sialadenitis, 345
Sialoliths, 330, *344*, 345
Sickle scaler, 183–184, *184*, *185*, *187*
proper use, 186–188
sharpening of, 215, *215*, *216*, *217*
Sinuses, 68–69
Sjögren's syndrome, 344
Skeleton, divisions, 35
Skin diseases, non-infectious, oral signs, 335–336
Skull, anatomy, 36, *36*, *41*
Smith, D. D., 440, 484
Smooth surface caries, 243, 246–251
Soft tissue trauma, dental tape or floss in, 201
Sordes, 229
Spiramycin, 269
Stains, 266, 354, 364–368, 474
bacteria in, 354
brown, 366
clinical significance, 366, 368
denture, removal, 202
fluorescent yellow, 366
green, 356, 365
Stains, metallic, 364, 365
orange, 356
plaque-disclosing, 243
removal, 194
abrasive strips in, 200
dental tape, 112
during prophylaxis, 356
tetracycline, 29, 364, 366
tobacco, 365, *365*
yellow to brown, 29
Standardization and calibration, survey, 466
Statistician, need for in surveys, 465
Sterile technique, 146–153
Stomatitis, diabetic, 337
gangrenous, *231*
Stones, sharpening, 211
Streptococci, 225, 233, 241, 270
Students, dental hygiene, number of, 489, 489*t*
Subclavian artery, *53*
Sucrose, 232, 246, 260
Suction apparatus, 208
Sulcus, gingival, 299, 373, 374
periodontal, 392
Superficial temporal arteries, 52
Surveys, dental, 464–470, 471
Sutton, Willis A., 441
Swallowing, difficulty in, 344
Swelling, postoperative, prevention, 205
Syphilis, congenital, 328

T

TAPE, dental, instruction in use, 31
Taste buds, 64
Taste pore, *305*
Teaching, 449, 455, 456, 457
formal approaches, 454–456
Techniques, polishing, 194–204
Teeth, abnormalities, 102
ages of completion, 301
anatomy, 70–83, *76*, *77*, *81*
attrition, 299
brown, 366
calcification, 293
carious, histologic study, 243
concrescence, 327
congenital absence, 324
contact points, 411, 412
dark and translucent, 366
deciduous, 288, 300, 301, *302*, 451, 466